Encyclopedia of
Food Engineering

other AVI books

Encyclopedia of Food Engineering

CARL W. HALL

Dean, College of Engineering
Washington State University

A. W. FARRALL

Professor and Chairman Emeritus
Agricultural Engineering Department
Michigan State University

A. L. RIPPEN

Professor, Food Science Department
Michigan State University

who were ably assisted by contributors

THE AVI PUBLISHING COMPANY, INC.

Westport, Connecticut

1971

©Copyright 1971 by
The Avi Publishing Company, Inc.
Westport, Connecticut

Registered at Stationers' Hall
London, England 1971

Library of Congress Catalog Card Number: 70-137710
ISBN-0-87055-086-1

Printed in the United States of America
By The Mack Printing Company
Easton, Pennsylvania

iv

CONTRIBUTORS

DALE A. CARLSON, Professor, Department of Civil Engineering, University of Washington, Seattle, Washington

J. M. DEMAN, Professor and Chairman, Department of Food Science, University of Guelph, Guelph, Ontario, Canada

DALE A. SEIBERLING, Manager, Equipment Engineering Department, Klenzade Products Inc., Beloit, Wisconsin

M. E. THORNER, Consultant, Lecturer, The Culinary Institute of America, New Haven, Connecticut

v

PREFACE

The purpose of this Encyclopedia is to bring together in one source, a useful collection of technical data relative to the application of modern engineering to the food processing industry. The Encyclopedia should be useful to the equipment designer, the operator and manager of food plants, students, and regulatory personnel.

Twenty years ago this book would have been almost impossible to assemble, at least in its present form. Much of the research work on which the book is based has been done in recent years. The great array of information now available makes it difficult for an engineer working in the food industry to have at his fingertips the latest information that would be sought, but what is usually needed in plant design, layout, and operation is summarized for easy use.

Subject headings have been selected on the basis of usage in the field. Whether an adjective or noun is used as the first word in the heading depends on the usage, closeness of other reference material, and amount of material available to cover a subject. Thus, a heading is provided for *Tunnel Dryers*, yet both acetylene and arc welding are included under *Welding*. Every attempt has been made by the authors to index, codify, and cross-reference subjects for easy and quick location.

The authors have emphasized equipment and facilities used in food handling, manufacture, and transportation. Material is included on food and food products, but the emphasis in on the equipment. Thus, the headings are *Agitators*, *Mixers*, etc., rather than Agitation, Mixing, etc.

Research publications, trade journals, and manufacturers' literature have provided much information. Every attempt has been made to acknowledge sources of information so that the inquiring person can study in more detail subjects of interest.

The authors have many years of both educational and industrial experience. They have been involved in finding new information through research and putting the information to use, either in new machines or by informing the industry of improved equipment, processes, and procedures. Because of the experience of the authors and availability of information, the book covers fluid products more completely than other product forms.

CARL W. HALL

July 1970

A

ABSOLUTE PRESSURE CONTROLLER

The absolute pressure controller maintains the vacuum in a vacuum pan or evaporator. The pressure within the pan or evaporator may be controlled by (a) regulating the flow of water to the condenser, (b) regulating the pressure-producing device, such as a vacuum pump, and (c) regulating the airflow into the vacuum pan space so that when air enters the pan, the absolute pressure is increased and the vacuum reduced. This operation is known as air-loading.

Gage Pressure

To convert from gage pressure (above atmospheric pressure) to absolute pressure, the atmospheric pressure when the instrument is read is added to the gage pressure reading. For example, at sea level if the nominal value of the atmospheric pressure (14.7 psia) existed when the gage was read, the absolute pressure (psia) is the gage pressure (psig) plus 14.7. Under vacuum conditions the absolute pressure is the atmospheric pressure minus the vacuum. The higher the vacuum the lower is the absolute pressure.

Absolute Pressure

The absolute pressure is measured and expressed using a perfect vacuum as the base or zero value. Thus, the "absolute" value of pressure is independent of atmospheric conditions. Vacuum and gage pressure measuring instruments measure the pressure or vacuum from the atmospheric pressure as a base.

Absolute pressure measuring elements, such as the bellows shown in Fig. A.1 or the U-tube in Fig. A.2, do not need to be compensated when used in atmospheric conditions because by design these units measure from a zero base (perfect vacuum). These elements are preferred for evaporator control.

Units of Pressure

Pressure is expressed in various units, equivalent values of which are: 14.7 psi = 33.9 ft of water = 29.9 in. of Hg = 76 cm of Hg = 760 mm of Hg.

Units of pressure must be consistent when calculating the absolute pressure from vacuum or gage pressure readings. Usual units for gage pressure are pounds per square inch, gage, (psig); for vacuum, inches of mercury (in. Hg); for absolute pressure, pounds per square inch, absolute (psia).

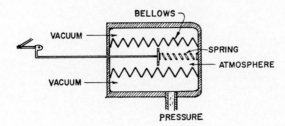

Fig. A-1.   Absolute pressure method using bellows

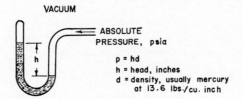

Fig. A-2.   Absolute pressure gage, U-tube

Reference

HALL, C. W., and HEDRICK, T. I. 1966. Drying Milk and Milk Products. AVI Publishing Co., Westport, Conn.

Cross-references: *Air; Pressure Element.*

ACCUMULATORS

Accumulators are widely used in the refrigeration industry as well as in many other processes for collecting a quantity of the product being handled. One purpose of the accumulator in refrigeration is to prevent slugs of refrigeration liquid from passing through the circuit which would otherwise cause difficulty in operation.

In continuous processing lines, an accumulator or accumulating table is often used to provide a temporary storage for packages from a continuous feed line. Thus, small interruptions in a system, such as ice cream hardening, will not require the shutting down of the main feed line. Filling machines often have a surge tank or accumulator to receive the continuous flow from the pasteurizer or the filling line to eliminate fluctuations in the feed line rate and to permit changes in the packaging line.

Operation

The accumulator in a flooded type refrigeration-evaporation type system is shown in Fig. A.3. Surges of liquid refrigerant passing through the coils are collected in the accumulator and recirculated. The liquid refrigerant is prevented from being drawn into the refrigeration compressor where damage could result. Refrigeration accumulators must be properly sized so that the accumulator will take care of any surge of liquid in the system.

The accumulator is often fitted directly with a refrigerant float valve to maintain a certain level of liquid in the system. Automatic control elements, such as pressure regulator and temperature regulator, are often attached to the accumulator.

The accumulator may be used on ice cream freezers or on room refrigeration systems or direct expansion type coolers.

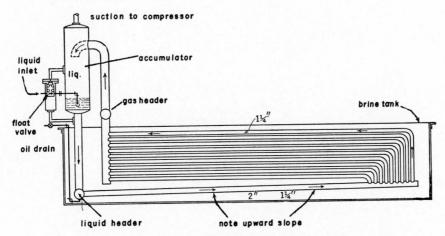

Fig. A-3.   Full flooded evaporating coil system with float control

Reference

FARRALL, A. W.   1963.   Engineering for Dairy and Food Products, 3rd Edition.   John Wiley & Sons, New York.

Cross-references: *Freezers, Ice Cream; Refrigeration, Principles, Flooded System; Surge Chamber.*

AERATION OR MECHANICAL COOLING

Aeration or mechanical cooling of grain must be distinguished from drying. For aeration much lower volumes of air of 0.1 cfm per bu or less are moved through the product for maintaining a uniform temperature. Damp grain may be cooled by (1) cleaning, removal of weed seeds, chaff, etc.; (2) turning, moving the grain from one bin to another; (3) natural ventilation, movement of air with wind pressure through the grain; or (4) by mechanical ventilation, using a fan with unheated air. Wheat with 20% moisture can be stored at 40° F without damage to its milling and baking qualities. Cold air can be moved through grain by mechanical means to reduce the temperature of high moisture grain and prevent spoilage. By using aeration safe storage can be provided for grain normally 1 to 2% above recommended moisture contents. An important use of cooling is to prevent the accumulation of moisture in certain layers because of moisture migration from warm to cold layers. About $^1/_2\%$ moisture is removed in cooling grain from 70° to 40° F. Undried grain can be held in cool weather with low airflow rates.

4. *Aeration or Mechanical Cooling*

Air Requirements

The quantity of air used for aeration is from $1/10$ to $1/60$ cfm per bu of grain. Recommended air flow rates are given in Table A.1. The static pressure encountered with these low air volumes in moving air through the grain is relatively low and it may be economical to move air through depths up to 150 ft. The static pressures of various products, based on different airflows for various depths, are presented in Table A.2. Most systems are designed for less than 15 in. (H_2O) static pressure.

TABLE A.1

AIRFLOW RATES USED FOR AERATION, CFM/BU[1]

	Southern States	Northern States
Farm storage	1/20 to 1/4	1/20 to 1/10[2]
Horizontal storage	1/20 to 1/4	1/20 to 1/10
Vertical storage	1/20 to 1/10	1/40 to 1/20

[1] Based on intermittent operation with suitable air conditions.
[2] For continuous operation, 1/60 to 1/30 cfm per bu.
Source: Hall (1957).

TABLE A.2

STATIC PRESSURES IN AERATION SYSTEMS* (NOT INCLUDING DUCT SYSTEM)

Airflow, Cfm/Bu	Depth of Storage, Ft	Static Pressure, in Water		
		Wheat	Shelled Corn	Rough Rice
1/10	50	4.0	1.5	2.65
	100	18.0	5.0	12.0
	150	42.0	12.0	27.7
1/20	50	2.0	0.5	1.25
	100	8.0	2.2	5.30
	150	19.5	5.25	12.5
1/30	50	1.4	0.32	0.90
	100	5.3	1.35	3.40
	150	12.0	3.30	7.95
1/40	50	1.0	0.23	0.65
	100	4.0	0.95	2.50
	150	9.0	2.25	5.93
1/50	50	0.80	0.20	0.50
	100	3.20	0.73	2.00
	150	6.60	1.50	4.65

* Some designers add 25 to 50% of the value to the above static pressures to account for fine material and packing.
Source: Hall (1957).

Horsepower

The horsepower requirements for a given airflow will depend on the quantity, depth, and kind of grain. Typical horsepower requirements are 1.5 hp for 35,000 to 40,000 bu flat storage for shelled corn, 1 hp for 20,000 bu flat storage, $1/2$ hp for 10,000 bu circular storage, and $1/8$ to $1/4$ hp for a 3,200 bu circular storage. A 60,000-bu silo

150 ft high, with 2,000 cfm, requires a 12-hp motor, and a 30,000-bu silo 60 ft high, with 3,000 cfm requires a 7.5-hp motor. For deep bins, the motor horsepower can be estimated by multiplying (0.0004) x (cfm) x (static pressure, inches of water) if the friction from ducts is not excessive.

Airflow

Usually the air is moved downward through the grain in aeration systems using a suction or exhaust system. Thus, the exhaust air which has been heated while passing through the grain is exhausted through warm grain thereby avoiding the possibility of condensation on the cold grain surface.

Equipment

The fan and the duct are much smaller for cooling than for drying a given quantity of grain. It is desirable to have a duct cross section of 1 sq ft for each 1,000 cfm of air flow (1,000 fpm velocity), although for short ducts of 25 ft or less, velocities up to 2,000 fpm are used. The minimum open surface area in square feet for a flat storage is cfm/20 and for an upright storage, cfm/50.

A very simple system for aeration of grain consists of installing a cylindrical duct vertically in the bin with the fan on the top of duct exhausting air from horizontal storages or vertical storages under 20 ft high. The length of the vertical duct can be changed according to the depth of the bin. An 8- or 12-in. diameter stove pipe can be used with a screen covered or perforated metal or slotted metal opening on the bottom half of the duct for air passage. Satisfactory operation can be obtained if the duct extends to the floor. Manufacturers use exhaust fans of either the centrifugal or the propeller type.

Horizontal ducts can be placed in the bottom of the grain bin and may be used with or without lateral or branch ducts. Branch ducts are necessary for shallow storages to obtain uniform air distribution. The ducts are usually made of 8- or 12-in. diameter perforated or slotted material. The duct systems used for drying can be used for cooling. A deep storage (over 20 ft) is usually cooled through 1 perforated pipe along the bottom of the bin. The fan can be moved from bin to bin or connected with air ducts and valves to direct the air to the appropriate bin. The temperature reduction is more rapid and more uniform by using the horizontal ducts as compared to the vertical ducts. The horizontal ducts can be adapted to any shape or size of bin (Fig. A.4).

Operation

The fan can be operated continuously with small flows of $1/20$ cfm per bu, or less when the air is at least 10°F cooler than the grain. Approximately 300 hr of fan operation are required to cool a deep bin of grain. It would be desirable to turn off the fan during periods of high humidity, rain, and heavy fog. A time or humidity control can be used to turn off the system during hours of high humidity. The labor required for manually controlling the operation of the fan usually does not justify the saving obtained in electricity. Humidity controls can also be used. Units which operate with $1/10$ to $1/20$ cfm per bu are often used for cooling the grain close to freezing and the fan moved to other bins for repeating the operation.

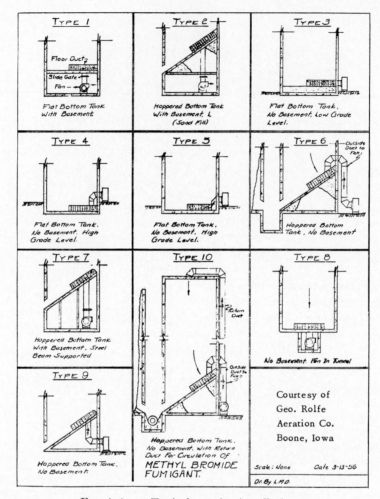

Fig. A-4.   Typical aeration installations

An aeration system is useful for fumigation.   The fumigant can be placed in the bin and recirculated for the recommended time.   The fumigant can then be flushed out.   If a vertical tube is used for fumigation, it is desirable that the tube extend to the floor to get complete and uniform distribution.

Reference

HALL, C. W.   1957.   Drying Farm Crops.   Edwards Brothers, Ann Arbor, Mich.

Cross-references: *Air Movement; Fans; Static Pressure.*

AGGLOMERATORS

Nationwide distribution of instantized nonfat dry milk was begun in 1954.   The response by retail customers was highly favorable and within a few years instantized nonfat dry milk replaced the regular spray-dried product on the retail market.

Purpose

The principal purpose of agglomeration, also called instantizing, is to improve the rate and completeness of the reconstitutability of dry products. This process affects wettability, sinkability, dispersibility, and solubility of the particles. However, total solubility is not improved by agglomeration.

Products

Instantizing has been successfully adapted to: dry milk, flours, starches, dry soups, cocoa products, dry puddings, sweetened flavored milk drinks, stabilizers, and other food products. Some of these products do not have adhesiveness when surface wetted, but are agglomerated by first blending with products that do, such as nonfat milk or sugar.

Systems

The major systems of agglomeration in the United States are the Peebles, Cherry-Burrell, Blaw-Knox, and Niro (Fig. A.5 A, B, C). The general features in common are: (1) wetting of surface of the particles with steam, atomized water, or a mixture of both, (2) agglomeration whereby the particles collide due to the turbulence and adhere to each other forming clusters, (3) redrying with hot air, and (4) cooling and sizing to eliminate the very large agglomerates and the very small particles.

In the *Peebles* process the nonfat dry milk pneumatically enters the agglomerating chamber. The particles are wetted to 10 to 15% moisture in the turbulent airstream zone and form agglomerates. These fall into the next zone or chamber which redries to approximately 4.0% by means of filtered air at 230° to 250°F. The product is cooled, sized with rollers, screened, and packaged. The fine particles are returned to be recycled through the agglomerating process.

The *A.R.C.S.* system of Cherry-Burrell consists of delivering dry milk at a uniform rate by air, screw, or vibrator to a horizontal tube. Wetting and agglomeration takes place in the moist rapidly moving air-product mixture which passes into a cyclone. Air returns from the top of the cyclone to recycle and the clusters drop into a filtered hot airstream at 270° to 300°F. The product is dried by this air while moving into the second cyclone. The air is exhausted from the top of the cyclone and the product clusters descend into a horizontal shaker through which cooling reduces the temperature from 160° to 180°F to about 100°F. The sifter removes the fine particles. The clusters pass through sizing rolls and are sifted and packaged. During wetting the moisture of nonfat dry milk increases to 6 to 8% and on redrying decreases to 3.5 to 4.5%.

In the *Blaw-Knox* Instantizer the dry milk is measured by a rotary-feed valve into a line and fed pneumatically into a small agglomerating tube. An alternative system uses a vibrating trough to control product entry into the agglomerating tube. Steam wets the particles to approximately 7% moisture as they fall between 2 jets. Ambient air entering through radial slots in the agglomerating tube maintains the turbulence necessary for the formation of aggregates. The agglomerated product drops onto a conveyor belt for conditioning and transport to vibrating redriers of the deck type. Two or more decks are common. There hot air dries the product to 4.0 to 4.5%. After the large agglomerates pass between sizing rolls the product is screened. Fine particles are reprocessed through the system.

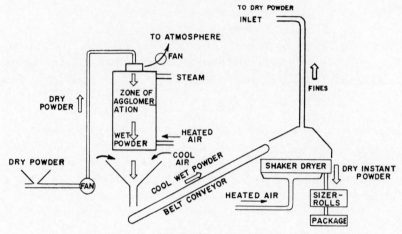

a.   The Peebles process.

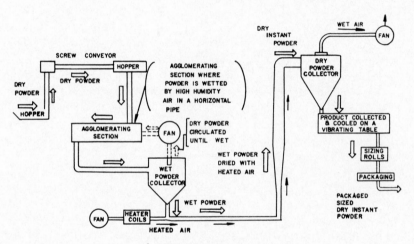

b. The ARCS systems.

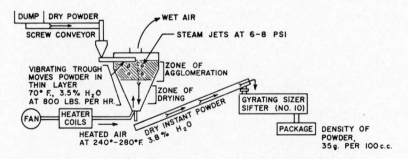

c.   The Blaw-Knox system.

Fig. A-5.   Processes for agglomerating dry milk

The *Niro* agglomerator is attached to the bottom of the vertical type drying chamber. Milk is dried to approximately 9% moisture in the drying chamber. A vibrator transports the product from the drier to the inlet of the Niro agglomerator. In the first section agglomeration takes place; in the second section, redrying with hot air occurs; and in the third, product is cooled to room temperature. Very fine mesh screens convey the product through the three sections. Air that passes up through the screens goes out the top of the agglomerator carrying the fine particles. These are returned to the drying chamber.

Factors Affecting Instantizing

Dry milk that is manufactured specifically for agglomeration usually gives the best results. Moisture content and particle size should be as uniform as possible. A minimum of fine particles with diameter less than 20μ is desired with the preferred particle range being 25 to 50μ. Nonfat dry milk for agglomeration should be low in fat content. Low-heat (6 mg or more of WPM) or medium-heat nonfat dry milk (less than 6 but more than 1.5 mg) is usually used.

The success of the instantizing operation depends upon adequate control of each step. The powder distribution into the wetting zone space must be uniform and at a constant rate. Moisture conditions must be uniform in all respects to avoid over- or underwetting of particles. Overwetted particles dissolve slowly and too little wetting permits excessive shattering during handling. The air movement has to be stabilized to assure optimum particle collision. Excessive movement causes product adherence to the equipment lining. Control of the *redrying* air temperature and its flow rate is necessary for adequate moisture removal without heat damage to the agglomerated product.

The fact that agglomeration lowers the density of dry milks is well-known. Usually flavor is not affected, but detrimental changes in flavor can occur as a result of agglomeration if the process is not carefully controlled.

Reference

HALL, C. W., and HEDRICK, T. I. 1966. Drying of Milk and Milk Products. AVI Publishing Co., Westport, Conn.

Cross-references: *Dry Milk, Properties; Spray Dryer.*

AGITATORS

Agitators of various types have many applications in the food industry. Mild agitation, as in a storage tank, or violent agitation, as in a high temperature heater or a freezer, may be used. Agitators are used for the food product, for air, and for fluids. The objective of agitation may be improved heat transfer, uniform heating or cooling, or preventing separation of various elements of the product being processed.

Types of Agitators

The simplest type is the propeller type agitator, Fig. A.6, which is usually driven at a relatively high speed, from 400 to 1200 rpm. Much agitation is secured with a small

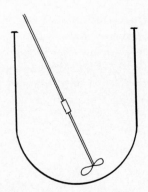

FIG. A-6.   High speed agitator for low viscosity fluids

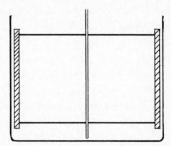

FIG. A-7.   Low speed agitator for high viscosity fluids

high-speed agitator which is used with fluids of low viscosity. A slow-speed type of agitator, which usually operates from 50 to 400 rpm, is used for liquids of high viscosity (Fig. A.7).   Agitators for high-viscosity fluids are usually of large cross section and may have paddles which operate in opposite directions, such as is usually found in the batch ice cream freezer.

Use of Agitator

A special type of agitator is the dasher or rotor in the small diameter coolers or heaters for viscous materials. This apparatus has a scraper for removing the product from the surface of the heat exchanger and also thoroughly agitates the product.

The agitation of viscous materials requires much energy which appears as heat, and in the case of the cooler, adds heat to the refrigeration load.

Most agitators are designed by the cut-and-try method since the many variables make it very difficult to design the agitator from formula except in unusual cases where the product has low viscosity. Overagitation not only wastes power but may injure the body and texture of the product being agitated. Agitation also may whip air into the product and cause undesirable results.

Air Agitation

Liquids of low viscosity such as fluid milk may be agitated by means of flowing clean sterile air into the product at the bottom.

The air must be sterile and procedures and equipment should meet 3-A specifications, if used for a food product. The air injector must be sanitary and easily cleaned. The air line must be fitted with a dependable sanitary check valve to prevent the product from getting into the air line. Special carbon ring compressors are available for air agitation units. Vapors from oil lubrication systems should be avoided in air agitation units. Figure A.8 shows the general principle of an air agitation system. The air must be applied with sufficient pressure to overcome the hydraulic pressure of the fluid in the tank being agitated.

Reference

U.S. Dept. Health, Education, Welfare. 1964. Milk and milk product equipment, a guide for evaluating sanitary construction.

Cross-reference: *Standards.*

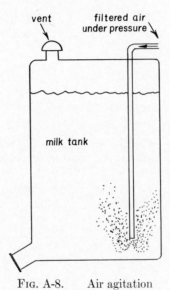

Fig. A-8. Air agitation

AIR

Air is a colorless, odorless gas consisting of a mixture of 78% nitrogen and 21% oxygen, plus several minor elements, and usually water vapor.

Air is important in processing plants as it relates to ventilation, agitation of product, pneumatic conveying, controls, as a means of energy supply through compressed air, for transfer of heat by cooling or heating, and as a supply of oxygen for aerobic processes. Air can be treated as a fluid for many applications. In many applications air, although a compressible fluid, can be considered as noncompressible.

Principles

Many calculations pertaining to air and other gases for a processing plant involve the effect of changes of pressure, volume, and temperature on the gas. Boyle's and Charles' Laws are combined in equation (1)

12.   *Air*

$$\frac{p_1V_1}{T_1} = \frac{p_2V_2}{T_2} = MR \tag{1}$$

where p = absolute pressure, psia, which is equal to the gage pressure plus 14.7, at atmospheric conditions

V = volume

T = absolute temperature, or temperature in $°F$ plus 460

M = molecular weight which is 29 for air

R = gas constant which is 53.3 for air

(See Table A.3 for R values for other gases.)

For isothermal conditions, that is, for constant temperature, $T_1 = T_2$ so

$$p_1V_1 = p_2V_2 \tag{2}$$

For adiabatic conditions, where there is no heat exchange

$$p_1V_1{}^k = p_2V_2{}^k \tag{3}$$

where $\qquad\qquad k = c_p/c_v$

which is approximately equal to 1.4 for air.

Density

The density of dry air at $70°F$ is 0.0729 lb per cu ft.   The density of saturated air per pound of dry air is slightly less.   Because air is compressible, as well as other gases, as the pressure increases the density increases in proportion to the absolute pressure ratio change.   To determine the density of gases at a pressure other than the stated pressure, multiply by the ratio of absolute pressure.   Assuming there is no change in pressure, the density will change inversely as the absolute temperature is changed. As air is heated through $1°F$, air will increase in volume by 1/492 of the original volume.

Other Properties

The specific heat of air for constant volume, c_v, is equal to 0.17 and for constant pressure, c_p, is equal to 0.24.

The value of k for adiabatic expansion is the ratio of c_p/c_v (Table A.3).

TABLE A.3
PROPERTIES OF GASES

	M Mol Wt	Density 68°F 1 Atm	R Gas Constant	C_p	(C_p/C_v)
Air	29.0	0.0753	53.3	0.241	1.4
Oxygen	32.0	0.0831	48.3	0.217	1.4
Natural Gas (avg)	19.46	0.0514			1.27
Nitrogen	28.0	0.07274	55.16	0.247	1.4
Hydrogen	2.0	0.00523	766.8	3.42	1.4
Steam	18.0		85.8	0.46	1.28
Carbon dioxide	44.0	0.1142	35.1	0.205	1.28
Sulfur dioxide	64.0	0.1663	24.13	0.154	1.25
Ammonia	17.0	0.0442	90.77	0.523	1.29
Ethylene	28.0	0.07280	55.11	0.40	1.22

Air is very seldom dry and therefore must be considered as a mixture containing water vapor. For the physical and thermal properties of air with moisture, see the section on humidity and psychrometric chart.

The critical temperature is that temperature above which a gas cannot be liquified. For air, the critical temperature is $-140°C$ (39 atm pressure), and for oxygen, is $-118°C$ (50 atm pressure).

The temperature rise with different heat inputs with different airflows is shown in Fig. A.9.

It is often necessary to measure the flow of air. The airflow is often determined indirectly by measuring the average velocity, and multiplying by the cross-sectional area to get the quantity of airflow. A pitot tube can be used (see static pressure); anemometers or orifices can be calibrated and used for determining airflow (Fig. A.10).

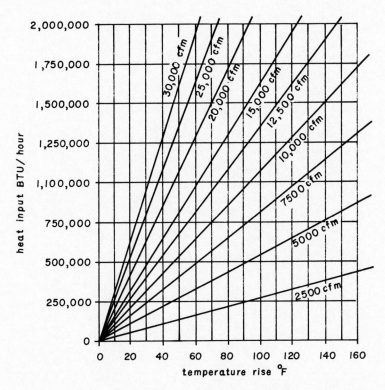

FIG. A-9. Temperature rise with different airflows and heat inputs

Piping Systems

Piping systems must be selected so as to minimize losses of pressure from the flowing fluid. In general, the size of piping must be calculated on the basis of the economics of cost of piping versus the cost of pumping the fluid. The loss of air pressure due to friction for an initial pressure of 100 psia is presented in Table A.4. In general, for the same quantity of free airflow, the loss of air pressure due to friction decreases as the initial pressure is increased. The pressure loss due to fittings and valves must also be considered. These losses are usually expressed in terms of equiva-

TABLE A.4

LOSS OF AIR PRESSURE DUE TO FRICTION, PSI IN 1,000 FT OF PIPE, AT 100 PSIG INITIAL PRESSURE

Cu Ft of Free Air per Min	Equivalent Cu Ft of Compression Air per Min	Nominal Pipe Diameter, In.										
		$\frac{1}{2}$	1	$1\frac{1}{2}$	2	3	4	5	6	8	10	12
10	1.28	6.50	0.28									
20	2.56	25.9	1.11	0.11								
30	3.84	58.5	2.51	0.26								
50	6.41		6.96	0.71	0.19							
80	10.24		17.8	1.83	0.49							
100	12.81		27.9	2.86	0.77							
200	25.62			11.4	3.06	0.37						
500	63.28			71.6	19.2	2.34	0.55					
1,000	126.6				76.9	9.3	2.21					
2,000	256.2					37.4	8.8	2.72	0.99	0.24		
3,000	384.6					84.1	20.0	6.0	2.26	0.53		
5,000	632.8						55.6	16.8	6.3	1.47	0.44	0.17
7,000	896.0							32.8	12.2	2.88	0.87	0.33
10,000	1,280							67.1	25.1	5.88	1.77	0.69
15,000	1,923								56.6	13.2	3.97	1.53
20,000	2,560									23.6	7.0	2.74
30,000	3,850									53.0	15.9	6.17

In general, for the same quantity of free air, loss of air pressure due to friction decreases as initial pressure is increased.
Source: Abbreviated from *Compressed Air Handbook*, Compressed Air and Gas Institute, New York (1947).

lent length of straight pipe (Table A.5). For pressure drops of air flowing under atmospheric conditions, see the section on ventilation.

The effect of altitude on air pressure and density of air must be considered for many operations. At sea level, the standard pressure is 29.92 in. Hg; at 2,000 ft, 27.82; at 4,000 ft, 25.84; at 6,000 ft, 23.98; at 8,000 ft, 22.22; and at 10,000 ft, 20.58 in. Hg.

References

COMPRESSED AIR AND GAS INSTITUTE. 1947. Compressed Air Handbook. New York.
CROCKER, S. 1946. Piping Handbook. McGraw-Hill Book Co., New York.

Cross-references: *Fluid Flow; Friction; Steam; Piping; Static Pressure; Air; Ventilation; Water Supplies.*

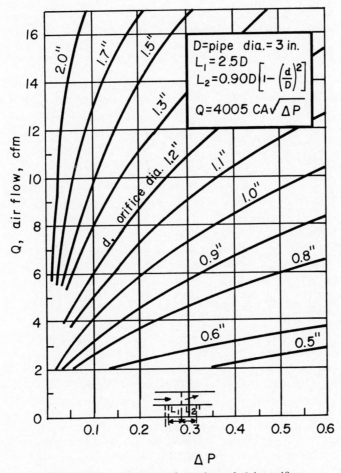

FIG. A-10.   Pressure drop through 3-in. orifice

AIR COMPRESSORS

Air compressors are widely used in the food industry for supplying air for many different purposes. Air under pressure is used for operating temperature control and

TABLE A.5

LOSS OF PRESSURE OF AIR, STEAM, AND GAS THROUGH SCREW PIPE FITTINGS, IN TERMS OF
EQUIVALENT LENGTHS OF STRAIGHT PIPE (SCHEDULE 40)

Nominal Pipe Size, In.	Gate Valve	Long Radius Ell	Standard Ell	Angle Valve	Close Return Bend	Tee Through Side Outlet	Globe Valve
$^1/_2$	0.36	0.62	1.55	8.65	3.47	3.10	17.3
1	0.61	1.05	2.62	14.6	5.82	5.24	29.1
$1^1/_2$	0.94	1.61	4.02	22.4	8.95	8.04	44.7
2	1.21	2.07	5.17	28.7	11.5	10.3	57.4
3	1.79	3.07	6.16	42.6	17.1	15.3	85.2
4	2.35	4.03	7.67	56.0	22.4	20.2	112
5	2.94	5.05	10.1	70.0	28.0	25.2	140
6	3.54	6.07	15.2	84.1	33.8	30.4	168
8	4.65	7.98	20.0	111.0	44.6	40.0	222
10	5.85	10.0	25.0	139.0	55.7	50.0	278
12	6.96	11.0	29.8	166.0	66.3	59.6	332

Source: Crocker (1946).

pressure control instruments.   Air is used for agitating materials, such as water in ice making and milk in milk plants.   Air is used for the operation of air-operated lifts.

Desirable features of compressed air operation is its flexibility, safety, and relatively low cost.   Air lends itself to throttling type controls.

Types of Compressors

Air compressors in the simple form are a single cylinder piston type pump with rings similar to those in a gasoline engine.   For higher pressures, piston-type pumps with multiple stages are more efficient.   It is customary to use multistage compressors for pressures above 50 psig.   Carbon rings are used for oil free air.

Rotary, lobe, or vane-type pumps are widely used for moderate pressures of up to 25 or 50 psi (Fig. A.11).   For extremely large airflow the multistage centrifugal compressor is favored.   Compressors can also be used for developing a vacuum.

Thermal Efficiency

The thermal efficiency of air compressors varies greatly with the type of pump and the pressure of operation.

The efficiency of high pressure compressors is greatly increased by the use of an intercooler (Fig. A.12) which cools the air between the stages.

Utilization

In most air pressure systems the collection of moisture could present a problem. This problem can be eliminated through the use of suitable moisture traps placed at strategic intervals in the line and immediately before air operated instruments.   Another problem is the accumulation of sediment and rust particles.   These materials are best eliminated through the use of a trap and filter ahead of instruments.

Pressure modulating valves are an important part of many compressed air systems.   These are usually of the diaphragm or piston type.   Small and moderate sized

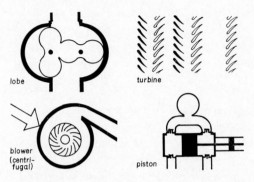

FIG. A-11.   Types of air compressors

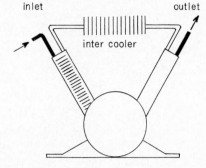

FIG. A-12.   Intercooler on compressor

valves are usually of the diaphragm type.   In this type of valve, a diaphragm whose movement is controlled by the low pressure side of the system is used to operate a modulating valve which feeds air into the system and maintains a predetermined temperature.

All air compressors should be fitted with a good air filter which will keep out particles of dust and foreign matter.   Also, the intake should be at a location where the air is free or reasonably free from dust, moisture, and contaminating vapors.

Maintenance

With a piston type compressor, the principal care is in maintaining clean and effective lubrication, keeping the pressure relief valve in proper operating order, removing water from the lubrication system, and in utilizing the oil recommended.

With lobe-type compressors, the principal care is in maintaining good lubrication with the correct lubricant and preventing foreign matter from getting into the pump.

With the centrifugal compressor, lubrication is important, particularly due to the high speed of centrifugal compressors.   Also, it is important to keep dust and foreign material out of the compressor through the proper use of air filters as excessive dust may cause buildup on the impellers of the compressor rotor.

References

NATIONAL SAFETY COUNCIL. 1967.   Cleaning air compressors and air receivers, Data Sheet *379*. Chicago, Ill.

CLEANING AIR COMPRESSORS AND AIR RECEIVERS. 1967.   Data Sheet *379*, National Safety Council, Chicago, Ill.

COMPRESSED AIR AND GAS INSTITUTE.   Various Bulletins.   Cleveland, Ohio.

Cross-references: *Air; Air Agitation; Static Pressure, Air.*

AIR CURTAINS

Considerable use has been made of air curtains in recent years to reduce refrigerated air losses from cold rooms and in the control of passage of insects at doorways. Essentially, there are two different types of fans for producing an air curtain.   Some are direct motor-driven propeller fans equipped with deflectors to direct the airstream.

The more recent models are somewhat more elaborate and incorporate the use of blowers encased in a cabinet which is equipped with carefully designed nozzles.   Depending upon the application, various air patterns are possible by adjusting the air velocity and characteristics of the fan discharge.

Insect Protection

Higher quantities and velocities are employed in producing air curtains for insect control.   The blower unit is mounted on the outside of the room or building above the doorway.   Some of the units are equipped with an automatic starting and stopping device to operate only when the regular door is open.   The pattern of the airstream and maximum velocities developed by one commercially available unit is illustrated in Fig. A.13.

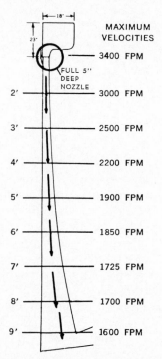

Fɪɢ. A-13.   Pattern of air stream and velocities for commercial air curtain

The velocity is gradually reduced as the distance from the fan nozzle is increased. Table A.6 illustrates the performance characteristics of various sizes of blower units used for insect control.

Customer Entrances

The velocity of air curtains for customer entrances for stores or other business establishments is much lower than that used for insect control.   At least 1 company designs the blower unit to produce a velocity of 650 fpm, 3 ft above the floor at a 6 ft 8 in. opening.   The air screen for this type of entrance is usually about 16 in. thick and completely blankets open doorways.   The continuously moving mass of air is pro-

TABLE A.6

PERFORMANCE OF VARIOUS SIZES OF BLOWER UNITS FOR INSECT CONTROL

Model	Width, In.	Motors, Hp	Run, Amps	Air Discharge Nozzle Area, Sq In.	Cfm at Nozzle	Cfm[1] Including Induced Air	Velocity	Shipping Weight Lb
H2016	20	One 1/3	6.0	100	2,640	4,200	Meets USDA to 12 high	60
H4016	40	Two 1/3	12.0	200	4,940	7,200	Meets USDA to 12 high	115
H6016	60	Three 1/3	17.4	300	7,600	13,500	Meets USDA to 12 high	160
H7216	72	Three 1/3	17.4	360	7,700	16,675	Meets USDA to 10 high	180

All models are available with 230v 1 phase or 230/460v 3 phase motors.
[1] Readings taken 5 ft from nozzle.

pelled downward, which also assists in insect control. Various patterns are illustrated in Fig. A.14.

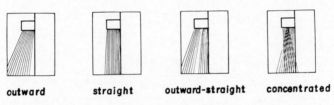

outward   straight   outward-straight   concentrated

FIG. A-14.   Patterns of air curtains for store entrances

Temperature Control

The refrigeration loss through an open door of a 38°F room was approximately 60,000 Btu per hr. when no circulating fan was used. With a small circulating fan operating in the room the loss was increased to about 72,000 Btu per hr. Conveyor passes located 30 in. above the floor resulted in a loss of approximately 9,000 Btu per hr. A conveyor pass 10 in. above the floor permitted a loss of about 12,000 Btu per hr. When the airstream discharged from a refrigeration blower unit was directed downward across the 36 in. doorway, the loss of refrigerated air was reduced to 12,000 Btu per hr., or about 20% of that experienced when no fan was in operation. The following sketch shows the principle of the directed airflow system used in the experiments by Williams and co-workers at Michigan State University.

Some design and operating characteristics of four sizes of a commercial unit are shown in Table A.7 and Fig. A.15. The unit is placed on the warm side of the cold room door and discharges air downward. The velocity is adjustable to accommodate openings up to 12 ft high. Careful consideration should be given to utilization and operation of air curtains which can play an important role in the operation of a food plant.

The U-value of an air curtain about 6 in. wide, at a velocity of 190–700 fpm is about 10–15.

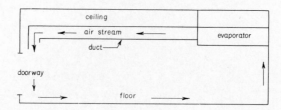

FIG. A-15.   Principle of directed airflow used in the experimental cooler

TABLE A.7

OPERATING CHARACTERISTICS OF FOUR COMMERCIAL AIR CURTAIN UNITS

Model	Width, In.	Motors, Hp	Run, Amp	Air Discharge Nozzle Area, Sq. In.	Cfm at Nozzle	Cfm[1] Including Induced Air	Velocity	Shipping Weight, Lb.
R1814	18	One ¹/₄	4.0	54	1,200	2,000	Adjustable	50
R3614	36	Two ¹/₄	8.0	108	2,500	4,200	Adjustable	90
R6014	60	Three ¹/₄	12.0	180	3,900	6,500	Adjustable	140
R7214	72	Three ¹/₄	12.0	216	4,200	7,200	Adjustable	160

All models are available with 230v 1 phase or 230/460v 3 phase motors.
[1] Readings taken 3 ft from nozzle.

References

FARRALL, A. W. 1963. Engineering for Dairy and Food Products, 3rd Edition. John Wiley & Sons, New York.

WILLIAMS, R., HEDRICK, T. I., and HALL, C. W. 1962. Directed air flow. Am. Milk Rev. *24*, No. 4, 25–26.

Cross-references: *Air; Air Filters; Air Movement.*

AIR FILTERS

The distribution of particle size in air and the manner in which the distribution is expressed may have a significant influence on the response expected from a filter. Filter efficiencies are normally determined by some standard method. The National Bureau of Standards (NBS) method measures discoloration of filter paper by various types of dust used to challenge the filter. Standard dust, fly ash, or atmospheric dusts are types normally used. The ASHRAE and AFI methods measure efficiency based on the weight of dust which passes through a test filter. The dioctyl-phthalate (DOP) test measures the concentration of 0.3μ particles passing through a test filter by light scattering in a smoke penetrometer.

None of the standard testing methods for filter efficiency measure actual numbers which may pass through a filter. The NBS and DOP methods measure surface area or stain, whereas the ASHRAE or AFI methods measure efficiency on a weight basis. The DOP test can be interpreted in terms of numbers since the aerosol particle size is constant 0.3μ; however, the method is used primarily on high and ultrahigh efficiency filters.

Selection

There are at least five basic factors which must be considered when selecting a filter for any application: (1) requirements for air cleanliness, (2) characteristics of the airborne particles, (3) concentrations of particles in the air, (4) volume of air to be cleaned, and (5) costs of installation, operation, and maintenance.

In dry food plant operations, the degree of air cleanliness may be somewhat difficult to establish without consideration of operation requirements. Air filters are available which will remove essentially all (99.97%) 0.3μ particles; however, the initial cost and operation at cost may not be justified. The concentration of airborne particles becomes important in using filters. High concentrations tend to load air filters rapidly resulting in high maintenance costs. This can be overcome by using the proper types and numbers of filters in sequence. The concentration of particles in air also influences the quality of filtered air. Since filters will remove a percentage of particles, higher concentrations in air entering the filter will result in higher concentrations in the filtered air. The latter situation is not of particular consequence when considering undesirable airborne bacteria. Airborne bacterial concentrations in most food plants are not high and the probability of a high concentration passing through an efficient filter is low. Most problems related to the volume of air to be filtered can be overcome by proper design of the selected filter.

Classification

Filters may be classified into 4 categories: (1) roughing filters, (2) medium efficiency or performance filters, (3) high efficiency or high performance filters, and (4) ultrahigh efficiency or absolute filters.

Roughing.—Roughing filters are the common type of air filter found in home air conditioners and furnaces. Roughing filters may be made of viscous coated fibers of metal, hair, or glass wool; or may be the dry type composed of loosely packed glass, cotton, or similar fibers. In general, the primary purpose of the roughing filter is to remove relatively large particles from the air. These filters will not have high efficiencies for small particles, such as airborne microorganisms.

Medium.—The medium efficiency of performance filter provides an improved efficiency for small particles by using compressed glass fibers, high quality paper fibers, and pleating of the media to maintain low media velocities at high flow rates. This type of filter is used to remove large particles and provide relatively clean air, but may be used as a prefilter for higher efficiency filter in some applications.

High Efficiency.—High efficiency or high performance filters will usually have efficiencies greater than 90%. The increased efficiency over the roughing and medium performance filters is attained by using smaller diameter fibers, decreasing porosity, and increasing the media pleating to maintain low media velocity.

Ultrahigh or Absolute.—The ultrahigh efficiency or absolute type filter will provide maximum removal of airborne particles. All filters in this category will have an efficiency of at least 99.9% or 0.3μ particles. Absolute filters are constructed of cellulose-asbestos fiber paper, glass and glass-asbestos fiber paper, and other similar materials. Although efficiencies of removal are high, prefilters must be used to prevent excessive loading of the ultrahigh efficiency filter.

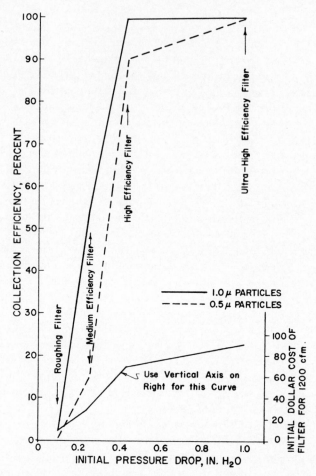

Fig. A-16.   Influence of filter efficiency on filter pressure drop

Operation

The increase in filter pressure drop encountered to attain higher filter efficiencies is illustrated in Fig. A.16.   The pressure drop values represent the response at the time of installation and the pressure drop of filters increases during use.

The important influence of particle size is also illustrated in Fig. A.16.   Roughing filters have a very low efficiency for 0.5 and 1μ particles, but their efficiency increases to over 98% for 10μ particles.   The influence of particle size is very pronounced when considering the medium efficiency filter, which has only 15% efficiency for 0.5μ particles and 58% efficiency for 1μ particles.   The efficiency of high efficiency filters is influenced significantly when considering particle sizes less than 1μ.   Removal efficiencies of greater than 90% cannot be expected without using a high efficiency or performance air filter.   This efficiency can be attained at an initial pressure drop of just over 0.4-in. water.   In order to receive the benefits of the ultrahigh efficiency filter, pressure drops in excess of 1-in. water are encountered.

A somewhat better basis for evaluation may be attained by consideration of initial filter costs and horsepower requirements presented in Fig. A.16 and Table A.8.

TABLE A.8
CHARACTERISTICS OF AIR FILTERS TO HANDLE 1,200 CFM

Filter Type	Initial Pressure Drop, In. H_2O	Approximate Operating Pressure Drop, In. H_2O	Approximate Horsepower of Fan Motor	Approximate Initial Cost of Filter, $
Roughing	0.09	0.4	0.15	10
Medium efficiency	0.25	0.6	0.23	30
High efficiency	0.43	0.75	0.3	70
Ultrahigh efficiency	0.94	1.5	0.56	90

This information will apply only to a filter handling 1,200 cfm of air. The initial costs are for the filter only and do not include installation. The horsepower calculation is based on an approximate operating pressure drop, which is a value between the initial pressure drop and the pressure drop at which the filter is replaced.

Other Air Treatment Methods

Viable particles may be removed from or inactivated in air by several other methods in addition to fibrous filters including: (1) air washing and scrubbing, (2) electrostatic precipitation, (3) air incineration, and (4) ultraviolet air sterilizers. In general, all of the above devices have efficiencies similar to the medium efficiency fibrous filters, and are not recommended to replace either high or ultrahigh efficiency filters. These methods will not maintain high efficiency levels under most field conditions.

Reference

HELDMAN, D. R., HALL, C. W., and HEDRICK, T. I. 1967. Air Filtration. Presented Am. Dry Milk Inst. Meeting, Chicago, Ill. Also J. Dairy Sci. *51*, 466–470, 1968.

Cross-references: *Air; Air Curtains.*

AIR MOVEMENT

The principles involved in the flow of air through a product for drying are the same for natural ventilation, forced ventilation, and heated-air drying. Basically, a drying system consists of a means of moving the air through the product, the wind for natural ventilation or a fan for mechanical ventilation, and ducts to distribute the air from the fan to the product. The main duct or manifold is the part of the system which distributes air or collects air from two or more smaller (lateral) ducts or perforated or slatted floor. In some cases, the floor acts as the main duct for distributing air to the product. The relationships among the volume of air moved through the product, the static pressure developed, and the depth of product over the air distribution system are important.

Terminology

The following terms are commonly used in air movement and drying.
Static Pressure (ΔP).—The resistance to flow of air through a product measured

in inches of water. The static pressure is negative for a drying system in which the fan is exhausting air.

cfm (*Q*).—The quantity of airflow in cubic feet per minute. The volume of air-flow is usually related to a specific volume of product in bin or cross-sectional area through which the air passes, as cfm per bu, cfm per cu ft, cfm per ton, or cfm per sq ft. A bushel is 1.25 cu ft of small grain or 2.5 cu ft of ear corn.

Forced Air Drying.—Natural air forced through grain or hay by a fan for drying products.

Heated Air or Heated Forced Air Drying.—Air to which heat is added prior to being forced through the product by a fan.

Reference

HALL, C. W. 1957. Drying Farm Crops. Edwards Brothers, Ann Arbor, Mich.

Cross-references: *Air; Fans; Static Pressure; Aeration or Mechanical Cooling.*

AIR-OPERATED CONTROLS

An air-operated control is designed to regulate the airflow to a control device which is usually a control valve regulating the flow of air, steam, product, or other controllable variable. In most food plants, air-operated controls are used for controlling temperature, pressure, and product flow.

System

An air-operated type of controller is an integral component of a control system which includes an air-operated regulating valve. The basic principles apply whether the sensing element measures pressure, temperature flow, or some other controllable variable. The air-operated controller is more sensitive than a self-acting type. The air-operated controller is usually required to operate a relay valve only in the air system which requires very little power. The air supplied by an air compressor does the work of opening or closing the regulating valve. The reduced air pressure from the controller is conveyed through tubing to the valve diaphragm.

One significant feature of an air-operated controller is its adjustable sensitivity. The sensitivity may be changed to suit the requirements of the apparatus on which it is used. The sensitivity is reflected in the distance which the control valve moves for a given change subjected on the sensing element. Principal elements of an air-operated control system are (1) the temperature controller in the case of a temperature regulated system, and (2) the diaphragm-control valve which moves in response to air pressure changes, thereby, controlling the temperature of the heating or cooling medium to the given equipment.

Sensitivity

The proper sensitivity of a controller is very important for satisfactory operation. With too high a sensitivity, the controller corrective action will be excessive and "hunting" will result. In practice, the sensitivity should be about $1/2$ of that setting which causes the controller to oscillate in a steady, rhythmical fashion. An adjustable sensitivity controller is set for applications where the magnitude of process changes is small or where deviations by the process control point and the set point are acceptable. One of the limitations of an adjustable sensitivity controller is that the control pen will always deviate from the set pointer which changes in process loads. The magnitude

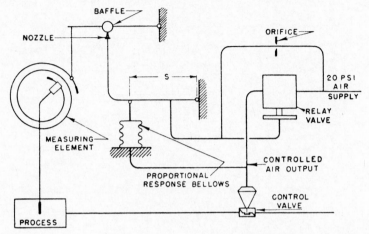

Courtesy of Milk Industry Foundation

Fig. A-17. Schematic layout of a proportional response controller

of the deviation depends on the extent of the load change and the sensitivity setting. Large load changes result in great offset. Smaller sensitivity settings for a given change in load produce a greater offset. Figure A.17 shows schematically the layout of the main components of a controller.

Reset

In more expensive air-operated controls offset is eliminated by the addition of an automatic reset system in the controller. In processes such as those experienced by the high-temperature, short-time (HTST) pasteurizer where load changes are great, the reset feature is a necessity. The automatic reset responds through a series of bellows to establish equilibrium conditions, wherein, the controller will maintain the control on the process with very small deviations. In specialized controllers designed for specific functions, the automatic reset mechanism is fixed rather than adjustable. Instead of utilizing an adjustable reset needle, a capillary interconnecting tubing between the bellows is used. Hence, the reset rate is not adjustable in the field. Illustrated in Fig. A.18 is the schematic layout of components of a controller having the automatic reset feature.

Maintenance and Use

Air-operated controllers should be protected against dust, and operated on a clean air supply with the filters blown out daily. Periodically, the air-relay valve should be cleaned according to the manufacturers instructions. If parts are washed in carbon tetrachloride, rubber gloves should be worn. The pins or pivots of the levers in the controllers should not be oiled. The manufacturer's instructions should be followed in resynchronizing the set pointer or recording pin.

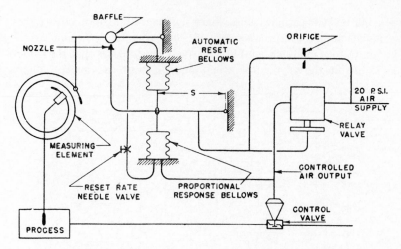

FIG. A-18. Schematic layout of a proportional response controller with automatic reset

Some causes of ineffective performance are (1) insufficient or widely fluctuating system air pressure, 20 to 25 psi should normally be supplied; (2) insufficient supply of heating or cooling media in systems where temperature is being controlled; (3) leaking bypass valves or air line leaks; (4) a clogged nozzle in the control, and (5) malfunctioning of the temperature-sensitive unit. In this latter case, repair of the controller by the manufacturer is indicated.

Air-operated controllers have been proved to be reliable for controlling many processes in food plants. Utilizing a clean air supply, the control system functions very satisfactorily under normal operating conditions. In a plant where humidity is high, air-operated control systems are among the most dependable of any known at the present time.

Reference

MILK INDUSTRY FOUNDATION. 1967. Manual for Milk Plant Operators, 3rd Edition. Washington, D.C.

Cross-references: *Air; HTST Pasteurization.*

ALLOYS FOR PROCESSING

Alloys are a physical mixture of two or more metals which are combined to form a new metallic material which has specific properties. The food industry uses alloys in the construction of most processing equipment. In addition to the basic metal needs, the industry finds it advantageous to use special alloys which are resistant to corrosion and have the minimum or in most cases no deleterious effect on the flavor of products which come in contact with them.

TABLE A.9

APPROXIMATE COMPOSITION OF METALS USED IN FOOD EQUIPMENT

Name of Metal	Percentage Composition										
	Copper	Nickel	Zinc	Tin	Lead	Iron	Chromium	Silicon	Manganese	Carbon	Mo
Copper	100	—	—	—	—	—	—	—	—	—	—
Nickel silver (German silver)	72	18	10	—	—	—	—	—	—	—	—
Monel metal	28	67	—	—	—	+	—	—	+	—	—
Ambrac	75	20	5	—	—	—	—	—	—	—	—
Bronze	85	—	2	9	4	—	—	—	—	—	—
Waukesha metal	55	—	28	+	—	+	—	—	+	—	—
Nickel bronze	65	20	5	5	5	—	—	—	—	—	—
Nickel	—	99	—	—	—	—	—	—	—	—	—
Solder	—	—	—	50	50	—	—	—	—	—	—
Stainless 302	—	8–10	—	—	—	71.10	17–19	1.00	2.00	0.15	0
Stainless 304	—	8–12	—	—	—	71.17	18–20	1.00	2.00	0.08	0
Stainless 316	—	10–14	—	—	—	68.17	16–18	1.00	2.00	0.08	2.00
Stainless 416	—	0	—	—	—	84.25	12–14	1.00	1.25	0.15	0.60
Stainless 440	—	0	—	—	—	79.95	16–18	1.00	1.00	0.60	0.75

Source: *Dairy Engineering.*

Types

There are two general types of alloys which are of most significance. The first is a so-called white metal of an approximate composition of copper, 66%; nickel, 20%; tin, 3%; lead, 4%; and zinc, 4%; and iron, 2.5%. This combination gives an excellent appearance, does not tarnish, and has very little effect on the flavor of food products, at temperatures up to 160°F.

The other and most important group of alloys are the stainless steels which are a mixture of chromium, nickel, and iron with usually a trace of some other elements added to give specific qualities.

Data

Table A.9 shows the characteristics and composition of a group of metals other than stainless steels which are used in the food industry. These materials are used in places where it is difficult to use stainless steel or where the expense of stainless steel makes its use prohibitive. Certain types of castings or special forms are very expensive if made of stainless steel.

The white metal is seldom used in sheets but is used for pipe fittings and special castings. This material is reasonably soft and can be readily machined and polished. It does not rust or corrode under normal conditions.

Stainless steels are manufactured for a wide variety of uses and with considerably varying specifications, to fit the particular use. However, those used in the food industry are generally of either the standard nonhardenable type or the hardening and tempering type.

Table A.10 shows the principal characteristics of types of 302, 304, 316, 416, and 440 types of stainless steel.

TABLE A.10

COMPOSITION OF STAINLESS STEEL

Chemical Composition, %									
C	Mn	P	S	Si	Cr	Ni	Mo	Se	

Type No. 302[1]

| 0.15 | 2.00 | 0.045 | 0.030 | 1.00 | 17.00 | 8.00 | | | |
| max. | max. | max. | max. | max. | 19.00 | 10.00 | | | |

Type No. 304[2]

| 0.08 | 2.00 | 0.045 | 0.030 | 1.00 | 18.00 | 8.00 | | | |
| max. | max. | max. | max. | max. | 20.00 | 12.00 | | | |

Type No. 316[3]

| 0.08 | 2.00 | 0.045 | 0.030 | 1.00 | 16.00 | 10.00 | 2.00 | | |
| max. | max. | max. | max. | max. | 18.00 | 14.00 | 3.00 | | |

Type No. 416[4]

| 0.15 | 1.25 | 0.060 | 0.15 | 1.00 | 12.00 | — | 0.60[5] | | |
| max. | max. | max. | max. | max. | 14.00 | | max. | | |

Type No. 416 Se[5]

| 0.15 | 1.25 | 0.060 | 0.060 | 1.0 | 12.00 | — | — | 0.15 | |
| max. | max. | max. | max. | max. | 14.00 | | | min. | |

Type No. 440[6]

| 0.60 | 1.00 | 0.040 | 0.030 | 1.00 | 16.00 | — | 0.75 | — | |
| 0.75 | max. | max. | max. | max. | 18.00 | — | max. | | |

[1] Type 302 is the general purpose austenitic chromium nickel stainless steel. Its corrosion resistance is superior to that of Type 301. Type 302 is the most widely used of the chromium nickel stainless and heat resisting steels. It is used largely in the annealed condition. It can be cold-worked to high tensile strengths but with slightly lower ductility than Type 301.

Type 302 is nonmagnetic when annealed, but is slightly magnetic when cold-worked.

[2] Type 304 is a low carbon austenitic chromium nickel stainless and heat resisting steel somewhat superior to Type 302 in corrosion resistance.

Type 304 is nonmagnetic when annealed, but is slightly magnetic when cold-worked.

[3] Type 316 is an austenitic chromium nickel stainless and heat resisting steel with *superior* corrosion resistance to other chromium nickel steels when exposed to many types of chemical corrodents, as well as marine atmospheres. It also has superior creep strength at elevated temperatures.

Type 316 is nonmagnetic when annealed, but is slightly magnetic when cold-worked.

[4] Types 416 and 416 Se are corrosion resisting chromium steels to which elements have been added to improve the machining and nonseizing characteristics. They are the most readily machinable of all the stainless steels and are suitable for use in automatic screw machines.

Both types are magnetic in all conditions.

[5] Optional.

[6] Type 440A is a hardenable chromium steel with greater hardness than Type 420 and with greater toughness than Types 440B and 440C.

Type 440A is magnetic in all conditions.

Source: American Iron and Steel Institute.

TABLE A.11
FINISH OF STAINLESS STEEL SHEETS

Unpolished Finishes

No. 1 Finish. Hot-rolled, annealed and descaled. Produced on hand sheet mills by hot rolling followed by annealing and descaling.

Generally used in industrial applications, such as for heat or corrosion resistance, where smoothness of finish is not of particular importance.

No. 2D Finish. A dull cold-rolled finish produced on either hand sheet mills or continuous mills by cold rolling, annealing, and descaling. The dull finish may result from the descaling or pickling operation or may be developed by a final light cold roll pass on dull rolls. The dull finish is favorable for the retention of lubricants on the surface in deep drawing operations.

This finish is generally used in forming deep drawn articles which may be polished after fabrication.

No. 2B Finish. A bright cold rolled finish commonly produced the same as No. 2D, except that the annealed and descaled sheet receives a final light cold-rolled pass on polished rolls.

This is a general purpose cold-rolled finish. It is commonly used for all but exceptionally difficult deep drawing applications.

This finish is more readily polished than No. 1 or No. 2D Finish.

Polished Finishes

No. 3 Finish is a polished finish obtained with abrasives approximately 100 mesh, and which may or may not be additionally polished during fabrication.

No. 4 Finish is a general purpose polished finish widely used for restaurant equipment, kitchen equipment, store fronts, dairy equipment, etc. Following initial grinding with coarser abrasives, sheets are generally finished last with abrasives approximately 120 to 150 mesh.

No. 6 Finish is a dull satin finish having lower reflectivity than No. 4 Finish. It is produced by Tampico brushing No. 4 Finish sheets in a medium of abrasive and oil.

It is used for architectural applications and ornamentation where a high luster is undesirable; it is also used effectively to contrast with brighter finishes.

No. 7 Finish has a high degree of reflectivity. It is produced by buffing of finely ground surface, but the "grit" lines are not removed. It is chiefly used for architectural and ornamental purposes.

No. 8 Finish is the most reflective finish that is commonly produced. It is obtained by polishing with successively finer abrasives and buffing extensively with very fine buffing rouges. The surface is essentially free of grit lines from preliminary grinding operations.

This finish is most widely used for press plates, as well as for small mirrors and reflectors.

Sheets can be produced with one or two sides polished. When polished on one side only, the other side may be rough ground in order to obtain the necessary flatness.

Source: American Iron and Steel Institute.

The stainless steel most commonly used in contact with food products is type 304, although type 302 is also quite widely used because of its good corrosion resistance and adaptability to deep drawing operations.

The type 440 hardenable type stainless steel alloy is a 17% chromium, 1% carbon alloy which is quite widely used for plungers on pumps and pump gears which must be very hard.

Finishes

Stainless steel sheets are obtainable in a number of finishes, in accordance with Table A.11.

For general purpose use in tank liners and for exterior purposes, a No. 4 finish is most widely used. The No. 7, which is a mirror finish, is recommended by some health departments but in most instances is not considered as worth the extra cost.   Experience indicates that the No. 7 finish is more difficult to keep looking good than the No. 4 finish due to its susceptibility to water spotting.

Under conditions of severe corrosion the type 316 or 316L stainless steel is recommended over the 302 or 304.

The basic type 302 which is the least costly of any of the mentioned types is recommended where appearance only is desired and the product does not come in contact with the food material.

A very important aspect of stainless steel is its susceptibility to welding, drawing, and finishing.   There are modifications of the basic type mentioned which will give improved results under certain conditions and these should be clarified with the stainless steel supplier.

Corrosion Resistance

Stainless steel is resistant to corrosion if properly handled.   It must be kept clean and not allowed to be in contact with acid and air.   Excessive strains will cause cracking and corrosion at joints.   Ordinary calcium or salt brine, unless kept neutralized, will also cause corrosion.   Laying wrenches on stainless steel surfaces may cause etching and corrosion.

The corrosion resistance of stainless steel is due to the formation of a chromium oxide layer which forms naturally on the surface when it is exposed to air.   This can be developed artificially by subjecting the surface to hot nitric acid 20–30% solution at 140°F for 30 min and removing the acid.   A highly polished surface is also more resistant to corrosion.

References

AMERICAN IRON AND STEEL INST.   Stainless and heat resisting steels Bull.   New York.
COMERFORD, W. J.   1964, 1965.   Selecting type of stainless steel.   Food Process. Catalog.

Cross-references: *Electrolytic Corrosion; Stainless Steel.*

ALUMINUM

Aluminum is widely used in some countries for the construction of dairy and food processing equipment.   Aluminum is particularly valuable in many uses because of its freedom from corrosion, light weight, and ease of fabrication.   Tremendous progress has been made in the use of alloys for special purposes where high strength is required.   However, for most food equipment uses, a high purity cast or aluminum sheet material is used.   The principal deterrents to the use of aluminum has been its lack of resistance to abrasion, and susceptibility to corrosion from cleaning solutions.

Physical Properties

Pure aluminum has an atomic weight of 26.97, density at 68°F of 168.56 lb per cu ft, melting point of 1220°F, coefficient of expansion 68° to 212°F, of 0.0000132, thermal conductivity of 1509 Btu/hr sq ft °F/in. thickness, tensile strength of 9,000 psi, hardness of 15, reflectivity for white light of 90%, and magnetic susceptibility (cgs units) of 0.00000058.

Many very excellent aluminum alloys have been developed, some having an ultimate strength of close to 50,000 psi.

Aluminum is very resistant to corrosion from atmospheric conditions. It is also resistant to distilled water, fruit juices, milk, air, and sulfur dioxide. However, it is quite readily dissolved by hydrochloric and hydrofluoric acids and particularly by caustic solutions. Alkali cleaners should not be used on aluminum because pitting and corrosion may result. Weak acid cleaners are used.

The resistance to corrosion of aluminum is due to a protective oxide film which is formed on its surface by natural oxidation. A very pure type of aluminum is most resistant to corrosion except that there are special aluminum alloys which are quite resistant. Nominal impurities in the aluminum may cause extensive corrosion.

Aluminum does not cause flavor problems with most food products and is excellent for use in contact with milk. Present cleaning methods limit use.

Aluminum may be cast, rolled, or spun. Aluminum may be heat treated, cold worked, and welded or soldered, although special fluxes and welding processes must be used. Special solders and fluxes may be used for soldering aluminum pieces.

Finishes

Many different types of finishes can be applied to aluminum. The finish may be ground, polished, buffed, colored, scratch-brushed, hammered, fluted sand blasted, or burnished. Aluminum may also be electroplated to give greater wear resistance to improve the finish, or to change the friction characteristics.

Special oxide coatings are applied to aluminum. Many different types of colored oxide coatings can be used to give a beautiful appearance, and also to improve corrosion resistance.

When painting aluminum, the paint adhesion will be greatly improved if the surface is prepared by treatment with a chromic acid solution or a phosphoric acid-alcohol mixture. Light sand blast treatment will also improve the adhesion.

Electric Conductor

Aluminum is now widely used as a conductor for high tension electric lines. Usually a cable of high strength steel reinforces the core of the strands of aluminum wire in order to provide extra strength.

In many installations, the cost of aluminum conductors for high-line service may be less than for copper.

References

Hunziker, O. F., Cordes, W. A., and Nisson, B. H. 1929. Metals in dairy equipment. J. Dairy Sci. *12*, 140–189, 252–284.

White, A. H. 1948. Engineering Materials. McGraw-Hill Book Co., New York.

Cross-references: *Alloys for Processing; Building Materials; Butter Churn; Carton Forming and Filling; Electric Wiring; Electricity; Electrolytic Corrosion.*

ANALOG COMPUTER

An analog control or analog computer operates on systems which are analogous to one another. Quantities are represented by mechanical devices or electrical components. Mechanical computers might consist of gears, lever arm, or slide rule. Electrical computers would have circuits analogous to the systems with resistance, current, and voltage as variable components. Analog computers provide a continuous output. With digital computers there are discreet numbers with spaces between the numbers.

On the analog computer, physical quantities such as weight, temperature, or area are represented by voltages. The voltage is the electrical analog of the variable being analyzed. Arbitrary scale factors are established to relate the voltages in the computer to the variables in the problem being solved. For example, 1 v might equal 100°F or 100 lb. The name analog comes from the fact that the computer solves by analogy using physical quantities to represent numbers.

Uses

Analog computers are especially useful in solving the dynamic behavior of temperature or motion of a system, which can be expressed in the form of a differential equation. An analog computer is useful for solving problems of radioactive decay, chemical reaction, heat flow, hysteresis, etc.

Developing the model to prototype relationships involves skill, practice, and imagination. An analog is a model which does not resemble the prototype but obeys an equation identical in form to that which governs the prototype. When corresponding boundary conditions are imposed, the results obtained on the analog may be converted to represent corresponding results for the actual system. The electric analog for analog computers is quite commonly used.

A characteristic of an analog computer of the electric type is the high gain direct current amplifier. With the proper combinations of input and feedback resistors or capacitors, it is possible to construct a circuit that will perform a variety of mathematical functions. The circuits which will perform these functions are shown below.

Multiplication by a constant is performed by using different values of input resistor, R_i, and feedback resistor, R_f (Fig. A.19).

Output

Output from an analog computer might be used to control a process operation. The output signal usually would be fed through an amplifier component to provide an adequate signal for making the necessary control. If numbers (digital) are needed on the output, either for calculations or control, an analog-to-digital converter might be used. The unit selects information from the continuous analog signal and prints out numbers corresponding to the information selected. Thus, numbers could be obtained every 10th, 100th, or 1,000th of a second, according to the information desired, and these numbers placed on an appropriate magnetic tape, punched tape, or cards, which in turn could be used for a control or computing operation.

Reference

MURRAY, F. J. 1961. Analog Devices. Columbia Univ. Press, New York.

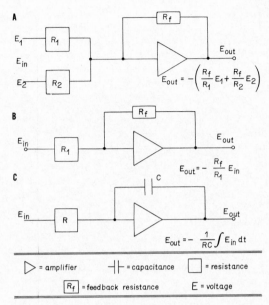

Fig. A-19. Analogs for circuits: A—sum or difference circuit; B—multiplier circuit; C—integrator circuit

Cross-references: *Automation; Digital Computer.*

ANTIOXIDANTS

Substances capable of slowing the rate of oxidation in autoxidizable materials are referred to as antioxidants.   They are used to prolong the shelf-life or keeping quality of food products particularly those containing fats.   Antioxidants are usually aromatic compounds which are phenolic or amine in character.   Selecting an antioxidant for a given purpose will require an evaluation of the characteristics of the system and some of the legal aspects in the use of the substances.   An antioxidant has certain features which make it acceptable for food use, including (1) does not impart undesirable flavor or other characteristics to the system in which it is used, (2) convenient to use, (3) safe to handle, (4) low in cost, and (5) effective in low concentrations.   Antioxidants are available both as synthetic compounds and naturally occurring substances.   For food uses it has been considered desirable in past years to use those antioxidants occurring in nature.   In more recent years, however, some of the synthetic compounds are favored because of their excellent antioxidant qualities.

Stringent regulations are enforced in the United States and in most European countries relative to the types and maximum quantities of antioxidants permitted in fats, fat-containing foods, and packaging materials for foods.   In the United States, the use and approval for use of antioxidants falls under the regulatory agencies of the Federal Food, Drug, and Cosmetic Act, the Federal Meat Inspection Act, and/or the Federal Poultry Inspection Act.   The agencies operating under the various acts have stipulated the quantities of the various compounds with antioxidant properties

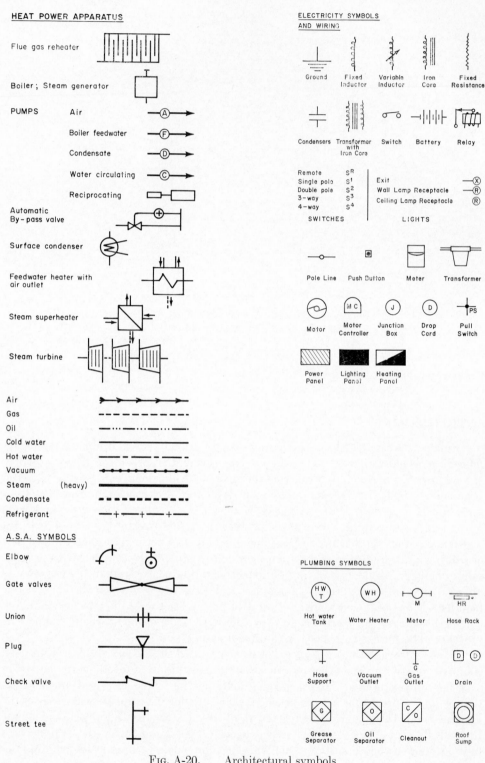

FIG. A-20.   Architectural symbols

which may be used in several food products. Among the most important of the antioxidants approved are the following compounds:

BHA—Butylated hydroxyanisole
BHT—Butylated hydroxytoluene
PB—Propyl gallate
THBP—Trihydroxybutyrophenone
TDPA—Thiodipropionic acid
DLTDP—Dilauryl thiodipropionate
        Tocopherols
        Gum guaiac

In addition to the compounds listed above, distearyl thiodipropionate is approved for use in food packaging materials. BHA, BHT, and PG are very commonly used in the United States at the present time. THBP is a rather recent antioxidant and is gradually finding commercial use in the food industry.

One of the most desirable characteristics of an antioxidant is its ability to "carry through" the heat treatment process. This property permits the antioxidant to be effective in the food product after processing and in the channels of marketing. The first compound with antioxidant properties that possessed carry through was gum guaiac. Other antioxidants also possess good carry through properties, namely BHA and BHT as well as a few others.

The synergistic effect of antioxidants in combination has been well established in the food industry. For example, BHA in combination with propyl gallate is a very powerful antioxidant. This combination is used particularly in fat systems designed for long periods of storage. One of the disadvantages encountered in the use of propyl gallate is its reaction with soluble iron causing a dark discoloration in the product. Citric acid in combination with BHA and BHT exhibits a synergistic effect. This combination is particularly effective in stabilizing commercial shortenings which are on the market. The acid synergists chelate metals which may be present in trace amounts in a product. By chelating the metals, the inactivation results so far as the oxidizing catalytic effect is concerned. Not all of the synergism brought about through combinations of antioxidants is achieved through the action of metal chelation.

An enzyme system known as glucose oxidase-catalase is listed as an antioxidant because it removes oxygen from hermetically sealed containers. By oxygen removal, the deteriorative reaction due to oxygen is eliminated. As can be realized, the system of preventing oxidation and off-flavors is different from the other chemicals listed as antioxidants.

Examples of allowable levels of BHA and BHT in specific food products are as follows: Up to 1,000 ppm BHA only in active dry yeast, up to 50 ppm BHA + BHT in dry breakfast cereals, up to 10 ppm BHA only in dry mixes for beverages or desserts, up to 200 ppm BHA + BHT in emulsion stabilizers for shortenings, and up to 10 ppm BHA + BHT in potato granules. In dairy products, BHA and PG, as well as some combinations of these are capable of inhibiting the development of rancidity. For a specific application, it is necessary to determine the approved antioxidant for the food product while achieving effective results economically.

References

ANON. 1965. Antioxidants. Food Process. *26*, No. 5, 121–139.
DUGAN, L. R., JR. 1963. Antioxidants. *In* Kirk Othmer Encyclopedia of Chemical Technology. Interscience Publishers, New York.
EASTMAN KODAK CO. 1967. Methods of analysis for food-approved phenolic antioxidants, Bull. *G-154*. New York.

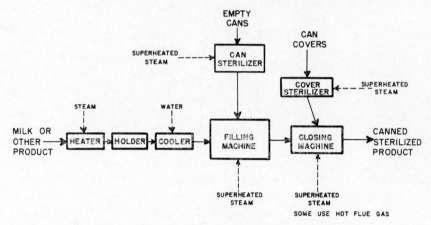

FIG. A-21.   Flow chart for Dole aseptic canning system

ARCHITECTURAL SYMBOLS

Plans of buildings and facilities usually use symbols to represent standard components or methods. The American Standards Association has assembled many such symbols for regular use.

Some symbols are especially developed and used by consulting engineers and architects. The symbols used for a drawing are usually placed and identified on the drawing. Some of the commonly used symbols are shown in Fig. A.20.

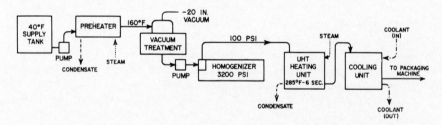

FIG. A-22.   Sterilization of milk for aseptic packaging

ASEPTIC PROCESSES

The general requirements for aseptic canning have been known for some time. Three methods have been advanced commercially: HCF, Avoset, and Dole.

The Dole system is now most widely used in the United States. Aseptic canning provides the primary advantage of improved product quality because foods are less subject to severe heat.   The heat treatment for the product is given before the canning process.   By using a HTST heat treatment ahead of canning, there is less heat effect on the product than if sterilization is done in the container.   It is possible to use this procedure because the temperature coefficient of destruction of bacteria is about five times the temperature coefficient for some of the heat sensitive constituents of the product.   Thus, aseptic canning describes the systems whereby the food product is sterilized prior to filling, in contrast to sterilizing in the container after packaging.

Principle

The product is sterilized and cooled before the canning operation.   The thermal process used to sterilize whole milk is usually in the range of $F_0 = 10$ to 12 min, disregarding the accumulated lethal effect during heating and cooling.   A typical process would be used to heat the product to 285°F, hold for 0.13 min, and cool.   Another process consists of heating to 300°F, followed by flash cooling to 212°F.   The product is cooled to 60°F as it enters the aseptic canner.

Three types of heat exchanger equipment are used to transfer heat to the product prior to sterilization, and to remove heat after sterilization.   These are the tubular or modified tubular, plate surface, and direct steam injection heaters.   In general, the equipment available for heating dairy products to 280° or 300°F is identical to that used for ultrahigh temperature (UHT) pasteurization.

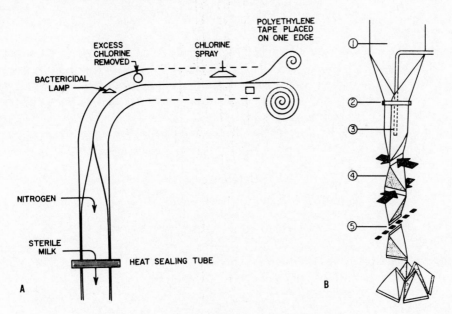

Fig. A-23.   Aseptic filling and packaging system

The Dole system (Fig. A.21) used lacquered metal cans which are sterilized by jets of superheated steam, produced by internal gas-fired steam superheaters at temperatures over 400°F.   The sterilized cans are filled with sterilized milk in a sealed chamber which is filled with superheated steam under positive pressure.   The covers are sterilized in a similar manner, placed on the cans, and sealed under vacuum. Thus, a sterile atmosphere is maintained within the unit during filling and closing (Fig. A.22).

The Tetra-Pak system (Fig. A.23) is designed to package sterilized milk aseptically in paper or plastic containers. The sterile milk is fed into a flexible tube in the presence of nitrogen under pressure. The packaging material is sprayed with chlorine or hydrogen peroxide; the excess chlorine is removed with an absorbing roll, and then the packaging material treated with ultraviolet by a bactericidal lamp. A sterile polyethylene tape is placed on the edge of the container to prevent contamination from organisms that might be in the packaging material itself.

Operational Practices

(1) Slightly over the minimum heat treatment is used to sterilize the product and to minimize heat effects on the product. For milk a typical treatment would be exposure up to 285° to 300°F, and then cool as quickly as possible by flashing or with a thin film plate exchanger.

(2) The product is fed under pressure to the canning system.

(3) The product is transferred to the can in a sterile environment, usually produced by superheated steam, hot gas, or ultraviolet radiation.

(4) A positive pressure is maintained on the chamber in which the canning is done so that organisms cannot move into the chamber and into the can.

(5) For metal containers, the lids must be treated in a manner similar to the can. If tin is used, the temperature should not exceed 425°F because tin begins to melt at 450°F.

(6) The space between the lid and the product should be filled with sterile superheated steam or high temperature gas to minimize the possibility of living organisms being in the space and to minimize the inflow of organisms during the canning process.

(7) To avoid creating an extremely high vacuum in the head space at the time of sealing, steam is often mixed with flue gas.

(8) The possibility of poststerilization contamination is minimized if the product and its container are as near to room temperature as possible when leaving the system.

References

HALL, C. W., and TROUT, G. M. 1959. High temperature treatment of milk. Dairy Eng. *76*, No. 10, 275–279.

PFLUG, I. J., HALL, C. W., and TROUT, G. M. 1959. Aseptic canning of dairy products. Dairy Eng. *76*, No. 11, 328–331.

Cross-references: *Heat Tranfer; Heating Systems for HTST; Pasteurization; Sterilizers; UHT Equipment.*

ATOMIZATION

The purpose of atomization is to obtain many small particles with a large surface area, preferably uniform in size, and generally ranging from 50 to 150 μ in diameter. Uniform particles provide: (1) superior instantizing product, (2) reduced product losses, (3) less over- and underdrying, and (4) more efficient drying. Large drops are more difficult to dry and require a longer time or a higher temperature, or both. The large surface area provides easy transfer of heat to the droplet and transfer of moisture

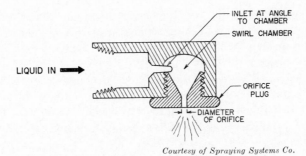

Courtesy of Spraying Systems Co.

FIG. A-24.   Pressure nozzle with swirl chamber

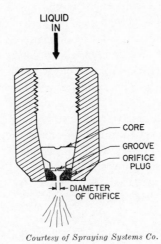

Courtesy of Spraying Systems Co.

FIG. A-25.   Centrifugal pressure nozzle with grooved core insert

away from the droplet.   The atomization of 1 gal. of product to 50 μ in diameter will produce 200,000 sq in. of surface area.

The type and efficiency of atomization affects the desired design (size, air temperature, exposure time, evaporation rate, and efficiency).   The atomization also affects the product properties, such as air content, moisture, bulk density, particle size (range and average), and ability to reconstitute.

The pattern produced by the atomizer must be directed so that the particles will be dried before hitting the surface of the drying chamber.   Otherwise, an accumulation of partially dried product will occur on the drier.   There are three major methods of atomizing: pressure nozzle, spinning disc, and pneumatic.

Pressure Nozzle

Pressure spray nozzles include the swirl nozzle (called whizzer or centrifugal pressure nozzle), the solid cone spray nozzle, and the fan nozzle.   The pressure spray nozzle is most common in the United States for milk and food product atomization for spray drying.   Pressures from 1,500 to 5,000 psi are used.   A high pressure pump such as the 3- or 5-piston homogenizer pump is commonly used.   For products which are preheated to a high temperature, it is important that a pump be used which does not operate at too high a speed to avoid cavitation in the pump cylinders.   The spray from a nozzle may range in shape from a flat sheet to a 120° cone.   The following describes the pressure spray nozzle.

(1)   As the viscosity increases, the cone angle decreases.   For example, when increasing from 1 to 100 centipoise viscosity, with a 0.036 in. diam orifice, the cone angle decreases from 60° to 42° in a nearly linear relationship.   Also, the capacity may increase or decrease at a given pressure with a change in viscosity, depending upon the formation of the air core.

(2)   Large core angles provide soft sprays and do not penetrate as far in the drier as hard sprays.

(3)   With an increase in pressure there will be only a small increase in core angle.

(4)   As the tangential velocity increases, the core angle increases, being 55° at 10 ft per sec and 76° at 46 ft per sec for a 0.031 in. diam orifice.

(5)   The drop size (a) will change inversely to the square root of the pressure, (b) will increase approximately as the square root of the viscosity, (c) will increase approximately directly as the surface tension, and (d) will increase approximately directly with the density.

The pressure nozzle with a swirl chamber (Fig. A.24) and the centrifugal pressure nozzle, with a grooved core insert to impart a spin or circular motion, are popular for drying of milk and milk products (Fig. A.25).   A conical spray pattern usually results, made up of small droplets with a hollow spherical core.   The pressure nozzle is made of two parts, the core which is identified by a number by most manufacturers, and an orifice also designated by a number (Table A.12).

TABLE A.12

CAPACITY AND ANGLE OF PRESSURE NOZZLES OPERATING AT 4,000 PSI

Orifice No.	Diameter, In.	Core Insert No.	Capacity, Water Lb per Hr	Grooves No.	Spray Angle, °
80	0.0135	10	66.6	2	56
76	0.02	16		2	
72	0.025	16	148.3	2	70
68	0.031	20		2	
65	0.035	20	452	4	68
60	0.040	17	533	4	73
55	0.052	21	702	4	75
52	0.0635	27	1400	4	75

Source: Spraying Systems Co.

One large nozzle or several small nozzles may be used.   Nozzles made of hardened stainless steel will show wear after 15 hr if a small orifice is involved.   By using tungsten carbide, the nozzles will have as much as 25 to 30 times the life of hardened steel.

Strainers or filters usually precede the spray nozzle to prevent clogging and excessive wear of the nozzle.   Nozzle capacities are usually rated on the basis of flow of water.   The output of various food products which have a higher viscosity would be a little less and it is suggested that a conversion factor for 40 to 24% solids be 70 and 80% of the flow of water, respectively.

When several nozzles are used, they must be arranged so that the spray patterns do not overlap. If spray patterns overlap, the droplets may combine and uneven drying or other difficulties result.

Centrifugal Spinning Disc

The spinning disc is particularly useful for viscous materials and for materials in a suspension. The spinning disc is used more for the drying of milk in Europe and England than in the United States.

Various types of centrifugal spinning discs consist of a radial-vaned disc (vanes placed between 2 discs), multiple discs (3 or more discs), and a bowl or hemispherically shaped liquid chamber through which the product moves (Fig. A.26). The product

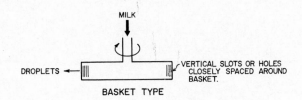

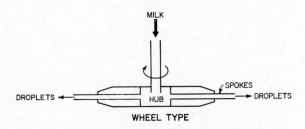

Fig. A-26.   Centrifugal disc atomizers

may be ejected from the spinning disc over a lip or through a slot, hole, or other opening. The disc atomizer permits considerable variation in capacity of from ±25% of the design capacity. The pattern produced by the disc is in the shape of an umbrella, although for very fine droplets a mist or cloud is formed. The drop size produced by the disc atomizer decreases with an increase in speed up to about 400 ft per sec for the product coming from the atomizer. The centrifugal unit is used in a vertical drying chamber.

Energy is used to rotate the nozzle, often at high speeds instead of putting energy in a pump for converting pressure energy to velocity as is done for the pressure nozzle. Small diameter discs of approximately 2 in. may be driven at 50,000 rpm and a large 30 in. diam disc may run at as low as 3,500 rpm. Peripheral speeds from 250 to 600 ft per sec are involved with capacities up to 60,000 lb per hr.

At speeds above 4,000 rpm, additional energy is required for moving air, so that the equation must be used with judgment.

Conflicting reports have been given on the comparative power requirements for the centrifugal disc as compared to the pressure nozzle for atomization. The power requirements for the rotating disc is about twice that for the pressure nozzle. Marshall (1954) reports that for comparable conditions approximately the same amount of power is required for discs or nozzles.

Pneumatic or Two-Fluid Atomization

The specific weight of dry milk prepared with a centrifugal disc atomizer is dependent on the specific gravity of the concentrated milk, which is not true for dry milk prepared with high pressure atomizers. The decrease in air content of powders with increasing solids of the concentrated milk is much more pronounced with the centrifugal

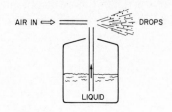

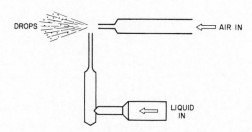

Fɪɢ. A-27.   Two fluid atomizers

as compared to the high pressure atomizer. The organoleptic properties of dry milk produced by the 2 methods remain the same when gas packed and stored for 1 yr at 60° to 70°F. Bulk density of powdered milk can be varied greatly by varying the pump and product pressure.

The fluid atomization is produced by passing compressed air or steam over an opening leading to the liquid, usually a pipe. Energy released from the fluid vaporizes the liquid. The unit operates similar to a perfume atomizer or sprayer. The principle is usually used for small flow rates, such as mentioned above, or for laboratory sprayer systems, and is particularly useful for providing uniform small droplets of 15μ or less.

Units may be classified as external mixing 2-fluid systems or internal mixing 2-fluid systems (Fig. A.27). A pneumatic unit is available in which air or steam is passed through a venturi when a liquid stream is injected into it, thereby causing droplet formation.

The two-fluid system is inexpensive in initial cost, but expensive to operate. It is particularly useful for highly viscous materials. During atomization, the droplets cool because of the expansion of the air or steam. Air and steam can transfer more energy per pound of fluid than is obtained by the increase in pressure of the liquid in the pressure nozzle system.

The major disadvantage of the pneumatic atomizer is the large amount of energy required.   In general, 2 to 3 times as much energy is required for the 2-fluid or pneumatic atomizer as with the pressure spray nozzle.

Comparison of Methods of Atomization

The amount of energy required to produce droplets is considerably higher than the theoretical calculated value.   For example, one analysis suggests that to atomize 1 gpm of water to 50-μ drops requires only 5 ft lb per min theoretically, as compared to 80,000 ft lb per min with the pressure nozzle.   This tremendous difference is attributed to energy for overcoming the friction of the air and for dispersing the droplets inside the drier, in addition to the small energy required for producing new surface area by overcoming surface tension.   The heating effect of the liquid during atomization is a measure of the efficiency of formation of droplets.   The greater the temperature increase the lower the efficiency of atomization.

References

HALL, C. W., and HEDRICK, T. I.   1966.   Drying of Milk and Milk Products.   AVI Publishing Co., Westport, Conn.

MARSHALL, W. R., JR.   1954.   Atomization and spray drying.   Inst. Chem. Eng. Monograph Ser. *50*, No. 2.   New York.

Cross-references: *Foam Spray Dryer; Spray Dryer.*

AUTOMATION

Industrial evolution has proceeded from manual; to manual with tools; to mechanization including tools, machines, and controls; to automation.   Automation is more technologically advanced than mechanization.   With mechanization the product moves into a process which is under certain control, such as temperature, pressure, or humidity, and the product moves out at the appropriate temperature.   If the desired condition is not reached, the product is rejected.   With automation, material moves to the process, which is controlled by a signal of a sensing element at the output of the material.   A procedure known as feedback changes the treatment of the product according to the preset program.

The productivity of labor usually increases with the evolution from machine to automation.   The dairy plant increased productivity 5 times in the last 30 yr.   From 1925 to 1930, productivity was from 25 to 30 gal. per manhour; in 1960, 120 gal. of pasteurized bottled product per manhour; and in 1967 in some plants, over 200 gal. per manhour.

Seldom can an entire plant operation be completely automated in one step.   Usually, segments of the system or small operations are automated.   Then other operations are automated.   The final step is to tie the entire system of operations together under automatic control with a feedback of information to provide automation.

Automation should be used as a method of making the best possible use of the 5 elements of production: money, men, material, machines, and management.   These are interrelated, and just as the functioning of automation components are inter-related, so utilizing the proper relationships of these 5 elements of production must be properly evaluated. The same procedures which have been used for making economical analysis for manual or mechanization can be used for automation.

Practices and Principles

(1) Obsolescense of new equipment used in automation may be much earlier than in old equipment. Often 5 yrs or less is the life of automatic equipment.

(2) Labor cost per hour of operation will probably be higher for automation.

(3) A major difficulty of making an analysis of automation operations is that many of the costs of automation systems have not been established. Such costs as maintenance, repairs, replacement of parts, and effect on down time, are not readily available.

(4) With an automated system, the ratio of capital investment per employee and per dollar sales will probably increase.

(5) An automation system may involve one or more computers to follow preset instructions.

(6) Plant operators going to automation will need to study very carefully the number of products and minimize the number of products handled by a particular plant. It will also be necessary to standardize on some components such as containers, materials, size, shape, and labels.

(7) A major need and problem in automation is the sensing element for measuring the variable of food product involved. Instruments are needed for measurement of various types of quantity and quality control which will provide the automation system with proper instructions to produce the product desired.

Reference

MICHIGAN STATE UNIV. 1962. Proc. 10th National Dairy Eng. Conf.

Cross-references: *Air Operated Controls; Analog Computer; Controllers; Digital Computer.*

B

BACTOFUGATION

Bactofugation is a process of removing up to 99% of the bacteria in milk by centrifugal force. The method is claimed to triple the shelf-life of market milk. The process consists of removing the bacteria from milk with two centrifugal separators in series. Milk is heated to 170°F to reduce its viscosity, after which it moves to the first centrifugal unit operating at a velocity of 20,000 rpm. Two small holes in the outside of the bowl shell allow continuous discharge of bacteria and about 1.5% skim milk. After the first centrifugal treatment, 90% of the bacteria have been removed. Milk then passes to the second centrifugal unit where 90% of the remaining bacteria are removed to achieve a total bacteria elimination of 99% of the raw feed. The process is considered as supplementary to pasteurization. It is necessary to destroy the bacteria not removed. With bactofugation the bacteria are removed rather than kept in the product. The procedure might find application in cottage cheese production for removing yeast and mold, and in sterile milk production by removing the bacteria prior to sterilization to provide a shorter heating and holding time.

Reference

Anon. 1963. Bactofugation. Food Proc. 24, No. 1, 127.

Cross-references: *Centrifugal Separators; Pasteurization.*

BAG FILLERS

Bags available in a wide variety of sizes and types provide an efficient and satisfactory means of merchandising many food products. With the advent of plastics and the combination of several materials to form a package, a wide range of characteristics can be achieved in packaging with bags. The common materials used include paper, cloth, plastic film, and mesh. For protection of dehydrated products against moisture infusion, multiwall bags incorporating plastic materials or metallic films are quite satisfactory. Plastic films are also suitable for vacuum packaging with or without the heat-shrinkable feature. A wide variety of closures are available to meet the needs of a given product. Some of these include sewn seams, metal clips, twisted wire, heat seals, glue seals, and taped seams.

Filling

Bag-filling equipment will usually weigh the product and stop the feed at the desired weight. Some bag fillers are equipped with a revolving head to increase ca-

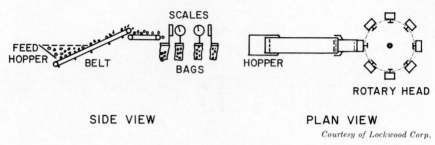

SIDE VIEW PLAN VIEW

Courtesy of Lockwood Corp.

FIG. B-1. Rotary head bagger

pacity. These units generally require two or more people to operate. A typical rotary bag fiiller is shown in Fig. B.1.

Packing

Packing units for citrus fruits and vegetables, such as potatoes or onions, are used in conjunction with sizing and sorting equipment. A typical combination of these machines is illustrated in Fig. B.2. To increase the output of a single filler head a continuous conveying system supplying a surge hopper just ahead of a weighing hopper is very effective. A schematic sketch of this principle is noted in Fig. B.3.

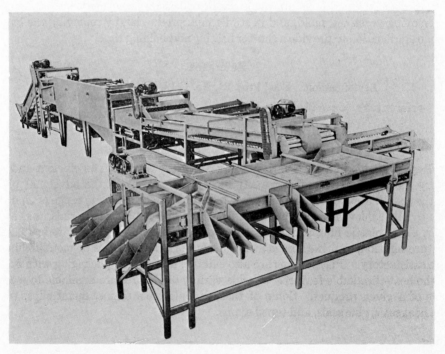

Courtesy of Aeroglide Corp.

FIG. B-2. Produce machine for sizing, sorting, and bagging

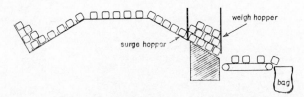

Fɪɢ. B-3.   Continuous weighing and packaging system

The capacity of one of these units on products such as oranges and potatoes is as follows:

Weight of Bag	Bags per Hour
3	750
5	700
8	650
10	600
15	500

Effective use of surge hoppers for bagging operations will usually result in a smoother operation.

Sealing

For certain products requiring extreme sanitation, special handling and sealing are necessary.   With the use of a multiwall polyethylene lined bag and a heat-sealing tape placed over a sewed seam, a very sanitary package is obtained.   Equipment used for stitching and sealing a 100-lb bag of nonfat dried milk is illustrated in Fig. B.4.

Coders are available for efficient coding of seams on bags.

As new materials and combinations become available, bags will probably continue to be used for a wide variety of food products.

References

Aᴇʀᴏɢʟɪᴅᴇ.   Produce Weigh-Packer, Sales Bull. *106*, Raleigh, N.C.
Lᴏᴄᴋᴡᴏᴏᴅ Gʀᴀᴅᴇʀ Cᴏʀᴘ.   1962.   Machinery Catalog.   Gering, Neb.

Cross-reference :   *Filling.*

BAKING

Progress has been particularly rapid in the development of mechanical processes for bakery products such as bread, cakes, pastries, biscuits, etc.   The bulk handling of flour, sugar, shortenings, and certain other ingredients is increasing.   Advances in packaging materials and techniques continue to be made.   There has been an increased emphasis on automation, particularly in relation to the application of automatic control for mixing and handling operations, oven conditions, and product characteristics.

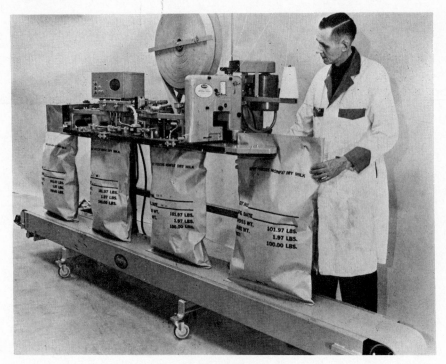

Courtesy of Doughboy

FIG. B-4.   Sealing unit with sealing and stitching heads

Raw Materials

In general the baking industry makes use of flour, sugar, shortenings, fat, eggs, and yeast as basic ingredients. Instantized flour used for bakery products is produced by moistening ordinary flour, the particles of which are stuck together and subsequently dried by heating. The final product has free-flowing properties and mixes well with water. Also, flour milled from steam-treated wheat has negligible amylase activity, and produces pastes with higher and more consistent viscosity than normal flours. Microwave treatment of flour for periods up to 3 min inactivates amylase and destroys gluten-forming properties. As a result, a considerably increased paste viscosity is obtained, the water absorption of the protein is increased, and the mesophile count is reduced. Gluten properties of flour may be modified by the addition to the flour of supplementary protein such as throlated gelatin. In this way a flour suitable for biscuit manufacture can be obtained, whereas the untreated would be unsuitable. The irradiation of cake flours results in the deterioration of white layer cake made with these flours. Changes in the starch and protein can occur as the result of irradiation. Generally unpasteurized whole egg is used in the baking industry with an increasing use of pasteurized egg. In some locations, regulations do not allow the use of unpasteurized eggs. The use of pasteurized egg in certain baked products has resulted in a problem, due to the presence of Salmonella organisms. This is particularly true with some sponge goods, choux paste, and baked custards. However, the freeze-dried whole egg will probably be an acceptable alternative to liquid whole egg in many applications.

In addition to many liquid shortenings, pure butterfat is being made available for food manufacturing purposes. The butterfat appears to be suitable for use in biscuits and fruit cakes, although for sponge cakes the fat must be "texturized." Mixed crystals of glycerol monostearate and propylene monostearate disperse readily in water and retain this property for a long time. The water dispersions enable sponge cakes to be produced with improved volume and texture. Also the crystals are effective emulsifiers in cake mixes and bread.

Yeasts are added in the bakery products during the production process to increase the loaf volume.

Bakery Products

Many different baking products are available on the market. These differ in taste, texture, size, shape, and manufacturing process. Here the brief discussion of only a few of these products will be presented.

Bread

The modern bread-making techniques make use of machines. The process has become continuous and rapid thus replacing the usual dividing, proving, and molding stages. Conventionally prepared and fermented dough is fed into a hopper, and a screw device transfers the dough into a developer section where gas is expelled or forced into solution, and the dough structure rendered homogeneous.

The important role of fat in mechanical development process of bread-makeup continues to receive much attention. The results of one investigation indicate the need of fat systems which will partially crystallize or congeal at the higher dough temperatures encountered in mechanical development processes. It is postulated that the fat crystals in the dough act as reservoirs to supply liquid fat during the baking process. This fat may function to prevent coalescence of gas cells and escape of gas.

The use of nonfat dried milk in continuous bread-making processes at levels greater than 2% of flour weight results in a loss of bread volume, a darker crumb color, and often a coarsening of crumb grain. Oxidation requirements of continuous mix bread increases as the nonfat milk content increases.

The addition of 1% pentosan-rich fraction to the flour increases its absorption, but is without significant effect on amylogram and extensogram characteristics. Increasing levels of pentosans lower bread volume and give rise to a coarsening of crumb grain.

A fairly new process of baking bread in cellulose film is being tried in a few countries. The dough is placed on a sheet of cellulose film folded to enclose a space three times the volume of dough piece. After proof, the dough is baked at 420°F and swells to fill the wrapper.

Confectionery

Cakes of various variety are generally grouped under flour confectionery. Water concentration has a critical effect on the extent of starch gelatinization during baking, and thus on the crumb structure of the final cake. The maximum volume is obtained at the liquid level producing a rounded cake contour, but the crumb structure is best at a slightly higher liquid level. The milk solids and egg protein have definite absorption requirements and the water bonded by them is not available for starch gelatinization. Varying the specific gravity of white, yellow, and devil's food cake affects their tenderness, grain, and texture.

Biscuits

A new method of making cookies uses a cream of fat, sugar, and less water than usual with flour to produce a granular dough that only adheres together on compression or baking. A technique of preventing cookies from absorbing moisture consists of spraying the product after baking with fat, and applying a secondary coating of suitable edible solids and fats.

Based on present knowledge it is possible to manufacture cream crackers with a satisfactory structure from an unfermented dough. The flavor of such crackers is comparable to that of crackers made by a conventional process.

Plant and Equipment

Continuous bread-making plants having a throughput rate of 150–300 lb per hr of dough are quite common.

Hearth-baked goods are automatically produced continuously at a rate of 1,800 one-pound loaves per hour.

An electronic baking oven for cakes using microwave energy piped through wave guides to numerous positions in the oven has been developed in the United Kingdom.

An experimental automatic bread-baking oven using combined high frequency and convection heating combined with high-speed mixing and a high-fermentation temperature makes it possible to make a loaf in 1 hr.

Convection and radiation are both important factors in cake cooling and the efficiency of this process, and the moisture retention of cake depends to a large extent on the temperature and velocity of cooling air. The optimum cooling method for an average cake consists of cooling the cake in still air after depanning, and then passing it through a cooling tunnel containing radiant reflectors.

Radiation

Wheat irradiated for disinfestation purposes is considered safe for consumption. The effect of such wheat irradiation on food within limited dose and energy would not be detrimental to wholesomeness. It is also expected that radiation will find application in disinfesting grain and destroying salmonellae in egg products. Incidence of *Salmonella* food poisoning has been associated with the use of unpasteurized egg by bakeries. Ultraviolet irradiation of liquid whole egg gives rise to severe off-flavors and should not be employed.

References

MATZ, S. A. 1960. Baking Technology and Engineering. AVI Publishing Co., Westport, Conn.

VALENTYNE, P. H. 1959. Heat balance in dough mixing. Baker's Dig. *33*, No. 1, 33, 35, 40, 41, 65.

Cross-references: *Agitators; Dough Mixing.*

BATTERIES

The *dry cell* battery is dry only to the extent that it is not necessary to add water or liquid.   The dry cell is based on the ionization of ammonium chloride usually called sal ammoniac.   The construction of the dry cell involves the use of a zinc can or container on the inside of which is a felt saturated with ammonium chloride.   The next layer is a mixture of manganese dioxide and carbon granules, and in the center is the carbon electrode.   The outside is covered with a paper container sometimes enclosed with steel to protect the paper that shields the zinc.

FIG. B-5.   Multi V-belt drive

Construction

One terminal is on the zinc container and the other on the central carbon electrode.   The surface area of zinc and carbon determines the amount of current that can be obtained.   When a wire is connected across the two terminals the zinc becomes the negative terminal and slowly dissolves to produce zinc ions and zinc chloride, displacing the ammonia and liberating hydrogen which is absorbed by the manganese dioxide.   Continued use of the battery results in depletion of the zinc and the end of its useful life.   The voltage of a new dry cell is about 1.5 v.   To obtain higher voltage, several cells are hooked in series by connecting the positive terminal on one cell with the negative terminal on the next cell.   A series of 4 cells will yield 6 v.   When cells are hooked in parallel the voltage remains at 1.5 v, but the current is multiplied 4 times.

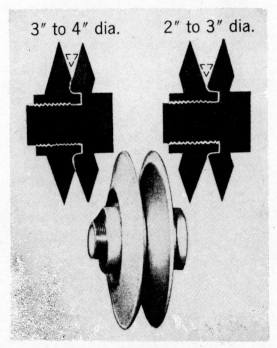

3″ to 4″ dia. 2″ to 3″ dia.

Fig. B-6. Adjustable speed pulley
The effective diameter of a pulley of this type is changed by merely screwing the
two sheaves closer together or farther apart. Speed can be changed from 25 to
50%, depending on the size of the pulley.

Storage batteries operate with different chemicals on a similar principle, but can be recharged by forcing an electric current into the cells. The common storage battery has positive lead plates coated with peroxide of lead. The negative plates are placed between the positive plates and are filled with a spongy type of metallic lead. The electrolyte is sulfuric acid. When electricity is drawn from the battery, the lead ions and the sulfate ions combine to form lead sulfate which is deposited on the plates. The hydrogen ions and the oxygen combine to form water. In this exchange electrons are released to produce the electric current which flows when the terminals are connected. The voltage produced by this type of cell is about 2 v compared to the dry cell's 1.5 v. Like the dry cells, the storage cells can be connected in series to increase the voltage. Sometimes cells are connected in series, and then two or more sets of series cells are connected in parallel to increase both the voltage and amperes.

Recharging

Eventually most of the sulfate and hydrogen ions are used, and the battery is exhausted. It can be recharged by forcing direct current into the battery with the positive pole of the generator connected to the positive pole of the battery and the negative to the negative. Electrons flow into the cells reversing the chemical action and removing the sulfate from the plates back to solution, and the oxygen from the solution back to the plates. Batteries that have been discharged or almost discharged contain mostly water for the electrolyte and freeze in cold weather, bursting the cell walls. Some water may evaporate during the course of time because of vapor pressure differences, so it is necessary to add water occasionally to keep the plates covered. When recharging the battery, it is obvious that when all of the sulfate has been returned to solution in the recharging process, no further value can come from additional charging. Most storage battery systems are equipped with regulators to control the charging rate according to the need of the battery. This is especially useful on engines where the generator operates regardless of whether the battery needs charging.

Cross-reference: *Electricity.*

BELTS

Belts are widely used in the food industry for transmitting power from one shaft to another. Belts are simple, relatively inexpensive, and quiet. They also provide a cushion which minimizes shocks and strains on machinery.

The principal types of belts relative to form are the flat belt and the V-belt. The V-belt may also be made in a multiple type construction.

The simplest type of belt is the plain flat belt which runs over the flat or slightly crowned set of pulleys. These belts are usually made of leather, but may be of rubber composition or balata which is used for very high speed and where great flexibility is required. Most belts must be kept dry.

Flat belts may slip off easily and the pulleys should be in perfect alignment for best results. A slight crown on the pulley helps to keep the belt in its proper location on the pulley.

V-belts (Fig. B.5) have become very widely used because they are trouble free, have great load-carrying capacity, and are all-round very satisfactory.

V-belts require special grooved pulleys (Fig. B.6) and the tension should be approximately correct; however, it is not as critical as with flat belts. Most V-belts are made of a composition of rubber and cords. Many of the newer heavy-duty belts contain metal flexible multiwire cords, which prevent the belt from stretching, and enable it to carry a much heavier load than otherwise. The carrying capacity of V-belts is listed by the manufacturers and a standard is set for the different size belts in sizes A, B, C, D, and E. The E-size belt is the largest. The carrying capacity is a function of the speed of the belt and its size plus a number of factors. The higher speed enables the belt to carry a greater horsepower.

Speeds of belt driven shafts are readily calculated by the formula

$$\text{Rpm-driver} \times \text{Diam-driver} = \text{Rpm-driven} \times \text{Diam-driven}$$

Thus, for example

$$\text{Rpm-driven} = \frac{\text{Rpm driver} \times \text{Diam-driver}}{\text{Diam-driven}}$$

V-Belt Standards and Performance Data

Engineering standards for V-belt drives have been established jointly by the Mechanical Power Transmission Association and the Rubber Manufacturers Associa-

TABLE B.1
STANDARD BELT DIMENSIONS
V-BELTS

V-BELTS

Nominal V-belt Cross Sections

Cross Section	b_b In.	h_b In.	h_{bb} In.	s_g In.
A	0.50	0.31	0.41	0.625
B	0.66	0.41	0.50	0.750
C	0.88	0.53	0.66	1.000
D	1.25	0.75	0.84	1.438
E	1.50	0.91	1.03	1.750

JOINED V-BELTS

tion. They cover 3 types of belts, namely (1) small single V-belts using 2L, 3L, 4L, and 5L; (2) classical multiple V-belts A, B, C, D, and E cross section; and (3) synchronous V-belts XL, L, H, XH, and XXH, cross section. This belt has teeth cast in it which match teeth in the pulleys, thus giving a positive drive with no slippage.

Classical or Standard V-Belt Drives

This standard covers V-belt drives used primarily for power transmission in industrial applications. One or more V-belts may be used on a drive as required to transmit the horsepower load. In general the drives are in the integral-horsepower class as distinguished from light duty fractional horsepower drives.

This Standard covers the five classical V-belt cross sections and sheave groove sizes designated A, B, C, D, and E.

Dimensions of V-belts and sheaves together with basic design data are covered in this Standard. The special requisites for the use of these belt sections in the joined form are covered in appropriate tables. This Standard does not include certain drives for automotive, agricultural, and light duty fractional horsepower applications for which other standards exist.

V-Belt Cross Sections

Nominal dimensions of the five cross sections are given in Table B.1. Because of different constructions and methods of manufacture, the cross-sectional shape, dimensions, and included angle between the sidewalls may differ with different manufacturers. However, all belts of a given cross section shall operate interchangeably in standard grooves designated by the same letter, but belts of different manufacturers should never be mixed on the same drive.

Service Factors

The selection of a V-belt drive for any application should be based on the nature of the load and the type of driving unit. Service factors for different kinds of driven machines combined with different types of driving units are shown in Table B.2. The

TABLE B.2

SUGGESTED SERVICE FACTORS FOR V-BELT DRIVES

Types of Driven Machines	Types of Driving Units					
	AC Motors: Normal Torque, Squirrel Cage, Synchronous and Split Phase DC Motors: Shunt Wound. Multiple Cylinder Internal Combustion Engines			AC Motors: High Torque, High Slip, Repulsion-Induction, Single Phase, Series Wound and Slip Ring DC Motors: Series Wound and Compound Wound. Single Cylinder Internal Combustion Engines. Line Shafts. Clutches		
	Intermittent Service (3–5 Hr Daily or Seasonal)	Normal Service (8–10 Hr Daily)	Continuous Service (16–24 Hr Daily)	Intermittent Service (3–5 Hr Daily or Seasonal)	Normal Service (8–10 Hr Daily)	Continuous Service (16–24 Hr Daily)
Agitators for liquids Blowers and exhausters Centrifugal pumps and compressors Fans up to 10 hp Light duty conveyors	1.0	1.1	1.2	1.1	1.2	1.3
Belt conveyors for sand, grain, etc. Dough mixers Fans over 10 hp Generators Line shafts Laundry machinery Machine tools Punches—presses—shears Printing machinery Positive displacement rotary pumps Revolving and vibrating screens	1.1	1.2	1.3	1.2	1.3	1.4
Brick machinery Bucket elevators Exciters Piston compressors Conveyors (drag—pan—screw) Hammer mills Paper mill beaters Piston pumps Positive displacement blowers Pulverizers Saw mill and woodworking machinery Textile machinery	1.2	1.3	1.4	1.4	1.5	1.6
Crushers (gyratory—jaw—roll) Mills (ball—rod—tube) Hoists Rubber calenders—extruders—mills	1.3	1.4	1.5	1.5	1.6	1.8

Note 1. The use of a service factor of 2.0 is recommended for equipment subject to choking.

Note 2. For devices used in grain and milling properties, refer to Mill Mutual Fire Prevention Bureau Bulletin VB-601.

driven machines are representative samples only. Select a driven machine whose load characteristics most closely approximate those of the machine being considered.

If idlers are used, the belt horsepower ratings must be reduced to reflect the detrimental effect of the additional bending stresses introduced on the V-belt. Refer to Rubber Manufacturer's Technical Information Bulletin No. 8, "Effect of Idlers on V-belt Performance," for general information and for specific horsepower rating correction factors.

TABLE B.3

STANDARD PITCH LENGTHS FOR V-BELTS

Standard Length Designation[1]	Standard Pitch Lengths, In.					Permissible Deviations from Std. Pitch Length, In.	Matching Limits for One Set, In.
			Cross Section				
	A	B	C	D	E		
26	27.3	—	—	—	—	+0.6 to −0.6	0.10
31	32.3	—	—	—	—	+0.6 to −0.6	0.10
35	36.3	36.8	—	—	—	+0.6 to −0.6	0.10
38	39.3	39.8	—	—	—	+0.7 to −0.7	0.10
42	43.3	43.8	—	—	—	+0.7 to −0.7	0.10
46	47.3	47.8	—	—	—	+0.7 to −0.7	0.10
51	52.3	52.8	53.9	—	—	+0.7 to −0.7	0.10
55	56.3	56.8	—	—	—	+0.7 to −0.7	0.10
60	61.3	61.8	62.9	—	—	+0.7 to −0.7	0.10
68	69.3	69.8	70.9	—	—	+0.7 to −0.7	0.10
75	76.3	76.8	77.9	—	—	+0.7 to −0.7	0.10
80	81.3	—	—	—	—	+0.7 to −0.7	0.20
81	—	82.8	83.9	—	—	+0.7 to −0.7	0.20
85	86.3	86.8	87.9	—	—	+0.7 to −0.7	0.20
90	91.3	91.8	92.9	—	—	+0.8 to −0.8	0.20
96	97.3	—	98.9	—	—	+0.8 to −0.8	0.20
97	—	98.8	—	—	—	+0.8 to −0.8	0.20
105	106.3	106.8	107.9	—	—	+0.8 to −0.8	0.20
112	113.3	113.8	114.9	—	—	+0.8 to −0.8	0.20
120	121.3	121.8	122.9	123.3	—	+0.8 to −0.8	0.20
128	129.3	129.8	130.9	131.3	—	+0.8 to −0.8	0.20
144	—	145.8	146.9	147.3	—	+0.8 to −0.8	0.20
158	—	159.8	160.9	161.3	—	+1.0 to −1.0	0.30
173	—	174.8	175.9	176.3	—	+1.0 to −1.0	0.30
180	—	181.8	182.9	183.3	184.5	+1.0 to −1.0	0.30
195	—	196.8	197.9	198.3	199.5	+1.1 to −1.1	0.30
210	—	211.8	212.9	213.3	214.5	+1.1 to −1.1	0.30
240	—	240.3	240.9	240.8	241.0	+1.3 to −1.3	0.30
270	—	270.3	270.9	270.8	271.0	+1.6 to −1.6	0.30
300	—	300.3	300.9	300.8	301.0	+1.6 to −1.6	0.40
330	—	—	330.9	330.8	331.0	+2.0 to −2.0	0.40
360	—	—	360.9	360.8	361.0	+2.0 to −2.0	0.40
390	—	—	390.9	390.8	391.0	+2.0 to −2.0	0.40
420	—	—	420.9	420.8	421.0	+3.3 to −3.3	0.50
480	—	—	—	480.8	481.0	+3.3 to −3.3	0.50
540	—	—	—	540.8	541.0	+3.3 to −3.3	0.60
600	—	—	—	600.8	601.0	+3.3 to −3.3	0.60
660	—	—	—	660.8	661.0	+3.3 to −3.3	0.60

[1] To specify belt size use the Standard Length Designation prefixed by the letter indicating cross section, for example: B 890.

Table B.2 also gives suggested service factors for different type of loads.

Table B.3 shows the standard pitch lengths for V-belts of various sizes. Note that the pitch length is the actual length as determined by twice the distance between the 2 pulleys plus the 2 lengths of the belt which wrap around the 2 pulleys, measured at the pitch diameter of the belt when on the pulley.

Horsepower Rating

The general horsepower rating of a V-belt as given by the RPM method which is the one now most widely used is given by the following rating formulas.

The general horsepower rating formulas are:

RPM METHOD

| *Cross Section* | *Formula* |

$$A \quad P_r = \left[0.7927(rd)^{-0.09} - \frac{1.394}{d} - 0.000244(rd)^2 \right] rd + 1.394r \left(1 - \frac{1}{K_{SR}} \right)$$

$$B \quad P_r = \left[1.399(rd)^{-0.09} - \frac{3.655}{d} - 0.000420(rd)^2 \right] rd + 3.655r \left(1 - \frac{1}{K_{SR}} \right)$$

$$C \quad P_r = \left[2.597(rd)^{-0.09} - \frac{10.163}{d} - 0.000746(rd)^2 \right] rd + 10.163r \left(1 - \frac{1}{K_{SR}} \right)$$

$$D \quad P_r = \left[5.549(rd)^{-0.09} - \frac{36.050}{d} - 0.001522(rd)^2 \right] rd + 36.050r \left(1 - \frac{1}{K_{SR}} \right)$$

$$E \quad P_r = \left[8.116(rd)^{-0.09} - \frac{68.864}{d} - 0.002193(rd)^2 \right] rd + 68.864r \left(1 - \frac{1}{K_{SR}} \right)$$

where P_r = the maximum horespower recommended at 180° arc of contact for a belt of average length (for other lengths and arcs of contact the horsepower obtained from the formula must be multiplied by the appropriate correction factors for length and arc of contact)

d = pitch diameter of small sheave, in.

r = rpm of faster shaft/1,000

K_{SR} = speed ratio factor

Note: The RPM method is the preferred method for presenting horsepower data. The combination FPM-RPM horsepower rating formulas and associated data are sometimes used in older presentations.

Table B.4 shows the nominal horsepower rating of "B" section size V-belts by the RPM method. Rating for other size belts can be obtained from a V-belt manufacturer or from the Mechanical Power Transmission Association.

References

FARRALL, A. W. 1963. Engineering for Dairy and Food Products, 3rd Edition. John Wiley & Sons, New York.

RUBBER MANUFACTURERS ASSOC., 444 Madison Ave., New York, N.Y. Mechanical Power Transmission Assoc., 3525 Peterson Road, Chicago, Ill.

Cross-reference: *Pulley Speed Controls.*

BLANCHING

Blanching is a process of heating fruit or vegetables prior to freezing. Sometimes blanching is used prior to canning. The purpose of blanching is to achieve several

TABLE B.4

HORSEPOWER RATINGS FOR "B" SECTION V-BELTS—RPM METHOD

SECTION 1

RPM of Faster Shaft	Rated Horsepower per Belt for Small Sheave Pitch Diameter																	
	4.6	4.8	5.0	5.2	5.4	5.6	5.8	6.0	6.2	6.4	6.6	6.8	7.0	7.2	7.4	7.6	7.8	8.0
870	1.74	1.93	2.12	2.31	2.49	2.68	2.87	3.05	3.24	3.42	3.60	3.79	3.97	4.15	4.33	4.50	4.68	4.86
1,160	2.12	2.36	2.61	2.85	3.09	3.32	3.56	3.80	4.03	4.26	4.49	4.72	4.94	5.17	5.39	5.61	5.83	6.05
1,750	2.72	3.06	3.39	3.72	4.05	4.37	4.69	5.01	5.32	5.62	5.92	6.22	6.51	6.80	7.08	7.36	7.63	7.90
200	0.57	0.62	0.67	0.72	0.77	0.82	0.87	0.92	0.97	1.02	1.07	1.12	1.17	1.22	1.27	1.32	1.36	1.41
400	0.97	1.07	1.16	1.26	1.35	1.45	1.54	1.64	1.73	1.82	1.91	2.01	2.10	2.19	2.28	2.37	2.47	2.56
600	1.32	1.46	1.60	1.73	1.87	2.01	2.14	2.28	2.41	2.54	2.68	2.81	2.94	3.07	3.20	3.33	3.46	3.59
800	1.63	1.81	1.99	2.16	2.34	2.51	2.69	2.86	3.03	3.20	3.37	3.54	3.71	3.88	4.05	4.21	4.38	4.54
1,000	1.91	2.13	2.34	2.56	2.77	2.98	3.19	3.40	3.61	3.81	4.02	4.22	4.42	4.62	4.82	5.02	5.22	5.41
1,200	2.17	2.42	2.67	2.92	3.16	3.41	3.65	3.89	4.13	4.37	4.60	4.84	5.07	5.30	5.53	5.75	5.98	6.20
1,400	2.39	2.68	2.96	3.24	3.52	3.79	4.07	4.34	4.61	4.87	5.13	5.39	5.65	5.91	6.16	6.41	6.66	6.90
1,600	2.59	2.91	3.22	3.53	3.84	4.14	4.44	4.74	5.03	5.32	5.61	5.89	6.17	6.44	6.72	6.98	7.25	7.51
1,800	2.76	3.11	3.45	3.78	4.12	4.45	4.77	5.09	5.40	5.71	6.02	6.32	6.61	6.90	7.19	7.47	7.74	8.01
2,000	2.90	3.28	3.64	4.00	4.36	4.71	5.05	5.39	5.72	6.04	6.36	6.68	6.98	7.28	7.57	7.86	8.14	8.41
2,200	3.02	3.41	3.80	4.18	4.56	4.92	5.28	5.63	5.98	6.31	6.64	6.96	7.27	7.57	7.87	8.15	8.42	8.69
2,400	3.11	3.52	3.93	4.32	4.71	5.09	5.46	5.82	6.17	6.51	6.84	7.16	7.47	7.77	8.05	8.33	8.59	8.84
2,600	3.16	3.59	4.01	4.42	4.82	5.21	5.58	5.95	6.30	6.64	6.96	7.28	7.58	7.86	8.13	8.39	8.63	8.86
2,800	3.19	3.63	4.06	4.48	4.88	5.27	5.65	6.01	6.35	6.68	7.00	7.30	7.58	7.85	8.10	8.33	8.54	8.73
3,000	3.18	3.63	4.06	4.48	4.89	5.28	5.65	6.00	6.33	6.65	6.95	7.23	7.48	7.72	7.94	8.13	8.31[1]	8.46[1]
3,200	3.13	3.59	4.02	4.44	4.84	5.22	5.58	5.92	6.24	6.53	6.80	7.05	7.27	7.47[1]	7.65[1]	7.80[1]		
3,400	3.05	3.51	3.94	4.35	4.74	5.11	5.45	5.76	6.05	6.32	6.55	6.77[1]	6.95[1]	7.10[1]				
3,600	2.93	3.38	3.81	4.21	4.58	4.92	5.24	5.53	5.78	6.01[1]	6.21[1]	6.37[1]						
3,800	2.77	3.21	3.62	4.00	4.35	4.67	4.96	5.21	5.42[1]	5.60[1]								
4,000	2.57	3.00	3.39	3.74	4.07	4.35	4.60[1]	4.80[1]	4.96[1]									
4,200	2.33	2.73	3.10	3.42	3.71	3.95[1]	4.15[1]											
4,400	2.04	2.42	2.75	3.04	3.28[1]	3.47[1]												
4,600	1.70	2.05	2.34[1]	2.59[1]														
4,800	1.32	1.63[1]	1.88[1]															
5,000	0.88[1]	1.15[1]																
5,200	0.40[1]																	

[1] Belt speed above 6000 feet per min, special sheaves may be necessary.

TABLE B. 4

SECTION 2

	Additional Horsepower per Belt for Speed Ratio								
Rpm of Faster Shaft	1.00 to 1.01	1.02 to 1.04	1.05 to 1.08	1.09 to 1.12	1.13 to 1.18	1.19 to 1.24	1.25 to 1.34	1.35 to 1.51	1.52 to 1.99	2.0 and Over
870	0.00	0.04	0.09	0.13	0.17	0.21	0.26	0.30	0.34	0.38
1,160	0.00	0.06	0.11	0.17	0.23	0.28	0.34	0.40	0.45	0.51
1,750	0.00	0.09	0.17	0.26	0.34	0.43	0.51	0.60	0.69	0.77
200	0.00	0.01	0.02	0.03	0.04	0.05	0.06	0.07	0.08	0.09
400	0.00	0.02	0.04	0.06	0.08	0.10	0.12	0.14	0.16	0.18
600	0.00	0.03	0.06	0.09	0.12	0.15	0.18	0.21	0.24	0.26
800	0.00	0.04	0.08	0.12	0.16	0.20	0.24	0.27	0.31	0.35
1,000	0.00	0.05	0.10	0.15	0.20	0.25	0.29	0.34	0.39	0.44
1,200	0.00	0.06	0.12	0.18	0.24	0.29	0.35	0.41	0.47	0.53
1,400	0.00	0.07	0.14	0.21	0.27	0.34	0.41	0.48	0.55	0.62
1,600	0.00	0.08	0.16	0.24	0.31	0.39	0.47	0.55	0.63	0.71
1,800	0.00	0.09	0.18	0.26	0.35	0.44	0.53	0.62	0.71	0.79
2,000	0.00	0.10	0.20	0.29	0.39	0.49	0.59	0.69	0.78	0.88
2,200	0.00	0.11	0.22	0.32	0.43	0.54	0.65	0.75	0.86	0.97
2,400	0.00	0.12	0.24	0.35	0.47	0.59	0.71	0.82	0.94	1.06
2,600	0.00	0.13	0.26	0.38	0.51	0.64	0.76	0.89	1.02	1.15
2,800	0.00	0.14	0.27	0.41	0.55	0.69	0.82	0.96	1.10	1.24
3,000	0.00	0.15	0.29	0.44	0.59	0.74	0.88	1.03	1.18	1.32
3,200	0.00	0.16	0.31	0.47	0.63	0.78	0.94	1.10	1.25	1.41
3,400	0.00	0.17	0.33	0.50	0.67	0.83	1.00	1.17	1.33	1.50
3,600	0.00	0.18	0.35	0.53	0.71	0.88	1.06	1.24	1.41	1.59
3,800	0.00	0.19	0.37	0.56	0.75	0.93	1.12	1.30	1.49	1.68
4,000	0.00	0.20	0.39	0.59	0.78	0.98	1.18	1.37	1.57	1.76
4,200	0.00	0.21	0.41	0.62	0.82	1.03	1.24	1.44	1.65	1.85
4,400	0.00	0.22	0.43	0.65	0.86	1.08	1.29	1.51	1.73	1.94
4,600	0.00	0.23	0.45	0.68	0.90	1.13	1.35	1.58	1.80	2.03
4,800	0.00	0.24	0.47	0.71	0.94	1.18	1.41	1.65	1.88	2.12
5,000	0.00	0.25	0.49	0.73	0.98	1.23	1.47	1.72	1.96	2.21
5,200	0.00	0.26	0.51	0.76	1.02	1.27	1.53	1.78	2.04	2.29

objectives: (1) soften the tissue to facilitate packaging; (2) avoid damage to the product; (3) eliminate air from the product; (4) preserve the natural color; (5) destroy or retard certain undesirable enzymes; and (6) help preserve natural flavor.

Principles

Blanching is achieved in hot water for a short period of time or in an atmosphere of steam. In water blanching the product is moved through water usually maintained at a temperature between 190° and 210°F. The product is carried on a belt through a steam chamber in the case of steam blanching into which live steam is constantly injected. The steam chamber is hooded and equipped with an exhaust and also a drain for the condensate. The time and temperature are regulated for each specific product to achieve the desired enzyme inactivation, color preservation, and other characteristics. As a guide, the operator utilizes either the catalase or the peroxidase tests to determine the adequacy of blanching. Currently the peroxidase test is commonly used in the industry. For the most part, a negative peroxidase test is

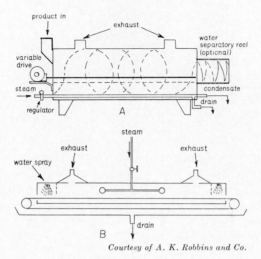

Courtesy of A. K. Robbins and Co.

Fig. B-7. Blanchers
A—Water type rotary blancher. B—Steam blancher for leafy products.

necessary to prevent the development of undesirable characteristics in the finished product.

Immediately after blanching, vegetables are quickly cooled usually in cold water which often serves as a flume to convey the product to the next operation. A rod-type cylindrical reel connected to the discharge of the blancher and equipped with water sprays also serves as an excellent cooling system.

Equipment

Blanchers of steam or rotary hot water types are designed to be automatically fed and equipped for continuous discharge. Both types are available with variable speed drive to permit adjustment to a range of line speeds. The rotary hot water blancher receives the product through a hopper normally just above the drive end. The product is conducted into a spiral unit which conveys it to the opposite end. In the case of the hooded live-steam blancher which has a perforated wire belt, the blancher serves as a conveyor making it very adaptable to any system.

Rotary hot water and steam blanchers are shown in Fig. B.7 A and B. The rotary water blancher is sometimes constructed of a steel frame with a galvanized sheet-metal tank and cast-iron ends. However, use of stainless steel construction is expected to expand during the years ahead. The blanching compartment is equipped with clean-out doors on the ends. The revolving drum is made of perforated galvanized sheet metal. A typical commercial water blancher would be slightly over 6 ft in height with an overall length of approximately 21 ft. The unit would possess a cylinder 4 ft in diameter and 18 ft long. A blancher of this size would be driven with a 5 hp motor with a capacity of approximately 5,100 lb per hr of peas.

The screw conveyor heat exchanger has been successfully used for blanching. This equipment is known commercially as the "thermascrew" and consists of a revolving auger submerged in a long, low-bottom trough. The auger propels the product through the hot water. Heating with this unit may be indirect or with direct steam

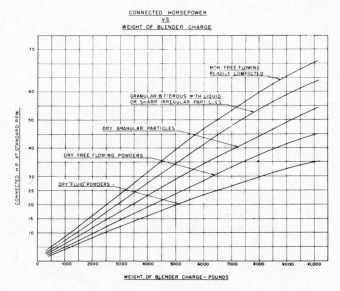

CONNECTED HORSEPOWER
VS
WEIGHT OF BLENDER CHARGE

F IG. B-8. Horsepower requirements for ribbon blenders

injection. Direct steam injection is frequently used with this type of heater, as well as, with the rotary water blancher. Typical operating conditions on mushrooms with the screw heat exchanger are as follows: Steam blancher 3 to 5 psi, 3.5 min exposure, capacity 2,500 lb per hr, 12 in. diam screw with 9 in. pitch at 5 rpm.

Some processors seem to prefer a steam blancher for leafy vegetables such as spinach, turnip greens, collard, etc. The steam blancher consists of a metal frame with a galvanized sheet metal steam chamber. The unit is frequently equipped with both water and steam sprays to increase its versatility as a scalder blancher. The lower belt of the hooded chamber is pitched to a central drain outlet for condensate removal. A typical commercial steam blancher is approximately 20 ft long, 4 ft wide, and 4 ft high. The unit is equipped with two 1 in. water inlets and two 2 in. steam inlets. Water spray pipes, as well as the steam spray pipes, are usually $1/2$ in. The drain outlet is 3 in. The unit is powered with a 3 hp motor often utilizing a variable speed drive.

Practices

Prior to freezing, some fruit is blanched, however, fruit does not require blanching to the same degree as vegetables. In fact, in most cases, fruit is not blanched. Sulfur dioxide is very often used in treating fruit to prevent browning caused by enzymes during freezing and storage. Apples, for example, may be dipped for about 1 min in a solution containing 0.2 to 0.25% of available sulfur dioxide at 2.8 to 3.0 pH. For fruits, blanching may cause undesirable softening, consequently, other treatments are frequently used.

Blanching time will vary between products. The condition or size of a product will also influence blanching time. Table B.5 gives typical blanching time for special vegetables to be frozen.

TABLE B.5

BLANCHING TIMES FOR VEGETABLES TO BE FROZEN

Product	Heating Medium	Blanching Time, Min
Asparagus	Live steam	3.5–5 depending upon stalk diameter
Broccoli	Live steam	3.5
Brussels sprouts	Live steam	5–6
Carrots	Water at 210°F	2–3
Cauliflower	Live steam	4–5
Corn on the cob	Live steam	6–11
Cut corn	Live steam	3
Lima beans (Fordhook)	Live steam	3–4
Lima beans (baby)	Water at 210°F	2.5
Peas (green)	Water at 210° to 212°F	50–60 sec
	Live steam	2–3
Snap beans (crosscut)	Live steam or water at 210°F	2–4
Snap beans (frenched)	Live steam	2–4
Spinach	Live steam	2–3

Because the product comes in contact with steam boiler water it must be of culinary quality. Boiler-treatment compounds must be limited to those approved by the Food and Drug Administration or other regulatory agencies if the steam is to be used for steam blanching. A rotary water-type blancher may be equipped with heat coils or an indirect heat exchanger to avoid direct steam injection into the blanching water. This method may permit the use of boiler treatment compounds which otherwise would be unacceptable. In most food plants the use of cyclohexylamine, octadecalamine, or morpholine are not recommended.

One should select a size of blancher which will handle the line capacity without being overcrowded. Overcrowding can occur particularly with the live steam blancher by depositing too thick a layer on the belt. A certain amount of penetration time is required to heat through the product. This is more critical in the case of the live steam blancher than with the water type because in the water-type unit the product receives a certain amount of agitation as it is being conducted through the water. Overloading a blancher can be one of the more serious mistakes made by the operator.

Maintenance of the unit should be on a regular basis to be certain that all of the automatic controls will perform properly. The use of a check thermometer to ascertain the accuracy of the one installed on the unit is a good practice.

Reference

JOSLYN, M. A., and HEID, J. L. 1964. Food Processing Operations, Vol. 3. AVI Publishing Co., Westport, Conn.

Cross-references: *Dewaterers; Washing and Blanching.*

BLENDERS

One of the most diversified pieces of equipment in the food industry is the blender. Most products require some mixing or blending in some stage of the process.

Blenders are designed for mixing dry or liquid ingredients or combining liquid and dry products. Four blenders used for dry products are the ribbon, tumbling or revolv-

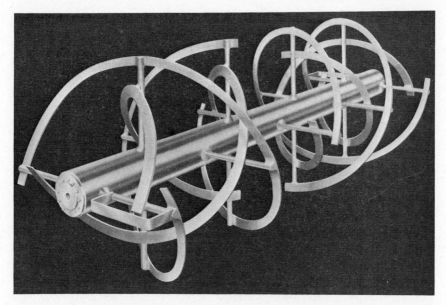

Courtesy of Strong-Scott Mfg. Co.

FIG. B-9.   Ribbon blender agitator

ing, air mixing, and vertical shaft propeller types.   One of the most commonly used is the ribbon type.   These are available with many modifications to permit mixing under vacuum as well as under pressure with applied heat.   Most ribbon blenders have a horizontal shaft with a U- or cylindrical-shaped vessel.   The horsepower for a ribbon blender is generally a function of the total weight of the charge.   Dry materials often vary substantially in their resistance to movement.   Horsepower demands, therefore, will vary accordingly.   A typical ribbon blender operating at recommended speed will require power according to Fig. B.8.

Typical power requirement for a U-shaped blender having a maximum working capacity of 200 cu ft is 25 hp with a shaft speed of 18 rpm.   A commonly used mixing element in a ribbon blender is illustrated in Fig. B.9.

A revolving blender will frequently have a Y-shape as illustrated in Fig. B.10. This unit is effective in combining a wide variety of dry ingredients.

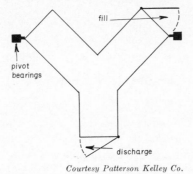

Courtesy Patterson Kelley Co.

FIG. B-10.   Y-shaped blender particularly suited for dry ingredients

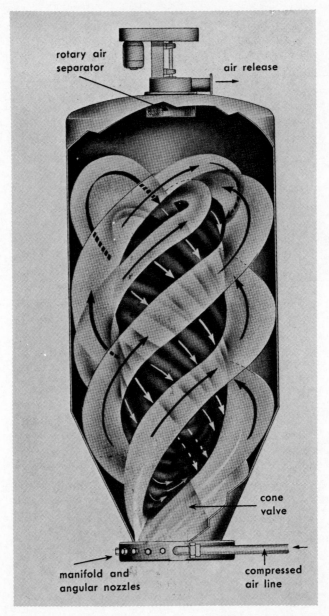

Courtesy of Sprout Waldron

Fɪɢ. B-11.   Air-pulsed mixer

A newer, more novel type blender for dry ingredients may be termed an air-pro-pelled blender.   This unit is illustrated in Fig. B.11.   These units commonly operate with compressed air at about 200 psi with short blasts introduced at the bottom of a cylindrical chamber which is equipped with a cone.   The exhaust is controlled with a rotary air separator to minimize product loss.   A typical air mixing blender has the following characteristics:

Working capacity	300 cu ft
Total capacity	472 cu ft
Body height	20 ft
Body diameter	70 in. total
Cylinder height	15 ft plus dome
Cylinder wall thickness	11 gage exhaust
Duct diameter	8 in.
Operating pressure range	150–225 psi

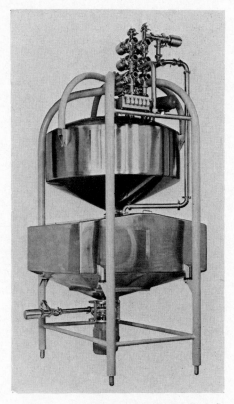

Courtesy of Ladish Tri-Clover Co.

FIG. B-12.   Automatic batch weigh system

Liquid Blenders

Liquid blenders are often basically a centrifugal pump or a propeller blade in the base of a container. Because liquid ingredients can be pumped, considerable automation can be incorporated into blending systems. For example, some ice cream plants are now utilizing programmed circuitry with air operated sanitary valves to feed ingredients to a weight tank used in conjunction with a blending tank. This system is illustrated in Fig. B.12. An inline blender is shown above the weight tank. A blending pump is also used at the base of the blend tank. This system feeds a pasteurizer continuously and is fully automatic.

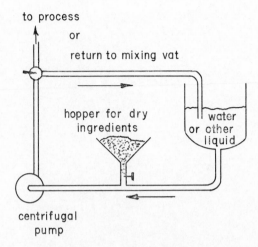

to process
or
return to mixing vat

hopper for dry
ingredients

water
or other
liquid

centrifugal
pump

FIG. B-13.   Blending system for reconstituting nonfat dry milk

Problems are commonly encountered when incorporating dry ingredients into liquids. A blending system utilizing a tapered funnel or hopper to direct nonfat dry milk or products into a liquid line ahead of a centrifugal pump has been used very successfully. The hook-up for this system is simple as shown in Fig. B.13.

Some manufacturers have designed equipment for combining dry ingredients with a liquid to form a slurry. These vessels may be equipped with a multispeed motor and a special agitator. This type unit is illustrated in Fig. B.14. The agitator in this vessel operates at about 400 rpm. A squirrel cage-propeller combination agitator creates a deep vortex into which the added dry ingredients are drawn. The dry particles are efficiently dispersed forming a uniform slurry. These units are made of stainless steel to achieve a high degree of sanitation and may be cleaned with CIP methods.

The fruit, nut, and flavoring feeder shown in Fig. B.15 also serves as a blender of the ingredients into a continuously flowing pipeline of ice cream. The unit may be utilized for other products as well.

References

ASSOCIATED DAIRY EQUIPMENT MFR. 1966. Adem Continuous Mix Processing System, General Bull. *93*. Everett, Mass.

CHEMICAL PROCESS. 1968. Product Uniformity up 300%. April.

CP DIVISION ST. REGIS. Dry Ingredient Incorporator, Bull. *B-1-225*. Chicago, Ill.

LADISH CO. TRI-CLOVER DIV. Tri-Clover Automatic Batch Weigh System. Kenosha, Wis.

SPROUT-WALDRON AND CO. Airmix Mixer, Bull. *255-C*. Muncy, Pa.

THE STRONG SCOTT MFG. CO. 1966. Catalog *RB-19*. Minneapolis, Min.

Cross-references: *Agitators; Dough Mixing.*

BOILERS

The food industry processes certain foods with heat which may involve boiling temperatures. The equipment may be open or enclosed types and may be heated by steam jacket, or by direct injection of steam. Normally, the product is treated in batches; however, there are continuous type cookers available for large operations.

FIG. B-14.   Dry ingredient incorporators

The equipment might be called a kettle, retort, cooker, or possibly a blancher depending upon its use and type.   The construction of the apparatus depends upon the particular use.   The principal points of management are to make certain that the steam jacket is properly drained of condensate by a trap and to provide a safety relief valve on the heating chamber.   Temperature control can be made automatic if desired.   Care of the vessel also includes protection of the jacket and the food contact surface from corrosion.

A boiler or steam generator is a pressure vessel for producing steam, usually at atmospheric pressure or above.   Most steam for a processing plant is produced by a central boiler and associated system.   Smaller boilers are often used for remote locations, and for plant expansion.

Operation

The boiler is a device with appropriate controls and accessories for transferring thermal energy from fuel (gaseous, liquid, or solid) to water to form steam.   The accessories essential for efficient operation are fuel supply;   water supply;   pressure control;   draft control;   method of adding water, either pump or injector;   and a firebox. To increase the efficiency of a boiler, the water might be preheated, the air preheated, or heat removed from the exhaust stack to heat incoming air or water.   Pumps may be used to circulate the water in the boiler to increase the rate of heat transfer.

Boilers may be classified as fire tube, water tube, or shell type.   In the fire tube, water surrounds the tube with the heated gases going through the interior.   The reverse

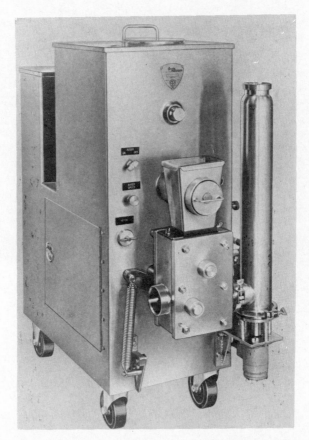

Fig. B-15.   Continuous flow blender

is true for the water-tube boiler. The shell tube consists of a shell with heating elements, often electrical for adding heat to the water. Fire-tube boilers are commonly used for smaller boilers. Boilers are rated according to: boiler horsepower, which is equivalent to the evaporation of 34.5 lb of water per hr at 212°F, or 33,472 Btu per hr; heating surface (HS) in square feet on the hot side of the tubes, where from 5 to 8 lb per hr-sq ft of water is evaporated; or by equivalent direct radiation (EDR), where 242 Btu per hr sq ft is figured for steam boilers and 150 Btu per hr-sq ft for water heaters. There is no relationship between boiler horsepower and mechanical horsepower as used for motive vehicles. In general, the term boiler horsepower is not being used greatly because of various conditions under which the rating may be obtained. Another definition for 1 hp is 10 sq ft of boiler heating surface designated on the hot side.

The present ASME power code suggests that the rating of boilers for size only should be in square feet of heating surface.

To decrease floor space required for boilers, the number of passes of the gas through the tubes is accomplished by stacking groups of tubes in the boiler. With the single pass boiler, heated air passes once through the boiler with long tubes to provide time for transfer of heat from the air to the water. Double-, triple-, and quadruple-pass boilers have been developed. With the 4-pass boiler approximately $1/4$ of the usual length of tube is required, with the gas passing through 4 different groups of tubes going to the stack.

An important aspect of boiler operation is to maintain efficient combustion of the fuel. In general, approximately 15,000 Btu per lb are obtained from coal, 19,000 Btu per lb from oil, and 950 to 1,130 Btu per cu ft for natural gas (approximately 22,520 Btu per lb of natural gas). Liquid petroleum gas varies from 500 to 1,000 Btu per cu ft. A measure of the efficiency of combustion is the temperature and composition of the stack gas. The temperature varies greatly depending upon the boiler, location of taking the temperature, type of fuel, etc., and is usually specified by the manufacturer for most efficient operation, but will vary from 400° to 600°F. The stack gases are analyzed by an Orsat apparatus which can be used for determining the carbon monoxide, carbon dioxide, and oxygen. In general, the carbon dioxide should be high with the carbon monoxide low. Incomplete combustion is indicated with high carbon monoxide. If too much air is supplied for combustion, however, a cooling effect occurs. An excess of air is supplied to the burner to permit as close to complete combustion as possible. In general, with gaseous fuels, approximately 10% air in excess of that required for complete combustion, is utilized, whereas for liquid fuels about 20%, and for solid fuels about 30%.

Electric Boiler

An electrically heated boiler may be used to produce hot water or steam. An electric boiler may be economical to install for locations remote from plant or boiler facilities and utilize for short peak loads where electricity is inexpensive compared to other energy sources.

The electrical energy is supplied through heating elements immersed in the water. Thus, conventional tubes are replaced by electric heating elements, such as those used in water heaters. The elements are normally placed near the bottom of the pressure container. These units are simple to operate, easy to control, and do not give off products of combustion.

The quantity of electricity to heat the water is calculated on the basis of 3,412 Btu per 1 kwh of electricity. To heat 1 lb of water from 62° to 338°F (at 100 psi) requires 1,158 Btu (see Steam). Thus, 1 kwh of electricity will provide about 2.9 lb steam at 100 psi from 62°F.

Principles and Practices

(1) Steam traps are necessary to maintain pressure and temperature in the steam line. These should operate so that there is not excessive steam loss to the atmosphere.

(2) For low-temperature processing operations, low-pressure steam, below 1 atm, may prove to be more economical than high-pressure steam, and provide less expensive operations because of reduced technical manpower required for operation as specified by various state laws, less problem of control and maintenance of traps, and other auxiliary equipment.

(3) It is usually economical to return the condensate from the process as feedwater to the boiler. This water has been heated, has a high heat content, and has been treated.

(4) Boilers should operate in the range of 70 to 80% efficiency as heat converters.

(5) There should be a continuous monitoring of the temperature and composition of the exhaust gases to evaluate the combustion efficiency of the boiler, usually through an Orsat or continuous measuring and recording devices.

(6) Water can be treated ahead of the boiler or in the boiler. For specific recommendations, particularly for unusual water conditions, specialists should be consulted to consider the problem and to make recommendations. The most common treatment ahead of the boiler is the zeolite treatment. Compounds may be added to the boiler to reduce scale. It is important to follow instructions to permit workers to operate safely and to prevent damage to the equipment.

(7) In addition to treating the water, the boiler should be "blown-down" periodically according to the amount of sludge accumulated.

(8) A vapor heater is placed on the steam outlet side of a boiler for heating steam to provide superheated steam.

(9) Entrainment of water droplets and carry-over of liquid in the steam may be due to excessive steaming rates, or an undesirable method of water treatment. Carry-over of water droplets should be avoided as the quality of steam is reduced.

(10) Most States and insurance companies have set certain specifications standards, and codes with respect to operation of steam boilers. These should be consulted.

Economical Operation

Economical steam boiler operation is achieved by the following.

(1) Heating surfaces should be kept clean on both the water side and the fire side. On the water side, water treatment may be carried out, either before the boiler or in the boiler. Blow-down can be practiced to remove sludge from the boiler. The fire side of the tube on a fire tube boiler should be kept clear of soot contamination by periodically scraping the flues.

(2) The fuel should be burned properly. Generally $\frac{1}{10}$ lb of coal is required to produce 1 lb of steam at 100 psi. An excess of oxygen (air) is provided to assure complete combustion. To assure complete combustion an excess of about 10% air, based on theoretical need, is provided for gas, 10 to 15% for fuel oil, and 15 to 30% for coal. Adding too much air causes excessive cooling and heat loss. The burning efficiency can be checked through analysis of stack gases, using an Orsat apparatus, with the carbon dioxide running 9 to 11%, and through stack temperature, which should be 400 to 600°F, depending on the boiler, fuel, etc. Check manual for instructions.

(3) The boiler should be fired according to load. This is particularly applicable to the coal fired boiler although important for all types. Fuel, oil, and gas burners are easier to provide on-off immediate withdrawal or application of heat than the coal boiler. The boiler should be fired so as to avoid excess blow-off. Excess blow-off means loss of steam, and therefore heat.

(4) Avoid excessive heat losses. These are represented primarily, as far as operation is concerned, as heat loss from steam leaks at valves and other accessories. Properly insulate steam pipes and be sure that steam traps operate properly to maintain pressure in the system. Also, the condensate should be returned to the boiler.

Reference

BABCOCK and WILCOX CO. 1955. Steam—Its Generation and Use. New York.

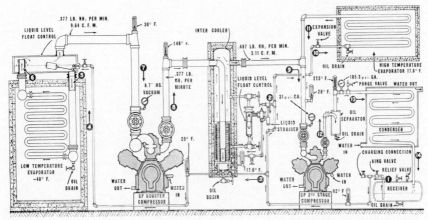

Courtesy of St. Regis Corp.

Fig. B-16.   Booster compressor on ammonia refrigeration system
Hookup for a booster in connection with a two-stage compression system, such as
is used for low-temperature refrigeration.

Cross references: *Culinary Steam Production; Energy; Evaporation; Evaporators; Insulation; Piping; Sensible and Latent Heat; Steam.*

BOOSTER COMPRESSOR

A booster compressor might be used on a refrigeration system or on an air compression system. It is a pump usually made to handle a large volume of gas or vapor at a relatively low pressure. Booster compressors are of particular use and advantage in refrigeration systems which operate at extremely low temperatures, 0°F or less, also on air compressor systems exceeding 50 psig.

Principle

The booster compressor is designed to take a vapor or gas at low pressure and high specific volume and compress the material to a moderate pressure. In a refrigeration system for example, as shown in Fig. B.16, ammonia at a temperature of −20°F is drawn from the evaporating coils and is raised by the booster compressor to a pressure of about 15 psi. The refrigerant is then discharged into an intercooler, and being partially compressed, is drawn into the regular high-pressure compressor. This system thermodynamically is considerably more efficient than if the high-pressure compressor were used to raise the −20°F vapor in one step to the condensing pressure. It also has the advantage that the low-pressure or booster compressor can be built much lighter than the regular high-pressure compressor, since it is subjected to lower operating pressures.

Practices

The booster compressor should be considered for use on any refrigeration system which operates at − 10°F or lower. It should also be considered in a multitemperature system in which part of the load is at temperatures such as −20° to −40°F, and part of

72. *Booster Compressor*

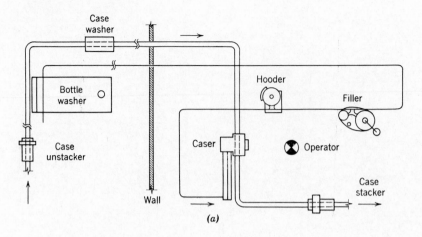

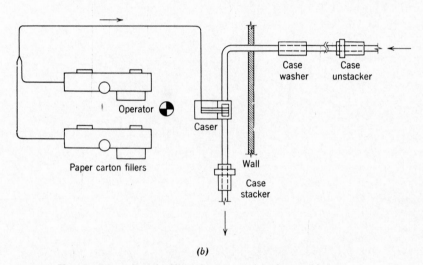

Fig. B-17. Bottle filling layouts: (a) glass; (b) paper

the load is above 0°, usually up to 20°–30°F. The low-temperature load can be connected directly to the booster compressor and the high-temperature load can be connected directly to the regular high-pressure compressor. If this were not done, the entire load would need to be carried by the high-pressure compressor. This would result in a very expensive machine which would of necessity need to operate at the lowest system pressure thus greatly decreasing the efficiency of compression.

Booster compressors for refrigeration systems are frequently of the rotary type design and extremely large units often are centrifugal multistage compressors.

In the operation of a booster compressor it is always important to start the high-pressure pump first, and to balance the operating pressures of the system to achieve the desired results most economically.

For extremely high air pressures, booster compressors may be built with more than two stages with increased efficiency. The increased efficiency of a booster compression refrigeration system depends upon the difference in the low-temperature side of the system and the high side. The greater the difference the greater is the increase in efficiency. The efficiency of a multistage air compressor is greatly increased by use of an intercooler between the stages.

Cross-references: *Air Compressors; Refrigeration Principles.*

BOTTLE FILLERS, CLOSERS, CAPPERS

Bottle fillers are used to place liquids such as milk, juices, carbonated and non-carbonated beverages, beer, soft drinks, and other low viscosity liquids in glass and plastic containers. Glass bottles are the containers most commonly filled by bottling equipment. Bottle fillers and cappers are normally designed with adjustments to fill several bottle sizes. Some bottle fillers are capable of handling bottles ranging in size from $^1/_2$ pint to 1 gal. Fillers are usually equipped with capper heads for applying a single closer cap. In some instances, an additional piece of equipment called the hooder receives the filled and capped bottles from the bottler and places an outer hood on the bottle. Hooders will apply various types of closures including plastic films or laminated materials.

Principles

Bottle fillers depend upon the accuracy of the container to determine quantity. Bottlers operate on the principle of displacing a given amount of liquid below the cap seat. Therefore, the volume of the container must be within close tolerances because it serves as a liquid measure. A bottle during filling has the air withdrawn through a vent tube. In the case of gravity-type bottle fillers, the air moves up the vent tube and is discharged above liquid level in the filler bowl. Greater capacity is obtained with vacuum type automatic bottle fillers. These units frequently operate at about 14 in. water vacuum. Most all bottle fillers are designed with a round bowl which rotates continuously during operation. Bottles are fed onto the pedestal beneath each valve with a special bottle spacing infeed mechanism. A conveyor normally supplies bottles to the fillers and removes the filled containers. The liquid level in the filler bowl is maintained at a constant level by means of a float or other regulating device.

System

A bottle washing, filling, and casing system is usually found in fluid bottling plants. In the system the bottler is regarded as the pacesetter to which the capacity of the other equipment is regulated. The washer, hooder, and casing equipment should be sized slightly faster than the bottle filler. This increased capacity allows for "catch-up" time in the case of production disruption and will allow for the bottler to fill without interruption for a short time. A certain amount of bottle conveyor should be included in the system to allow for brief stoppages of the washer, hooder, and casing equipment without causing a shutdown of the filler.

The arrangement of the bottle filler, hooder, and casing equipment should be convenient for the operator who can normally supervise all of this equipment (Fig. B.17).

Specifications

Vacuum-type bottle fillers will usually handle 5 to 8 quart bottles per minute per valve. Vacuum readily removes air from the bottle, as well as some foam from the product. With some vacuum fillers, a chipped cap seat or lip on the bottle will admit air and prevent the bottle from being filled.

The filling speed is affected by the type and viscosity of the product. For example, a 28 valve vacuum-type filler has a maximum production rate per minute for various products (Table B.6).

The temperature of the product being filled should also be considered. The volume relationship of 4% milk and 25% butterfat cream at various temperatures as compared with 68°F is given in Table B.7.

TABLE B.6

PRODUCTION OF VACUUM BOTTLE FILLER

Product	Production in Bottles per Minute			
	$^{1}/_{2}$-Gallon	Quarts	Pints	$^{1}/_{2}$-Pints
Homogenized milk	120	160	165	170
Chocolate milk	—	130	140	140
20% Cream	—	120	135	135
40% Cream	—	110	125	125
Buttermilk	—	110	125	125

TABLE B.7

EFFECT OF TEMPERATURE ON VOLUME OF MILK AND CREAM

Filling Temperature, °F	Volume of 4% Milk	Volume of 25% Cream
68	1.000	1.000
60	0.9985	0.9970
50	0.9975	0.9925
35	0.9967	0.9835

Practices

To the plant operator it is very important to fill containers accurately. Underfilling, of course, is illegal; whereas, overfilling a milk bottle, for example, at the rate of 0.05 oz on a 100,000 qt per day operation result in a loss of approximately 53,100 qt of milk per year. Checking the accuracy of fill on each valve of a bottle filler about once a week is good assurance to the operator that he is not over- or underfilling.

Products containing air cannot be accurately filled on most bottle fillers. This is especially true in the case of heavy-bodied products such as cultured buttermilk. Liquids containing air will result in glass bottles lacking the familiar sharp ringing sound when bumped together lightly. A dead insulated sound occurs if air is in the product when the bottles are tapped together lightly.

A bottle conveyor feeding filler and hooding equipment should be properly lubricated. Insufficient conveyor lubricant may cause excessive bottle breakage at the filler infeed, especially if there are a large number of empty bottles on the conveyor ahead of the filler.

TABLE B.8

MILK BOTTLE TOLERANCE

| | Tolerances on Individual Capacity | | | |
| | In Excess | | In Deficiency | |
Nominal Capacity	Fluid Drams	Cubic Inches	Fluid Drams	Cubic Inches
10 Fluid ounces or less	2.25	0.50	1.25	0.28
1 Pint	3.00	0.68	2.00	0.45
1 Quart	4.00	0.90	3.00	0.68
1/2 Gallon	6.00	1.35	5.00	1.13
1 Gallon	10.00	2.26	8.00	1.80
2 Gallons	18.00	4.06	12.00	2.71

Source: Milk Industry Foundation.

If the distance between the bottle washer and filler is especially long, such as 100 ft, it is often helpful to install a bottle retarder on the conveyor about 15 ft ahead of the filler. This reduces bottle pressure on the in-feed star wheel reducing breakage.

Reference

MILK INDUSTRY FOUNDATION. 1967. Manual for Milk Plant Operators. Washington, D.C.

Cross-references: *Bottles and Cartons; Bottle Washers; Vacuum Filler.*

BOTTLES AND CARTONS

Glass bottles are often used to serve as containers of legal measure for food products. For dairy products the bottle serves as a legal measure and the carton capacity must be permanently marked on the side. If a glass bottle for such products as salad dressing carries an applied label, the bottle need not be permanently marked relative to its capacity. Where the glass bottle serves as a unit of measure as the milk bottle, it must conform to the standards published in the National Bureau of Standards Handbook 44, Second Edition. The fill-point of a milk bottle is specified at $1/4$ in. below the plane of the sealing surface if the internal diameter is 2 in. or less. If the internal diameter at the sealing surface is greater than 2 in., the fill-point is specified at $1/8$ in. below the cap seat. Other items required on and for milk bottles are: (1) the last two digits of the year of manufacture; and (2) water at 68°F plus or minus 5°F is used to determine capacity. Tolerances permitted for the average capacity of milk bottles, as well as the individual milk bottle tolerance, are shown in Table B. 8.

A given lot of milk bottles shall be considered as failing to meet the tolerance requirements when (1) the average error of a sample of 25 or more bottles exceeds the tolerance values, or (2) the error in 20% or more of the individual bottles in the sample is greater than the appropriate tolerance for individual bottles.

The amount of glass in a bottle will vary somewhat with its shape. There has been a tendency to reduce the weight of glass to obtain advantages in shipping without impairing strength. Square bottles generally contain less glass than round bottles. Also the distribution of glass through a bottle is important for strength. Glass bottles must pass a number of impact and different shock tests. Careful control is maintained by the manufacturer regarding cooling rates after blowing. Brittleness must be avoided.

Blown Plastic Containers

In recent years considerable interest has been shown in blown plastic containers. Most of these are of the high density polyethylene type. Some containers have been made with polypropylene and polystyrene. The high density polypropylene containers can be of the returnable or nonreturnable types. Because retailers prefer the nonreturnable container, considerable emphasis has been placed on the lightweight (approximately 54 gm) nonreturnable $1/_2$-gal. size. Manufacturers have made for the dairy and other segments of the food industry blown plastic container machines for a variety of sizes and shapes. A returnable plastic $1/_2$-gal. milk container will weigh about 95 gm. When returnable containers are used, most States require an automatic inspection device which is sealed by the health officer to determine the presence of volatile contaminates. The filling of lightweight, nonreturnable plastic containers has been somewhat of a problem, and it has been necessary to modify filling valves and capping heads. Nonreturnable containers tend to collapse under vacuum in filling which reduces the capacity. Placing a restrictor in the suction line to the blower permitting only a $1/_2$-in. opening in the line, which reduces the vacuum to about 10 in. of water, has proved quite satisfactory.

In blow molding high-density polyethylene, a cycle of about 10 sec per container is required. The major delay in blow molding is due to the cooling time required to set the plastic before releasing from the mold. Refrigerated water is usually used as the coolant for the blow molding heads. Lower temperature coolants such as refrigerated propylene glycol have not proved to be a major advantage over 34°F water, because condensation forms on the mold when opened to the atmosphere. Moisture on the blow mold surface causes a bubble resulting in the pinhole and a defective container. Reducing the humidity in the blow mold room assists in correcting the moisture condition.

Blow mold machines require considerable refrigeration for cooling of the heads and also a clutch mechanism. An example of this requirement is stated by one manufacturer who suggests a 20 hp condensing unit to handle the refrigeration load of a 5 head, 30 per min, $1/_2$-gal. machine. The heat requirements are mainly for liquifying the polyethylene at a temperature of 425° to 450°F for blow molding.

Cartons

Cartons for food products will vary widely in size, shape, and type. Some need not be sufficiently tight to hold liquids while others such as milk cartons must have excellent seals. All cartons for use in the food industry should be carefully stored in a room of relatively low humidity. In general, a temperature of 70° to 75°F and 30 to 40% RH have proved satisfactory. The storage area should be clean, well ventilated and free from strong odors. It is a good practice to store cartons on spacers above a floor and at least 6-in. clearance from walls. All cartons should be carefully handled to prevent cracking of the plastic or paraffin coating. Milk cartons which are among the most difficult to form and properly seal in a food plant are most satisfactory with a moisture content of about 5%. For these cartons, a storage room of 30% RH is recommended. The plastic coated paper cartons are heated with electrical or fuel gas heaters to melt the plastic which is then bonded under pressure to form the seals.

For packaging most food products in bottles and cartons, the special characteristics of a given product must be considered. However, the package should be designed and constructed to make it tamperproof during marketing. All packages must carry the legal label requirements for a given product and must be considered in package design.

References

NATL. BUR. STD. HANDBOOK 44. Washington, D.C.
MILK INDUSTRY FOUNDATION. 1967. Manual for Milk Plant Operators. Washington, D.C.

Cross-references: *Bottle Fillers, Closers, Cappers; Bottle Washers; Carton Forming and Filling; Packages; Vacuum Filler.*

BOTTLES, WASHERS

Mechanical bottle washing is necessary to reduce the cost of processing and handling, and to insure a more uniform and perfect washing operation. Washers are made in sizes from the small hand operated to the large completely automatic soaker-type washers.

Types

The simplest type of hand washer usually consists of a motor-driven brush mounted above a small wash tank. The operator lifts the bottles and places them over the brush which is rotated and this action together with the sloshing action of the operation removes any foreign matter from the bottle surface. Rinsing and sterilizing is a separate operation. The second type of washer is the so-called, automatic jet-type of washer. This type of washer has a traveling chain which supports and carries the bottles to the different stations in the washer where the bottle is subjected to high-pressure jets of wash water sterilizing solution and in some cases an air blast. This washer is relatively inexpensive and is fairly satisfactory if the soil on the bottles is of a type which comes off easily. Jet washers range from small sizes to those handling 120 bottles per min or more.

The soaker type washer consists of a traveling carrier with pockets for the bottles. This carrier which is mounted on a chain moves the bottles in rows through the different treatments. In the latest type of washers the bottles are fed automatically, move to rinse position, and then to a soak and wash position at which the bottles are subjected to a strong alkali treatment for approximately 20 to 30 min. The bottles are then rinsed with clean sterile water and ejected to be conveyed to fillers. A number of variations of this type of washer include a mechanical brush or the so-called air brush which is a high-pressure air jet which loosens the soil. The principal advantages of the soaker type washer are that bottles are thoroughly sterilized and even tenacious residue is usually removed. Because of the extended exposure of the bottles to the hot alkali in the soaking position. The cost of operation of this type of washer is usually lower than the jet type because less steam, water, and pump power are needed.

Figure B.18 shows a diagram of one type of soaker washer.

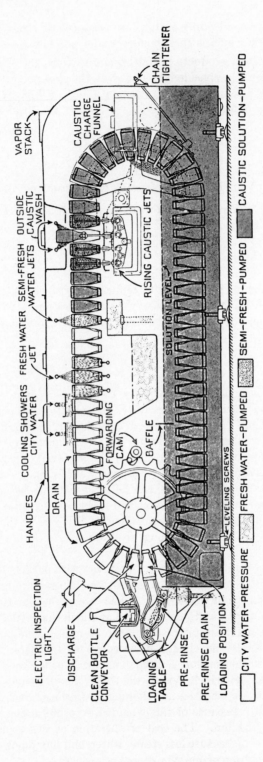

Courtesy of St. Regis Corp.

FIG. B-18.   Soaker-type bottle washer showing various treatments to which bottles are subjected as they move through the machine

Management

Management of the jet-type washers consists mainly in keeping the jets clean and free from deposits, keeping the strainers and filters clean, and maintaining proper temperatures and solution strengths. Strict adherence to the directions of the manufacturer is important, as carelessness with temperatures may result in extreme breakage of bottles. The pumps which circulate the solution for the jets must be kept clean and the stuffing boxes or packing glands kept in good repair. Motors must be of the waterproof type or protected from moisture.

With the soaker type washers maintenance of soaker solution temperature and strength are the two most critical points. Rinse nozzles and rinse water circulation systems must be kept clean and in good operating condition also. It is important to clean all strainers each day.

Auxiliary Equipment

The principal auxiliary equipment in connection with bottle washers are automatic solution strength controls, clean bottle inspection, and illumination devices. It is customary to supply special lighting for the inspection of clean bottles usually with a light intensity of 100 lumens.

Good ventilation around the bottle washers is desirable to remove the excess steam and vapor which would otherwise cause condensation and make the bottle washing area a very undesirable place to work. Proper drainage of the floor around the bottle washer is necessary. An important auxiliary of bottle washing is the materials handling system consisting of conveyors, casers, stackers, unstackers, and counters.

References

ANON. 1967A. Keep sanitary standards high. Food Eng. *39*, No. 2, 92–94.
ANON. 1967B. Dry-feeds detergents directly into solution. Food Eng. *39*, No. 4, 174.
ANON. 1965. Cleaning materials and methods. Food Manuf. *40*, No. 11, 50–55.
FARRALL, A. W. 1963. Engineering for Dairy and Food Products, 3rd Edition. John Wiley & Sons, New York.

Cross-references: *Bottle Fillers, Closers, Cappers; Cleaning of Equipment.*

BRINE REFRIGERATION

Brine is a solution of a salt such as sodium chloride or calcium chloride in water. It is widely used in the food industry as a cooling medium. Brine can be used at temperatures below 32°F for the transmission of heat, because the freezing point of the brine is depressed by the salt.

In the early days of refrigeration, brine was very widely used. With newer developments of accurate controls for direct expansion refrigeration, brine is less important. Brine is also used as a safety method, where direct expansion cooling might be hazardous.

Today numerous solutions, e.g., ethylene glycol widely used in the cooling systems of automobiles, are used for transmission of refrigeration at low temperatures.

TABLE B.9

BRINE TABLE—SODIUM CHLORIDE BRINE

Specific Gravity at 39°F	Degrees Baumé at 60°F	Degrees Salometer at 60°F	Pounds of Salt per Gallon of Solution	Pounds of Salt per Cu Ft	Percentage of Salt by Weight	Freezing-Point, °F	Specific Heat	Weight per Gallon at 39°F
1.007	1	4	0.084	0.628	1	31.8	0.992	8.40
1.015	2	8	0.169	1.264	2	29.3	0.984	8.46
1.023	3	12	0.256	1.914	3	27.8	0.976	8.53
1.030	4	16	0.344	2.573	4	26.6	0.968	8.59
1.037	5	20	0.433	3.238	5	25.2	0.960	8.65
1.045	6	24	0.523	3.912	6	23.9	0.946	8.72
1.053	7	28	0.617	4.615	7	22.5	0.932	8.78
1.061	8	32	0.708	5.295	8	21.2	0.919	8.85
1.068	9	36	0.802	5.998	9	19.9	0.905	8.91
1.076	10	40	0.897	6.709	10	18.7	0.892	8.97
1.091	12	48	1.092	8.168	12	16.0	0.874	9.10
1.115	15	60	1.389	10.389	15	12.2	0.855	9.26
1.155	20	80	1.928	14.421	20	6.1	0.829	9.64
1.187	24	96	2.376	17.772	24	1.2	0.795	9.90
1.196	25	100	2.488	18.610	25	0.5	0.783	9.97
1.204	26	104	2.610	19.522	26	1.1	0.771	10.04

Sodium Chloride

Sodium chloride brine is used where temperatures need not be carried below 4° of 5°F. Sodium chloride brine is relatively inexpensive, and not unduly corrosive if the solution is kept free from excessive air, and if the strength of the solution is maintained at a high level. Sodium chloride brine made from 20% salt by weight, has a specific gravity of 1.115, a specific heat of 0.829, and a freezing point of 6.1°F.

Table B.9 shows the important characteristics of sodium chloride brine.

Calcium Chloride

Calcium chloride brine is used for moderately low temperature and is essential for temperatures of 50°F below zero. Calcium chloride brine is very corrosive if it is in an acid condition. If kept free from air and properly neutralized, the corrosive action is fairly slight.

A 20% by weight solution of calcium chloride brine requires approximately 3.4 lb of salt per gallon of solution, has a specific gravity of 1.179, a specific heat of 0.73, and a freezing point of −1.4°F. See Table B.10 for specific freezing points, etc. of calcium chloride brine.

Brine systems must be kept at the proper strength. The freezing point of the brine must be lower than the operating temperature. Also, brines must be kept neutralized to maintain a noncorrosive condition. The greatest cause of corrosive brine is through air absorption which causes an acidic reaction.

Neutralization

Acid brines should be neutralized by the addition of lime water on caustic soda solution until the pH is between 7 and 8. Systems having iron only in contact

TABLE B.10

BRINE TABLE—CALCIUM CHLORIDE BRINE

Degrees Baumé 60°F	Specific Gravity 60°–66°F	Degrees Salometer 60°F	Percentage CaCl₂ by Weight	Pounds CaCl₂ per Gallon of Solution (Approx.)	Freezing Point, °F	Specific Heat
0	1.000	0	0	0	+32	1.00
1	1.007	4	1	—	31.1	0.99
2.1	1.015	8	2	—	30.4	0.97
3.4	1.024	12	3	$1/2$	29.5	0.96
4.5	1.032	16	4	—	28.6	0.94
5.7	1.041	22	5	—	27.7	0.93
6.8	1.049	26	6	1	26.6	0.91
8	1.058	32	7	—	25.5	0.90
9.1	1.067	36	8	—	24.3	0.88
10.2	1.076	40	9	$1 1/2$	22.8	0.87
11.4	1.085	44	10	—	21.3	0.86
12.5	1.094	48	11	—	19.7	0.84
13.5	1.103	52	12	2	18.1	0.83
14.6	1.112	58	13	—	16.3	0.82
15.6	1.121	62	14	—	14.3	0.815
16.8	1.131	68	15	$2 1/2$	12.2	0.795
17.8	1.140	72	16	—	10	0.78
19	1.151	76	17	—	7.5	0.77
20	1.160	80	18	3	4.6	0.755
21	1.169	84	19	—	+1.7	0.74
22	1.179	88	20	—	−1.4	0.73
23	1.188	92	21	$3 1/2$	4.9	0.72
24	1.198	96	22	—	8.6	0.71
25	1.208	100	23	—	11.6	0.70
26	1.218	104	24	4	17.1	0.69
27	1.229	108	25	—	21.8	0.685
28	1.239	112	26	—	27	0.68
29	1.250	116	27	$4 1/2$	32.6	0.67
30	1.261	120	28	—	39.2	0.665
31	1.272	124	29	—	46.2	0.66
32	1.283	128	30	5	−54.4	0.65

with brine may operate with pH as high as 10 or 11 without harm. Those systems containing both iron and zinc, such as with galvanized cans in an iron tank, should be held at a pH not higher than 8. The pH determination of brines is made by means of a direct reading indicating electrometer such as the Coleman pH electrometer or the Beckman pH meter. For routine plant control where extreme accuracy may be unnecessary, color indicators can be used.

With color indicators a sample of brine to be tested is placed in each of two test tubes and a few drops of phenolphthalein indicator added to one. If this tube on being compared with the other shows a pink coloration, the true pH of the brine is higher than 8.0; if no coloration occurs, a sample of the brine is placed in each of three tubes supplied with a block comparator. The one with the indicator such as phenol red is placed in the center. Comparison is then made with color standards.

To increase the pH value of a brine, add a small quantity of caustic soda pre-

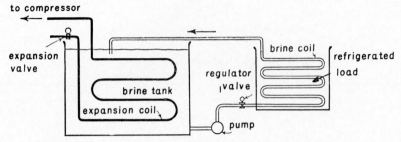

Fig. B-19.   Coil arrangement of a brine refrigeration system

viously dissolved in water.   Caustic soda should be added in very small amounts and the brine allowed to circulate for a time to assure thorough mixing.

To reduce the pH of brine, a mild acid is usually added.   Carbonic acid gas obtained from a cylinder of liquid carbon dioxide is often used.

Corrosion

One of the best corrosion retarders for calcium chloride brines is sodium bichromate.   Bichromate is simply dissolved in water with a suitable quantity of caustic soda, and added to the brine.   One plan is to use 70 to 125 lb of commercial sodium bichromate ($Na_2 Cr_2 O_7 2H_2O$) per 1,000 cu ft of brine.   In practice, 100 lb of the commercial sodium bichromate in about 20 gal. of water plus 30 lb of caustic soda are mixed together.   This solution is then added to 1,000 cu ft of brine, being careful to add this material to the brine gradually and at a point of fairly rapid circulation.

Freshly prepared brines of calcium chloride may be treated directly with sodium bichromate without the addition of caustic soda.   Brines treated with chromate may cause an irritation known as chrome itch from repeated contact with the skin.   Workmen should wear rubber or oil saturated gloves when handling brine covered cans.

Electrolytic action can be minimized with brines by the following: (1) avoid combinations of unlike metals in the system;   (2) avoid using metals having different degrees of purity;   (3) avoid using poor quality metal;   (4) prevent a state of strain in metals in the system;   and (5) prevent stray electric currents in the system. The system should be grounded.

Foam can be prevented by keeping air out of the system.   It is also caused by the presence of iron rust and insoluble particles.   Temporary relief can be obtained by the addition of a small quantity of denatured alcohol.

Brine systems in new plants often accumulate excessive sediment which should be cleaned out regularly.   Ammonia leaks will cause the formation of sediment very rapidly if the brine has much magnesium in it.   Calcium brine which is free from magnesium should be used.   Ammonia is removed from brine by heating it to a fairly high temperature (170°F).   The addition of some caustic soda may also be of assistance.   If a brine is heavily contaminated with ammonia it is better to use a new charge of brine.

System

Brine systems may be of the circulating type, the storage type, or the congealing type.   In the circulating system, the brine is cooled to the proper temperature by

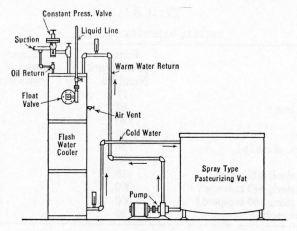

FIG. B-20.   Sweet water cooling system

direct expansion coils and is then circulated by a pump through coils in a cold storage room, a freezer milk cooler, or other apparatus where it absorbs heat, and returns back to the direct expansion system where the heat is extracted (Fig. B.19). There is practically no storage of brine in this type system. It is used primarily for safety or health reasons where it is undesirable or not permitted to use a direct expansion refrigeration system. The formula for refrigerating effect of this type is

$$Q = W\text{B} \times C \times (T_1 - T_2)$$

where $W\text{B}$ = weight of brine circulated, lb per hr

    Q = Btu heat removed per hr

    C = Specific heat of brine

    T_2 = temperature of brine at inlet

The brine storage system is used where it is undesirable to store and use a large quantity of refrigeration in a short time, but operate a small refrigeration system for a long period of time. The refrigeration stored in the brine may be calculated by the formula

$$Q_P = W \times C \times (T_1 - T_2)$$

where Q = Btu available in the brine

    W = weight of brine in the tank

    C = specific heat of the brine

    T_1 = final temperature of the brine

    T_2 = temperature of the brine at the beginning

The congealing tank system of refrigeration is used for storing refrigeration as ice which forms on the coils in the tank. Since each pound of frozen water stores 144 Btu, a large amount of refrigerant can be stored in a small amount of space. The brine must be weak enough so that the ice will freeze on the coils.

Sweet Water System

A sweet water cooling system uses plain water to carry the refrigeration (Fig. B.20). Since water freezes at 32°F, it is suitable only for cooling to approximately

TABLE B.11

BRINELL HARDNESS NUMBERS

	Some Typical Brinell Numbers	Corresponding Rockwell Numbers with Small Tip
Cast iron	77	40
Wrought iron	37	—
Brass	120	73
Aluminum	44	0
Aluminum, annealed	16	—
Copper	180	93
Stainless steel, 302 series	150	90
Stainless steel, 440 annealed	200	95
Stainless steel, 440 tempered	500	120
Aluminum casting	20	—

34° to 33°F.   There is a safety factor, however, with a temperature above freezing. This system is widely used for cooling milk and other substances which might be injured by freezing.   A modification of the sweet water system is similar to the congealing tank brine system in that some of the water is frozen into ice on the coils of the refrigeration system.   This is the ice bank system, which stores a large amount of refrigeration in a small volume.

Reference

FARRALL, A. W.   1963.   Engineering for Dairy and Food Products, 3rd Edition.   John Wiley & Sons, New York.

Cross-references: *Milk Cooling; Refrigeration Principles.*

BRINELL HARDNESS

The ability of a metal to withstand mechanical penetration is a measure of a type of hardness.   The test procedure consists of forcing a hardened sphere against the material.   The load divided by the surface area produced gives a Brinell number representing the pressure, kg per mm².   Thus, soft materials have a small number identifying them.   Typical values are presented in Table B.11.

Rockwell Method

The Rockwell method involves relating the depth of penetration of a spherical or conical indentor with various loads on the surface.   The harder the material the less the penetration and the higher the Rockwell number.

The hardness values are used to indicate properties of materials to be used for manufacture or for properties of equipment.   Empirical relationships can be established between strength, fatigue properties, machining properties, and impact strength.

Cross-references: *Graphite; Homogenizers.*

BRITISH THERMAL UNIT (BTU)

The British thermal unit (Btu) is a measure of heat energy. Generally, the heat content value is used to represent the change of heat energy between two conditions or states of a material, or the heat energy above some arbitrary benchmark. Theoretically, there would be zero heat at zero degrees absolute, a temperature which can be approached but not reached. The benchmark for the heat energy in steam such as in the steam tables is 32°F. Instruments are not available for measuring the thermal energy content directly. The temperature, state, mass, and material must be considered. A British Thermal Unit is defined as the amount of heat to change the temperature of 1 lb of water by 1°F at 60°F. Likewise, one calorie is the amount of heat required to change the temperature of 1 gm of water 1°C at 15° C. One thousand calories equal one Calorie (large calorie) which is sometimes stated as 1,000 gm-cal are equivalent to 1 kg/cal.

The British thermal unit basis of energy representation is commonly used in engineering work. In countries using the metric system the large or kilo-cal unit is used. The equivalent of 1 Btu is 252 gm-cal or 0.252 kg-cal. The mechanical equivalent of heat is 778 ft-1b equals 1 Btu.

British thermal units are invisible and have no weight. The important feature is the amount of energy and the effect on environment, products, chemical processes, etc.

Cross-references: *Boilers; Calorie; Insulation; Sensible and Latent Heat; Specific Heat.*

BUILDING MATERIALS

Exterior Walls

The exterior walls of food plants can be made of the following materials: (1) brick, concrete block, or hollow tile with cement plaster inside; (2) brick, concrete block, or hollow tile faced with structural or ceramic tile inside; (3) concrete block with a glazed finish on one side for interior wall finish; (4) concrete with cement plaster inside; (5) concrete faced with structural or ceramic tile inside; and (6) double-faced ceramic block.

Walls of wooden materials are generally unsatisfactory in food processing plants because moisture will enter causing mildew and dry rot in a relatively short time.

Interior surfaces may be coated with commercial materials such as ceramic which is a hard vitreous substance costing between 50 to 75¢ per sq ft when applied. Other special compounds may be used to provide a sanitary vitreous surface for the interior walls of dairy plants. Structural tile is the most durable and requires the least amount of maintenance.

Ceilings

Most dairy plant ceilings are plastered which in general is quite satisfactory. Cement plaster will not withstand much abuse from bumping. During recent years, precast slabs are being used to a great extent for ceiling and upper floor construction.

These precast slabs of concrete are reinforced and will withstand considerable abuse and carry heavy loads. A ceiling and floor is erected at the same time through the use of these materials.

Floors

A milk plant floor must be smooth and impervious so they can be easily cleaned and maintained. Floors must resist the attack of lactic acid in milk and cleaning solutions. Hot water or steam condensates spilling on the floor also have attacking properties. Floors must withstand the force of blows from cans and other tools. The floor should slope toward drains with not less than $1/4$ in. per ft in processing rooms. In cold storage rooms where case storage occurs the slope should be limited to $1/8$ in. per ft. Excessive slope will cause stacks of cases to lean excessively. Consideration should be given to nonslip characteristics of floors. Particles of emery embedded in concrete exposing the upper portion of the particles develop a nonslip characteristic which is quite effective.

Dairy plant floors may be of three general types.

(1) Vitreous brick or tile laid with acid-proof bed and joints. This type of floor is installed by many companies with various acid-proof materials. If laid with the proper materials and workmanship, this floor is undoubtedly the best obtainable to date for hard dairy service. It is also the most expensive in initial cost, because of the cost of materials and time for installing the acid-proof bed and joints.

(2) Vitreous brick or tile laid with mortar bed and with cement joints which contain added hardening and waterproofing solution or compound. This type of floor costs less than the type 1 floor, but the joints are somewhat susceptible to erosion by lactic acid in milk. Regrouting must be done rather frequently. Joints in vitreous brick or tile floors should be $1/8$ to $1/4$ in. wide. The wider joints, while requiring more grouting, appear to minimize the danger of grout bridging over. The brick or tile should be selected as to size before shipment, or very accurately sized on the job. Brick or tile must come from a manufacturer whose products stand up well in service and will not chip or develop soft spots which cause uneven wear. Replacing brick or tile in a floor is rather difficult and usually quite expensive.

(3) Concrete floors, with special, hard, selected, and graded aggregates. When laid by contractors specializing in such work, these floors are satisfactory for dairies. This type of floor is cheaper than the other two types, however, the entire floor is subject to attack and disintegration caused by lactic acid and other chemicals. A brick or tile floor having joints not exceeding $1/4$ in. in width, has only 5% of the floor which may be attacked. When a concrete floor is poured after the plant has been built, care should be taken to prevent the occurrence of cracks between the floor and walls.

For sanitary reasons, all dairy floors should have a 5-or 6-in. high cove or base at all walls and partitions. The radius of the cove may be $3/4$, 1, or 2 in. depending upon local health regulations. Where a brick or tile floor is used, the cove base should be of the same or similar material as the floor, because it will stand more abuse than the wall material.

In refrigerated milk storage rooms it is desirable to build the finished base 3 or 4 in. away from the wall and 5 to 8 in. high. The top of the base should taper back to the wall at an angle not less than $45°$. This serves as a bumper section to protect the wall surface from damage from cases, cans, and dollys.

The modern cold storage room may have a welded steel four-way plate floor having formed steel plate curves at all columns and walls. This type of floor construction goes very well with in-floor chain conveyor systems. The installation of an in-floor conveyor and its companion welded steel plate floor necessitates careful planning and layout. All conveyor pans should be leveled and anchored to a subfloor or a 6-in. concrete pad approximately 24 in. wide and 4.5 in. below the finished floor. Conveyor pans when anchored in place will act as screens for a poured 6-in. concrete floor. This floor should be reinforced with 6 in. by 6 in. number 10 gage wire mesh and have a smooth troweled finish with no low spots.

After the slab has cured, 4 ft × 8 ft sheets of $^1/_4$ in. floor plate having beveled edges may be placed. Care should be taken to minimize plate warping due to heat generated during welding. Warping can be counteracted through the use of explosive driven studs for anchoring the plate. Care must be taken to weld all studs after they have been ground. Formed steel plate curbs should have a 2-in. radius cove, 6 in. high, 4 in. wide, and a sloping top to the wall. The top surface should extend 1 in. into a slot cut into the inner layer of insulation. Gutters, power units, and shunt pit should have 3 by 3 by $^3/_8$ in. angle frames securely anchored into the concrete slab. When the four-way steel plates are welded to this frame it will serve as a waterproof termination to the floor. Gutters and pits must be covered with a movable grating or plate. Twelve inch square steel plates laid in epoxy bed forms a durable waterproof floor, which is also finding considerable application in refrigerated rooms.

Brick or tile floors in processing rooms should have a waterproof membrane laid down when the floor is built. This membrane may be built in 2 layers of 15-lb felt mopped with liquid, preferably hot, asphalt, and turned up at least 3 in. above the high point of the walls and partitions. Where acid-proof joints are used, the membrane should be mopped with an acid-proof material. The membrane should be applied to and slope with the floor fill. If so installed, it will stop leakage through a floor, and lead to the flashing flange to the nearest floor drain, then through the flange weep holes into the drain itself. By sloping the membrane in this manner, leakage is localized and does not become general over the entire floor slab.

Interior Walls

Walls must be built of smooth, impervious material which can easily be cleaned and maintained. They are not subjected to the same hard wear and attack from chemicals as are floors. There are four general types of wall construction used in milk plants today.

(1) *Structural ceramic tiles*. These are hard-burned, glazed clay or shale tile units, with two 5 in. by 8 in. or 6 in. by 12 in. face and obtainable either in 1.75 in. or 3.75 in. thickness. They can be built into the wall or partition or with wall ties built in as the wall is constructed. In some cases the wall may be built first and the tile applied later as a finish facing. Joints are $^1/_4$ in. wide. Tile is obtainable in white or various colors, and this type is generally used in processing rooms, bottle washing, and case storage rooms. In milk cooler rooms where appearance may be less important, a cheaper grade known as salt-glazed tile is frequently used.

(2) *Ceramic tile*. These are also hard-burned, glazed clay or shale units, generally 4 in. by 4 in. or 6 in. by 6 in. They are spotted on the back with the setting material and applied as a facing with joints about $^1/_{16}$ in. wide which are then filled and rubbed.

(3) *Cement plaster*. This product is applied in three coats: brown, scratch, and finish. They may be applied on steel stud and metal lath partition construction; and two coats, scratch and finish, on concrete brick, hollow tile, or concrete blocks. The final coat has either a sand or smooth trowled finish. A plastered wall requires three coats of paint: priming, second, and finish coat. It is cheaper in first cost than either of the other types but will require occasional paint. A 6 by 6 by $3/8$ in. ceramic tile for a 5-ft high wainscot may be used in processing rooms and also other areas to protect the plastered wall. This practice reduces the cost below that of a wall faced entirely with ceramic tile, and reduces the maintenance costs. Cement plaster is quite easily damaged by equipment, hand trucks, and dollys.

(4) *Double faced ceramic*. For interior partitions especially, the use of double faced ceramic tile makes it possible to construct the partition and finish both sides in one operation.

Roofs and Roofing

Roofs are usually classified as flat, semisteep, and steep depending upon the rise in inches per horizontal foot. Flat roofs are those in which the rise per horizontal foot varies from 0 (level) to 3 in. Semisteep roofs vary from 3.25 to 12 in. rise per horizontal foot. Steep roofs vary from 13 to 24 in. rise per horizontal foot. In general food plant roofs are flat of semisteep.

For flat roofs, gravel surfaced built-up roofing using base sheets or felts may be used. Cap sheet roofing with a mineral-surface or smooth-surface cap sheet may be used between the slopes of $3/4$ to 3 in. per horizontal foot. Roofing built up in layers and given a cold protective coating may also be used.

For semisteep roofs, from 3.25 to 9 in. rise per foot, gravel surfaced built-up roofing would not be used due to the tendency for the asphalt on hot days to creep, thus causing the gravel to loosen.

Roofs which rise greater than 9 in. per horizontal foot, may have asphalt or asbestos shingles. Slate, shingle tile, or curved tile over built-up roofing is also very satisfactory, but quite expensive.

For less expensive roof construction, corrugated iron, aluminum, or transite sheets may be used on slopes over 3 in. rise per horizontal foot. If used on lesser slope the end and side laps of all sheets must be well-sealed against driving rain or snow.

Roof decks may be constructed of ribbed steel plate, spot welded to supporting metal construction beneath. Such panels have a flat plate on top of the rib, to which insulation is applied. A built-up roofing is laid on top.

Where built-up roofing finishes against parapet walls, a cant-strip should be installed at the intersection of the roof deck and the inner face of the parapet. The flashing should be run up the cant-strip to proper height on the wall and properly attached so as to be secure and watertight, and cap flashed with metal or other flashing material recessed into the parapet and solidly caulked.

The roof deck under built-up roofing should generally be insulated, particularly in colder climates.

Where wood sheathing is used for decking it is desirable to use $1/2$ or 1 in. thick rigid insulation board on top of the deck before the application of the roofing. This will make a smooth deck with no board edges projecting to cut the roofing plies. This also contributes to the insulation of the roof.

It is usually more effective and desirable to put insulation above the ceiling rather than on top of the deck. This is particularly true where the building is in warm climates where, even though there may be a louvre-ventilated open space between ceiling and roof, the air will become extremely warm. Much of this heat passes through the ceiling construction to the rooms below unless insulation is placed above the ceiling construction.

A few important items to follow in construction of a roof are as follows. (1) Never apply roofing materials during inclement weather. (2) If insulation is used, it must be kept dry continuously until it is sealed within the roof. (3) Roofing materials with a high moisture content should not be used. (4) Concrete decks must be sealed off by a vapor seal course or positive surface seal before applying the final roof materials. (5) A vapor seal course must be used over all decks in cold climates where high inside humidities are present. (6) All felts should be thoroughly "broomed down" as quickly as possible after the bitumen roofing compound is applied.

A light-colored roof will reflect much of the solar heat, and thus a lower roof temperature is maintained during bright summer days. A black roof may reach a temperature of 160°F, whereas a light-colored roof would attain about 110°F under the same conditions. White- or light-colored broken stones are being used to replace gravel or dark-colored broken stones as a top surfacing in many plants.

Doors, Windows, and Skylights

Door frames of welded steel should be galvanized or covered with stainless steel to avoid corrosion. Doors with wood cores should be thoroughly dried out and the metal covering and hardware applied. All openings in the covering should be soldered to avoid accumulation of moisture and eventually rot. All-metal doors are preferred for dairy plant use rather than a metal-clad wooden door.

Aluminum sash is becoming competitive with steel sash for industrial construction. Aluminum is not subject to rust or corrosion and it requires no painting. The putty of the sash should be on the outside.

Glass block for windows has the advantages of being sanitary, giving good light distribution, and being low in maintenance cost. Metal ventilating units in standard sizes fit with the blocks and can be built into the windows. There should bo no window sills. But if used, sills should be sloped down at an angle of 50° to 60° to prevent dirt accumulation and the placing of objects on the sill. Glass blocks are desirable because of their insulating value, and because they may be obtained in color, and light-diffusing and light-directing characteristics. They also become part of the structure of the building by being an integral part of the wall.

Insulated Rooms

Refrigerated milk storage rooms are subject to a great deal of wear, therefore, a heavy duty floor is required. Vitreous brick floors are satisfactory. However, the steel plate floor may be used when installing a new conveyor system. The interior face of the insulated walls of refrigerated rooms may be finished with cement plaster and scored in 4- or 5-ft squares. The wall may be faced with glazed tile either structural or plain ceramic. Glazed tile is higher in first cost, however, it is preferable inasmuch as it eliminates painting. A mastic finish on the walls will not give the protection provided by materials possessing a hard finish. If cement plaster is to be used as the finish on the insulated ceiling, it should be specified that it be applied over well-anchored metal lath. Due to the weight of the plaster, a number of plants are not using this type of construction. If used, it is of utmost importance that the insulation of the ceiling be installed properly and the various layers well-bonded together. Mastic emulsion is generally used as a finish on the ceiling insulation. This has been found to be very satisfactory and is applied in 2 coats each $1/8$ in. thick. It is much lighter than plaster and may be obtained in white or dark colors. White mastic dries white and requires no painting. Above a 5-ft high wainscoat, the mastic may be used on the wall as well as the ceiling.

Reference

MILK INDUSTRY FOUNDATION. 1967. Manual for Milk Plant Operators. Washington D.C.

BULK BINS

Portable bulk bins may be used to hold nonfat dry milk a few days prior to usage in the plant. These bins also are gaining in usage as a container for shipment to industrial users. The bins are fabricated from different metals or alloys including stainless steel. Aluminum is most often used by the dry milk industry, costing about $1/2$ as much and being lighter than those made from stainless steel. One common size is about 3.5 by 4 by 6 ft with a capacity of approximately 74 cu ft and a tare weight of about 225 lb. The bin is designed for transfer by a forklift. The advantages are mainly in reduction of labor and bag costs with possibly a reduction in dust problem.

Automatic conveying equipment is available to fill a group of these bins, each in succession when properly positioned. They are airtight and can be stacked. The bins are emptied into a hopper by elevating and tilting the product flow, or by inversion to allow the product to flow through an iris-type outlet valve. The bins may be easily cleaned by the recirculation spray-ball system. Powder stored in bulk bins cools very slowly, about 2°F per day.

Reference

HALL, C. W., and HEDRICK, T. I. 1966. Drying Milk and Milk Products. AVI Publishing Co., Westport, Conn.

Cross-references: *Dry Milk Physical Properties; Forklift Trucks; Materials Handling; Pneumatic Conveying; Storage Design.*

BULK TANKERS

Insulated, cylindrical tanks mounted in a horizontal position on trailer wheels or on the truck are used for pickup of bulk milk. The tanker driver is responsible for sampling, weighing, checking quality, and handling the milk. Some of the operations formerly done at the dairy plant are now done by the tanker driver. In some areas the tanker driver must be licensed by the state for bulk pickup.

The trend is to every-other-day pickup of bulk milk. Thus in initial planning a 2,000-gal. tanker usually is selected to replace two 100-can (10 gal.) routes. However, the size should be selected on the basis of an efficient bulk milk route, rather than as replacing two can-truck routes. Most of those who purchased 1,750-and 2,000-gal. tanks now find a larger one is more economical for a complete bulk handling operation. The tank may be mounted on tandem axles or a single axle. In many northern areas, a load of 1,700 gal. can be carried on single axles and for larger loads a tandem axle is needed. Requirements vary in different States because of load restrictions on the highways during the spring. The laws should be checked before purchasing a tank and deciding whether single or tandem axles are to be obtained. Tandem axles provide a transport which is difficult to get stuck.

Three-A standards have been established for tankers. The outer surface of the outer covering may be of steel which is jointed, stainless steel, aluminum, or plastic. The tank is usually constructed as 1 compartment, but there may be 2 compartments which would be desirable if 2 grades of milk are to be picked up. There is a trend to use the tank without baffles.

A rear compartment contains a pump. It is desirable to have either a positive or centrifugal pump rated at 75 gal. per min. The positive pump is best for all round use under many different conditions. It is belt-driven from an electrical motor and operates between 400 and 500 rpm. The centrifugal pump is connected directly to an electrical motor and operates at 1,800 rpm. A pump which is too small requires the tanker driver to wait too long to move the milk from bulk tank to tanker. An electrical outlet must be provided at the farm for 230 v service for the motor.

A sample tray or box is also provided in the rear compartment in which ice or some coolant may be placed to keep the sample cold. Composite samples are utilized in which samples for several days are collected before a butterfat test is made. Plastic or rubber hoses are provided for conveying the milk from the milkhouse. In some locations the length of the hose is restricted.

Agitation in the truck tanker can be done by pump (recirculation), propeller (portable), air, or manual. Determining the quantity of milk in the tank can be done by weighing on a scale or by measuring the height of the milk in the tank when setting on a level platform.

With a properly arranged route on every-other-day (EOD) pickup, the cost of pickup for a tanker will normally be less than for cans.

Reference

HALL, C. W. 1963. Processing Equipment for Agricultural Products. Edwards Brothers, Ann Arbor, Mich.

Cross-reference: *Cooling Milk.*

BUTTER CHURN

The butter churn has been used for hundreds of years and up until the past 20 yr was a relatively simple device in which cream could be agitated violently to cause the separation of the butterfat from the serum portion of the cream. Numerous attempts have been made to develop a so-called continuous churn beginning in the 1930's.

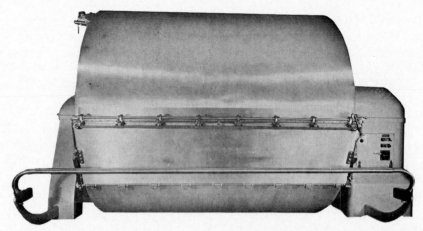

Fig. B-21.   Metal churn

Since 1960 the progress has been particularly rapid and today there are hundreds of continuous churns in use throughout the world.   There are, however, still thousands of old type churns in use.   Butter making is still an important part and at one time was the most important element of the dairy industry.   The use of butter substitutes has greatly affected the butter market and some of the modern machinery used for butter substitutes and spreads can with modifications be used for the manufacture of butter.

Principles

An early principle of churning consisted of agitating or stirring the cream sufficiently to cause a rupture of the fat globule membrane which surrounds each butterfat globule, thereby causing the fat globules to stick together.   Cream is an emulsion in which the butterfat phase is the discontinuous phase in a continuous phase of serum. When cream is churned into butter the result is a reversal of the phase in which the butterfat is the continuous phase, and the small amount of serum is the discontinuous phase.

Continuous Butter Machine

Several types of continuous butter machines have been developed.   The Creamery Package system starts with cream of 30 to 45% fat, separates it to about 80% fat content, then utilizes a homogenizer to break the emulsion of the high fat cream, after which the almost pure fat is drawn off by a gravity separator.   This is then standardized, and color and salt are added to give the proper butter composition.   The product then passes to a chilling tube and a butter worker, from which the finished butter is extruded continuously.

The Cherry-Burrell process starts with cream of 40 to 45% fat content, passes it through a desludging centrifugal separator which discharges it at 88–90% fat.   It then passes to a standardizing vat where salt, color, and water are added to give the proper composition.   This is followed by chilling in a refrigerated agitator type cooling

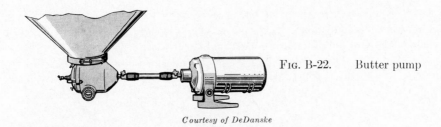

Fɪɢ. B-22.   Butter pump

Courtesy of DeDanske

tube of small diameter.   The final step is to pass the chilled butter through a "worker" after which it is extruded continuously.

The third and most widely used system is a modification of the so-called "Fritz" process.   Essentially this machine has a drum fitted with a high-speed agitator which serves to break the emulsion of cream.   The butterfat globule and serum then pass to a separating screen which allow the buttermilk to flow off.   The butter granules are forced into a third compartment where a certain amount of water passes over the butter and washes away excess serum.   The butter then passes to a working device which is usually a single or double auger which further collects or solidifies the butter mass, and then forces it through a perforated plate to give the proper texture.

The butter is extruded into either a bulk filling nozzle and box filler or it goes directly to an automatic butter packaging machine.

In the new continuous type churns this same reversal of the phase is accomplished by agitation at a given temperature, but the whole process takes place in a few seconds as compared to the old churning method which required 30 to 40 min of agitation.

With the continuous churn in order to maintain the proper composition of the butter, it is very essential to have the cream at a certain percentage of butterfat and to have it ripened and held at a uniform temperature for usually 8 or 10 hr.   Considerable experience is required on the part of the operator to obtain uniform results.   The speed of the dasher, temperature of the wash water, and speed of the working rolls are all important factors in the composition and fat loss in the manufacture of butter with this system.

The texture of the finished butter is controlled almost entirely by the temperature of the butter and by the amount of working by the working rolls or medium.

In churning butter, there are many important technical details, including control of temperature and acidity of the cream, and the amount of working of the butter to give the proper texture.

Practices with Batch-type Churn

Figure B.21 shows a standard metal churn in common use.   The churn drum is made of a special aluminum or stainless steel alloy which has a roughened surface to which the butter does not stick.   Some of the churns are made with special cooling facilities and some operate under vacuum or pressure.   Usually some special unloading means is provided for either pumping or dropping the butter out of the churn drum after the serum portion or buttermilk has been drawn off.   Provision is also made for adding water to wash the excessive serum solids away from the fat.

The operator usually finds it necessary to standardize the cream and to adjust the acidity to the proper point.   In many instances, the cream is also ripened or held at a specified temperature for a certain length of time to properly condition the butter-fat globules. The churning or breaking of the emulsion usually takes 35 to 40 min, after which the buttermilk or serum portion is drawn off, then the butter is washed by means of fresh cold water during which the churn barrel is rotated 3 of 4 times. The percentage of moisture in the butter is controlled by the temperature of the water and the number of revolutions made with the churn during the washing operation. Salt

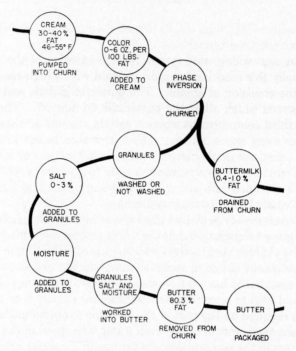

FIG. B-23.   Outline of conventional butter making

is added after the washing process. The butter is then removed by means of either a pump (Fig. B.22) or by dropping it into a large receptacle which will hold the entire batch of butter.

References

FARRALL, A. W.   1963.   Engineering for Dairy and Food Products, 3rd Edition.   John Wiley & Sons, New York.

HUNZIKER, O. F.   1940.   The Butter Industry, 3rd Edition.   Published by the author.   La Grange, Ill.

TOTTMAN, C. C., McKAY, G. L., and LARSON, C.   1939.   Butter, 4th Edition.   John Wiley & Sons, New York.

WILSTER, G. H.   1957.   Practical Butter Making, 8th Edition.   OSC Cooperative Assoc., Corvallis, Ore.

Cross-references: *Butter, Whipped; Butter Manufacture; Butter Wrapping Machines; Freezers, Ice Cream.*

BUTTER CUTTERS

Butter cutters form a class of machines which are widely used in the dairy industry and in the margarine industry to automatically or semiautomatically cut a slab or ribbon of the butter into desired portions.

The basic principle of the butter cutter is that a small diameter stainless piano wire, approximately $^1/_{16}$ to $^1/_{32}$ in. in diameter is forced through the butter. Bulk butter is usually cut into 1- or $^1/_4$-lb portions and wrapped for the retail trade.

Special machines are made which cut the butter into individual portions about 1.25 in. square and $^1/_4$ in. thick. Some machines automatically extrude the butter through a die and eject it onto a special small waxpaper or plastic sheet. Some machines also make a fancy imprint on one side of the butter patty.

The new type continuous butter machines use the same basic principle of cutting off the slab of butter by a wire. The butter is extruded for slabs of 50 lb or more for the bulk butter trade.

In using butter cutters the butter must be at the right body and texture for cutting. If it is too stiff, trouble will result with the breaking of wires, dies do not fill properly and excessive strain results on the mechanisms. On the other hand, butter which is too soft will not cut cleanly and the particles will not hold their shape. When stored at temperatures of 0°F or below for extended periods, the butter must be tempered at a temperature of approximately 40°F for several days before cutting.

Normally butter does not cut readily immediately after it is churned because it is too soft. If stored overnight at a temperature of 40°F, the fresh butter will cut easily.

BUTTER MANUFACTURE

Conventional

The cream is tempered and pumped into the churn from the holding vat (Fig. B.23). The desired churning time is 30 to 45 min so cream churning temperature is established accordingly. It can vary from 46° to 50°F during the warm months and 50° to 56°F during the winter. Cream warmed to 113°F and then cooled to churning temperature and held for 30 min, churns at a lower temperature in the same time as cream warmed from 36°F to churning temperature and held 30 min.

The churn is usually filled just under $^1/_2$ full or approximately 40 to 48% of the capacity. It is important not to fill the churn too full, because foam will reduce the agitation which will prolong the churning time. Churning with too little cream is less efficient.

The speed of the churn should be such as to provide maximum agitation within reasonable limits. A speed of 15 to 30 rpm is used depending upon the type of churn. Some modern churns are provided with as many as eight speeds to meet the needs of the various steps in the churning operation.

The churn, which is revolved to obtain the agitation, may be classified as to shape, for example, a cylinder, a cube, a cone, or a double cone. Churns may be grouped as: roll type—single, double, and multiple; roll-less—cylindrical and rectangular or box type; combined churns and butter workers or churns without butter workers; and wood or metal. Metal churns (aluminum or stainless steel) have replaced the wooden churn in many creameries in the United States. The advantages of metal over

Courtesy General Dairy Equipment Co.

FIG. B-24.   Continuous butter maker

wooden churns are: ease of cleaning and sanitizing, relatively little maintenance, and improved keeping quality of the butter.

When the churn is ready, it is revolved until the "break" occurs and the granules attain such a size as to become visible.   This is shown by the clearing of the sight glass which otherwise is covered with cream and the granules are wheat kernel to pea size. Some factors affecting the churnability of cream are: temperature and time held before churning; composition of the butterfat; agitation, kind and extent; and percentage fat in cream.

Most common cause of overchurning is too high a temperature of the cream for churning.   This may result in composition control difficulty.   The large butter granules or mass cannot be chilled properly; thus the body is likely to be leaky or greasy, and the keeping quality may be jeopardized.

Buttermilk

The buttermilk is drained as soon as the granules have reached the desired size. The buttermilk is drained quickly by gravity through a strainer into a container from which it is usually pumped to a storage tank.

A practice, common among some creameries, is to sell the buttermilk for stock feed in concentrate, high acid, or powder form.   Much of the sweet cream buttermilk is dried and used in food products for human consumption.

For each 100 lb of butter produced from 35% cream, there are available approximately 150 lb of buttermilk.   The fat content in the buttermilk usually ranges from

0.5 to 1.0%. In addition to the fat, typical sweet cream buttermilk will contain about 3.5% protein, 4.8% sugar, 0.7% ash, and the remainder is water and minor constituents.

The fat losses in the buttermilk are due mainly to: churning low-testing or excessively high-testing cream; improper neutralization, partial churning during pumping; improper pasteurization; improper cooling and holding of cream before churning; too high a churning temperature; and overloading the churn.

Washing the Granules

Butter granules are washed after the buttermilk has drained. Some operators prefer to spray water over the granules at 0°–10°F below the churning temperature while allowing the water to drain until it is clear. The drain valve is closed and the churn is filled with water to the same level as the cream was or at least enough water to cover the granules. The temperature of the wash water used depends upon the condition of the granules, i.e., soft or hard. The softer the granules, the lower the water temperature should be.

One washing should be enough for average or high-quality butter. Butter granules churned from low-quality cream may be washed a second time in an effort to improve the flavor.

The number of revolutions and the speed of the churn for washing depends upon the construction of the churn. Ten to fifteen revolutions at a low speed are generally sufficient.

The water is then drained. If the butter granules are too soft, it may be desirable to hold them in the cold water before draining.

Water should be of the highest quality since it comes in contact with the butter granules. The water should have no objectionable taste and be free from undesirable chemical compounds bacteria and extraneous matter.

Filtering of the wash water is a safeguard against adding sediment to the butter. If the microbiological content of the wash water is not satisfactory, pasteurization or chemical treatment is necessary. Exposure to ultraviolet ray treatment is less common for reduction of the microorganisms.

Case Against Washing

The principal purpose of washing the butter granules is of course to reduce the buttermilk content. Secondly body and texture are influenced if tempering the granules is necessary in order to work the butter sufficiently without developing stickiness. With off-flavored cream, washing may slightly improve the flavor.

The need for washing butter granules has been questioned by numerous individuals both in research and industry for many years. They contend that washing may endanger the keeping quality, is time consuming, and adds to waste disposal problems. The washing of the butter granules may be a time honored custom which is practiced more out of tradition than for good and sufficient reason.

Disadvantages of not washing butter granules are: butter is too soft immediately upon being removed from the churn; the lower temperature required for churning may prolong the churning time considerably; and soft granules may not drain properly.

Studies of the curd content showed that nonwashed butter contains between 0.3 to 0.53% more curd than in washed butter.   In comparing nonwashed and washed butter for flavor quality before and after storage there is no significant difference.

In making nonwashed butter the following steps should be taken: churn as cold as is practicable to obtain firm granules, thoroughly drain the buttermilk, and adjust the moisture content using buttermilk from the same churning.

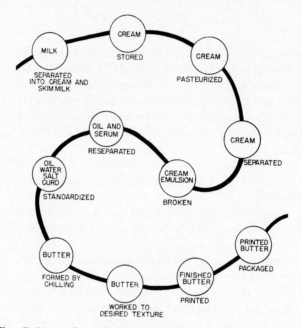

Fig. B-25.   Steps in continuous butter making (one type)

Adding Salt

Salt (sodium chloride) may be added after the wash water has been completely drained.   The amount added depends primarily on the market requirements and may range from 0 to 3%.   An example of salt calculation is given.

Assume 2% salt is desired in butter containing 80% fat from 850 lb. of milk fat

$$\frac{2.0 \times 1.25 \times 850}{100} = 21.25 \text{ lb of salt}$$

where 2.0 = lb of salt in 100 lb of butter
1.25 = lb of butter from 1 lb of fat
850 = lb of fat in churn

Methods of adding salt to butter are dry salting, wet salting, and brine salting. The method used most is the dry method.   The salt is sprinkled evenly over the butter or placed in a trench formed by a ladle.   The churn is revolved in low speed to distribute the salt uniformly through the the butter.

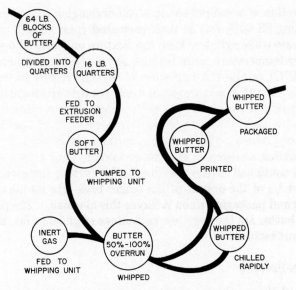

FIG. B-26.   Continuous process of making whipped butter

Working the Butter

"Working" is the term applied to the process of incorporating the salt, dispersing the moisture, and compacting the granules into the familiar form.   Butter was worked outside the churn in butter workers prior to the invention of the combined churn and butter worker in 1892.   Then churns had internal mechanisms such as wooden rolls between which the butter passed with each revolution.   Most churns at the present time have no internal mechanical apparatus to work the butter, but depend on shelves (ribs or vanes) to cause tumbling or folding of the butter as the churn rotates to provide the working action.

Removing Butter from Churn

In the conventional method of churning, the removal of butter has been an area of concern to public health officials.   The normal practice is to transfer the butter manually using either wooden or metal paddles.   Recently, churns have been designed so that the butter may be removed mechanically.   A butter boat is wheeled into position and the churn slowly revolved so that the butter falls into it.   The butter pump is not used extensively in the United States.   One reason may be that the design of most churns is cylindrical.   With the development of the cream separator, several machines were tried as a means of converting cream to butter (1880–1899). These machines were no competition for the conventional method of churning because of their low output and the nature of the resulting product.   About 1930 a new attempt at manufacturing butter by continuous means was begun (Fig. B.24 and 25), and a number of processes have been developed.

Continuous Butter Making

Cream with 40–45% fat is mechanically treated during heating so that the emulsion state of the fat is weakened.   During the succeeding separation the emulsion is broken. Reseparation is accomplished in a self-desludging separator. The fat concentrate (containing 88–90% fat) is then vacreated (pasteurized) and accumulated in standardizing vats while agitators keep the mixture uniform. To avoid crystallization of the fat the temperature must be kept above the melting point usually 115°–120°F (46.1°–48.9°C) or else the formation of crystals results in mealiness. While in the liquid state, the pH, color, water, and salt content are standardized. Cooling and partial working are performed in the chiller-worker which consists of two jacketed tubes equipped with scrapers and agitators (modification of continuous ice cream freezer). The temperature of the merging butter is 39.2°–46.4°F. A means may be provided for adding nitrogen in the chiller-worker. For better spreadability the butter working is continued in the "texturator." Further improvement is attained by recycling about $1/3$ of the output of the chiller back into its inlet. The butter is ready for printing and packaging when it leaves this machine. The principal physical properties in this butter are the very low percentage of globular fat, the coarser water dispersion, and short texture.

Creamery Package Process

In this method the emulsion is broken by homogenization after reseparation of cream to 80% or higher fat. The resulting mixture of serum and butter oil flows to a settling tank where the serum is fed back into the balance tank for 40% cream while the supernatant layer containing 98% of the fat is pumped to a vat for standardizing.

Water, salt, color, and culture are added to attain the desired butter composition. The butter mix is thoroughly agitated to insure uniformity and pumped to the "worker-chiller" at pressures up to 325 psi. While in the chiller the butter mixture is worked and the temperature reduced to approximately 40°F. Working continues in the crystallizer from which the butter is discharged at a temperature of approximately 50°F. The increase in temperature of 10°–12°F is due to the heat of crystallization. The butter is ready to be printed or bulk packaged.

Fritz Process

This is a continuous process originally developed in Germany and now widely used. Cream of approximately 50% butterfat is produced by separating. The cream is pasteurized and cooled. Butter is churned by high-speed vanes in a cylinder. Two rotating screws receive the buttermilk and granules. The buttermilk is removed and the butter is forced through a perforated plate.

Advantages

The advantages of continuous buttermaking may be summarized as: continuous operation, close composition control, reduced chances for bacterial contamination, less air incorporated, reduced oxidative changes, improved butter score with sour cream, and more efficient.

Overrun

When cream is churned into butter, certain amounts of nonfat constituents such as moisture and curd are incorporated into the finished product as well as salt. The difference between the amount of butter produced and the amount of butterfat churned is known as overrun and is expressed as a percentage.

Overrun may be calculated in three ways, each providing a check on the butter-making process. Overrun calculated on the basis of pounds of butterfat paid for and the pounds of butter sold is known as "actual overrun." The calculation of this overrun accounts for all kinds of losses. The following is an example of this calculation

1,000 lb butter made and sold
830 lb butterfat purchased
———
170 lb overrun

$$\frac{170 \times 100}{830} = 20.5\% \text{ overrun}$$

Frequently the butter maker desires to check the efficiency of the churning process. This is calculated from the amount of butterfat actually present in the vat of cream which is to be churned and the amount of butter removed from the churn as in (1) below.

Also, an overrun may be calculated on the basis of the composition of the finished butter as in (2) below.

100% butter
80% butterfat
———
20% overrun $\hspace{4cm}$ (1)

$$\frac{20(100)}{80} = 25\% \text{ overrun} \hspace{4cm} (2)$$

Fat Losses

The overrun attainable is affected by the losses of butterfat occurring during the different processes involved in the manufacturing of butter. The losses begin to occur immediately as the cream or milk is received. Accurate weighing of the full and empty can is necessary. A small loss on each can will result in considerable losses in cream for large churnings. Careless testing is another source of loss. The test on the cream must be carried out correctly to ensure against losses.

If whole milk is purchased the fat losses in the skim milk due to poor separation will reduce the amount of butter produced. Skim milk should not test more than 0.01-0.02% fat.

Butterfat losses in the buttermilk are unavoidable. However, these losses can be kept to a minimum by proper attention to: (1) the temperature of the cream at churning, (2) correct neutralization, (3) pasteurization, and (4) fat content of the cream. Controlling the composition of the butter to 80% fat (or as close as possible) will also increase overrun.

Other losses occur when cream is not adequately drained from cans, rinsed from vats, pumps, and pipes. Leakage, spillage, and overage in packaging also reduce the maximum overrun attainable.

Test for Composition

Butter is analyzed by the Kohman method in the United States creameries. It is sampled in a roll or mass by a trier sampling in at least three representative places in the churn. After a thorough mixing by stirring of the sample, 10 gm of butter is weighed into a special aluminum cup which has been previously cleaned, heated, cooled, and weighed. The sample is heated until a light brown sediment develops. The cup and contents are cooled and reweighed. From the difference in weight, the percentage moisture is calculated. A special balance shows the percentage moisture directly.

After the moisture test is completed, 50 ml of petroleum ether is added to the residue in the cup. The contents are mixed with a rotary motion and then the cup is allowed to set at an angle for 3 min. All but a few drops of the liquid are poured off and the process repeated. After the second fat extraction, the cup is heated gently until all traces of the petroleum ether has disappeared. It is cooled, reweighed, and the percentage of fat computed.

The residue from the fat test is used for the salt test. It is rinsed from the cup by 3 successive 25-ml portions of warm 140°F distilled water into a 250-ml flask. The flask is filled to the 250 ml mark with distilled water. Then 25 ml of this solution is pipetted into a white cup. Three drops of 5% aqueous solution of potassium chromate indicator is added. The solution is titrated with silver nitrate solution (29.05 gm in 1 liter of water) until a brick red color appears. The percentage of salt in the butter is equal to the number of milliliters required to attain the end point.

The percentage of curd in the butter is obtained by subtracting the percentage of moisture, fat, and salt from 100. If the percentage of curd is abnormally high or low, an error may have been made in the testing of the moisture, fat, or salt. The curd in butter has a normal range of 0.5 to 2.0.

Reference

HALL, C. W., HEDRICK, T. I., and HANCK, R. 1963. Technical aspects of butter manufacture in the U.S.A. Dairy Ind. *28*, No. 11, 818–824.

Cross-references: *Butter Churn; Butter Cutter; Butter, Physical Properties; Butter, Whipped.*

BUTTER, PHYSICAL PROPERTIES

Butter is composed of milk fat, moisture, curd, and often salt. Small amounts of air are contained. The curd is composed of minerals, lactose, phospholipids, acids, and other minor compounds. The milk fat is composed of a mixture of triglycerides. The milk fat is the most important and plentiful constituent, making up 80%.

The fat in butter exists in globular and free forms. Fat is in the globular form in milk. Fat globules vary in size from less than 1 to 20μ. The membrane covering the fat globule has a negative charge, which decreases as the acidity increases. Free fat is the result of fat globules uniting after the membrane is removed from churning.

The normal melting point range of milk fat is 88° to 97°F. For milk fat the temperature of solidification is between 66° and 76°F. The apparent specific heat of butter, which includes some latent heat, is 0.512 at 32°F; 0.527 at 59°F; 0.556 at 104°F; and 0.580 at 140°F.

The density of milk fat is 0.91 to 0.95 at 94°F, and about 0.896 at 140°F.
The viscosities of milk fat at different temperatures are as follows:

°C	Poise	°C	Poise
30	0.258	70	0.071
40	0.173	80	0.059
50	0.124	90	0.049
60	0.093	100	0.042

The air pressure required to move butter at 60°F through a 1.5 in. diam stainless steel tubing is represented by

$$\text{Psig} = (5.6 \times +4.4) \pm 1.3x$$

where x is the length of tube in feet.

The spreadability is largely dependent on temperature. Many mechanical devices have been used for measuring the hardness and spreadability. The addition of edible substances is done to improve spreadability, particularly at refrigerator storage temperature.

Whipped butter is produced by incorporating nitrogen or air from 50 to 100% in volume.

Butter is stored at 35° to 40°F for a few days; 0° to −20°F for several weeks.

References

HALL, C. W., HEDRICK, T. I., and HANCK, R. C. 1963. Technical aspects of butter manufacture in the U.S.A. Dairy Ind. *28*, No. 10, 740–744; *28*, No. 11, 818–824; *28*, No. 12, 882–885.

HALL, C. W., HEDRICK, T. I., and HANCK, R. C. 1964. Technical aspects of butter manufacture in the U.S.A. Dairy Ind. *29*, No. 1, 26–31.

Cross-references: *Butter Manufacture; Butter, Whipped; Fat, Physical Properties; Specific Heat.*

BUTTER, WHIPPED

Whipping may be accomplished as either a batch or continuous process (Fig. B.26). In the batch process, the butter is normally tempered at a temperature of 62°–70°F prior to cutting into slabs. The tempered slabs are placed in a 60- to 80-quart whipper. Air is incorporated into the butter during the whipping until an overrun of 50 to 100% is obtained.

Untempered Butter

Two continuous methods are used for whipping butter. One involves the use of untempered butter. Blocks of butter are cut into four pieces and softened by augering. The softened butter is then pumped to the continuous whipping unit where the volume is increased by 50 to 100% in the presence of nitrogen or air. The whipped butter is packaged in rigid containers and chilled rapidly in the cooler. Numerous modifications to this method are used in many states to meet specific plant operating conditions. One such modification involves the tempering of the butter 65°–70°F which eliminates the need for softening by augering.

Melted Butter Oil

The second continuous method utilizes melted butter or butter oil at 100°–115°F. If butter oil is used, it is standardized to the composition of butter. The product is pumped to a continuous butter whipper. An inert gas, such as nitrogen, is often metered into the product instead of air. Metering provides control of the overrun greater than that usually possible in the batch method.

Cooling

Due to the energy input the butter is too soft after being whipped to be handled by the molding and wrapping equipment. The product tends to degas if handled in this state. A scraped surface heat exchanger with special feature has been designed to cool the whipped butter. The mutator shaft is not centered in the cylinder of the unit, but is set off on an axis parallel to the cylinder axis. As a result, the blades move in and out as the shaft revolves which improves the intermixing and reduces the product buildup on the shaft. The advantages of this design over conventional concentric design are a high rate of heat transfer and a reduced power load when handling very viscous product.

Whipped butter has become a popular product in recent years. Prior to 1942 very little butter was whipped. Whipped butter is manufactured to improve spreadability and to some extent it affords a means of meeting the competition of lower priced substitutes because of the greater volume while retaining the desirable characteristics of flavor, general appearance, body and texture, and color. Advocates of whipped butter emphasize the lower calorie content and price per unit volume. They also stress that whipping provides a product having better spreadability at cooler temperatures than regular butter and some other spreads.

Reference

HALL, C. W., HEDRICK, T. I., and HANCK, R. C. 1963. Technical aspects of butter manufacture in U.S.A. Dairy Ind. *28*, No. 12, 882–885.

Cross-references: *Butter Churn; Butter Manufacture.*

BUTTER WRAPPING AND PRINTING MACHINES

Butter is molded mechanically by most print forming machines utilizing stainless alloy augers to force slabs of butter through a molding head. After the proper width and height are formed, the extruded butter is cut mechanically into proper lengths. The two principal styles of prints are Elgin and Western. Butter is usually printed in $1/4$-lb and 1-lb solid prints in each of the styles. One-fourth pound Elgin prints are 1.25 by 1.25 by 4.75 in. Western $1/4$-lb pound prints are 1.5 by 1.5 by 3.25 in. One 1-lb prints of Elgin style are 2.5 by 2.5 by 4.75 in. The Western style solid pound prints are $1^1/_2$ by $3^1/_{16}$ by $6^1/_2$ in. Cartoning is usually 4 quarters or 1-lb solid print. Cartoning machines are available, however, for cartoning two Elgin quarters. Printing and packaging equipment is available to print and wrap small table size patties or $1/_2$-lb patties.

Principles

Butter may be printed from bulk boxes or directly from a continuous churn or, as in the case of margarine, directly from the Votator. The principle involved is to pass the product through a molding head resulting in an extrusion of proper width and height dimensions. Butter is cut with a stainless steel wire. The molding head is water jacketed for tempering with circulating water. The operating temperature range for the water is 70° to 100°F. In handling butter from the cold storage room, it is first precut mechanically. The slabs are then automatically sent to the print-wrap machine then to the cartoner and finally to the overwrap or caser.

Specification

The precutter designed to handle butter about 40° to 50°F is equipped with a hydraulic system for forcing the block through the wire cutters. This pump will usually develop 500 psi hydraulic pressure. Printing speeds will affect, to a large extent, the size of the print. A machine will print and wrap 3,600 lb per hr in $1/4$-lb prints. Most manufacturers design equipment so the capacities of the precutter, print wrapper, carton machine, and the overwrapping equipment will synchronize at the same capacity. The cartoning machine, as well as the wrapping machine, are quite flexible in the types of cartons and wrapping materials being used. The carton may be the tuck or tuckless type and may be heat-sealed. The overwrap machine will handle various types of overwrap material which may be cellophane, foil, glassine, or other heat-sealable products. A tear-tape for rapid package opening is sometimes applied to the overwrap.

Practices

The four steps involved in cutting, printing, and packaging butter are synchronized, and in most cases linked together with sanitary belt conveyor. The precutter and print former are generally closely coupled together. There should, however, be some distance between the printer and cartoner and also between the cartoner and overwrap machine. This allows for minor interruptions of one machine in the line without forcing a complete shutdown each time some difficulty is experienced. The machines are designed so that forming at the printer does not overwork the butter. Overworking cold butter results in a loss of moisture which is usually undesirable. To reduce labor, more of the modern plants are utilizing continuous butter churns which discharge into a hopper, which in turn, extrudes the butter to the print wrapper. Continuous churns discharge butter at a temperature and consistency suitable for printing and wrapping in one continuous operation. Central butter packaging plants are in operation and account for a large portion of butter distributed in the United States.

One important step involved in the plant packaging operation is that of check weighing each unit. The operator on the print wrapper can adjust the size of a print to the desired quantity. Properly operated, this equipment maintains a high degree of uniformity between units. The operator should provide for a slight amount of weight loss due to moisture evaporation from the surface of the prints.

References

HUNIZKER, O. F. 1940. The Butter Industry, 3rd Edition. Published by the author, La Grange, Ill.

LYNCH CORP. Butter, margarine, and other products, Packaging Automation Bull. Anderson, Ind.

Cross-references: *Butter Churn; Butter Cutter; Butter Manufacture.*

C

CALIBRATION

The process of ensuring that the value indicated by a measurement represents the value measured is known as calibrating the instrument. Too often the indicated values of instruments are taken as being correct. This is particularly true of many expensive instruments, which the user may think are accurate. Also, a simple glass tube thermometer may need to be calibrated.

Calibration consists of comparing the instrument to a known standard, whether it be temperature, pressure, or length. National Bureau of Standards thermometers are available, graduated to 0.01°F, covering a wide temperature range with a series of thermometers, which can be obtained for checking thermometers over the temperature scale. A deadweight gage is used to check pressure gages. The physical properties of a substance may be used for calibrating certain points on the scale, such as the boiling point of water at 212°F and freezing point at 32°F at sea level.

Instruments may be supplied with a scale on which numbers are read, but which do not represent direct values being measured. The values read must be converted to the true value being measured, usually with a calibration graph or table supplied with the instrument. The standard procedure is to place the instrument reading on the abscissa and the accurate reading on the ordinate. The correction factor, such as + or − degree is usually placed on the ordinate (Fig. C.1).

The correction factor for instruments with uniform scales is usually made in terms of percentage of the full scale. Another common procedure is to express calibration errors in terms of a percentage of the reading.

Cross-reference: *Moisture Measurement.*

CALORIE

The quantity of heat required to change the temperature of 1 gm of water from 14.5° to 15.5°C is referred to as a small calorie. The mean calorie is $^1/_{100}$ of the amount of heat required to raise 1 gm of water from 0° to 100°C. The large calorie, Calorie, is 1,000 small calories.

The British thermal unit is the amount of heat required to increase the temperature of 1 lb of water at its maximum density by 1°F. Two-hundred fifty-two small calories are equivalent to 1 Btu.

Among other factors, the nutrition of people and animals is often evaluated in terms of large calories. The human daily calorie requirements decrease as adults get older, are less for women than for men, and increase from birth to adulthood (Table C.1).

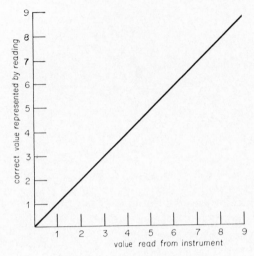

Fig. C-1.   Calibration chart

Cross-reference: *British Thermal Unit.*

TABLE C.1

HUMAN DAILY CALORIE REQUIREMENTS

	Age, Yr	Weight, Lb	Calories
Men	25	155	3200
	45	155	3000
	65	155	2550
Women	25	130	2300
	45	130	2200
	65	130	1800
Children	1–3	30	1300
	4–6	40	1700
	7–9	60	2100
	10–12	80	2500

CAN WASHERS

Most milk is brought from farms to the processing plant in the United States for fluid milk purposes by means of large tank trucks. The milk is pumped out of the farmer's bulk milk tank, where it has been collected, hauled to the city, and emptied into large receiving tanks at milk receiving stations or the processing plant. Some farmers, however, use the 10-gal. milk cans for the collection of milk, and these cans are then taken to the milk receiving station or processing plant. A very important factor in the bacteria count and quality of milk is the cleanliness of the cans. Normally, the 10-gal. cans are drained and washed at the milk receiving station after which they are returned to the farm.

If only a few cans are handled, they are usually manually washed with a hand brush and small tank. However, all large processors use a mechanical can washer. There are also many other applications where mechanical can washers are used.

Principles

The following are eight important points for proper can washing.

(1) Drain product which remains in the can.

(2) Rinse thoroughly with clean water to remove most of the product film which remains in the can.

(3) Use some method, such as a high-velocity warm or hot solution to soak loose and dislodge any material which may adhere to the can.

(4) Rinse with recirculated hot water.

(5) Follow with clean hot sterile unused water to remove all traces of washing solution.

(6) Follow by steaming with dry saturated steam to sterilize the can.

(7) Follow by treatment with hot air blast to remove the remaining moisture.

(8) Locate washing powders and solutions near the area of use.

For small and relatively inexpensive washers the circular or rotary washer is frequently used. This is a semiautomatic machine and the cans are usually placed in the machine by hand and removed by hand. Automatic unloading machines are available.

The straight-away type of washer (Fig. C.2) is used for large capacities. These washers may be fed automatically, although usually the operator sets the cans in the washer. An oscillating rack moves the can by steps and automatically unloads it and replaces the cover at the outlet end. The forward motion of the carriage moves the can to the next treatment in the washer. Usually, the washing is in 2 treatments and the drying may be with 2 or 3 identical treatments.

Auxiliary Equipment

The principal auxiliary equipment used with can washers includes can dumpers, weigh and receiving tanks, and automatic samplers of the milk. Auxiliary ventilation equipment is often used to remove the steam and vapor from the vicinity of the washers.

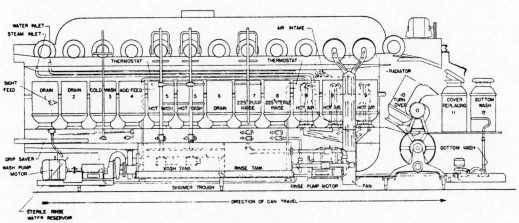

Courtesy of Lathrop Paulson

Fig. C-2.   Straight-away can washer

An important auxiliary attachment is an automatic device for maintaining the strength of solution in the wash tanks.   Another attachment often used is a special draining attachment for improving the drainage of milk from the can before washing.   Most can washers of the straight-away type have an automatic relidding device, since the cans and lids are discharged at a temperature which is too hot for the operator to handle manually.   Further attachments include special conveyors, automatic can counting devices, and auxiliary air systems for giving improved drying.

Management

The following items are important in the care and management of can washers:

(1) Jets must be kept clean so that the washing solution is applied at full pressure and proper volume.

(2) Automatic opening valves must be kept in good operating condition to allow full flow of the liquid and to shut off tightly when a can is not in washing position.

(3) Can washer solutions must be kept at the proper temperature as determined by the requirements of the particular washer and solution.   Generally, for a 2-tank unit, the washing solution is kept at a temperature of approximately 140°F in the first tank and about 180°F in the second.

(4) Steam sterilization jets must be kept free and open at the right time.   A properly operating trap on heating coils for the hot air system is necessary or the air will not heat properly and the can will not dry.

(5) The strength of alkali in the washer must be maintained at the proper level. Some washers use so-called acid cleaners, others use alkali cleaners.

(6) Drying of the cans requires proper temperature of the air, usually 300°F. The can must be steamed to the proper temperature before reaching the drying position or it will not dry properly.

Cleaning

Can washers must be kept clean.   Stoppage of jets on either the washing or the sterilizing system will prevent satisfactory operation.   Most washers have a strainer on the inlet of the solution wash pump which should be cleaned daily.   The wash tanks need to be cleaned daily if used for heavy duty operation.

Detergents and cleaning compounds are important elements in any food processing plant, since cleanliness and cleaning efficiency greatly affect the quality of the finished product.   Cleaning compounds are also important in that, if improperly used, they may seriously damage expensive processing machinery.   The food plant engineer is interested in both aspects of detergents and cleaning materials.

There are two broad types of cleaning materials in use in the food industry: the alkali types which are represented by trisodium phosphate, which is the basis of many important cleaners;   also there are the acid type cleaners which are frequently used and are particularly valuable for cleaning aluminum surfaces.

Properties

The properties of individual cleaners vary tremendously depending upon the exact composition.   Usually cleaners are designed for specific categories of service by the manufacturers. The broad categories of cleaners and their properties are given in Table C.2.

TABLE C.2

CLEANERS AND THEIR INGREDIENTS

Ingredients of Common Detergents

Basic Alkalies
    Caustic soda
    Soda ash
    Trisodium phosphate
    Sodium
    Metasilicate
Organic Compounds
    Chelating agents
    Wetting agents
    Organic acids
    Mineral acids
Complex Phosphates
    Sodium tetraphosphate
    Sodium tripolyphosphate
    Sodium Hexametaphosphate
    Tetrasodium pyrophosphate

The properties of cleaners are affected by (1) the temperature at which they are used, (2) the nature of the surface which is to be cleaned, and (3) the type of product which is processed on the equipment. No one cleaner can be best for all purposes.

Management

The selection and use of a particular cleaner should be based on the composition of water with which it is to be used. Attention must also be given to whether the application of the cleaner and detergent is for a short period or a soaker type of opera-

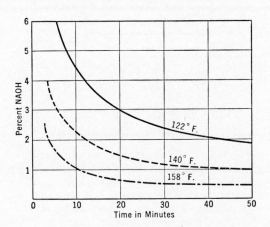

FIG. C-3. Bactericidal efficiency of alkali

tion.   The strength of an alkali type solution is rated in comparison to that of saturated solution of sodium hydroxide.

The effectiveness of detergents is greatly affected by the temperature.   This can
be either too high or too low depending upon the type of detergent.   Excessive temperature will cause heavy deposits.   In most automatic washers, provisions must be
made for the maintaining of the strength of the solution by the addition, either constantly or periodically, of additional cleaning elements.   The relationships of time,
temperature, and strength of alkali for equal bactericidal efficiency of alkali solutions
are shown in Fig. C.3.

Excessive strength of alkali in a bottle washer or a can washer may cause etching
on bottles or removal of tin from tinned cans.

Modern methods of cleaned-in-place cleaning systems require accurate control of
the strength and temperature of cleaning solution.

References

Farrall, A. W.   1963.   Engineering for Dairy and Food Products, 3rd Edition.   John Wiley
& Sons, New York.
Milk Industry Foundation.   1967.   Manual for Milk Plant Operators, 3rd Edition.   Wash-
ington, D.C.

Cross-references: *CIP Systems; Cleaning of Equipment; Sanitation.*

CANNING

Community canning centers or community kitchens were developed during and
after World War II as a means of assuring processed food for human consumption
(Fig. C.4) and some are still in operation.   The boiler is a major piece of equipment
for the community cannery.   The boiler installation must meet the safety, fire, and
insurance regulations.   About a 15 bhp (boiler horsepower) boiler operating at 100
to 110 psi is usually needed.   One boiler horsepower will evaporate 34.5 lb per hr of
water at 212°F.

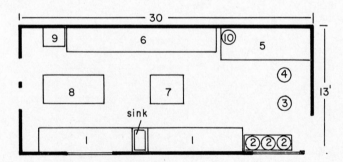

Fig. C-4.   Floor plan of community kitchen
1—Stainless steel table (homemade): $^3/_4$-in. pipe legs 40 in. apart and 36 in. high;
for dishpans, colanders, scoops, knives, slicers, etc.   2—Cooling tanks.   3—
Blancher.   4—Washer.   5—Utility wooden table for sugar, etc.   6—Board top
table (covered with oilcloth; sawhorses for legs) for scale, sealer, funnel, frames,
fillers, stamps, etc.   7—Cutter for asparagus, beans.   8—Pea huller.   9—Rack
for frozen food.   10—Sugar.

Operations

The sequence of operations for food preparation for vegetables, such as carrots, is as follows: (1) vegetables are washed and placed in line for canning; (2) the produce is then placed on a metal preparation table; (3) skins are removed and carrots cut into the desired shapes and placed in the cans to within about $1/2$ in. of the top, and salt and other seasoning are added; (4) the filled cans are then moved to the filling table where boiling water is poured into each can to within $1/2$ in. of the top; (5) the filled cans are placed in the exhausting vat and heated to 180°F after which the cans are ready to be sealed as rapidly as possible; (6) the cooking process is accomplished primarily in retorts where heat sufficient to kill spoilage bacteria can be obtained with steam heat. As the steam pressure is increased the temperatures increase, which at 10 psi is 240°F; 15 psi, 250°F; and at 21 psi, 260°F. Time and temperature processing varies greatly with different products (Tables C.3 and C.4).

TABLE C.3

PROCESSING TIME FOR VEGETABLES AT 240°F, 10 PSI, MIN

Food	No. 2 Can	No. 3 Can	Pint Glass	Quart Glass
Asparagus	30		30	35
Beans				
Dried kidney	70	85	80	90
Lima	40	50	50	55
Snap	25	30	30	35
Beets, baby	30	30	30	35
Carrots	30	30	30	35
Corn, whole kernel	50	65	60	70
Peas				
Black-eyed	40	50	50	55
Green	40		45	
Sweet potatoes	95	115	95	120
Tomatoes	25	30	25	35
Vegetable soup	50	65	60	70

For altitudes over 2,000 ft, add 1 psi for each additional 2,000 ft.
Cool tin cans immediately after processing.
Based on Farmers Bull. *1762*, U.S. Dept. Agr.
Source: Hall (1963).

Auxiliary Equipment

Auxiliary equipment and mechanical aids for the processing kitchen consist of cherry pitter, apple peeler, apple slicer, strawberry slicer, cutting boards, asparagus cutter, bag opener, pea and lima bean huller, power driven cutter for snap beans, asparagus and rhubarb, power cherry pitter, power fruit slicer, corn cutter, sorting table or belt, a portable work area, and the usual kitchen utensils.

Reference

HALL, C. W. 1963. Processing Equipment for Agricultural Products. Edwards Brothers, Ann Arbor, Mich.

TABLE C.4

PROCESSING TIME FOR FRUITS AND VEGETABLES AT BOILING WATER AT 212°F, MIN

Food	Pack	Pt and Qt Glass Jars	No. 2 and 3 Tin Cans	Half Gallon Glass Jars
Apples	Boil, hot pack in syrup	15	10	20
	Boil, hot pack dry	20	15	25
	Hot pack applesauce	5	5	10
Apricots	Cold pack, cover with hot syrup	25	No. 2–15	30
	Precook and hot pack	15	15	20
Beets, pickled	Hot pack	30		35
Blackberries	Cold pack, cover with hot syrup	20	15	25
	Precook and hot pack	5	5	10
Blueberries	Cold pack, cover with hot syrup	20	15	25
	Precook and hot pack	5	5	10
Cherries	Cold pack, cover with hot syrup	25	20	30
	Precook and hot pack	5	5	10
Fruit juices	Pack at 160°–170°F, process at 180°F	20		25
Fruit purée	Pack at 160°–170°F, process at 212°F	20		25
Peaches	Cold pack, cover with hot syrup, firm	35	30	40
	Precook and hot pack	15	15	20
Pears	Cold pack, cover with hot syrup		No. 20	
	Precook and hot pack	20	20	25
Pineapple	Pack raw, cover with hot syrup	30	25	35
Plums	Cold pack, cover with hot syrup	20	15	25
	Precook and hot pack	5	5	10
Rhubarb	Precook and hot pack	5	5	10
Sauerkraut	Precook and hot pack	pt 25	No. 2–15	35
		qt 30	No. 3–30	
Strawberries	Precook and hot pack	5	5	10
Tomatoes	Cold pack	45	35	50
	Precook and hot pack	5	5	10
Tomato juice	Hot pack		5	

For altitudes above 1,000 ft, add 20% time for each additional 1,000 ft.
Process immediately after packing.
Cool tin cans in cold water immediately after processing.
Cold pack refers to raw pack.
Source: Hall (1963).

Cross-references: *Cans; Retort; Sterilizer; Hydrostatic.*

CANS

The basic type can used in the canning industry has been the tin container made from sheets of steel covered with a thin layer of tin. Several methods are employed to coat the steel with tin. The finished cans from each method are designed for special purposes. For some foods, tin containers have the inside coated with a special enamel. The so-called "standard enamel" is used for red-colored fruits and vegetables to prevent color fading. For foods containing sulfur, a can lined with "C enamel" is recommended. This type of container should be used for corn and baked beans whose sulfur content reacts with plain tin to form a harmless but undesirable black discoloration. Other types of enamels are used to line the interior of cans to be used for special foods including citrus juices, wine, beer, soups, and meats. Some of the general properties of can-lining resins currently in use are given in Table C.5.

Table C.5

PROPERTIES OF CAN LINING RESINS

Coating-type Resin	Flavor	Flexi-bility	Adhe-sion	Color	Cost	Solder Damage Resis-tance	Steril-ization Resis-tance	Acid Resis-tance	Alkali Resis-tance
Acrylics	1[1]	1	1	1	3	1	1	1	1
Alkyds	3	2	1	2	1	2	2	2	3
Epoxy-amine	1	1	1	1	2	1	1	1	1
Epoxy-ester	2	1	1	2	2	2	1	1	2
Epoxy-phenolic	1	1	1	3	2	1	1	1	2
Oleoresinous	2	1	1	2	1	2	1	1	3
Phenolic	2	2	1	3	1	1	1	1	3
Polybutadiene	2	2	1	2	1	1	1	1	1
Vinyl	1	1	2	1	3	3	2	1	1

[1] Rating scale: 1 = good, 2 = fair, 3 = poor.
Source: *Modern Packaging.*

Can Description

Cans for the food industry come in many styles, shapes, and dimensions. The container must have sales appeal, possess easy handling characteristics, and above all, adequately preserve the food. Table C.6 shows the dimensions, capacity, uses, and some special features of several styles of cans. The manufacturer is usually very helpful in suggesting can styles for various products.

Each dimension of a can is expressed by a number having three digits. The left-hand digit states the number of whole inches while the two right-hand digits give any additional as a fraction of the dimension in sixteenths of an inch. The first number given for a can size is the diameter and the second number the height. Dimensions are "overall" with the diameter measured to the outside of the double seam and the length including the entire seam at each end of the can. In the case of rectangular cans the first two sets of digits refer to the base dimensions and the third number designates the height.

Cans must be able to perform effectively at filling speeds as high as 1,100 cans per min. The can must also withstand the high processing temperatures needed for product sterilization.

Can Specification

There has been a gradual trend toward the reduction or elimination of the amount of tin applied to steel plate. Research has been stimulated to develop exterior coatings. Considerable progress has been made in the development of high-speed printing techniques and applications of lithographic illustrations in as many as six colors. Containers may be embossed which present a raised surface increasing the attractiveness and design of a can.

TABLE C.6

TYPICAL CAN SIZES, USES AND SPECIAL FEATURES

| Style | Common Size Range | | Some Uses | Special Convenience Features |
	Dimensions[1]	Capacity		
Round, multiple friction cans	208x203–610x708	$^{1}/_{32}$–1 gal	Paint and related products	Large opening; firm reclosure; ears and bails for easy carrying of large sizes
Round, single-friction cans	213x300–702x814	To 10 lb	Paste wax; powders; grease	Good reclosure
Oblong I-style cans	214x107x406–610x402x907	$^{1}/_{16}$–1 gal	Varnish; waxes; insecticides	Pour spout and screw cap closure
Sanitary or open-top can	202x214–603x812	4 oz–1 gal	Fruits; vegetables; meat products	Tamperproof; ease of handling; large opening
Aerosol cans	202x214–300x709	3–24 oz	Foods; nonfoods	Designed for fit of standard valve cap
Flat-top cylinders	401x509–610x908	1–5 qt	Oil; antifreeze	Unit of use capacities; tamperproof since it can't be reclosed
	211x413 or 604	12 and 16 oz	Beer; soft drinks	
	211x306	8 oz	Malt liquor	
	211x300	8 oz	Cat food	
	300x407	15 oz	Dog food	
Crown cap, cone top can	200x214–309x605	4–32 oz	Chemical additives	Tamperproof closure; easy pouring
Spice can, oblong	Wide range	1–16 oz	Seasonings	Dredge top. Various dispenser openings
Key-opening, reclosure cans	307x302–502x608	$^{1}/_{2}$–2 lb	Nuts; candy; coffee	Lugged cover reclosure
	401x307.5–603x712.5	1–6 lb	Shortening	Lid is hinged
	211x301–603x812	$^{1}/_{4}$–5 lb	Dried milk	Good reclosure
Key-opening, nonreclosure cans	Wide range of sizes and shapes		Sardines; large hams; poultry; processed meats	Contents can be removed without marring product
Oval and oblong, with long spout	203x014x112–203x014x503	1–4 oz	Household oil; lighter fluid	Small opening for easy flow control
Hinged-lid pocket-type can	Wide range of sizes		Tobacco; strip bandages	Firm reclosure
Flat, round cans	213x013	$1^{1}/_{2}$ oz	Shoe polish	Friction closure
Flat, hinged-lid tins	112x104.5x004–212x205x003.75	12–30 tablets	Aspirin	Easy opening and reclosure
Square, oval and round-breasted containers	Wide assortment of shapes and sizes		Powders	Perforations for dispensing; reclosure feature
Slip-cover cans	Wide range of sizes—straight side and flaring		Lard; frozen fruit; eggs	Simple reclosure

[1] Can dimensions: 610x814 means that the can is (nominally) $6^{10}/_{16}$ in. in diameter and $8^{14}/_{16}$ in. high. In the case of rectangular cans the first two sets of digits refer to base dimensions; the third set to can height.
    Source: Modern Packaging Encyclopedia (1967).

In the food industry most metal cans still require a can opener for opening. Significant progress has been made on easy-open metal cans which are particularly applicable for beverages. Some cans are equipped with a narrow metal band for opening with a key opener which is manually propelled permitting removal of the lid. The reclosable feature is an advantage for food products consumed over a period of time.

Aluminum cans, some of which are fabricated in the processor's plant, are also making considerable impact in the industry. The citrus and beverage industries have used the aluminum can to a considerable extent.

Cans used for canned meats are coated with tin and the weight of tin is designated as 0.5 to 1.5% of the total weight. Cold-rolled steel plate dipped in molten tin is the most common type. Hot-dipped tin plate carries a greater percentage of tin than electrolytic tin plate. The electrolytic process permits close control of the amount of tin applied to steel. This tin plate is usually known as 0.5 plate and is satisfactory for many of the nonacid foods. Often the 0.5 tin plate can will have a specially designed inside enamel. Canned meats are packed to some extent in the hole-and-cap can having a soldered side seam. The meat is put through a hole in the top and the can is closed with a cap which is soldered on. The cap is vented and protected on the underside by a cleat which prevents the product from plugging the vent during processing. This type can is usually rectangular or pyramidal in shape.

Each food must be considered separately when cans are selected. For example, apples present the problem of releasing gases (oxygen, carbon dioxide, and nitrogen) during processing and can cause troublesome pinholing. Plain, unenameled cans are recommended for apples to avoid pinholing and hydrogen swells. Other products have characteristics which will have a bearing on the choice of can needed for a successful operation.

References

ANON. 1967. Mod. Packaging Encyclopedia *40*, No. 13A. McGraw-Hill, New York.
CAMPBELL, C. H. 1950. Campbells' Book, A Manual on Canning, Pickling and Preserving, 3rd Edition. Vance Publishing Corp., Chicago.
National Canners Assoc. 1966. Processes for Low Acid Canned Foods in Metal Containers, 10th Edition, Bull. *26L*. Washington, D.C.

Cross-references: *Canning; Conversion Values.*

CARBON DIOXIDE

Carbon dioxide is one of the widely used gases in the food industry. It is a colorless and odorless gas, usually produced as a by-product of the coke industry or by special burners.

Carbon dioxide can be obtained in relatively pure form for use in making carbonated beverages, and for filling cans of powdered products, where it is desired to keep oxygen out of the product to prevent oxidation.

Carbon dioxide is also widely used as a refrigerant. Its properties as a refrigerant are given in Table C.7.

TABLE C.7

PROPERTIES OF CO_2 AS A LIQUID REFRIGERANT

Boiling point—Sea level	−108.4°F
Gage Pressure PSIG @ 86°F	1024.3
Gage Pressure PSIG @ 5°F	319.7
Heat content of sat. vapor in 5°F evaporator, Btu/lb	102.14
Heat content leaving 86°F condenser, Btu/lb	45.45
Btu refrigerating effect/lb	56.69
Pounds of refrigerant per min/ton	3.528
Btu refrigeration/ft^3 piston displacement	212.0
Toxicity	None (however, will not support life)

Liquid carbon dioxide is chilled to make a solid carbon dioxide, which is known as Dry Ice. Its properties are given in Table C.8. It is customary for Dry Ice to be

TABLE C.8

PROPERTIES OF SOLID CO_2 (DRY ICE)

Temperature: $-103.3°F$ in a CO_2 atmosphere
$-123.0°F$ in a 50% CO_2 atmosphere
Density: 50 to 55 lb per 10 in. cube
Refrigeration effect per lb (heat of sublimation from a
solid at $-109.3°F$ to a gas) = 246.3 Btu

delivered in 50-lb cakes which can be stored in an insulated cabinet. It is cut into slabs of the proper size for use with a band saw. Dry Ice is used where (1) lightness in weight is essential, (2) extremely low temperatures are required, and (3) it is desired to obtain refrigeration without moisture.

Reference

FARRALL, A. W. 1963. Engineering for Dairy and Food Products, 3rd Edition. John Wiley & Sons, New York.

CAROTENE STABILIZATION

The carotene content of hay is practically all destroyed during curing in the sun. The carotene loss can be prevented by dehydrating alfalfa with high temperature air. Alfalfa can be blanched in heat by passing it between heated rolls to stabilize the carotene. Even though the carotene is preserved through drying or blanching by passing between heated rolls, the carotene continues to be lost during storage and 50% or more may be destroyed after 6 months. The storage loss of carotene can be prevented by sealing hay in an oxygen-free atmosphere, and/or the use of refrigeration.

Reference

HALL, C. W. 1957. Drying of Farm Crops. Edwards Brothers, Ann Arbor, Mich.

CARTON FORMING AND FILLING

This section is concerned with paper carton forming and filling, and does not include form-seal packages produced from thermoplastic materials. In the food plant a wide variety of cartons are formed depending upon the nature of the product to be packaged. Other factors determining the package material to be used, aside from whether the product is a liquid or dry material, are the effects of oxygen and the hygroscopicity of the product. Some products require a very low oxygen atmosphere which affects the type of packaging materials as well as the equipment for forming and sealing which can be used.

Principles

In most large operations, the stock material is in a large roll or in flat paper blanks. Some paper milk cartons are shipped to the processing plant in three separate pieces.

They are formed on the mandrel where the bottom piece is applied. The separate top is added after filling, and all joints are heat sealed. Other type cartons have the blanks precut at the paper plant where the sidewall is sealed. With this carton, the bottom flaps are heat sealed, as well as the top, after filling.

Cartons for dry products, such as cereals, are usually glued at the time of forming on the mandrel. Dry cereal carton boxes require a suitable interliner to protect the product from excessive moisture absorption. The interliner will normally have a relatively low gas and water vapor transmission rate. Gas transmission rates of some packaging films for several gases are given in Table C.9.

TABLE C.9

AMOUNTS OF DIFFERENT GASES TRANSFERRED IN 24 HR BY DIFFERENT FILMS AT ROOM TEMPERATURE

Cubic centimeters per 100 sq in. of film at 15 lb pressure differential

Type of Film	Temp.—RH Variations	Nitro-gen	Oxygen	Carbon Dioxide	Air	Ethyl-ene	Ethyl-ene Oxide	Sulfur Dioxide
Cellophane (MSAT)[1,2]	—	32.0	43.0	111.0	35.0			
Cellophane (MSAD)[5]	2% RH	—	6.30	37.04				
	100% RH	—	205.4	346.8				
Vinylidene[1] (Cryovac)	—	3.1	11.1	27.1	5.1			
Cellulose Acetate[3]	25°C	—	352.5	1,912.0	—	549.2	19,500	18,510
(P-903)	0°C	—	132.2	809.0	—	—	5,590	7,848
Cellulose Acetate[3]	25°C	—	250.0	932.0	—	112.7	4,560	5,445
(P-912)	0°C	—	112.7	421.0				
Rubber Hydrochloride[4]								
(Pliofilm 100 FMI)	—	—	144.0	924.0				
0.0005 in. Polyester[5]	2% RH	—	18.67	24.65				
(Mylar)—	100% RH	—	49.67	86.50				
0.0005 in. Polyester[5]								
(Mylar)—	2% RH	—	7.70					
0.002 in. Polyethylene	100% RH	—	15.52					

[1] Values by Cryovac Co., Food Processing *17*, No. 8 (1956).
[2] With moist gas at high relative humidity.
[3] Values by Celanese Corp. on two types of film differing in flexibility and toughness (converted from investigator's values expressed in cc per sq. meter per 24 hr. per cm. mercury pressures).
[4] Values by Goodyear Tire and Rubber Co.
[5] Values by Nagel and Wilkins (1957) converted from investigator's values expressed in grams per sq meter per hr.
Source: Joslyn and Heid (1963).

Aluminum foil alone will often have pinholes which are more numerous in thin foils such as 0.00035 in. The water transmission rate is much lower through foil laminates than through plain foil. The water transmission rate of some typical laminates are given in Table C.10.

The efficiency of a package is often regarded as the ratio of the water vapor transmission rate, "WVTR," of the completely filled package to that of the flat barrier material. Machine fabricated packaging materials which have been formed into a complete package usually have a more reduced barrier property level than that of the original material. The type of material will affect the extent barrier properties are lost during carton formation. A rather brittle waxed paper, for example, may lose its barrier properties to a considerable degree. The method of handling a product, as well as its nature affects the package requirements.

TABLE C.10

WATER VAPOR TRANSMISSION OF ALUMINUM FOIL LAMINATES[1]

Material	Thickness, In.		WVTR Gm/100 Sq In./24 Hr; 100°F; 100% RH	
	Foil	Laminant	Flat	After Creasing[2]
Al foil laminated to moistureproof Cellophane	0.00035	0.0009	0.00	—
			0.01	0.03
			0.01	0.01
Al foil laminated to cellulose acetate	0.00035	0.0012	0.01	—
			0.02	0.07
Al foil laminated to rubber hydrochloride	0.00035	0.0008	0.01	0.01
			0.01	—
Al foil laminated to vinyl polymer	0.00035	0.0012	0.01	0.02
			0.02	0.01
Al foil laminated with wax to 30-lb glassine	0.00035	—	0.00	0.04
Al foil BEIS-O	0.00035	—	0.07	0.42
Al foil laminated to moistureproof Cellophane	0.001	0.0009	0.00	0.00
Al foil laminated to vinyl polymer	0.001	0.0012	0.00	0.00
Al foil laminated with wax to 35-lb glassine	0.001	—	0.00	0.02
Al foil BEIS-O	0.001	—	0.00	0.40

[1] Alcoa aluminum foil—its properties and uses (1953). Each value is the average of measurements on 2 or 3 test pieces.

[2] "Creasing" means creased with 4 equidistant parallel folds and then with 4 more folds at right angles to the first.

Source: Joslyn and Heid (1963).

System

In the food plant most large operations will fold the packages from flat material just prior to filling. Small companies may find the form and seal equipment to be too expensive, therefore, will purchase preformed cartons from the manufacturer. Because of the bulkiness of preformed cartons, large operations will generally have lower carton costs than smaller companies who must rely on preforming at some distant plant. With improvements in plastic coated paper, most milk cartons are heat sealed. Wax-coated cartons have been replaced in recent years by the plastic-coated packages. The carton forming and filling are frequently accomplished with one machine. In some products, however, such as flour or cereal packaging, the "former" and filler are two separate machines linked together with a package conveyor. For cereals, the package closer is usually coupled to the filler.

Carton forming and filling speeds are synchronized to make a continuous operation. New machines being developed are steadily increasing the rate of cartons handled. Milk carton forming and filling of the half-pint size is accomplished at a rate of 160 per min.

Practices

Cartons should be stored in a room with a comparatively low humidity for efficient forming. Excessive moisture in the paper board will result in bubbles when heat is applied at the seal. If the carton is to be used for liquids, a perfect seal is obviously required. Operators should provide a clean, dry storage for all plastic-coated blank packaging materials. In some cases it may be necessary to install heaters and humidifying equipment in the storage room. Blank cartons and roll stock materials should not be stored on damp concrete floors. Placing such materials on strips of wood will assist in keeping the moisture content low by reducing absorption from the floor.

Most cartons are formed on a mandrel to achieve the proper dimensions and to hold the blank securely for either heat sealing or gluing. In some instances, the carton interior may be sprayed with a chemical such as hydrogen peroxide to destroy bacteria. In these instances heat is usually applied to dry the carton. This may be in the form of sterile, heated air applied in an enclosed chamber. Cartons containing liquid products are usually filled with a volumetric metering valve. In some cases the quantity placed in the carton may be determined gravimetrically. Dry cereals are often fed into a carton through a vibrating trough which is controlled gravimetrically. Cartons of cake mixes are filled by weight control. These usually employ a vibrating feeder to place approximately 90 to 95% of the contents in the package at the first stage of filling. The remainder of the fill is accomplished with a smaller more accurate vibrating feeder to deliver the exact amount as determined with a preset weight control.

For sanitary reasons, the idea of preforming large quantities of packages in advance of filling is discouraged. The carton former and filler capacity should be closely synchronized for continuous operation. Where the preformer and filler are two separate machines, a slightly larger capacity is desired in the carton former than in the filler.

References

JOSLYN, M. A., and HEID, J. L. 1963. Food Processing Operations, Vol. 2. AVI Publishing Co., Westport, Conn.

FARRALL, A. W. 1963. Engineering for Dairy and Food Processing, 3rd Edition. John Wiley & Sons, New York.

Cross-reference: *Conversion Values.*

CASE COMBINERS, STACKERS AND DESTACKERS

The purpose of case destackers, combiners, and stackers is to reduce manpower requirements used to perform relatively menial tasks in materials handling. This equipment is used in conjunction with other equipment including fillers and casers. The advent of infloor conveyors made practical the use of destackers, combiners, and stackers. The systems have increased productivity per man-hour, and provided less damage to cases and higher line efficiency. Mechanical handling of cases is especially applicable to large volume plants. Very small operations probably cannot justify the capital investment in extensive materials handling systems. Of special significance is the saving through the reduction of labor requirements.

Principles

In materials handling systems uniformly sized packages and cases generally result in a smoother operation than when various size packages and cases are used.

The combiner is designed to accumulate cases on a conveyor line until a predetermined number have been collected to form a stack usually 5 or 6 high. With a combiner, 1 stacker might serve 2 or 3 filling lines of various products if the fillers are of such low capacity so as not to overcrowd the stacker.

System

In a dairy plant the package handling system may operate on glass, paper cartons, or blown plastic bottles. A typical system would include in-floor conveyors, destacker, and case washer in the empty case room. For glass bottles, the washer would also be in this room. Stacks of empty cases are manually pulled onto the in-floor conveyor. These cases are automatically conveyed to the destacker. Single cases are ejected from the destacker and in the case of glass bottles conveyed to the bottle washer. If the line is a paper carton filling system, the cases are sometimes inverted, passed through a case washer, and reinverted before moving to the caser in the packaging area. Glass bottles from a filler or paper cartons from the carton filler are automatically cased with a caser. The filled cases are fed through a combiner or directly to the stacker for mechanical stacking usually 5 or 6 high. The stacks move into the storage area on in-floor conveyors. The systems have increased productivity per man-hour, decreased case damage, and given higher line efficiency.

In a system involving case and package handling equipment, the filler is usually the pace setter. The capacity of the various pieces of equipment is closely synchronized and usually adjustable for a given line speed. Most of the associated machines are set to operate slightly faster than the filler to allow for "catch up" time in the event of minor shutdowns. Designing some conveyor length between the individual pieces of equipment in the system will permit package or case accumulation in the event of minor operational disruptions of any piece of equipment.

Destacker Types

Case destackers consist of two types both of which are adjustable to accommodate various case widths. The two types are: the bottom-up destacker and the lay-down destacker. These units usually are either hydraulic or air operated. In the bottom-up unit a stack of cases is lifted slightly above one case height to enable clamps to hold all but the bottom case which is lowered to the injection conveyor at the base of the unit. Bottom-up destackers will unstack up to 20 cases per minute when 6-high stacks are used. To gain capacity, the destackers are usually equipped with a short high-speed belt or discharge conveyor to eject the cases from the machine.

The lay-down destacker is not set for handling cases containing glass bottles. They are adaptable primarily to handling empty cases to be filled with paper cartons, blown glass bottles, or perhaps some other type package. The lay-down destacker has a lower initial cost than the bottom-up machine. A stack of cases is received at the infeed of the unit by a double chain conveyor. The conveyor transfers the stack onto a cradle which lays the cases on their side. As the cases move up the cradle a high-speed belt separates them by removing the one upper-most in the stack. Cases may be discharged inverted or right side up depending upon whether or not they are to be washed. It is desirable to discharge the cases in an inverted position to empty any foreign material and permit washing. A lay-down destacker will successfully operate at speeds up to 30 cases or more per minute. The capacity of the unit is dependent upon the stack height and conveyor speed. Lay-down stackers having a smoothe hain on the incline will have a minimum discharge height of about 15 in. above the through conveyor. The incline of the destacker has a minimum of 1.5 in. per ft. Lugs are necessary on the chain if steeper inclines are required.

Case Combiners

The case combiner is used to automatically count, group, and release cases in the desired number to produce a uniform stack of products from two or more filling lines feeding a single case stacker. The combiner permits the stacker to automatically assemble a stack of cases of like products. The stacker can handle more than one filler provided its rated capacity is not exceeded. Traffic control is a relatively simple mechanical device used at the point of converging conveyor lines to prevent cases from jamming between the conveyor side rails. The first case to reach the traffic control is permitted to pass through while the second case from the other line is held until the first case passes the jamming point. In higher speed plants combiners are not often used because the capacity of larger fillers are sufficient to utilize the rated capacity of a stacker.

Case Stacker

Case stackers are of two general types: bottom-up and top-down. The bottom-up stacker is the most common because it lends itself to more plant layouts. It operates on the common floor level either with in-floor or standard above floor conveyor. Bottom-up stackers are operated by air, hydraulic, mechanical, or a combination of these. In the dairy plant milk cases enter the bottom of the stacker and are raised individually to build the stack from the bottom until 5 or 6 cases have been accumulated. The entire stack is then lowered to the conveyor and released. The top-down stacker lends itself to two-story buildings where filling and casing is on the second floor with the storage area on the first floor. Cases are then placed on top of the stack as they are lowered and the stack is discharged at the lower level. Some of the stacker models are as follows: (1) top stacking, front entry, front discharge; (2) top stacking, rear entry, front discharge; (3) bottom stacking, rear entry, front discharge; (4) bottom stacking, left-side entry, front discharge; and (5) bottom stacking, right-side entry, front discharge.

The feed-discharge schematics are illustrated in Fig. C.5.

Practices

Some caser-stacker units are combination machines and are being used successfully. These units are somewhat more expensive than either the caser or the stacker, however, the cost is usually less than two single units. There is a space saving achieved with the combination caser-stacker. Some modifications have been made using individual casers and stackers by coupling together very closely, perhaps the distance of only one case. This system results in economy in floor space and performs satisfactorily.

Several stackers can discharge stacks of filled cases into a common conveyor system leading to the storage area. In some instances, the stacks of products are

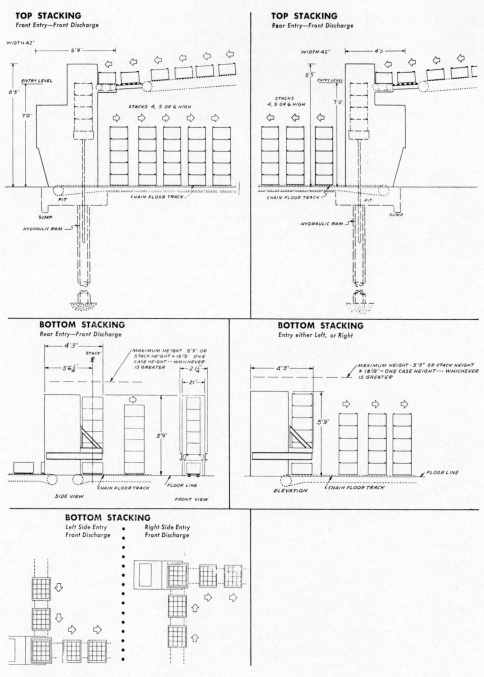

Courtesy of FMC Corp.

FIG. C-5.   Schematics of methods of feed discharge of cases

moved directly to the truck loadout stations for immediate shipment.

When considering the investment in materials handling equipment, the greatest saving will usually be made in the reduction of manual labor for handling many small

Courtesy of Mojonnier Bros. Co.

FIG. C-6.   Unitized load of cases

items. In many operations destackers, combiners, and case stackers have returned the original investment to the owner in less than 2 years.

References

FARRALL, A. W. 1963. Engineering for Dairy and Food Products, 3rd Edition. John Wiley & Sons, New York.

MILK INDUSTRY FOUNDATION. 1963. Manual for Milk Plant Operators, 3rd Edition. Washington, D.C.

CASE STORAGE

Case storage in a plant operation should be considered as an integral part of a materials handling system. Inefficient methods employed in the storage of cases can lead to excessive labor costs through rehandling. Effective use of space is necessary in case storage to lower capital investment and overhead costs. In a milk processing plant, cases for paper cartons and milk bottles should be handled in stacks or multiples which may be accomplished with conveyor or palletized systems.

Requirements

In considering case storage, a plant operator must carefully evaluate the type of cases to be used. Weight and strength are important. More recently, plastic cases are being employed by the dairy industry. Their sanitary characteristics have some merit. Cases should be easily cleanable and stackable with good stability for multiple handling. Uniformity of size is extremely important in the mechanized handling of cases in any type of food processing plant.

Combining conveyors with palletizing or unitizing systems is being done in several modern plants. Cases may be handled with a forklift very effectively in large cold storage rooms and where wholesale trailers are loaded with a forklift. Figure C.6 shows the 6 stack-30 case unitized load on the tines of a forklift ready for placing in the storage area of a cold room. To avoid handling of pallets, the unitization of cases is finding wider acceptance in the industry.

Plant Layout

In developing a plant layout adequate storage must be provided to achieve efficiency and a smooth materials handling system. This is true for storage of both empty and filled cases. Empty cases may be stored on a dock and exposed to atmospheric conditions; however, a roof over the area is recommended. In colder climates an enclosed case storage is suggested both for the comfort of the operating personnel and to facilitate cleaning of the cases.

Courtesy of Rapistan, Inc.

Fig. C-7.   Flow rack in meat cooler

Types

A relatively new innovation for case storage includes a roller bed consisting of long parallel rollers about 3 in. in diameter which revolve propelling the entire mass of cases from one end of the roller bed to the other. The infeed and discharge from the roller bed may be made fully automatic which will supply the casing operations. The roller bed system may also be employed in refrigerated rooms for the storage of filled cases. Discharge from this roller bed would be controlled by the demand of truck loading activities.

The conveyorized flow rack is finding many applications in the food and other industries. Cases of various sizes may be placed on a flow rack for storage. The system has the advantage of making an assortment of products readily available for convenient and rapid loadout of trucks. When a case or carton is removed from one of the conveyors in the flow rack the remaining supply automatically rolls forward to the discharge position. The flow rack is illustrated in Fig. C.7.

Flow racks are now engineered with flexibility utilizing conveyor systems. Flow racks are especially useful in warehouses containing packaged goods.

Layout and Utilization

Grocery warehouses are frequently laid out to employ pallets stacked 3 or 4 high in racks. A grocery warehouse for storing cases of packaged goods will frequently

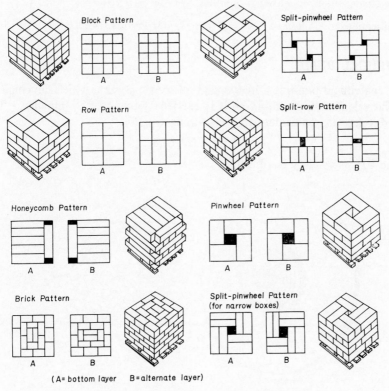

(A= bottom layer   B=alternate layer)

FIG. C-8.   Loading patterns for cases

vary from 50,000 to 250,000 sq ft of floor area. The usual minimum ceiling height is 22 ft. Some warehouses are built with ceiling heights up to 26 ft with the idea of adding another pallet in the vertical storage space. Aisles in a modern grocery warehouse are generally $6^{1}/_{2}$ or 7 ft wide. The additional aisle width permits two of the straddle-type trucks to pass comfortably in the aisle.

In storing cases of supplies or finished goods on pallets several types of loading patterns may be used. The size and shape of the case must be considered in selecting the pallet loading pattern. The types of patterns commonly used are block, row, pinwheel, honeycomb, brick, split-row, and split-pinwheel. These loading patterns are illustrated in Fig. C.8.

Case storage areas must be designed to carry the heavy load which is often imposed on this section of a plant. Cognizance of this fact is important when designing a new plant or when converting an area of an older plant into case storage. In some instances buildings have had to be reinforced to serve adequately and safely as a storage area.

References

JUHREND, E. F. 1965. Pallet and unitized case handling systems. Paper presented at Milk Industry Foundation, Montreal, Can., Oct. 18.

LEWIS-SHEPARD PRODUCTS. Grocery warehousing, Bull. Application Analysis *152*. Watertown, Mass.

RAPISTAN, INC. 1966. Materials handling equipment and services. Grand Rapids, Mich.

RAYMOND CORP. A. B. C. of pallet handling. Greene, N.Y.

Cross-references: *Conveyors; Forklift Trucks; Materials Handling.*

CENTRIFUGAL PUMP

The centrifugal pump is a high-speed rotary type pump which develops pressure due to the velocity of the liquid as it is carried around by the impeller. The head which is developed is determined by the formula

$$VH = V^2/64.4$$

where the VH = velocity head in feet

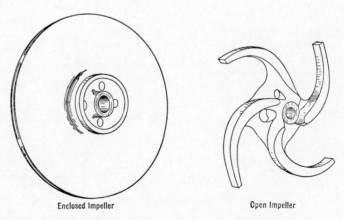

Enclosed Impeller   Open Impeller

FIG. C-9.   Centrifugal pump impellers

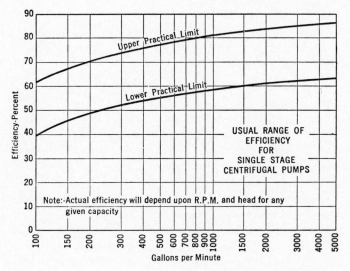

FIG. C-10.   Efficiency of centrifugal pumps

V^2 = the square of the velocity of the water in ft per sec at the periphery of the impeller

Centrifugal pumps are very widely used in the food industry for pumping water and many kinds of fluid food products. Centrifugal pumps are simple, relatively inexpensive, and require very little upkeep. They are not self-priming, although they can be made self-priming by means of a check valve in the suction line.

Description

Centrifugal pumps are built in all sizes from tiny units up to those with many thousands of gallons per minute capacity. They are also built with various numbers of stages. A single stage unit is quite limited in pressure. However, by the use of multiple stages, pressures of hundreds of pounds per square inch can be obtained. They are also built with various types of rotors or impellers for specific purposes. The open impeller, Fig. C.9, is less efficient than the closed impeller type. However, the open impeller will handle solid particles and debris without plugging.

Centrifugal pumps are usually direct-connected to a motor. The speeds may be from 900 to 3,600 rpm depending upon conditions with 1,200 or 1,800 rpm as the usual pump speed for small- or medium-sized pumps.

Centrifugal pumps can be built of sanitary construction so that they may be easily and quickly taken apart for cleaning, or may be of the standard bolted type which is seldom dismantled.

The usual water pumps are built of cast iron or bronze. However, those for handling food products are usually built of stainless steel or white metal.

The efficiency of centrifugal pumps varies greatly. Small units of 5 to 10 gal. per min capacity may have efficiency of 25 or 30%. Extremely large pumps designed for a certain purpose may have an efficiency of over 90%.

The centrifugal pump can be designed to be very efficient for a specific set of conditions, but if these conditions are changed the efficiency drops off quite rapidly.

Characteristics

An important characteristic for the centrifugal pump with respect to the food industry is that it is more foolproof than most any other type of pump. For example, if the discharge valve is closed the pressure will build up only to a certain point, and it is not likely to damage the system such as would happen if a positive pump were used. Also, it is possible to regulate the flow of a centrifugal pump reasonably accurately by throttling the discharge line. One of the disadvantages is that the centrifugal pump has a tendency to overagitate or churn liquids particularly if pumping against considerable pressure. The centrifugal pump is not self-priming except certain special designs, and its performance is impaired by small air leaks in the suction side. This condition may cause extreme foaming when some materials are pumped. Figure C.10 shows the usual range of efficiency for centrifugal pumps of 100 gal. per min or greater capacity. Sanitary centrifugal pumps are normally less efficient than regular industrial centrifugal pumps, since the clearances are greater and the dismantling feature makes it difficult to use the most efficient shapes.

Modern sanitary type centrifugal pumps are frequently mounted directly on the motor shaft making a very compact unit (Fig. C.11). Modern practice also includes the use of a rotary metallic seal rather than packing on the pump shaft (Fig. C.12).

Sanitary centrifugal pumps should be made to comply with the 3-A standards. The standards cover the features of the pump, the method of mounting the motor, the type of motor, and the type of legs which support the pump and motor.

Cross-reference: *H.T.S.T. Pasteurization.*

Courtesy of Ladish Tri-Clover Co.

Fɪɢ. C-11.   Sanitary-type centrifugal pump

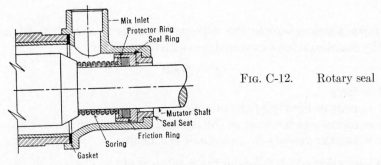

FIG. C-12.   Rotary seal

Courtesy of Cherry-Burrell Corp.

CENTRIFUGAL SCREENS

In the processing of many food products, such as fishmeal, oil seed meal, soya protein, beet sugar processing, and in the freeze concentration of juice, the screening centrifuge is widely used. This device with high basket speeds produces up to 2,000 times the force of gravity. It uses a conveyor spiral for positive displacement of solids across the screening basket.

A centrifuge device for separating solids from liquids has capacities of from a few pounds per hour up to 50 tons per hour with coarse materials. It works well whether the solids are lighter or heavier than the liquid to be separated.

Separation is accomplished by a conical or cylindrical screening drum or perforated plate. The screening medium works with a conveyor spiral which rotates in the same direction but at a slightly different speed.

A mixture of solids and liquids is introduced at the end of the screening drum. Solids are retained somewhat by the screen inclination, assisted in some applications by the conveyor. Liquid is discharged through the openings in the screening medium as a result of centrifugal force.

Solids are discharged through a narrow opening in the end and can be removed by a belt or a similar conveyance. In some applications a knife is directed across the face of the basket to remove the solids.

Reference

ARTHUR G. MCKEE AND CO., 721 N. Bee St., Sacramento, Calif.

CENTRIFUGAL SEPARATORS

Centrifugal separators are important in the food industry. They are special rotating machines designed to use centrifugal force to cause a stratification, and thereby enable the separation of elements in a mixture of materials having different specific gravity. The most widely used equipment for this purpose is the centrifugal cream separator. There are, however, numerous other centrifugal machines such as the clarifier, and the numerous special types of separating machines. Some centrifugal devices collect the material in a rotating basket which must be emptied manually; in others the collected material is automatically ejected by means of a scraper blade.

Principle

The force which separates the different elements in a centrifugal machine is generated by centrifugal force in accordance with the equation

$$F = Mrw^2$$

where F = force
  M = mass or density of the product
  r = distance of the mass of the material to the center of rotation
  w = angular velocity in revolutions per minute

Stoke's equation which indicates the movement of the material is

$$V = 2r^2 \frac{(d_p - d_f)A}{9\Gamma}$$

where V = the rate of movement of fat globules in centimeters per second
  r = radius in centimeters of the fat globule
  Γ = viscosity of the milk
  d_p and d_f = density of the serum and the fat, respectively
  A = acceleration, the gravitational constant, and is numerically equal to 980 dynes

This equation can also be used to calculate the velocity of movement of fat globules through serum due to the centrifugal force of the separator. The following equation gives the values of A' when the acceleration is due to centrifugal force

$$A' = \left(4\pi^2 n^2 \times \frac{R}{60^2} \right)$$

where n = rpm of bowl
  R = distance of globule from axis of rotation

Several factors in the equation are numbers which may be represented by a numerical constant of the value 0.00244.   The equation then becomes

$$V = 0.00244 \times \frac{(d_p - d_f)r^2 n^2 \times R}{\Gamma}$$

The rate of fat globule separation is increased by: (1) greater difference in density of the milk serum and the fat, (2) greater speed of centrifuge, (3) greater radius of the fat globule, (4) greater distance from the rotational center, and (5) lower viscosity of the milk serum.

Milk and Cream Separators

There are three principal types of separators which are mechanically driven.   The first is the air tight or pressure fed type which is fully enclosed and equipped with a hollow driving spindle which conveys milk or other products into the bowl.   Milk is fed to the separator or clarifier by means of a positive displacement pump.   Regulation of the fat content of the cream is accomplished by an external valve which can be adjusted while the machine is operating.   This type machine operates in a very steady manner and one of its principal advantages is that it does not cause foam.

The second is the gravity type enclosed separator. In this machine, the fluid completely covers the intake opening of the collector, and thereby liquid seals entering milk or cream which also eliminates foam. Approximately 40 psi pressure is produced which can be used to move products.

A third type of machine is fed by gravity and discharges the product at atmospheric pressure. These machines are less expensive than the other two. The production of foam is a disadvantage.

Clarifier

The centrifugal clarifier, which is used to remove small extraneous material from fluids such as milk, is made almost the same as the cream separator. The machine separates only heavy extraneous matter which is allowed to collect in the outside portion or peripheral portion of the centrifugal bowl. At the end of the run this deposit is removed manually. Thus, a clarifier can operate only for a few hours at a time before it becomes ineffective and must be cleaned. In large plants which require continuous operation, two machines are set in parallel so that one can be cleaned while the other is operating without stopping the entire operation. Machines recently developed are available for removing sediment while in operation.

Management

One important factor in the operation of centrifugal equipment is that they must be set level and be solidly bolted to the floor. If this is not done, the high-speed machines may cause excessive vibration and damage may result.

The ideal temperature for separating milk, for example, in most separators is from 85° to 100°F. For certain purposes they may be operated at temperatures as low as 40°F or as high as 140° or 150°F. Uniform operating pressure, uniform speed, and uniform temperatures are needed to give efficient operations. A good milk separator should not pass in excess of 0.25% fat in the skim milk.

Many variations of the standard cream separator are used for industry. They are used for separating blood serum. They are used for separating water from oil. Machines may be obtained with capacities of a few hundred pounds per hour up to 20,000 lb per hr.

Special centrifugal equipment can also be obtained for separating cream to a test as high as 80 or 90% butterfat. Supercentrifuges are also available for removing impurities from oil and special solutions up to 99.9%. Special centrifuges are made with automatic unloading devices which will remove the collected solids from the bowl without stopping. Basket-type centrifuges are so made that they will collect large amounts of solid material from the liquid which is passed through them. The separating force in a centrifuge may become many times stronger than gravity in accordance with the centrifugal force equation.

Cross-references: *Bactofugation; Butter Churns; Clarifiers; Ultracentrifuge.*

CHAINS

Chains are widely used in the food industry as a means of driving shafts. The chain has the feature that it gives a positive drive so that operations can be accurately timed.   It is a relatively inexpensive type of drive, and there are many types of chains available.   The ones most commonly used in the industry are the roller-chain and the silent chain.   Standard specifications for chains for different purposes are available, and recommendations for use should be closely followed.

Chains are much more noisy than belts.   However, chains operate at relatively low speeds, and thus if the chain is enclosed and runs in oil, it can be very quiet.

Exposed chains subjected to dusty or corrosive atmospheres wear rapidly.

In the care and operation of chains, the following are of great importance: (1) the chains should be adapted to the job; (2) the chain speed should be within the manufacturers' limits; (3) chains should be kept clean and free from dirt and grit; (4) chains should be kept well-lubricated; (5) chains should be kept at proper tension; and (6) sprockets must be properly aligned.

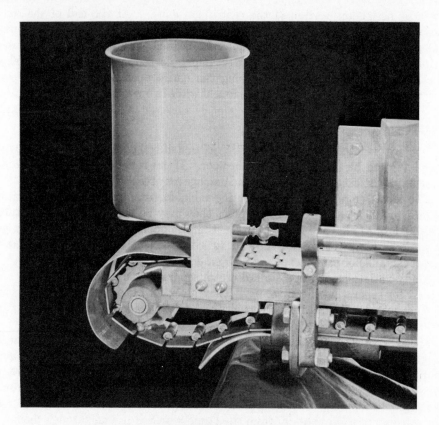

Courtesy of Cherry-Burrell Corp.

Fig. C-13.   Above: Drip-type lubricator.   Below: roller lubricator

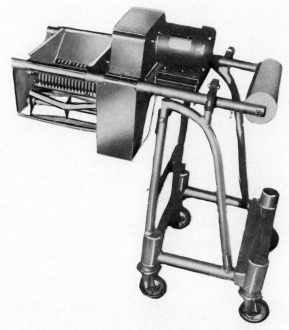

Fig. C-14.   Curd mill with portable stand

The speed of a shaft driven by chains and sprockets is given by the formula

Rpm driver × number of teeth of driver = rpm driven × number of teeth driven

Many special types of chains are available for use as conveyors.   Some conveyor chains are used to support small platforms; others carry hooks on which animal carcasses can be hung and transported.

Lubrication of conveyor chains is accomplished by dripping a soap solution or other lubricant on the chain, (Fig. C.13.A), or the chain may be drawn through a shallow lubricating pan, or it may be lubricated by lubricating rollers as shown in Fig. C.13.B.

Special hardened chain links of alloy steel are used where wearing conditions are severe.

CHEESE CURD MILL

In the manufacture of cheddar and some other types of cheeses, it is necessary to cut the slab of curd into relatively small pieces or chunks (milling), so that the whey will properly drain from the curd.   Milling also enables the curd to be washed thoroughly and provides an opportunity for salt to become more thoroughly mixed with the curd.

The basic principle of the curd mill is that of a rotating cylinder on which sharp discs are mounted in such a manner that the livery slab of cheese is run through it thereby cutting it into strips about $^5/_8$ in. wide.   A cutter at right angles cuts these strips into $^5/_8$-in. lengths in the other direction.   The result is that a cube of cheese of $^5/_8$-in. dimension is produced.   Several different sizes of cuts can be obtained, how-

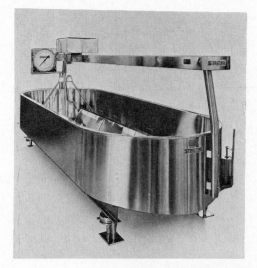

FIG. C-15.   Draining and creaming vat

Courtesy of Stoelting Bros.

Courtesy of Grace Machinery Co.

FIG. C-16.   Dual mixing and creaming unit on load cells

ever, the $^5/_8$-in. cube is standard.   Figure C.14 shows a modern cheese curd mill mounted on a portable stand.   Special types of curd mills utilizing the above principle, but with different detail construction are used for the new semicontinuous methods of manufacturing cheddar-like cheese.

Reference

FARRALL, A. W.   1963.   Engineering for Dairy and Food Products, 3rd Edition.   John Wiley & Sons, New York.

Cross-references: *Cheese Handling Equipment; Cheese Vats.*

CHEESE HANDLING EQUIPMENT

The manufacture of cheese over the years has been accomplished to a considerable extent with manual or semimanual methods. More recently cheese equipment manufacturers and the industry have been putting forth special effort to mechanize some of the operations. Attempts are now being made to clean cheese vats with mechanical cleaning-in-place methods.

Pumping

Several advances have been made in mechanizing the manufacture of cottage cheese by pumping the curd suspended in whey or wash water to draining vats equipped with load cells. This method permits an accurate determination of curd quantity so that the proper amount of creaming mixture may be added. Mechanical stirrers or agitators are efficient for mixing cream with the curd in a creaming vat (Fig. C.15 and C.16).

Creamed cottage cheese curd may be pumped through stainless steel tubing or plastic lines having a minimum of about 3-in. diameter. The pump should be the type which will avoid extensive mashing or distortion of the curd particles. These are usually low rpm rotary impeller or sliding vane type pump. Carton fillers for cottage cheese vary in design ranging from a revolving turret to a positive displacement piston arrangement. Cottage cheese carton filling of 1-lb size may now be accomplished at speeds of about 150 units per min. Packaging is quite highly automated except for casing of cottage cheese cartons. During the next few years development of equipment for mechanizing cottage cheese carton casing will undoubtedly occur.

Draining

Special equipment is also available for draining wash water from the curd in portable drums. The drained curd is then handled mechanically by lifting the drums for discharging the contents into a blender for creaming. The creamed curd then moves from the blender directly to the carton filler.

In the Cheddar cheese industry, equipment has been developed to make and handle the product quite automatically (Fig. C.17). The curd is milled in an end unloading finishing vat which is separate from the cooking vat. This curd is then transferred mechanically into the molds which are conveyed to the presses.

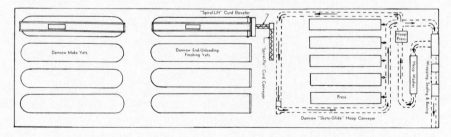

Courtesy of Damrow Bros. Co.

FIG. C-17.   Schematic product flow with mechanical handling of cottage cheese

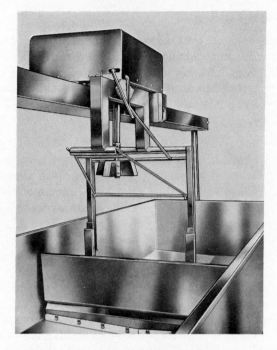

Fig. C-18.   Curd pusher

Equipment Modifications

The various modifications for handling cheese are designed with the thought of improving efficiency and result in a more uniform product. A typical example of such a modification is the curd pusher which may be attached to the cheese vat agitator to push the curd to the outlet end (Fig. C.18).

Efforts will continue to further improve cheese manufacturing procedures and equipment.

References

DeLaval Separator Co.   Ched-O-Matic Brochure.   Poughkeepsie, N.Y.
Grace Machinery Co., Oakland, Calif.
Stoelting Brothers Co.   Draining and Creaming Vat, Bull. *1700-15.3.*   Kiel, Wis.

Cross-references: *Cheese Curd Mill; Cheese Vats.*

CHEESE, PHYSICAL PROPERTIES

Cheese is classified as nonripened, ripened, or hard and soft cheese. A typical example of nonripened cheese is cottage cheese, whereas, Cheddar and most hard types are considered ripened varieties. The physical properties of cheese will vary considerably depending upon method of manufacture, composition, and degree of aging. The composition of a single cheese varies with the time held in the curing room. Because of the many varieties of cheese it is very difficult to generalize on the physical properties. Some of the data pertaining to ten distinct types of natural cheese classified by a distinguishing difference in processing are shown in Table C.11.

TABLE C.11

TYPES OF NATURAL CHEESE CLASSIFIED BY DISTINGUISHING DIFFERENCES IN PROCESSING

Distinctive Processing	Distinctive Characteristics	Typical Varieties of Cheese
Curd coagulated primarily by acid[1]	Delicate, soft curd	Cottage cheese, cream, Neufchatel
Curd particles matted together	Close texture,[2] firm body	Cheddar, Cheshire
Curd particles kept separate	More open texture	Colby, Monterey, Edam, Gouda
Presence of small amount of copper from copper cheese kettle or vat	Granular texture; brittle body	Grana—hard grating types: Parmesan or Reggiano, Romano or Sardo
Stretched curd	Plastic curd; threadlike or flaky texture	Provolone, Caciocavallo, Mozzarella
Bacteria ripened throughout interior with formation of eyes[3]	Gas holes or eyes throughout cheese	Emmentaler or Swiss (large eyes); Gruyere, Asiago (small eyes)
Mold ripened throughout interior	Visible veins of mold Typical piquant, spicy flavor	Blue, Roquefort, Stilton, Gorgonzola
Surface ripened principally by mold	Edible crust; soft, creamy interior Typical pungent flavor	Camembert, Brie
Surface ripened principally by bacteria and yeast	Surface growth; soft, smooth, waxy body Typical mild to robust flavor	Bel Paese, Brick, Limburger, Muenster, Port du Salut
Protein of whey or whey and milk coagulated by acid and high heat	Sweetish flavor of whey	Whey Cheese: Gjetost, Sap Sago, Mysost, Primost, Ricotta

[1] In contrast to coagulation by acid and enzymes or in whey cheese, by acid and high heat.

[2] Close texture means no mechanical holes within the cheese; open texture, considerable mechanical holes.

[3] In contrast to ripening by bacteria throughout interior without eye formation.

Characteristics

The origin and several of the characteristics of common varieties of natural cheese are given in Table C.12.

Two important cheese varieties processed by utilizing mold originated in France, namely the Camembert and Roquefort. Cheddar constitutes the largest variety of hard cheese produced in the United States. Cheese consumption per capita has been increasing indicating the desirable qualities obtained for a menu through the use of cheese.

Reference

NATIONAL DAIRY COUNCIL. 1967. Newer Knowledge of Cheese, 2nd Edition. Chicago, Ill.

Cross-references: *Cheese Curd Mill; Cheese Handling Equipment; Cheese Vats; Chlorination.*

ORIGIN, CHARACTERISTICS AND MODE OF SERVING

Cheese	Origin	Consistency and Texture	Color and Shape
Asiago	Italy	Hard to hard grating; granular, tiny gas holes or eyes	Light yellow; cylindrical
Bel Paese	Italy	Soft; smooth, waxy body	Slightly gray surface, creamy yellow interior; small wheels
Blue	France	Semisoft; visible veins of mold, pasty, sometimes crumbly	White, marbled with blue-green mold; cylindrical
Brick	United States	Semisoft; smooth, waxy body	Light yellow to orange; brick-shaped
Brie	France	Soft; thin edible crust, creamy interior	Whitish crust, creamy yellow interior; medium and small wheels
Caciocavallo	Italy	Hard; compact, flaky	Light tan surface, light interior; tenpin shape, bound with cord
Camembert	France	Soft; thin edible crust, creamy interior	White crust, creamy yellow interior; small wheels
Cheddar (American)	England	Hard; smooth, firm body	Light yellow to orange; varied shapes and styles, with rind and rindless
Colby	United States	Hard type but softer and more open in texture than Cheddar	Light yellow to orange; cylindrical
Cottage	Uncertain	Soft; moist, delicate, large or small curds	White; packaged in cuplike containers
Cream	United States	Soft; smooth, buttery	White; foil-wrapped in rectangular portions
Edam	Holland	Hard type but softer than Cheddar; more open, mealy body	Creamy yellow with red wax coat; cannonball shape
Gjetost	Norway	Hard; buttery	Golden brown; cubical and rectangular
Gorgonzola	Italy	Semisoft; visible veins of mold, less moist than Blue	Light tan surface, light yellow interior, marbled with blue-green mold; cylindrical
Gouda	Holland	Hard type but softer than Cheddar; more open, mealy body like Edam	Creamy yellow with or without red wax coat; round and flat

C.12

COMMONLY USED VARIETIES OF NATURAL CHEESE

Flavor	Basic Ingredient	Ripening Period	Mode of Serving
Piquant, sharp in aged cheese	Cows' milk, whole or partly skimmed	2–6 months for table use; 12 months minimum for grating	As such; as seasoning (grated) when aged
Mild to moderately robust	Cows' milk, whole	6–8 weeks	As such (dessert); on crackers; in sandwiches
Piquant, spicy	Cows' milk, whole	2 months minimum; 3–4 months usually; 9 months for pronounced flavor	As such (dessert); in dips; in cooked foods; in salads
Mild	Cows' milk, whole	2 weeks or longer	As such; in sandwiches salads
Mild to pungent	Cows' milk, whole	4–8 weeks	As such (dessert)
Sharp, similar to Provolone	Goats' or cows' milk, whole or partly skimmed	3 months minimum; 12 months or longer for grating	As such; as seasoning (grated) when aged
Mild to pungent	Cows' milk, whole	4–5 weeks	As such (dessert)
Mild to sharp	Cows' milk, whole	2–12 months or longer	As such; in sandwiches; in cooked foods
Mild	Cows' milk, whole	1–3 months	As such; in sandwiches; in cooked foods
Mild, slightly acid	Cows' milk, skimmed; cream dressing may be added	Unripened	As such; in salads; in dips; in cooked foods
Mild, slightly acid	Cream and cows' milk, whole	Unripened	As such; in sandwiches; in salads; on crackers
Mild, nutlike	Cows' milk, partly skimmed	2 months or longer	As such; on crackers; with fresh fruit
Sweetish, caramel	Whey from goats' milk	Unripened	As such; on crackers
Piquant, spicy, similar to Blue	Cows' milk, whole or goats' milk or mixtures of these	3 months minimum	As such (dessert)
Mild, nutlike, similar to Edam	Cows' milk, partly skimmed but more milk fat than Edam	2–6 months	As such; on crackers; with fresh fruit

(Continued)

TABLE C.12

Cheese	Origin	Consistency and Texture	Color and Shape
Gruyere	Switzerland	Hard; tiny gas holes or eyes	Light yellow; flat wheels
Limburger	Belgium	Soft; smooth, waxy body	Creamy white; rectangular
Monterey (Jack)	United States	Semisoft; smooth, open texture	Creamy white wheels
Mozzarella (Pizza cheese)	Italy	Semisoft; plastic	Creamy white; rectangular and spherical
Muenster	Germany	Semisoft; smooth, waxy body	Yellow, tan or white surface, creamy white interior; small wheels and blocks,
Neufchatel	France	Soft; smooth, creamy	White; foil-wrapped in rectangular retail portions
Parmesan (Reggiano)	Italy	Hard grating; granular, brittle body	Light yellow with brown or black coating; cylindrical
Port du Salut (Oka)	Trappist Monasteries France and Canada	Semisoft; smooth, buttery	Russet surface, creamy yellow interior; small wheels
Primost	Norway	Semisoft	Light brown; cubical and cylindrical
Provolone	Italy	Hard; compact, flaky	Light golden-yellow to golden-brown, shiny surface bound with cord; yellowish-white interior; pear, sausage and salami shapes
Ricotta	Italy	Soft; moist and grainy, or dry	White; packaged fresh in paper, plastic or metal containers, or dry for grating
Roquefort	France	Semisoft; visible veins of mold, pasty and sometimes crumbly	White, marbled with blue-green mold; cylindrical
Sap Sago	Switzerland	Hard grating; granular	Light green; small, cone-shaped
Stilton	England	Semisoft; visible veins of mold, slightly more crumbly than Blue	White, marbled with blue-green mold; cylindrical
Swiss	Switzerland	Hard; smooth, with large gas holes or eyes	Rindless blocks and large wheels with rind

(*Continued*)

Flavor	Basic Ingredient	Ripening Period	Mode of Serving
Nutlike, sweetish	Cows' milk, usually partly skimmed	3 months minimum	As such (dessert)
Robust, highly aromatic	Cows' milk, whole or partly skimmed	1–2 months	In sandwiches; on crackers
Mild	Cows' milk, whole	2–6 weeks for table use; 6–9 months for grating	As such; in sandwiches
Mild, delicate	Cows' milk, whole or partly skimmed	Unripened	As such; in pizza and other cooked foods
Mild to mellow, between Brick and Limburger	Cows' milk, whole	2–8 weeks	As such; in sandwiches
Mild	Cows' milk, whole	Unripened	As such; in sandwiches; in dips; in salads
Sharp, piquant	Cows' milk, partly skimmed	14 months minimum to 24 months or longer	As such; as seasoning (grated)
Mellow to robust, between Cheddar and Limburger	Cows' milk, whole or slightly acid	6–8 weeks	As such (dessert); with fresh fruit
Mild, sweetish, caramel	Whey with added buttermilk, whole milk or cream	Unripened	As such; in cooked foods
Mild to sharp and piquant, usually smoked	Cows' milk, whole	2–12 months	As such; in cooked foods
Bland but semisweet	Whey and whole or skim milk, or whole or part skim milk	Unripened	As such; in cooked foods; as seasoning when dried
Sharp, spicy piquant	Sheeps' milk	2 months minimum to 5 months or longer	As such (dessert); in salads; on crackers
Flavored with clover leaves, sweetish	Cows' milk, skimmed and soured plus buttermilk and whey	5 months minimum	As such; as seasoning (grated)
Piquant, spicy, but milder than Roquefort	Cows' milk, whole with added cream	2–6 months or longer	As such (dessert); in cooked foods
Sweetish, nutlike	Cows' milk, partly skimmed	2 months minimum to 9 months or longer	As such; in sandwiches; with salads

CHEESE VATS

Many kinds of cheese manufactured require a cheese vat to accomplish (1) setting of the curd with a starter culture of bacteria and usually an enzyme, and (2) cooking of the curd. Vats may be round with a round bottom, such as those used for making Swiss cheese. More commonly cheese vats are long, relatively narrow, low and rectangular in shape. The shape and size of the cheese vats have been changing somewhat in recent years with the adoption of automated equipment and other accessories. With mechanical agitators, some of the new cheese vats are deeper than older styles where the milk was hand stirred. The basic steps performed in the cheese vat include holding the milk at a constant temperature during the setting period, cooking and agitation of the curd, draining of the whey, and in many cases washing of the finished curd. Some dairy plants add salt and creamed dressing to cottage cheese curd for mixing in the cheese vat prior to packaging.

Principles

A cheese vat is a jacketed vessel equipped with hot and cold water supply for heating and cooling. The vat must heat the product uniformly and usually at a slow even rate during cooking. The setting temperature of the milk and skim milk are dependent upon the kind of cheese to be made and the time desired to achieve the proper acidity development prior to cutting the curd. Usually the setting temperature will range from 70° to 85°F. The final cooking temperature will usually range from about 110° to 135°F. During the cooking period the acid-forming bacteria will continue to produce lactic acid up to a temperature of approximately 105°F. Further elevation of the temperature causes a firming of the curd particles by expulsion of the whey.

System

Because of the many varieties of cheese produced there is considerable variation in utilization of a cheese vat. Cheddar cheese plants are currently using the cheese vat for setting and cooking several batches per day to fully utilize the equipment. After the curd is set and cooking begins, stirring is accomplished with a mechanical agitator. Following cooking, the whey and curd particles are pumped to a special finishing vat for cheddaring, milling, washing, and draining. Mechanical pushers mounted on the agitator frame assist in emptying the cheese vat of whey and curd. From the finishing vat, the milled and salted curd is transferred to the pressing molds. After pressing, the formed blocks of curd are wrapped and cured.

For cottage cheese manufacture, the cheese vat may serve only to set and cook the product which is then transferred with the whey or first wash water to a draining and creaming vat. Usually the curd must be washed in the cheese vat following cooking to sufficiently firm the curd to permit pumping in the final wash water without shattering. In the draining vat, which is mounted on load cells to assist in determining the amount of creamed dressing to add, the curd is thoroughly mixed with the dressing. The creaming vat is of round-end design to permit full contact with the sweep of the revolving agitator. From the creaming vat the curd is pumped through 3- or 4-in. diam pipe lines to the carton filling machine.

In the case of Cheddar cheese, cheddaring may be done in the cheese vat. For cottage cheese, the final draining of chlorinated wash water may be accomplished in the cheese vat. In several plants, cottage cheese curd is creamed in the cheese vat following removal of the wash water. The vat may be equipped with a curd pusher to assist in product removal.

Specifications

The capacity of cheese vats will range from 100 to over 2,500 gal. A typical 1,200-gal. cheese vat will be supported on 8 legs, and the inside dimensions will be $17^1/_2$ ft long and 58 in. wide. The average height of the inside of the vat will be 2 ft. A 2,500-gal. vat will be supported on 12 legs, and will be 31.5 ft long and 62 in. wide. The average inside height will be approximately 25 in. The overall length of this vat is 33 ft which includes the water pump and control system. The innerliner of cheese vats is made of stainless steel usually 16 gage, type 302, with a no. 4 finish. A sanitary manually operated outlet valve is used. From $^1/_2$ to $1^1/_2$ hp will be used to circulate water through the jacket and spray pipes. The sidewall of the vat is sprayed with the heated water. Early models relied on direct steam injection into a water filled jacket equipped with an overflow. The newer spray type vats require less water for the heating medium which also heats more evenly and efficiently. Many of the new cottage cheese vats are equipped with a bottom "pod" outlet. The "pod" outlet facilitates removal of the product with a pump.

The purchaser of a cheese vat has several options, including round or square end styles; a liner of 18, 16, or 14 gage stainless steel; heating pipes of brass, galvanized iron, or stainless steel; and a jacket of stainless steel or mild steel which may be insulated or uninsulated, etc. Standard construction will often include 10 gage mild steel for the jacket which is covered with 20 gage no. 4 polished stainless steel. The stainless steel innerliner is commonly 14 gage with a no. 4 finish.

Automatic heat controls may be obtained by setting the time and temperature as required for different varieties of cheese. This equipment includes an indicator control, steam-control valve, air regulator, filter, steam strainer, 60-min timer with light and bell, and transformer. The controls are prewired at the factory and mounted on the panel board.

Practices

Selection of a cheese vat will require a knowledge of present and an estimate of anticipated future production volumes. For a cottage cheese operation, a 500-gal. vat is the minimum size recommended. As plants are becoming larger, vat sizes in the range of 2,000 to 3,000 gal. are common. In selecting a cheese vat, one should consider the advantages of the mechanical accessories which are available to reduce production costs.

Vertical cheese vats of 2,000-gal. capacity have been designed and some are in use. This type vat lends itself to a two-floor operation especially in the manufacture of Swiss cheese. A large vertical vat tends to be somewhat less practical for soft curd products such as cottage cheese.

The kind and size of cheese vat must be synchronized with the production schedule and associated equipment.

Cross-reference :   *Cheese Handling Equipment.*

CHLORINATION

Chlorine is one of the halogens and a commonly used chemical for destroying pathogenic bacteria in water supplies and on food contact surfaces.   On clean equipment, chlorine is a very effective sanitizer.   For treatment of iron bearing water, chlorine is often added to oxidize soluble ferrous iron to the insoluble ferric state. The iron can then be removed by filtration.   Other compounds in water may also be removed through the oxidizing properties of chlorine, followed by filtration.

Precisely how chlorine destroys bacteria is not completely understood.   However, studies indicate that an enzyme inhibiting action occurs which requires some contact time to accomplish bacterial destruction.   Oxidation is known to be an effective mechanism by which chlorine destroys bacteria.   The cell membrane also suffers injury when in contact with chlorine.   There is some evidence to indicate that chlorine reacts and combines with cell protein.   A combination of these various functions destroys not only vegetative cells, but also bacterial spores and other microorganisms.

Control of pathogens through chlorination prevents disease epidemics.   Municipalities and food plants using large volumes of water will usually meter chlorine gas into the water directly.   Special equipment is needed for this purpose because of the small quantity required.   City water supplies usually carry a chlorine residual of 0.3 to 0.5 ppm.   A normal contact time for chlorine in the water is 20 to 24 hr.   Since time is required to destroy bacteria, and as low levels are used in water supplies, the longer contact time becomes very important.

Food plants and water municipalities may purchase liquid chlorine in 150-lb cylinders or larger vessels for metering as a gas.   Chlorine can be vaporized from 150-lb cylinders at a rate of 35 lb per 24 hr.   Where greater feed rates are required, a suitable number of containers must be connected together to prevent freezing of the chlorine as a result of evaporation, which produces a cooling effect.   Liquid chlorine cylinders possess a pressure of 85 psi at 70°F.   Liquid chlorine boils at -30.1°F at 0 psig.   Chlorine as a gas has a yellowish-green color and is very active when moist, and will react with most all of the common metals except silver.

The highly reactive chlorine, which is a strong oxidizing chemical, will destroy over 99% of most disease producing bacteria in an exposure as low as 0.2 ppm for a contact time of 30 sec.   This concentration, although very low, will kill the coliform group of bacteria within 2 min at a pH of 6 to 7.   As the pH raises to 8, 4 min are required, and 6 min are necessary at a pH of 9.

In water, chlorine gas forms hydrochloric acid and hypochlorous acid.   Other chemicals when dissolved in the water, which has been chlorinated, form hypochlorites such as sodium hypochlorite, calcium hypochlorite, etc.   Chlorine in the form of gas, liquid, or dry powder, results in an available active chlorine when dissolved in water, because of the formation of hypochlorous acid and hypochlorite ions.   The combination of the hypochlorous acid and the hypochlorite ions in a water solution is equivalent to the oxidizing capacity of the active chlorine applied.   Sodium hypochlorite and calcium hypochlorite are commonly used as sanitizers in food plants.   Sodium hypochlorite is available in solutions containing up to 15% available chlorine.   The commonly available household bleach contains approximately 5.25% sodium hypochlorite, which is equivalent to 5.0% by weight of available chlorine. The amount of available chlorine per gallon of hypochlorite containing various percentages is as follows:

Hypochlo-rite (%)	Available Chlorine (%)	Weight per Gal. (Lb)	Lb of Chlorine per Gal.
1.0	1.0	8.4	0.08
5.25	5.0	8.9	0.44
10.5	10.0	9.7	0.97
15.75	15.0	10.5	1.57

A test commonly used to estimate with reasonable accuracy the free available chlorine residual is the orthotolidine-arsenite (OTA). This test eliminates some of the errors due to the presence of iron or manganese. For general plant work, the OTA test possesses satisfactory accuracy. However, for more precise measurements needed in research this test is generally regarded as inferior. A more accurate test is the amperometric titration method. Since this latter test utilizes an electrical end point, it is necessary to use an amperometric titrator. One of the main advantages of the titration method is the elimination of many of the factors contributing to errors with the orthotolidine test, such as temperature, time, iron, manganese, and nitrate. In water treatment plants the residual chlorine recorder controller is an instrument commonly used to provide a permanent record of chlorine strength in the water supply. Automatic control of chlorination to a preset level is possible by incorporating the controller in the system.

The activity of a hypochlorite solution on bacteria is increased with a lower pH. For example, the killing time of *Bacillus metiens* at 68°F using a 25 ppm hypochlorite solution is as follows: at pH 6, the killing time is 2.5 min; at pH 8, 5.0 min; and at pH 10, 121.0 min. Wash water for cottage cheese is usually acidified to increase the effectiveness of chlorination to render the water practically bacteria-free. For this purpose phosphoric acid is frequently used to reduce the pH to about 5.0. Temperature also greatly affects the activity of most chlorine sanitizers. A hypochlorite solution at 100°F will be more active than one at 50°F. Although the hypochlorite sanitizers are more active at higher temperatures, they are also more corrosive. Slower acting forms of chlorine, such as chloramines, are perhaps a desirable choice when sterilizing with high temperature solutions in the range of 160° to 175°F. The chloramines are more stable at this temperature as well as sufficiently active to achieve good sanitation.

For milk bottle chlorination between the final rinse jets of the washer and the filler, an exposure of a chlorine rinse containing 50 to 60 ppm available chlorine is very effective. For other plant operations, such as the prerinse of sanitary lines and equipment prior to use, 150 to 200 ppm available chlorine should be used. A material decrease in chlorine content of the sanitizing solution during the rinse operation indicates that organic matter is present on the equipment surfaces. For example, a drop in available chlorine from 200 ppm to 50 ppm indicates unsatisfactory cleaning of equipment. In most sanitizing rinses the decrease in chlorine strength should be no more than 25 ppm. When an operator is assembling a filler, he should wear rubber gloves in handling the parts.

Molds, bacteriophage, and bacterial spores are more difficult to destroy than vegetative cells. To kill moulds on walls and similar surfaces about 5,000 ppm of sodium hypochlorite is recommended. To achieve a lasting germicidal effect, some plant operators will follow the hypochlorite with a spray of quaternary ammonium compound at a strength also of 5,000 ppm. Cheese plants troubled by bacteriophage which destroys the cultures, may obtain some control by spraying equipment and culture rooms with 1,000 ppm available chlorine for a few days. Once the problem is under control, a regular daily spraying with 400 to 500 ppm chlorine solution will help alleviate the difficulty.

Certain chlorine sanitizers may lose strength during storage. Therefore, the effectiveness of a sanitizing and chlorination operation should be checked periodically by making an actual bacterial count of the equipment surfaces or of the component being chlorinated, such as water. The plant operator should not assume that going through a chlorination procedure will consistently achieve the desired results. Operating conditions could change so that destruction of bacteria is not achieved. A regular procedure of checking the efficiency and effectiveness of chlorinating equipment and sanitizing solutions in a processing plant should be followed.

References

HIRSCH, A. 1945. Manual for Water Plant Operators. Mechanical Publishing Co., New York.

KLENZADE PRODUCTS, INC. 1960. Klenzade Dairy Sanitation Handbook. Beloit, Wis.

MILK INDUSTRY FOUNDATION. 1967. Manual for Milk Plant Operators, 3rd Edition. Washington, D.C.

Cross-references: *CIP Systems; Cleaning of Equipment; Sanitation.*

CIP CLEANING

The term cleaning as related to the care and maintenance of equipment in the chemical processing industries generally refers to the procedure of physically or chemically removing depositions in the form of scale or sediment following prolonged use of a particular item of equipment or processing installation. By comparison, cleaning in the food processing industries (and in dairy products processing specifically) refers to the treatment given all product contact surfaces following each period of use to first remove all physical evidence of soil and to apply a bactericidal treatment to sanitize all surfaces. Nonproduct contact surfaces are given similar, though less rigorous, attention. The normal period of use is less than 1 day, and all tanks, vats, pipes, pumps, valves, heat exchangers, and packaging equipment are thus cleaned at least once every 24 hr. In some special instances, longer periods of continuous use of the piping system or certain tanks may reduce the frequency of cleaning to approximately once every third day.

Until recent years, cleaning of all milk processing equipment involved complete disassembly; manual cleaning by rinsing, brushing with solution, rinsing, and sanitizing; and reassembly followed by application of sanitizing solutions just prior to processing. The labor required for these procedures frequently constituted as much as 50% of the total labor required to handle all phases of a production operation from receiving through processing, packaging, and load-out.

Development of Mechanical-Chemical Cleaning

An early application of welded lines in 1951 was reported to "explode the common theory that all dairy pipelines must be dismantled for sanitary reasons." It was shown "that the permanent system provides fewer sources of bacterial contamination. And consequently, products processed through these lines are of uniform high quality." This initial welded installation utilized crosses with inspection ports at every change of direction, and the welding technique involved the use of filler rod followed by subsequent grinding and polishing of the inner surfaces of the weld.

A 12-month study using CIP in a medium-sized milk plant revealed labor reductions of as much as 75% as compared with manual takedown cleaning. This study also gave considerable attention to the factors of temperature, velocity, pressure, and cleaning materials.

Cleaning procedures in milk processing plants were historically subject to greater lack of uniformity and control than any of the other processing operations, because they were handled by less skilled and trained personnel, they were accomplished under undesirable working conditions and at night, and less supervision was provided as compared with production operations. Recognizing that CIP (Cleaned-in-Place) procedures could be automated to minimize some of these weaknesses, Seiberling applied automatic programming and chemical feed equipment to an installation in a small milk plant and further established criteria regarding engineering for CIP. Prior to 1955, most recirculation cleaning was accomplished with existing product pumps by using existing tanks or vats or small portable tanks as the solution tank for the recirculating procedure. In 1955 and 1956, several manufacturers introduced multitank CIP systems of packaged design incorporating a rinse water tank, solution tank, sanitizing tank, pump, heating controls, programming controls, and air blow-down equipment to facilitate recovery of solution.

Early applications of in-place cleaning were restricted to piping systems, and generally to only the longer piping systems. But, results achieved suggested that even greater benefits could be obtained if similar procedures could be applied to the cleaning of vessels such as tank trucks, storage tanks, processing vats, and valves. Seiberling and Harper obtained bacteriological evidence supporting the ability to satisfactorily spray clean storage tanks and tank trucks in early 1957, and followed this with a report of radioisotope evaluation of the cleanability of an air-operated valve of CIP design later the same year.

During the past decade, experience has shown that CIP has provided the key to open the doors to many other changes in dairy and food products processing technology. The ability to ensure controlled sanitation through mechanical-chemical cleaning has led to extensive development of all welded product piping systems, application of air-operated valves, appreciable increases in the sizes of processing and storage tanks as compared with vessels that had to be cleaned manually, significant increases in processing flow rates and packaging machinery capacity, and approaches to plant design and arrangement not previously feasible. The total cleaning problem involves far more than pumps, tanks, sprays, and controls. The design of a food processing plant for today and tomorrow requires consideration of materials and methods of construction, equipment layout, specialized cleaning equipment, design of processing equipment, and, finally, the design of the process.

CIP Procedures and Equipment

In-place cleaning as applied today is essentially chemical in nature. Processing equipment and CIP appurtenances are designed to permit solution to be brought into intimate contact with all soiled surfaces and continuously replenished. The results achieved are dependent upon the combined effects of time, temperature, and concentration, all of which may be placed under automatic control. Since relatively high volumes of solution must be brought into contact with the soiled surface for periods of time ranging from as little as 10 min to as much as 1 hr, recirculation of the cleaning solution is essential to maintain economic operation.

CIP systems are available in two different forms. Multitank recirculating units utilize the same wash solution for a large number of cleaning operations during the production day, adding to this solution as required to maintain strength and cleaning ability. Single tank, single use systems operate on the basis of making up smaller volumes of solution automatically to the required concentration, using it once at the lowest possible strength, and discharging it to the sewer at the end of each cycle.

The two systems are comparable with respect to program control equipment. Multi-tank systems require more space and utilize more parts in the form of tanks, valves, level controls, and temperature controls and require added attention during the operating day to check solution condition or to dump and recharge the tanks. The multitank systems also lack flexibility in that a single combination of temperature and concentration must be used for all equipment to be cleaned with the system. The single tank system is smaller in size, simpler in design, lower in initial investment, and more flexible in application. All chemicals are fed automatically and in the proper proportions from the containers or from bulk storage.

In addition to pumps, tanks, and valves, the CIP system will further include some type of program control equipment and chemical feed equipment. Then, a CIP supply-return system will be installed to permit the recirculation of flushing, washing, rinsing, and sanitizing solutions through various piping circuits and different items of processing equipment throughout the production period. In the dairy industry, both regulations and operating requirements have made it necessary to utilize make-break connections between cleaning supply-return piping and the various items of equipment to be cleaned in position. No valves are utilized to separate product containing circuits or vessels from solution containing piping. In some other industries, this requirement has not been mandatory, and, in fact, the larger sizes of lines and valves in use have made it impossible to consider such approaches. In this instance, leak protected valving is developed to prevent intermixing of product and solutions, and it is generally agreed that certain minimal portions of the piping will not be cleaned to optimum conditions. Complex piping systems of several thousand feet in length can be easily cleaned in a single operation. Prerinsing with cold or tempered water is continued until the effluent runs nearly clear; then recirculation of the cleaning solution is accomplished for periods of time ranging from 10 min to as much as 1 hr. Temperatures may vary from 130° to 180°F or more. Chlorinated alkaline cleaners may be utilized alone or in the desired sequence with acid detergents. Where air-operated valving is utilized, the cleaning circuits will be developed to permit valves to be operated throughout the cleaning process so as to thoroughly clean all ports and all connecting lines. Following the solution recirculation, cold or tempered water is utilized as a postrinse, and this is generally followed with either an acidified recirculated final rinse or a sanitizing rinse with a chlorine or iodophor based sanitizing solution.

Successful spray cleaning of storage tanks and processing vats is dependent upon properly designed tanks, and properly applied spray devices. Some general comments regarding tank design are given in a later section.

The permanently installed fixed-ball spray has gained favor over rotating and oscillating spray devices. Its advantages include: (1) there are no moving parts; (2) it can be made completely of stainless steel; (3) its performance is not affected greatly by minor variations in supply pressure; (4) a properly established installation will continue to provide satisfactory service; and (5) it sprays all of the surface all of the time.

Fixed ball-type sprays are available with a variety of characteristics in terms of flow rate, discharge pressure, and pattern of coverage. Experience has indicated that cylindrical and rectangular tanks can be adequately cleaned if sprayed at 0.1 to 0.3 gal./min/sq ft of internal surface, and patterns are arranged to spray the upper $1/3$ of the tank. If considerable appurtenances exist in the tank, such as heating or cooling coils and complex agitators, some special patterns may be required to cover these surfaces with resultant increases in the total flow rate required.

Vertical silo-type tanks may be cleaned satisfactorily at flow rates of 2.5 to 3.0 gal./min/lineal foot of tank circumference. Nonclogging disc sprays are used in vessels of this type because of the relative difficulty in reaching the spray devices for occasional inspection and cleaning.

Although the major portion of all spray cleaning is conducted with relatively standard sprays, special devices in the form of ring sprays, spray sticks, and disc sprays are available for specific applications in evaporators, dryers, vacuum chambers, and other vessels having unique design characteristics to meet special processing requirements.

Tank cleaning programs involving the use of spray devices differ from line cleaning programs in that prerinsing and postrinsing are generally accomplished by using a burst technique. Water will be discharged in 3 or more bursts of 15 to 20 sec duration, and the tank will be drained completely between successive bursts. This procedure is more effective in removing sedimentated soil and foam than is continuous rinsing and can be accomplished with much less water. The successful mechanical-chemical cleaning of heat exchange equipment is dependent in part upon proper operation of the equipment during production processes. For instance, the use of high-pressure steam and high heating rates with inadequate agitation, or turning steam on before all heat transfer surfaces are covered with product may produce burn-on which is nearly impossible to remove by spray cleaning with normal programs. As a result, time, temperature, and concentration must all be increased to cope with this problem, at extra expense for the cleaning procedure. Or, similar results may be experienced through repetitive use of equipment without cleaning between operations. In most instances food processing equipment has an optimum operating period beyond which further operation without shutdown results in reduced efficiencies and increases the cleaning problems.

The basic procedures outlined above have been applied in fluid milk plants, ice cream plants, cheese plants, edible soybean processes, brewery operations, and various types of food processing operations with uniform success. It is generally possible to design and apply equipment and programs which can produce surfaces that are physically clean and nearly free of all bacterial contamination. Standard swab tests on spray cleaned equipment should yield sterile plates in 75 to 80% of the samples, and plates showing not more than 3 to 5 colonies on the remaining samples when sampling is done immediately following cleaning and before sanitizing. If equipment is properly handled, there should be no positive coliform counts on any swab taken from surfaces cleaned by in-place cleaning procedures.

Process Equipment Design

Dairy, food, and beverage processing plants generally utilize a combination of tanks, pipes, valves, pumps, and heat exchange equipment to accomplish the various production processes. Dairy equipment in the United States has for may years been constructed or installed in compliance with Sanitary Standards or Accepted Practices formulated jointly by the International Association of Milk, Food, and Environmental Sanitarians, the United States Public Health Service, and the Dairy Industry Committee. On occasion, representatives of other food processing industries have viewed these standards as unnecessarily rigid. However, 20 yr ago milk seldom required more than 2 days to make the trip from the farm to the plant and to the ultimate consumer, whereas today 2 or 3 days may be involved between production and receiving at the processing facility, several more days may pass before it enters a distribution channel, and an additional 5 to 7 days may go by before it reaches the ultimate consumer. The quality of milk has improved tremendously during these years, largely because of improved sanitation practices at all levels starting at the farm, continuing through processing, including packaging.

Perhaps some of the requirements such as inspectability, surface finish, and minimum radii are not as necessary with the advent of mechanical-chemical cleaning as previously, but most of the design practices are based on long-range experience and will be reviewed here for the benefit of those concerned with the purchase or design of equipment for other food processing operations.

Tanks

Storage tanks for raw or finished materials are generally of three different designs. Rectangular horizontal tanks (Fig. C.19) are susceptible to proper in-place cleaning if they meet the following criteria.

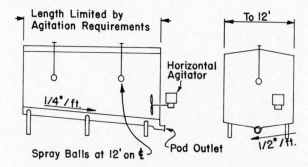

Fig. C-19.   Rectangular horizontal tank

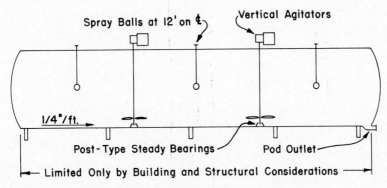

Fig. C-20. Cylindrical horizontal tank

(1) The bottom should pitch not less than $^1/_4$ in./ft from the rear to front, and $^1/_2$ in./ft from side to center.

(2) The outlet should be of a pod type of design.

(3) Mechanical agitators of the horizontal type should be limited to a location near the manhole for ease of removing the impeller and cleaning the seal assembly.

(4) The top of the tank should pitch approximately $^1/_2$ in./ft from the center to the sidewall.

(5) A minimum radius of 1 in. diam is desirable at all corners.

Cylindrical horizontal tanks (Fig. C.20) have been used in various sizes ranging from 6 ft 6 in. to 12 ft in diameter and from 8 to 65 ft in overall length. The installation should provide for pitch of $^1/_4$ in./ft to a pod type of outlet. If multiple vertical agitators are utilized, mechanical seals are preferred at the top to avoid loss of cleaning solution, and if steady bearings are required, they must provide only point or line contact with the shaft so as to respond to CIP operations.

Horizontal rectangular and cylindrical tanks can be satisfactorily cleaned with fixed-ball type sprays installed not more than 12 ft apart and developed to provide patterns in accordance with recommendations stated previously.

Silo-type tanks (Fig. C.21) will store appreciably larger quantities of products in a limited amount of ground area, generally on the outside of the processing structure. A properly designed tank of this type is actually easier to spray clean than cylindrical or rectangular horizontal tanks of appreciably less capacity. The tanks must be set and leveled properly, and the flat bottoms must pitch not less than $^3/_4$ in./ft to a pod type of outlet. Proper overflow protection and a provision of clean air for venting requires the provision of a vent-overflow line which terminates in the production area, generally in the tank alcove. The supply line to the disc type of spray may serve as the revent line to stop siphoning action following overflow. If mechanical agitation is utilized, the horizontal agitator should be located near the manhole for ease of manual cleaning of the impeller and seal assembly.

Vertical processing tanks (Fig. C.22) seldom exceed 2,000 gal. in capacity and differ from storage tanks in that heating and cooling surfaces are generally supplied on the major portion of the bottom and sidewall. Sweep type of agitators are used in conjunction with an adjustable baffle, and the presence of this additional equipment on the inside of the tank requires a double ball type of spray to properly clean both sides of the baffle and its supporting brackets. A mechanical seal is recommended on the agitator shaft, and the manhole cover should be gasketed to the tank to prevent loss of solution during the cleaning operations.

The following are some general design considerations applicable to all tanks.

(1) A pod or depressed type of outlet is beneficial in permitting fast and complete emptying of product and efficient operation of cleaning return pumps with a minimum solution level in the tank.

(2) Tank bottoms should be pitched to provide rapid drainage.

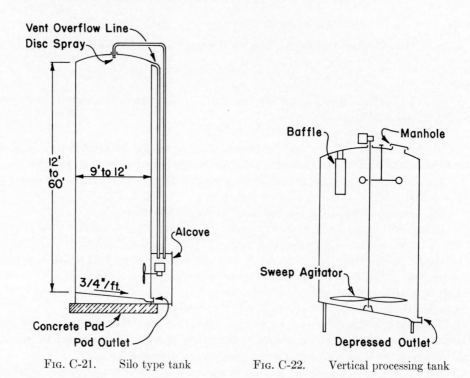

FIG. C-21.   Silo type tank   FIG. C-22.   Vertical processing tank

(3) Legs or foundation structure should provide adequate height to establish a minimum static head on the inlet of product and CIP return pumps of not less than 12 and preferably 18 in.

(4) The tank must be equipped with an adequate permanent vent to protect the vessel against all changes in pressure or vacuum resulting from filling and emptying and heating and cooling associated with the cleaning operations.

(5) Mechanical seals should be used for agitators, and if steady bearings are required, they should provide only line or point contact and serve mainly to provide guiding only, rather than support.

(6) Diaphragm type of pressure sensors are recommended in combination with manometer systems to determine level, weight, or volume of tank contents.

(7) Projectile type of thermometer wells are acceptable for use with filled tube temperature indicating and recording systems. Thermocouples installed so as to sense only the temperature of the tank surface provide an even more satisfactory installation from the standpoint of cleanability.

Pumps

The most widely used pumps include those of centrifugal design, positive displacement (gear type) design, and high-pressure reciprocating piston type of design. Centrifugal pumps have their greatest applicability as transfer pumps where precise control of flow is not necessary. Gear type of positive displacement pumps are used to handle viscous fluids, to operate against discharge heads beyond the capabilities of the sanitary type of centrifugal pumps, as timing pumps, and as metering pumps. High pressure piston type pumps are used most widely as homogenizers or as the supply pump for spray drying systems.

Of the three types, the centrifugal pump is most readily designed for effective CIP cleaning. High speed (3,000–3,600 rpm) pumps are capable of moving large volumes of product at relatively high discharge pressures. Low speed pumps (1,500–1,800 rpm) are most satisfactory for CIP return pump applications, filler supply pumps, and handling of products which are susceptible to churning under extreme agitation.

Centrifugal pumps equipped with properly designed internal mechanical seals or external seals of pulse-shaft design can be incorporated in CIP circuits and need only occasional disassembly for inspection and seal replacement.

Where process requirements demand the use of gear type of positive displacement pumps, rubber or plastic coated rotors are more desirable than metal rotors, and the pump must be physically installed to permit easy removal of the gears during CIP operations.

The piston types of high-pressure pumps are susceptible in part to CIP cleaning, but certain appurtenances such as the homogenizing valve and the suction strainer must be removed daily for manual cleaning and reinstallation.

Heat Exchangers

Shell and tube heat exchangers equipped with return-bend connections of CIP type of construction can be incorporated in CIP piping circuits or may be cleaned independently as a separate operation. Triple tube heat exchangers are available only in CIP design and have a further advantage in that they can be installed so as to be completely self-draining. Plate type heat exchangers are more widely used than either of the tubular units, however, because of ease of inspection, flexibility of design with respect to proper streaming for desired velocities and pressure losses, and ease of adaptation to new applications. Plate type heat exchangers are being designed for increasingly higher operating pressures, but in some instances are not capable of withstanding the pressures required for associated line CIP operations at flow rates required to produce adequate velocity in the piping system. Satisfactory performance can be achieved under these conditions by utilizing a booster pump downstream of the plate heat exchanger to reduce back-pressure on the plate unit or by using split flow cleaning hookups to reduce velocity, and hence pressure loss, through the various sections of the plate heat exchange unit.

Product Valves

The plug type of valve of either 2-way or 3-way configuration is the valve most commonly used in food plant piping systems. Prior to 1960, such valves were available only with metal plugs and metal seats and generally failed to provide tight shut-off and dripped continually when handling fluid products of low viscosity. Rubber coated or plastic coated plugs have eliminated these problems. However, the plug valve cannot be cleaned in position, and the plug must be removed following the pre-rinsing operation so that both the body and plug can be manually cleaned and sanitized prior to reassembly, after which the remainder of the in-place cleaning operation is completed.

Diaphragm-type valves have been used to eliminate the necessity for manual cleaning, but have the disadvantage of being available only in two-way shutoff configurations. Hence, it is necessary to use 3 individual valves to achieve the same degree of flow control as is possible with a single 3-way plug valve. And, these valves must be installed with the diaphragm in a near vertical position to achieve proper drainage of the body cavity.

Disc-type valves have been used in some brewery applications. These valves can be cleaned effectively with exception of the shaft seal area if left in the open position. But, they cannot be used as shutoff valves to close a port in a piping circuit which is being recirculation cleaned, for the areas beyond the valve disc will not come into contact with cleaning solution.

The most satisfactory valve for CIP application is the compression type of valve with a molded rubber valve disc or a Teflon O-ring seal on a stainless steel disc. O-rings are used for the valve stem seal, and the piping system design provides for inclusion of all ports of the valve in the CIP circuit. Then, valve sequencing or cycling equipment is used to operate the valves in proper combinations throughout the cleaning program, causing water to first pass through the piping system in 1 direction, then another, in as many as 6 or 8 different manners. Every valve will be operated 2 or 3 times during the prerinse, 4 to 6 times during the wash, and 3 or 4 times during the postrinse. All portions of every valve and every part of the piping system are thus exposed to equivalent mechanical-chemical treatment. The operation of the valve causes the stem O-ring to pump some cleaning and rinsing solutions into this area, effectively cleaning the seal, stem, and gland area.

Note that where air-operated valving is used in extensive food plant piping systems, the complete system or substantial portions of the system must be cleaned at one time, as some of a group cannot be cleaned while others are being used for process operations.

Air-operated valves may be installed in header systems but the most common practice involves grouping valves into manifold assemblies or clusters. This approach has the following advantages.

(1) Large numbers of valves can be shop fabricated into a single unit. Jigs and fixtures are more readily available to provide and maintain proper alignment, and welding and polishing operations are all more easily supervised than during field installation.

(2) The remaining piping work involves mostly point-to-point connections.

(3) Utilities in the form of air and electrical connections are concentrated in fewer conduits and fewer locations, reducing installation cost and facilitating maintenance and troubleshooting.

Piping Systems

Three different types of construction are now employed for in-place cleaned piping systems. The different types of connections include: (1) inert-gas welded

Fig. C-23. Timed program controller

joints for permanent connections, (2) clamp type of joints of CIP design for semi-permanent connections, and (3) threaded joints with hexagon nuts and CIP gaskets for those connections opened daily for processing and cleaning procedures.

Some general recommendations regarding piping system design and installation include the following.

(1) All parts of the piping system must be pitched $^1/_{16}$ in. to $^1/_8$ in./ft to drain points such as removable elbows, valves, or special openings provided for draining purposes.

(2) The support system should be of rigid construction to maintain pitch and alignment, and should be designed so as to preclude electrolytic action between the support(s) and pipeline(s).

(3) A complete piping system may be cleaned in a single circuit, but normally it should be developed into two or more circuits compatible with startup and shutdown of production operations.

(4) The generally accepted minimum velocity for CIP operations is 5 ft/sec. However, satisfactory results have been achieved at velocities as low as 3 ft/sec, and in excess of 10 ft/sec. Total circuit length must be controlled so as to achieve these velocities with the available CIP supply pumps and within the pressure limitations imposed by other equipment.

(5) Dead-ends such as capped tees are undesirable, and, if mandatory, all branches of tees should be located in a horizontal position and should be limited in length to not more than 1.5 pipe diameters. Vertical dead-ends are undesirable because entrapped air prevents cleaning solution from reaching the upper portion of the fitting.

(6) The piping system design should provide for inclusion of the maximum amount of piping in the CIP circuit(s). It is better to install 1 or 2 small jumpers than to remove and manually clean 5 or 6 short lengths of piping. Mechanical-chemical cleaning is much more rigorous and is subject to better control than manual cleaning.

In summary, many different types of processing equipment are now being designed with special attention to making them cleanable by CIP procedures. The major criteria include noncorrosive materials of construction, relatively smooth product contact surfaces, freedom from crevices, ability to confine cleaning solutions, and a reasonable degree of inspectability of each specific item of equipment or CIP circuit.

Process Design

Though most food processing procedures involve the operations of heating, cooling, holding, mixing, blending, and mass transfer, the sequence in which these operations are applied varies appreciably, and process design cannot be discussed in the same simple manner as equipment design. The timing and sequence of operations can be automatically controlled (Fig. C.23). However, some general recommendations based on experiences in a number of food processing operations would include the following.

(1) The number of vessels provided for storage or processing should be minimized by using the largest sized vessel possible. This will reduce the number of connections, valves, and instruments required, as well as cleaning and maintenance needs.

(2) Continuous heat treatment systems are more readily cleaned in-position than batch-type systems of comparable capacity. For instance, a plate heat exchanger and holding tube is more readily cleaned-in-place than a large number of processing kettles or vats required to accomplish the same heat treatment. Furthermore, the capital cost for instrumentation, valving, and controls will be less for the continuous process.

(3) Although other materials may ultimately find increased application in food processing systems, stainless steel is the most suitable material of fabrication at the present time.

The design of the plant in which the processing equipment is installed may also affect the degree of sanitation ultimately achieved. Floor, wall, and ceiling surfaces must be of smooth, hard, and durable materials which will resist the effects of the product, cleaning materials, and water. Hallways, vestibules, and other small rooms should be reduced to an absolute minimum, as such areas are frequently collectors of dirt and debris. Proper lighting in all areas of the plant will aid in maintaining sanitary conditions by making the need for cleaning obvious.

Prepared by DALE A. SEIBERLING

References

SEIBERLING, D. A. 1968. Chem. Eng. Progr. Symp. Ser., *64*, No. 86, 94–104.
SEIBERLING, D. A. 1970. Master Brewer's Assoc. of America Tech. Quart. Contents *7*, No. 1, 73–80.

Cross-references: *Can Washers; Chlorination; Cleaning Equipment; Sanitation.*

CLARIFIERS

The clarifier is used to remove sediment and other usually undesirable material from milk and food products. The clarifier is very similar to the separator in design, construction, and operation except that there is no cream spout. Sediment removed from the product is collected inside the bowl and must be removed periodically.

Principle

Not until the introduction of homogenization did leucocytes play a significant role in bottled milk. Since fat clustering and rising are inhibited by homogenization, the fat globules can no longer sweep the leucocytes normally present in all milk into the cream layer. Thus, the heavier leucocytes are free to settle, thereby forming a grayish, oil-like sludge at the bottom of the bottle. Any sediment in bottled milk is objectionable, including that in homogenized milk. Clarification is the practical means of rendering homogenized milk sediment free. As homogenized milk commands most of the milk sales, virtually all milk processed in America today is clarified. Several clarifier installations are possible, including: (1) between the bulk tank and receiving room, raw-milk storage tank at 40°F; (2) between the storage tank and preheater at 40°F; (3) between preheater and pasteurizer at 90° to 120°F; (4) after pasteurization but before homogenization at (145°F and above); and (5) after pasteurization and after homogenization at 145°F and above.

Likewise, the milk may be clarified at a wide range of temperatures. Several factors must be considered in selecting the best installation and procedure to follow. Commercial operations and laboratory trials have demonstrated satisfactory clarification of raw milk at 40°F. Clarification of the incoming milk at this temperature has the following advantages. (1) One essential step of processing is completed when the milk is in the storage tank; (2) the clarified stored milk is ready for pasteurization without further treatment; (3) the clarifier may be used longer without dismantling when clarifying cold; (4) if disassembly becomes necessary, the pasteurization operation would not be disrupted; and (5) the clarifier does not become a potential contributor to postpasteurization contamination.

Operation

Removal of white blood cells by centrifugal clarification is more efficient at temperatures of 90° to 135°F than at 40°F. At best, single clarification removes an average of 41 to 50% of the leucocytes. However, this percentage removal is sufficient to prevent sedimentation in homogenized milk in most cases. Milk having leucocyte counts ranging from 80,000 to 200,000 per ml may be homogenized nonclarified, and yet be free of the sediment problem. Nevertheless, all normal milk to be homogenized and having leucocyte counts ranging from 50,000 to 500,000 per ml should be clarified to eliminate the possibility of sediment formation. Unquestionably, mastitic milk, colostrum milk, and milk from long-lactating cows with leucocyte counts from 500,000 to 5,000,000 per ml or above should be clarified if the milk is to be homogenized.

The nature and amount of clarifier slime from raw and pasteurized milk differ widely. Apparently, the denaturing of some of the milk proteins upon heating makes them more susceptible to centrifugalizing.

The clarifier bowl clogs more quickly when clarifying pasteurized milk than when clarifying cold raw milk. Generally, a clarifier may be operated from 2 to 8 hr on 40°F milk as contrasted to 1 to 4 hr at 135°F.

Early research showed that clarification was more effective in overcoming sedimentation when done after rather than before homogenization. Since then, homogenizers have been so improved that they are virtually free from being a contributor to sediment. Nevertheless, care must be taken that no extraneous matter gets into the homogenized product.

Centrifugal separators or separator-clarifiers are used effectively for clarifying milk. Regardless of the type of centrifuge, the efficiency decreases rapidly when the slime space in the bowl becomes filled. Adequate data support the soundness of clarifying milk cold at 40°F before pasteurization.

System

Normally in the high-temperature short-time system the milk may be clarified cold, just ahead of the pasteurizing system; or may be clarified hot, as the product leaves the regenerator section with the temperature of the milk about 135°F. In one method when the clarifier is in conjunction with a homogenizer, the milk flows from the regenerator to the following in order: timing pump, clarifier, homogenizer, heater, and holding tube (Fig. C.24). A more recently used method consists of installing a clarifier or clarifier-separator after pasteurization with milk leaving the pasteurized

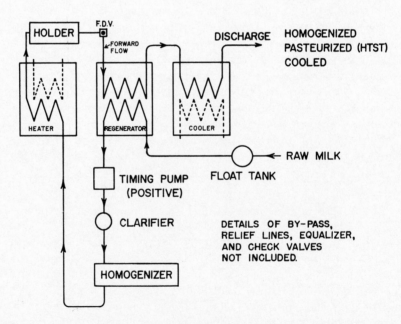

Fɪɢ. C-24.   Homogenization and clarification of regenerated milk before HTST pasteurization

side of the regenerator going to the centrifugal machine, and then returning to the heat exchanger for final cooling.

With some units the clarifier is fed by a pump. The clarifier may continue to operate when the timing pump is stopped. However, if the clarifier should stop, the timing pump should be electrically connected so that it will stop also. A clarifier operating at 12,000 rpm will produce a back pressure of about 50 psi (U.S. Public Health Serv. 1966).

Modern clarifiers may be obtained with a bowl designed for periodic desludging automatically during operation. In large volume plants this feature permits many hours of operation without losing clarifying efficiency. A preset timer regulates the intervals for desludging the bowl. This unit also lends itself to CIP cleaning which results in labor saving and overall economy.

Reference

U.S. Public Health Serv. 1966. Milk ordinance. Publ. *229*.

Cross-reference: *Centrifugal Separators.*

CLEANING OF EQUIPMENT

A vat should be rinsed immediately after use with cold water to remove milk and loose solids. It should then be partially filled with hot water and a cleaning solution. After cleaning, the solution should be removed and the tank rinsed with cold water. Sterilization of the surfaces with a chlorine solution should take place before use, preferably no more than 30 min before, rather than after use. With the 300 series of stainless steel a cleaning solution of 200 ppm should not be in contact with the surface more than 30 min to avoid subsequent corrosion or pitting.

The cleaning of plate or the tubular heat exchanger equipment is not normally carried out as an entirely manual operation. A circulation method for moving the cleaning solution through the heat transfer equipment is commonly used. "Alternate" pumps especially to clean the equipment should be used, rather than the milk pumps. For milk pumps, hardened stainless steel is normally used for the impellers or plungers. The hardened stainless steel corrodes more easily than regular stainless steel.

After the unit is rinsed with warm water, it is cleaned by continuous circulation from the pump. Either a base or acid cleaner is used, sometimes changing from day to day or from week to week according to the material to be removed and characteristics of the water used for cleaning. Normally, the system will be cleaned by circulation for about 30 min, and then flushed and finished with a cold water rinse. The heat transfer unit is then checked to see that all food particles or deposits have been removed, and if not, manually cleaned to assure proper sanitation. The equipment is flushed with a chlorine solution of about 200 ppm prior to the next processing operation.

With plate heat exchangers the additional precaution of preventing damage to the gaskets must be kept in mind. The heat exchanger should be cooled to room temperature before cleaning to prevent the gaskets from loosening from the plate. The pressure of the plates against the gaskets should be relieved periodically to prevent the gaskets from being forced into a permanent set.

Recommendations

To decrease the time requirements for manual cleaning, the following recommendations should be followed.

(1) Eliminate excessive rinsing of parts, particularly the outside portions.   (2) Handle parts of equipment as little as possible.   (3) Place parts on a wash rack as the parts are disassembled and washed.   The water should be convenient for cleaning and rinsing.   Materials and equipment should be close to the work area.   (4) Place the water hose on a self-winding reel.   From 3 to 4 min are required to wrap the hose after use without a reel.   (5) Avoid crossing an alley with the water hose.   The movement of carts and trucks is hampered by a water hose across an alley.   (6) Place a water valve on the discharge end of the hose to save labor and water.   (7) Locate equipment so that it can be easily washed without ladders, steps, etc.   (8) Avoid scratching of plates.   If an abrasive is needed, (a) use a mild abrasive, such as Bon Ami, or (b) use a stainless steel sponge for more severe corrosion.   Do not use a sponge made of dissimilar material, as specks of the dissimilar metal on the surface will cause deterioration of the surface and corrosion of the stainless steel.

One of the most important steps in satisfactory cleaning of processing equipment is inspection of food contact surfaces after the cleaning steps have been performed. An operator should not assume that because a CIP system has been energized or manual steps taken that the cleaning was adequate.   Before the next processing run, sufficient inspection of equipment and parts should be made to be certain of the adequacy of cleaning.

Cross-references: *Bottle Washers; Can Washes; Chlorination; CIP Systems; Pumps; Sanitation; Stainless Steel.*

COEFFICIENT OF EXPANSION

During heating, gases, liquids, and solids usually increase in length or volume. The notable exception is liquid water, which will decrease in volume to a temperature of approximately 4°C and then increase in volume with an increase in temperature. The total change in length of a solid from absolute zero temperature to the melting point is about 2% of the total length.   The ratio of the change in length per degree centigrade to the length at 0°C is known as the coefficient of linear expansion.   The equation representing the relationship is

$$l_t = l_0(1 + \alpha t)$$

where l_0 = length at 0°C
t = temperature, °C
α = linear coefficient of expansion, 1 per °C

Likewise, the coefficient of volumetric expansion can be expressed by the equation

$$V_t = V_0 (1 + \beta t)$$

where V_0 = volume at 0°C
t = temperature, °C
β = cubical coefficient of expansion, 1 per °C

These equations can also be expressed in terms of the Fahrenheit temperature scale. The cubical or volumetric expansion is approximately three times the linear coefficient of expansion. The cubical coefficient of expansion for water vapor is 0.0042, of water is 0.000207, and of ice is 0.000113 (Table C.13). The coefficient of volume expansion

TABLE C.13

COEFFICIENT OF THERMAL EXPANSION OF MISCELLANEOUS MATERIALS
(RANGE 32° TO 212°F), 1/°C

Gases (Cubical) (β)		
Air	0.00367	
Ammonia	0.00379	
Carbon dioxide	0.00372	
Chlorine	0.00383	
Ethylene	0.00373	
Hydrogen	0.00366	
Oxygen	0.00367	
Water vapor	0.0042	
Solids (Linear) (α)		(Cubical) (β)
Iron	0.000012	0.000035
Aluminum	0.000025	
Copper	0.0000165	0.00005
Ice (before freezing)	0.000051	0.000113
Glass	0.0000085	0.000026
Wood, across fiber	0.00004	
Monel metal	0.000016	
Stainless steel	0.000012	
Rubber		0.000487
Liquids (Cubical) (β)		
Water	0.000207	
Mercury	0.000181	
Ethyl alcohol	0.00112	
Acetic acid	0.00107	
Petroleum	0.000955	

Source: *Smithsonian Institute Tables.*

for gases is about the same, and is 0.00367 per 1°C (Table C.13). To obtain the coefficients in terms of °F, multiply by $5/9$. Thus, the cubical coefficient of expansion of gases is 0.00204 per °F. For engineering purposes, the cubical expansion of milk and similar liquids can be considered the same as for water.

A pipe made of steel, wrought iron, or cast iron expands upon heating or contracts during cooling. Pipe installations are normally made at room temperature. Pipe expands due to heating when steam is added. If any of these materials were installed at 32°F, the pipe would lengthen approximately $1/2$ in. per 100 ft of length at 100°F; 1.3 in. per 100 ft of length at 200°F; and 2.2 in. per 100 ft of length at 300°F; and 3.0 in. per 100 ft of length at 400°F. The joints or design must permit expansion of the pipeline without breaking. Expansion joints made of flexible material, slip joints or loops in the pipe may be utilized to permit expansion of the pipe. Similar arrangements can be made for contraction at low temperatures. Considerable force is exerted because of expansion or contraction during temperature changes. An iron bar of 1 sq in. cross section, heated from 0° to 100°C will exert a force equal to the weight of about 13 tons.

COFFEE ROASTING

Processing of the coffee beans starts as soon as possible after harvest and continues until the seeds have about 12 to 15% moisture dry basis. Either the dry or the wet process may be used. Dry processing is often used where water is scarce and production is underdeveloped. Wet processing (Fig. C.25) produces a superior dried product.

Coffee for the market must be roasted in order to develop the proper flavor and to kill certain organisms which might be present. This process may be either batch or continuous type and in general is accomplished by heating the coffee bean for a specified time and temperature depending upon type of bean and the flavor desired. The development of a particular flavor is very largely dependent upon the accurate and exact control of time and temperature. The moisture control is also important. Figure C.26 shows the basic design of a batch roaster and a continuous type roaster.

References

HALL, C. W. 1963. Processing Equipment for Agricultural Products. Edwards Brothers, Ann Arbor, Mich.

SIVETZ, M., and FOOTE, H. E. 1963. Coffee Processing Technology, Vols. 1 and 2. AVI Publishing Co., Westport, Conn.

COLLOID MILLS

The colloid mill is a rotary device which is used for extremely fine grinding or homogenizing of fluid products. Colloid mills are widely used in the baking, canning, and candy industries. They are also used in the manufacturing of certain types of peanut butter.

Principles

The principal feature of the colloid mill is that it can thoroughly mix and grind even coarse gritty materials when mixed with a liquid phase.

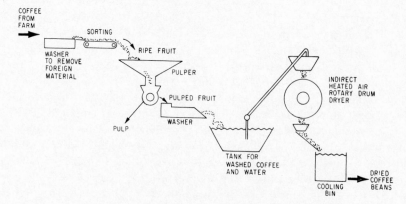

FIG. C-25.   Mechanized coffee bean processing

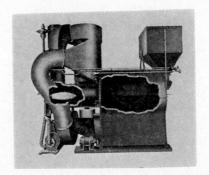

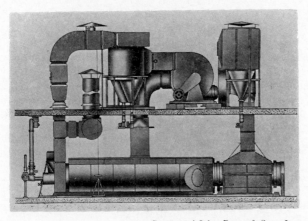

Courtesy of Jabez Burns & Sons, Inc.

Fɪɢ. C-26.   Above—Batch type coffee roaster. Below—Continuous type coffee roaster

The principle of operation is simple. The product passes between a rapidly rotating rotor and a stator which are separated by a few thousandths of an inch. The shearing action of the rapid movement of the product film which adheres to the moving surface reacting with the stationary surface material film causes a grinding, shearing, and mixing action.

Types

There are two principal types of colloid mills. One is the so-called smooth surface colloid mill in which the rotor and the stator are both very smooth. The second type of mill has a fluted rotor which may have a fluted stator. This fluted arrangement gives a much more rigorous treatment and grinding action than the smooth surfaced machine. The fluted surface mill is used more for materials in which there is considerable grinding as compared to a situation in which merely a strong intimate mixing action is desired. Figure C.27 shows the principle of the colloid mill.

Circular Continuous Tube Type

Colloidal material may also be produced in a hollow circular continuous tube. The material is introduced to the space in the presence of steam or compressed air. The material is propelled around the tube at high speeds and reduced in size by impact

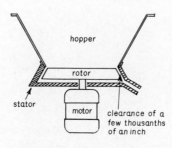

F<small>IG</small>. C-27.   Colloid mill

of particle against particle and particles against the side of the wall.   The material is removed when reduced to the desired size.

Cross-references: *Grinders; Size Designation.*

COLOR METERS

The adoption of standard colors for different foods and establishing of workable color standards are important goals.   Color uniformity is an important part of quality control for most food products.   Such products include flour, tomatoes, catsup, beans, and beer.

Color is of interest to the consumer.   It is of interest to the manufacturer because proper color can influence sales.   Color is an indication of uniformity of product and certain colors are associated with certain undesirable as well as desirable qualities.

For many years color matching was done on a visual basis only.   Deficiencies in the method were that people saw different colors differently depending upon their individual sensitivity and upon the intensity and type of light in which the product was exhibited.

In recent years, electronic color meters have been developed which use controlled light sources and are independent of the person reading the meter.

The Munsell Color Dictionary has been used for many years.   It provides a visual comparison method in which hundreds of small color discs on the pages can be used for direct comparison.   With this method the variables of type of light, light sensitivity of the person, and possible fading or changing color of the disc can be factors for error or lack of uniformity.

The Macbeth Munsell Disc Colorimeter is a visual matching system which is widely used in comparing the color of tomatoes, cherries, or cotton fibers.

The Agtron Colorimeter is an instrument which reads the degree of color of the product.   It is usually built with a filter and specifically adapted to a particular product such as tomatoes or flour.   It will give a direct reading on the degree of color and indicate to the observer whether the sample is within a specified range of redness or whiteness.

Difference Meter

The latest and most sophisticated type of meter is called the "Color Difference Meter" of which there are several makes including the Gardner and the Hunter.

This meter can be used for practically all types of products and it is electronically operated. It is not affected by individual personal differences and gives a definite reproducible reading.

The principle of the Color Difference Meter is that it exposes the sample to three different wavelengths of controlled illumination, and measures (1) the lightness, that is the degree of black and white, (2) the degree of hue or color, and (3) the intensity of the color.

The instrument reads the values directly since it computes electronically the various values. This equipment is quite widely used at present where extremely accurate color measurements are needed.

In all color comparison work, the sample should be properly selected and standards of maximum and minimum established. In those methods which depend upon visual observation, it is important that the operator have a good eye for color, and if possible a standardized illumination be used. Color discs which are used as standards must be stored in such a manner that they will deteriorate as little as possible.

Reference

MACKINNEY, G., and LITTLE, ANGELA C. 1962. Color of Foods. AVI Publishing Co., Westport, Conn.

Cross-reference: *Lighting.*

COMPOSITION OF FOOD PRODUCTS

Food products vary sufficiently in composition to make a balanced diet possible. With the need for many nutrients in the diet, it is imperative that selections are made to provide nutritional requirements. Palatability and convenience as well as physical characteristics also influence the acceptance of foods by consumers.

The major categories of foods include meat, poultry, dairy products, bakery goods, fruits, and vegetables. The composition of a product affects its physical and chemical characteristics. Bacteriological considerations are extremely important in preservation. Processing, which usually involves heating, causes changes in physical characteristics of many foods. A textural change is one of the most noticeable resulting from processing. In many cases, the changes are desirable such as increasing tenderness of meat by cooking. Enzymes also produce changes in many food products.

The components of foods are often sensitive to light as well as heat. Exposure to sunlight affects vitamin content and the flavor of milk. Contact with copper bearing metals produces an off-flavor in dairy and other products. Because of changes in flavor, texture, and other factors resulting from processing or handling of foods, it is necessary to carefully observe recommended practices.

The composition of some common food products is given in Table C.14.

Many modern processed foods are combinations of several basic commodities. In these foods the composition is varied by compounding of ingredients. The composition of products such as cheese will vary during the aging process, and is readily noticeable by flavor changes.

The nutrients contributed by major food groups are of interest to nutritionists, processors, and consumers. The percentage of nutrients contributed by the major food groups is shown in Table C.15.

TABLE C.14

COMPOSITION OF SOME COMMON FOODS

	Amount	% Water	Food Energy Calories	Protein, Gm	Fat (Total Lipid), Gm	Carbohydrate, Gm	Calcium, Mg	Iron, Mg	Vitamin A value, IU	Thiamine, Mg	Riboflavin, Mg	Niacin, Mg	Ascorbic Acid, Mg
Apples	1, 150 gm	85	70			18	8	0.4	50	0.04	0.02	0.1	3
Beef—lean and fat	3 oz	53	245	23	16	0	10	2.9	30	0.04	0.18	3.5	0
Butter, 2 sticks	1 cup, 227 gm	16	1,625	1	184	1	45	0	7,500				0
Carrots, raw, whole 5½ x 1 in.	1 carrot, 50 gm	88	20	1		5	18	0.4	5,500	0.03	0.03	0.3	4
Chicken, cooked, flesh only, broiled	3 oz	71	115	20	3	0	8	1.4	80	0.05	0.16	7.4	
Corn flakes, plain	1 oz	4	110	2		24	5	0.4	0	0.12	0.02	0.6	0
Cottage cheese, creamed	1 cup, 225 gm	78	240	31	9	7	212	0.7	380	0.07	0.56	0.2	0
Eggs, cooked, boiled, shell removed	2 eggs, 100 gm	74	160	13	12	1	54	2.3	1,180	0.09	0.28	0.1	0
Flour, enriched, sifted	1 cup, 110 gm	12	400	12	1	84	18	3.2	0	0.48	0.29	3.8	0
Grapefruit, 4½ in. diam, white	½ grapefruit, 285 gm	89	55	1		14	22	0.6	10	0.05	0.02	0.2	52
Ham, light cure, lean and fat roasted	3 oz	54	245	18	19	0	8	2.2	0	0.40	0.16	3.1	
Lettuce, iceberg	1 head, 220 gm	96	60	4		13	91	2.3	1,500	0.29	0.27	1.3	29
Milk; fluid, whole (3.5% fat)	1 cup, 244 gm	87	160	9	9	12	288	0.1	350	0.08	0.42	0.1	2
Oranges, Florida 3 in., raw	1 orange, 210 gm	86	75	1		19	67	0.3	310	0.16	0.06	0.6	70
Peas, green, cooked	1 cup	82	115	9	1	19	37	2.9	860	0.44	0.17	3.7	33
Potatoes, baked, peeled after baking	1 potato, 99 gm	75	90	3		21	9	0.7		0.10	0.04	1.7	20
Sugar, granulated (cane or beet)	1 cup, 200 gm		770	0	0	199	0	0.2	0	0	0	0	0
Tuna fish, canned in oil, drained in oil	3 oz	61	170	24	7	0	7	1.6	70	0.04	0.10	10.1	

Source: *Nutrition*, 7th Edition. 1966. Houghton Mifflin Co., Boston.

TABLE C.15

PERCENTAGE OF TOTAL NUTRIENTS CONTRIBUTED BY MAJOR FOOD GROUPS, 1966[1]

Food Group	Per Cent											
	Food Energy	Protein	Fat	Carbo-hydrate	Cal-cium	Phos-phorous	Iron	Vitamin A Value	Thi-amine	Ribo-flavin	Niacin	Ascorbic Acid
Dairy products, excluding butter	12.5	23.6	14.5	7.4	76.7	38.1	2.3	12.1	10.4	44.5	1.8	5.0
Eggs	2.2	5.7	3.4	0.1	2.4	5.8	6.0	6.5	2.5	5.6	0.1	0
Meat (including pork fat cuts), poultry, and fish	18.9	38.6	33.5	0.1	3.3	23.8	28.6	21.3	26.9	23.1	44.6	1.1
Fats and oils, including butter	16.7	0.1	41.2	[2]	0.4	0.2	0	8.8	0	0	0	0
Dry beans and peas, nuts, and soya flour	3.0	5.2	3.6	2.3	2.7	5.9	7.1	[2]	6.1	1.9	6.8	[2]
Potatoes and sweet potatoes	2.8	2.4	0.1	5.4	1.0	3.9	4.4	7.5	6.6	1.8	7.4	21.0
Citrus fruits	0.7	0.4	0.1	1.4	0.7	0.5	0.7	1.1	2.1	0.4	0.7	21.1
Other fruits	2.4	0.7	0.3	5.2	1.2	1.2	4.0	6.5	2.0	1.6	2.0	12.1
Dark green and deep yellow vegetables	0.3	0.5	[2]	0.5	1.5	0.6	1.7	20.6	0.9	1.1	0.7	9.2
Other vegetables, including tomatoes	2.4	3.2	0.4	4.3	4.6	4.8	9.0	15.2	7.1	4.4	6.1	30.6
Flour and cereal products	21.0	19.2	1.5	37.2	3.4	13.0	28.1	0.4	35.3	14.7	24.0	0
Sugars and other sweeteners	16.3	[2]	0	35.5	1.0	0.2	5.4	0	[2]	0.1	[2]	[2]
Coffee and cocoa[3]	0.8	0.4	1.4	0.7	1.0	1.9	2.8	[2]	0.1	0.8	5.8	0
Total[4]	100.0	100.0	100.0	100.0	100.0	100.0	100.0	100.0	100.0	100.0	100.0	100.0

[1] Percentages were derived from nutrient data which include quantities of iron, thiamine, riboflavin, and niacin added to flour and cereal products; quantities of vitamin A value added to margarine and milk of all types; quantities of ascorbic acid added to fruit juices and drinks.

[2] Less than 0.05%.

[3] Chocolate liquor equivalent of cocoa beans.

[4] Components may not add to total due to rounding.

Source: U.S. Dept. Agr.

TABLE C.16

STORAGE, FREEZING, HEAT PROCESSING DATA

Storage Temperature, Humidity, Shelf-Life, Water Content, Freezing Point, Specific Heat

	Storage Temp., °F	Relative Humidity, %	Approximate Storage Life	Water Content, %	Average Freezing Point, °F	Specific Heat Above Freezing	Specific Heat Below Freezing	Water Content, %	Specific Heat Above Freezing	Specific Heat Below Freezing	Ref.
Vegetables											
Artichokes											
Globe	31–32	90–95	1–2 wk	83.7	29.6	0.87	0.45	90	0.93		1
Jerusalem	31–32	90–95	2–5 mo	79.5	27.5	0.83	0.44				
Asparagus	32	90–95	3–4 wk	93.0	30.4	0.94	0.48				
Avocados	45–55	85–90	4 wk	65.4	30.0	0.72	0.40				
Beans											
Green or snap	45	85–90	8–10 days	88.9	30.2	0.91	0.47	90	0.92		3
Lima beans	32–40	85–90	10–15 days	66.5	30.8	0.73	0.40	65.5	0.73	0.40	
Fresh								90	0.92		3
String beans								88.9	0.91	0.47	4
Dried beans								12.5	0.30	0.24	4
Beets											
Bunch	32	90–95	10–14 days	87.6	29.2	0.90	0.46				
Topped	32	90–95	1–3 mo	89.9	30.3	0.92	0.47				
Broccoli, sprouting	32	90–95	7–10 days	84.9	30.2	0.88	0.46				
Brussels Sprouts	32	90–95	3–4 wk								
Cabbage											
Late	32	90–95	3–4 mo	92.4	30.5	0.94	0.47				
White, fresh								90–92	0.93		1
Carrots											
Bunch	32	90–95	10–14 days	88.2	28.8	0.90	0.46	86–90	0.93		1
Prepackaged	32	80–90	3–4 wk								
Topped	32	90–95	4–5 mo								
Boiled								92	0.90		1
Cauliflower	32	85–90	2–3 wk	91.7	30.2	0.93	0.47				
Celeriac	32	90–95	3–4 mo	88.3	30.2	0.91	0.46				
Celery	32	90–95	2–4 mo	93.7	30.9	0.95	0.48				
Corn											
Sweet	31–32	85–90	4–8 days	73.9	30.8	0.79	0.42	75.5	0.80	0.43	3
Green								10.5	0.28	0.23	3
Dried								97	0.98		1
Cucumbers	45–50	90–95	10–14 days	96.1	30.5	0.97	0.49				
Eggplants	40–45	85–90	10 days	92.7	30.4	0.94	0.48				
Endive	32	90–95	2–3 wk	93.3	31.1	0.94	0.48				

TABLE C.16 (*Continued*)

	Storage Temp., °F	Relative Humidity, %	Approximate Storage Life	Water Content, %	Average Freezing Point, °F	Specific Heat		Water Content, %	Specific Heat		Ref
						Above Freezing	Below Freezing		Above Freezing	Below Freezing	
Frozen-pack vegetable	−10 to 0		6–12 mo								
Garlic, dry	32	70–75	6–8 mo	74.2	28.0	0.79	0.42				
Kale	32	90–95	3–4 wk	86.6	30.7	0.89	0.46				
Kohlrabi	32	90–95	2–4 wk	90.1	30.0	0.92	0.47				
Leeks, green	32	90–95	1–3 mo	88.2	30.4	0.90	0.46	92	0.95		1
Lettuce	32	90–95	3–4 wk	94.8	31.2	0.96	0.48				
Lentils								12	0.44		1
Mushrooms											
Fresh	32–35	85–90	3–5 days	91.1	30.0	0.93	0.47	90	0.94		1
Dried								30	0.56		1
Mushroom Spawn											
Manure spawn	34	75–80	8 mo								
Grain spawn	32–40	75–80	2 wk								
Okra	50	85–95	7–10 days	89.8	28.6	0.92	0.46				
Onions	32	70–75	6–8 mo	87.5	30.1	0.90	0.46	65–95	0.76–0.97		1
Parsley											
Parsnips	32	90–95	2–6 mo	78.6	29.8	0.84	0.46				
Peas											
Dried								9.5	0.28		3
Green	32	85–90	1–2 wk	74.3	30.1	0.79	0.42	76	0.81	0.22	3
Air dried								14	0.44		1
Peppers											
Sweet	45–50	85–90	8–10 days	92.4	30.5	0.94	0.47				
Chili (dry)	32–40	65–75	6–9 mo	12.0	30.9	0.30	0.24				
Popcorn, unpopped	32–40	85		13.5		0.31	0.24	75	0.84		1
Potatoes											
Early crop	50–55	85–90		77.8	30.0	0.82	0.43				
Late crop	38–50	85–90		68.5	29.8	0.75	0.40				
Sweet potatoes	55–60	90–95	4–6 mo		29.2	0.92	0.47				
Pumpkins	50–55	70–75	2–6 mo	90.5	29.9						
Radishes											
Spring, bunched	32	90–95	10 days	93.6	30.1	0.95	0.48				
Spring, prepacked	32	90–95	10 days	93.6	30.1	0.95	0.48				
Winter	32	90–95	2–4 mo	93.6		0.95	0.48				
Rhubarb	32	90–95	2–3 wk	94.9	29.9	0.96	0.48				
Rutabagas	32	90–95	2–4 mo	89.1	29.7	0.91	0.47				
Sorrel								92	0.96		1

TABLE C.16 (Continued)

	Storage Temp., °F	Relative Humidity, %	Approximate Storage Life	Water Content, %	Average Freezing Point, °F	Specific Heat Above Freezing	Specific Heat Below Freezing	Water Content, %	Specific Heat Above Freezing	Specific Heat Below Freezing	Ref.
Salsify	32	90–95	2–4 mo	79.1	29.6	0.83	0.44	85	0.90		1
Spinach	32	90–95	10–14 days	92.7	31.3	0.94	0.48	93	0.94		3
Squash											
Acorn	45–50	75–85	4–5 wk		30.0						
Summer	32–40	85–95	10–14 days	95.0	30.4	0.96					
Winter	50–55	70–75	4–6 mo	88.6	29.8	0.91					
Tomatoes											
Mature green	55–70	85–90	2–5 wk	94.7	30.4	0.95	0.48	85	0.89		
Ripe	32	85–90	7 days	94.1	30.4	0.95	0.48				
Turnips	32	90–95	4–5 mo	90.9	29.8	0.93	0.47				
Fruit											
Apples	30–32	85–90		84.1	28.2	0.87	0.45	75–85	0.89–0.96		1
Apple pulp								85	0.89		3
Jonathan, Grimes	30–31		2–3 mo								
Golden, McIntosh	30–31		2–3 mo								
Golden delicious	30–31		3–4 mo								
Cortland, R.I. Greening	30–31		3–4 mo								
Baldwin, Delicious	30–31		4–5 mo								
Stayman, Winesap	30–31		4–5 mo								
York Imperial, Arkansas	30–31		4–5 mo								
Northern Spy	30–31		4–5 mo								
Rome Beauty, Ben Davis			4–5 mo								
Yellow Newton			5–7 mo								
Apricots	31–32	85–90	1–2 wk	85.4	29.6	0.88	0.46				
Bananas		85–90		74.8	29.6	0.80	0.42				
Dates											
Dried				20.0	–4.2	0.36	0.26				
Fresh				78.0	27.1	0.82	0.43				
Dried Fruits	32	50–60	9–12 mo			0.30–0.32					
Figs											
Dried	32–40	50–60	9–12 mo	24.0	27.1	0.39	0.27				
Fresh	28–32	85–90	5–7 days	78.0		0.82	0.43				
Grapefruit	32–50	85–90	4–8 wk	88.8	28.6	0.91	0.46				
Lemons	32,55–58	85–90	1–4 mo	89.3	29.0	0.92	0.46				
Limes	48–50	85–90	6–8 wk	86.0	28.2	0.89	0.46				
Mangoes	50	85–90	2–3 wk	81.4	29.4	0.85	0.44				

TABLE C.16 (*Continued*)

	Storage Temp., °F	Relative Humidity, %	Approximate Storage Life	Water Content, %	Average Freezing Point, °F	Specific Heat Above Freezing	Specific Heat Below Freezing	Water Content, %	Specific Heat Above Freezing	Specific Heat Below Freezing	Ref
Melons											
Canteloupe, Persian	45–50	85–90	1–2 wk	92.7	29.9	0.94	0.48				
Honey Dew, Honey Ball	45–50	85–90	2–4 wk	92.6	29.8	0.94	0.48				
Casaba	45–50	85–90	4–6 wk	92.7	29.9	0.94	0.48				
Watermelons	36–40	85–90	2–3 wk	92.1	30.6	0.97	0.48				
Nectarines				82.9	29.0	0.90	0.49				
Oranges	32–34	85–90	8–12 wk	87.2	28.0	0.90	0.46				
Papayas	45	85–90	2–3 wk	90.8	30.1	0.82	0.47				
Peaches	31–32	85–90	2–4 wk	86.9	29.6	0.90	0.46				
Pitted								90	0.91		3
Pears	29–31	85–90									
Bartlett	30–31		1½–3 mo	82.7	27.7	0.86	0.45				
Comice, Hardy, Kieffer	30–31		2–3 mo								
Bosc	30–31		3–3½ mo								
Anjou	30–31		5–6 mo								
Winter Nelice			6–7 mo								
Persimmons	30	85–90	2 mo	78.2	27.5	0.84	0.43				
Pineapples											
Mature green	50–60	85–90	3–4 wk	85.3	29.1	0.88	0.45				
Ripe	40–45	85–90	2–4 wk	85.7	29.7	0.88	0.45				
Plums (and fresh Prunes)	31–32	80–85	3–4 wk		28.7	0.88	0.45	81	0.87		3
Dried								28–35	0.53–0.59		1
Pomegranates	34–35	85–90	2–4 mo		26.5	0.88	0.45				
Quinces	31–32	85–90	2–3 mo	85.3	28.1	0.90	0.46				
Tangerines	31–38	90–95	3–4 wk	87.3	29.5	0.90	0.46				
Berries											
Blackberries	31–32	85–90	7 days	84.8	29.4	0.88	0.46				
Blueberries	31–32	85–90	3–6 wk	82.3	28.6	0.86	0.45				
Cherries	31–32	85–90	10–14 days	83.0	27.7	0.87	0.45				
Cranberries	36–40	85–90	1–3 mo	87.4	30.0	0.90	0.46				
Currants	32	80–85	10–14 days	87.4	30.2	0.88	0.45				
Dewberries	31–32	85–90	7–10 days	88.9	29.2	0.90	0.46				
Gooseberries	31–32	80–85	3–4 wk		30.0						
Grapes											
American type	31–32	85–90	3–8 wk	81.9	29.4	0.86	0.44				
European type	30–31	85–90	3–6 mo	81.6	27.1	0.86	0.44				

TABLE C.16 (*Continued*)

	Storage Temp., °F	Relative Humidity, %	Approximate Storage Life	Water Content, %	Average Freezing Point, °F	Specific Heat Above Freezing	Specific Heat Below Freezing	Water Content, %	Specific Heat Above Freezing	Specific Heat Below Freezing	Ref.
California grapes											
Emperor Ohanez, Lavalle			3–5 mo								
Malaga, Castica, Cornichon			2–3 mo								
Sultanina											
(Thompson Seedless)			1–2½ mo								
Tokay, Alexandria (Muscat)			1–1½ mo								
Eastern Grapes											
Concord			4–7 wk								
Niagara			3–6 wk								
Delaware			4–7 wk								
Catawba			5–8 wk								
Worden			3–5 wk								
Moore			3–6 wk								
Logan Blackberries	31–32	85–90	7 days	82.9	29.5	0.86	0.45				
Raspberries											
Black	31–32	85–90	7 days	80.6	29.4	0.84	0.44				
Red	31–32	85–90	7 days	84.1	30.3	0.87	0.45				
Frozen (black, red)	−10 to 0		1 yr								
Strawberries											
Fresh	31–32	85–90	7–10 days	89.9	30.2	0.92	0.42	91	0.96		3
Frozen	−10 to 0		1 year	72.0							
Dairy Products, Eggs											
Butter	32–36	80–85	2 mo	16.0		0.33		15	0.64	0.30	2
Frozen	−10 to −20	80–85	1 year	16.0			0.25	16	0.50		4
Cheese, nonfat	35			37–38	28.0	0.50	0.31	50	0.64	0.35	3
Cheeses		65–70						30	0.44	0.29	2

	Storage Temp., °F Ideal	Max.	Average Freezing Point, °F
Brick	30–34	50	16.3
Camembert	30–34	50	
Cheddar	30–34	60	8.8
Cottage	32–34	45	29.8
Cream	32–34	45	
Limburger	30–34	50	18.7
Neufchatel	32–34	45	

TABLE C.16 (*Continued*)

	Storage Temp., °F	Relative Humidity, %	Approximate Storage Life	Water Content, %	Average Freezing Point, °F	Specific Heat Above Freezing	Specific Heat Below Freezing	Water Content, %	Specific Heat Above Freezing	Specific Heat Below Freezing	Ref.
Process American	40-45	75			16.6						
Process Brick	40-45	75									
Process Limburger	40-45	75									
Process Swiss	40-45	75			17.5						
Roquefort	30-34	50			3.7						
Swiss, domestic	30-34	60			14.0						
Swiss, imported					14.7						
Cream											
Sweetened	-15		Several mo	73	28	0.85	0.40	75	0.85	0.50	2
40% fat	59								0.92		
15% fat	59								0.93		
30% fat	59								0.99		
60% fat									0.70	0.30	
Sour cream								57-73	0.70	0.45	2
Cream Cheese				58-66	27	0.78	0.45	80			2
Ice Cream											
Milk											
Whole				87.5	31	0.93	0.49	87.5	0.92	0.60	
Skim	40							91.0	0.95		
Dried	35		Several mo	3.5		0.23					
Sweetened	32-40		Several mo								
Powdered			Several wk					12.5	0.93	0.49	4
Whey						0.31			0.97		
Eggs											
Shell	29-31	85-90	8-9 mo	67.0	28.0	0.74	0.40	74.0	0.76		3
Shell, farm cooler	40-45	75		67.0	28.0	0.74	0.40	76.0	0.41	0.41	2
Frozen	-10 to 0	Minimum	Over 1 year	73.0	28.0		0.42	70	0.76		
Dried, whole	35	Minimum	6-12 mo	5.0		0.25	0.21				
Dried, yolk	35	Minimum	6-12 mo	3.0		0.22	0.21				
Dried albumen	35	Minimum	6 mo	Up to 6%		0.25					
Fermented albumen	Room temp.	Minimum	Over 1 year	3-15		0.22-0.32					
Meat, Poultry											
Bacon											
Cured, farm style	60-65	85	4-6 mo	13-29		0.30-0.43	0.24-0.29				
Cured, packer style	34-40	85	2-6 wk								
Frozen	-10 to 0	90-95	4-6 mo								

TABLE C.16 (Continued)

Product	Storage Temp., °F	Relative Humidity, %	Approximate Storage Life	Water Content, %	Average Freezing Point, °F	Specific Heat Above Freezing	Specific Heat Below Freezing	Water Content, %	Specific Heat Above Freezing	Specific Heat Below Freezing	Ref.
Beef											
Fresh	32–34	88–92	1–6 wk	62–67	28–29	0.70–0.84	0.38–0.43				
Frozen	−10 to 0	90–95	9–12 mo								
Bones									0.40–0.60		1
Fat beef								50	0.60	0.35	2,4
Lean beef								70–76	0.76	0.41	2
Dried								5–15	0.22–0.34	0.19–0.26	
Mincemeat									0.84		1
Hams and Shoulders											
Fresh	32–34	85–90	7–12 days	47–54	28–29	0.58–0.63	0.34–0.36				
Frozen	−10 to 0	90–95	6–8 mo								
Cured	60–65	50–60	0–3 years	40–45		0.52–0.56	0.32–0.33				
Fat Backs	38–40	85–90	0–3 mo								
Kidneys									0.86		1
Lamb											
Fresh	32–34	85–90	5–12 days	60–70	28–29	0.68–0.76	0.38–0.51				
Frozen	−10 to 0	90–95	8–10 mo								
Lard	−10 to 0	90–95	3–4 mo						0.38		4
Livers, frozen	−10 to 0			70.0							
Mutton								90	0.93		1
Pork											
Fresh	32–34	85–90	3–7 days	35–42	28–29	0.48–0.54	0.30–0.32				
Fresh, fat								39	0.62		1
Fresh, non-fat								57	0.73		1
Frozen	−10 to 0	90–95	4–6 mo								
Smoked								57	0.60	0.32	
Sausages											
Fresh					26			65	0.89	0.56	4
Dried		85–90			26			65.5	0.89	0.56	4
Smoked	40–45	85–90			25			60	0.86	0.56	4
Franks	40–45				29			60.0	0.86	0.56	4
Sausage Casings	32–34	90–95	5–10 days	70–80	28–29	0.76–0.84	0.42–0.51				
Veal											
Cutlets								72	0.82		1
Cutlets, fried								58	0.74		1
Venison								70	0.81		1

TABLE C.16 (*Continued*)

	Storage Temp., °F	Relative Humidity, %	Approximate Storage Life	Water Content, %	Average Freezing Point, °F	Specific Heat — Above Freezing	Specific Heat — Below Freezing	Water Content, %	Specific Heat — Above Freezing	Specific Heat — Below Freezing	Ref.
Poultry											
Fresh	32		1 wk	74	27.0	0.79		60–70	0.68–0.76	0.38–0.41	2
Frozen	−10 to 0		6–9 mo				0.37				
Frozen, eviscerated	−10 to 0		9–10 mo								1
Goose, eviscerated								52	0.70		
Rabbits											
Fresh	32–34	90–95	1–5 days								
Frozen	−10 to 0	90–95	0–6 mo								

Meat Products

	Storage Life (Months) At 10°F	At 0°F
Beef	4–12	6–18
Beef, chopped	3–4	4–6
Beef livers	2–3	2–4
Ham, Bacon		
Smoked	1–3	2–4
Uncured	2	4
Lamb	3–8	6–16
Pork	2–6	4–12
Pork sausage	1–2	2–6
Veal	3–4	4–14

Fish

	Storage Temp., °F	Relative Humidity, %	Approximate Storage Life	Water Content, %	Average Freezing Point, °F	Specific Heat — Above Freezing	Specific Heat — Below Freezing	Water Content, %	Specific Heat — Above Freezing	Specific Heat — Below Freezing	Ref.
Fresh	33–40	90–95	5–20 days	62–85	26.0	0.80	0.40				
Frozen	−10 to 0	90–95	8–10 mo			0.70	0.39				
Smoked	40–50	50–60	6–8 mo			0.76	0.41				
Brine Salted	40–50	90–95	10–12 mo					16–20	0.41–0.44		
Dry Salted											
Mild Cured	28–35	75–90	4–8 mo			0.76	0.41				
Fat								60	0.68	0.38	2
Nonfat								75–80	0.80	0.43	2
Iced											
Cod				78	28	0.76	0.41				
Haddock				78	28	0.82	0.43				
Halibut				75	28	0.80	0.43				

TABLE C.16 (*Continued*)

	Storage Temp., °F	Relative Humidity, %	Approximate Storage Life	Water Content, %	Average Freezing Point, °F	Specific Heat Above Freezing	Specific Heat Below Freezing	Water Content, %	Specific Heat Above Freezing	Specific Heat Below Freezing	Ref.
Herring											
Kippered				70	28	0.76	0.41				
Smoked				64	28	0.71	0.39				
Salmon				64	28	0.71	0.39				
Menhaden				62	28	0.70	0.38				
Tuna				70	28	0.76	0.41				
Fillets											
Haddock, Cod				80	28	0.84	0.44				
Ocean Perch				80	28	0.84	0.44				
Whiting				82	28	0.86	0.44				
Pollock				79	28	0.83	0.44	82	0.82		3
Mackerel				57	28	0.66	0.37				
Shellfish											
Scallop meat				80	28	0.84	0.44				
Shrimp				83	28	0.86	0.45				
American Lobster				79	28	0.83	0.44				
Oysters, Clams				87	28	0.90	0.46				
Caviar								50–56	0.70	0.31	2
Sugar, Sweets, Miscellaneous											
Bread											
White								44–45	0.65–0.68		1
Brown								48.5	0.68		1
Dough											
Flour				13.5		0.38	0.28	12–13.5	0.45–0.52		1
Grains								15–20	0.43–0.45		1
Gelatin									0.45–0.48		4
Macaroni								13	0.31		1
Nuts	32–50	65–70	8–12 mo	3–6		0.22–0.25	0.21–0.22		0.44–0.45		1
Dried				3–10		0.21–0.29	0.19–0.24				
Oils (Vegetable)	35		1 year								
Oleomargarine	35	60–70	1 year	15.5		0.32	0.25	75–90	0.47–0.50	0.35	2
Olives, fresh	45–50	85–90	4–6 wk	75.2	28.5	0.80	0.42				
Pearl Barley									0.67–0.68		1
Porridge (Buckwheat)									0.77–0.90		1
Raisins								24.5	0.47		1
Rice								10.5–13.5	0.42–0.44		1
Salt									0.27–0.32		1
Sugar						0.20	0.20				

TABLE C.16 (*Continued*)

	Storage Temp., °F	Relative Humidity, %	Approximate Storage Life	Water Content, %	Average Freezing Point, °F	Specific Heat Above Freezing	Specific Heat Below Freezing	Water Content, %	Specific Heat Above Freezing	Specific Heat Below Freezing	Ref.
Maple Sugar				5		0.24	0.21				
Maple Syrup				36		0.49	0.31				
Yeast	31–32			70.9		0.77	0.41				
Coffee, green	35–37	80–85	2–4 mo	10–15							
Chocolate, ground										0.63	4
Cacao, ground										0.63	4
Cocobutter										0.60	
Candy (Storage life at temperature over 32°F)											
Sweet Chocolate		40	3–6 mo								
Milk Chocolate		40	2–4 mo								
Lemon Drops		40	2–4 mo								
Chocolate Covered Peanuts		40–45	2–4 mo								
Peanut Brittle		40	1–1½ mo								
Coated Nut Roll		45–50	1½–3 mo								
Uncoated Peanut Roll		45–50	1–2 mo								
Nougat Bar		50	1½–3 mo								
Hard Creams		50	3–6 mo								
Sugar Bonbons		50	3–6 mo								
Cocoanut Squares		50	2–3 mo								
Peanut Butter Taffy Kisses		40	2–3 mo								
Chocolate Covered Creams		50	1–3 mo								
Chocolate Covered Soft Creams		50	1½–3 mo								
Plain Caramel		50	3–6 mo								
Fudge		65	2½–5 mo								
Gum Drops		65	3–6 mo								
Marshmallows		65	2–3 mo								

References

Columns 1 to 7 of Table C.16 are from the Air Conditioning and Refrigerating Data Book 1956–1957. Footnotes to the Data Book table refer for further details to various chapters of the same book. These details have been filled in to complete the table.

Used by courtesy and permission of the American Society of Heating, Refrigerating and Air Conditioning Engineers.

Data in columns 8–10 are based mainly on research performed by Russian institutions. Figures in column 11 refer to the following sources:

1. Researches of the Institute for Mass Feeding at Kiev. Quoted from W. G. Ordinanz, Food Industries, December 1946.
2. M. W. Tuchschneid, Die Kaeltebehandlung schnellverderblicher Lebensmittel, Hamburg 1957, a German Translation of a Russian book.
3. Ulmann's Encyclopaedie der Technischen Chemie, Vol. XI, Berlin-Munich 1960.
4. A. L. Rapoport and L. B. Sosnovsky. Technology of Confectionery (Russian), Moscow, 1957.

Source: *Food Engineering*, Mar. (1962).

TABLE C.17

PH VALUES OF FOOD PRODUCTS[1]

Food Product	pH	Food Product	pH
Vegetables			
Artichokes	5.6	Okra, cooked	5.50–6.4
Canned	5.7–6.0	Olives	3.6–3.8
Asparagus	5.6; 5.4–6.0	Onions	
Canned	5.2–5.3; 4.4	Red	5.3–5.8
Buds	6.7	White	5.4–5.8
Stalks	6.1	Yellow	5.4–5.6
Beans	5.3; 5.7–6.2	Parsley	5.7–6.0
String beans	4.6	Parsnip	5.3
Lima beans	6.5	Peas	6.0–6.5;
Beets	5.3; 4.9–5.6		5.8–6.4;
Sugar beets	4.2–4.4		7.0
Canned beets	4.9	Frozen	6.4–6.7
Broccoli	6.5	Canned	5.7–6.0
Brussel sprouts	6.3	Dried	6.5–6.8
Cabbage	5.2–6.0	Pepper	5.15
Green	5.4–6.0	Pimentos	4.6–4.9
White	6.2	Potatoes	6.1
Savoy	6.3	Potato tubers	5.7
Red	5.4–6.0	Sweet	5.3–5.6
Carrots	4.9–5.2; 6.0	Optimum	5.5–6.0
Canned	5.18–5.22	Pumpkins	4.8–5.2
Juice	6.4	Radishes	
Cauliflower	5.6	Red	5.8–6.5
Celery	5.7–6.0	White	5.5–5.7
Cereal	6.4–6.2	Rhubarb	3.1–3.4
Chives	5.25–6.10	Canned	3.4
Corn	6.3; 6.0–6.5	Rice	
Canned	6.0	Cooked brown	6.2–6.7
Sweet	7.3	Cooked white	6.0–6.68
Cucumbers	5.1	Cooked wild	6.0–6.4
Dill pickles	3.2–3.5	Sauerkraut	3.6; 3.4
Eggplant	4.5	Sorrel	3.7
Gherkins	5.8	Spinach	5.5–6.0; 6.8
Hominy grits, cooked	6.0	Cooked	6.6–7.2
Horseradish	5.35	Frozen	6.3–6.5
Kale, cooked	6.4–6.8	Squash	5.0–5.4
Kohlrabi, cooked	5.7–5.8	Tomatoes	
Leeks, cooked	5.5–6.0	Whole	4.9; 4.2–4.3
Lettuce	6.0	Paste	3.5–4.7
Lentils, cooked	6.32–6.83	Canned	3.5–4.7
Marrows	4.7–5.6	Juice	4.1–4.2
Mushrooms, cooked	6.2	Turnips	5.2–5.5
Fruits			
Apples	2.9–3.3	Honey dew	6.3–6.7
Delicious	3.9	Persian	6.0–6.3
Golden delicious	3.6	Nectarines	3.9
Jonathan	3.33	Oranges	3.1–4.1
McIntosh	3.34	Juice	3.6–4.3
Newtown	3.30	Marmalade	3.0

TABLE C.17 (*Continued*)

Food Product	pH	Food Product	pH
Northern spy	3.37	Papaya	5.2–5.7
Winesap	3.47	Peaches	3.4–3.6
Apple juice	3.4–4.0	In jars	4.23
Apple sauce	3.33–3.36	In cans	4.09
Apple purée	2.85–2.45	Pears	3.9–4.9
Whipped purée	2.40	In jars	4.23
Apricots	3.3; 3.6–4.0	In cans	4.89
Dried	3.6–4.0	Compot	4.5
Canned	3.74	Persimmons	5.4–5.8
Bananas	4.6; 4.5–4.7	Pineapples	3.5; 4.7–5.2
Cantaloupe	6.17–7.13	Canned	3.5
Dates	6.3–6.6	Plums	2.8–4.6
Figs	4.6	Blue	2.8
Grapefruit	3.0–3.3	Green	3.6
Canned	3.1–3.32	Red	3.6
Juice	3.03	Yellow	3.9
Guavas, canned	3.70	Damson	2.9
Lemons	2.2–2.4	Frozen	3.22
Canned juice	2.32	Pomegranates	3.0
Limes	1.8–2.0	Prunes	3.1–5.4
Mangos	3.9–4.6	Quince, stewed	3.1–3.3
Melons		Tangerines	4.0
Cassaba	5.5–6.0	Watermelons	5.18–5.6

Berries

Food Product	pH	Food Product	pH
Blackberries	3.2–4.5	Currants, red	2.9
Blueberries	3.7	Gooseberries	2.8–3.1
Frozen	3.11–3.35	Grapes	3.4–4.5
Cherries	3.2–4.1	Raspberries	3.2–3.7
Cranberries		Strawberries	3.0–3.5
Sauce	2.4	Frozen	2.3–3.0
Canned juice	2.3–2.5		

Meat, Poultry

Food Product	pH	Food Product	pH
Beef		Pork	5.3–6.9
Ground	5.1–6.2	Canned w/beans	6.5
Pink color optimum	6.0	Veal	6.0
Ripened	5.8	Chicken	
Unripened	7.0	Fillet	6.5–6.7
Canned	6.6	Ragout	6.5–6.8
Tongue	5.9	Turkey, roasted	5.72–6.8
Ham	5.9–6.1		
Lamb	5.4–6.7		
Tongue	5.9		

Fish

Food Product	pH	Food Product	pH
Fish, most species just after death	6.6–6.8	White fish	5.5
		Fish	
Clams	6.5	White sturgeon	5.5–6.0
Crabs	7.0	Zander	5.3–5.7
Oysters	4.8–6.3	Bullheads	5.3–5.7
Tuna fish	5.2–6.1	Gadoid	6.3–7.0
Shrimp	6.8–7.0	Herring	6.1–6.4
Salmon	6.1–6.3	Fresh water fish	6.9–7.3

TABLE C.17 (*Continued*)

Food Product	pH	Food Product	pH
		Dairy Products, Eggs	
Butter	6.1–6.4	Edam	5.4
Buttermilk	4.5	Roquefort	5.5–5.9
Casein	4.6	Swiss Gruyer	5.1–6.6
Milk	6.3–6.5–8.5;	Eggs	
	6.1	Egg white	7.0–9.0
Acidophilus	4.0	Yolk	6.4
Cream	6.5	Freshly laid, egg white	7.6–8.0
Cheeses		Freshly laid, egg yolk	6.0
American, mild	4.9	Egg albumen	4.6
Camembert	7.44	Egg solids, whites	6.5–7.5
Cheddar	5.9	Yolks	6.2–6.8
Cottage	5.0	Whole	7.1–7.9
Cream cheese	4.88	Frozen	8.5–9.5
		Bakery Products	
Bread	5.4; 5.3–5.8	Pound cake	6.6–7.1
Best for bread	5.0	Sponge cake	7.3–7.6
Eclairs	4.4–4.5	White layer	7.1–7.4
Napoleons	4.4–4.5	Yellow layer	6.7–7.1
Biscuits	7.1–7.3	Flour	
Crackers	7.0–8.5	Normally	6.1–6.2
Angel food	5.2–5.6	For cake	5.0–5.2
Chocolate cake	7.2–7.6	Optimum	6.0–6.3
Devil's food	7.5–8.0		
		Miscellaneous	
Caviar, American	5.4	Lime	2.0–2.25
Cider	2.9–3.3	Orange	3.3–4.3
Cocoa		Pineapple	3.4–3.6
Ground	6.3	Prune	3.7
Cocoa butter	6.6	Mayonnaise	4.2–4.5
Corn syrup	5.0	Molasses	5.0–5.4; 5.5
Corn starch	4.0–7.0	Blackstrap molasses	5.8
Ginger ale	2.0–4.0	Raisins	3.8–4.0
Guava jelly	3.7	Sugar	5.0–6.0; 5.5
Hominy	6.9–7.9	Liquid sugar	5.2–6.8
Honey	3.9	Sugar cane juice	5.2–6.2
Jams, Jellies	3.1–3.5	Vinegar	2.0–3.4
Juices		Yeast	3.0–3.5
Lemon	2.32		

[1] In this Table, pH values are compiled for a variety of food materials and ingredients. Sources of information include various reports of measurements performed and published by scientific, institutional, private and industrial research sectors.

Values (pH) for the same product obtained from various sources cannot be equal since samples, their characteristics, and the external conditions of the experiments could not have been identical.

Therefore, a few figures are often given in the table for each product showing values derived from various sources, under various conditions. Expressions such as 4.3 to 3.7 mean that pH values available fluctuate between 4.3 and 3.7.

References

1. Chemistry and Technology of Foods and Food Products. Ed. Morris B. Jacobs. Interscience Publishers, New York, 1951.
2. Advances in Food Research, Mrak & Stewart, editors, Academy Press, New York, 1957.
3. Am. Journal of Digestive Diseases and Nutrition, M. A. Bridges and M. R. Mattice, 1939, Vol. 6. This is the most complete report available.
4. Bakery Technology and Engineering, S. A. Matz. AVI Publishing Co., 1961.
5. Handbook of Food Preparations, American Home Economics Association, 1961. Used by permission of the Association.
6. Composition of Cane Juice and Cane Final Molasses. Scientific Report No. 15 of Sugar Research Foundation, Inc., New York, 1953.
7. Various publications and data of Industrial Research Laboratories placed at our disposal by courtesy of American Maize Products Corp. and Western Condensing Co.
8. Articles in the magazine Food Technology, 1961.

Data were also checked and completed by figures from Russian reports. Among those used:

1. Articles of Tchistiakov, Rogatchev, Spiridonova, Noscova and Zacharova in the Problems of Conservation, A. M. Yemelianov (Russian), Moscow, 1937.
2. T. S. Inikhov, Biochemistry of Milk (Russian), Moscow, 1956.
3. D. I. Lobanov, Technology of Food Preparing (Russian), Moscow, 1951.
4. A. I. Ostrowsky, Technochemical Control in the Bread Baking Industry (Russian), Moscow, 1949.
5. A. Nikolajev and Y. Sorokin, Processing of Hard Cheeses (Russian), Moscow, 1952.
6. L. V. Metlitzky, Storaging of Vegetables (Russian), Moscow, 1949.
7. A. L. Rapoport and L. B. Sosnovsky, Technology of Confectionery (Russian), Moscow, 1957.

Source: *Food Engineering*, Mar. (1962).

The composition of food products affects storage conditions, freezing characteristics, heat processing requirements, and shelf-life. Storage, freezing, and certain heat processing data for a number of products are presented in Table C.16.

Knowledge of pH values of food products is important in quality control. Since variations will exist between samples of a food product or material, more than one pH value is given in Table C.17 as reported by different investigators.

For detailed composition of virtually all food products the reader is referred to U.S. Dept. Agr. Handbook *8*.

References

CHANEY, M. S., and Ross, M. L. 1966. Nutrition, 7th Edition. Houghton Mifflin Co., Boston.
LEVIN, D. N. 1962. How to calculate heat processes. Food Eng. *34*, No. 3, 89–104.
MILK INDUSTRY FOUNDATION. 1967. Milk facts. Washington, D.C.

CONCRETE

Concrete is a structural material made of cement and water plus appropriate aggregates to provide a material which will flow when mixed, and which will solidify upon curing. Cement is a heated limestone clay product.

Requirements

It is usually desirable to provide a structure or structural member which is watertight, strong, and durable. These requirements can be met by using a proper water-cement ratio. Further, it is necessary to (1) properly select, (2) proportion and mix ingredients, (3) place the fluid mixture in properly shaped and supported forms, (4) finish the surface, and (5) cure the concrete.

The ingredients for concrete consist of water, cement, sand, and gravel, with the last 3 of these identified by a ratio, such as 1:2:3, which represents a ratio of cement, sand, and gravel by volume. One bag or sack of cement is 1 cu ft and weighs 94 lb. From 4.5 to 5 gal. of water per cubic foot or sack of cement should be used. This fact is often overlooked and operators often consider only the mixture of cement, sand, and gravel, and add water to provide the consistency of mix. A procedure for making good concrete consists of measuring or metering out the water and cement, then adding the sand and gravel to get the appropriate consistency of mixture.

Aggregates must be free of organic matter. If the aggregates contain water, the amount of water added externally to provide the proper cement-water ratio must be reduced.

Mixing must continue until the concrete is placed. Forms must be adequately designed to withstand the weight of the concrete in the fluid state. Also they should not absorb an excess of moisture from the concrete which would decrease the strength of the concrete. The concrete must be worked into the forms to obtain a uniform density throughout. The exposed edges are worked and it is important that walls, floors, etc. are built continuously avoiding breaks between partially cured and fresh concrete. The incorporation of calcium chloride and air into cement is used for many applications, particularly during winter weather. Reinforcement may be added to provide strength. Preformed members often reinforced with prestressed reinforcement rods are becoming quite common for construction.

Curing should continue for some time, usually considering that the maximum strength is obtained in four weeks. Measures must be taken to avoid too rapid curing, which causes a weaker concrete.

Practices

(1) Avoid adding too much water in relation to the cement. In general, 4.5 to 5 gal. per cu ft of cement is added, depending on the amount of moisture on the aggregate.

(2) Be sure that the aggregates are clean. Sand and gravel often need to be washed.

(3) Avoid curing or drying concrete too rapidly. The concrete can be covered and water added periodically to avoid too rapid drying.

(4) The component parts of the concrete combine to make less than the sum of the parts. Thus, a 1:2:3 cu ft mixture would make about 4.5 cu ft of concrete, depending upon the size of aggregates.

(5) Reinforce structural members where concrete is intended. Reinforcing members should be covered with at least $3/4$ in. of concrete over the rod.

(6) Prestressed members are made to put the reinforcing materials under tension to give the members strength. This principle utilizes the strong compressive characteristics of concrete.

(7) Do not finish or work a floor or walk while a water cover is over the curing concrete. If worked during this time, the cement moves to the top, does not provide the strength required in the concrete, and will provide a "dusty" concrete when cured.

(8) Provide adequate contraction and expansion joints for temperature changes to avoid cracking of concrete. Provide joints about every 10 ft with the number and location dependent upon the thickness of concrete, its density, the temperature changes which the concrete must withstand, and relationship to surrounding members.

Reference

PORTLAND CEMENT CO. Several handbooks and bulletins.

Cross-reference: *Building Materials.*

CONTROLLER FOR HEATING WATER

Hot water is normally used to heat the milk to the pasteurization temperature in a plate high-temperature short-time unit. The hot water may be supplied by either (1) steam introduction at a mixing tee, or (2) steam injection into a water tank, or (3) enclosed water heating and circulating unit. The water is usually heated 2° to 3°F above the pasteurization temperature. Compressed air at 20 psi is used to actuate the regulating valves.

During start-up and diverted flow of the high-temperature short-time unit, the diaphragm valve (1) (Fig. C.28) is wide open permitting steam to move directly to diaphragm valve (2). Because the water is cold, the temperature sensing element and

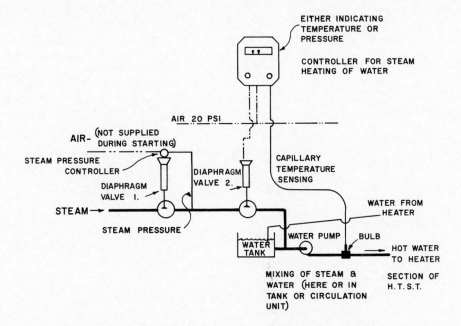

DIAPHRAM VALVE I. AIR-TO-CLOSE FOR MAINTAINING UNIFORM
STEAM PRESSURE (DIRECT ACTING)

DIAPHRAM VALVE 2. AIR-TO-CLOSE FOR SUPPLYING STEAM TO
WATER BEING PUMPED TO HEATER

FIG. C-28. Steam heating of water

capillary tube signal the indicating temperature controller to permit air to pass to the diaphragm valve (2), which opens the valve (air-to-open), and steam is added to the water to bring it to the temperature set on the controller.

During forward flow of the product, the steam pressure controller operates the diaphragm valve (1) to maintain a constant steam flow for heating water, regardless of the fluctuation of the steam pressure in the line caused by boiler or equipment demands. Air is supplied to close the valve to the preset position. When forward flow is reached, air is supplied to the steam pressure controller.

The hot water temperature is sensed by the thermometer bulb, and the response sent through the capillary tube to the temperature controller. Heating will continue until the temperature comes to the preset value at the controller. At this time, air entering the controller is partially bled off through an orifice and used to maintain a diaphragm motor in a position to furnish a constant steam supply. The term "motor" applies to the air-operated diaphragm device which maintains the valve position.

Temperature controllers should be checked against mercury bulb thermometers to determine accuracy.

The sensitivity of the temperature controller is adjustable. The sensitivity should be set so that just enough steam is supplied to heat the water without overheating. The setting should achieve steady temperature regulation at the control point. With a lower sensitivity the diaphragm valve movement is less for a given temperature variation.

Maintenance and operation of valves consist of (1) providing proper packing around the valves, (2) supplying clean air to the unit at uniform pressure and flow rate, and (3) checking the accuracy of the temperature as indicated by the control.

Cross-references: *Controllers; H.T.S.T. Pasteurization.*

CONTROLLERS

Controllers in the food industry play a very important role in regulating temperature, pressure, flow rates, and other controllable variables. Solution strengths and time intervals are also controlled by automatic controllers. Some of the type controllers used are self-acting, pressure, conductivity, and level controls.

Self-Acting Controller

The self-acting controller is automatic and usually utilized in controlling temperature. A common use is controlling the solution temperature of a bottle washer, circulating clean-in-place tank, blancher, and similar applications. The self-acting temperature controller is quite acceptable where extreme sensitivity is not required. They utilize a hermetically sealed bulb and flexible tubing system. The temperature-sensitive element must be properly installed according to manufacturers instructions. If placed horizontally in a solution tank, the ferrule will often carry the word "top" to designate correct installation. It is usually more desirable to install the controller in a horizontal line with the activating mechanism above the valve body. Recognizing the inlet and outlet connections to the valve body to obtain the correct direction of product flow through the valve is very important. Adjustment of the temperature-control point is accomplished by changing the spring-adjusting nut on most controllers.

Maintenance

Good maintenance of a controller requires checking of the packing around the valve stem and tightening the packing nut only enough to prevent leakage. Excessive tightening of a packing nut must be avoided. The valve stem on some controllers is equipped with a grease-sealed lubricator which should be turned about $1/4$ turn at least once a week. If the control is not equipped with the special lubricator, lubricating the valve stem with heavy oil once a week is a good practice. In some cases, a preformed, dry lubricated packing is used which requires no lubrication. Controllers should be protected against excessive corrosion. The connecting tubing should be free of sharp bends and not subjected to excessive vibration.

If a controller valve leaks, the difficulty can sometimes be corrected by replacing the removable seat. A self-acting temperature controller should be protected with a strainer, up stream. When installing the controller, a bypass should be included for manual operation in emergencies.

The thermal system can be checked for proper functioning by placing the bulb alternately in cold and hot water having at least 100°F difference. If no movement of the valve stem can be noted under these conditions, it is apparent that the thermal element is inoperative and the controller is in need of repair.

Pressure Controller

Various types of pressure controllers may be found in a food plant depending on the process. One simple air-operated pressure controller often used in conjunction with a diaphragm valve is installed directly above the diaphragm. This controller on the steam valve is used principally for reducing steam pressure. For reducing steam pressure, a reverse acting controller is generally used with an air-to-open steam valve. If the steam pressure increases, a capsular chamber expands throttling the air supply to the instrument. Air on the diaphragm of the valve flows out through a bleed screw closing the valve, and thus decreasing the steam pressure. The steam pressure desired may be set with a control knob on the instrument.

If this type of instrument fails to function, the air supply should be turned off and the set point adjustment knob removed so that the number of threads which are exposed can be noted and the adjustment knob replaced to the proper position. Since this is an air-operated controller, clean orifices are necessary. Regular maintenance is suggested.

Thermal Limit Recorder Controller

The thermal limit recorder controller is employed on the high-temperature, short-time pasteurizer used in the dairy industry. It controls the action of the important flow-diversion valve of the unit. In achieving control of the flow-diversion valve, the controller determines the temperature at which the supply air is admitted to the diaphragm forcing the valve into forward flow. The sensing element of the controller is installed in the milk line immediately up stream from the flow-diversion valve. The forward flow cut-in temperature is carefully determined and the controller contact box is sealed at the plant by the health officer to prevent underpasteurized milk from entering pasteurized products. As the name implies this controller is also a recorder. Recording the pasteurization temperature and position of the flow diversion valve are functions performed by this instrument.

Conductivity Controller

The conductivity controller usually consists of two electrodes which are exposed to a solution and respond to the degree of conductivity of the solution. These instruments may be adjusted to operate either on an acid or alkaline solution. They are used extensively for maintaining the strength of solutions for can washing.

Conductivity controllers may also be used for maintaining the liquid level of food products. They are frequently used to sound an alarm when a vat or tank is full. The liquid level control is used on the constant level tank of high-temperature short-time pasteurizers and is connected to an air operated valve that regulates the flow to the tank.

Liquid Level Controller

By installing a lightweight rubber diaphragm known as an air type liquid level controller in the bottom or lower side of a vessel, a modulating valve or signal device may be controlled. An inlet and outlet nozzle located in a chamber on the opposite side of the diaphragm responds to a change in pressure caused by a variation in liquid level height. This type of relatively simple sanitary pressure sensing element has proven satisfactory in controlling liquid level within narrow limits.

Time Controller

The time controller is usually an integral part of a system that controls the time of a process or processes. Such controllers are adjustable and flexible to meet time requirements.

Relief Controller for Air Systems

The relief controller for air systems has been used to control the amount of air entering an ice cream freezing chamber. The regulator allows excess air to bypass through a relief valve to the atmosphere and permit only the amount desired to enter the product. Permitting excess compressed air to escape into the atmosphere is a disadvantage economically.

Reference

MILK INDUSTRY FOUNDATION. 1967. Manual for Milk Plant Operators, 3rd Edition. Washington, D.C.

Cross-references: *Absolute Pressure Controller; Air Operated Controls; HTST Pasteurization; Level Measurement and Control.*

CONVERSION VALUES

The need to convert from one measure or unit to another is ever present in the food industry. Quantities of length, area, and volume may be expressed in many different units; thermal quantities of various designations may be used; density and weight may be expressed in different forms; and metric and English units may be used. Consistent units must be used throughout an analysis. To avoid serious errors, units should be carried along with figures in calculations. To assist in converting from one framework of units to another, standard constants, as listed in Tables C.18 to C.23 are useful.

Table C.18

CONVERSION FROM ENGLISH TO METRIC UNITS

Table of Equivalents

Customary Weights and Measures with Metric Equivalents		Metric Weights and Measures with Customary Equivalents	
Length		**Length**	
1 inch	= 2.54 centimeters	1 millimeter	= 0.03937 inch
1 foot	= 30.48 centimeters	1 centimeter	= 0.3937 inch
	= 0.3048 meter	1 meter	= 39.37 inches
1 yard	= 0.9144 meter		= 3.281 feet
1 mile	= 1609.34 meters		= 1.094 yards
	= 1.609 kilometers	1 kilometer	= 0.6214 mile
Area		**Area**	
1 square inch	= 6.452 square centimeters	1 square centimeter	= 0.155 square inch
1 square foot	= 0.0929 square meter	1 square meter	= 1.196 square yards
1 square yard	= 0.8361 square meter		= 10.764 square feet
1 acre	= 0.4047 hectare	1 hectare	
1 square mile	= 259.0 hectares	(10,000 m^2)	= 2.471 acres
Capacity or volume		1 square kilometer	= 0.386 square mile
1 cubic inch	= 16.387 cubic centimeters		= 247.1 acres
1 cubic foot	= 0.0283 cubic meter	**Capacity or volume**	
1 cubic yard	= 0.7646 cubic meter	1 cubic centimeter	= 0.061 cubic inch
1 fluid ounce (U.S.)	= 29.573 milliliters	1 cubic meter	= 35.315 cubic feet
1 liquid pint (U.S.)	= 0.4732 liter		= 1.308 cubic yards
1 liquid quart (U.S.)	= 0.9463 liter	1 milliliter	= 0.0338 fluid ounce (U.S.)
1 gallon (U.S.)	= 3.7853 liters	1 liter	= 33.81 fluid ounces (U.S.)
1 quart dry (U.S.)	= 1.012 liters		= 2.1134 pints (U.S.)
Weight			= 1.057 quarts (U.S.)
1 ounce (avdp.)	= 28.50 grams		= 0.2642 gallon (U.S.)
1 pound (avdp.)	= 453.592 grams	1 kiloliter	= 264.18 gallons (U.S.)
	= 0.4536 kilogram	**Weight**	
1 ton (short)	= 0.907 ton (metric)	1 gram	= 0.03527 ounce (avdp)
1 ton (long)	= 1.016 ton (metric)	1 kilogram	= 35.274 ounces (avdp)
	= 1016.05 kilograms		= 2.205 pounds (avdp)
Volume per unit area		1 metric ton	
1 gallon (U.S.)/ acre	= 9.354 liters/hectare	(1,000 kg)	= 0.984 ton (long)
Weight per unit area			= 1.102 tons (short)
1 pound (avdp.)/ square inch	= 0.0703 kilogram/ square centimeter		= 2204.6 pounds (avdp)
		Volume per unit area	
1 pound (avdp.)/ acre	= 1.121 kilograms/ hectare	1 liter/hectare	= 0.107 gallon (U.S.)/acre
Area per unit weight		**Weight per unit area**	
1 square inch/ pound (avdp.)	= 14.22 square centi- meters/kilogram	1 kilogram/square centimeter	= 14.22 pounds (avdp)/ square inch
		1 kilogram/hectare	= 0.892 pound (avdp)/ acre

Pressure per unit area
1 pound per square inch = 703.1 kilogram per square meter
1 pound per square inch = 0.0703 kilogram per square centimeter
1 pound per square inch = 70.3 grams per square centimeter
1 pound per square foot = 4.88 kilogram per square meter
1 pound per square foot = 0.488 gram per square centimeter

Miscellaneous
1 British thermal unit	= 252 calories (gram)r = .252 kilocalories
1 foot pound	= 0.138 kilogram mete
1 cubic foot	= 28.3 liters
1 inch	= 25.4 millimeters = 2.54 centimeters
1 foot	= 30.48 centimeters = 0.3048 meter
1 yard	= 91.44 = 0.9144 meters
1 square inch	= 645.2 square millimeters
1 square foot	= 0.029 square meter
1 square yard	= 0.8361 square meter
1 cubic inch	= 16,387 cubic millimeters = 16.387 cubic centimeters
1 cubic foot	= 28,320 cubic centimeters = 0.0283 cubic meter
1 pound	= 0.4536 kilogram = 453.6 grams

TABLE C.19

CONVERSION FACTORS FOR AGRICULTURAL PRODUCTS

Product	Unit	Approximate Equivalent
Apples	1 lb dried	8 lb fresh
	1 barrel	3 bu baskets
	1 case 24 No. $2^1/_2$ cans	1.4 bu fresh
Applesauce	1 case 24 No. $2^1/_2$ cans	1.2 bu fresh
Apricots	1 lb dried	5.5 lb fresh
Beans, lima	1 lb shelled	2 lb unshelled
Beans, snap or wax	1 case 24 No. $2^1/_2$ cans	$1/_{100}$ tons fresh
Buckwheat flour	100 lb	3.47 bu buckwheat
Calves	1 lb live	0.555 lb dressed
Cattle	1 lb live	0.549 lb dressed
Cane syrup	1 gal.	5 lb sugar
Cherries, sour	1 case 24 No. $2^1/_2$ cans	0.023 tons fresh
Chickens	1 lb live	0.72 lb ready-to-cook
Corn	56 lb shelled	70 lb husked ear corn
Corn, sweet	1 case 24 No. 2 cans	0.038 tons fresh
Cornmeal, degermed	100 lb	3.16 bu corn
Cornmeal, non-degermed	100 lb	2 bu corn
Cotton	1 lb ginned	3.26 lb seed cotton
Cottonseed meal	1 lb	2.10 lb cottonseed
Cottonseed oil	1 lb	5.88 lb cottonseed
Dairy products		
Butter	1 lb	21.1 lb milk
Cheese	1 lb	10 lb milk
Condensed milk, whole	1 lb	23 lb milk
Dry cream	1 lb	19 lb milk
Dry milk, whole	1 lb	7.6 lb milk
Evaporated milk, whole	1 lb	2.14 lb milk
Nonfat dry milk	1 lb	11 lb liquid skim milk
Ice cream	1 gal	15 lb milk

TABLE C.19 (*Continued*)

Product	Unit	Approximate Equivalent
Eggs	1 case	47 lb
Eggs, shell	1 case	39.5 lb liquid whole
Eggs, shell	1 case	10.8 lb dried whole
Figs	1 lb dried	3 lb fresh, California
		4 lb fresh elsewhere
Flaxseed	1 bu	$2^{1}/_{2}$ gal. oil
Grapefruit, Florida	1 case 24 No. 2 cans	0.83 box fresh fruit
Hogs	1 lb live	0.569 lb dressed, not including lard
Linseed meal	1 lb	1.56 lb flaxseed
Linseed oil	1 lb	2.80 lb flaxseed
Malt	1 bu (34 lb)	1 bu barley (48 lb)
Maple syrup	1 gal.	8 lb maple sugar
Nuts		
Almonds		
Imported	1 lb shelled	$3^{1}/_{2}$ lb unshelled
California	1 lb shelled	2 lb unshelled
Brazil	1 lb	2 lb unshelled
Cashews	1 lb	4.55 lb unshelled
Chestnuts	1 lb	1.19 lb unshelled
Filberts	1 lb	2.5 lb unshelled
Pecans	1 lb	2.5 lb unshelled
Pistachios	1 lb	2 lb unshelled
Walnuts		
Black	1 lb	$8^{1}/_{3}$ lb unshelled
English	1 lb	2.56 lb unshelled
Oatmeal	100 lb	7.6 bu oats
Oranges, Florida	1 case juice 24 No. 2 cans	0.63 box fresh
Peaches		
California, freestone	1 lb dried	$6^{1}/_{2}$ lb fresh
California, cling	1 lb dried	$7^{1}/_{2}$ lb fresh
Clingstone	1 case 24 No. $2^{1}/_{2}$ cans	1.0 bu fresh
Peanuts	1 lb shelled	$1^{1}/_{2}$ lb unshelled
Pears	1 lb dried	$5^{1}/_{2}$ lb fresh
Bartlett	1 case 24 No. $2^{1}/_{2}$ cans	1.1 bu fresh
Peas, green	1 lb shelled	$2^{1}/_{2}$ lb unshelled
	1 case 24 No. 2 cans	$^{1}/_{100}$ tons
Prunes	1 lb dried	$2^{1}/_{2}$ lb fresh, California
		3 to 4 lb fresh elsewhere
Raisins	1 lb	4 lb fresh grapes
Rice, milled	100 lb	152 lb rough or unhulled rice
Rye flour	100 lb	2.23 bu rye
Sheep and lambs	1 lb live	0.477 lb dressed
Soybean meal	1 lb	1.28 lb soybeans
Soybean oil	1 lb	5.45 lb soybeans
Sugar	1 ton raw	0.9346 ton refined
Tomatoes	1 case 24 No. 2 cans	0.027 tons fresh
Turkeys	1 lb live	0.80 lb ready-to-cook
Wheat flour	100 lb	2.3 bu wheat
Wool, domestic shorn	1 lb greasy	0.45 lb scoured

Source: *Agricultural Statistics*, U.S. Dept. Agr. (1961).

TABLE C.20

WEIGHTS AND MEASURES OF FRUITS AND VEGETABLES

Fruit or Vegetable	Unit	Approximate Weight, Lb
Apples	Northwest box, $10^1/_2$ x $11^1/_2$ x 18 in.	44
	Eastern box, 11 x 13 x 17 in.	54
Apricot	Lug, $4^5/_8$ x $12^1/_2$ x $16^1/_8$ in.	24
	Crate, $4^1/_2$ x 16 x $16^1/_8$ in.	24
Asparagus	Crate	30
Avocados	Lug, $4^1/_2$ x $12^1/_2$ x $16^1/_8$ in.	12–15
Bananas	Box, 13 x 12 x 32 in.	40
Beans		
Lima, dry	Bushel	56
Unshelled	Bushel	32
Snap	Bushel	30
Beets		
Topped	Bushel	52
Bunched	Crate, 8 x 12 x 22 in.	40
Berries, frozen pack	50-gal. barrel	380
Blackberries	24-qt crate	36
Cabbage	Wire bound crate, vary	50
	Western crate, 13 x 18 x $21^5/_8$ in.	80
Cantaloupe	Jumbo crate, 13 x 13 x $22^1/_8$ in.	83
Carrots		
Topped	Bushel, open mesh bag	50
Bunched	Western crate, 13 x 13 x $22^1/_2$	75
Cauliflower	$1^1/_2$-bu crate	37
Celery, crate	Crate	60
Cherries	Lug, $4^1/_8$ x $11^1/_2$ x 14 in.	16
Cranberries	Barrel	100
Cucumbers	Bushel	48
Grapefruit		
Florida, Texas	Box, 12 x 12 x 24 in.	80
California (desert)	Box, $11^1/_2$ x $11^1/_2$ x 24 in.	64
California (other)	Box, $11^1/_2$ x $11^1/_2$ x 24 in.	67
Grapes	4-qt basket	6
	12-qt basket	18
	Lug, $5^3/_4$ x $13^1/_2$ x $16^1/_2$ in.	28
	4-basket crate, $4^3/_4$ x 16 x $16^1/_8$ in.	20
Lemons	Box, $9^7/_8$ x 13 x 25 in.	76
	Carton, $10^1/_4$ x $10^{11}/_{16}$ x $16^3/_8$ in.	70
Lettuce	Crate, 13 x 18 x $21^5/_8$ in.	70
Limes	Box	80
Olives	Lug, $5^3/_4$ x $13^1/_2$ x $16^1/_8$ in.	25–30
Onions		
Dry	Sack	50
Green	Crate, 13 x 18 x $21^5/_8$ in.	50–55
Oranges		
Florida, Texas	Box, 12 x 12 x 24 in.	90
California, Arizona	Box, $11^1/_2$ x $11^1/_2$ x 24 in.	75
Peaches	Bushel	48
Peanuts, unshelled		
Virginia	Bushel	17
Runners	Bushel	21
Spanish	Bushel	25

TABLE C.20 (*Continued*)

Fruit or Vegetable	Unit	Approximate Weight, Lb
Pears		
California	Bushel	48
Other	Bushel	50
Western	Box, $8^1/_2$ x $11^1/_2$ x 18 in.	46
Peas		
Green, unshelled	Bushel	30
Dry	Bushel	60
Peppers	Bushel	25
	Crate, $13^3/_8$ x 11 x 22 in.	50
Pineapples	Crate, 12 x $10^1/_2$ x 33 in.	70
Plums and prunes	$^1/_2$ basket	28
	4-basket crate	20–29
Potatoes	Bushel	60
	Barrel	165
	Bag	50
Quinces	Basket	48
Raspberries	24-qt crate	36
Rutabagas	Bushel	56
Spinach	Bushel	20
Strawberries	24-qt crate	36
Sweet potatoes	Bushel	55
Tangerines, Florida	$^1/_2$ box	45
Tomatoes	Bushel	53
	Lug box, $5^3/_4$ x $13^1/_2$ x $16^1/_8$ in.	32
Turnips, topped	Bushel	54

Source: *Agricultural Statistics*, U.S. Dept. Agr. (1961).

CONVEYORS

Conveyors are mechanical devices used to assist in the movement of articles or products from one location to another without using a vehicle such as truck, forklift, cart, or similar device. Conveyors are of two basic types: gravity and power. A wide variation exists in many characteristics between conveyors of the gravity or the power type.

The chief advantages attributed to a conveyor is greater production realized in a manufacturing plant or warehouse because of the large reduction in labor, heavy lifting, and carrying. Conveyors of one type or another will be found in virtually every food processing plant today. The emphasis on increased productivity per man hour will practically dictate the need for installing materials handling equipment.

Principles

Conveyors are often manually fed at some point in the system, and in some operations the products at the discharge end of the conveyor are removed manually. In certain situations a mechanical device or transfer is installed on the end of a conveyor section.

TABLE C.21

WEIGHT OF GRAIN AND SEEDS PER BUSHEL[1]

Product	Weight, Lb	Product	Weight, Lb
Alfalfa	50	Milo	56
Barley	48	Navy beans	60
Bermuda grass	35	Oats	32
Bluegrass seed	22	Orchard grass seed	14
Bran	20	Osage orange	36
Broomcorn seed	44–50	Pea beans (Navy)	60
Buckwheat	48–52	Popcorn, on ear	70
Cane seed	50	Popcorn, shelled	56
Castor beans	46	Poppy seed	46
Clover seed	60	Rapeseed	50, 60
Corn, shelled	56	Red top seed	50, 60
Corn in ear, shucked	70	Rice, rough	45
Corn in ear, with husks	74	Rye	56
Corn meal	50	Salt	50
Cotton seed	32	Sesame seed	46
Cowpeas	60	Sorghum or cane seed	50
Flaxseed	56	Soybeans	60
Grain sorghums	56	Sudangrass seed	40
Hemp seed	44	Sunflower	24, 32
Hickory nuts	50	Sweet clover	60
Hungarian seed	48, 50	Timothy	45
Kaffir corn	56, 50	Velvet beans, hulled	60
Malt	38	Vetch	60
Meadow fescue seed	24	Walnuts	50
Millet seed	48–50	Wheat	60

[1] 1 bushel = 2150.4 cu in.

TABLE C.22

RAW PRODUCT NEEDED TO YIELD A GIVEN NUMBER OF PINT PACKAGES[1]

Fruits	Amount of Fresh Fruit	Approx Number Packages	Vegetables	Amount of Fresh Vegetables	Approx Number Packages
Apples	1 bu (42–44 lb)	40	Asparagus	10 lb	8
Berries	24 qt case	30	Beans (Snap)	25 lb	25
Cherries	25-lb lugs	22	Beans (Lima)	10-lb in pod	4
Cranberries	1 pk (8 lb)	12	Broccoli	25 lb	20
Grapes	1 bu	35	Carrots	1 bu	35
Peaches	1 bu (48 lb)	40	Cauliflower	1 lb	1
Pears	1 bu (50 lb)	40	Corn	6 ears (cut)	1
Plums	1 bu (50 lb)	40	Greens	1 lb	1
Rhubarb	1 pound	1	Peas	30 lb in pod	12
Strawberries	24-qt case	24	Squash	10 lb	10

[1] While the table shows the approximate amount of produce required to fill a given number of pint packages, many patrons may prefer to pack some of the fruits, or bulky vegetables such as asparagus, broccoli and cauliflower, in quart containers. Those who do can easily calculate the amount of produce necessary to fill a given number of quarts. Levin and Gaston (1950).

Source: Levin and Gaston (1950).

Table C.23

COMMON CAN SIZES USED FOR FRUITS AND VEGETABLES

Can Name	Designation of Size	Approx Net Weight Lb Oz	Number of Cupfuls	Number of Cans per Case
No. 1 tall	301 x 411	1 —	2	24
No. 303	303 x 406	1	2	12, 24
No. 2	307 x 409	1 4	$2^1/_2$	12, 24
No. 2 cylinder	307 x 512	1 10	3	24
No. 2 tall	307 x 604	1 10	$3^1/_4$	12, 24
No. 3 cylinder	404 x 700	3 2	$5^3/_4$	12
No. 5	502 x 510	3 10	$6^1/_2$	12
No. 10	603 x 700	6 10	12	6

Can designation: first digit represents inches, next two the extra fraction expressed as sixteenths of an inch. The first number is diameter and second is height.

Source: *The Canned Food Reference Manual,* American Can Company (1949).

The flexibility of conveyors and their versatility in handling a wide variety of products makes them extremely useful in moving products or packaging materials from one operation to another including transfers to different floor levels. With proper design, conveyors are suitable for low or high temperature and indoor or outdoor applications.

Systems

Processing operations in a manufacturing plant are frequently linked together with a conveyor. The conveyor, as a result, becomes an integral part of the total materials handling system. Materials handling equipment, such as casers and case stackers, are designed especially for use with a conveyor. Bottle washers and fillers are also good examples of equipment linked together by conveying equipment.

Rather complicated control systems which may employ cybernetics can be utilized in an automated conveyorized materials handling system. The controls become important in segregating a wide variety of products moving either into or out of storage.

Many types and adaptations have been made to utilize conveyors for specialty products. As a result, some of the types of conveyors in existence are: wood slat, metal chain, metal or rubber belt, roller, wheel, bucket, plate, flight, oscillating, monorail, flexible spiral, and air conveyor. Most chain and belt conveyors of the power-driven type are made up of four basic parts: (1) the supporting frame, (2) the belt or chain take-up unit, (3) the belt or chain, and (4) power unit. Some belt and also wheel conveyors are extendable for ease in loading or unloading trucks.

Chain Conveyors

It is common practice, particularly in dairy and food plants, to use powered chain conveyors of either the in-floor or above-floor type. Usually the chain links are hardened chromium steel containing 5 to 7% manganese. This makes a very durable chain link. This type of conveyor is usually designed so that the actual load does not exceed $^1/_6$ of the rated conveyor capacity. A typical example would be to have a 24,000-lb system which would be capable of handling 4,000 lb for a single chain conveyor or 8,000 lb if it is a double chain.

When calculating the horsepower requirements, the load on a chain begins in the drive unit at the slack point of the chain and accumulates in the direction of chain travel to the point where force is applied. The factors making up the load are (1) the weight of the chain per foot of conveyor, (2) the average weight per foot of packages per foot of conveyor, (3) the number and type of curves, (4) pitch of the conveyor, (5) coefficient of friction, (6) speed of chain in feet per minute, and (7) length of conveyor in feet. When packages on a conveyor are blocked in position by a conveyor stop, the weight of the packages or load on the section should be doubled. The formula for calculating horsepower is

$$\text{Hp} = \frac{\text{lb chain pull} \times \text{chain speed in ft per min}}{33,000}$$

where lb chain pull = (average weight per ft of package + weight of chain per ft)
$\times$ length of conveyor in feet $\times$ coefficient of friction

For single and multiwheel curves
30° to 90° = 5 ft straight conveyor equivalent
90° to 180° = 10 ft straight conveyor equivalent
For bar curves
20° to 45° = use 40% of accumulated load to the curve
46° to 90° = use 50% of accumulated load up to the curve
For slope or pitch factor add 10% to chain pull (in pitched section only) for each $^1/_2$ in. per foot increment above level
A coefficient of friction of 0.33 is often used

Belt Conveyors

Belt conveyors made of Neoprene or similar products such as Hycar have many uses in the food plant. There are several working formulas which apply in the design and consideration for a belt installation. Several of these working formulae and other belt data are as follows.

BELT LENGTH

when pulleys are the SAME SIZE

$$L = \frac{D + d}{2} \times 3.1416 + 2C$$

when one pulley is LARGER

$$L = \frac{D + d}{2} \times 3.1416 + 2C + \frac{(D - d)^2}{4C}$$

BELT SPEED
in ft per min

$$S = D \times \text{rpm} \times 0.2618 \times 1.021$$

MAXIMUM PRODUCT WEIGHT
on belt at any one time

when load is known per sq ft or per cu ft basis

$$P = K_1 \times C \text{ (in ft)} \times W \text{ (in ft)}$$

when load is known by lb per hr or tons per hr

$$P = \frac{K_2}{S \times 60 \text{ (min)}} \times C \text{ (in ft)}$$

HORSEPOWER
to drive flat belt conveyor

for LEVEL conveyors

$$\text{Hp} = \frac{F \times S \times (P + M)}{33,000}$$

for INCLINED conveyors

$$\text{Hp} = \frac{(P \times B) + (P + M) \times F \times S}{33,000}$$

EFFECTIVE TENSION
(which is a relation of weight and friction)

$$F = F \times (P + M)$$

or

$$T_1 - T_2 = \frac{P \times 33,000}{WNS}$$

BELT PLIES NEEDED

$$N = \frac{T}{W \times U}$$

where B = sine of angle of incline
$\quad C$ = center to center distance, in.
$\quad D$ = diameter drive pulley, in.
$\quad d$ = diameter tail pulley, in.
$\quad E$ = effective tension, lb
$\quad F$ = coefficient of friction (See Table)
Hp = horsepower
$\quad K_1$ = load per sq or cu ft, lb
$\quad K_2$ = load per hr, lb
$\quad L$ = belt length, in.
$\quad M$ = belt weight, lb
$\quad N$ = number of plies
$\quad P$ = product weight, lb

rpm = revolutions per minute
S = speed ft per min
T = total maximum tension, lb
T_1 = tight side tension, lb ply per in. of width
T_2 = slack side tension lb. ply per in. of width
U = unit working tension of belt, per in. per ply (see Table)
W = belt width, in.

Belt Weight, Oz per Sq Ft

Series 8, 3 ply	8.5
Series 15, 3 ply	18
Series 15 friction surface, 2 ply	8
Series 16, 3 ply	11.5
Series 25, 2 ply	9.5

Other plies, weight in proportion

Roller Conveyors

Roller conveyors are available in a variety of sizes varying from a few pounds to several tons. Roller diameters range from 1 to 6 in., and roller lengths from 6 in. to 3 or 4 ft. Roller capacities will normally range from 35 to 8,000 lb per roller. The bearings are available in virtually every type which is used in the industry. Relationships for roller loads are given in Table C.24.

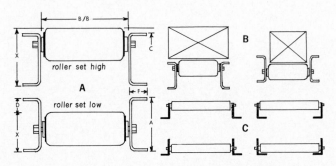

Courtesy of E. W. Buschman Co.

Fig. C-29.   Frames for roller conveyors
A—Two positions of rollers. B—High and low roller positions with load. C—Rollers mounted on angle frames, (l) with angles turned out, (r) with angles turned in.

Rollers are set high or low. Rollers in the high position will convey packages of a width greater than the roller lengths. When the roller is set low only packages which will fit between the frame can be conveyed. The various types of frames for roller conveyors may be seen in Fig. C.29.

Roller specifications and load rates are usually based on the standards adopted by the Conveyor Equipment Manufacturers Association for a surface speed of 60 fpm for gravity operation. For other surface speeds, the roller load rating may be multiplied by a service factor. For speeds lower than 60 fpm, the multiplication factor is

TABLE C.24

ROLLER ASSEMBLY WEIGHT AND WIDTH CHART TO DETERMINE ROLLER LOAD FRAME MUST CARRY[1]

Diam of Roller	Length															
	6 In.	8 In.	10 In.	12 In.	14 In.	16 In.	18 In.	20 In.	22 In.	24 In.	26 In.	28 In.	30 In.	36 In.	42 In.	48 In.
1 In.	0.53	0.66	0.79	0.91	1.04	1.17	1.30	1.42	1.55	1.68	1.81	1.94	2.07	2.46		
1 3/8 In.	0.86	1.06	1.26	1.46	1.66	1.86	2.06	2.26	2.46	2.66	2.86	3.06	3.26	3.86		
1.9 In.	1.82	2.24	2.66	3.07	3.49	3.90	4.32	4.73	5.15	5.56	5.98	6.39	6.81	8.06		
2 1/8 In.	1.18	1.47	1.76	2.04	2.33	2.61	2.90	3.18	3.47	3.75	4.04	4.33	4.61	5.47		
2 1/2 In.	2.04	2.49	2.94	3.39	3.84	4.30	4.75	5.20	5.65	6.11	6.56	7.01	7.46	8.82		
2 1/4 In.	3.2	3.9	4.6	5.3	6.0	6.6	7.3	8.0	8.7	9.4	10.1	10.8	11.5	13.6		
2 9/16 In.	4.6	5.6	6.6	7.6	8.6	9.6	10.6	11.6	12.6	13.6	14.6	15.6	16.6	19.6	22.6	25.6
3 1/2 In.	6.1	7.2	8.3	9.4	10.5	11.7	12.8	13.9	15.0	16.1	17.2	18.4	19.5	22.8	26.2	29.5
3 1/2-5/16 In.	10.2	12.5	14.8	17.0	19.3	21.5	23.8	26.0	28.3	30.5	32.8	35.0	37.3	44.1	50.9	57.7
4 1/4-1/2 In.	17.0	21.1	25.2	29.3	33.4	37.5	41.6	45.7	49.8	53.9	58.0	61.2	66.2	78.5	90.8	103.1
5 In.	25.7	32.3	38.9	45.5	52.1	58.7	65.3	71.9	78.5	85.1	91.1	97.7	104.9	124.7	144.5	164.3

[1] Weights shown in lb according to length of roller. Covers one roller, one shaft, and two bearings.
Source: E. W. Buschman Co.

greater than 1.0, and for speeds greater than 60 fpm, the multiplication factor is less than 1.0. For a surface speed of 20 fpm, a factor of 1.44 may be used; for 40 fpm, the factor is 1.14; for 80, 100, and 120 fpm, the factors are 0.91, 0.84, and 0.79, respectively. Where rollers are subjected to shock loads, the load rating per roller should be reduced

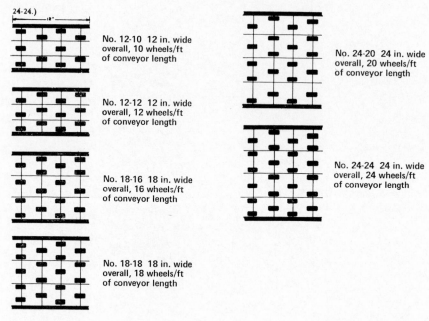

Courtesy of Rapistan Inc.

FIG. C-30.   Configurations of wheel conveyors

by 50%. This design may require closer roller spacing or heavier rollers at loading points. The roller specifications are given in Table C.25.

Wheel Conveyors

Wheel conveyors find many uses for handling packages in food plants. They are very adaptable because of their lightweight and portability in storage rooms and in truck loading and unloading operations. Most manufacturers will produce both aluminum and steel frames. A typical comparison of the capacities of the two types of wheel conveyor frames are shown in Table C.26.

Approximately 20 different wheel patterns are available from most manufacturers. Special patterns for specific carrying needs determine the wheel spacing of a wheel conveyor. Some of the more common wheel patterns are illustrated in Fig. C.30.

Principles and Practices

In selecting conveyors of the two basic types, gravity and power, comparison factors may be listed as follows:

Gravity	Power
Lower initial cost	Higher cost
Limitations for elevation	Positive drive
Lightweight	Can be designed for variety of service
Often portable	More maintenance
Electric power not necessary	
Suitable for live storage	

In choosing the proper conveyor, such factors as flexibility, safety, labor saving, suitability for the entire system, and overall satisfactory service should be considered. A conveyor must suit the specific needs relative to roller spacing and wheel spacing.

In calculating the capacity of roller conveyors, divide the weight of the commodity with the greatest weight per length ratio for the number of rollers supporting the package. The importance of roller spacing is illustrated in Fig. C.31.

The inclines of gravity roller conveyor systems are very important for successful operation. In Table C.27, the pitch recommendations for various commodities are given. All conveyors require proper installation and maintenance. Proper and regular lubrication are essential. Quite often when trouble occurs, one may use a trouble-shooting chart such as Table C.28 for chain-type conveyors. Central lubrication systems are satisfactory and easier to operate and control than manual control of several stations.

References

E. W. BUSCHMAN Co. Engineering data book, *60B*. Cincinnati, Ohio.

FARRALL, A. W. 1963. Dairy and Food Products Engineering, 3rd Edition. John Wiley & Sons, New York.

MILK INDUSTRY FOUNDATION. 1967. Manual for Milk Plant Operators, 3rd Edition. Washington, D.C.

MOLINE MALLEABLE IRON, INC. Conveyor Chain Manual Design Engineers' Handbook. St. Charles, Ill.

THE RAPIDS-STANDARD Co. Rapid Wheel Conveyor, Cat. *5*. Grand Rapids, Mich.

Cross-references: *Drum Handling; Lubricants; Materials Handling.*

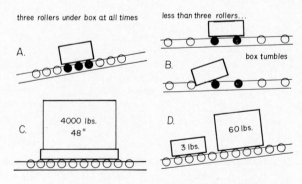

Courtesy of E. W. Buschman Co.

FIG. C-31.   Spacing and loading of conveyor
A and B—Minimum length package determines spacing of rollers;   C and D—
Maximum load per ft determines size of rollers.

TABLE C.25

ROLLER SPECIFICATIONS AND LOAD RATINGS

Roller Diameter, In.	Axle Size, In.	Bearing Type	Load Rating
1	$1/4$ Hex.	Plain	85
$1^5/_{16}$	$3/8$ Hex.	Plain	150
$1^3/_8$	$1/4$ Hex.	Plain integral	90
$1^3/_4$	$7/_{16}$ Hex.	Plain	270
$1^3/_4$	$7/_{16}$ Hex.	Dustproof	270
$1^3/_4$	$7/_{16}$ Hex.	Grease packed for life	270
$1^3/_4$	$7/_{16}$ Hex.	Grease packed, Teflon seal	270
$1^3/_4$	$7/_{16}$ Hex.	Pressure lubricated	270
$1^3/_4$	$1/_2$ Rd.	Oilite bronze	300
1.9	$3/8$ Hex.	Plain integral	170
1.9	$7/_{16}$ Hex.	Plain	270
1.9	$7/_{16}$ Hex.	Dustproof	270
1.9	$7/_{16}$ Hex.	Grease packed for life	270
1.9	$7/_{16}$ Hex.	Grease packed, Teflon seal	270
1.9	$7/_{16}$ Hex.	Pressure lubricated	270
1.9	$1/_2$ Rd.	Oilite bronze	300
2	$7/_{16}$ Hex.	Plain	270
2	$7/_{16}$ Hex.	Dustproof	270
2	$7/_{16}$ Hex.	Grease packed for life	270
2	$7/_{16}$ Hex.	Grease packed, Teflon seal	270
2	$7/_{16}$ Hex.	Pressure lubricated	270
2	$1/_2$ Rd.	Oilite bronze	300
$2^1/_4$	$3/8$ Hex.	Plain integral	180
$2^1/_4$	$7/_{16}$ Hex.	Plain	280
$2^1/_4$	$7/_{16}$ Hex.	Dustproof	280
$2^1/_4$	$7/_{16}$ Hex.	Grease packed for life	280
$2^1/_4$	$7/_{16}$ Hex.	Grease packed, Teflon seal	280
$2^1/_4$	$7/_{16}$ Hex.	Pressure lubricated	280
$2^1/_4$	$1/_2$ Rd.	Oilite bronze	300
$2^1/_2$	$7/_{16}$ Hex.	Plain integral	180
$2^1/_2$	$7/_{16}$ Hex.	Plain	290
$2^1/_2$	$7/_{16}$ Hex.	Dustproof	290
$2^1/_2$	$7/_{16}$ Hex.	Grease packed for life	290
$2^1/_2$	$7/_{16}$ Hex.	Grease packed, Teflon seal	280
$2^1/_2$	$7/_{16}$ Hex.	Pressure lubricated	280
$2^1/_2$	$1/_2$ Rd.	Oilite bronze	300
$2^1/_2$	$11/_{16}$ Hex.	Plain	575
$2^1/_2$	$11/_{16}$ Hex.	Dustproof	575
$2^1/_2$	$11/_{16}$ Hex.	Grease packed for life	575
$2^1/_2$	$11/_{16}$ Hex.	Pressure lubricated	575
$2^9/_{16}$	$11/_{16}$ Hex.	Plain	575
$2^9/_{16}$	$11/_{16}$ Hex.	Dustproof	575
$2^9/_{16}$	$11/_{16}$ Hex.	Grease packed for life	575
$2^9/_{16}$	$11/_{16}$ Hex.	Pressure lubricated	575
$3^1/_2$	$11/_{16}$ Hex.	Plain	680
$3^1/_2$	$11/_{16}$ Hex.	Dustproof	680
$3^1/_2$	$11/_{16}$ Hex.	Grease packed for life	680
$3^1/_2$	$11/_{16}$ Hex.	Pressure lubricated	680

TABLE C.25 (*Continued*)

Roller Diameter, In.	Axle Size, In.	Bearing Type	Load Rating
3¹/₂	1¹/₁₆ Hex.	Plain	1,700
3¹/₂	1¹/₁₆ Hex.	Dustproof	1,700
3¹/₂	1¹/₁₆ Hex.	Grease packed for life	1,700
3¹/₂	1¹/₁₆ Hex.	Pressure lubricated	1,700

Source: E. W. Buschman Co.

TABLE C.26

MAXIMUM TOTAL CAPACITIES[1] OF CONVEYOR FRAMES, LB

Type of Conveyor	5-Ft Section	10-Ft Section	10-Ft Section Supported on 5-Ft Centers
Steel Frame 2¹/₂ In. Channel	1600	800	3200
Steel Frame 3¹/₂ In. Channel	2000	1000	4000
Steel Frame 4 In. Channel ("Low" wheels only)	2500	1250	5000
Aluminum Frame 2¹/₂ In. Channel	1050	525	2100
Aluminum Frame 3¹/₂ In. Channel	1470	735	2940

[1] Distributed load capacity using entire length of section.
Source: Rapistan.

COOLING MILK AND OTHER LIQUIDS

To control the growth of bacteria, raw milk is cooled immediately after milking on the farm. After reaching the processing plant it is usually cooled a few degrees in the storage tank prior to processing. Following pasteurization, milk is again cooled and held at a low temperature until consumed. Milk is often cooled in the final package since it is exposed to warm temperatures during distribution. In all, milk is frequently cooled 3 to 5 times during handling and processing.

Factors Affecting Cooling

Milk and other fluid products have a variable specific heat with a maximum at 67°F. The specific heat of whole milk is between 0.93 and 0.94 at 67°F. Skim milk has a specific heat of 0.95. The specific heat of cream possessing various amounts of butterfat is compared with those for whole milk, whey, and water in Fig. C.32.

Can Coolers

When milk and juices which have been cooled over a surface cooler, the cans might be placed in a dry-refrigerated storage. If the product has not been cooled over a surface cooler, the rate of heat loss from a can in dry storage is too slow, since the loss amounts to about a 5°F temperature drop in the first hour after storage in a 50°F room.   The cans may be placed in refrigerated water in tanks known as immersion coolers.   Water is normally used in immersion coolers and such water can be from a spring, well, or cooled by ice or by mechanical refrigeration systems.   To get milk to 50°F or lower in 2 hr after milking, it is necessary to use mechanical refrigeration with agitation or stirring of the water.   Approximately 1 to 1.5 kwh of electricity is required per can of milk per day, for cooling to 45° to 50°F.   The refrigeration capacity must be capable of removing the heat.   Insulation should be provided in the box so that the water extends above the milk level, and about 1.5 to 1.67 gal. of water storage for each gallon of milk are required to get adequate cooling.   The water may be circulated by the propeller, by pump, or by air agitation.

Rapid cooling of liquid products in containers is obtained with units which spray cold water that provides essentially rapid agitation of the cooling medium over the surface of the can.   With these units, doors can be provided at floor level of the cooler so that it is not necessary to lift the cans for moving into or out of the cooler.   From the operational standpoint the holes which distribute the cold water over the surface of the cans should be checked to make sure that water is uniformly distributed.   Scale, straw, soil, and other impurities tend to clog these openings.

To cool four 10-gal. cans of milk per day from 92° to 42°F requires a $1/_3$ hp motor on a mechanical refrigeration compressor, and from 40 to 60 ft of $1/_2$ in. diam copper tubing for coil.   Approximately a 10°F temperature difference occurs between the bottom and top of a 10-gal. can during cooling with the warmest milk at the top.   Stirring the milk mechanically will increase the rate of cooling and decrease the temperature difference between the top and bottom.   When handled in cans, warm fresh

TABLE C.27

INCLINES FOR ROLLER CONVEYORS

	Approx. Inches of Drop Per Foot	
Object Conveyed and Approx. Weight	Plain or Dustproof Ball Bearing In.	Grease-Packed Ball Bearing In.
Cartons—1 to 5 lb	$7/_8$	
Cartons—5 to 15 lb	$3/_4$	
Cartons—15 to 50 lb	$5/_8$	$3/_4$
Empty milk cans—18 to 25 lb	$5/_8$	1
Wood cases—20 to 50 lb	$1/_2$	$3/_4$
Baskets with wood runners—50 to 70 lb	$1/_2$	$3/_4$
Cartons—50 to 75 lb	$1/_2$	$3/_4$
Lumber (std. boards)	$1/_2$	$3/_4$
Wood cases—50 to 150 lb	$7/_{16}$	$5/_8$
Milk cans (Full)—75 to 100 lb	$7/_{16}$	$5/_8$
Steel and wood beverage cases (Full)	$7/_{16}$	$5/_8$
Wood cases—150 to 200 lb	$3/_8$	$5/_8$
Steel drums (empty)—50 to 100 lb	$3/_8$	$5/_8$
Steel tote boxes (smooth riding surface) 15 to 50 lb	$3/_8$	$5/_8$
Steel oil drums (smooth bottom) 300 to 750 lb	$5/_{16}$	$1/_2$
Tote pans—50 to 100 lb	$7/_{16}$	$5/_8$
Tote pans—100 to 250 lb	$3/_8$	$1/_2$
Tote pans—250 to 500 lb	$5/_{16}$	$7/_{16}$

TABLE C.28

TROUBLE-SHOOTING CHART FOR CHAINS

Symptoms	Causes	Remedies
Excessive noise	Misalignment	Check alignment and correct
	Too little or too much slack	Adjust chain centers for proper slack
	No or improper lubrication	Lubricate
	Loose casings or bearings	Draw up all bolts and brace casings if necessary
	Chain or sprockets worn	Reverse[1] or replace if necessary
	Excessive speed	Consider shorter pitch chain or larger sprocket
Wear on chain, sidebars, and sides of teeth	Misalignment	Remove chain and correct alignment of the sprockets and shafts
Chain climbs sprockets	Poorly fitting sprockets	Turn sprockets and chain[1] or replace if necessary
	Severe overloads	Reduce load if possible, lubricate to reduce operating friction
	Chain worn overlength	Replace with a new chain
Broken pins and rollers	Chain speed too high for pitch	Use chain with shorter pitch of equivalent or greater strength
	Shock or suddenly applied loads	Avoid shocks, easy starts give long life
	Corrosion fatigue	Use plated or corrosion resistant materials, improve lubrication
Chain clings to sprockets	Incorrect or worn sprockets	Turn sprockets and chains[1] or replace if necessary
	Heavy and tacky lubricants	Clean chains and sprockets and lubricate correctly
	Sprocket may be oversize	
Chain whip	Long centers or high pulsating loads	Reduce centers when possible
	Too much slack	Install chain take-up, idler sprocket or wooden runway
Chain gets stiff	Misalignment	Check alignment and correct, replace damaged chain
	Improve lubrication	Remove chain, clean and relubricate
	Excessive overloads	Reduce load when possible
	Corrosion	
	Material packed or frozen in joints	Protect chain with case if possible, or clean and relubricate regularly
Broken sprocket teeth	Obstruction or foreign material in chain case	Check chain clearances
		Drain and clean chain case
Cotters come out	Vibration and centrifugal force	Turn chain over so heads of cotters are on inside nearest shafts

[1] Reverse chain only if it does not have rollers. May be of help with roller chain when OD of bushings is worn.

Source: Moline Malleable Iron Co.

milk should not be mixed with cold milk, because the addition of the warm milk raises the temperature and hastens bacterial growth and might induce rancidity.

Immersion or spray coolers holding from 1 to 16 cans are available which have motors on the mechanical compressors from $1/4$ to 2 hp and an electrical requirement of about 1 kwh per 10-gal. can. For an immersion tank a water to milk ratio of 5 to 1 is preferred.

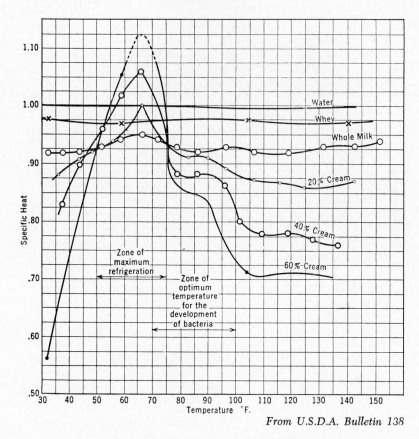

From U.S.D.A. Bulletin 138

Fɪɢ. C-32.　The specific heat of milk products

Bulk Milk Coolers

Bulk milk handling developed first on the West Coast early in the 1940's. Early in the 1950's the dairy regions of the Midwest began to adopt bulk milk handling on the smaller farms as compared to those in areas of the West. New tanks were specially-designed and about 15 to 20 manufacturers now make refrigerated bulk milk tanks. These tanks are used for various liquid products.

The 3-A standards have been established to aid manufacturers in developing a piece of equipment that would be easy to clean and which would also establish certain minimum standards of performance. Tanks meeting the 3-A standards must cool milk to 50°F within 1 hr, and to 40°F within 2 hr after milking. A period of 1.5 hr is provided for placing milk in the tank in not less than 5 equal increments evenly spaced. According to the above standards, for an everyday tank, the unit must cool $1/_2$ of the tank capacity and for an every-other-day tank, the unit must cool $1/_4$ of the tank capacity. Some States have adopted cooling requirements more stringent than these requiring the product be cooled to 45°F within 1 hr after milking. In some areas it is also required that the milk not exceed 50°F when warm milk is added (known as the blend temperature) to the tank at the following milking. Milk is normally held below 40°F.

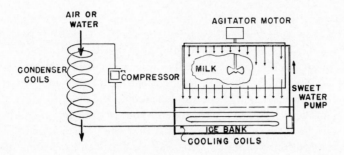

a. ICE BANK

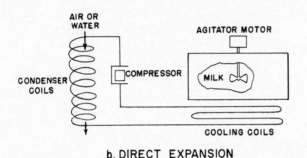

b. DIRECT EXPANSION

FIG. C-33.   Ice bank and direct expansion bulk tank

Classification of Tanks

Tanks may be classified according to their method of refrigeration: direct expansion or ice bank. With the direct expansion system the product is cooled directly by the cooling coils which extend around the bottom of the tank. With the ice bank system, a bank of ice is frozen around coils and water is circulated around the ice bank and around the tank to cool the milk. Some tanks are cooled by a combination of these two methods (Fig. C.33).

Tanks may be classified according to the regularity of pickup: everyday (ED), or every-other-day (EOD). The every-other-day pickup tanks predominate, although in many areas even though the routes are every-other-day pickup, every-day tanks are used to assure that the tanks have adequate refrigeration capacity for the milk that might be placed in them.

Tanks may be classified as atmospheric or vacuum tanks which latter tanks are often used with pipeline milking systems.

The size of the tank is designated in gallons capacity when full. It is difficult to select the proper size of tank because usually a dairyman will increase production after converting to bulk handling. The most common size is from 250 to 500 gal. in the Midwest, although 2,500 gal. tanks are used. For irregular milk production, the tank should be chosen on the basis of the peak production. For every-other-day, the tank should be 2.5 times the daily peak production. With a daily peak production of 100 gal., the tank should be 150 gal. for every-day, and 250 gal. for every-other-day pickup.

Bulk handling systems normally have a higher initial cost than can handling systems. Not only an additional cost for the tank is involved, but the milkhouse will require a major remodeling for about 20% of the farms.

The possibilities of increased return to justify the added cost of a bulk system are as follows: (1) gains for measuring milk on the farm, (2) elimination of can cost, (3) savings in hauling costs, and (4) premiums paid by the plant for bulk milk.

The ice bank type has a refrigeration compressor and motor unit which operate several hours per day—up to 20. During this time the ice bank is built which is available for subsequent cooling of milk. Off-peak electricity, if available, may be used for building the ice bank. With the direct expansion system, the cooling must be done by the compressor during filling and after milking which reduces the number of hours for cooling. Thus, the compressor motor is larger for a direct expansion than for the ice bank system. The direct expansion system is usually more costly than the ice bank, but does not require as much electricity for cooling (Table C.29).

TABLE C.29

CHARACTERISTICS OF TWO TYPES OF BULK MILK TANKS

Item	Direct Expansion (DX)	Ice Bank (Sweetwater) (IB)
Inner milk liner cooled by	Refrigerant (Freon)	Chilled water
Size of compressor, per 100 gal. of milk daily	$2/3$ to 1 hp	$1/3$ to $1/2$ hp
Electric motors for operating unit	Compressor, agitator	Compressor, agitator, chilled water pump
Hours of operation per day	3 to 6	12 to 20
Electrical requirements, kwh per 100 lb, EOD[1]	0.80 to 1.1	1.3 to 1.6
Original cost	Usually higher for capacities under 500 gal.	Usually lower for capacities under 500 gal.

[1] Every-other-day pickup.
Source: Hall (1963).

Agitator

An agitator is provided for thorough mixing of the product and to achieve a fast rate of cooling. There are many different agitator designs. Agitators normally run 30 to 50 rpm and are powered with a $1/8$ to 1 hp electric motor. They may be two-speed, multiple-speed, or variable speed. The agitator normally runs slow, but where quick agitation before emptying the tank is required by the tanker driver, the fast speed is used. Complete agitation should be provided in 3 to 5 min. The agitator will normally run when the compressor runs for the direct expansion tanks or when the circulating water pump operates for the ice bank tanks. Because of the infrequent amount of operation required after the milk is cooled, stratification will often occur with the lower temperature on the bottom and higher temperature on the top where the butterfat accumulates. To prevent the stratification some milksheds require that a time clock be used to operate the agitator periodically.

Agitation should not splash milk onto the lid of the bulk tank cooler. Some agitators have two sections, one at the bottom and one at the top to help avoid splashing. Milk splashed on the top tends to cake, is not refrigerated, and is not easily washed from the tank. Agitation should not be so violent that the butterfat globules clump together. If the agitator runs too rapidly, churning will result and flakes of butterfat or butter may be noted in the tank.

Some agitators are provided with a variable speed drive or motor which can be operated at the desirable speed for regular mixing, rapid mixing, or for use in cleaning the tank.

Electrical Requirements

The cost of electricity for operating a bulk tank depends upon (1) the type of tank, (2) whether the tank is air or water cooled, or features combined air-water cooling, (3) whether the tank has an air-water cooled condenser, and (4) the air temperature with an air-cooled condenser. There is a close relationship of cost of operation and the season of the year. If water is available for cooling the condenser at a low cost, and of good quality which will not cause excessive scaling, the use of water or air-water condenser is recommended. From 0.8 to 1.1 kwh per 100 lb of milk are required for direct expansion and from 0.9 to 1.3 kwh per 100 lb for the ice bank tanks for every-other-day pickup. A part of the electricity for the ice bank tank can be purchased on off-peak rates, and it is quite possible that the cost of electricity would be about the same as the direct expansion unit which used a lower amount of electricity. Caution must be exercised in operating an ice bank tank on off-peak, because in some cases the tank might not build sufficient ice to cool the milk during the following loading.

Good ventilation must be provided for an air-cooled condenser to keep the refrigeration costs to a minimum. Approximately 500 cfm of air are required for each 1 hp driving the compressor. A water-cooled condenser requires from 1.5 to 2.5 gal. of water for each 1 gal. of milk to be cooled. Electrical costs can be reduced about 15% by using water cooling, as compared to air cooling. Air-cooled units are available up to approximately 5 hp, and water-cooled units are normally available beginning at 2 hp.

Installation of Bulk Tank

A clearance of 2 ft around the sides of the tank and 3 ft at the outlet end is usually required. The milkhouse should have a door which can be opened up to 4 ft wide for moving the tank into the milkhouse. The required clearance around the tanks will vary in different milksheds so it is important to check with local authorities. A 230 v electrical outlet should be provided for the bulk tank, an electric water heater, and the truck tanker pump. The bulk tank is calibrated at the factory and a graduated stick is provided for determining the quantity of milk. Quantity determinations are made with the tank in a level position. Levels of various types, including bullseye, plumb bob, and scribe marks on the tank, help in getting the tank near a level position. It is necessary to check the calibration of the tank by placing water in the tank, usually in 5-gal. increments. A tank must be installed and kept level in the milkhouse. A floor is required which will withstand the concentrated load. A desirable floor will consist of a layer of 12 in. of gravel or crushed rock covered with 5 in. of concrete, reinforced with No. 6 wire installed near the bottom of the floor. An opening about 8 in. by 8 in. must be provided in the wall for extending the hose from the tanker. In some areas the opening must be 3 ft above the ground level.

Quantity

The quantity of milk in the tank is determined by reading the graduated rod and referring to a calibration chart. The graduated rod may be divided into increments from $1/64$ to $1/4$ in. Care must be exercised in reading the amount of milk in the tank. Attempts have been made to use milk meters. No meter is available which provides the accuracy required for bulk tank pickup on the farm. The principal difficulty encountered in existing meters is the incorporation of air at the beginning and at the end of the metering cycle. Foam eliminators are being developed to improve the accuracy of metering devices.

Surface gages are also used to determine the quantity of product. A surface gage provides a method of measuring by moving a rod until it touches the surface of a product, from which a reading is taken at a fixed point. One unit utilizes two electrodes which, when both make contact with electrical current going through, will light a small lamp, making it quite easy to determine accurately the elevation of milk in the tank. Tanks are calibrated on the basis of 8.60 or 8.61 lb per gal. of milk. The tolerance for farm bulk tanks ranges from 0.2 to 0.5% of the volume of milk in the tank, depending upon the size of the tank.

The acceptable tolerance for measuring the gallons in a bulk milk tank for (1) 500 gal. or less tank is plus or minus 1 gal.; (2) 501 to 1,000 gal., plus or minus 2 gal.; and (3) 1,001 to 1,500 gal., plus or minus 3 gal. On a particular tank the acceptable tolerances applied shall not be smaller than the smallest volume corresponding to a graduate interval at any point on the gage rod or surface gage.

In general, the tanker driver is responsible for rinsing the tank and the farmer is responsible for cleaning and sanitizing. Because the tank is refrigerated, there is some question regarding the necessity of rinsing the tank after milk is removed.

Cooling in the Processing Plant

Milk transferred to the dairy plant may or may not pass through a plate-type heat exchanger while being transferred to a raw milk storage tank to await processing. Some plants rely on the temperature of the incoming raw milk to be sufficiently low so as to require no further cooling. Raw milk will generally be received below 42°F. For long periods of storage of up to 72 hr, the temperature should be lowered to about 34° or 35°F. This may be done with a cold-wall tank if a plate heat exchanger is not used. The cold wall may be refrigerated with direct expansion ammonia, Freon, or ice water. In purchasing a new raw milk storage tank, the plant operator should consider one having cooling capability. Surface type heat exchangers are also used.

Most modern plants use the high-temperature short-time pasteurization system consisting of a plate-type heat exchanger. This unit utilizes regeneration to accomplish about 75 to 80% of the temperature reduction after pasteurization. The plate unit will often have an overall U-value of 300 to 400. Final cooling of the pasteurized product is accomplished in the cooler section of the press. The coolant in most cases is refrigerated water. The ratio of water to milk volume in the cooler section may vary from about 3:1 to 6:1. Ice water will usually lower the temperature of whole milk to about 37°F in an efficient plate cooler section. In certain cases, the operator may choose to use propylene glycol instead of refrigerated water to reach lower final temperatures. The propylene glycol in this case is recirculated through a direct expansion heat exchanger for cooling. Brine also accomplishes the same purpose; however, the tendency to corrode pipe lines and equipment is a disadvantage.

A few modern plants are utilizing direct expansion tubular coolers to achieve final cooling of milk after the product leaves the regenerator. This equipment usually employs an ammonia circulating pump which sprays the tubes with chilled refrigerant. Temperatures just above freezing are obtainable with this type of equipment.

Another method of cooling is achieved in a number of plants through flash cooling equipment. This is the result of developing a vacuum on a chamber for removal of undesirable odors in the product. The amount of cooling will depend upon the temperature entering the vacuum chamber and the absolute pressure maintained in the chamber. If milk is steam treated to elevate the temperature to about 200°F, flash cooling may be in the range of 30° to 40°F.

Cooling in the Package

Whole milk and other fluid dairy products are generally cooled a few degrees after packing in the refrigerated room. Freshly washed glass bottles, as well as cartons, formed immediately before filling, will generally be higher in temperature than the product. This results in an increase in temperature making cooling in the final package desirable. Air should be circulated in the cooled storage room and the refrigerating capacity of the evaporator coil and condensing unit should be carefully sized for adequacy. Good refrigerated storage and maintaining the product at a temperature within 3° or 4°F above freezing help measurably in the control of psychrophilic bacteria, thereby, increasing shelf-life.

References

FARRALL, A. W. 1963. Engineering for Dairy and Food Products, 3rd Edition. John Wiley & Sons, New York.

HALL, C. W. 1963. Processing Equipment for Agricultural Products. Edwards Brothers, Ann Arbor, Mich.

MILK INDUSTRY FOUNDATION. 1967. Manual for Milk Plant Operators, 3rd Edition. Washington, D.C.

Cross-references: *Bulk Tanker; Cryogenic; Heat Exchanger; Heating Systems for HTST.*

COOLING POWDER

Warm powder, such as that coming from the dryer, may hold heat for some time, particularly if placed in a container. Prolonged heating may cause damage and a decrease in quality of the product. The k-value for dry products is about 0.15 to 0.25 Btu per bu sq ft °F per ft. Some cooling will take place in the dryer if an air brush is used to remove the product. Three principles of cooling the product outside the dryer are: (1) conduction cooling in which the product is cooled in a water jacketed screw conveyor; (2) convection cooling where room air or refrigerated air is used to cool to 100°F, or by moving conditioned air over the product or through the conveyor handling the product; and (3) radiation cooling in which a cold evaporator surface is placed in view of the warm product. This method has not been exploited by the dry milk industry.

The outlet of a cyclone separator can be surrounded by a chamber through which cold air is moved to cool the product. The material moves on to an entrainment separator for separation of solids and air. A vibratory conveyor for moving dry powder permits cooling as the product moves through the surrounding air.

Oxygen can be removed more easily from warm powder than cold, when an inert gas, such as nitrogen, is used for packaging.

The amount of heat to be removed is given in Btu by multiplying the specific heat by the weight (in pounds) times the difference in temperature (°F). A specific heat of approximately 0.25 to 0.28 Btu per °F lb may be used for dry milk powder. The density of drum-dried milk is 0.3 to 0.5 gm per ml, and for spray-dried milk is 0.5 to 0.6 gm per ml. The true density of nonfat dry milk is 1.4 to 1.5 gm per ml. Some drying occurs in the cooling process. About $^1/_3$ to $^1/_2$ of the heat removed in the cooling process is used in vaporizing water. Thus 2,000 Btu will remove about 1 lb of water.

Reference

HALL, C. W., and HEDRICK, T. I. 1966. Drying of Milk and Milk Products. AVI Publishing Co., Westport, Conn.

Cross-references: *Heat and Mass Transfer; Droplets; Heat Transfer.*

COPPER

Copper is one of the most useful metals in industry. It is nonmagnetic, has high ductility, high electrical conductivity, relatively high resistance to corrosion in most atmospheres, and is easily formed and soldered.

Copper has an electrode potential of 0.344, which is lower than tin, and is therefore protected by tin.

Copper has been widely used in the food industry for making pans and kettles. It has been very largely displaced by stainless steel because stainless steel is more inert and therefore causes less flavor problems with food products.

For many years when considerable copper was used, it was found that if the copper surface was kept polished and scrupulously cleaned, the flavor effect was minimized. The modern food industry stores food longer and today people are more sensitive to off-flavors, therefore, wherever possible stainless steel is used in contact with the product.

Copper is very useful for conducting fluids of a nonfood nature such as in pipes or tubes used for water and air. Copper is very rapidly attacked by ammonia and ammonia fumes.

Copper alloys are used in plates and in bearings. It is by far the most used material for conducting electricity.

Properties

The properties of annealed copper are as follows: relative electrical resistance near 20°C = 1; temperature coefficient of resistivity near 20°C per °C is 0.00393; density (gm per cm³) at 20°C = 8.89; thermal conductivity near 20°C = 3.91; melting point = 1083°C.

The ASTM specifications for properties of copper wire are shown in Table C.30.

TABLE C.30

ASTM PROPERTIES OF COPPER WIRE

Diam-In.	Hard Drawn Wire		Medium Drawn Wire			Soft Annealed Wire	
	Tensile Strength, Min.	Elongation % in 60 In. Min.	Tensile Strength Psi		Elongation % in 60 In. Min.	Tensile Strength Psi Max.	Elongation % in 10 In. Min.
			Min.	Max.			
0.460	49,000	3.75[1]	42,000	49,000	3.75[1]	36,000	35
0.325	54,500	2.40[1]	45,000	52,000	3.00[1]	36,000	35
0.229	59,000	1.79[1]	48,000	55,000	2.25[1]	36,000	35
0.162	62,100	1.14	49,000	56,000	1.15	37,000	30
0.114	64,300	1.02	50,000	57,000	1.06	37,000	30
0.081	65,700	0.95	51,000	58,000	1.00	38,500	25
0.057	66,400	0.89	52,000	59,000	0.94	38,500	25
0.040	67,000	0.85	53,000	60,000	0.88	38,500	25
Electrical Resistivity Ohms (mile pound)	910.15		905.44[2]			891.58	
Micro ohms per cm cube	1.7930		1.7837			1.7544	

[1] Elongation in 10 in. gage length.
[2] On wire below 0.324 in. diam, 896.15 for larger wire.
Source: Based on ASTM Specifications.

Alloys

Copper is one of the most useful alloying metals. Copper is used in making brass, bronze, and many other useful alloys. Many of the uses of copper alloys involve plates, tubes, and castings. Table C.31 shows the values of allowable working stresses for nonferrous materials as recommended by ASTM unfired pressure vessel code.

Reference

MARKS, L. S. 1958. Mechanical Engineers Handbook, 6th Edition. McGraw-Hill Book Co., New York.

CORROSION

A protective or passive layer will build up on clean, dry stainless steel surfaces exposed to air (oxygen). The protective layer may be removed by erosion caused by the product, scratching of the surface during cleaning, action of strong chemicals, or a flow of electric current. The flow of electricity may be due either to dissimilar metals or stray electric currents. Corrosion of the active stainless steel may occur if the protective layer is removed. The proper care of stainless steel consists of minimizing the possibility of removal of the protective layer, as follows.

(1) Remove accumulated products from plates after use at the end of each operation.
(2) Avoid circulating a cleaning solution which is stronger than recommended for

TABLE C.31

MAXIMUM ALLOWABLE WORKING STRESSES FOR NONFERRIC MATERIALS

ASME Unfired Pressure Vessel Code, Table U.4 (Condensed)

Material	Equivalent ASTM Specification	Stresses, Psi for Temperatures Not Exceeding °F					
		Up to 150	250	350	400	450	500
Muntz metal condenser	B 43-33	5,000	4,000	2,500			
Tubes and brass pipe	B 111-37 T						
Red brass tubes	B 43-33	6,000	5,500	5,000	4,500		
Copper plates, tubes and pipe	B 11-33 B 13-33 B 42-33	6,000	5,000	4,500	4,000		
Admirality condenser Tubes and pipe	B 43-33 B 111-37 T	7,000	6,500	6,000	5,500	4,500	
Copper-silicon alloy Plates types A and C	B 96-36 T	10,000	10,000	5,000			
Monel annealed tup 70,000 psi tensile	B 98-36 T	14,000	14,000	14,000		13,500	13,000
Cast steam bronze 88-6-1.5-4.5	B 61-36	6,800	6,300	5,800	5,400	5,000	4,200
Cast steam bronze 85-5-5.5 (ounce metal)	B 62-36	5,500	5,000	4,500	3,500		
Cupronickle (70/30 and 80/20)	B 111-37 T	10,000	10,000	9,000	8,400	7,500	6,300

longer than necessary. Rinse cleaning solution from plates. (3) Remove rust particles which might be carried over from steam, cold water, and water remaining on the surface. (4) Separate heat transfer plates and leave open to provide complete drainage and exposure to air. (5) Keep the brine which contacts stainless steel neutral or slightly alkali. Test weekly. The brine should be at a pH between 7.5 and 8.0. If the brine is too strongly acid, due usually to carbon dioxide from the air mixing into the brine, add a solution of caustic soda to neutralize. If the brine solution is too alkaline from other than dissolved ammonia, add sodium dichromate to neutralize. (6) Wash brine off plates at the end of each day's operation. Leave plates exposed to air to rebuild the passive layer.

Cross-references: *Brine; Can Washers; CIP Systems; EMF Series; Stainless Steel.*

CRYOGENICS

The cryogenic industry dates to about 1906 when Carl Von Linde, Hampson, and Claude independently developed techniques for the liquefaction of air. Air was first liquified in smaller quantities in 1885 by Dewar in England and Olszewski in Poland when both men used the cascade evaporation system. About 20 yr later low temperature liquification of air was done commercially.

Principles

Cryogenic engineering has been employed to separate various elements in air and other gaseous mixtures. Hydrogen and helium are commonly liquified for industrial process.

In the food industry liquid carbon dioxide and liquid nitrogen are finding broader acceptance for cooling food products and refrigerated spaces. The use of these products as a refrigerant achieves rapid freezing rates and may produce desirable effects for the food product. For example, the color of poultry meat improved with a rapid chill in liquid nitrogen. Rhubarb has been rapidly frozen with carbon dioxide resulting in a very acceptable product.

In very low temperature cooling, the paramagnetic and diamagnetic materials are used. Paramagnetic materials are attracted to a magnetic pole, whereas diamagnetic materials are repelled. When some of the paramagnetic materials are cooled to low temperatures their molecular motion nearly stops. These particles are usually not subjected to a strong magnetic field and then demagnetized. The demagnetization of the material reduces the temperature of the region about it. The result is called adiabatic cooling. In cryogenic engineering, when extremely low temperatures are desired, the cooling is accomplished in stages to achieve greater economy. In the first stage a paramagnetic material may be chilled by evaporating liquid helium. This is followed by applying a strong magnetic field to the material. The next stage involves extraction of the helium gas while maintaining the material under a strong magnetic field. The fourth stage involves demagnetization of the material which produces very low temperatures. The method of magnetic cooling is used extensively in the liquefaction of helium. Frequently, in commercial practice the use of ammonia or Freon-12 is employed to accomplish the first step of precooling. The boiling point temperature, freezing point, critical temperature, latent heat, and other qualities of several cryogens are given in Table C.32.

Applications

Liquid nitrogen is receiving considerable attention for refrigerating truck bodies used to transport food products at temperatures above freezing. Several milk truck bodies are refrigerated with liquid nitrogen controlled by a thermostat to maintain a set temperature of about 38°F. A typical liquid nitrogen refrigerating system for a truck body is shown in Fig. C.34 (see also Fig. N.2). Low temperature truck boxes used for transporting frozen foods and ice cream are also being refrigerated through the direct injection of liquid nitrogen. To avoid loss of gas, a truck body in good condition is recommended. Some cost values have been compared using the traditional compression gas system versus a cryogenic system for long and short distance hauling. In the study conducted by the Transportation and Facilities Branch of the U.S. Dept. of Agr., mechanical refrigeration was considered to be somewhat less costly than liquid carbon dioxide refrigeration. Semitrailers were used in the study and the cost per trip was determined to be $138.00 higher for carbon dioxide refrigerated trailers than for conventional units. The trailers were carried piggy back for 18 trips between Pueblo, Colo., and Philadelphia, Pa. Each contained 26,000 lb of frozen meat. The trailer equipped with CO_2 cooling had a heat transmission rate of 7,350 Btu per hr. Improvements in truck body construction will probably help in lowering costs of cryogenic cooling methods.

The use of liquid nitrogen for freezing poultry products, shrimp, certain vegetables, and meats appears to be quite practical and desirable from the production

TABLE C.32

DATA ON CRYOGENS

Argon (A)

Boiling point, normal, °F	−302.6
Freezing point, °F	−309.0
Critical temp., °F	−187.5
Critical pressure at critical temp., psia	705.0
Vol. at 70°F and at atmospheric, cu ft per lb	9.67
Molecular weight	40.0
Liquid density, normal, lb per cu ft	87.0
Latent heat, Btu per lb	70.0
Gas density at 70°F and 14.7 psia	0.1034

Deuterium (D₂)

Boiling point, normal, °F	−417.4
Freezing point, °F	−426.0
Critical temp., °F	−391.0
Critical pressure at critical temp, psia	239.0
Vol. at 70°F and at atmospheric, cu ft per lb	96.0
Molecular weight	4.0
Liquid density, normal, lb per cu ft	10.7
Latent heat, Btu per lb	135.0
Gas density at 70°F and 14.7 psia	0.0104

Ethane (C₂H₆)

Boiling point, normal, °F	−127.6
Freezing point, °F	−297.9
Critical temp., °F	+ 90.1
Critical pressure at critical temp., psia	708.0
Vol. at 70°F and at atmospheric, cu ft per lb	12.77
Molecular weight	30.1
Liquid density, normal, lb per cu ft	33.8
Latent heat, Btu per lb	209.8
Gas density at 70°F and 14.7 psia	0.0783

Ethylene (C₂H₄) Refr. 1150

Boiling point, normal, °F	−154.8
Freezing point, °F	−272.5
Critical temp., °F	49.1
Critical pressure at critical temp., psia	735.0
Molecular weight	28.05
Liquid density, normal, lb per cu ft	35.2
Latent heat, Btu per lb	207.4
Gas density at 70°F and 14.7 psia	0.729

Fluorine (F₂)

Boiling point, normal, °F	−306.6
Freezing point, °F	−363.0
Critical temp., °F	−200.0
Critical pressure at critical temp., psia	807.0
Vol. at 70°F and atmospheric, cu ft per lb	12.4
Molecular weight	38.0
Liquid density, normal, lb per cu ft	93.8
Latent heat, Btu per lb	74.0
Gas density at 70°F and 14.7 psia	0.0983

Helium (He)

Boiling point, normal, °F	−452.10
Freezing point, °F	−455.8
Critical temp, °F	−450.2
Critical pressure at critical temp, psia	33.0
Volume at 70°F and atmospheric, cu ft per lb	96.7
Molecular weight	4.0

Neon (Ne)

Boiling point, normal, °F	−411.0
Freezing point, °F	−415.4
Critical temp, °F	−379.8
Critical pressure at critical temp, psia	395.0
Vol. at 70°F and atmospheric, cu ft per lb	19.2
Molecular weight	20.18
Liquid density, normal, lb per cu ft	75.35
Latent heat, Btu per lb	37.2
Gas density at 70°F and 14.7 psia	0.05215

Nitrogen (N₂)

Boiling point, normal, °F	−320.5
Freezing point, °F	−345.91
Critical temp, °F	−232.9
Critical pressure at critical temp, psia	492.2
Vol. at 70° F and atmospheric, cu ft per lb	13.5
Molecular weight	28.0
Liquid density, normal, lb per cu ft	50.46
Latent heat, Btu per lb	85.7
Gas density at 70°F and 14.7 psia	0.07245

Nitrous Oxide (N₂O)

Boiling point, normal, °F	−127.2
Freezing point, °F	−131.6
Critical temp, °F	+ 97.7
Critical pressure at critical temp, psia	1054.0
Vol. at 70°F and atmospheric, cu ft per lb	8.73
Molecular weight	44.0
Liquid density, normal, lb per cu ft	76.8
Latent heat, Btu per lb	162.0
Gas density at 70°F and 14.7 psia	11.46

Ozone (O₃)

Boiling point, normal, °F	−169.4
Freezing point, °F	−314.5
Critical temp, °F	40.2
Critical pressure at critical temp, psia	791.0
Vol. at 70°F and atmospheric, cu ft per lb	8.0
Molecular weight	48.0
Liquid density, normal, lb per cu ft	101.8
Latent heat, Btu per lb	128.6
Gas density at 70°F and 14.7 psia	0.124

Oxygen (O₂)

Boiling point, normal, °F	−297.3
Freezing point, °F	−361.8
Critical temp, °F	−181.1
Critical pressure at critical temp, psia	737.0
Vol. at 70°F and atmospheric, cu ft per lb	12.18
Molecular weight	32.0
Liquid density, normal, lb per cu ft	71.3
Latent heat, Btu per lb	91.6
Gas density at 70°F and 14.7 psia	0.0828

Refrigerant 13 (CCl₁F₃)

Boiling point, normal, °F	−114.6
Freezing point, °F	−294.0
Critical temp, °F	839.0
Critical pressure at critical temp, psia	561.0
Vol. at 70°F and atmospheric, cu ft per lb	12.45

TABLE C.32 (*Continued*)

Liquid density, normal, lb per cu ft	7.798	Molecular weight	104.5
Latent heat, Btu per lb	9.9	Liquid density, normal, lb per cu ft	95.0
Gas density at 70°F and 14.7 psia	0.01034	Latent heat, Btu per lb	63.9
		Gas density at 70°F and 14.7 psia	0.273

Hydrogen (H₂)

Boiling point, normal, °F	−423.0
Freezing point, °F	−434.5
Critical temp, °F	−399.8
Critical pressure at critical temp, psia	188.0
Vol. at 70°F and at atmospheric, cu ft per lb	192.3
Molecular weight	2.0
Liquid density, normal, lb per cu ft	4.42
Latent heat, Btu per lb	195.0
Gas density at 70°F and 14.7 psia	0.0052

Refrigerant 14 (CF₄)

Boiling point, normal, °F	−198.5
Freezing point, °F	−299.2
Critical temp, °F	− 49.9
Critical pressure at critical temp, psia	542.0
Volume at 70°F and atmospheric, cu ft per lb	2.9
Molecular weight	88.0
Liquid density, normal, lb per cu ft	122.4
Latent heat, Btu per lb	57.0
Gas density at 70°F and 14.7 psia	0.228

Krypton (Kr)

Boiling point, normal, °F	−244.0
Freezing point, °F	−250.9
Critical temp, °F	− 82.8
Critical pressure at critical temp, psia	796.0
Vol. at 70°F and at atmospheric, cu ft per lb	4.6
Molecular weight	84.0
Liquid density, normal, lb per cu ft	150.5
Latent heat, Btu per lb	46.2
Gas density at 70°F and 14.7 psia	0.217

Xenon (Xe)

Boiling point, normal, °F	−162.5
Freezing point, °F	−169.2
Critical temp, °F	+ 61.9
Critical pressure at critical temp, psia	855.0
Vol. at 70°F and atmospheric, cu ft per lb	2.93
Molecular weight	131.30
Liquid density, normal, lb per cu ft	191.0
Latent heat, Btu per lb	41.4
Gas density at 70°F and 14.7 psia	0.342

Source: Woolrich (1965).

and quality standpoint. Both poultry and shrimp are being frozen commercially. Shrimp frozen with liquid nitrogen approximates the cost per pound of production equal to the cost per pound of liquid nitrogen. The total heat absorbed by a pound of liquid nitrogen is approximately 165 Btu. Theoretically, the cost of liquid nitrogen should be lower to accomplish the chilling effect per pound of product. Meat patties have been frozen in an atmosphere of liquid nitrogen and some of the equipment available handles the product at a rather rapid rate. Less maintenance costs and lower

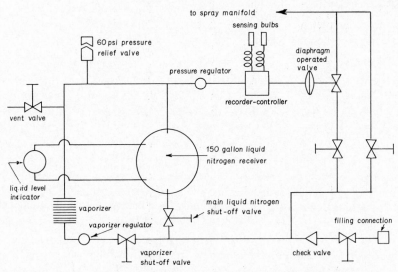

FIG. C-34.   Schematic of liquid nitrogen truck refrigeration system

labor requirements are attributed to the use of liquid nitrogen. These costs will often offset higher refrigerant costs when the entire system is considered.

When poultry is frozen rapidly there is not the darkening of the bone which normally occurs with slow freezing. The darkening is due to freezing the product after the hemoglobin moves to the surface of the bone. The light, slightly bleached color of poultry is desirable for merchandising. Equipment is available to achieve a rapid chill of poultry pieces in packages by lowering the temperature from about 45° to 28°F. This equipment consists of a series of compartments into which liquid nitrogen is fed and regulated by a thermostat. While passing through the system the product is subjected to lower temperatures. The atmosphere in each compartment is circulated with a fan. With improved technology and greater advances in the application of cryogenics, wider acceptance in processing foods can be anticipated.

References

AIR REDUCTION SALES. 1961. The use of liquified gases in the ice cream industry. Tech. Data Proc. Bull. *ADE 900.* Madison, Wis.

ANON. 1966. Basic aspects of cryogenic engineering, Refrig. *10,* No. 9, 224–226.

GUILFOY, R. E. 1964. Transportation of perishable foods. Food Eng. Conf. Proc., Michigan State Univ.

WOOLRICH, W. R. 1965. Handbook of Refrigerating Engineering, 4th Edition, Vol. 1. AVI Publishing Co., Westport, Conn.

Cross-references: *Nitrogen; Liquid; Cooling; Refrigeration Principles.*

CRYOSCOPES

The freezing point of a liquid is lowered by the addition of dissolved solutes. When water is added to milk the dissolved salts are diluted and the freezing point is raised. The change in freezing point is a direct function of added water. In the case of fluid milk, the freezing point is sufficiently sensitive to detect the addition of water in very low quantities. The adulteration of raw milk with 1% added water causes a rise in the freezing point of approximately 0.00542°C.

Application

Fresh raw milk containing no added water has a relatively constant narrow range of freezing points, about 0.555° to about 0.535°C. Different areas of the country will frequently have milk with some variation in the freezing point. The average is approximately 0.542°C.

Several methods have been used to determine the freezing point of milk. One of the most common commercial cryoscopes in use is the Fiske. The instrument is calibrated with 2 standard solutions of sucrose or 2 solutions of sodium chloride. Both the sucrose and sodium chloride solutions are carefully compounded to produce standards with freezing points of 0.422° and 0.521°C. The sucrose solutions consist of 7 and 10 gm of sucrose diluted to 100 ml solution with distilled water. The standard sodium chloride solutions result in the same equivalence as the sucrose and contain 0.6892 and 1.0206 gm of sodium chloride per 100 gm of water. The cryoscope dial is adjusted so that it reads the freezing temperature of each of the solutions correctly for standardization before determining the freezing point of milk.

The time required to perform the freezing point test is determined by the crystallization return of the sample after freezing. If milk samples are prechilled in ice, the total test time for screening purpose is about 3 min per sample. To obtain more precise results, a test time of at least 4 min is necessary. To obtain the higher degree of precision, the time will vary from one milk sample to another. The percentage of added water on the Fiske milk cryoscope can be read directly on the galvanometer scale. The standard sample size is 3 ml. The size of the sample need not be exactly 3 ml to obtain accurate and reliable results.

An example of the use of cryoscope in determining adulteration of milk with water is as follows. Assume that samples of milk taken directly after milking with a dry dipper average 0.542°C. Water added at level of 1% to this milk will raise the freezing point about $T/100$ or 0.00542°C. Therefore, the formula for percentage added water is

$$(T - T')/(T/100)$$

and if $T' = 0.532$°C and $T = 0.542$°C
then

$$\frac{(0.542 - 0.532)}{0.00542} = \frac{0.010}{0.00542} = 1.84\% \text{ approximately}$$

The freezing point of milk is affected by souring. A titratable acidity higher than 0.18% expressed as lactic acid should be viewed with caution. Developed lactic acid will depress the freezing point and result in erroneous readings.

Other Cryoscopes

Cryoscopes in addition to the Fiske include the Hortvet Cryoscope. In the Hortvet method the actual freezing point is determined after checking the accuracy of the thermometer using standard sucrose and salt solutions. The following formula is used to ascertain the percentage of added water in the milk sample.

$$W = \frac{100 \ (T - T')}{T}$$

where W = percentage of added water
  T = the average freezing point of normal milk
  T' = the actual freezing point on a given sample

A semiautomatic cryoscope modification has been developed by Shipe, Dahlberg, and Herrington. This laboratory method was first reported in 1953 and utilizes a small Freon compressor unit connected to an evaporator coil in a glycerol-water solution (14.4% by weight of pure glycerine). The solution freezes at -3.0°C. The sample is frozen in this solution under agitation and the thermometer is tapped in the sample to determine the freezing point. Other recognized methods for determining the freezing point of milk are the acetic serum, sour serum method, and copper serum method.

With the freezing point of a sample of milk of 0.550°C, Table C.33 may be used

TABLE C.33

TABLE FOR DETERMINING ADDED WATER IN MILK BY MEANS OF FREEZING-POINT DEPRESSION
(BASED ON WINTER TABLE[1])

(For practical purposes added H_2O results may be expressed to nearest decimal.)

Freezing Point of Sample Below Zero °C	Added Water % by Volume	Freezing Point of Sample Below Zero °C	Added Water % by Volume	Freezing Point of Sample Below Zero °C	Added Water % by Volume	Freezing Point of Sample Below Zero °C	Added Water % by Volume
0.550	0.00	0.520	5.45	0.490	10.91	0.460	16.36
0.549	0.18	0.519	5.63	0.489	11.09	0.459	16.54
0.548	0.36	0.518	5.82	0.488	11.27	0.458	16.73
0.547	0.54	0.517	6.00	0.487	11.45	0.457	16.91
0.546	0.73	0.516	6.18	0.486	11.64	0.456	17.09
0.545	0.91	0.515	6.36	0.485	11.82	0.455	17.27
0.544	1.09	0.514	6.54	0.484	12.00	0.454	17.45
0.543	1.27	0.513	6.73	0.483	12.18	0.453	17.64
0.542	1.45	0.512	6.91	0.482	12.36	0.452	17.82
0.541	1.63	0.511	7.09	0.481	12.54	0.451	18.00
0.540	1.82	0.510	7.27	0.480	12.73	0.450	18.18
0.539	2.00	0.509	7.45	0.479	12.91	0.449	18.36
0.538	2.18	0.508	7.64	0.478	13.09	0.448	18.54
0.537	2.36	0.507	7.82	0.477	13.27	0.447	18.73
0.536	2.54	0.506	8.00	0.476	13.43	0.446	18.91
0.535	2.72	0.505	8.18	0.475	13.64		
0.534	2.91	0.504	8.36	0.474	13.82		
0.533	3.09	0.503	8.54	0.473	14.00		
0.532	3.27	0.502	8.73	0.472	14.18		
0.531	3.45	0.501	8.91	0.471	14.37		
0.530	3.64	0.500	9.09	0.470	14.54		
0.529	3.82	0.499	9.27	0.469	14.73		
0.528	4.00	0.498	9.45	0.468	14.91		
0.527	4.18	0.497	9.64	0.467	15.09		
0.526	4.36	0.496	9.82	0.466	15.27		
0.525	4.54	0.495	10.00	0.465	15.45		
0.524	4.73	0.494	10.18	0.464	15.63		
0.523	4.91	0.493	10.36	0.463	15.82		
0.522	5.09	0.492	10.54	0.462	16.00		
0.521	5.27	0.491	10.72	0.461	16.18		

[1] *Chem. News*, 110, 283 (1914).

to determine added water in milk based on freezing point change. The values would have to be adjusted to suit the milk supply if the freezing point were found to be higher or lower than 0.550°C with a range from 0.513° to 0.565°C, an average of 0.539°C may be used if experience shows the value in the middle of the range to represent an average of several samples.

Conclusion

Dairy plant operators find the cryoscopic method of determining adulteration a very useful test in laboratory control. Herds with a high incidence of mastitis will usually produce milk with abnormal freezing points. The cryoscopic test is useful in screening the raw milk supply for this abnormality also.

References

MILK INDUSTRY FOUNDATION. 1959. Laboratory Manual, 3rd Edition. Washington, D.C.
SHIPE, W. F., DAHLBERG, A. C., and HERRINGTON, B. L. 1953. A semi-automatic cryoscope
for determining the freezing point of milk. J. Dairy Sci. *36*, 916–933.

Cross-reference: *Cryogenics.*

CULINARY STEAM PRODUCTION

The use of steam obtained directly from the boiler is often not permitted for
heating milk and food products, because chemicals may be present from previous
water treatment which would be damaging to the product. However, steam may be
supplied to a heat exchanger to heat potable (drinkable) water to form culinary (food)
steam for heat treatment of milk (Fig. C.35). There is no mixing of the steam supply
of the plant and the culinary steam produced. The culinary steam can be used for
direct injection into the product. Thus, only that portion of the steam which is to be
used for direct food treatment need be put through the heat exchanger, and the remainder of steam requirements can be produced and utilized in the conventional
manner.

Heat in the plant steam entering the heat exchanger is transferred through a coil
to potable water which becomes the culinary steam. Additional heat will raise the
temperature of the steam still higher to produce superheated steam. Leaving the
heat exchanger through bare pipe about 40 ft in length permits loss of heat from the
culinary steam to provide nearly dry saturated steam to the process.

Water heating can also be carried out as shown in Fig. H.15.

Cross-references: *Boilers; Steam; Water.*

CURDOMETER

Various samples of milk have properties which result in varying coagulation

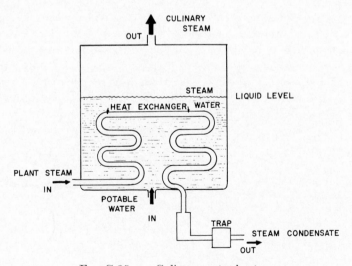

FIG. C-35.   Culinary water heater

characteristics.   A sample of milk may be treated with an enzyme which has been acidified and the strength of the resulting curd measured with a curdometer.

Principle of Operation

Milk which has been curdled is subjected to the shearing force of a calibrated plate which registers the force in grams.   The sample must be tempered by the enzyme pepsin and with hydrochloric acid to coagulate the milk.   The curd tension is usually determined on the coagulum after 10 min in the 95°F water bath.

Specifications

A curdometer is equipped with a radial dial which registers the curd tension force in grams.   The special curd knife consists of 8 radial plates each having $9/16$ in. of lineal cutting edge and being 0.02 in. thick.   The plates are spaced equally and enclosed by a circular ring plate which is 1.75 in. od, $3/16$ in. high, and 0.031 in. thick. The radial plates are attached to the inside of the ring plate and extended upward from it a distance of $2^1/16$ in.   The radial plates are reduced to a radial of $5/32$ in. above the ring plate.   The upper ends are curved inward and attached to the central spindle which is $5/16$ in. diam.   The cutting edge of the ring plate is tapered from the outside at an angle of 30° to the knife edge.   The lower and cutting edges of the radial plates are tapered on each side at an angle of 15° to a dull knife edge.   The cutting edges of the radial plates and the ring plate must be in approximately the same plane deviating not more than $1/32$ in.   The total lineal cutting edge of the knife must be 9.8 in. ± 0.10.   All joints must be soldered smooth and the knife made of noncorrosive metal.

A curdometer (tensiometer) must impart automatic movement to the knife and travel at the rate of 1 in. in 7 to 8 sec.   The instrument must be sufficiently sensitive to enable obtaining readings of an accuracy of ±1.10 gm.

Procedure

In the American Dairy Science Association method, 100 ml of milk to be tested is pipetted into a heavy-wall jar 3 to 4 in. high with approximately $2^3/8$ in. id.   To the sample which has been tempered to 95°F is added 10 ml of coagulant.   The coagulant is made by adding 450 mg of dry pepsin to 100 ml of 0.08 N hydrochloric acid. The curd tension should be made on the sample at the end of a 10-min period ±30 sec. The 95°F water bath results in a satisfactory coagulum for curd tension measurements. The readings are recorded as the maximum obtained when the knife penetrates the surface.   A sufficient number of tests should be made so that 2 or more will check within 10%.   The average of these readings is regarded as the curd tension value.

Reference

MILK INDUSTRY FOUNDATION.   1959.   Laboratory Manual, 3rd Edition.   Washington, D.C.

Cross-reference: *Cheese Handling Equipment.*

CYCLONE SEPARATOR

The centrifugal force acting on the particle for removing the product from the air is

$$CF = (m)\,(a) = \left(\frac{w}{g}\right)(a) = \frac{wV^2}{gr}$$

where CF = force on the particle, lb

g = acceleration due to gravity, 32.2 ft per sec

w = weight of particle, lb

V = velocity of particle, ft per sec

r = radius, ft; i.e., the radius from the center of the cyclone to the particle position or the radius of rotation in ft

$m = w/g$

The centrifugal force on the product is exerted toward the edge of the cyclone. The weight of the particle is effective vertically in the direction of the outlet.

Arrangement

Cyclones can be used individually or in combination to provide multi-cyclone units. Units of 96 tubes or cones have been used to get high efficiency of separation in which cyclones were arranged in 2 elements, each with 48 cyclones in rows of 6 and each mounted at a 45° angle. However, the trend is toward fewer, larger cyclones to remove fines from air.

Velocity

High air velocity is needed to separate small, lightweight materials from air. A high air velocity is obtained by small diameter cyclones, several of which may be placed in parallel. Cyclones can be placed in series with a small diameter high-velocity unit at the end to remove small particles in the stream. With a higher velocity there is a greater pressure drop and thus is more costly to remove the product. The cost of obtaining the separation must be balanced against the value of the product obtained, assuming that the minimum requirements are met from the standpoint of loss of product and contamination of the environment.

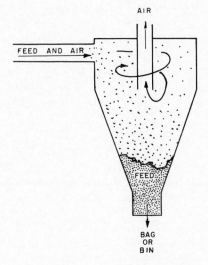

Fig. C-36.   Cyclone separator

224.   *Cyclone Separator*

The general arrangement of a cyclone separator is given in Fig. C.36.

Characteristics

The following characteristics identify the cyclone separator.

(1) The separation is a function of the difference in diameter and density of the product and air with the larger values giving more efficient separation.   (2) The velocity of the inlet is one of the main factors in controlling efficiency as it is related to the cyclone diameter.   Velocities may approach 100 ft per sec.   (3) A smaller diameter cyclone at a fixed pressure drop will have a higher efficiency than a larger diameter one. (4) The diameter of the inlet is usually about $1/4$ of the diameter of the cyclone.   (5) The collection efficiency can be increased by reducing the air outlet diameter, which at the same time will increase the pressure drop.   A major problem in operation for a unit with these design characteristics is the leaking of air in at the outlet of the unit causing vacuum.   The design must incorporate a change in cross section entering the cyclone.   (6) A smaller gradual and outlet result in separation of smaller particles. The practical limit is set by the permissible and economical pressure drop of the system. (7) The pressure drop to the cyclone decreases as powder or dust is incorporated in the air.   (8) The pressure drop of the system decreases as the concentration increases for the same airflow in cubic feet per minute.

Reference

HALL, C. W., and HEDRICK, T. I.   1966.   Drying of Milk and Milk Products.   AVI Publishing Co., Westport, Conn.

Cross-references: *Grinders; Spray Dryers.*

D

DAIRY PLANT LAYOUT AND DESIGN

It is very difficult to "detail" a definite step-by-step plan for developing a *perfect* plant layout. The ideas of several persons are usually sought and future requirements are estimated as accurately as possible. The anticipated plant volume in 5 to 10 yr, products to be made, types of packages, method of distribution, materials handling and load out facilities, and office space are examples of items to be considered in planning. The total layout coordinates all functions and labor utilization and may be thought of as two interrelated parts: equipment layout and room arrangement.

Objectives

Some of the objectives in developing a plant layout are to: (1) improve or facilitate production operations; (2) minimize materials handling; (3) maintain flexibility of the operation for alterations and expansion; (4) minimize investment in equipment; (5) make economical use of floor area; (6) promote effective utilization of the labor force; and (7) provide for employee convenience and comfort.

Improving production operations involves the arrangement of equipment for efficient processing and smooth flow of product. Major emphasis should be given to planning the path of products and supply items through the plant, so there will be coordination at critical points in processing and overall production. Much has been said about "straight line" flow of products. This is basically sound, however, the flow often is not "straight," and need not be. An important consideration is to have a minimum of backtracking and to provide for a smooth operation. The flow might well be U- or L-shaped, or some other pattern.

Materials handling is emphasized in a good layout. A good layout provides for reducing materials handling to a minimum and utilizes mechanical devices wherever practicable. The plant operator must use considerable judgment in determining when it becomes practical to invest in more elaborate materials handling equipment. Volume handled, anticipated labor savings, investment, and other factors must be considered in materials handling problems.

Maintaining flexibility of a plant operation becomes important when a new product must be made, production increased, new methods and new equipment introduced, or other changes made. Locating services and utilities conveniently allows for equipment rearrangement with minimum expense. In the original layout, provision for future expansion is always important. Expansion may be thought of as the amount of increased production possible in the original building, and secondly, expansion of the building itself at some future time.

Investment in equipment can be a big variable depending upon the size of the operation and products made. In the layout, careful consideration should be given

225

the utilization of equipment. Part-time use of 2 similar machines is costly and wherever practicable the products should be scheduled for processing with 1 machine.

Floor area is obviously expensive (Table D.1). Each area of a plant should be scrutinized in the planning stage to make sure it will be used to advantage. Wasted or idle floor area will naturally be a burden on the rest of the plant. It is now a common practice to design dairy plants with milk storage tanks located alongside the building with only the fronthead inside. Corridors and partitions should be held to a minimum for more efficient use of floor space.

The utilization of labor can be enhanced by a good plant layout. The following should be considered. (1) Will the layout reduce handling of materials to a minimum, especially avoidable rehandling? (2) Have the walking requirements been minimized? Are materials and controls accessible? Is necessary operating information readily available without walking? (3) Has the layout provided for effective supervision? The supervisor has a walking problem too, therefore, he should be headquartered close to the operation to increase his effectiveness.

Employee comfort requires building into the plant a satisfactory atmosphere and conveniences. Attention must be given to light, ventilation, heat, safety, humidity, dust, etc. The lack of parking facilities could be a major problem and requires consideration.

Equipment Layout for Fluid Milk

Unless the plant is specializing in a few items, the equipment in the processing area should be arranged to correlate the processing of by-products with the fluid milk operation. For example, the high-temperature short-time pasteurizer may be used in conjunction with a separator. Conveniences for the operator need special attention in planning the arrangement. Control valves, thermometers, control panels, etc., should be conveniently located. The equipment arrangement should permit maximum use of in-place cleaning. An effective layout will allow cleaning of lines and the HTST with solution from a central circulating tank. Some short pipes and fittings may be placed in the tank, and cleaned by the circulating solution as the circuit is cleaned.

TABLE D.1

RECOMMENDED SPACE REQUIREMENTS FOR AREAS IN FLUID MILK PLANTS

Area	Floor Area
Total plant area	1.5 to 2.0 sq ft per gal. per day; up to 3.0 sq ft per gal. per day for small plants
Refrigerated milk storage room	For round bottles, $5\frac{1}{4}$ gal. per sq ft For square bottles, $7\frac{1}{2}$ gal. per sq ft For paper cartons, 11 gal. per sq ft (stacked 5 high)
Bottle washing room	Area of refrigerated storage plus space for equipment and conveyors
Processing room	About 5 times the area occupied by equipment
Dry storage	25% of total plant area
Refrigeration compressor room	0.6 to 1.0 sq ft per cwt. of milk handled
Boiler room, not included fuel storage	0.40 to 0.80 sq ft per cwt. of milk handled

The filling area should not be divided more than necessary by conveyors. Utilizing a corner or end of a room will minimize the amount of conveyor in the filling area. The system for handling filled cases, whether paper cartons or glass, will depend largely upon the size and type of operation. Dollys are satisfactory for most small plants. For medium size and larger plants a conveyor system is desirable. Installing casers and case stackers with in-floor conveyor offers sizable labor savings when prop-

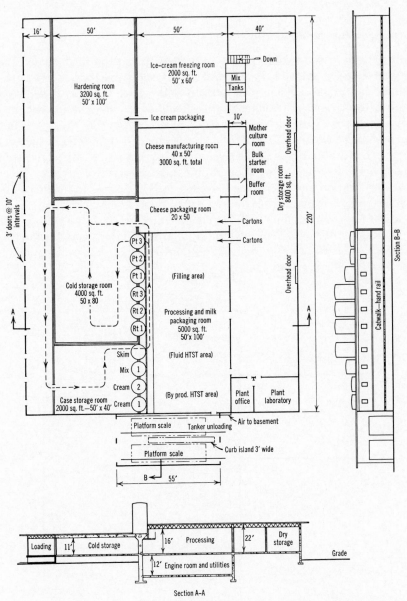

Courtesy of Klenzade Products Co.

FIG. D-1.   Modern milk, cheese, and ice cream plant

erly utilized.   The greater investment and floor area needed for automatic equipment can be justified in larger operations by increased output per man-hour.

In bottle washing rooms two things seem important in the equipment layout. First, provide, if possible, sufficient empty case conveyor to permit filling the washer without causing excess cases to be stacked on the floor.   Changing to different bottle sizes during operation can be troublesome with a short case conveyor.   Secondly, the case washer should be located near the bottle washer to take advantage of overflow water for case washing.

Room Arrangements for Fluid Milk

Arrangement of the various rooms and areas depends on their related functions, amount and shape of available land, truck traffic, accessibility to streets, presence of retail store, and others.   Some principles to follow are: (1) plan flexibility for less costly future expansion; (2) traffic patterns should be smooth and prevent congestion; (3) size operational areas large enough to handle a reasonable expansion in volume without enlarging the building; (4) dry and cold storage room should handle a moderate volume increase and permit relatively easy expansion; (5) the processing room should not open directly to out-of-doors, but into less critical areas; (6) centralize the laboratory and production manager's office; and (7) correlate the flow of products and supplies with the equipment layout for a minimum of handling.

A layout for a modern fluid milk, ice cream, and cottage cheese plant is illustrated in Fig. D.1.   By utilizing automation the labor productivity is very high in this plant. Elevating the silo tanks for both raw and pasteurized products permits gravity flow to processing and packaging equipment.

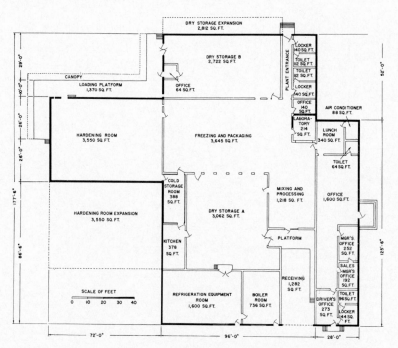

FIG. D-2.   Layout for an automated plant manufacturing one million gal. of ice cream

TABLE D.2

ASSUMED SALES, PRODUCTION, AND INVENTORY IN A PLANT HANDLING 1 MILLION GALLONS
OF ICE CREAM AND 250,000 GALLONS OF NOVELTIES, BY MONTH

Month	Production, Gal.	Sales, Gal.	Inventory at end of month,[1] Gal.
December			30,000
January	80,000	76,250	33,750
February	80,000	80,000	33,750
March	100,000	95,000	38,750
April	110,000	102,500	46,250
May	120,000	115,000	51,250
June	135,000	132,500	53,750
July	135,000	141,250	47,500
August	135,000	133,750	48,750
September	110,000	116,250	42,500
October	90,000	95,000	37,500
November	80,000	80,000	37,500
December	75,000	82,500	30,000
Total	1,250,000	1,250,000	

[1] Does not include truck inventory of about 10,000 gal.

TABLE D.3

JOB CLASSIFICATION AND WORKERS NEEDED IN THE AUTOMATED PLANT MANUFACTURING
1 MILLION GALLONS OF ICE CREAM AND 250,000 GALLONS OF NOVELTIES ANNUALLY

Job Classification	No. of Workers Needed
Supervision	1
Receiving, mix assembly, and processing	1
Freezer operation, maintenance	2
Novelties and packaging	6
Crating and conveying	1
Dry storage	$1/2$
Hardening room and loading	2
Cleanup	1
Laboratory and records	1
Loading out	$1^1/_2$
Engineers	3
Total	17

An effective layout will also increase operating efficiency in ice cream plants. The assumed monthly volumes are given in Table D.2 for a model plant of $1^1/_4$ million gallon annual production. Major components of the plant are shown in Fig. D.2. These components are organized with consideration to product and container flow, floor space utilization, labor utilization, centralized supervision, and future expansion. The plant dimensions of 177.5 ft wide and 196 ft long provide 22,494 sq ft of usable floor space. The equipment layout with legend is shown in Fig. D.2 and D.3. This operation is highly automated and requires 17 plant workers whose job classifications are described in Table D.3.

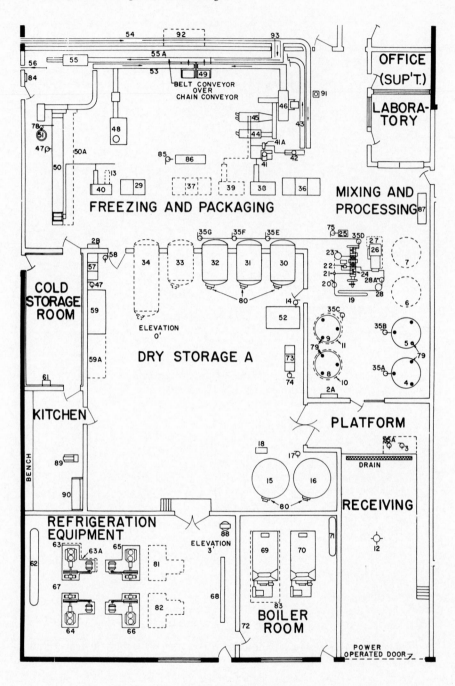

SCALE OF FEET

0   5   10   20

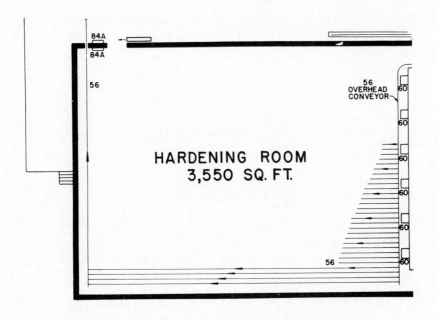

1   CONTROL PANEL
2A, 2B CIP CONNECTING STATIONS
3   RECEIVING PUMP 150 GPM
4   RAW CREAM TANK 1,500 GAL.
5   CONCENTRATED SKIM MILK TANK 1,500 GAL.
6   FUTURE CREAM TANK 1,500 GAL.
7   FUTURE CONCENTRATED SKIM MILK TANK 1,500 GAL.
8   MIX ASSEMBLY TANK 300 GAL.
9   MIX ASSEMBLY TANK 300 GAL.
10, 11 FUTURE MIX ASSEMBLY TANKS 600 GAL. EACH
12 CIP TRANSPORT TANK WASHER ON HOIST
13 FUTURE 1-CYLINDER CONTINUOUS FREEZER 180 GPH
14 CENTRIFUGAL PUMP FOR ICE WATER 100 GPM
15 CORN SIRUP TANK 2,800 GAL.
16 LIQUID SUGAR TANK 2,800 GAL.
17 CENTRIFUGAL PUMP FOR LIQUID SUGAR 50 GPM
18 ROTARY SIRUP PUMP 30 GPM
19 PASTEURIZER 30-SECOND HOLDING TUBE
20 STEAM INFUSER HEATER
21 FLOW DIVERSION VALVE
22 POSITIVE DISPLACEMENT TIMING PUMP 10 TO 20 GPM
23 INFEED BALANCE TANK
24 PLATE PASTEURIZER 600 GPH
25 WATER HEATER FOR PLATE PASTEURIZER
26 HOMOGENIZER 600 GPH
27 FUTURE HOMOGENIZER 1,200 GPH
28 VACUUM DEAERATOR
28A VACUUM DEAERATOR DISCHARGE PUMP
29 MIX FLAVOR TANK WITH TWO 125-GAL. COMPARTMENTS
30–32 MIX STORAGE TANKS 1,500 GAL. EACH
33 FUTURE MIX STORAGE TANK 1,500 GAL.
34 FUTURE MIX STORAGE TANK 3,000 GAL.
35 SANITARY CENTRIFUGAL PUMPS:
        A, B, E, F, G—50 GPM
        C—25 GPM
        D—10 GPM
36 MIX FLAVOR TANK WITH THREE 250-GAL. COMPARTMENTS
37 FUTURE MIX FLAVOR TANK WITH THREE 250-GAL.
        COMPARTMENTS
38 3-CYLINDER CONTINUOUS FREEZER 900 GPH
39 FUTURE 3-CYLINDER CONTINUOUS FREEZER 900 GPH
40 1-CYLINDER CONTINUOUS FREEZER 180 GPH
41 FRUIT FEEDER 10 TO 120 GPH
41A BLENDER
42 BULK CAN FILLER
43 ASCENDING CONVEYOR FOR BULK CANS IN BASKETS
44 ½-GAL.-CARTON FILLER
45 PINT-CARTON FILLER
46 OVERWRAP MACHINE
47 BRINE CIRCULATING PUMP 250 GPM
48 CUP FILLER AND BOXER

49 PACKAGE GROUPER
50 STICK NOVELTY BRINE TANK SYSTEM
50A FUTURE STICK NOVELTY BRINE TANK SYSTEM
51 CHOCOLATE CIRCULATING UNIT 10 GPM
52 12,000-LB. ICE BUILDER
53 GROUPING CONVEYOR
54 WIRE-BASKET CONVEYOR
55 PACKAGE CRATER
55A CRATER INFEED BELT
56 OVERHEAD CONVEYOR SYSTEM
57 3-TANK CIP UNIT
58 CIP CIRCULATING PUMP 160 GPM
59 SHELL AND TUBE NOVELTY BRINE COOLER
59A FUTURE SHELL AND TUBE NOVELTY BRINE COOLER
60 —20° F. COOLING UNIT, 5.5 TON, WITH FAN AND
        ELECTRIC DEFROST
61 40° F. COOLING UNIT
62 AMMONIA RECEIVER
63 AMMONIA BOOSTER COMPRESSOR 30 TONS
63A FUTURE AMMONIA BOOSTER COMPRESSOR 60 TONS
64 AMMONIA BOOSTER COMPRESSOR 69 TONS
65 AMMONIA COMPRESSOR 53 TONS
66 AMMONIA COMPRESSOR 75.4 TONS
67 LIQUID AMMONIA INTERCOOLER
68 ELECTRIC PANEL BOARD
69 STEAM BOILER 50 BHP
70 STEAM BOILER 50 BHP
71 HOT WATER TANK
72 BOILER FEED WATER SYSTEM
73 CIP SYSTEM
74 CIP CIRCULATING PUMP 160 GPM
75 HOT WATER CENTRIFUGAL PUMP FOR HTST 100 GPM
76 EVAPORATIVE CONDENSER 130 TONS
77 FUTURE EVAPORATIVE CONDENSER 130 TONS
78 CENTRIFUGAL PUMP FOR CHOCOLATE 10 GPM
79 LOAD CELLS
80 LEVEL TRANSMITTER
81 FUTURE BOOSTER COMPRESSOR 68.85 TONS
82 FUTURE COMPRESSOR 113.70 TONS
83 FUTURE BOILER 100 BHP
84, 84A CONVEYOR SELECTOR SWITCHES
85, 85A PORTABLE CIP RETURN PUMPS
86, 87 PORTABLE CLEANUP TANKS
88 AIR COMPRESSOR
89 EXPERIMENTAL COUNTER-TYPE ICE CREAM FREEZER
90 ICE CREAM STORAGE CABINET
91 2½-GAL. CAN FORMING MACHINE
92 HEATING AND VENTILATING UNITS MOUNTED ON ROOF
93 AUTOMATIC BASKET DIVIDER

FIG. D-3.   Layout of equipment in the receiving area, mix assembly and processing area, freezing and packaging area, storage areas, and boiler and refrigeration equipment

As equipment, controls, marketing methods, and other procedures change with new developments, plant layouts will also change to best utilize the components for greater efficiency.

References

FARRALL, A. W. 1963. Engineering for Dairy and Food Products, 3rd Edition. John Wiley & Sons, New York.

MILK INDUSTRY FOUNDATION. 1967. Manual for Milk Plant Operators, 3rd Edition. Washington, D.C.

SLADE, F. H. 1967. Food Processing Plant, Vol. 1. Chemical Rubber Publishing Co. Cleveland.

TRACY, P. H. 1966. Layouts and operating criteria for automation of dairy plants manufacturing ice cream and ice cream novelties. U.S. Dept. Agr. ARS 750.

Cross-references: *Architectural Symbols; Materials Handling Systems; Plant Layout; Poultry Processing; Shipping Docks; Slaughter House Design.*

DEFROSTING

Defrosting of refrigeration coils and rooms is an important procedure in maintaining the efficiency of refrigeration apparatus and cold storage rooms.

When a cooling surface is at a temperature below 32°F and in the presence of air containing moisture, the moisture will deposit and collect as frost on the surface of the cold coil or plate. In many situations, the accumulation of $1/4$ to $1/2$ in. of frost will decrease the heat transfer so seriously that not only is the cost of operation increased very greatly, but it may be impossible to obtain the desired low temperature in a room.

It may be possible to prevent the formation of the frost by using a sufficiently large amount of evaporator surface with a higher temperature so that moisture collects as condensate which can be drained. This is possible, however, only in rooms where the temperature of the surface of the coil can be allowed to rise to a temperature above freezing part of the time.

Methods

There are three principal methods of removing the frost from the cold coil or surface. The simplest method is to open the doors on the refrigerated room or space and allow warm air to enter. This method is seldom used however, because the warm air not only warms the coils and melts the ice, but it also warms the food materials stored in the room and may cause some product deterioration or spoilage.

The second method is to mechanically or manually chip the ice off the surface. This is a laborious job and there is a danger of causing leaks in the circuit.

The third and the preferred method for defrosting is to pump hot gas from the compressor directly to the expansion coil. The hot gas loosens the ice very quickly and it can be easily removed from the room. Figure D.4 shows the principle of the hot gas defrosting line. It is essential when using the hot gas line to shut off the liquid refrigerant line to the coil and to open the defrosting line slowly so that an excessive amount of liquid is not pumped back into the compressor in a slug.

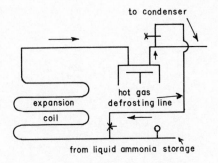

Fig. D-4.   Hot gas defrosting

Water sprays, warm air, electric heating elements and other modifications are also employed to accelerate defrosting where expedient to do so.

Cross-reference: *Refrigeration Principles.*

DEHYDRATING AGENTS

An absorbent or dehydrating agent such as calcium chloride or activated alumina can be used for reducing the vapor pressure of the drying air and decrease the necessity of using heated air for drying.   Most of the research work in this field has been done with calcium chloride because it is an inexpensive dehydrating agent.   The chemical cost for reducing the moisture content of feed from 31.5 to 16%, db with calcium chloride at 2 cents per pound was about 11 cents per 100 lb of combined feed, and required 24 hr.   To reduce the moisture content from 17.3 to 13%, db, the cost was 6 cents per 100 lb of feed.

Dehydrating agents are often placed in packaged food or pharmaceutical products to maintain low moisture levels.   Dehydrating agents are usually placed in a permeable membrane to provide physical separation of the product and dehydrating agent.

Acids such as HCl or H_2SO_4 can also be used for absorbing moisture.

Desiccants for Packaging Subsistence

In-package desiccation of dehydrated foods is often desirable for shelf-life extension.   The success of in-package dessication must depend substantially upon the success of the package in excluding moisture vapor from the package contents.

Certain dehydrated food products packaged for military use requiring the use of a desiccant must meet the specifications set forth for this type of packaging.   The desiccant, calcium oxide, shall be calcined or recalcined lime.   A minimum of 28.5% by weight moisture absorption capacity is required of the desiccant when held in a desiccator for 7 days at 24°C.   In powdered, pelletized, or granular form the calcium oxide must pass through a U.S. Standard No. 3 sieve.

A desiccant must be packaged in small bags not to exceed 4 oz. to be acceptable to the military.   The bags are to be made from heat-sealable creped Kraft paper having a 2 way stretch of at least 15%.   Seals must be a minimum of $5/16$ in. wide and continuous.   Bags must be marked with FDA acceptable ink as follows:

"Important
Throw This Bag Away
Contents Not Edible
This Bag Is Used Solely
to Absorb Moisture"

The amount of desiccant to be used per package is calculated as follows

$$Wd = \frac{Wp \times \% \text{ water} \times 3.5}{100}$$

where Wd   = weight of desiccant in ounces
     Wp   = weight of product in ounces
     % water = percentage of water to be removed after package is sealed

Desiccant bags should be distributed throughout the container for effective moisture absorption.

The user of a container having bags of calcium oxide desiccant should be marked:

"Caution—Desiccant
Keep Container Closed
Open Only to Withdraw Contents
Limit Quantity to That Intended To Be Used
Tightly Reseal Immediately After Any Withdrawal"

Pellets of absorptive materials are available commercially; however, the acceptability of a material should be ascertained before attempting to use the product in a food package.

Reference

U.S. Army. 1968. Military Spec., Desiccants and Desiccation, Method of: For Packaging Subsistence. *MIL-D-43266A*.

Cross-references: *Antioxidants; Packages.*

DEHYDROFREEZING

Dehydrofreezing is the method of processing in which a considerable portion of the moisture in a product to be frozen is first removed by ordinary drying methods employing heat; the product is then frozen using a standard freezing procedure. In some products, such as apples, from 20 to 50% of the moisture can be removed with little expense using normal heat drying, thus greatly reducing the amount of water which must be frozen. There is also considerable saving in shipping and storage of the product, and product quality is not seriously damaged.

The process merely substitutes a more rapid and less expensive normal heat-drying process for a part of the rather expensive freezing operation, and removes as much of the water as can be removed without serious damage to the product.

This process is not adapted to all types of products. The heat-drying part of dehydrofreezing may cause considerably more product deterioration than if the product was simply frozen. Dehydrofreezing is used where quality is not impaired by the method. Careful attention must be given to the temperature during the heat drying step and to the percentage of moisture which is removed by the drying procedure.

Most extensive use of dehydrofreezing in the United States has been for processing of apples to be used in making pies. Dehydrofrozen material is stored at the usual low temperatures used for frozen products.

Cross-reference: *Refrigeration Principles.*

DENSITY CONTROL

The product concentration can be controlled on vacuum pans or recirculating evaporators. Control is accomplished by measuring the final product concentration and varying the discharge rate from the vacuum pan or last effect of the evaporator. In order for the product concentration control system to work properly, however, adequate automatic level control is necessary.

Techniques

Three techniques for measuring product concentration for automatic control can be successfully applied. The first is based on *density* and is accomplished by using a bubble tube-sample column combination with the appropriate pressure measuring instrument. Since the sample column provides a constant height of liquid, the bubble tube back pressure is then a measure of the density. The second approach uses a *density transmitter* where the sample is run through a constant volume chamber or section of pipe and the weight of this sample is then measured by appropriate means. This is essentially the pycnometer method of density measurement. Several instruments are available based on this principle which can accurately measure density for a milk evaporator. The third method is a continuous industrial process *refractometer*. Such a refractometer is designed to be inserted in a product discharge sample line. It has an electrical output which can easily be amplified and transduced, if desired, to be compatible with conventional pneumatic control instrumentation.

Utilization

The prime advantage of the latter two product composition measuring approaches over the bubble tube-sample column approach, is that they are more easily cleaned-in-place and do not require that air be purged through the product.

If the absolute pressure of the pan or final effect of the evaporator is adequately controlled, temperature compensation of the product concentration measuring system is not required. If the absolute pressure is not controlled, the product temperature for a given composition will vary. Temperature compensation is then required.

The specific gravity of an evaporated or condensed (sweetened) product can be calculated by the following equation

$$SG_{evap} = \frac{100\%}{\dfrac{\% \text{ fat}}{SG_{fat}} + \dfrac{\% \text{ snf}}{SG_{snf}} + \dfrac{\% \text{ H}_2\text{O}}{SG_{H_2O}} + \dfrac{\% \text{ sugar}}{SG_{sugar}}}$$

at 60°F the SG of fat $= 0.93$
SG of snf $= 1.608$
SG of water $= 1.00$
SG of sugar $= 1.589$

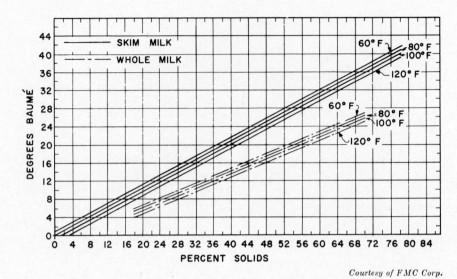

Fig. D-5.   Solids versus Baumé reading

The equation shows the effect of various solids on the specific gravity of the mixture.   The percentage fat and percentage sugar in the evaporator feed must be constant if density of the final concentration is to have any correlation with the percentage solids-not-fat.   This is also true when using refractive index as a measure of concentration.

On single pass evaporators density control by the means previously discussed does not apply, since the product flow through the evaporator is controlled from the feed end.   Density control can sometimes be achieved in this type of evaporator depending on the specific type of evaporator involved (Fig. D.5).

The specific gravity is often measured with the Baumé hydrometer.   For products heavier than water, a specific gravity of 1 is equivalent to a Baumé reading of 0° and a specific gravity of 1.1 equivalent to 13.18 Baumé degrees.   The conversion scale from Baumé to specific gravity is

$$SG = \frac{145}{145 - \text{Bé}}$$

where Bé = Baumé hydrometer reading, degrees.

The Baumé reading can also be used to determine solids content.

Refractive Index

Another reliable means of measuring product concentration is by refractive index. The refractometer is an optical device for determining the total solids based on the refraction of light from a sodium source or a filtered white light.   A high degree of accuracy can be achieved.   These units can be used for evaluation of a sample or for continuously checking the total solids of the product discharging from the evaporator. The refractive index obtained is temperature dependent, so the sample must be cooled to the standard (usually 68°F) or corrected.   To convert the refractive index (RI) to total solids, T (percent) the following equations are used

$T = 70 + 444 \ (RI - 1.4658)$ for sweetened condensed whole milk
$T = 70 + 393 \ (RI - 1.4698)$ for sweetened condensed skim milk

Refractometers may be installed between evaporators of a multiple effect system to continuously check the rate of evaporation of water. It is desirable to check the accuracy of the refractometer quite frequently.

Cross-references: *Density of Milk; Evaporators; Refractometer.*

DENSITY OF MILK

The purchase of milk is based upon the butterfat test and the pounds of product at an established quality standard. Because of the decrease in demand of butterfat, milk is being purchased on a total solids basis in some areas. It is normally accepted that to be milk, over 3.0% butterfat must be contained. As the percent butterfat increases as produced from the cow, the solids-not-fat (SNF) also increases. The density of milk changes with the butterfat, solids, and the temperature. For naturally-produced milk, as the percentage butterfat increases the weight per gallon (or the density) increases (Fig. D.6). As the temperature is increased the density is decreased or the weight per gallon is decreased. Milk or cream which has been standardized by adding more cream to obtain a higher percentage butterfat will have a reduction in weight per gallon as the percentage fat is increased (Fig. D.7). In the calibration of bulk milk tanks where the milk is naturally produced on the farm, an increase in density results with an increase in butterfat. In the dairy plant where milk is standardized to obtain certain butterfat tests a decrease in density results with an increase of butterfat. Equipment must be provided so that the weight of the milk can be properly determined and a representative sample obtained for butterfat tests.

Reference

Hall, C. W. 1963. Processing Equipment for Agricultural Products. Edwards Brothers, Ann Arbor, Mich.

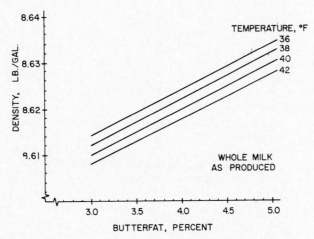

Fig. D-6.   Approximate density of whole milk as produced

Cross-reference: *Specific Gravity.*

DENSITY OF POWDERED PRODUCTS

Particle density is influenced principally by the amount of entrapped air. One of the main processing factors that contributes to particle density is viscosity and air incorporation into the concentrate ahead of drying. The type of spray atomization has an effect on the air retention. Centrifugal spray dry milks have more entrapped air than pressure spray products.

True density refers to the air free solids and may be calculated from the formula

$$\text{density} = \frac{110}{\dfrac{\%\ \text{fat}}{0.93} + \dfrac{\%\ \text{snf}}{1.6} + \dfrac{\%\ H_2O}{1.0}}$$

The true density of nonfat dry milk is 1.44 to 1.48 gm per ml, and of dry whole milk 1.26 to 1.32. The moisture content and the ratio of solids-not-fat to fat are the two chief variables affecting true density. In a dry high fat product an increase in moisture reduces density and the opposite is true for nonfat dry milk. A decrease in fat will increase true density.

With the occluded air plus the space in the interstices, dry milk offers an opportunity for compression. The application of 100 to 150 psi. to dry whole milk can

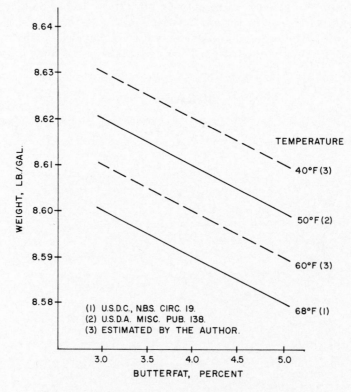

Fig. D-7. Approximate density of standardized milk

eliminate $1/2$ or more of the space. Densities of drum-dried or spray-dried products were increased to 1.1 or above. A bulk density of 0.45 is obtained by compressing foam spray nonfat dry milk at 500 to 600 psi. The addition of nondairy ingredients, e.g., sucrose, to milk before drying will affect the bulk density of the dry product. Certain additives including sodium aluminum silicate and calcium silicate will increase the bulk density of dry whole milk.

Commercial product density averages for nonfat dry milk are: foam spray, 0.32 gm per ml; instant, 0.26; and regular, 0.591.

Reference

HALL, C. W., and HEDRICK, T. I. 1966. Drying of Milk and Milk Products. AVI Publishing Co., Westport, Conn.

Cross-references: *Conversion Values; Density Control; Evaporators; Refractometers.*

DETERGENTS AND CLEANING

The main purposes of cleaning are to make available to the consumer nutritious and wholesome food products free of foreign matter, and to prevent disease transmission. Some other objectives are to improve product flavor and keeping quality, achieve esthetic values, and improve equipment performance, e.g., better heat transfer, and assist in corrosion control.

Steps followed in cleaning most food processing equipment are as follows.

(1) Rinse. Rinsing is an extremely important phase of cleaning. Proper temperature will conserve water. Warm water 100°–110°F is usually more effective than 50°F water. Avoid circulating rinse water containing food solids. Prompt rinsing to prevent "drying-on" of solids is important.

(2) Properly compounded detergent solutions must be applied properly to soil that is to be removed. The time of contact and solution strength must be adequate for thorough cleaning.

Properties and functions of cleaning solutions include displacement of the soil involving various mechanisms, some of which are: penetration and wetting; saponification of fat; peptization of proteins; and dissolving of minerals and soluble compounds. Also, soil must be dispersed in solution involving deflocculation (holding of insoluble particles in suspension, including sequestering and chelating functions) and emulsification of unsaponified fats.

(3) Give a final rinse to prevent redeposition of soil on the cleaned surface.

A good cleaner for a food processing plant also possesses properties including good solubility, nontoxic, noncorrosive, stable upon storage, economical, noninjurious to hands in the case of hand cleaners, and noncaking.

Chemical Cleaning Compounds

There are two basic cleaners—alkaline and acid types. Alkaline cleaners consist of the basic alkalies and usually contain polyphosphates and wetting agents. Combinations of compounds often result in a synergistic effect making the blended product a more effective detergent. The basic alkalies commonly used in food plant cleaners are caustic soda, soda ash, trisodium phosphate, and sodium metasilicate.

Some Properties of Basic Alkalies

Product	Properties
Caustic soda	High germicidal action; dissolves proteins; good saponifying ability; poor rinsability; burns skin; poor mineral deposit control; poor as deflocculant
Soda ash	Fair saponifying value; good as a buffer; fair water softening ability; best used in combination with phosphates
Trisodium phosphate	Good deflocculation and emulsification ability; good rinsability; relatively corrosive on tin
Sodium metasilicate	High deflocculating and emulsifying value; good dispersion ability; protects metal from corrosive action of other compounds; some saponifying ability

Complex phosphates improve the detergency properties of cleaners; hence, are found in most high quality detergents. They have good rinsability and are noncorrosive.

Some Properties of Complex Phosphates

Product	Properties
Sodium tetraphosphate	Good sequestrant of magnesium and calcium; good emulsifying, dispersion, and peptizing ability
Sodium tripolyphosphate	Very good sequestrant of Mg and Ca; good emulsification, dispersion, and peptization
Sodium hexametaphosphate	Excellent sequestrant of calcium; poor sequestrant of magnesium; good emulsification, peptizing, and dispersion ability
Tetrasodium pyrophosphate	Sequesters magnesium very well, but not as effective on calcium; least effective of the complex phosphates in emulsification, dispersion, and peptizing ability, but still valuable in cleaners

Acid cleaners used in the food industry are usually the organic type. However, certain inorganic acids are useful in milkstone removal particularly.

Organic acids with wetting agents form a balanced cleaner and when included in a cleaning program aid materially in preventing milkstone. Organic acids are useful in controlling mineral precipitates from hard water, thus reducing film formation.

Chelating Compounds and Wetting Agents

Chelating agents form a complex with metallic ions which serves an important function in cleaning solutions. Various compounds differ in their ability to sequester metals such as calcium, magnesium, and iron. Chelating agents are effective water softeners and assist in control of mineral deposits on equipment.

Wetting agents have been called "surface active agents." There are three general types; namely, anionic, nonionic, and cationic. The anionic is the most commonly used type. They are quite neutral; and although many combinations may exist, the sulfated alcohols and alkyl aryl sulfonates are most common. Either acid or alkaline solutions are suitable for these wetting agents.

Nonionic wetting agents do not ionize and may be used with anionic or cationic compounds. This group is finding more use in the market.

Cationic wetting agents include the quaternary ammonium compounds and are not as active a wetter as the anionics for example. They serve a germicidal function also.

Factors in Cleaning

Various factors need adjusting to satisfactorily produce the desired results in cleaning equipment over a period of time. Time, temperature, detergency, and physical action are employed in cleaning processing equipment. The results achieved are the criteria for evaluating a cleaning program for a given situation. An example of guideline suggestions for a dairy plant may be given as follows.

(1) Hand washing method: use mild alkaline general purpose cleaner about 120°F and pH of 9 to 10.

TABLE D.4

SPECIFICATIONS FOR VIBRATING DEWATERER

Model No.	136A	138A
Maximum width of feed and discharge chutes, in.	36½	36½
Size of screening area—length and width, ft.	3 x 6	3 x 8
Overall height—horizontal position, in.	33	33
Overall length of screening body, including receiving and discharging lips, in.	92	116
Overall width, including shaft, in.	48	48
Overall length of mounting frame, in.	84	108
Overall width of mounting frame, in.	44	44
Slope of screen	From 10° to 30° depending upon material and results wanted	
Center of drive sheave to end of box, in.	36	48
Frame material	Consists of 2–5 in. I-beams and 2–6 in. channels	
Screen body material	10 in. x 6 ft	10 in. x 8 ft
J and L junior channels	or	or
	12 in. x 6 ft	12 in. x 8 ft
Approximate speed of machine	800 to 1800 Rpm— depending upon materials and results wanted	
Operating horsepower	1	2
Weight—Domestic shipment, lb	1100	1200
Cu ft packed for export	119	149
Weight packed for export, lb	1300	1450
No. of decks	1	1

Source: A. K. Robbins.

(2) Clean in place method:
  (a) For cold milk lines use chlorinated alkaline cleaner 130° to 140°F for 15 to 20 min.
  (b) For hot milk lines use an acid cleaner about 175°F for 20 min, then alkaline detergent 160°F for 40 min.
  (c) Small parts washers 155° to 160°F for 15 to 20 min.
  (d) Spray-cleaning milk tanks or tankers use chlorinated alkali about 135°F for 10 to 15 min.

Satisfactory cleaning procedures must be developed for each operation in food processing plants. From time to time changes occur which may necessitate a change in cleaning methods. Inspection of equipment after cleaning to ascertain whether or not the cleaning has been done satisfactorily cannot be overemphasized.

Cross-references: *Chlorination; CIP Systems; Cleaning of Equipment; Sanitation.*

DEWATERERS

Dewatering commonly involves two major operations in a fruit and vegetable processing plant, namely, remove water and separate water from solids. This equipment in the processing operation is usually used in connection with a flume system. Dewatering is accomplished either with a revolving reel or vibrating screen. In most cases the screen and rods of the reel are made of stainless steel. A typical vibrating screen consists of $1/16$ in. diam stainless steel wires spaced $1/8$ in. apart, and welded to $3/8$ in. diam steel rods located on 3-in. centers. The vibrating screen is pitched at a slight angle to discharge the product uniformly. Specifications for one vibrating type of dewaterer are given in Table D.4.

Two of the no. 138 dewatering units mounted over a concrete pit have been used to separate 800 gal. per min from the product pumped over the screens. Cannery waste is commonly dewatered and the solids are disposed of separately, quite often utilized in fertilizer. A typical dewatering screen is shown in Fig. D.8. The dewatering reel illustrated, Fig. D.9, is equipped for adjustable pitch and is suitable for a

Courtesy of A. K. Robbins and Co.

Fig. D-8.   Dewatering screen for cannery wastes

variety of vegetables including peas, lima beans, whole kernel corn, etc. Its use is effective at the end of flumes or other equipment. Specifications for the dewatering reel shown are given in Table D.5.

The dewatering reel may be attached to the discharge end of a blancher. In this case it is equipped with fresh water sprays to achieve washing and cooling of the blanched product being discharged from the blancher. Water drained from the reel is not returned to the blancher.

Cross-references: *Blanching; Centrifugal Separation; Extractor; Strainers; Various Drying Methods; Washing and Blanching.*

DICERS

Dicers, strip cutters, and slicers are used widely in food processing.

The products handled in these machines include apples, asparagus, beans, cheese, meat, tomatoes, and an extremely wide variety of food products. Table D.6 lists the type of product and the dicing-slicing and miscellaneous treatments provided by these machines.

Strip cutters used to cut potatoes are made with impeller spaces of different widths to position and hold the potatoes lengthwise while centrifugal force holds them firmly against stationary slicing knifes which cut the slabs from the length of potatoes. Usually the machines are used for cutting slices $1/2$ in. as maximum width. A machine with this type design for cutting potatoes into French fries or julienne cuts has a capac-

Courtesy of A. K. Robbins and Co.

Fig. D-9.   Dewatering reel or roll washer

TABLE D.5

SPECIFICATIONS FOR REEL-TYPE DEWATERER

Specifications		Construction
Length overall	3 ft 9 in.	Frame welded steel
Width overall	2 ft 3 in.	Reel support gray iron casting
Height (maximum)	3 ft 6 in.	Catch basin, splash guards
Height (minimum)	2 ft 10 in.	and drive guard sheet steel
Length of reel	3 ft 0 in.	Reel stainless steel rod welded
Diameter of reel	1 ft 2 in.	spirally to longitudinal
Rod spacings in reel, in.	$^9/_{64}$	stainless reinforcing rods
Height to feed inlet (maximum)	2 ft $5^1/_2$ in.	Opening between rods—
Height to feed inlet (minimum)	1 ft $9^1/_2$ in.	$^9/_{64}$ in.
Height to discharge outlet (maximum)	1 ft 4 in.	Gears—totally enclosed
Height to discharge outlet (minimum)	1 ft 3 in.	Drive—motor only
Distance from floor to drain connection, in.	$7^3/_4$ in.	
Drain outlet, in.	ips 3 in.	
Motor hp required	$^1/_4$	
Shipping weight, lb	350	

ity of from 1,200 to 4,000 lb per hr. The strips can be cut with a square cross section of $^5/_{32}$, $^1/_4$, $^5/_{16}$, $^3/_8$, or $^1/_2$ in.

A green bean cutter for cross cutting beans, asparagus, okra, celery, and rhubarb feeds the product into a set of tapered packets which form the cutting chamber. The hopper and cutting chamber revolve together and carry the product past a set of stationary cutting knives. The knives cut the product into uniform clean cut lengths. The capacity of a typical machine on straight green beans is approximately 3,000 lb per hr.

A typical machine may be used for dicing, strip cutting, and slicing potatoes, apples, mushrooms, onions, cabbage, and celery. The different models vary in the size of cubes they cut and also in the size of the products they will handle. One model, for example, cuts $^3/_4$-in. cubes of beets, potatoes, sweet potatoes, pineapples, cabbage, pickles, melons, and apples at capacities up to 15 tons per hour (Fig. D.10).

A different dicer is used on products such as boned chicken and turkey, peppers, celery, and citrus peel. In operation the product is rolled flat by passing between the feed drum and the companion feed roller which is slotted for engagement of the circular knife assembly, stripping the product, and ejecting it over a shear plate and into the rotating cross cut assembly where it is cut into squares. The capacity of a machine of this type is from 1,000 to 3,000 lb per hr.

Numerous special dicers and strippers are made for specific purposes. Most of them are continuous in operation and have capacities from 3,000 to 10,000 lb per hr depending on the product. Most have interchangeable parts or adjustments.

A somewhat similar type machine is called the scarifier, which is designed to scarify or to place small slits in the surfaces of all types of round products. Machines are available which will make either plain, flat, or corrugated potato chip surfaces at capacities up to 7,000 lb per hr input. Special machines are available for specific products including meat.

The horsepower required to operate these machines is nominal, being from a fraction of a horsepower to 5 hp.

It is desirable to obtain the machines with 18-8 stainless steel materials which contact the product. The slicing knives are made of either a hardened stainless steel or other hardened rust-resistant steel.

The knives of a slicer must be kept sharp. A motor-driven special knife sharpener is available for assisting in this operation. Usually knives must be sharpened after each 8 hr if good results are to be obtained. It is very important in the operation of equipment of this type to have the products thoroughly washed and free from gravel, pieces of metal, or other foreign material. Magnetic devices for separation of metal may precede dicers.

Reference

Food Machinery and Chemical Corp. Canning Machinery Div. Cat. *160*.

DIELECTRIC HEATING

Dielectric heating is used to heat materials of low thermal conductivities. A product to be dried is heated by placing it in a strong electrostatic field produced by high frequency. The effect is principally caused by a high voltage with a low current. The material to be heated is placed between the plates of a condenser which are con-

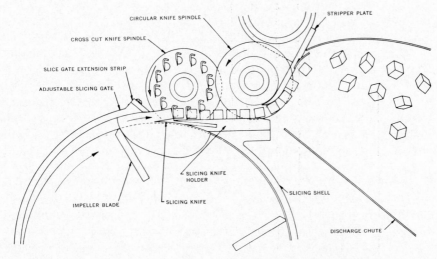

Courtesy of Urschel Laboratories

Fig. D-10.   Vegetable cutter

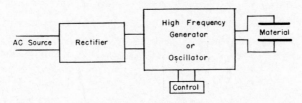

Fig. D-11.   Circuit for high frequency dielectric dryer

nected to a high-frequency generator or oscillator. The plates are alternately charged, positively and negatively, causing a changing stress on the molecules of the material being dried. The rapid moving electric field generates heat by molecular friction in the wet material.

Dielectric heating will heat the product uniformly, thus offering an advantage for drying products such as rice, peanuts, and beans which crack very easily with uneven heating of forced heated air drying. The rate of drying must be controlled, however, because rapid heating will explode the kernel. To evaporate 1 lb of water requires $2/3$ Kwh. From other applications it appears that frequencies of 10 to 30 mc and a voltage of 15,000 v or less across the product are desirable (Fig. D.11). The higher the frequency (Fig. D.11) the lower the voltage required to obtain the same heating.

DIGITAL COMPUTER

The digital computer works with numbers according to instructions provided, and is usually referred to as a general purpose computer.

The basic components of a digital computer are input, which permits information to be placed into the computer; output, which permits information to be taken from the computer; memory, which permits information to be stored; an arithmetic unit, which performs the calculations as instructed and required; and control and analysis, with instructions from the memory unit to employ the arithmetic unit to take the appropriate action and then call for additional instructions from the memory unit.

The digital computer processes data according to a memory unit or stored program; input data are read from punched tapes, magnetic tapes, discs, punched cards, or tapes. Information from cards, tapes, etc. is translated into magnetic or electrical impulses and the machine stores and handles information as digits (numbers).

The digital computer must be given a set of instructions. A stored program means that the set of instructions is placed in the memory unit of the machine and remains there until the problem is solved or instructions are given to remove the stored information.

To solve a problem the computer must be given a list of very specific instructions which outline in a step-by-step fashion all operations which must be done to solve a given problem. Different methods of programming may be required. In general, the fortran, algol, or PL-1 methods are used for programming the mathematical equations, scientific and engineering problems, although many special purpose programs are used. The program and the computer must be compatible.

The binary number system is often used. The binary system of numbers has the following characteristics. (1) Express numbers in powers of 2. (2) Omit the powers of 2 when writing numbers. (3) Insert zeros for powers of 2 not required.

In binary notation, 25 is expressed as

$$25 = 16 + 8 + 1$$
$$= 1 \times 2^4 + 1 \times 2^3 + 0 \times 2^2 + 0 \times 2^1 + 1 \times 2^4$$

so 25 can be expressed in terms of 1 and 0, as a binary, $= 11001$

TABLE D.6

TYPICAL APPLICATIONS DICERS, STRIP CUTTERS, SLICERS

Product	Dicing	Slicing	Miscellaneous
Apples	×[1]	×	
Asparagus		Cross cut	
Bamboo shoots		×	
Bananas		Cross cut	
Beans		French style	
		Cross cut	
Beef	×	×	
Beets	×	×	Strip cut
			Crinkle cut
Bread croutons	×		
Broccoli	×	Cross cut	
Cabbage	×		
Carrots	×	×	Strip cut
			Crinkle cut
Cauliflower	Sweet pickles		Quartering
	Fine relish		
Celery	Fine relish	Cross cut	
Cheese	×		
Cherries	×	×	
Chicory	×		
Chicken	×	×	
Citron	×		
Clams	Clam dicer		
Coconut		×	
Corn		×	
Cranberries	×	×	Scarifying machine
Eggplant	×	×	Strip cut
Fish		Cross cut	
Frankfurters		Cross cut	
Garlic		×	
Ginger Root		Cross cut	
Greens	×		Strip cut
Leeks		Cross cut	
Lettuce	×		
Meat	×		
Melon	×		Crinkle cut
Melon rind	×		
Mushrooms	Condiments	×	
Okra		Cross cut	
Onions	Fine relish	×	
Oranges	×	×	
Papaya	×		
Parsley			For chopping
Peaches	Baby food	×	
Pears	Baby food		
Peas			Scarifying machine
Peel, citrus	×		Strip cut
Peppers	Fine relish	Cross cut	Strip cut
Pickles		Cross cut	Strip cut
		Lengthwise slicing	Quartering and halving machine

TABLE D.6 (*Continued*)

Product	Dicing	Slicing	Miscellaneous
			Crinkle cut
			Sweet, mixed pickles
Pineapple	×	×	Crinkle cut
Pork		×	
Potatoes	Hash brown	Cross cut	Crinkle cut
Potato chips		×	
Radishes		×	
Rhubarb		Cross cut	
Rutabagas	×		
Squash	×	Cross cut	
Strawberries		×	
Sweet potatoes	×		
Tomatoes		×	
Turkey	×		
Water chestnuts		×	
Zucchini		Quartering	

[1] Denotes applicable.
Source: Urschel Lab. Inc.,Valpariso, Ind.

In the binary number system

$0001 = 1$
$0010 = 2$
$0011 = 3$
$0100 = 4$
$0101 = 5$
$0110 = 6$
$0111 = 7$
$1000 = 8$
etc.

The decimal system of numbers may be used on the output and is similar to the binary except the numbers are in powers of 10 instead of 2.   The usual Arabic number system is set up on the decimal system.   The computer may be used to (1) keep inventories of supplies, materials, and finished products at economical levels; (2) maintain proper spare parts inventory and to assist in maintenance of equipment; (3) make more accurate sales analyses, which will quickly pinpoint trouble spots in a product or sales region, (4) compute minimum cost ingredient in formulas that meet quality, standards, legal restrictions, and process requirements; (5) assure accurate automatic control and recording in batching of ingredients; (6) schedule production for minimum labor and equipment costs; (7) provide for more accurate and comprehensive evaluations of production equipment and performance; (8) solve complex design problems particularly those involving mathematical equations; and (9) perform company business operations, such as payroll.

Reference

MURRAY, F. J. 1961. Digital Computers. Columbia Univ. Press, New York.

Cross-reference: *Analog Computer.*

DOUGH MIXING

Dough mixing is a major operation in the United States. A total of approximately 11 billion pounds of bread dough is mixed each year. Most of this is mixed in horizontal batch type mixers. In the past few years, there has been much interest in continuous dough mixers. It is likely that the proportion of continuous mixers will grow rapidly in the future due to lower labor costs and more uniform control.

Most of the batch mixers are of the horizontal type with various sizes as in Table D.7.

Operation

In the operation of the usual horizontal mixer, 2 to 3 min is required for the flour to become wetted; then 10 to 12 min is required for the process in which the agitator folds, kneads, stretches, shears the raw dough, and disperses and moistens dry lumps, and also disperses the gas bubbles quite uniformly. Four batches per hour can be obtained from commercial equipment. An important aspect of operation is the maximum power required by the agitator is at the point where completion of the mixing has arrived. Beyond this point, there is a breakdown of gluten and less power is required. This principle is useful in instrumenting the operation.

The horizontal mixers handle all types of yeast-raised dough for bread, sweet rolls, and sweet goods. During the mixing, heat is developed so that the temperature is raised up to 100°F. In order to keep the temperature below this level, chilled water is used in mixing the ingredients. In addition the jacket of the mixer bowl or body is cooled with refrigerated water.

For mixing cakes and similar materials, a special mixer called a Hobart mixer is often times used. This is a much less sophisticated mixer usually set vertical and requires less horsepower to drive.

A new type of mixer called a Daymadic has been introduced recently. This is a vertical type mixer and the mixing bowl is mounted on casters so that the batch can be rolled under the mixer agitator and out again for the respective treatments. This mixer is built much like a cake mixer. The feature of the Daymadic mixer is that it uses short mixing cycles with rest periods between. For example, the cycle is as follows: (1) short mixing cycle 15 sec slow speed, (2) short mixing cycle 18 to 30 sec, high speed, (3) stand with no agitation, 2.5 hr, (4) sugar and salt added and batch agitated for 15 sec, slow speed, (5) agitation 3 min, high speed, and (6) stand with no agitation, 15 min. The capacity of this type of unit is about 6,000 lb per hr.

TABLE D.7

DOUGH MIXERS

Mixer Size No.	10	13	16	20
Maximum, lb	1,000	13,000	16,000	20,000
Minimum, lb	500	650	500	
Agitation, hp	15/30	20/40	25/50	37.5/75
Agitation, rpm	57–75	35/70	35/70	35/70
Compressor, hp	15	15	20	20
Bowl vol, cu ft	41.2	50.6	61.6	79

Continuous Bread Mixing

Several manufacturers have developed large capacity continuous bread mixing machines which are suitable for plants making over 100,000 lb of dough per week. The system covers scaling, premixing, fermentation, mixing, depositing, and panning.

The two principal parts of this machine are the premixer and incorporator, and the final mixing or developer stage. In the premixer three streams of product are fed into the unit, namely, (1) a liquid ferment or so-called liquid sponge, (2) liquid shortening, and (3) flour. The residence time of the product in this part of the system is about 1 min.

The U.S. Army Quartermaster Corps has developed a small continuous dough mixing setup for field mixing use which has a capacity of from 150 to 300 lb per hr. This machine is quite simple and uses no artificial cooling. It is lightweight and easily transported. It uses a chemically leavened bread mix. The finished dough is extruded into the bread pans directly.

References

ABBOT, J. A. 1963. Continuous mixing, Food Eng. *25*, No. 8, 64–65, 134.
STRAHMANN, H. 1959. Apparatus for making bread and pastry dough. U.S. Pat. 2,868,143. Jan. 13.

Cross-reference: *Mixer.*

DRAINS

Floor drains in food processing plants are important from the standpoint of sanitation and ease of operation of the plant.

Types

The standard type of industrial drain is shown in Fig. D.12, which consists of a cup-shaped receptacle and an inverted bell cap with perforated cover which may be removed. The drain is made so that it functions as a trap, always maintaining a liquid seal in the line.

In addition to this type of drain, which is usually made of cast iron, the drainage lines are also equipped with a trap. The trap is very important from the standpoint of keeping foul odors in the sewage system from backing into the room.

Location

Two different procedures relative to location of drains may be considered. One

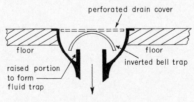

FIG. D-12.   Floor and drain

arrangement is that drains be placed at regular intervals throughout the processing floor usually on about 20-ft centers and particularly with a drain close to the location of machines which require much washing down. With this system there are no drains near the outside walls.

The second type arrangement is to have a shallow ditch adjacent to the side walls of the room into which water will drain from the manufacturing floor. Each of these ditches then has a proper drain and trap. This arrangement provides a floor which is usually drier than one in which the drains are placed at regular intervals throughout the manufacturing floor. Some operators feel that it gives a more satisfactory working floor, and less chance for accumulation of water around the machines. This system, however, can only be used on relatively narrow rooms, since in a large room it would be necessary to have drains placed at least every 40 ft even with this system.

All manufacturing floors which require drainage, and where there is water on the floor must have a slope of approximately $1/4$ in. per ft toward the drain.

References

FARRALL, A. W. 1963. Engineering for Dairy and Food Products, 3rd Edition. John Wiley & Sons, New York.

Cross-reference: *Floors.*

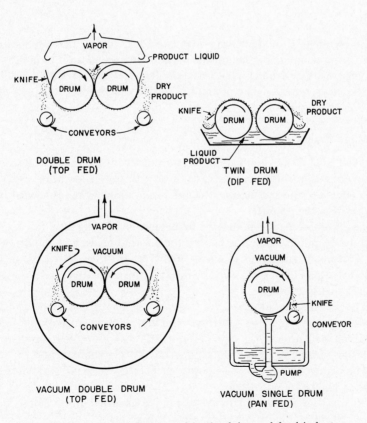

FIG. D-13. Drum driers used in the dairy and food industry

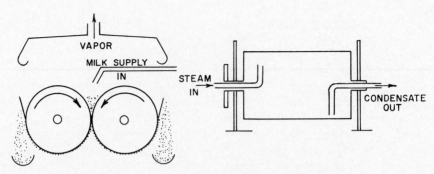

Fig. D-14.   Steam and condensate flow for a drum dryer

DRUM DRYER

The drum dryer provides a method of removing moisture from viscous materials. The process is used for making foods and chemicals. A limitation on use of the drum dryer is the sensitivity of the food for heat, and the effect on solubility of the product. These units may be classified as single or double drum, and atmospheric or vacuum. Small applicator rolls may be used to apply materials on large diameter drums.

Operation

The precondensed product from 3 to 1, 5 to 1, or the raw product is placed in a thin film from a liquid storage on the exterior surface of an internally steamheated rotated metal drum or drums. The dried product is scraped from the rolls after about $^3/_4$ revolution of the roll. The product is usually removed at less than 5% moisture content (Fig. D.13 and D.14).

Principles and Practices

(1) The product is precondensed, often from 5 to 1 ahead of the dryer, to provide economical operation. Precondensing is done with the evaporator. The greater the number of effects of the evaporator, the less steam input which is needed to evaporate 1 lb of water from the product.

(2) The product may be preheated to increase the drying rate.

(3) A 100% quality steam is desired for internal heating of the drum. The surface temperature of the drum is about 300°F to provide efficient transfer; proper venting and suction of the steam, and removal of the condensate from the internal area of the drum must be provided.

(4) The speed of rotation of the drum must be regulated and is based on the temperature, density, diameter of drums, and gap adjustment between rolls.

(5) Homogenization of the input product may be desirable to prevent breakdown of fat emulsion of milk or to prevent separation of other components.

(6) The drums must be kept smooth. It is often necessary to refinish the drums after 1,000 or 3,009 hr of operation.

(7) Flexible knives should be used to remove the dried film. These knives should be easily adjustable and must fit tightly against the rolls.

(8) High moisture of dry product may be due to low temperature of the surface, a thick film, high total solids, or drum revolving too rapidly (Table D.8).

(9) About 1.5 lb of steam are required to evaporate 1 lb of water.

(10) The optimum output for most food products is about 3 to 5 lb per sq ft per hr of dry product from the drum.

Evaporation

The constant rate period of drying during evaporation from a drum dryer is represented by

$$R = 2.45V^{0.8}\Delta p$$

where R = evaporation rate, lb per hr sq ft
V = velocity, ft per sec
$\Delta p = (p_s - p_a)$, atm
p_s = saturation vapor pressure
p_a = air vapor pressure

References

HALL, C. W., and HEDRICK, T. I. 1966. Drying of Milk and Milk Products. AVI Publishing Co., Westport, Conn.

HUNZIKER, O. Z. 1949. Condensed Milk and Milk Powder. Published by the author, LaGrange, Ill.

DRUM HANDLING

Several mechanical methods are available for handling empty or full drums containing dry or liquid materials. Some devices are practical for handling only a few drums daily while conveying systems or fork trucks may be used where a large number are involved. In the interest of safety some means must be provided the workers for handling drums. Drums because of their shape are difficult to handle manually except for rolling in certain instances.

For some operations the manually operated drum handler is satisfactory. The unit enables 1 man to transport short distances, drums weighing up to 800 lb. A crank on the equipment allows the operator to draw clamps tighly around the drum. A manually operated hydraulic lift pedal raises the drum which can then be tilted at any angle for pouring of contents.

TABLE D.8

EFFECT OF INCREASING VARIABLES ON PERFORMANCE OF A DOUBLE DRUM ATMOSPHERIC DRYER

	Variables			
	Steam Pressure	Feed Temperature	Drum speed, Rpm	Distance Between Drums
Film thickness	Increase	Increase	Decrease	Increase
Evaporation between drums	Increase	Decrease	Increase	Decrease
Evaporation on drum	Increase	Increase	Decrease	Increase
Total heat transfer	Increase	No change	No change	No change
Moisture content of powder	Decrease	Decrease	Increase	Increase
Production of dried product	Increase	Increase	Increase	Increase

Forklift

More elaborate drum handling methods are employed utilizing a variety of attachments on a standard forklift. Several variations are available in the principle used for gripping one or more drums for moving with a forklift truck. In some cases the drums are gripped top and bottom, whereas others apply clamps around the middle of the drum. Some systems also achieve drum rotation for emptying the contents. An attachment which carries the drum close to the vertical structure achieves greater load stability and maneuverability than those on the end of the times. A lifting device which mounts on a fork truck with the capability of lifting four drums is illustrated in Fig. D.15.

Eight jaws on the unit close on the beads of the drum so the heavier the drum the tighter the grip.

Conveyors are often the most practical in plants where a large number of drums are handled. Roller and chain conveyors are quite adaptable and may be constructed with special cradles for drums.

Vertical conveyors operate efficiently for moving drums between floors or levels. They work particularly well on containers of uniform size. (Fig. D.17).

Cross-references: *Conveyors; Forklift Trucks; Materials Handling.*

DRY ICE

Dry Ice is the trade name for solid carbon dioxide. Dry Ice is mainly a by-product of industry. Carbon dioxide, when purified, is liquified and expanded to form

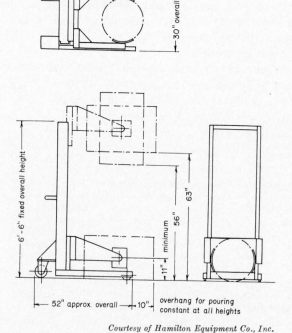

Courtesy of Hamilton Equipment Co., Inc.

Fig. D-15.   Fifty-five gallon drum handling equipment

a snow which is then pressed into blocks. Dry Ice is quite widely used for preserving foodstuffs between the retailer and the home. It is also used where an extremely low temperature is desired in a small storage box. One of the principal features is that dry ice passes directly from a solid to a gas without the liquid stage or phase.

Data and Specifications

Dry Ice has the following general characteristics: temperature, $-109.3°F$ in a CO_2 atmosphere; temperature, $-123°F$ in a 50% CO_2 atmosphere; density is 50 to 55 lb per 10-in. cube; cost 3 to 5¢ per lb; refrigerating effect per pound from a solid at $-109.3°F$ to a gas at atmospheric temperature equals 246.3 Btu.

Courtesy of Alvey Ferguson Co.

FIG. D-16.   Keg and barrel chain conveyor system

Dry Ice is a white, solid substance commercially delivered in 50-lb cakes. The cakes are usually sawed into slabs or strips which are packed in insulated bags along with the food product which is to be delivered. Special cardboard shipping containers are used which keep the dry ice from direct contact with the food product.

Dry Ice is also used to cool refrigerated trucks.

The principal management points for handling Dry Ice are (1) store in a well-insulated box where the heat loss will be moderate; (2), handle so that workmen do not get frost damage; and (3) provide for control of temperature so that the food product is not cooled to too low a temperature. This can be accomplished by wrapping the Dry Ice in paper or light insulation, or by a thermostatic damper to control the flow of gas and air. Provision must be made for escape of the CO_2 gas.

Reference

FARRALL, A. W. 1963. Engineering for Dairy and Food Products, 3rd Edition. John Wiley & Sons, New York.

Cross-references: *Carbon Dioxide; Refrigeration Principles.*

Courtesy of Alvey Ferguson Co.

FIG. D-17.   Vertical conveyor for drums

DRY MILK, PROPERTIES

Physical Properties

To meet the needs in designing equipment and developing new processes considerable research is now in progress to determine the physical properties of dry milk powder. These properties vary considerably with manufacturing procedures and subsequent environmental conditions such as temperature, moisture, and humidity.

Frictional Properties

Frictional properties are useful in the development of materials handling devices (Table D.9).

Thermal Conductivity

The thermal conductivity of dry milk powder is particularly important in regard to cooling the powder as it is removed from the dryer. The product may be cooled by radiation, moving room or cool air through the product, and moving the product over cooled conveyors. Thermal conductivity properties are quite useful in determining a change of temperature of these products during handling and storage. Typical values for thermal conductivity are given in Table D.10.

Salmonella

Salmonella comprises a group of microorganisms which in some people cause gastrointestinal disturbances. Epidemics relating to this undesirable organism in food have recently occurred in various locations in the United States. The *Salmonella* organism enters food products through the air. Recent outbreaks of salmonellosis (1966) were traced to nonfat milk solids. In the drying of this product, *Salmonella* can enter through the drying air and cooling air. Air may be filtered to reduce contamination. It is believed that the major source of contamination is involved with the purchasing operation. Considerable attention is being given to reducing the possibility of contamination of the air and nonfat milk solids from animals, insects, and people.

Equilibrium Moisture

Equilibrium moisture content (EMC) values are used to determine changes of the dry milk in relation to the surrounding environment (Table D.11). It is standard practice in the United States to dry to 5.0% for nonfat milk, Table D.11 and 4.5% for dry whole milk.

TABLE D.9

COEFFICIENT OF FRICTION OF NONFAT DRY MILK AT ROOM TEMPERATURE

Moisture Content, %	Coefficient of Friction	Moisture Content, %	Coefficient of Friction
0	0.53	4	0.62
2	0.58	6	0.66

TABLE D.10

RELATIONSHIP OF TEMPERATURE AND MOISTURE ON K-VALUE OF FINE NONFAT MILK POWDER

Temperature, °F	Moisture Content, %	k, Btu/hr-ft-°F	Temperature, °F	Moisture Content, %	k, Btu/hr-ft-°F
102°	4.2	0.242	130°	5.8	0.351
132°	4.2	0.300	130°	6.9	0.374
150°	4.2	0.336			

TABLE D.11

EQUILIBRIUM MOISTURE CONSTANTS OF DRY MILK (1965)

High-heat Nonfat			Medium-heat Nonfat			Low-heat Nonfat		
Temp., °F	RH %	EMC % DB	Temp., °F	RH %	EMC % DB	Temp., °F	RH %	EMC, % DB
100	4.00	8.35	102	6.50	8.00	101	3.00	7.14
144	1.50	5.50	141	2.00	5.30	147	0.80	4.74
191	0.50	3.83	192	0.65	3.25	194	0.25	1.89
233	0.20	2.50	241	0.10	1.60	238	0.15	0.13
273	0.05	1.75	272	0.05	1.00	270	0.10	0.03

References

HALL, C. W., and HEDRICK, T. I. 1966. Drying of Milk and Milk Products. AVI Publishing Co., Westport, Conn.

HAYASHI, H., HELDMAN, D. R., and HEDRICK, T. I. 1967. Internal friction of nonfat dry milk. ASAE Paper, Saskatchewan, Can.

HELDMAN, D. R., HALL, C. W., and HEDRICK, T. I. 1965A. Equilibria moisture of dry milk at high temperatures. Trans. ASAE *8*, No. 4, 535–541.

HELDMAN, D. R., HALL, C. W., and HEDRICK, T. I. 1965B. Vapor equilibrium relationships in dry milk. J. Dairy Sci. *48*, No. 7, 845–851.

OJHA, T. P., FARRALL, A. W., DHANAK, A. M., and STINE, C. M. 1966. Determination of transfer through powdered food products, ASAE Paper *66-823*, Chicago, Ill.

Cross-references: *Powder Handling Equipment; Vapor Pressure.*

DUST EXPLOSION

The danger of explosion from fine particles of dust should be considered in the design and operation of granaries and elevators. There are three basic requirements for an explosion: (1) a suitable mixture of dust and oxygen, (2) a spark, and (3) a confined area. Explosions are most likely to occur when very fine particles are suspended in the atmosphere. If a spark occurs in a confined area, an explosion is more likely to occur if the surrounding air is not moving. The building regulations, insurance requirements, and national fire code are established to prevent explosions. Explosions are prevented by providing a well-ventilated building equipped for dust removal, and special dustproof electrical equipment and lights, with the equipment properly grounded to prevent sparks from static electricity. Certain construction features provide an exit for explosive power so that the force is not confined within the building which could cause extensive destruction.

The possibility of explosion is designated on the basis of concentration of organic products in the air. A concentration of organic dust of 5 gm per cu ft or less is usually considered safe from explosion.

References

EDWARDS, P. W., and LEINBACK, L. R. 1935. Explosibility of agricultural and other dusts as indicated by maximum pressure and rates of pressure rise. U.S. Dept. Agr. Tech. Bull. *490*.

NATIONAL FIRE PROTECTION ASSOC. 1946. National Fire Codes, Vol. 2, The Prevention of Dust Explosions. Boston.

Cross-reference: *Explosion.*

E

EFFICIENCY

Efficiency is a much used and often abused term. In engineering analysis, it is most commonly applied as a measure of the input which results in output of useful work. One law of thermodynamics is that it is impossible to utilize 100% of the energy in a transfer because energy is used to overcome friction and changes due to heat. Energy is lost from a high temperature body as heat. Another law of thermodynamics states that energy can be neither created nor destroyed. Energy or power can be measured or represented in Btu, Btu per unit time, Btu per unit volume, or Btu per unit weight.

$$Input = output + loss$$

Lost energy is unavailable to the process, and therefore results in an inefficiency. The efficiency in percent is obtained by dividing the output by the input and multiplying by 100. Some typical values of the efficiency of energy conversion are given in Table E.1.

Cross-references: *Electric; Energy; Fans; Fuels; Gears; Generators; HTST Pasteurization; Spray Dryers.*

EGG HANDLING

The method of processing eggs varies greatly according to the circumstances of production and marketing. When a farmer consumes eggs from his own farm, little or no processing is involved. The movement of eggs through market channels and the amount of processing varies considerably from one geographical area to another. Eggs which are exported involve considerable processing. Considerable processing is involved when a change in physical form is required, such as separation of albumen and yolk, drying, or freezing.

Egg Characteristics

The following characteristics of eggs are important in handling shell eggs: (1) the shell is very fragile and cannot resist large mechanical stresses, so eggs cannot be handled roughly in bulk; (2) eggs do not have a uniform round shape and vary in size, thus their ellipsoid shape poses problems of mechanical handling in a continuous system; (3) the air, humidity, and temperature affect the quality of the egg yolk and albumen and changes from chemical and bacteriological reactions; and (4) the inside quality as well as the external appearance have an effect on the market price.

259

TABLE E.1

EFFICIENCY OF ENERGY CONVERSION

Transfer of heat in steam to mechanical energy of engine—maximum efficiency about 15%
100 watt tungsten filament gas filled lamp = efficiency of conversion of electrical energy to light energy, 16%
Thermal efficiency of a fuel oil engine = approximately 20%
Thermal efficiency of a gasoline engine with a compression ratio of 10:1 = about 60% maximum
Steam boilers = 70 to 80%
100 watt fluorescent tube, efficiency of conversion of electricity to light = 40%
Electric heat exchangers to liquids = above 90%
Electric energy to single phase electric motors = 75 to 85%
Steam to fluid in heat exchangers = 70 to 80%
Radiant heating = 60 to 70%

TABLE E.2

CANDLED INDEX AND TIME TO COOL EGGS IN DIFFERENT CONTAINERS WITH EGGS

Container	Time to Cool Eggs from 78° to 65°F, Hr	Candled Index[1] After		
		3 Days	7 Days	14 Days
Egg on wire mesh	$1/3$	1.4		
Round wire basket	3	1.5	1.6	1.9
Galvanized 3 gal. pail	6.4	1.5	1.4	1.9
Ventilated wire case	15.1	1.4	1.6	2.0
Wooden case	21.0	1.5	1.5	1.9
Rectangular wire case	22.2	1.3	1.5	2.0
Precooled cardboard case	26.7	1.7	1.5	1.9
Cardboard case	31.6	2.0	1.9	3.0

[1] Grade AA = 1, A = 2, B = 3, C = 4, newly laid index = 1.4.

Maintenance of Quality

Maintenance of quality of eggs begins as soon as the eggs are laid. Eggs should be gathered regularly, at least twice per day, and cooled quickly after gathering. Mechanical handling of the eggs from the nest to the egg room is helpful for rapid gathering of the eggs. Eggs should be maintained at from 50° to 60°F in a high relative humidity of at least 75%. Eggs will be cooled quite rapidly if air circulation is provided around each egg. Eggs will be cooled more rapidly and quality maintained if they are placed in an open wire basket so that the cool air can circulate. Several hours are required for eggs at the center of a crate to cool from body temperature to storage temperature (Table E.2).

A burlap screen evaporative cooler with a pan above can be used to keep a room cool (10°F above water temperature) and with a high relative humidity (70–75%). A small fan moving air through the burlap is desirable. The air velocity through the burlap screen should be 125 to 175 fpm. It is necessary to periodically wash the burlap to remove dirt and to kill mold which accumulates. An evaporative cooler requires approximately 1.27 kwh of electricity per case.

If eggs get wet, mold may enter through the shell and spoil the eggs. To avoid condensation on the surface, eggs should not be cooled below the dewpoint.

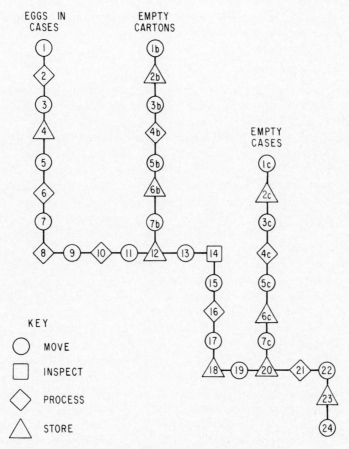

Fig. E-1. Flow for egg grading center

1—Eggs in cases moved from receiving trucks via chutes to scales. 2—Eggs weighed in crates when brought in by trucks. 3—Eggs in cases moved to storage by dollies. 4—Refrigerated storage of newly arrived eggs. 5—Eggs moved to washer and drier. 6—Eggs removed from case; eggs washed and dried. 7—Eggs placed on conveyor belt and taken to sizing machines. 1b—Egg cartons brought into plant unassembled. 2b—Unassembled egg cartons stored until needed. 3b—Unassembled egg cartons moved from storage to carton assembly. 4b—Egg cartons assembled by machine. 5b—Assembled cartons placed in chutes overhead the candlers. Cartons move down chutes by gravity. 6b—Assembled cartons stored overhead until candler needs them. 7b—Candler moves cartons in front, into which are placed candled eggs. 1c—Unassembled cases brought into plant. 2c—Unassembled cases stored until needed. 3c—Unassembled cases moved from storage to assembly area. 4c—Cases assembled. 5c—Assembled cases placed near rotary packing table. 6c—Assembled cases stored until egg cartons are ready to be packed in cases. 7c—Cases moved to rotary packing table to be filled. 8—Eggs physically separated into specific size groups by weight. 9—Eggs roll down an incline to candler. 10—Candling: a manual-visual operation to determine the thickness of albumen, presence of spots in albumen or yolk, roundness or flatness of yolk, condition of shell and stability of air cell. 11—Eggs placed in carton manually. 12—Eggs placed in egg cartons until filled, then moved to conveyor. 13—Eggs placed on conveyor manually. Cartons then moved to the inspector. 14—An inspection to insure that the proper grade cartons go to the correct case packer. 15—Cartons moved from inspector to sealer. 16—Cartons closed and sealed with date stamped on them. 17—Cartons moved from sealer to rotary packing table. 18—Cartons stored on rotary packing table. 19—Cartons placed in cases manually from rotary packing table. 20—Cartons stored in cases until the case is full. 21—Cases sealed with staples. 22—Cases moved to cold storage by dollies. 23—Cases moved into cold storage until shipped. 24—Cases moved from cold storage to truck.

Hatching eggs should be cooled to 40° to 65°F, with 55°F recommended, to prevent development of the embryo.

Grading

The grading of eggs involves sorting as to quality and condition of the product including cleanliness of the surface and candling for internal qualities and for size determination (Fig. E.1).

Cleaning of eggs consists of dirt removal by abrasive action using a light sandpaper or by washing and drying. Washing with water 160° to 170°F for about $1/3$ min will give rapid cleaning, and no more than 2°F increase in egg temperature which also aids in subsequent drying. Lower temperatures are often used for a longer time and detergent-germicide combinations added to improve the keeping qualities. Pasteurization of cleaned eggs in the shell can be done by agitating the eggs in a water bath at 144°F for over 2 min. After washing, the eggs can be dried by moving unheated or heated air over the eggs.

After cleaning and drying, the eggs may be given an oil or plastic coating to close the pores of the shell so that air, water vapor, and bacteria cannot enter and contaminate the eggs. Sealing of the eggs helps maintain a carbon dioxide percentage equivalent to that in a fresh egg of about 10%. By maintaining the carbon dioxide level the movement of water from the albumen into the yolk is inhibited.

Classes of egg quality range from AA (the highest), A, B, to C (the lowest edible quality). The different sizes are jumbo, extra large, large, medium, small, and peewee. Thus, eggs are identified by a combination of weight-quality, i.e., Large AA, Small AA, etc. The size is based on the weight of 1 doz eggs such as 24 oz which means that 12 eggs or 1 doz are required to make 24 oz.

An egg grading center is described (Fig. E.2). Eggs are delivered daily to the processing plant by refrigerated trucks. The eggs are moved off the truck on a metal chute. The egg cases move by gravity along the chute to a set of scales, where they are then weighed. The weight is recorded and the date of entry is stamped on the case.

PERSONNEL

1-8	CANDLERS
9-10	LOADERS
11	CASE HANDLER
12	CARTON PACKER
13	INSPECTOR
14	CARTON SUPPLIER

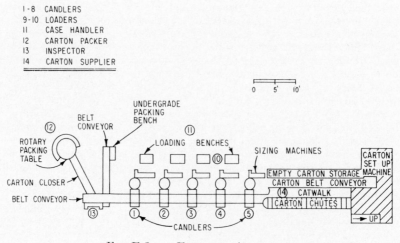

Fɪɢ. E-2.   Egg processing center

The eggs are moved from the scales by dollys to the cold storage where they remain until needed. This storage period is usually less than one day. The eggs are removed from cold storage on dollys and taken to the egg washer and dryer. An air agitation machine using a mild detergent is often used for washing.

A belt conveyor transfers the washed eggs to the egg weighing machine. The eggs roll down an incline from the sizing machine to the candlers. The candlers grade the eggs into the grades of A, B, C, and checks. These grades are assigned on the basis of the amount of thick or thin albumen, roundness or flatness of the yolk, condition of the egg shell, and the stability of the air cell.

The eggs are placed in cartons and conveyed to an inspector, who sends them to the correct case packer. The cases are sealed and often date stamped on the seal before cased.

Candling

Candling of the eggs consists of placing them before a light which shines through the shell. The position and size of the yolk, the air sack, and presence of foreign materials such as blood cells can be seen from the candling examination (Fig. E.3). A worker can candle from 30 to 40 cases of eggs per 8-hr day. A case contains 24 doz eggs. Half-cases are sometimes used. Equipment is now available for automatic weighing of eggs rapidly and without damage. Electronic methods of grading are being developed for evaluation of those properties now done through manual candling.

Cold Storage

During some seasons of the year, production of eggs exceeds consumption. Eggs produced during this time can be removed from the shells and placed in cold storage at 0°F or lower and kept for several months. The eggs may be broken out of their shells and stored as scrambled eggs in metal or glass containers. Another storage method is to separate the eggs and yolks and store separately under refrigerated conditions. Less storage space, about $1/6$ that required for whole eggs in the case, is required for dried eggs. A spray dryer is used for drying eggs. Whole eggs for drying are preheated to 140°F, forced through nozzles under a pressure of 2,000 to 6,000 psi, and dried with air at 250° to 300°F to 4 to 5% moisture content.

Cross-reference: *Refrigerated Storage.*

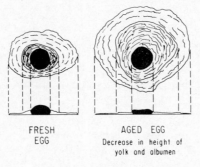

FRESH
EGG

AGED EGG
Decrease in height of
yolk and albumen

Fig. E-3.   Comparison between body of fresh and aged eggs

ELECTRIC MOTORS

An electric motor converts electrical energy to mechanical energy on a rotating shaft. Motors used in food processing plants are usually induction motors. The larger motors above 50 hp are synchronous. With an induction motor, the speed of the shaft is slightly less than synchronous speed.

Induction motors are normally of the single-phase or three-phase type. The single-phase has a special winding arrangement for starting the motor. The 3-phase does not have a special starting mechanism and consequently is 15 to 25% less expensive to build, has slightly more efficiency, and requires less maintenance. After the starting operation, both single-phase and three-phase motors run by induction. A 2-pole motor will run from 3,450 to 3,500 rpm, a 4-pole 1,725 to 1,750 rpm, and a 6-pole motor 1,150 to 1,165 rpm.

Principles

Three major types of single-phase induction motors are used: the split phase start, the capacitor start, and the repulsion start. Each has varying characteristics according to starting torque, starting current, and effect on line voltage (Table E.3).

Induction motors may be designed for 2 different voltages, such as 115 or 230. To reverse the motor, the connections to the starting winding are reversed. For a repulsion start induction run motor, with dual voltage, there are two running windings, with the starting winding in the rotor or armature.

Protection

Protection is needed that will permit the motor to draw enough current for starting on normal load, yet providing the motor protection against an overcurrent that will cause excess heating after the motor has been operated for some time (Fig. E.4). A

TABLE E.3

CHARACTERISTICS OF MOTORS

Single-phase, 60-cycle A-C, 115 and 230 V

	Horse-power	Rpm Rated Speed	Starting Torque	Reversibility	Starting Current	Comparative Cost	Applications
Shaded-pole	Up to $1/10$	1,500 1,000	Low	No	High	50%	Portable fans, ventilating fans, agitators, and low starting load equipment
Split-phase general purpose	Up to $1/3$	3,450 1,725 1,140 865	Medium	Yes	Medium	85%	Fans, blowers, oil burners where frequent starting is required
Capacitor-start induction	$1/8$-$3/4$	3,450 1,725 1,140 865	High	Yes	Low	100%	Refrigerators, pumps, compressors. Dual voltage
Repulsion-start induction	$1/4$-10	3,450 1,725 1,140	High	Yes (brush)	Low	105%	Same as above
Universal	Up to $3/4$	500-15,000 (variable)	High	No	Low	150%	Vacuum cleaners, food mixers, etc., single voltage, DC or AC current

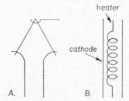

Fɪɢ. E-4.   Heated cathode: A—direct heated; B—indirect heated

heater coil in the starter switch provides motor protection. The usual capacity is 125 to 140% of the ampere rating on the motor nameplate. Single-phase control will have 1 heater coil, and a 3-phase control 2 heater coils. A circuit which is used for lighting only can use specially designed plug fuses sold under the name of Fustron or Fusestat to avoid breaking the circuit with the normal fuse during the normal starting time with the motor.

Motor Maintenance

The following items should be checked to properly maintain motors in operation. (1) Protect motors from moisture. (2) Be sure that motor is large enough for the job. (3) Use only proper size of fuse and overload relay. (4) Use proper electrical connections. A single-phase connection on three-phase motor may cause motor to fail. (5) Use proper or adequate size of wires to avoid excessive voltage drop. In general, the wire should be large enough so that there will not be in excess of 2% voltage drop to the motor (Table E.5). (6) Properly lubricate bearings, neither over- nor under-lubricating them. (7) Be sure motor is properly aligned. (8) Avoid unnecessary starting and stopping and running of motors. (9) Provide adequate ventilation so that the motor does not overheat. Clean surroundings help extend motor life.

Economics

For most economic operation, motors should operate close to full load (Table E. 6). A high power factor should be maintained. Three-phase motors provide better power factor characteristics than single-phase motors. Operating cost is kept at a minimum by larger size of copper wire to minimize voltage drop.

Cross-reference: *Electric Wiring.*

ELECTRIC WIRING

Electric current is the flow of electrons. Electric conductors are used to provide for the efficient flow of electrons. Good conductors, including metals such as copper and aluminum, have a low resistance to flow of electrons. Insulators such as rubber, porcelain, oil, and air which help keep the electrons in the conductor, have a resistance to flow of electrons. Electric wiring is basically a conductor mounted on insulators or a conductor covered with insulation.

The more power (based on amperes) carried, the larger is the wire as designated by gage number (Tables E.7 and E.8). The higher the voltage the more insulation or insulator for bare wire is needed. As electric current flows through the wire heat

TABLE E.4

OVERCURRENT PROTECTION FOR MOTORS

Full Load Current Rating of Motor, Amp	For Running Protection of Motors		Max. Allowable Rating of Branch Circuit Protection Devices Single Phase, Squirrel Cage, Synchronous	
	Max. of Nonadjustable Devices	Max. of Adjustable Devices	Fuses	Overload Trip
1	2	1.25	15	15
2	3	2.50	15	15
3	4	3.75	15	15
4	6	5.0	15	15
5	8	6.25	15	15
7	10	8.75	25	20
8	10	10.0	25	20
10	15	12.5	30	30
15	20	18.75	45	40
20	25	25.00	60	50
30	40	37.50	90	100
40	50	50.00	125	100
50	60	62.50	150	125
60	80	75.00	200	150
70	90	87.50	225	175
80	100	100.00	250	200
90	110	112.50	300	225
100	125	125.00	300	250
110	150	137.50	350	300
120	150	150.00	400	300
130	175	162.50	400	350
150	200	187.50	450	400
175	225	219.00	600	500
200	250	250.00	600	500
250	300	313.00	800	700

Source: National Electrical Code.

is produced. It is desirable to keep the heat loss to a low economical value by a small resistance from the wire. Resistance to flow of electric current in a particular conductor is represented by voltage drop. Acceptable voltage drops usually found are 1 to 3% in lighting circuits, and up to 5% in motor circuits. With an input of 230 v, the output of the circuit for a 2% voltage drop is 225.4 v.

The insulation and material around the wire must permit transfer of heat away while containing the electrons. Insulation varies depending on voltage of the circuit; exposure such as outdoor, indoor, or buried; moisture conditions; abrasive possibilities; and temperature.

Cross-references: *Aluminum; Electricity; Electric Motors; Energy.*

ELECTRICITY

Electricity is always a part of each molecule. All materials have an electrical potential or charge. The flow of an electric current is caused by adjustments in

TABLE E.5

WIRE SIZES FOR INDIVIDUAL SINGLE-PHASE OR THREE-PHASE MOTORS BASED ON 2% VOLTAGE DROP
ON FULL LOAD CURRENT

Motor Hp	Volts	Approx. Fl. Ld. Amp	Length of Run in Feet							
			50	100	200	300	400	500	800	1,000
$1/20$	115	2.4	14	14	12	10	10	8	6	6
$1/12$	115	2.6	14	14	12	10	10	8	6	6
$1/8$	115	2.8	14	14	12	10	8	8	6	6
$1/6$	115	3.2	14	14	12	10	8	8	6	4
$1/4$	115	4.6	14	12	10	8	6	6	4	2
$1/3$	115	5.1	14	12	10	8	6	6	4	2
$1/2$	115	7.4	14	10	8	6	4	4	2	1
$3/4$	115	10.2	12	10	6	4	4	2	1	0
$1/6$	230	1.6	14	14	14	14	14	14	12	10
$1/4$	230	2.3	14	14	14	14	12	12	10	8
$1/3$	230	2.6	14	14	14	14	12	12	10	8
$1/2$	230	3.7	14	14	14	12	10	10	8	6
$3/4$	230	5.1	14	14	12	10	10	8	6	6
1	230	6.5	14	14	12	-10	8	8	6	4
$1 1/2$	230	9.2	14	-12	10	8	6	6	4	2
2	230	12.0	14	-12	8	6	6	4	2	2
3	230	17.0	10	-10	8	6	4	4	2	1
5	230	28.0	10[a]	8	6	4	2	2	0	-00
$7 1/2$	230	40.0	8[b]	6	4	2	1	0	000	0000
10	230	50.0	6[a]	6[a]	2	1	0	00	-0000	250M[1]

[1] M = circular mils.

electrical potential toward equilibrium. In order to understand electricity, it is necessary to visualize the electron, the basic unit of electric current. Once the electron is in mind, almost all common electrical devices can be visualized as masses of electrons performing according to the force exerted upon them.

Electrons

Physicists and chemists are not in complete agreement as to the status of the electron in the atom. The chemists often think of the atom as composed of a dense nucleus surrounded by one or more stationary electrons while the physicists think of the electrons as moving about the nucleus much as planets move about the sun. However it may be, it seems certain that the atom is mostly space with a dense nucleus as heavy as if a grain of sand weighed a ton, and the electron as far from the nucleus proportionately as the planets are from the sun.

Each atom has a normal number of satellite electrons about it, beginning with 1 for hydrogen, 2 for helium, and so on up through the scale of elements to the heaviest atoms such as uranium. Although each element has a normal number of electrons when it is in electrical equilibrium, it often happens that an element loses some of its electrons or gains extra ones because of friction, heat, magnetism, or differences in electrical potential. If electrons are displaced, the material has a positive charge; if extra electrons are gained, it has a negative charge. If may happen that two materials both have extra electrons in which case the material with the least extra electrons

TABLE E.6A

FULL LOAD CURRENTS IN AMPERES

Direct Current Motors[1]

Hp	115V	230V	550V
$1/4$	3	1.5	
$1/3$	3.8	1.9	
$1/2$	5.4	2.7	
$3/4$	7.4	3.7	1.6
1	9.6	4.8	2.0
$1^1/_2$	13.2	6.6	2.7
2	17	8.5	3.6
3	25	12.5	5.2
5	40	20	8.3
$7^1/_2$	58	29	12
10	76	38	16
15	112	56	23
20	148	74	31
25	184	92	38
30	220	110	46
40	292	146	61
50	360	180	75
60	430	215	90
75	536	268	111
100	—	355	148
125	—	443	184
150	—	534	220
200	—	712	295

[1] Values of full-load currents are for motors running at usual speed.
Source: National Electric Code.

TABLE E.6B

FULL LOAD CURRENTS IN AMPERES

Single Phase Alternating Current Motors[1]

Hp	115V	230V	440V
$1/6$	4.4	2.2	
$1/4$	5.8	2.9	
$1/3$	7.2	3.6	
$1/2$	9.8	4.9	
$3/4$	13.8	6.9	
1	16	8	
$1^1/_2$	20	10	
2	24	12	
3	34	17	
5	56	28	
$7^1/_2$	80	40	21
10	100	50	26

[1] Values of full-load currents are for motors running at usual speeds and motors with normal torque characteristics. Motors built for especially low speeds or high torques may have higher full-load currents, in which case the name and current ratings should be used.

To obtain full-load currents of 208- and 200-volt motors, increase corresponding 230-volt motor full-load currents by 10 and 15%, respectively.

Source: National Electric Code.

will be positive in respect to the material with the most electrons. Electrons are seldom lost. The nature of the power of attraction between an electron and the nucleus is not clearly defined, but it is very much like the gravitational pull between the earth and the moon, or the earth and the sun in which the mass is balanced with the velocity with which the system revolves. With this concept it is possible to visualize matter as consisting of mostly space with a multitude of atoms each with electrons which are sometimes shifted from one atom to the other.

Current

Direct electrical current is believed to be a parallel flow of electrons in the same direction among the atoms of a substance. Electrons can be forced into a circuit in which they flow from one atom to another. Sometimes, as in static electricity, there is no circuit and electrons are knocked out of one material and accumulated in another material with no place to go. Alternating current is like direct current except that the direction of the electron flow is constantly swinging back and forth like a pendulum. The ability of different materials to conduct electricity varies greatly. The conductivity is usually better at low temperatures. At ordinary temperatures, mercury is the poorest of metallic conductors, and silver is the best being about 66 times as good as

TABLE E.6C

FULL-LOAD CURRENT

Three-Phase AC Motors

	Induction Type Squirrel-Cage and Wound Rotor, Amp					Synchronous Type Unity Power Factor, Amp			
Hp	110V	220V	440V	550V	2300V	220V	440V	550V	230V
$1/2$	4	2	1	.8					
$3/4$	5.6	2.8	1.4	1.1					
1	7	3.5	1.8	1.4					
$1\frac{1}{2}$	10	5	2.5	2.0					
2	13	6.5	3.3	2.6					
3		9	4.5	4					
5		15	7.5	6					
$7\frac{1}{2}$		22	11	9					
10		27	14	11					
15		40	20	16					
20		52	26	21					
25		64	32	26	7	54	27	22	5.4
30		78	39	31	8.5	65	33	26	6.5
40		104	52	41	10.5	86	43	35	8
50		125	63	50	13	108	54	44	10
60		150	75	60	16	128	64	51	12
75		185	93	74	19	161	81	65	15
100		246	123	98	25	211	106	85	20
125		310	155	124	31	264	132	106	25
150		360	180	144	37		158	127	30
200		480	240	192	48		210	168	40

For full-load currents of 208- and 200-volt motors, increase the corresponding 220-volt motor full-load current by 6 and 10 per cent, respectively.

Source: National Electric Code.

mercury. Copper is next best being about 94% as good as silver. As a conductor of electricity, aluminum is 51% as good as silver and 55% as good as copper. When aluminum is used for transmission lines, the size of wire must be increased to make up for its lower conductivity. Also iron strands may be added to provide strength. Iron has only 16% of the conductivity of copper, and lead has less still, being only 8% as good as copper.

The flow of electricity is much like the flow of water with electrons flowing along the path of least resistance, and with electrons easily influenced by magnetic forces.

Magnetism

Magnetism is a phenomena that everyone knows about but seldom understands. It is not quite clear as to what the basic material comprises. However, just as infrared radiation is a constant phenomena of molecular and atomic motion, so is magnetism a constant phenomena of electron motion. For example, when an electric current flows in a wire, the wire is surrounded by magnetic lines of force. When looking along the wire in the direction in which the current is flowing, the lines of magnetic force circle the wire in a clockwise direction. If the wire is made into a coil and each coil insulated from every other coil, the lines of magnetic force are combined in strength according to the number of coils.

The magnetic lines of force meet less resistance through some materials than others. Air offers considerable resistance to magnetic force whereas iron offers very little resistance, and some kinds of iron can be made into permanent magnets radiating their own lines of force just as if an electric current were flowing in the iron. Soft iron will not hold permanent magnetism, but can be made into a temporary magnet by placing it in the magnetic field of an electric coil, thus becoming an electromagnet.

If a wire is moved through a magnetic field against the lines of force, then electricity is induced to flow in the wire. Thus an electric generator can be made by arranging wires or bars through the lines of force of permanent magnets as in a magneto. It might seem that the magnet would soon use up its magnetism, but this is not the case. Instead, the energy to produce the electrical current comes from the

TABLE E.7

BRANCH CIRCUIT REQUIREMENTS[1]

Circuit Rating	15 Amp	20 Amp	30 Amp	50 Amp
Conductors (Min. Size)				
Circuit wires	14	12	10	6
Taps	14	14	14	12
Overcurrent Protection	15 Amp	20 Amp	30 Amp	50 Amp
Outlet Devices				
Lampholders permitted	Any type	Any type	Heavy duty	Heavy duty
Receptacle rating	15 Max. amp	15 or 20 Amp	30 Amp	50 Amp
Maximum Load	15 Amp	20 Amp	30 Amp	50 Amp

[1] Type R, RW, RU, RUW, RH-RW, SA, T, TW, RH, RUH, RHW, RHH, and THW conductors in raceway or cable.

Source: National Electric Code.

TABLE E.8

ALLOWABLE CURRENT-CARRYING CAPACITIES OF INSULATED COPPER CONDUCTORS IN AMPERES[1]

Size AWG MCM	Rubber Type R Type RW Type RW Type RUW (14-2) / Type RH-RW Thermoplastic Type T Type TW	Rubber Type RH RUH (14-2) / Type RH-RW Type RHW Thermoplastic Type THW	Paper Thermoplastic Asbestos Type TA SA / Var-Cam Type V Asbestos Var-Cam Type AVB / MI Cable RHH[2]	Asbestos Var-Cam Type AVA Type AVL	Impregnated Asbestos Type AI (14-8) Type AIA	Asbestos Type A (14-8) Type AA
14	15	15	25	30	30	30
12	20	20	30	35	40	40
10	30	30	40	45	50	55
8	40	45	50	60	65	70
6	55	65	70	80	85	95
4	70	85	90	105	115	120
3	80	100	105	120	130	145
2	95	115	120	135	145	165
1	110	130	140	160	170	190
0	125	150	155	190	200	225
00	145	175	185	215	230	250
000	165	200	210	245	265	285
0000	195	230	235	275	310	340
250	215	255	270	315	335	...
300	240	285	300	345	380	...
350	260	310	325	390	420	...
400	280	335	360	420	450	...
500	320	380	405	470	500	...
600	355	420	455	525	545	...
700	385	460	490	560	600	...
750	400	475	500	580	620	...
800	410	490	515	600	640	...
900	435	520	555	...	...	...

Correction Factors, Room Temps. Over 86°F

°C	°F						
40	104	.82	.88	.90	.94	.95	...
45	113	.71	.82	.85	.90	.92	...
50	122	.58	.75	.80	.87	.89	...
55	131	.41	.67	.74	.83	.86	...
60	140	...	.58	.67	.79	.83	.91
70	158	...	...	.52	.71	.76	.87
75	167	...	...	.43	.66	.72	.86
80	176	...	...	.30	.61	.69	.84
90	194	...	...	...	.50	.61	.80
100	212	...	...	...	...	.51	.77
120	248	...	...	...	...	...	.69
140	284	...	...	...	...	...	.59
°C	°F						

[1] Not more than three conductors in raceway or cable or direct burial (based on room temperature of 86°F).

[2] The current-carrying capacities for Type RHH conductors for sizes AWG 14, 12 and 10 shall be the same as designated for Type RH conductors in this Table.

Source: National Electric Code.

force required to move the wire against the magnetic field. Everyone who has tried to turn a hand operated magneto as in some of the older telephone systems, knows that it requires force to turn the crank. Most generators use the magnetic field from energized electromagnets rather than permanent magnets for production of electricity. Electric motors operate like generators, except in reverse.

By considering electrons and magnetism together, one can better visualize electricity in solids: a picture of electrons speeding through space surrounded by their lines of magnetic force, or at home in their appointed positions in the outer orbit of an atom until the near approach of other electrons force them out of position, or the absence of an electron nearby leaves an abyss into which one falls.

Electrical Measurement

Amperes are units of electric current and are proportional to the number of electrons flowing. Amperes may be compared to gallons of water flowing through a pipe. The diameter of the pipe determines to a large extent the volume of water that can be forced through the pipe in a minute. The diameter and conducting capacity of a wire determine the number of amperes that pass through the wire. The coulomb is the unit of electrical quantity and each ampere is equal to one coulomb per second. Although of no importance here, the coulomb is the amount of electrical energy required to electroplate the negative terminal in a solution with 0.001118 gm of metallic silver. The coulomb represents an actual number of electrons passing through the electroplating solution. As amperes flow through a wire or other conductor, they meet a resistance similar to ordinary friction and some of the electrical motion is converted to heat. An extreme example of this is in the filament of a lamp where the resistance in the filament is so intense that the tungsten glows white hot. Electrical friction or resistance has a special name and one unit of resistance is called an ohm.

Voltage is the force or potential difference that pushes the amperes past the ohms. The amount of force that will push one ampere through a resistance of one ohm is one volt. Volts, amperes, and ohms must always be in balance. In calculations, volts = ohms × amperes in an algebraic equation or some algebraic rearrangement of this formula. The measure of electrical work is the watt hour, the watt being the unit of electrical power. A watt is one ampere flowing at one volt pressure (volts × amperes = watts). In work, one watt is equal to 44.4 ft-lb per min or 746 watts are equal to 1 hp. Conversion factors include 1,000 watts equals 3,412 Btu per hr or 1 Kwh equals 3,412 Btu per hr.

Coils

The electric coil is extensively used and, as explained under magnetism, multiplies the magnetic field according to the number of turns and arrangement of the turns.

The electromagnet consists of an iron core surrounded by an electrified coil which concentrates magnetic lines of force in the iron. Soft iron is used because as soon as the electric current is stopped, the iron loses its magnetism. The power of the electromagnet varies with the number of amperes as well as the number of turns. Electromagnets are much used for operating switches and safety devices. Voltage regulators, low voltage switches, and relays are usually electromagnetic devices. By bending the soft iron core in the form of a horseshoe, the two poles of the magnet are brought closer together and the power of the magnet is increased. Horseshoe type electromagnets are used for lifting iron, picking iron out of grain and feed, and for other situations requiring quick powerful action. Electromagnets are rather simple to make, but the wire must be the proper gage for the volume of current and carry enough insulation to keep the coil from shorting.

Induction coils are a basic device for use with alternating current. Alternating current flows first in one direction and then in the other. Most power stations supply an alternating current that make 60 cycles per second. It is obvious that when alternating current flows through a coil, the magnetic lines of force will form and fade away in one direction, and then repeat the process in the other direction as the flow of current alternates. If another coil is placed near the first coil and arranged to form an independent circuit, the lines of magnetic force cut across the conductors and induce a current.

Power Factor

For alternating current electricity the apparent power is the volts, E, times amperes, I, or $E \times I$. The true power will be different than the apparent power if the voltage and amperage are not in phase with each other. The true power (watts) can be determined with an appropriate wattmeter. The apparent power (watts) can be determined from the product of volts and amperes of the circuit. The power factor is the true power divided by the apparent power. The power factor is 1 or less and is

$$\frac{\text{watts}}{\text{volts} \times \text{amperes}}$$

Electronic Oven

Uniform rapid heating can be obtained with an electronic oven. Commercial units operate at approximately 2,450,000,000 cycles per second. Heating is obtained by molecular movement caused by alternating current.

Cross-references: *Batteries; Electric Motors; Electric wiring; Energy; Graphite; Lighting.*

ELECTROLYTIC CORROSION

It is normal to think of a battery as being a commercial product of certain size and shape, but batteries are often unwittingly provided by combinations of susceptible materials.

An electrolyte can be formed by acids or salts that occur in almost all water and dew. Moisture falling or condensing from the air contains carbonic acid formed by the absorption of carbon dioxide from the air. Air near the sea, usually contains salt from the sea which drifts with the dust in the air. Ground water from ditches, wells, creeks, and springs also contains acids or salts to some degree.

Applications

When two metals are both moistened by the same solution, the more active metal tends to displace the other. The most common example of this occurs with galvanized roofing and pipes. The zinc used to galvanize the iron being more active than iron always takes precedence and reacts with salts and acids in adjacent moisture and prevents the iron from acting. Eventually, all the zinc will have gone into solution and then the iron will begin to dissolve whenever it has opportunity to displace something less active. Iron usually displaces hydrogen in the acids that occur in soil, organic materials, and in rain water. Iron in alkaline solutions is more durable because most of the salts forming alkaline solutions are higher than iron in the activity series.

Pipelines, water tanks, and other iron work in moist places can be protected from ionic corrosion by furnishing coatings or attachments of higher metals for which magnesium and zinc are much used. Tin being below iron in activity does not protect the iron from electrolysis. The protection by tin is merely a fencing operation to keep solutions away from the iron. Once moisture gets through the tin to the iron, corrosion quickly follows. Metals like tin, gold, silver, and copper are so slow to form ions that they have long been recognized for their durability.

Recent trends toward the use of aluminum, magnesium, and many other metals have increased the possibility for electrolytic corrosion by providing opportunities for one metal to displace another.

When aluminum roofing is nailed with iron nails, the aluminum tends to displace the iron and eventually corrosion destroys the security of the fastening. This situation is overcome by the use of aluminum nails.

Ionization is not responsible for all metallic destruction. Oxygen and chemical fumes attack some metals and destroy them, but unless moisture and carbon dioxide are present, the process is usually slow.

Another opportunity for electrolytic corrosion occurs when two different metals are joined together and an electric current tends to flow and electrons pass from the more active metal to the less active metal. As long as all junctions between the two metals are the same temperature the flow will be neutralized, but if a junction between two metals is heated, the flow of electrons will be increased at the heated junction, and enough voltage will be developed to overcome the back flow at cooler junctions. This principle is used extensively in thermocouples to measure temperatures at remote or dangerous locations and to measure temperatures in furnaces. It is possible because the flow of current is proportional to the temperature at the junction. It is obvious that in metal work on roofs, downspouts, and in piping that the use of combinations of metals may result in a flow of current that may aid electrolysis.

Cross-references: *Batteries; Electricity; EMF Series.*

ELECTRONICS

The field of electronics is based on a substantial body of literature. Years of study can be devoted to the subject. The purpose of the following material is to acquaint the reader with some of the basic principles which will help understand some of the phenomena involved. Specially trained technicians are needed to service most electronic equipment in a food plant.

Electronics refers to the study involving the flow of electrons through gas-filled tubes, vacuum tubes, and transistors, etc., with the accompanying circuits and controls.

Cathode

The most elementary tube consists of a cathode from which electrons are emitted, as water is evaporated from the surface of a lake. The cathode may be caused to emit electrons by heating the cathode, by directing light radiation on the surface, or by placing a high magnetic field around the cathode to "pull" the electrons off. Heat is commonly used. The heat may be applied directly, by heating the filament using electricity, alternating current or direct current, or indirectly, using a heater element near the cathode. Symbolically, these may be represented as shown in Fig. E.4A and B.

The diode (two electrodes) is one of the simplest of units, which consists of a cathode, which is an electron emitter, and an anode, called a plate, which collects electrons and is positively charged (Fig. E.5). The current will flow in the diode only when the plate is positive with respect to the cathode. Current will flow only in one direction. The diode can act as a switch or valve, starting or stopping current flow depending on the plate charge. This characteristic provides the ability to rectify alternating current to direct current by cancelling $1/2$ of the cycle. Various electron tubes (diodes) respond differently depending on material, area of cathodes and plate, heating, gas, and voltage on the plate. Graphs and tables furnished by the manufacturers present these relationships. Tubes are selected to accomplish a certain response.

Triode

Elements can be added of various types to alter the response of the basic tube. A third element, a control grid, may be added to make a triode. The control grid is placed between the cathode and plate closer to the cathode. The control grid does not obstruct the flow of electrons, but when a small voltage is applied to the control grid, there is a large variation in the plate current through the tube.

A triode (Fig. E.6) has three operating voltages: the voltage on the plate is positive, on the heater is alternating current or direct current, and the direct current

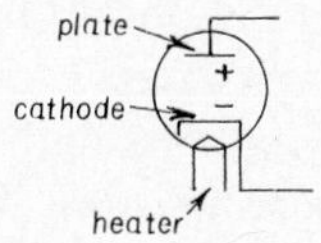

FIG. E-5.   Diode

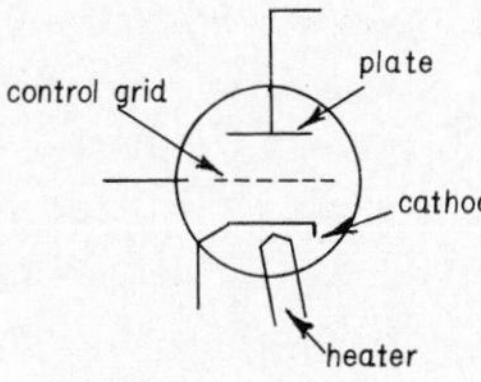

FIG. E-6.   Triode

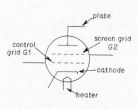

FIG. E-7.   Tetrode

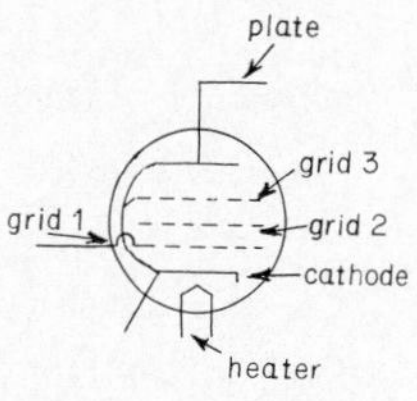

FIG. E-8.   Pentrode

voltage on the grid slightly negative from cathode. A signal voltage is the name given to the alternating voltage imposed on the grid. The characteristics of the tube are based on the grid wire size and spacing, and the grid and plate dimensions. An important use of the triode is to obtain voltage amplification, such as from a voice microphone.

Tetrode

A tetrode is formed by inserting a screen grid between the control grid and the plate of a triode (Fig. E.7). The screen grid is an effective electrostatic shield which presents feedback of energy. In schematic diagrams the control grid is represented by G1 and the screen grid by G2.

Pentode

A fifth element, a third grid, G3, added to the tetrode makes a pentode (Fig. E.8). The G3 grid is added between the screen grid G2 and the plate. G3 is called the suppressor grid because it reduces the effects of secondary emission by directing these secondary electrons back to the plate rather than letting them go to the screen grid. The suppressor grid may be connected, or grounded, to the cathode.

Transistors

Transistors replace electronic tubes for many applications. Transistors have no heater element, longer life, less heat dissipation, and usually are smaller. Transistors are generally not used for high voltages.

Transistors are made of semiconductors. A charge carrier moves through a solid pure material. The most popular semiconductors are germanium, silicon, and selenium. Each atom of a pure metal made with germanium will have four electrons in the outer orbit. The pure material may be "doped" with a substance like arsenic or antimony, which has five electrons (called donors) in the outer orbit. The pure material may be "doped" with indium or gallium, which has three electrons (called acceptors) in the outer orbit. The germanium "doped" with arsenic is an N-type, negative, because the fifth electron does not find a place in the structure and is free to roam, and when an electric field is applied, electrons go to the positive pole. It is called N-type because the negative charge carries. If the impurity has only three electrons in the outer shell, it is known as a P-type where the current is carried on by the holes, equivalent to a positive charge. The P- and N-elements may be connected in various manners to produce the same effects as certain vacuum tubes (Fig. E.9).

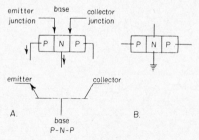

Fig. E-9.   P- and N-elements: A—triode (here charge carriers are holes) and
B—tetrode

EMF SERIES

The relative activity of materials is represented by the electromotive force (EMF) series as follows with the most active ions or material highest on the list:

calcium	nickel	copper (Cu^{2+})
sodium	410 stainless steel	oxygen (O_2)
aluminum	50–50 solder	copper (Cu^+)
zinc	300 stainless steel	bronze
chromium	tin	silver
steel	lead	mercury
cast iron (Fe^{2+})	hydrogen	chlorine
	brass	

Practices and Principles

(1)   A material in the preceding list will replace a material below it.

(2)   If aluminum and stainless steel are in contact with an electrolyte between, the aluminum will go into solution or be deposited on stainless steel.

(3)   Aluminum bars in a chlorine solution can be used to protect a steel tank.

(4)   Stainless steel 400 series will corrode more rapidly than 300 series in a chlorine solution.   (The EMF difference between the metals and chlorine is greater for the 400 series.)

(5)   Some materials, such as lead, would be toxic.

(6)   The closer together on the preceding list two materials appear, the less likely corrosion will develop.

Cross-references: *Batteries; Corrosion; Electricity; Electrolytic Corrosion; Stainless Steel.*

ENERGY

Energy is the capacity to do useful work.   Energy may be used for providing light, heat, motion, chemical reaction, etc.   Energy sources might be considered in order of their availability to perform desirable tasks.   Electricity might be considered at a higher level than other energy sources, because energy is available from electricity for carrying out most desirable functions, such as light and heat.

Heat on the other hand, such as in a hot body from the heating element, a friction member, or steam, is at a low level source, because it is available to provide heat units to a lower temperature source, which might be used for motion but probably not for light.   Thus, energy sources could be listed in order of availability: solar, nuclear, electric, chemical, fossil fuel, motion, and heat.

Passing electricity through a conductor may be done so as to provide considerable heat, but is difficult, although not impossible, to produce a large flow of electricity by heating a conductor.   The flow of energy is in the direction of less availability, that is, toward heat.

Mechanical Energy

Energy may be available from a mechanical device.   A moving body possesses energy because of its motion, known as kinetic energy (KE)

$$KE = \frac{wv^2}{g^2}$$

where KE = kinetic energy, ft lb
  w = weight of body, lb
  g = acceleration, 32.2 ft per sec^2
  v = velocity of the body, ft per sec
  1 mph = 1.46 ft per sec

A rotating device has kinetic energy because of its motion

$$KE = \frac{IW^2}{2}$$

where I = inertia in lb-ft^2
  W = angular velocity in radians per second

where 2π radians = 360°
  or 1 radian = 57.3°

Energy may be available from a body because of its position, and is known as potential energy (PE)

$$PE = W \times h$$

where h = vertical height, ft
  W = weight of the body, lb

Energy may be obtained from compressed gas. The amount of energy available from a compressed gas (E) is

$$E = W_a RT \ln \frac{P_1}{P_2}$$

where E = energy in ft-lb per lb
  W_a = weight of air used to move a pound of product or to atomize a pound of liquid
  R = gas constant
  T = absolute temperature, °R
  P_1 = initial pressure, psia (abs)
  P_2 = final pressure, psia (abs)
absolute
  pressure = gage pressure + 14.7 psi at sea level

This relationship can be used for determining the amount of energy available to atomize a liquid with a pneumatic atomizer, and to move a product through fluidization or pneumatic handling. The amount of energy available in a compressed air tank could be determined by this relationship. The value of the gas constant varies with gas involved.

Useful gas constants or R-values are as follows:

air	53.3	hydrogen	76.7
carbon dioxide	4.9	nitrogen	55.1
carbon monoxide	55.1	oxygen	48.3

Electricity for Heating

As electrons (electricity) flow through a conductor, heat is produced. In a conductor for lighting circuits, the quantity of energy utilized in heating is kept small with usually less than 2% voltage drop permitted. In a heating unit, the electrical conductor is designed to produce a large amount of heat. A small diameter conductor provides a high resistance to flow of electrons and heat is produced. The power (p) in watts, used for heating is

$$P = I^2R$$

where I = rate of electrical current flow in amperes
R = resistance of conductor in ohms

Energy is the power, (p) times the time, (t) so that electrical energy, (E) is equal to

$$E = I^2Rt$$

where energy, joules is converted into heat in time, (T)

$$E_B = 0.000948\ I^2Rt \text{ Btu}$$

The energy equivalent for electricity is that 1 kwh = 3412 Btu, or 1.34 hp hr, or 26.56×10^3 ft-lb.

Practically all of the energy of electricity is effective in heating. There are no combustion losses. The only losses occur through the insulation of the wire due to transfer of heat produced in the wire to the surrounding atmosphere. Electricity is more expensive in most localities as a heating source. It is a high level of energy, which can degrade into light and then into heat energy.

Heat from Fuel

During combustion of a fuel, heat is given off. The quantity is known as the heat of combustion or heating value. Fuels may be classified as gas, liquid, or solid. The heating value of a fuel may be classified as (1) net or low heating value and (2) gross or high heating value. The net heating value is obtained by subtracting the heat

TABLE E.9

HEATING VALUE OF TYPICAL FUELS

Fuel	High Heating Value Btu/lb
Coal	11,000 to 14,000
Oil	18,000 to 19,500
Natural gas	700 to 1,000
Saturated hydrocarbons (C_nH_{2n+2})	21,000 to 23,000
Unsaturated hydrocarbons (C_nH_{2n})	18,000 to 21,000
Lignite (dry)	6,000 to 7,000
Bagasse (dry)	8,000 to 9,000
Gasoline	20,200
Kerosene	19,900
Fuel oil	18,500
Hardwoods	8,100 to 8,900
Softwoods	8,400 to 11,000

needed to vaporize moisture from the moisture formed when a fuel burns. Approximately 1,000 Btu are required for each pound of water evaporated which comes from the moisture present in the fuel or the moisture formed during combustion. Water is formed during combustion if hydrogen is present in the fuel. Equations used to determine the gross heating value in Btu per lb of fuel are

Liquid fuel

$$Q = 13,500 \text{ C} + 60,890 \text{ H Btu/lb}$$

Solid fuel

$$Q = 14,500 \text{ C} + 62,000 \text{ H} \frac{0}{8} + 4,500 \text{ S}$$

where Q = Btu/per lb heating value
  C = % carbon in the fuel, written as a decimal or fraction
  H = % hydrogen, written as a decimal or fraction
  O = % oxygen
  S = % sulfur as a decimal or fraction

A rule-of-thumb is to consider that approximately 1 gal. of water is produced per each 1 gal. of fuel oil burned. The quantity of heat produced can be calculated roughly on the basis of amount of carbon, hydrogen, or sulfur burned. The total heat produced in oxidizing carbon to carbon monoxide is 4,400 Btu per lb; and for carbon to carbon dioxide, 14,000 Btu per lb; for oxidizing of hydrogen 62,000 Btu per lb; for oxidizing and sulfur 4,020 Btu per lb.

TABLE E.10

FUEL VALUES OF MILK AND PRODUCTS

	Cal/100 gm
4.0% Milk	71.6
Nonfat milk	37.5
Ice cream	208
18% BF cream	201
40% BF cream	381
Buttermilk	36.4
Sweetened condensed	335
Unsweetened condensed	172

Natural gas will produce approximately 1000 Btu per cu ft, but ranges from 700 to 2,500 Btu per cu ft. Heating values of typical fuels are presented in Table E.9.

To provide for the complete oxidation of fuel, it is necessary that the proper amount of oxygen, usually through air supply, be provided. It is the usual practice to provide from 10 to 50% more air than is required to assure complete combustion. At the same time, more air than is necessary should not be supplied to avoid excessive cooling of the flame, and therefore low efficiency.

Fuel Valve of Foods

Foods when consumed or oxidized release energy. The fuel values of milk and milk products are presented in Table E.10.

Cross-reference: *Horsepower.*

EQUILIBRIUM MOISTURE CONTENT

Equilibrium moisture content relates directly to the drying and storing of hygroscopic materials. The equilibrium moisture content is useful to determine whether a product will gain or lose moisture under a given set of temperature and relative humidity conditions. A product is in equilibrium with its environment when the rate of moisture loss from the product to the surrounding atmosphere is equal to the rate of moisture gain of the product from the surrounding atmosphere. The atmospheric conditions are defined by temperature and relative humidity. The moisture content of the product when it is in equilibrium with the surrounding atmosphere is called the *equilibrium moisture content* or *hygroscopic equilibrium.* The relative humidity of the surrounding atmosphere is known as the equilibrium relative humidity at the particular temperature. Thermodynamically, equilibrium is reached when the free energy change for a material is zero. The adsorption process is accompanied by a decrease in entropy. The equilibrium moisture content of a particular product varies with the relative humidity and the temperature, and may be expressed on either a wet or a dry basis. For use in mathematical calculations it is customary to express the moisture content on a dry basis.

The relationship between the moisture content of a particular material and its equilibrium relative humidity at the particular temperature can be expressed by means of equilibrium moisture curves or by tables (Table E.11 and E.12). These curves are sometimes referred to as isotherms because the values plotted for each curve usually correspond to a specific temperature. Unless stated otherwise, equilibrium moisture content curves are commonly plotted for a temperature of 77°F (25°C).

The composition of the product determines the adsorption of moisture. With feedstuffs, the relative amounts of soluble carbohydrate and protein largely determine the equilibrium moisture curve. At 63% RH the water adsorption varies directly with the carbohydrate content and inversely with the protein content, and at 90% RH the relationship is reversed.

Determination of Vapor Pressure

The equilibrium moisture content information can be used for determining the vapor pressure of the material. If the vapor pressure of the material is higher than the vapor pressure of the surrounding atmosphere, moisture will move from the material to the atmosphere. Conversely, if the vapor pressure of the material is lower than the surrounding atmosphere, moisture will move from the atmosphere to the material. The vapor pressure of the material in question can be readily determined by superimposing equilibrium moisture content data on a psychrometric chart. If the vapor pressure of the product is below that of the atmosphere, the product will gain moisture and may gain enough moisture to permit mold growth in storage to the extent that the product is damaged.

Cross-references: *Moisture Content; Moisture Measurement; Vapor Pressure.*

EVAPORATION

Evaporation occurs when molecules obtain enough energy to escape as a vapor

TABLE E.11

GRAIN EQUILIBRIUM MOISTURE CONTENT, PERCENT, WB

Material	Temp., °F	Relative Humidity, %									
		10	20	30	40	50	60	70	80	90	100
Barley	77	4.4	7.0	8.5	9.7	10.8	12.1	13.5	15.8	19.5	26.8
Buckwheat	77	5.0	7.6	9.1	10.2	11.4	12.7	14.2	16.1	19.1	24.5
Cottonseed	77				6.9	7.8	9.1	10.1	12.9	19.6	
Dry beans											
Mitchelite	40						12.8	14.4	17.0		
	50						13.8	15.3	18.0		
	77	5.6	7.4	8.6	9.8	11.2	12.9	14.9	17.5[1]		
	100						12.0	14.2	17.1		
	130						12.4	14.3	18.5		
Red Mexican	77	6.0	7.5	8.6	9.8	11.0	12.8	15.2	18.6[1]		
Great Northern	77	5.9	7.4	8.5	9.6	10.9	12.6	15.0	18.0[1]		
Light red kidney	77	6.1	7.5	8.7	9.9	11.1	12.9	15.1	18.5[1]		
Dark red kidney	77	5.4	7.2	8.4	9.6	10.7	12.5	15.0	18.6[1]		
Flat, small white	77	6.0	7.1	8.3	9.6	11.0	12.6	15.0	18.1[1]		
Pinto	77	6.1	7.4	8.5	9.8	11.0	12.6	15.2	18.2[1]		
Flaxseed	77	3.3	4.9	5.6	6.1	6.8	7.9	9.3	11.4	15.2	21.4
	77				6.1	6.8	7.9	9.3	11.4	15.7	
Oats	77	4.1	6.6	8.1	9.1	10.3	11.8	13.0	14.9	18.5	24.1
Rice											
Whole grain	77	5.9	8.0	9.5	10.9	12.2	13.3	14.1	15.2	19.1	
	100	4.9	7.0	8.4	9.8	11.1	12.3	13.3	14.8	19.1	
Milled	77	5.1	7.6	9.0	10.3	11.5	12.6	13.8	15.4	18.1	23.6
Rough	80				9.2	10.4	11.7	13.2	15.0	17.1	
	111						10.3	12.3	14.3	16.5	
	77	5.2	7.6	8.7	9.9	10.9	12.2	13.5	15.7	20.6	26.7
Rye	40	6.3	8.6	9.8	11.0	12.4	13.8	15.7	17.6	21.5	
Shelled corn	60	7.5	7.8	9.0	10.3	11.3	12.4	13.9	16.3	19.8	
YD	86	4.4	7.4	8.2	9.0	10.2	11.4	12.9	14.8	17.4	
	100	4.0	6.0	7.3	8.7	9.0	11.0	12.5	14.2	16.7	
	122	3.6	5.5	6.7	8.0	9.2	10.4	12.0	13.6	16.1	
	140	3.0	5.0	6.0	7.0	7.9	8.8	10.3	12.1	14.6	
WD	77	5.1	7.2	8.5	9.8	11.2	12.9	13.9	15.5	18.9	24.6
Shelled popcorn	77	5.6	7.4	8.5	9.8	11.0	12.2	13.1	14.2	18.4	23.0
Sorghum	77	4.4	7.3	8.6	9.8	11.0	12.0	13.8	15.8	18.8	21.9
Kafir	40	6.8	8.5	9.7	11.0	12.3	13.7	15.3	17.3		
	70	6.0	7.7	9.1	10.3	11.5	12.8	14.2	16.0	19.0[1]	
	90	5.0	7.0	8.4	9.6	10.8	12.0	13.2	14.7	17.0[1]	
Soybeans	77		5.5	6.5	7.1	8.0	9.3	11.5	14.8	18.8	
	77				7.0	8.0	10.1	12.2	16.0	20.7	
Sugar beet seeds	40			10.0	11.5	12.7	13.9	15.3	17.6	22.6	
	60			9.0	10.0	11.5	13.5	14.1	16.2	19.9	
	80			8.0	9.1	10.4	11.6	12.9	14.7	18.0	
	100			7.0	8.3	9.2	10.4	11.5	13.2	15.8	
Wheat											
Soft red winter	20				11.3	12.8	14.1	15.6	17.0		
	32				11.0	12.2	13.5	14.7	16.2		
	50				10.2	11.7	13.1	14.4	16.0		
	70				9.7	11.0	12.4	14.0			
	77	4.3	7.2	8.6	9.7	10.9	11.9	13.6	15.7	19.7	25.6

TABLE E.11 (*Continued*)

Material	Temp., °F	Relative humidity, %									
		10	20	30	40	50	60	70	80	90	100
Hard red winter	77	4.4	7.2	8.5	9.7	10.9	12.5	13.9	15.8	19.7	25.0
Hard red spring	77	4.4	7.2	8.5	9.8	11.1	12.5	13.9	15.9	19.7	25.0
White	77	5.2	7.5	8.6	9.4	10.5	11.8	13.7	16.0	19.7	26.3
Durum	77	5.1	7.4	8.5	9.4	10.5	11.5	13.1	15.4	19.3	26.7
Wheat	77	5.8	7.6	9.1	10.7	11.6	13.0	14.5	16.8	20.6	
	122	4.0	5.8	6.7	8.1	10.0	10.8	12.6	15.1	19.4	

[1] Unreliable because of mold growth.

Source: Hall (1957).

from a solution, a solid, or nonvolatile liquid. The rate of escape of the surface molecules depends primarily upon the temperature of the liquid, the temperature of the surroundings, the pressure above the liquid, surface area, and type of evaporator (rate of heat transfer to product). Heat is taken from the surroundings as water molecules escape from the surface. The liquid will continue to evaporate until it is gone from an open container. In a closed container with air space above the liquid, evaporation will continue until the air is saturated with water molecules. Removal of water from a liquid product by evaporation is enhanced by adding heat and by removing the saturated air or wet air above the liquid. This is done by forcing air over the liquid or by decreasing the pressure by placing a vacuum on the surface. To avoid excessive entrainment of droplets in the exhaust vapor for an open container, the rate of evaporation should not exceed 30 ± 10 lb per hr sq ft based on surface area of evaporator.

Latent Heat

The quantity of heat required to change 1 lb (or 1 gm) of liquid water to 1 lb (or 1 gm) of gas vapor is known as the *latent heat* of evaporation or vaporization. The latent heat value varies for different liquids and depends upon the temperature of evaporation, which is controlled by the pressure (Table E.13). As the temperature (or pressure) of evaporation is increased, the quantity of latent heat is decreased. The sensible heat required to reach a certain higher temperature is increased and the total heat (sensible plus latent heat), is greater for a higher temperature of evaporation, except as the critical properties are approached.

Boiling

Boiling is evaporation which occurs throughout a liquid as contrasted to a surface phenomenon. Heat is normally added to the bottom of a container in which a liquid is placed. The bubbles form next to the heat source, rise to the top of the liquid, and, as heating continues, the entire mass is heated and the vapor bubbles continue rising to the top of the liquid surface. When this occurs, boiling results. Agitation occurs as a result of the formation of bubbles at the heated surface and their movement through the liquid. The extent of agitation depends on the rapidity of heating. Even though the speed of heating is increased, the temperature of boiling does not increase, but the rate of evaporation is increased. During boiling, the pressure of the vapor in the liquid must exceed the air pressure by an infinitesimal amount. At

TABLE E.12

OTHER AGRICULTURAL MATERIALS EQUILIBRIUM MOISTURE CONTENT, PERCENT, WB

Material	Temp., °F	Relative humidity, %									
		10	20	30	40	50	60	70	80	90	100
Bran	70–80							14.0	18.0	22.7	38.0
Bread	77	0.9	1.8	3.1	4.4	6.1	7.7	10.3	12.3	16.0	
Bone meal	70–80							14.1	10.8	12.4	22.0
Cabbage	32	3.1		4.1		7.3		15.5	22.1		
Air-dried	77	1.3		4.7		9.1		16.0	23.3		
Scalded, savoy	99	1.7		4.7		8.6		16.5	22.7		
Carrot	50	3.2	3.7	4.5	6.3	8.8	12.5	17.4	24.7		
Scalded	77	2.1		4.4		9.5		18.2	26.6		
Air-dried	140	1.2	2.3	4.4	6.4	9.4	13.0	19.1	29.2		
Cotton cloth	77	2.4	3.6	4.7	4.8	6.3	7.8	9.1	10.4	12.0	
Crackers	77	1.5	2.4	3.3	4.0	4.9	7.0	7.8	10.0	11.9	
Eggs, spray-dried	50	2.8	3.8	5.1	6.1	7.3	8.7	10.7			
Eggs, spray-dried	99	2.3	3.4	4.3	5.6	6.5	8.3	10.0			
	176	1.2	2.0	2.7	3.4	4.5	5.8	6.7			
Fibre	70–80				4.5	5.5	6.5	9.0	12.2	26.5	
Flax	77	2.5	3.9	4.8	5.9	7.0	7.8	9.1	11.1	13.1	
Flour	77	2.0	3.6	5.2	5.7	7.5	9.6	11.2	13.7	16.0	
Linen	77	1.7	2.9	3.9	4.8	5.7	6.6	6.9	8.1	9.5	
Linseed coke	70–80							13.5	17.5	23.5	40.5
								14.5	21.9	35.0	51.0
Locust beans	70–80										
Lumber	77	2.8	4.2	5.7	7.0	8.4	10.1	12.2	14.8	18.0	23.1
White spruce	77	3.5	5.2	6.5	8.3	9.8	12.6	12.0	15.6	20.0	25.4
Macaroni	77	4.8	6.6	8.1	9.5	10.8	12.0	13.8	15.6	18.1	
Manila hemp	77	2.7	4.3	5.9	7.0	7.8	9.2	10.6	12.0	13.9	
Milk											
Powder	50	2.7	3.0	3.4	4.8	7.0	6.5	7.6			
Full-cream	99	2.6	3.3	4.1	4.0	4.5	6.5	7.9			
Spray-dried	176	1.2	1.8	1.6	2.3	2.4	4.3	7.7			
Oats	70–80							13.1	15.4	18.5	31.4
Peaches, dried	75	0.7	1.5	2.6	4.6	7.3	11.0	16.8	25.1		
Peas, whole		6.6		9.0		11.2		14.1	17.1		
Potatoes	50	4.9		7.3		10.7		14.3	19.8		
Scalded	99	4.3		6.9		9.6		13.4	16.7		
Air-dried	176	3.1		5.5		7.2		10.6	13.8		
Prunes, dried	75	2.1	3.9	6.6	9.5	12.7	16.1	20.7	27.7		
Raisins	75	2.9	5.4	8.2	11.3	14.5	18.6	23.1			
Reclaimed rubber	77		0.8	0.9	1.0	1.1	1.2	2.0	2.9	3.7	
Scotch beans	70–80							13.8	17.0	22.0	33.9
Sheepskin	77		7.8	9.8	11.1	12.2	13.3	15.7	22.4		
Sisal hemp	77	3.2	4.7	5.4	6.6	7.4	8.7	10.2	11.5	13.4	
Starch											
2 Parts protein, 1 part	70–80				9.0	10.5	11.5	13.0	14.7	17.7	31.5
1 Part protein, 2 parts	70–80				8.5	9.0	10.8	12.0	14.1	17.7	35.5
Starch	70–80				10.0	11.0	12.2	14.1	15.5	17.7	26.5
Straw	70–80				9.0	10.5	12.0	14.0	17.0	24.5	36.0
Tanned leather	77	7.9	10.4	11.7	13.1	13.9	14.7	16.1	18.5	23.1	

TABLE E.12 (*Continued*)

Material	Temp., °F	Relative humidity, %									
		10	20	30	40	50	60	70	80	90	100
Tobacco											
Cigarette	77	6.4	8.3	10.0	11.6	13.8	16.1	19.3			
N.C. leaf	77	6.7	9.9	12.2	14.2	16.5	18.7	21.3	24.9		
Bright strip	80	1.6	2.9	4.0	5.2	7.1	10.0	13.8	17.6		
	100	1.4	2.7	3.7	4.9	6.6	9.2	12.9	16.6		
	120	1.2	2.4	3.5	4.6	6.0	8.4	12.0	15.5		
	140	1.1	2.1	3.1	4.2	5.6	7.7	11.1			
Turkish	80	2.5	3.5	4.6	6.2	8.3	11.0	15.1			
	100	2.1	3.1	4.0	5.4	7.4	10.1	13.7			
	120	1.8	2.7	3.2	4.5	6.4	8.9	12.3	17.8		
	140	1.5	2.2	2.8	3.7	5.4	7.9	11.0	15.8		
Burley strip	80	3.4	5.0	5.6	6.3	7.4	9.5	13.3			
	100	2.6	4.3	5.2	6.0	6.6	8.3	11.4	16.5		
	120	1.8	3.5	4.7	5.5	6.2	7.3	9.7	13.8		
	140	12.0	2.7	4.1	5.1	6.0	6.8	8.5	11.9		

Source: Hall (1957).

normal atmospheric conditions at sea level, the atmospheric pressure is 760 mm Hg or 14.7 psia (0 psig); which is the same pressure for boiling at 212°F. If the pressure above the liquid is decreased, as through a vacuum, the pressure of vapor in the liquid at boiling is less, and the boiling temperature is lower. However, the quantity of heat required to evaporate a given amount of liquid at a lower pressure is greater. A vacuum is utilized to remove water at lower temperatures from products which are heat sensitive and might decompose at higher temperatures.

The boiling point of a solution is greater than the boiling point of water at the same pressure. The elevation of the boiling point due to dissolved solutes is related to the molecular weight of the solute. The addition of 1 gm molecular weight of substance to 1,000 gm of water increases the boiling point of water 0.9°F at 760 mm pressure. The vapor produced above a solution which boils at 215°F and 14.7 psi will, however, be at 212°F.

Cross-references: *Boilers; Evaporators; Refrigeration Principles; Sensible and Latent Heat; Spray Dryers; Vapor Pressure.*

EVAPORATORS

The first step in a commercial drying operation is to remove the bulk of the water (50 to 80%) in an evaporator; the second step is to remove the remainder of the surface-adsorbed water in the drier. At some moisture content (20 to 40%) the behavior of a material becomes more characteristic of a solid than of a liquid. The water changes from the continuous to discontinuous phase at about 15% moisture content in milk.

Milk and milk products may be treated in the evaporator for removal of moisture to obtain an end product such as concentrated, condensed, evaporated milk, or other milk products. Water is usually removed from liquid milk products in the evaporator before the drying operation. The cost of removing moisture in the evaporator is normally less than in the subsequent conventional drying operation. Milk products

TABLE E.13

SATURATION TEMPERATURE, PRESSURE, AND LATENT HEAT OF VAPORIZATION OF WATER

°C	Cal per Gm	Pressure, Mm Hg	°F	Btu per Lb	Pressure, Psia
0	595.9	4.6	32	1075.8	0.09
10	590.4	9.2	50	1065.6	0.18
20	584.9	17.5	70	1054.3	0.36
30	579.5	31.8	90	1042.9	0.70
40	574.0	55.3	110	1031.6	1.28
50	568.5	92.5	130	1020.0	2.22
60	563.2	149.4	150	1008.2	3.72
70	557.5	233.7	170	996.3	6.0
80	551.7	355.1	190	984.1	9.4
90	545.8	525.8	212	970.3	14.7
100	539.5	760.0	230	958.8	20.8
110	532.9	1074.6	250	945.5	29.8
120	525.7	1489.1	270	931.8	41.9
130	518.5	2126.2	290	917.5	57.6
140	511.1	2710.9	310	902.6	77.7
150	503.5	3570.5	330	887.0	103.1
160	495.6	4636.0	350	870.7	134.6
170	487.2	5940.9	370	853.5	173.4
180	478.6	7520.2	390	835.4	220.4

Source: Hall and Hedrick (1967).

are normally condensed from an initial solids content of 9 to 13% down to a final concentration of 40 to 45% total solids before the product is pumped to the drier.

Evaporation systems may be single effect or multiple-effect with 2, 3, 4, or more evaporator bodies or vacuum units. In the dairy industry, the single-effect evaporator is often called a vacuum pan. Four units in a multiple-effect evaporator are the maximum commonly used. In the multiple-effect evaporator, the units operate at decreasing pressure in the direction the product moves through the units.

The usual practice for milk and other food products is to operate the evaporators at a vacuum, so that the temperature of evaporation and boiling is lower than it would be at atmospheric pressure. With lower temperatures of evaporation, there is less heat damage to some products.

Horizontal Tube Evaporator

A simple unit, not used to a great extent on new installations, is the horizontal tube evaporator (Fig. E.10). Horizontal tubes from $^3/_4$ to $1^1/_4$ in. diam extend across the bottom of a cylindrical chamber from 3 to 10 ft diam and 8 to 15 ft high. Steam enters a chest on one end of the tubes, moves through the tubes, and the condensate is removed from the chest at the opposite end. The vapor is removed from the top of the cylindrical chamber.

Vertical Short-tube Evaporator

Tubes carrying the steam internally are placed vertically in the bottom of the cylindrical evaporator chamber (Fig. E.11). It is easier to clean the tubes in a verti-

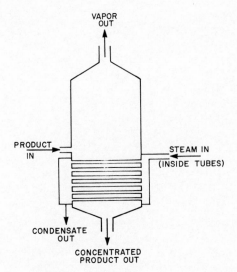

FIG. E-10.　　Horizontal tube evaporator

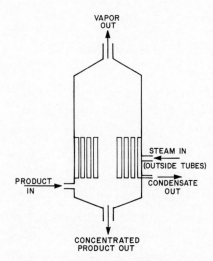

FIG. E-11.　　Vertical tube (short) evaporator

cal unit than in a horizontal tube evaporator. This type of unit is known as the Roberts evaporator in Europe and as the Calandria evaporator in the United States.

In a basket type evaporator the tubes may be placed in the shape of a ring. This unit provides an open space in the center so that the liquid may circulate more freely through the coils, with the liquid moving up through the coils as it is heated and the colder product moving down through a cylindrical volume in the center.

Forced Circulation Evaporator

In natural convection evaporators, the velocity of the fluid is usually less than 3 or 4 ft per sec. It is difficult to heat viscous materials with a natural circulation unit. Therefore, the use of forced circulation to obtain a velocity of liquid up to 15 or 16 ft per sec at the entrance of the tubes is desired for more rapid heat transfer. Forced circulation or agitation can be applied to either horizontal or vertical tube units. The liquid head above the heat exchanger is usually great enough to prevent boiling in the tubes. A centrifugal pump is normally used for circulation of milk products, but a positive pump is used for highly viscous fluids.

Vertical Long-tube Evaporator

The long-tube vertical (LTV) evaporator uses natural circulation with the flow of product either upward or downward. With upward flow, the unit is known as the climbing or rising liquid film evaporator (Fig. E.12, 13, 14), and with the downward flow it is known as the falling film evaporator. The Kestner is a specific type of LTV evaporator with rising film circulation and with the vapor head concentric with the tube chest. A deflector plate or umbrella on top of the tube bundle is required to deflect the liquid and to reduce entrainment.

Tubes of $1^1/_4$ to 2 in. diam and 12 to 20 ft long are used to move liquid on the inside. These are placed in a steam chest so that steam heats from the outside of the tube. The LTV evaporator is normally used with the heating element separate from

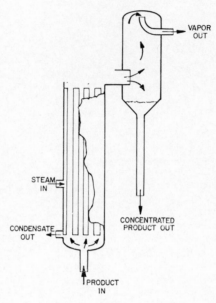

Fig. E-12.   Long tube vertical rising film evaporator

the liquid-vapor separator.   The product enters the bottom of the evaporator body and as it is heated by steam condensing on the opposite side of the tube, the product moves rapidly to the top of the tube and then into a separation chamber.   Vapor is removed and the concentrated product removed or recirculated through the evaporation chamber again, depending on the concentration desired.

Falling Film Evaporator

The falling film evaporator is used to reduce the amount of heat treatment or exposure to heat of the product.   The tubes are from 1.5 up to 2 in. in diameter and up to 30 ft long in the falling film evaporator.   The product is sprayed or otherwise distributed over the inside of the tubes which are heated with steam.   Moisture removed moves downward to the vapor separator as does the concentrated product. The product may be recirculated for another concentration or removed from the system.   The Reynolds number of the falling film should exceed 2,000 for good heat transfer.   The falling film evaporator is gaining popularity in the United States and Europe.

Plate Evaporator

A recent development in the evaporation of water from milk and milk products is the use of a plate evaporator (Fig. E.15).   It operates on the same principle as a vacuum pan.   The unit consists of a plate heat exchanger with low pressure steam between every other plate and the product in the alternate positions.   The steam is fed into top openings.   The product moves into a space from the bottom of the unit and moves up between the plates, operating on much the same principle as a rising film tube evaporator.   Two units may be connected and operated as a two-stage unit.

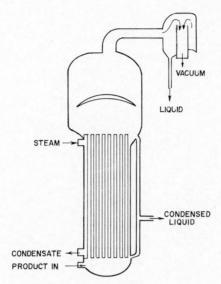

Fɪɢ. E-13.   LTV rising film evaporator

Multiple-effect Evaporator

The vapor produced through evaporation in the vacuum pan contains considerable latent heat. The vapor from the vacuum pan may be used in much the same way to heat another vacuum pan as steam is used to heat the unit. Thus, two or more effects can be utilized in the evaporator to provide a method of utilizing the useful heat in the vapor and to improve economy of the operation. A common multiple-effect evaporator is the triple-effect system. Each effect can consist of any of the types of several units discussed previously. Figure E.16 illustrates the principle involved and the flow of product and steam, but any of the units can be replaced with a film or other type evaporator. In the multiple-effect evaporation system, the vapor removed from the first effect at a high temperature moves to the heating coils or tubes of the second effect, which is at a lower temperature. Likewise, the vapor removed from the second effect is directed to the heating coils or tubes of the third effect, which is at a still lower temperature. The temperature must decrease in the direction of flow of the vapor so that the heat will flow from the vapor to the product. Thus, the temperature of evaporation of the product must decrease from the first to the third or final effect. The decrease in the evaporation or boiling point is obtained by maintaining a higher vacuum or providing a lower pressure at the third or final effect as compared to the first effect. A temperature drop of at least 12° to 15°F is needed to justify the next effect.

The multiple-effect evaporation system is often erroneously given credit for having a larger capacity than a single-effect unit. A triple-effect system operating with the difference in temperature of 90°F between the first and third effect will have approximately the same capacity as the single-effect unit with the same temperature difference.

The major advantage of the multiple-effect evaporator is that it requires less steam per pound of water evaporated. The major disadvantage is that more investment is required. The cost of the additional equipment and its operation and

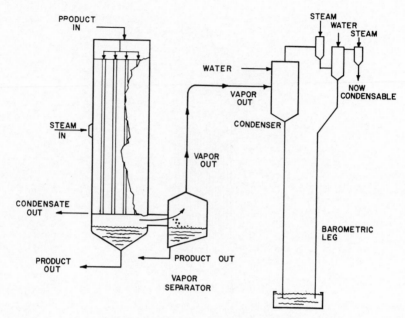

Fig. E-14.   LTV vertical falling film evaporator

maintenance must be justified on the basis of the saving in steam for heating. The optimum number of effects is arrived at by an economic analysis. A single-effect unit will require about 1.2 lb of steam to evaporate 1 lb of water in the evaporator body; the double-effect, 0.6 lb of steam per pound of water evaporated; for a triple-effect, 0.4 lb of steam per pound of water evaporated; and for a quadruple-effect, 0.3 lb of steam per pound of water evaporated. These figures should be considered as a rule of thumb (Table E.14). The exact amount of steam required depends upon the design, flow of the system, and many other factors.

There are three basic methods of feeding (supplying product) in or to a multiple-effect evaporator. The forward feed, backward feed, and parallel feed (Fig. E.16) or combinations thereof, may be used for connecting the various effects and for directing product, steam, and vapor flow. In the forward flow, the product and vapors move in the same direction through all three effects. Milk evaporators normally use

TABLE E.14

APPROXIMATE QUANTITY OF STEAM REQUIRED TO VAPORIZE 1 LB OF WATER IN AN EVAPORATOR, LB

No. Effects	Range	Average
Single	1.33–1.00	1.17
Double	0.63–0.50	0.57
Triple	0.40–0.34	0.37
Quadruple	0.30–0.26	0.28
Quintuple	0.24–0.22	0.23
Sextuple	0.20–0.18	0.19
Septuple	0.18–0.16	0.17

Source: Hall and Hedrick (1967).

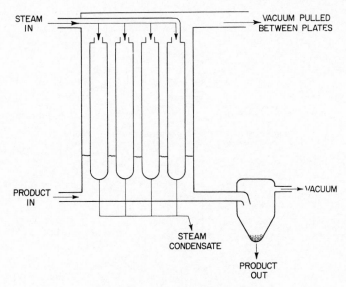

Fɪɢ. E-15.   Plate evaporator

forward flow systems.   In the backward flow, the vapor moves from the first to the third effect, and the product enters the third effect and leaves at the first effect.   In the parallel feed, the vapor moves from the first to third effect, but the feed is sent directly to each effect with no transfer of material from one effect to another. Thus, only the vapor moves through all three effects.   The forward feed is most common, primarily because of its simplicity in that fewer pumps are required. The backward flow is generally more expensive and used in connection with highly viscous products which enter cold.

Considerable labor is required to maintain and clean multiple-effect evaporators for milk and food products.   Multiple-effect evaporators have been available for many years.   Only recently have evaporators been designed for handling large quantities of milk over practically a 24-hr day operation, so that the multiple-effect can be justified.   Cleaning-in-place systems have decreased labor requirements for cleaning.

Agitated Film Evaporator

Effective heat transfer for vaporization, without damage to the product, is related to exposure for a short time for a particular temperature, and the existence of a turbulent thin film next to the heating surface.   The agitated film evaporator provides an approach to meeting these conditions.   The entering product is moved to the outer edge of the chamber by centrifugal force of the rotating blades.   The chamber is heated around the circumference.   Both the vapor and condensed product move vertically downward and are removed and separated by conventional means.   The unit is particularly suited to products of high viscosity.

Swept or Scraped Surface Evaporator

The scraped surface heat exchanger, such as is used for ice cream freezing or product heating, can be utilized as an evaporator.   Low pressure steam surrounds the

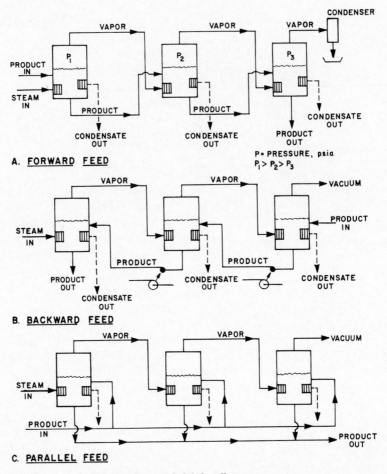

FIG. E-16.   Multiple effect evaporator

chamber, and a vacuum can be maintained in the chamber.   The scrapers or knives assist in moving high viscosity products from the heating surface.   A product of 70 to 80% solids can be obtained.

Centrifugal Evaporator (Centri-therm)

The centrifugal equipment consists of a stack of rotating cone elements which preceded the development of the expanding flow evaporator.   Each cone element is made up of stainless steel walls with a hollow section into which steam is supplied through the hollow spindle which supports the elements.   The product to be condensed is sprayed onto the heated surfaces of the cone elements.   The centrifugal force developed by the rotation which provides up to 200 gm spreads the liquid in a thin layer over the inner surface.   The product is about 0.004 in. thick over the surface.   The centrifugal force keeps the lower surface inside the cone element free from condensate.

The conditions at the heating surface are such to provide good heat transfer and to assist in vaporization. The condensate is discharged immediately by the centrifugal force from the steam heated surface. The thin product layer and the turbulence of the product provide rapid heat transfer and little resistance to heat transfer due to vapor. The concentrate accumulates around the outer diameter of the cone and is displaced upward where it is removed. Evaporating vapors are removed under a vacuum through a large side outlet. The steam condensate is collected under a steam jacket. A standard unit provides a vaporization of 1,800 lb per hr of water with concentration up to 35% solids. The unit can be cleaned-in-place.

Evaporator with Conical Heating Surfaces

A recent design utilizes heating surfaces comprised of inverted nested stainless steel cones known as an expanding flow evaporator. Alternate passages are connected with the product inlet with the other passages connected with the steam inlet. Steam enters and rises, then flows down through every other passage between the cones and leaves as condensate. The product to be evaporated enters and is distributed by nozzles into the passages not occupied by the steam. The product is heated to boiling as it moves up and out over the heat surface. The vapor and droplets of the condensed product move into the shell surrounding the heating cones when the droplets move down. The vapor moves up, with the separation aided by a deflector, and leaves. The vapor leaving can be directed to the next effect or condenser.

Countercurrent flow of heat exchange mediums results with a larger cross section utilized for the larger volume of product and steam. A double-effect unit with a thermocompressor (11,000 lb per hr) of skim milk uses about 0.39 lb steam per pound of water evaporated.

Refrigeration Cycle Evaporation

The refrigeration cycle consists of a compressor, evaporator, condenser, and refrigerant. The refrigerant gas is increased in density at the compressor, after which the gas is condensed to a liquid by removal of heat at the condenser, is metered to the evaporator where it gains heat and the cycle is repeated. The heat given off by the refrigerant at the condenser is used for heating the product in a product evaporator where moisture is removed. A vacuum is pulled on the system, using the steam jet or mechanical vacuum pump. The vapors removed are directed to coils which are cold (the refrigerant evaporator of the refrigeration system) and the vapors condense out of the product system and are removed by a condensate pump.

The refrigeration cycle evaporator is particularly useful for removing water from heat sensitive products, in the temperature range of from 40° to 100°F. Food products so handled need to be pasteurized. From 60 to 100 hp per 1000 lb per hr of water evaporated is required for operating the electrical equipment for a refrigeration cycle evaporator.

Vapor Recompression

Vapor recompression offers a method of obtaining increased efficiencies in utilization of energy similar to a double-effect evaporator. Energy is added to the vapor removed from the evaporator. Energy is added by a mechanical compressor or a steam jet to provide mechanical vapor recompression or thermal steam jet vapor recompression (known as a thermocompressor). Consider 1 lb of saturated steam leaving a vacuum pan at 6 psia or 170°F. The steam or vapor will contain 1,134 Btu per lb of total heat, of which 996 Btu per lb are latent heat. The objective of vapor recompression is to increase the pressure and thereby the temperature of the vapor to a point above the condensation temperature so that the latent heat may be removed. In a vapor recompression system, the increase in temperature for a mechanical compressor is about 30°F which is equivalent to increasing the pressure about 5 psi and requires an addition of about 10 Btu per lb to the vapor. The compressed steam can be fed to the heating coils and used for heating the product.

Another approach is to mix incoming high pressure steam with the low pressure vapor being removed from the vacuum pan or evaporator. This provides a low pressure steam which has a higher temperature of condensation than the low pressure vapor being removed and which can be used for heating the product.

The compressors used for mechanical compression may be either reciprocating positive or centrifugal units. Rotary positive displacement units may be more economical for small capacities.

Principles and Practices in Operation of Evaporator

(1)   The unit may be operated either as a batch system or as a continuous system.

(2)   Unit should be sanitized before product is placed into the container.

(3)   Milk should be placed over the heating coils before steam is moved into the coil to prevent scorching of the product. Otherwise, the product would scorch should it splash on a preheated steam coil.

(4)   The product is held at a uniform level in the evaporator. The rate of moving milk into the evaporator should be such that water volume removed will be replaced.

(5)   Too rapid boiling will cause an increase in entrainment. A rule of thumb for design is to consider approximately 30 lb per hr sq ft surface area. High pressure steam should be avoided because with a higher temperature of condensation the product might be damaged. Units are normally designed for 5 psi steam pressure or less.

(6)   Economy of cooling water to a water condenser should be checked. No more water should be used than is necessary to condense the vapors being removed.

(7)   A measure of the economy of water use is the temperature difference between the cooling water and condenser discharge water, which should be about 5°F.

(8)   Air leaks in the system may cause a fluctuation in temperature in the evaporator or a large air leak may cause boiling to stop. Air leaks may occur around valves, fittings, joints, covers, and observation ports.

(9)   A vacuum pan or single-effect evaporator for milk is normally operated at a temperature of 130° to 140°F or 25 in. Hg vacuum.

(10)   To stop the evaporator follow proper order of events: (a) turn off the steam;   (b) turn off the water to the condenser;   (c) stop the vacuum pump;   and (d) open the relief valve to the vacuum chamber.

(11)   Dry saturated steam is more desirable for vacuum pan operation than wet or superheated steam.

(12)   Rule of thumb utility requirements for evaporation are as follows: 0.14 lb of steam per pound of milk for forewarming;   1.1 to 1.2 lb of steam per pound of water evaporated for single-effect operation;   0.2 to 0.7 lb of steam per pound of water

vapor for steam injector operation; and 13 to 18 lb of water per pound of water vapor for condenser operation.

(13) Decreased steam costs can be obtained with multiple-effect evaporators. Multiple-effect evaporators can be obtained by using two or more evaporators, a thermal compression, or mechanical recompression of vapors from the product. The additional cost of equipment and operation for a multiple-effect evaporation must be balanced against the savings in fuel.

(14) Commonly accepted overall heat transfer values range from 200 to 600 Btu per hr sq ft °F. Forced circulation systems may go to a U-value of 2,000. Manufacturers' literature should be consulted regarding specific evaporators.

Each installation for evaporation is especially designed according to the needs of the processor. The above values are presented only to give an indication of the steam, water, and other utility requirements, and each installation must be carefully figured on the basis of the operation, volume, labor requirements, number of effects, and specific products.

Reference

Abstracted from HALL, C. W., and HEDRICK, T. I. 1966. Drying of Milk and Milk Products. AVI Publishing Co., Westport, Conn.

Cross-references: *Density Control; Evaporation; Refrigerated Storage; Refrigeration Principles.*

EXPLOSION

Explosion caused by concentration of organic materials in the atmosphere depends upon the increase in temperature of the particles to the ignition point. The possibility of explosion usually is designated on the basis of concentration of the product in the air. It is generally considered that a concentration of organic dust of 5 gm per cu ft or less is safe from the standpoint of explosion. Adequate ventilation must be provided to maintain the concentration at a low level.

Cross-references: *Boilers; Dust Explosion; Refrigeration Principles; Safety.*

EXTRACTOR

Juice extractors are designed to separate juices from pulp, seeds, skin, etc. They are made in either batch or continuous type; however, the continuous worm type machine is generally used.

Usually the machines are built very heavy since high strains are involved in compressing the product to the point where the juice is adequately extracted.

Usually the product is fed into the machine in a crushed and preheated condition. Figure E.17 shows a common type of worm type juice extractor. Machines for modern industry must be of sanitary construction and usually all contact parts are made of polished stainless steel.

Principle

The principle of operation of these machines involves the use of the tapering

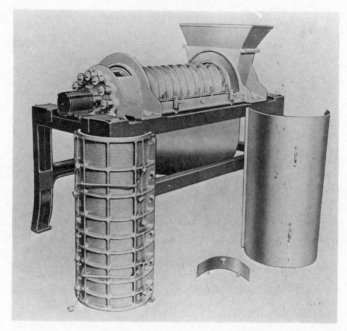

Courtesy of FMC Corp.

Fig. E-17.   Horizontal perforated screen type juice extractor

auger which moves and pushes the pulp along a gradually decreasing cross-sectional area.   High pressure is exerted and at the same time movement on the product, so that it will be forced out through a perforated screen while the fibrous material is continuously pushed forward and exhausted as a by-product.

Power

Extractors usually have large capacity and quite high electric power consumption. A typical extractor system has an input capacity of 110 to 120 gal per min, and will yield about 90 to 91% extraction based on 18 to 28% solids in extracting pineapple juice.   The horsepower requirement for the operation would be from 30 to 40 hp.

A tomato juice extractor operates at about 400 rpm and will handle 8 to 10 tons per hour of tomatoes from tomatoes that are crushed and preheated.   Special nickel-silver screens with 0.020-in. perforations are standard.   Screens with 0.027- and 0.033-diam perforations can be furnished.

Most extractors are built with a worm of constant outside diameter and an increasing root diameter in the direction of pulp travel.   This provides a gradually decreasing pulp area which serves to build up the pressure and force the juice from the pulp.

In operation, machines can be used as either single stage or multiple stage combinations.   The design of the worm is slightly different for tomato and for citrus applications.   The worm is a stainless steel casting.

Reference

FMC Chemical Corp. Canning Machinery Div., Cat. *160*.

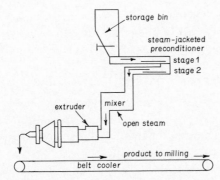

Courtesy Northern Regional Laboratory, U. S. Dept. Agr.

FIG. E-18.   HTST cooker-extruder
New cooking extrusion method prepared full-fat soybean flours of maximum stability and nutritive value. The system puff-cooks preconditioned material which is then cut into pieces for cooking and drying.

Cross-reference: *Extruder.*

EXTRUDER

Extrusion refers to the shaping of the products to the desired configuration size and consistency by forcing the material through a die usually under extremely high pressure. Extrusion has long been used in the food industry in the making of special shapes of food products, the filling of fancy ice cream packages, and the manufacture of cookies, cakes, etc. Extrusion equipment has been perfected greatly in the past 10 yr and is now used in such widely diverse activities as extruding aluminum and metal shapes and for compacting and pelleting various products. Extrusion equipment exists in various sizes, capacity, and sophistication. The simplest type of extrusion device would be a cookie maker or a fancy ice cream package filler. From this degree of simplicity, extremely sophisticated equipment involving automatic control, temperature adjustment, controlled mixing, and blending may be employed. Figure E.18 shows a typical extruder system.

Utilization

A very important feature of extrusion systems is the possibility of drastically reducing the cost of operation, because it is a continuous operation which can be highly mechanized and automated. In addition, the following are five important aspects relative to the product which are often available through an extrusion system.

(1)   Uniform product size, which is a must for efficient processing, packaging, and quality control.

(2)   Engineering physical traits because extrusion often provides greater strength, exposes more surface for faster processing, and permits variation in appearance of the product.

(3)   Waste reduction. Sliced peeled potatoes require screening out the fine trim-ends. By being worked into a plastic mass (trim-ends and all), the potatoes can be extruded without waste into uniform pieces looking much like the original slices.

(4)   Cookie bakers use extruders with wire cut-off machines and units for making

fruit filled pieces like fig newtons, rotary cookie machines, and bar cutters. Rotary molders for making 6,000 lb per hr of biscuits are also included under this group.

(5) Cheese processors extrude stretch-curd cheese to provide adjustable weight control of Italian specialities.

Procedure

In extrusion, the usual practice is to maintain uniform flow of material through the diehead. But many unusual effects can be achieved by using nonuniform flow such as rippled ribbons, scalloped edges, etc.

Another mixing technique, mill extruding, combines dry extrusion with roll making. Dry blending, in which intimate dispersion of some materials (color, flavor solutions) is accompanied by spray injection, offers another possibility. By introducing a vacuum section an extruder can be changed simply into a compounder-extruder. This unit simultaneously extrudes and extracts moisture from material before reaching the die.

Extrusion can also produce firmer products capable of withstanding shipment. One may use dehydrated potatoes as a raw material. After rehydration, the mass can be extruded and cut into chip form. In so doing, it builds greater strength into the chips and ensures size uniformity.

Quality Control

There are many ways by which the quality of the materials can be improved during the extrusion process. For example, the vacuum-operated extrusion process produces void-free macaroni and spaghetti superior in color to that made conventionally. The technique involves maintaining 23 in. Hg in a pressure chamber of a continuous kneader-extruder to remove air from the dough and produce smoother, firmer-textured goods. The procedure minimizes violent escape of entrapped air upon release of high extrusion pressure.

The locked-in flavor technique produces solid essential oil flavors. Cold-pressed citrus oils are incorporated into a plastic mixture (glycerol and corn syrup solids) to form solid filaments without fracturing.

An important use of the extrusion principle is in the filling of ice cream. The stiff, semiplastic ice cream is extruded through a die which shapes it to fit a paper carton, which in turn is hand placed under the die, and the product cut off by the edge of the die as the filled carton is removed.

Fancy center and multiflavor ice cream is made by extruding the different colors and flavors through a multiorifice die and directly into the package.

Types of extruders in use are (1) the hydraulic- or cam-operated plunger which forces the material through a die; (2) the spiral screw similar to a sausage stuffer is effective for some uses; and (3) a rotating blade or roller which mixes the material and forces it through openings in a perforated plate has many advantages for pasty or paste-type materials.

Cross-reference: *Extractor.*

F

FANS

Fans or blowers are used for nonpositive movement or displacement of air. Compressors are used for positive air displacement. The air may be moved for heating, cooling, or changing the conditions in a room.

The capacity of a fan is identified by the volume of air moved in cubic feet per minute or hour at a certain pressure or head. The head is made up of the static and velocity pressure. The static head is utilized in overcoming the friction of the air with its contents in the duct, and the velocity head is the pressure required to produce the flow.

Classification

Fans may be classified as radial flow (centrifugal) or axial flow (propeller). With radial flow fans, the air moves in the direction of the radius of the fan wheel, and with axial fans the flow is parallel to the axis of rotation of the blade. Radial flow fans can be constructed with blades which are straight, forward curved, or backward curved. The axial flow fans consist of other types with impellers, or propeller fans with an enlarged hub known as a disk fan (Fig. F.1, F.2, F.3, and F.4).

Other methods of specifying a fan are the following: whether air handling or product handling, dimensions of the fan, dimensions of the inlet or outlet, resistance of fans to spark, corrosion resistance, whether single or double acting, type of driver, and whether of sanitary construction.

Operating Characteristics

The mechanical efficiency of a fan is defined as the ratio of the fluid air horsepower output to the brake horsepower input to the fan, and is in the range of 40 to 70%. The motor horsepower to drive a fan is approximately 2 times the fluid horsepower of a fan, which represents 50% efficiency

$$\text{Fan fluid horsepower} = \frac{(\text{cfm}) \ (\text{SP})}{6,350}$$

$$\text{Motor horsepower} = 2 \times \text{fluid horsepower}$$

$$\text{Static efficiency} = \frac{(\text{cfm}) \ (\text{SP})}{(6,350) \ (\text{hp input})}$$

where cfm = airflow, cfm
SP = static pressure, in. H_2O

299

The usual variations in fan characteristics are approximately as follows: the capacity, (cfm), of the fan varies directly as the square of the speed ratio; and the horsepower varies as the cube of the speed ratio. Fans can be connected in tandem to increase the static pressure (SP) and in parallel to increase the capacity (cfm). In general these same relationships exist for both radial and axial flow fans.

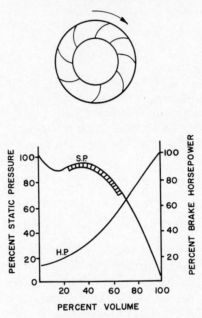

Fig. F-1.   Forward curved centrifugal fan characteristics

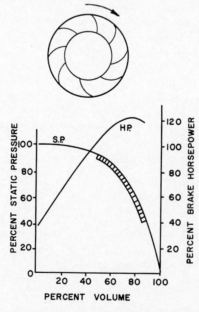

Fig. F-2.   Backward curved centrifugal fan characteristics

The volumetric efficiency of a centrifugal fan is equal to the volume of air delivered divided by the displacement of the fan wheel. Fans must be selected for a particular application. Seldom will a secondhand fan purchased at random meet specific needs. A reputable manufacturer will furnish the performance curves for any of his fans. In addition to performance characteristics, the fan selection should be based on space requirements, installation costs, initial costs, controls necessary, power requirements, method of driving, position of mounting, flexibility of use, hazards involved in use, maintenance requirements, and noise produced (Tables F.1 and F.2).

Radial or Centrifugal Fans

The radial flow or centrifugal fans consist of a wheel which is rotated in a spiral or circular housing. The air pressure at the center of the wheel is less than the surrounding air pressure. For design or operation, higher pressure is obtained with a centrifugal fan or blower by increasing the length of blades or by increasing the speed of operation to get greater centrifugal force.

Forward-curved Fans.—The forward curved centrifugal fan is constructed of curved blades mounted in the outer periphery of a revolving wheel in the housing.

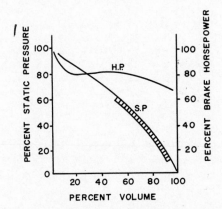

Fig. F-3. High speed propeller fan characteristics

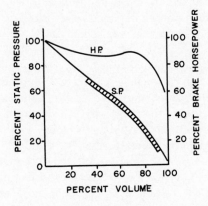

Fig. F-4. Vane axial flow fan characteristics

TABLE F.1

PERFORMANCE OF DIFFERENT TYPES OF FANS[1]

Fan Type	Free delivery, %	Horsepower, %	Static efficiency, %
Radial blade	30	40	68
Forward-curved	40	27	75
Backward-curved	56	98	82
Vane axial	66	83	65
Propeller	30–60	60–55	30

[1] Data at fan selection point of 100% SP.
Source: Air Conditioning and Engineering (1955).

TABLE F.2

CENTRIFUGAL FAN PERFORMANCE TABLE (FOR THESE FANS ONLY)

Size, Diameter, In.	Speed, Rpm	Motor, Hp	Cfm Delivered at Static Pressures of						
			$1/2$ In.	$3/4$ In.	1 In.	$1^1/_4$ In.	$1^1/_2$ In.	$1^3/_4$ In.	2 In.
32	2,040	3	14,500	13,000	11,500	9,800	7,800	5,300	2,500
32	2,360	5	18,100	16,900	15,700	14,400	13,100	11,700	10,300
36	1,640	3	16,000	14,200	12,000	8,800	5,200	1,800	
36	1,980	5	20,800	19,400	17,700	16,000	14,000	11,500	8,400
42	1,140	5	25,000	20,000	12,800	2,000			
42	1,510	5	24,000	22,000	19,400	16,400	12,200	7,600	3,600
42	1,740	$7^1/_2$	29,500	27,400	25,200	23,000	20,500	17,500	14,000

Source: Hall (1957).

There are often from 20 to 75 curved blades, with the curved blades so arranged that the leading edge of the blade is on the outer edge of the periphery. This fan is usually used in commercial ventilation work because it has a low periphery speed and is more quiet in operation than other fans.

The forward-curved fan must have a connected load to prevent overloading. The fan has the characteristic that the horsepower increases as the volume increases and, if not adequately designed and protected, the motor can easily be overloaded and damaged. These fans are normally designed to operate at low static pressure of 1 in. of water or less. The highest mechanical efficiency that can be obtained with this fan is about 80%.

Backward-curved Fans.—The backward-curved fan usually has less curved blades around the outer periphery for the same size wheel, and usually operates at a speed 1.5 to 2 times the speed of the forward-curved fan. The fan wheel is made with the leading edge of the curved blade on the inner edge of the periphery. This fan has a wide range of usefulness, but is generally used where a large variation in airflow volumes may occur. The high speed requires heavy construction and the volume occupied by the fan is larger than for the forward-curved fan. A mechanical efficiency as high as 80% may be obtained under best operating conditions. The straight-bladed fan is sometimes called the radial-blade or paddle-wheel fan because the blades of the fan are placed in the radius of the wheel. The radial fan is used for low volume displacement against high pressure. The radial fan consists of 5 to 12 blades and usually operates in a range of 500 to 3,000 rpm. It has a particular advantage where materials are carried in the air stream, which might otherwise damage blades around the periphery. This fan does not have blade sections around a periphery, but are mounted from the center axle.

Axial-flow Fans

Axial-flow fans consist of the propeller fan, vane-axial fan, and tube-axial fan.

Propeller.—A propeller fan consists of blades mounted on a hub with the blades at about a 15° pitch angle. Propeller fans are generally not designed to work against high resistances, although they can be multistaged for producing above 5 in. static pressure. Propeller fans are suited for ventilation of rooms and air ducts of low resistance. The propeller fan is characterized by excessive noises at high speeds. It requires a rather uniform horsepower over a wide range of volumes, with a reduction in horsepower as the fan approaches 100% volume output (at low static pressure).

Vane-axial Fans.—The vane-axial fan is distinguished by large hubs and short blades in addition to stationary straightening vanes on the discharge side of the fan to prevent rotation or swirling of the air. It is generally used for delivery of air for pressures up to 9 in. of water. It is used for ventilation systems where space is valuable or head room is limited.

Tube-axial Fans.—The tube-axial fan is similar to the vane-axial fan except that guide vanes are not used. The tube-axial fan is simpler and somewhat less efficient than the vane-axial fan. The horsepower and static pressure curves for axial-flow fans are very similar.

Practices and Principles

The following practices and principles apply in selecting fans.

(1) The range of operation of airflow volumes must be considered for the range in pressures required. These requirements are the prime considerations in selecting fans.

(2) For ventilation systems, where quiet operation is essential, the forward-curved blade fan is recommended because of its inherent low speed and desirable sound characteristics. Fans are available which will put out as many as 500,000 cfm and for static pressures as high as 15 in. of water.

(3) Fans may be controlled or their output controlled by dampers, into or out of the fan, inlet vanes to give proper direction to the air, variable speed drives, and/or fluid drives.

(4) In general, propeller fans are used where air is moved from one space to another at low resistance.

(5) Duct connections to and from the fan should be carefully designed to minimize pressure drop and pressure losses.

(6) Flexible connections should be placed between the fan and ducts.

References

AMERICAN BLOWER CORP. 1955. Air Conditioning and Engineering. Detroit, Mich.

MARKS, L. S. 1941. Mechanical Engineers' Handbook, 4th Edition. McGraw-Hill Book Co., New York.

PERRY, J. H. 1950. Chemical Engineers' Handbook, 3rd Edition. McGraw-Hill Book Co., New York.

Cross-references: *Air Movement; Blowers; Compressors; Friction; Static Pressure; Ventilation.*

FAT FRYERS

Deep-fat fryers designed for volume processing of seafood, poultry, meat items, and snack foods are available. This machinery is designed with an overhead flight submerged conveyor. The product is submerged in the frying oil and moves at an even speed through the length of the kettle. The conveyor speed can be varied as needed for precise control of the frying cycle. A coiled circulatory oil system with external heat exchanger is used to maintain precise temperature across the entire length and width of the kettle. A modulation control on the burner system auto-

TABLE F.3

MELTING POINTS OF COMMON FATTY ACIDS, METHYL AND ETHYL ESTERS, MONO-, DI-, AND TRIGLYCERIDES,[1] AND ALCOHOLS

Compound	Acid	Methyl Ester	Ethyl Ester	Mono-glyceride[2]	Diglyceride[3]	Triglyceride	Alcohol
Butyric	− 7.9	−95.0	−93.0	—	—	—	—
Caproic	− 3.4	—	—	19.4	—	−25.0	−51.6
Caprylic	16.7	−41.0	—	—	—	8.3	−16.3
Nonanoic	12.5	—	−44.0	—	—	—	− 5.0
Capric	31.6	−18.0	−20.3	53.0	44.5	31.5	6.9
Undecanoic	29.3	—	−15.0	—	—	—	15.9
Lauric	44.2	5.0	− 1.8	63.0	56.5	46.5	24.0
Myristic	54.4	18.8	12.3	70.5	65.5	57.0	38.3
Palmitic	62.9	30.6	24.4	77.0	72.5	65.5	49.6
Stearic	69.6	39.1	33.9	81.0	78.0	73.0	58.0
Arachidic	75.3	46.6	41.6	84.0	—	—	65.5
Oleic	16.3	−19.8	—	35.2	21.5	5.5	7.5
Elaidic	43.7	—	—	58.5	55.0	42.0	37.0
Erucic	33.4	—	—	50.0	46.5	30.0	—
Linoleic	− 6.5	—	—	12.3	− 2.6	−13.1	—
Linolenic	−12.8	—	—	15.7	−12.3	−24.2	—
Ricinoleic	5.5	—	—	—	—	—	—
α-Eleostearic	49.0	—	—	—	—	—	—
β-Eleostearic	72.0	—	—	—	—	—	—

[1] Melting point of the highest-melting, most stable polymorphic form is given.
[2] The nonsymmetrical (or α-) isomer.
[3] The symmetrical (or α,α'-) isomer.
Source: Swern (1964).

matically compensates for variations in the input load. Units are available which can give the following typical production capacities in pounds per hour: beef patties, 7,000; fish sticks, 6,000; onion rings, 3,500; poultry, 6,000; and French fries, 6,500 to 13,000.

Vegetable oil is normally used in these fryers. The oil flows by gravity to a strainer tank, and then passes through a fine mesh screen to the clean side of the strainer tank. From the tank it is pumped to the exchanger and then to the receiving end of the kettle.

TABLE F.4

VISCOSITY OF FATS AND OILS

Oil	Acid Number	Specific Gravity, 20°/4°C	Kinematic Viscosity, Centistokes		Saybolt Viscosity	
			100°F	210°F	100°F	210°F
Almond	2.85	0.9188	43.20	8.74	201	54.0
Olive	—	0.9158	46.68	9.09	216	55.2
Rapeseed	0.34	0.9114	50.64	10.32	234	59.4
Mustard	—	0.9237	45.13	9.46	209	56.9
Cottonseed	14.24	0.9187	35.88	8.39	181	52.7
Soybean	3.50	0.9228	28.49	7.60	134	50.1
Linseed	3.42	0.9297	29.60	7.33	139	49.2
Raw perilla	1.36	0.9297	25.24	6.85	120	47.6
Sunflower	2.76	0.9207	33.31	7.68	156	50.3
Castor	0.81	0.9619	293.4	20.08	1368	97.7
Coconut	0.01	0.9226	29.79	6.06	140	45.2
Palm kernel	9.0	0.9190	30.92	6.50	145	46.5
Lard	3.39	0.9138	44.41	8.81	206	54.2
Neatsfoot	13.35	0.9158	43.15	8.50	200	53.1
Sardine	0.57	0.9384	27.86	7.06	131	48.3
Cod liver	—	0.9138	32.79	7.80	153	50.7
Refined whale	0.73	0.9227	31.47	7.48	147	49.7
Sperm	0.80	0.8829	22.99	5.70	110	44.1

Source: Swern (1964).

Small batch type fryers are also available for the small operator.

The principal items of management and service are to keep foreign material out of the oil and to be sure that temperature measurement and control equipment are functioning properly. Oil tends to break down during use through hydrolysis causing formation of some free fatty acids which often impart off-flavors. Checking free fatty acid content periodically is necessary to ensure good flavor. Sanitation of the entire system is of utmost importance.

Cross-reference: *Fat, Physical Properties.*

FAT, PHYSICAL PROPERTIES

Fats and oils are substances of animal or plant origin which are often identified by their physical properties. Glyceryl esters of fatty acids, or triglycerides, comprise the main portion of these water-insoluble substances. Triglycerides which are normally semisolid at room temperature are ordinarily called a "fat." Those which exist as a liquid are usually referred to as an "oil." The combination of fatty acids in a triglyceride determines the properties of fats and oils. In nature fats vary considerably in their physical properties since their composition may be influenced by climate, soil, and variety for vegetable fats. Nutrition, breed, season, and other factors affect the properties of animal fats.

Common fats such as lard, tallow, butterfat, shortening, or margarine are mixtures of a solid phase with a liquid phase. Microscopic triglyceride crystals exist in the solid phase. Changing the proportions of the two phases will vary the plasticity of a product and affect other characteristics as well.

Melting Point

The melting point of a fat is often not sharp or always the same. Often a fat can be heated slowly so it becomes liquid and upon a further rise in temperature will again solidify. A second melting will occur at a higher temperature. By rapidly cooling the substance it will usually lower the melting point. This phenomenon is explained by polymorphism, the occurrence of more than one crystalline form.

As the chain length of fatty acids increases, the melting point is raised. Likewise, with more unsaturation the melting point is lowered. Melting points for the most stable forms of several fatty acids, esters and their glycerides, and alcohols are given in Table F.3. Combinations of fats from various sources are frequently used to develop a product for a specific purpose and with a satisfactory melting point.

Viscosity

Viscosity will vary with the extent of internal friction between molecules. The intermolecular attractions of the long chains in glyceride molecules account for the relatively high viscosities of oils. An increase in unsaturation usually lowers the

TABLE F.5

VISCOSITIES OF SATURATED FATTY ACIDS AND THEIR METHYL AND ETHYL ESTERS

Compound	Viscosity, Centipoises (Temperature, °C)		
	Acid	Methyl Ester	Ethyl Ester
Formic	1.782	0.367	0.413
Acetic	1.219	0.383	0.452
	0.622		0.269
Propionic	1.099	0.461	0.536
Butyric	1.538	0.572	0.666
	0.728	0.328	0.363
Valeric	2.30	0.711	0.836
Caproic	3.23	0.407	0.818
	1.279		0.537
Heptanoic	4.33		1.11
Caprylic	5.74	1.26	1.38
	2.62		0.716
	1.86		
Nonanoic	8.08		1.69
	3.79		
Capric	4.34	0.985	1.74
	2.56		0.999
Undecanoic	7.30		
Lauric	7.3	3.08	3.08
	3.84	1.13	1.23
Myristic			3.32
	5.06	1.53	1.64
Palmitic			5.76
	7.1		2.00
Stearic		2.36	3.75
	9.04		2.59

Source: Swern (1964).

viscosity of an oil. Oils containing short chain fatty acids will generally have a lower viscosity than the high molecular weight acids with an equivalent degree of unsaturation. Viscosities of several oils are given in Table F.4 at 100° and 210°F.

Fatty acids exhibit higher viscosities than their methyl or ethyl esters because of the intermolecular hydrogen bonding in the acids through the carboxyl group. Table F.5 gives viscosities of saturated fatty acids and their methyl and ethyl esters.

TABLE F.6

DENSITY OF COMMERCIAL FATS AND OILS[1]

Temp., °F	Ml/Gm	Lb/Ft^3	Temp., °F	Ml/Gm	Lb/Ft^3
0	0.942	58.8	260	0.848	52.9
10	0.938	58.5	270	0.844	52.6
20	0.934	58.3	280	0.840	52.4
30	0.931	58.1	290	0.837	52.2
40	0.927	57.9	300	0.833	52.0
50	0.923	57.7	310	0.829	51.7
60	0.920	57.4	320	0.826	51.5
70	0.916	57.2	330	0.822	51.3
80	0.913	56.9	340	0.819	51.1
90	0.909	56.7	350	0.815	50.9
100	0.905	56.5	360	0.811	50.6
110	0.902	56.3	370	0.808	50.4
120	0.898	56.0	380	0.804	50.2
130	0.895	55.8	390	0.801	50.0
140	0.891	55.6	400	0.797	49.8
150	0.887	55.4	410	0.793	49.5
160	0.884	55.1	420	0.790	49.3
170	0.880	54.9	430	0.786	49.1
180	0.877	54.7	440	0.782	48.9
190	0.873	54.4	450	0.779	48.6
200	0.869	54.2	460	0.775	48.4
210	0.866	54.0	470	0.772	48.2
220	0.862	53.8	480	0.768	47.9
230	0.858	53.8	490	0.764	47.7
240	0.855	53.3	500	0.760	47.5
250	0.851	53.1	550	0.742	46.3

[1] Figures given are average for cottonseed oil, iodine number about 110. For other oils containing principally C_{16} and C_{18} fatty acids, make corrections as follows:

Linseed oil, iodine number about 190: To value for ml/gm, add 0.013; to value for lb/ft^3 add 0.8.

Soybean oil, iodine number about 130: To value for ml/gm add 0.004; to value for lb/ft^3 add 0.3.

Hydrogenated vegetable oil or lard, iodine number about 70: From value for ml/gm subtract 0.006; from value for lb/ft^3 subtract 0.4.

Highly hydrogenated vegetable oil or other fat, iodine number about 10: From value for ml/gm subtract 0.010; from value for lb/ft^3 subtract 0.6.

For other fats and oils of similar composition, make corrections according to the appropriate iodine number.

Note: These values apply only to completely liquid oils, and not to partially solidified materials.

Source: Swern (1964).

Density

Density of fats is higher in the solid than in the liquid state and shows greater shrinkage on solidification and expansion on melting than thermal expansion of the solid or liquid phase. Significantly different densities are observed in the various polymorphic forms of triglycerides. In the liquid state the density of both fatty acids and glycerides is greater the lower their molecular weight and the higher their unsaturation.

Approximate density values for common fats containing mainly C_{16} and C_{18} fatty acids are shown in Table F.6 for several temperatures. In the temperature range between 150° and 500°F, the density change is approximately a linear variation with temperature, decreasing about 0.00064 for each 1°C or 0.000355 for each 1°F.

Density values for some liquid fatty acids, esters, and triglycerides are presented in Table F.7.

Molar volume (Vm) in the liquid state is the result of dividing the molecular weight of the oil by its density. The equations for correlating molar volumes of saturated fatty acids with number of carbon atoms (n) at 20° and 80°C are

TABLE F.7

DENSITY OF LIQUID FATTY ACIDS, METHYL AND ETHYL ESTERS, AND SIMPLE TRIGLYCERIDES

	Density (Temperature, °C)			
Compound	Acid	Methyl Ester	Ethyl Ester	Triglyceride[1]
Butyric	0.9292 (50)			
	0.9043 (75)	0.8359 (75)	0.8205 (75)	
Caproic	0.8796 (75)	0.8313 (75)	0.8198 (75)	
	0.8751 (80)	0.827 (80)	0.8141 (80)	
Caprylic	0.8662 (75)	0.8287 (75)	0.8191 (75)	
	0.8615 (80)	0.824 (80)	0.8148 (80)	
Undecanoic	0.8741 (50)			
	0.8505 (80)			
Capric	0.8583 (75)	0.8271 (75)	0.8196 (75)	
	0.8531 (80)	0.823 (80)	0.8151 (80)	0.8913 (80)
Nonanoic	0.8813 (50)			
	0.8570 (80)			
Lauric	0.8516 (75)	0.8259 (75)	0.8195 (75)	0.8801 (80)
	0.8477 (80)	0.822 (80)	0.8153 (80)	
Myristic	0.8481 (75)	0.8252 (75)	0.8197 (75)	
	0.8439 (80)	0.821 (80)	0.8156 (80)	0.8722 (80)
Palmitic	0.8446 (75)	0.8247 (75)	0.8198 (75)	
	0.8414 (80)	0.820 (80)	0.8158 (80)	0.8663 (80)
Stearic	0.8431 (75)	0.8244 (75)	0.8218 (75)	
	0.8290 (80)	0.821 (80)	0.8161 (80)	0.8632 (80)
Oleic	0.863 (60)	0.875 (25)		0.9078 (25)
	0.850 (80)	0.860 (45)		
Elaidic				0.8872 (55)
Linoleic		0.890 (25)		
		0.875 (45)		

[1] Change in density per degree Centigrade, 0.00067–0.00073.
Source: Swern (1964).

$$20°C \qquad Vm = 16.89n + 23.62 \qquad n \text{ varies 2 to 9}$$
$$80°C \qquad Vm = 17.25n + 28.88 \qquad n \text{ varies 4 to 18}$$

Characteristics for several triglycerides cooled to complete solidification are shown in Table F.8. Natural fats being mixtures of triglycerides do not exhibit the abrupt density changes in the solid state as do the pure substances.

Combustion

The heats of combustion for saturated fatty acids have been quite accurately determined. As the molecular weight increases so does the heat of combustion and varies from about 5,900 cal per gm for butyric acid to about 9,600 for stearic, and 9,800 for behenic. Values given for unsaturated fatty acids are somewhat unreliable due in part to the purity of the fatty acids. Triglycerides possess essentially the same heat combustion as the fatty acids of which they are composed. Lard and tallow are about 9,500 cal per gm. For a variety of fats the heat of combustion may be approximated by the equation.

$$\text{Heat of combustion} = 11,380 - (\text{iodine no.}) - 9.15 \text{ (saponification no.)}$$

The values given above are expressed in terms of constant volume at 15°C.

Specific Heat

Specific heats of some vegetable oils at several temperatures are given in Table F.9. As the temperature is raised the specific heat of fats in both the solid and liquid states becomes greater. Longer chain fatty acids have a higher specific heat than those with fewer carbon atoms.

Fats are poor conductors of heat and only limited data are available.

TABLE F.8

DENSITY AND THERMAL EXPANSIBILITY OF COMPLETELY SOLID FATS

Fat	Temperature, °C	Density	Specific Volume	Range, °C	Change in Specific Volume per 1°C
Trilaurin, β-form	−38.6	1.057	0.946	−38 to −24	0.00019
Trimyristin, β-form	−38.4	1.050	0.953	−38 to −22	0.00021
Tripalmitin, β-form	−38.2	1.047	0.955	−38 to −18	0.00022
Tristearin, β-form	−38.6	1.043	0.959	−38 to −20	0.00023
Tristearin, β'-form	−38.0	1.017	0.983	−38 to −33	0.00029
Tristearin, α-form	−38.0	1.014	0.987	−38 to −33	0.00032
Trielaidin, highest melting form	−38.7	1.017	0.983	−38 to −22	0.00018
Triolein, highest melting form	−38.7	1.012	0.988	−38 to −33	0.00038
HCSO,[1] highest melting form	−38.2	1.022	0.978	−38 to −20	0.00029
HCSO,[2] highest melting form	−38.6	1.000	1.000	−38 to −33	0.00039
Lard, highest melting form	−38.6	1.005	0.995	−38 to −33	0.00038

[1] Hydrogenated cottonseed oil, iodine number, 0.85; mp 62.5°C.
[2] Hydrogenated cottonseed oil, iodine number, 59.5; mp, 41.4°C.
Source: Swern (1964).

Conductivity

Thermal conductivity values for olive oil in Btu per hr ft² °F per ft are 0.097 at 66°F, and 0.093 at 160°F. The values for castor oil are 0.104 and 0.100 at 68° and 212°F, respectively.

Flash Point

The smoke, fire, and flash points are important when heating oils for cooking because they indicate thermal stability in contact with air. When smoke is first detected rising from an oil the temperature is noted and recorded as the smoke point. The temperature at which volatiles evolving from a heated fat will flash but not support combustion is known as the flash point. The fire point is the temperature at which the substance supports combustion. Data on smoke, flash, and fire points for several oils are presented in Table F.10.

Other physical properties have been determined on fats and oils. Some of these include electrical properties, absorption spectra, solubility, and boiling point.

TABLE F.9

SPECIFIC HEATS OF VEGETABLE OILS

Temperature			Temperature		
°C	°F	Sp. Heat	°C	°F	Sp. Heat
Hydrogenated Cottonseed Oil (Iodine Number 6.5)			Tung Oil		
79.6	175.3	0.520	21.5	70.7	0.435
119.8	247.4	0.544	37.3	99.1	0.463
160.4	320.7	0.570	79.3	174.7	0.486
201.4	394.5	0.584	120.5	248.9	0.515
219.4	426.9	0.595	160.3	320.5	0.535
270.3	518.5	0.643	190.6	375.1	0.549
Castor Oil (Iodine Number 83.0)			Linseed Oil (Iodine Number 172.1)		
29.9	85.8	0.495	30.2	86.4	0.463
79.8	176.7	0.539	70.7	159.3	0.491
120.9	249.6	0.565	110.4	230.7	0.510
172.4	342.3	0.588	150.2	302.4	0.537
209.8	409.6	0.603	191.1	376.0	0.554
219.7	427.5	0.595	240.1	464.2	0.591
250.7	483.3	0.633	270.5	518.9	0.636
271.2	520.2	0.657			
Perilla Oil (Iodine Number 186.2)			Soybean Oil (Iodine Number 128.3)		
6.4	43.5	0.414	1.2	34.2	0.448
36.9	98.4	0.436	38.6	101.5	0.469
79.9	175.8	0.454	80.4	176.7	0.493
151.5	304.7	0.481	130.9	267.6	0.526
199.6	391.3	0.515	172.3	342.1	0.558
270.4	518.7	0.575	209.6	409.3	0.590
			240.2	464.4	0.617
			271.3	520.3	0.666

Source: Swern (1964).

References

MEYER, L. H. 1960. Food Chemistry. Reinhold Publishing Corp., New York.

SWERN, D. (Editor). 1964. Bailey's Industrial Oil and Fat Products, 3rd Edition. Interscience Publishers, John Wiley & Sons, New York.

Cross-references: *Butter, Physical Properties; Butter, Whipped; Milk Fat Testing, Rapid.*

FEED WATER HEATER

Important economies and additional capacity can be obtained in a steam plant through the use of a feed water heater. The general principle of the feed water heater is that either direct or indirect heat is used to warm the incoming boiler feed water.

Types

There are several types of feed water heaters (Fig. C.36). One heater uses waste heat and exhaust steam or condensate return water from processes directly to heat the incoming feed water (Fig. F.5). An indirect type of feed water heater is also used to reclaim the heat from return water which has impurities or for some reason cannot be mixed with the cold feed water and injected into the boiler (Fig. F.6).

Fuel Savings

The savings in fuel with the use of a feed water heater can be accurately calculated if the quantity and temperature of the return water are known. Table F.11 gives an approximate percentage saving in the heat energy which must be supplied to a boiler if returning hot condensate water at given temperature condition is used. The capacity of the boiler is increased through the use of heated feed water at different temperatures in proportion to the energy saving.

TABLE F.10

SMOKE, FLASH, AND FIRE POINTS OF OILS

Oil	Smoke Points		Flash Points, Open Cup		Fire Points	
	°F	°C	°F	°C	°F	°C
Castor, refined	392	200	568	298	635	335
Castor, dehydrated	348	176	570	299	638	337
Corn, crude	352	178	562	294	655	346
Corn, refined	440	227	618	326	678	359
Linseed, raw	325	163	540	287	667	353
Linseed, refined	320	160	588	309	680	360
Olive, virgin	391	199	610	321	682	361
Soybean, expeller, crude	357	181	564	296	664	351
Soybean, extracted, crude	410	210	603	317	670	354
Soybean, refined	492	256	618	326	673	356
Perilla, raw	321	161	575	302	678	359
Perilla, refined	352	178	608	320	685	363
Perilla, refined	408	209	615	324	685	363

Source: Detwiler and Markley (1940).

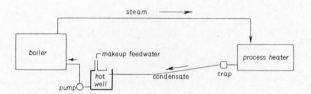

FIG. F-5.   Direct feedwater heater system

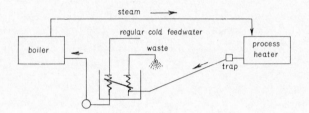

FIG. F-6.   Indirect feedwater heater system

Condensate Return

Where return condensate is added directly to the feed water to raise its temperature, the purity of the water should be checked carefully and no impurities be added that can injure the boiler or contaminate the products utilizing the steam.

Supplying warm or hot feed water to a boiler has an additional advantage since less strain results on the boiler because of the lower temperature change.

Cross-references: *Boilers; Steam.*

FILTERS

The product to be filtered may be passed through fine wire mesh, a perforated strainer, or woven cloth to remove dirt and slime. Milk is normally heated to about 90° to 110°F before filtering. There is less effect on the cream line of the milk when filtered as compared to clarified. Filtering has large acceptance in those areas where milk is not homogenized, largely outside of the United States. Units are available to connect directly on the high-temperature short-time system, after the preheater or regenerative section. These units using 40–90 mesh cloth are usually cylindrical in shape and look like a sock. The fluffy side of the filter pad should face the flow of milk. Usually two filters are attached but they are used one at a time. This permits continuous operation and the flow can be switched from one to the other while replacing a filter. A pressure gage may be attached to indicate when excessive buildup of sediment occurs, which is normally at about 10 psi for an APV unit. A higher pressure may break the cloth and stop filtering action.

Cross-references: *Air Filters; Bactofugation; Centrifugal Separators; H.T.S.T. Pasteurization; Ultrafiltration.*

TABLE F.11

FEED WATER HEATER ECONOMY

Feed Water, °F	Feed Water Heated, °F	Saving in Fuel, %
70	0	0.0
100	30	2.6
130	60	5.2
160	90	7.8

Saving in energy to generate steam at 100 psig—from 70°F normal feed water—if *feed water heater* is used to heat feed water with heat from return condensate at several temperatures.

FINISHES ON METAL

The American Iron and Steel Institute provides a standard for finish for sheet finishes, both hot rolled and cold rolled. The distinctions are made in the finishes of stainless and heat resisting steel sheets by numbers. The unpolished finishes are No. 1, No. 2D, and No. 2B. The polished finishes are described as No. 3, No. 4, No. 6, and No. 7, and No. 8. There is some variation in the finishes depending on the thickness of the sheet and the composition and method of manufacture. Generally the thinner the sheet, the smoother the surface. The chromium-nickel and chromium-nickel-manganese compositions have a somewhat different appearance than the chromium types for a coarse finish.

Appearance

The appearance, or color, of the finish of sheet No. 3, 4, 6, 7, and 8 may differ slightly among the 200, 300, 400 series of stainless and heat resistant steel types. Due to the variations, a standard which is based on smoothness or reflectance has therefore not been established.

Description

A description of the unpolished finishes is as follows

No. 1 Finish.—Hot rolled, annealed, and descaled. Produced on hand sheet mills by hot rolling followed by annealing and descaling.

Generally used in industrial applications, such as for heat or corrosion resistance, where smoothness of finish is not of particular importance.

No. 2D Finish.—A dull cold rolled finish produced by either hand sheet mills or continuous mills by cold rolling, annealing, and descaling. The dull finish may result from the descaling or pickling operation or may be by a final light cold roll pass on dull rolls. The dull finish is favorable for the retention of lubricants on the surface in deep drawing operations.

This finish is generally used in forming deep drawn articles which may be polished after fabrication.

No. 2B Finish.—A bright cold rolled finish commonly produced the same as No. 2D, except that the annealed and descaled sheet receives a final light cold rolled pass on polished rolls.

This is a general purpose cold rolled finish. It is commonly used for all but exceptionally difficult deep drawing applications.

This finish is more readily polished than No. 1 or No. 2D Finish.

A description of the polished finishes is as follows:

No. 3 Finish.—A polished finish obtained with abrasives of approximately 100 mesh, and which may or may not be additionally polished during fabrication.

No. 4 Finish.—A general purpose polished finish widely used for restaurant equipment, kitchen equipment, store fronts, dairy equipment, etc. Following initial grinding with coarser abrasives, sheets are generally finished last with abrasives approximately 120 to 150 mesh.

No. 6 Finish.—A dull satin finish having lower reflectivity than No. 4 Finish. It is produced by Tampico brushing No. 4 Finish Sheets in a medium of abrasive and oil.

It is used for architectural applications and ornamentation where a high luster is undesirable; it is also used effectively to contrast with brighter finishes.

No. 7 Finish.—Has a high degree of reflectivity. It is produced by buffing of finely ground surface, but the "grit" lines are not removed. It is chiefly used for architectural and ornamental purposes.

No. 8 Finish.—The most reflective finish that is commonly produced. It is obtained by polishing with successively finer abrasives and buffing extensively with very fine buffing rouges. The surface is essentially free of grit lines from preliminary grinding operations.

This finish is most widely used for press plates, as well as for small mirrors and reflectors.

Sheets can be produced with 1 or 2 sides polished. When polished on one side only, the other side may be rough ground in order to obtain the necessary flatness.

Cross-reference: *Stainless Steel.*

FLASH PASTEURIZER

Early pasteurization was accomplished by devices which either forced the product in a thin layer over the heating surface, or moved the product between two heated surfaces. The product is heated to as high as 185°F. The various units for accomplishing this treatment have since become known as flash pasteurizers. One of these units, the Danish heater, consists of a large central cylinder with a jacket. Steam in the central cylinder heats water between the cylinder and jacket. Milk is pumped into the bottom of the unit. The milk is moved by centrifugal force to the walls of the tank where it is heated. The heated product leaves through a pipe at the top, tangent to the tank linear. The unit acts somewhat like a pump lifting milk 10 to 15 ft. However, the unit is difficult to control for temperature. No particular holding is required as the product is heated to temperatures up to 185°F.

Another flash pasteurizer forces milk between two concentric heated cylinders to produce a pasteurized product. One type of unit employs a revolving arm which moves between the heating surfaces to keep product in motion. In another unit the inner cylinder, containing a spiral ridge, turns forcing the product through the unit. A heating medium of water, heated by steam, is usually used.

The principle of regeneration can be utilized by passing the outgoing warm product through a heat exchanger so as to transfer heat to the incoming cold product.

Cross-references: *Pasteurization; UHT Equipment.*

FLOORS

The floors of the processing plant provide one of the building features which is important for maintaining sanitary conditions and satisfactory environment for the workers.

Floors differ throughout the processing plant, depending on the use. A major consideration must be given to floors which will come into contact with the food or waste products associated with the processing operation. Floors provide an important impression, favorably or unfavorably, to the visitor of the plant.

Requirements

The following requirements must be considered in selection of material for the floors of the processing plant. These requirements consider chemical and mechanical operations, as well as worker relationships.

(1) A high degree of sanitation must be possible.

(2) There must be a resistance of the floor to food products, acids, greases, detergents, and sanitizing agents.

(3) The floor must withstand steam.

(4) The floor must withstand impact from bottles, cases, crates, pallets, and fork lift trucks in many areas.

(5) The floor must provide an attractive appearance.

(6) The floor must be free of undesirable odors. This may or may not be related to sanitation.

(7) The floors should provide a long service life.

(8) The total cost of the floor, both initially and for maintenance, must be considered in terms of the possible returns.

(9) Proper drainage must be provided which in general means a slope of $1/4$ in. per ft either toward center drains or along the edge of the room.

(10) The floor must wear evenly under different types of traffic maintained.

(11) The floor should not be excessively slippery where employees walk and work.

Area Requirements

There is a tendency to overbuild, that is to provide more floor area than can be economically used. On the other hand, provisions must be made for expanding the plant to sustain larger operations in the future. In the processing areas, the floor area provided is normally five times the area covered by the equipment. The importance of dry storage is often overlooked in plants; dry storage requirements vary tremendously with different sizes and types of processing operations. In general, there should be at least 25% of the total area of the plant devoted to dry storage. Equipment should be placed so that there is at least 3 ft of space between equipment where workers must move. For a dairy plant, for fluid milk processing, from 1 to 2 sq ft of space must be provided per gallon processed per day.

Types

Processing floors may be of the following:

(1) Concrete slab monolithic floors are most common. Although not as durable as others available, the economy, considering first cost and the usual length of life in service makes concrete one of the most economical. Concrete is affected by milk acids, grease, and some detergents, and is eroded in standard processing plant operations from cases and crates. The life of the material depends considerably upon the method of mixing and installing the concrete (see Concrete). The major requirement is that the concrete be dense and that the proper cement-water ratio be used as recommended. Surface hardeners may be used. Stone chips and iron filings may be added to provide a better wearing surface.

(2) Wood floors are not satisfactory in the presence of steam and most foods. The accumulation of food residues will often putrefy and produce unsanitary conditions with wood floors.

(3) Concrete floors may be supplied with a protective coating. Vinyl, styrene, or chlorinated rubber coatings are resistant to food acids, but do not withstand heavy traffic or steam cleaning.

(4) Tile floors made from packing house tile, but now applied to many food plants, perform quite satisfactorily if strong joints and a proper base for the tile are used. In general, the tile floor is only as good as the joint. Tile should be installed so that the joints can be easily grouted by machine and refinished. Portland cement can be used for the base of the tile and for the joints. However, for longer life, tile floors can be pointed with Furan or other plastics for the joints and support of the tile.

Tiles are normally 6 by 6 by $^1/_2$ or $^3/_4$ in. thick.

Brick pavers may also be used. A standard brick is 8 by $3^3/_4$ by $2^1/_4$ in. Many sizes are available. An important aspect of installing tiles or pavers is that an excellent subbase is necessary, as well as proper grouting of the brick or tile.

(5) Terrazo floors are excellent for areas where processing is not done. In general, acid or alkaline deterioration occurs around the terrazzo aggregates and causes a short life of an acceptable floor.

The following principles and practices apply to floors in processing plants.

(1) Concrete provides the least expensive floor based on installation and provides serviceability.

(2) A minimum quantity of water must be used for preparing the concrete as an excessive amount of water will lower the quality from the standpoint of denseness, wearability, and water absorption.

(3) Carborundum or carbon crystals may be mixed with the finish coat of concrete.

(4) The floor surface may be treated with a solution of sodium silicate, aluminum sulfate, or zinc sulfate to give the concrete increased resistance to food acids.

(5) Boiled linseed oil may be added when warm in about two coats. Also, enamels may be used in place of linseed oil. These help provide a hard abrasive resistant finish.

(6) Floors of unloading platforms, receiving, and shipping areas may be covered with metal plates. These may be placed in or over the floor.

(7) Metal-covered or metal floors are now being used widely in storage areas where the products or containers can be slid over the floor.

Cross-references: *Building Materials; Concrete; Drains; Ice Cream Hardening.*

FLOUR AGITATOR

Handling flour can be a dusty operation. When blending flour to obtain the maximum quality characteristics, enclosed blenders usually are the most successful. The revolving chamber type are quite satisfactory. Ribbon blenders agitate products such as flour quite effectively. However, the dust created can be objectionable unless adequately enclosed.

Bulk handling of flour using pneumatic conveying systems and bulk bins makes blending operations more efficient. Bucket elevators create dusty conditions and provide a place for insects to grow.

In the process of milling, conveying, sifting, blending, and bagging, flour undergoes considerable agitation and sanitation is important in all operations.

Reference

MATZ, S. A. (Editor) 1959. The Chemistry and Technology of Cereals as Food and Feed. AVI Publishing Co., Westport, Conn.

Cross-references: *Blender; Bulk Bins; Dry Mixer; Pneumatic Conveying.*

FLOW CHARTS

A flow chart can be used to illustrate the movement of materials in a system. An existing arrangement and proposed arrangements can be evaluated on the basis of such factors as cost, returns, time, layout, flexibility, equipment, and storage. An analysis of the flow of animals, feed, water, products, and man can be made.

The flow chart permits a rapid analysis of amount of handling and storage of products (Fig. F.7 and F.8).

Weak points can often be located by studying the flow diagram and analyzing each step in the process. Conveyors may be improperly sized. The grinder may not be used to capacity because of a slow elevating process. The mixer may be improperly sized. Improved operations can be obtained after analyzing the present arrangement, questioning the necessity of each step, trying alternative combinations, and evaluating possible changes. Applications to industrial and agricultural problems are available.

FLOWMETERS (SANITARY TYPE)

The use of sanitary flowmeters in the food industry has been growing. Some of the applications consist of measuring bulk liquids and food products, measuring water flow rates, determining the quantity of fluid products which are ingredients in a food mixture, and determining production schedules. The flowmeter measures volume. The accuracy is related to methods for compensating for the entrained air in the liquid being measured.

Desirable features of sanitary flowmetering systems are (1) sanitary construction for easy cleaning, (2) the error should be less than $\pm 0.5\%$ of actual reading, (3) capacity should be flexible up to nearly 300 gpm, (4) the unit should integrate, and (5) an air-eliminating device should be included in the system. Flow measurement can be classified by type of meter as positive displacement, turbine type, magnetic type, variable area, and timed flow.

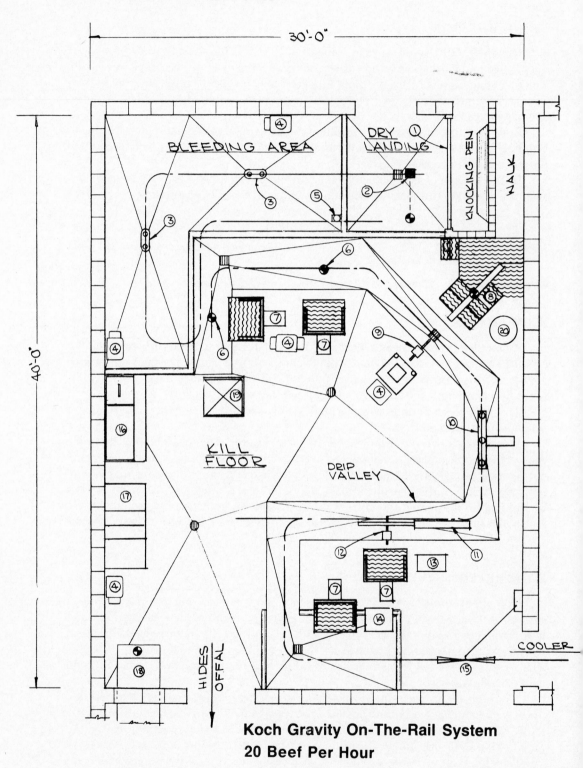

**Koch Gravity On-The-Rail System
20 Beef Per Hour**

Courtesy Koch Supplies,

Fɪɢ. F-7. Beef slaughtering operation
1—Revolving knocking pen door. 2—Hoist and lander. 3—Blood and water drain. 4—Lavatory and sterilizer. 5—Shackle lowerator. 6—Transfer device. 7—Elevating platform. 8—Hide stripper with platforms and stanchion. 9—Brisket saw. 10—Eviscerating drop. 11—Spreader. 12—Splitting saw. 13—Saw sterilizer. 14—Shroud tank. 15—Track scale. 16—Head table. 17—Pluck and gullet table. 18—Paunch dump. 19—Head flushing cabinet. 20—Hide drum.

Positive Displacement Meter

Positive displacement meters are of two general types. One of these meters consists of a calibrated measure chamber, a rotary piston, and a counter with a register. Figure F.9 illustrates the action which is based on continuous filling and emptying of the chamber with the rotating piston recording the motion through a magnetic coupling to the totalizer. The use of a magnetic coupling makes it possible for the back

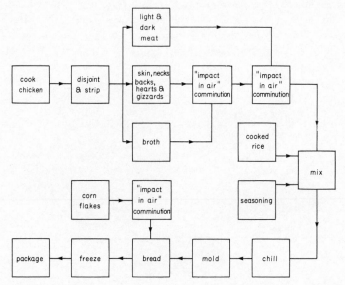

From "They Turned By-products Into Profitable Co-products" by G. M. Kovac and R. E. Morse

Fɪɢ. F-8. Chicken stick process flowsheet

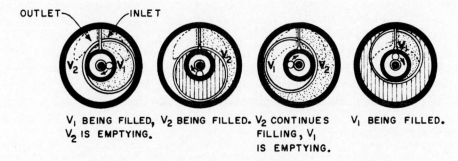

V₁ BEING FILLED, V₂ BEING FILLED. V₂ CONTINUES V₁ BEING FILLED.
V₂ IS EMPTYING. FILLING, V₁
IS EMPTYING.

Fɪɢ. F-9. Principle of operation of rotary piston fluid meter wall of the chamber to be of solid metal, eliminating the need for shaft seals or stuffing boxes. The piston is made of plastic material which is nontoxic, nonabsorbent, and resistant to cracking. The accuracy of the meter is affected by a wide change of temperatures. A temperature exceeding 104°F requires a different piston than that used for lower temperatures. The energy for the motion of the piston is derived from the product flow. The pressure drop through the unit is comparatively low, therefore, may be used with a positive or centrifugal type pump. The maximum operating pressure is considered to be 45 psi. The meter has been increased in size and is now capable of capacities of about 200 gpm. As with most meters, an air eliminator is necessary for reliable accuracy. The manufacturer guarantees an accuracy within ±0.5% of actual reading when operating under field conditions where an air eliminating device is used.

This positive displacement meter may be equipped with various types of measuring and recording devices. It is obtainable with an automatic proportioning system which may be preset for closing a valve, or it may be furnished with a mechanism for stopping the feed pump after a predetermined quantity has been delivered.

Another variation of the positive displacement type of sanitary flowmeter is the oval wheel meter. The dismantled meter showing the oval wheels and other parts is shown in Fig. F.10. A calibrated chamber inside of which the oval wheels revolve

Fɪɢ. F-10.   Oval wheel flow meter

displaces the revolving wheel function. The oval wheels have a gear train and are meshed very precisely in the instrument. The design of the teeth of the gear train is such that the oval wheels can be inserted in one manner only in the chamber. The revolutions of the oval wheels are transmitted to the counter mechanism through a magnetic coupling similar to that used in the rotary piston meter. The accuracy of this meter is similar to that of the rotary piston unit. A stainless strainer up stream from this meter is recommended to prevent damage.

Turbine Type Flowmeters

Sanitary turbine flow meters utilize a flow sensing element in the product as shown in Fig. F.11. A small multibladed rotor containing an Alnico magnet produces an ac

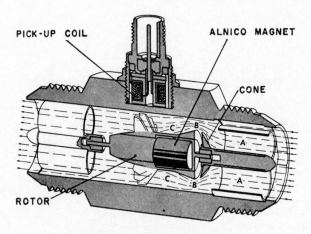

FIG. F-11.   Turbine flow meter

electrical output with a frequency directly proportional to flow rate. Calibrated instruments pick up the ac signal, amplify, and use it for recording flow rate, totalizing, or for input to other controls.   The turbine flowmeter system has, in addition to the flow sensing element, a frequency convertor and an electronic potentiometer.   The frequency convertor delivers a dc output directly proportional to the frequency of the ac input from the sensing element.   A digital counter of the roller type registers a proportion of the pulses from the sensing element.

Adjustment to handling products of various specific gravities is available for use with turbine flowmeters.   Calibration can be done automatically during operation for products varying in specific gravity from 9.6 to 1.6.   The accuracy of the system is within ±0.5% over most of the instrument range.   An advantage of this type flowmeter is that the dc output may be used with a dial type indicator at the location, and a recording instrument installed at another location.   The sensing element may be adapted to a variety of instrumentation which utilizes the ac output.

A unique feature of the sensing element is the low pressure area in which the rotor spins establish a hydraulically balanced rotor position.   A thrust bearing for the rotor is unnecessary.   Teflon guides keep the rotor spinning freely in the low pressure area.   Either horizontal or vertical lines are satisfactory for the sensing element.   The element may be cleaned-in-place and is not affected by minor variations in temperature or head pressures.   Because a small voltage is generated, this type of flowmeter lends itself to automation in food plants.   The instrumentation is sensitive to moisture and should be protected.

Electromagnetic Flowmeter

The electromagnetic flowmeter illustrated in Fig. F.12 is based on the principle of Faraday's Law which states that emf (voltage) is induced in a circuit by and during a change in the magnetic flux.   The system consists of a flow transmitter, an electrical insulated liner on the inside of the product tube, an electromagnetic which induces a magnetic field through the product tube, and two metallic electrodes which are flush with the inside surface of the insulating tube liner.   Teflon, neoprene, Kel-F, or glass are usually used for lining the product tube.   In order to measure product flow with

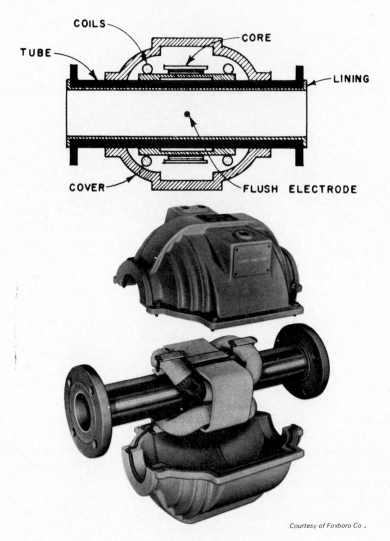

FIG. F-12.   Electromagnetic flow meter

an electric flowmeter, it is necessary that the product be a conductor of electrical current.   Most liquid foods are a sufficiently good conductor for this type flowmeter. The output of the flow transmitter is linear and directly proportional to the average velocity of the product flowing though it.   The very small voltage produced is a function of the flow between the two electrodes and may be measured in an instrument and the results recorded or totalized in a remote location.   Converting the voltage to digital readout or other function involves a certain degree of error.   The accuracy will normally be within ±1.0% of full scale or flow rate.   For example, if 80 gpm were the flow rate, an expected accuracy would lie within ±1.0% of 80 gpm.   Certain advantages may be cited for the electromagnetic flowmeters in that there are no obstructions in the product line which facilitates cleaning.   Another advantage lies in the fact that a wide variety of uses may be made of the voltage produced in the trans-

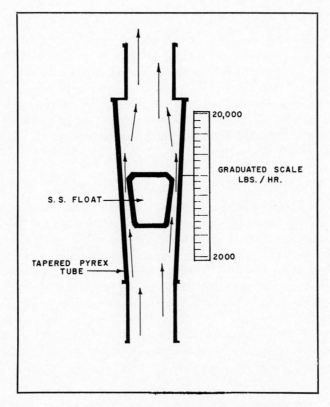

Fɪɢ. F-13.   Variable area meter—float movement indicates flow rate

mitter. This voltage when amplified may be used in multirecord instruments which are available and provide color and coded records of up to six different transmitters on one chart. Electrical alarm or automatic controls may be operated by the system. Highly automated plants may find application for this type meter in regulating product flow control. The meter is appreciably affected by normal variations in different density or viscosity. Turbulence of flow does not adversely affect the accuracy of the system. The instrument will include entrained air in the quantitative rates.

Variable Area Meter

A variable area meter is actually a rotameter or flow rate indicator. The uni serves a useful purpose to indicate the rate of product flow through various machine and to proportion ingredients such as those used for making ice cream mix. The principle of operation involves movement of a tapered stainless steel float in a tapered tube. As the flow increases, the float rises, increasing the cross-sectional area and indicating the flow rate on a graduated scale as illustrated in Fig. F.13. One commonly used variable area meter is graduated to rate from 2,000 to 20,000 lb per hr. Variable area meters usually do not integrate or totalize the volume of product passing through it in a given time. The instrument is useful in indicating solution flow rates in CIP circuits.

Timed Flowmeter

When a positive pump in good condition has been calibrated for delivery at a constant infeed and discharge pressure, the pump may be used as a metering device. The revolutions may be counted by inserting a magnet in the pump coupling and by merely counting the revolutions, the quantity delivered may be controlled. With the pump running at a constant rate, the delivery per unit of time also may be used to make the pump serve as a meter. Depending upon the many factors which affect volumetric measurements, the metering pump can be reasonably used in operations where extreme accuracy is not necessary.

Air Eliminator and Product Sampling

In recent years larger size and effective air eliminators have been produced. One of these eliminators utilizes air pressure inside the chamber and as the product flows over a weir, air is expended through the outlet port of the eliminator. To enhance the accuracy of volumetric metering, the air eliminator should be regarded as a must.

The flowmeter lends itself to increasing the accuracy of sampling a product. A schematic method of incorporating the sampling device in conjunction with the meter is shown in Fig. F.14. As product flow increases a larger sample is collected.

Volumetric flowmeters are generally not considered as accurate as gravimetric determinations. These do, however, provide the food plant operator with a comparatively inexpensive and flexible method of making quantity determinations useful in the operation of the food processing plant.

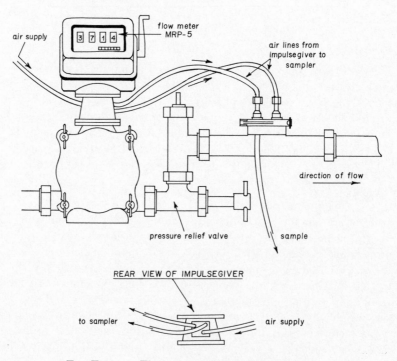

FIG. F-14.   Flow meter with automatic sampler

References

MILK INDUSTRY FOUNDATION. 1967. Manual for Milk Plant Operators. Washington, D.C.
RIPPEN, A. L., and HALL, C. W. 1958. Flowmeters and how they are used. Milk Plant
Monthly *47*, No. 5, 23–28.

FLUID BED DRIERS

The fluid bed drier is used for removing moisture from food products of granular or fibrous nature and moisture content of about 50% to about 2 or 3%, if desired.

The drier is rather simple in construction, compact, and can be quite efficient. The labor and power costs are usually quite low with respect to many other methods of drying.

Principle

This type of drier consists essentially of a compact drying chamber of tubular vertical design in which hot air is forced into the bottom at such a rate the particles are kept in a suspended state. Usually a cloth bag or other similar powder collecting device is used above the drying bed to collect and retain any real fine particles which otherwise might be lost in the discharge air.

Operation

The efficiency and drying rate of this drier are quite good. It is constructed so that it can be cleaned readily. Air preheaters of either steam or electricity are normally used and the air is filtered before it is passed into the fluidized bed.

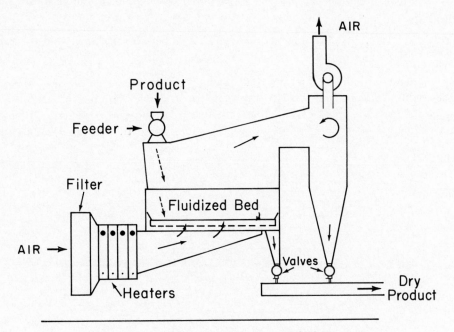

FIG. F-15.   Fluidized bed continuous drying system

Figure F.15 shows the construction of this type of drier. The rate of drying depends upon a number of variables such as air velocity, drying temperature, material properties, and size and shape of granules or fibers.

This drier can be obtained in sizes from 4 to 440 lb per batch in single models; however, multiple oven carousel type units are available that will dry up to 6,500 lb per hr of product with automatic control.

Cross-references: *Drier; Drum Driers; Spray Driers; Tunnel Driers.*

FLUID FLOW

A knowledge of the flow of fluids, liquids, and gases is necessary to determine the power required to move these fluids. Many of the products in a processing plant become fluidized at some stage of the processing operation.

Principles

The total mechanical energy of a fluid system includes elevation energy, pressure energy, and velocity energy. The friction due to fluid flow must also be overcome by the pump or other energy input to the system. The energy is usually represented in foot-pounds force per pound mass, or designated as feet of head of flowing fluid. The elevation is represented directly in feet of head. The pressure usually in pounds per square foot or pounds per square inch is converted to the equivalent in feet of head where for water 14.7 psi is equivalent to 33.9 ft of head. The velocity head is equal to the velocity squared divided by 2 times gravity, where gravity is 32.16 ft per sec².

The flow in a pipe or duct or other system is identified by Reynolds number in which a Reynolds number of 2,100 or less represents streamlined flow; 2,100 to 4,000, mixed flow; and 4,000 and above as turbulent flow.

$$\text{Reynolds number} = \frac{\text{diameter (ft)} \times \text{velocity (ft per sec)} \times \text{density (lb per ft}^3)}{\text{viscosity}}$$

For a noncircular fluid conductor or one in which the fluid does not fill the entire cross section, the hydraulic radius, R, is substituted in Reynolds number in which the hydraulic radius is the cross section of area divided by the wetted perimeter. Reynolds number, incorporating the hydraulic radius, is four times the hydraulic radius times

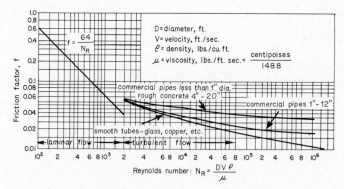

Fig. F-16. Relation of friction factor and Reynolds number

TABLE F.12

VISCOSITY OF LIQUIDS

Material	Temperature, °C	Density, Gm/Cc	Coefficient of Viscosity, Centipoise
Brine, CaCl₂, 25%	0		4.55
	20		2.4
	40		1.28
	60		0.72
Castor oil	10	0.969	2420
	20		986
	40		231
Ethyl alcohol	0	0.791	1.77
	10		1.45
	20		1.19
	40		0.86
Linseed oil, raw	10	0.942	58.0
	30		33.1
	50		17.6
	70		11.6
Methyl alcohol	0	0.810	0.813
	20		0.591
Olive oil	10	0.918	138.0
	20		84.0
	40		36.3
Soybean oil	30		40.6
	50		20.6
Sugar	125		190000
Turpentine	0	0.87	2.25
	20		1.49
	30		1.27
Water	0	1.00	1.60
	20		1.01
	40		0.71
	60		0.49
	80		0.36
	100		0.26

the velocity, times the density, divided by the viscosity. Most tables (Tables F.12 and F.13) give the viscosity of fluids in centipoises. These values can be converted to the units for Reynolds equation by dividing by 1,488.

Friction Head

Tables are available for reading the friction head directly under most conditions for transport of air or water, in a hydraulic or pneumatic system. However, for many food products, where there are varying physical properties, it is necessary to calculate the friction head based on the properties of the product. Darcy's equation is used for calculating the friction head for gases or liquids

$$F = f \times \frac{L}{D} \times \frac{V^2}{2g}$$

where f = friction factor

L = length, ft

D = diameter, ft

V = velocity, ft

g = gravity, 32 ft

The f is read from a figure or table as related to the roughness of the pipe, the physical characteristics of the fluid, and velocity as represented by Reynolds number (Fig. F.16 and F.17).

The velocity, V, is the average velocity throughout the cross section of the piping or tubing. For streamlined or laminar flow, the average velocity is $1/2$ of the maximum velocity at the center. For turbulent flow, the average velocity is approximately 0.8 of the maximum velocity.

The quantity of discharge, Q, is represented by $Q = A \times V$, in cubic feet per second.

Bernoulli's equation is used to represent the flow at two locations in a pipe based on the conservation of energy. This equation is

$$\frac{p_1}{w} + z_1 + \frac{V_1^2}{2g} = \frac{p_2}{w} + z_2 + \frac{V_2^2}{2g} + \text{lost head}$$

where w = density of fluid, lb per cu ft

p_1, p_2 = pressure head at two positions

V_1, V_2 = velocity heat at two positions

z_1, z_2 = elevation head at two positions

The velocity of efflux from an orifice in a tank is represented by $V = \sqrt{2gh}$. Because of frictional losses this is usually expressed as $V = c\sqrt{2gh}$ where c is the coefficient of discharge, and is 0.8 for a square orifice outlet and 0.95 for a round smooth orifice. The quantity of discharge is then equal to $A \times V$, that is the cross-sectional area times the average velocity.

For turbulent flow, the losses in friction head due to fittings and valves are usually significant, particularly as the velocity increases. In general, it is desirable to keep the velocity of liquids below 8 ft per sec so that the velocity head will be less than 1.

TABLE F.13

VISCOSITY OF GASES (AT A PRESSURE OF 1 ATM)

Gas	Density, Gm/liter	Temperature Range, °C	Coefficient of Viscosity, Centipoise
Air	1.293	0–100	0.01709
Ammonia	0.771	15–100	0.0096
Carbon dioxide	1.98	−20–140	0.0137
Carbon monoxide	1.25	15–100	0.1166
Chlorine	3.22	20–100	0.0129
Helium	0.18	−100–100	0.0187
Hydrogen	0.09	−183–21	0.0084
Methyl chloride	2.30	−15–300	−0.00988
Nitrogen	1.25	15–100	0.0166
Oxygen	1.43	17–100	0.0187
Sulfur dioxide	2.93	18–100	0.0117

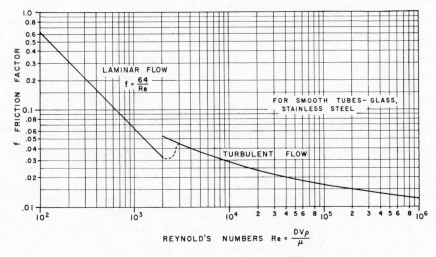

Fɪɢ. F-17.   Friction factor for different Reynolds numbers

In the final analysis, the costs involved in piping, pumping, etc. must be calculated to determine optimum flow.   The friction loss due to fittings can be expressed in feet of head $= K \times V^2/2g$, where $K = 0.15$ for a gate valve, and 7.5 for a globe valve. In general, K is about 0.5 for a smooth bend elbow with a radius of curvature of the elbow equivalent to the diameter of the pipe.   Also, the friction head loss due to fittings and valves may be expressed in terms of pipe diameters where $40 \times K$ is the length of the equivalent pipe which would be needed to provide the same friction loss as the fitting or valve.

Reference

Hᴇɴᴅᴇʀsoɴ, S. M., and Pᴇʀʀʏ, R.   1955.   Agricultural Processing Engineering.   John Wiley & Sons, New York.

Cross-references: *Air; Air Movement; Friction; Piping; Steam; Viscosity; Ventilation.*

FLY, INSECT AND RODENT CONTROL

Under the U.S. Food, Drug, and Cosmetic Act, food plant conditions must be sufficiently sanitary to render food products free from suspicion of contaminants. Wording in the act is such that conditions whereby a product may have become contaminated with filth or may have been rendered injurious to health is interpreted to mean that only suspect conditions leading to possible contamination need be found by the inspector.   Actual product contamination need not be proved.   This means that food plant operators must keep the plant and premises in satisfactory condition including a program which will control insects and rodents.

Flies

Flies are best controlled by employing a program of prevention.   Elimination of the breeding places or areas of filth which attract flies is the most effective control.

If the fly population in or around a food plant is great, unsanitary conditions are indicated. The local health department may be helpful in eliminating breeding places in the vicinity of the plant on property owned by others. Careful cleaning of garbage cans or using single service plastic liners is a must. Storing the containers on concrete platforms which are easily cleaned is effective in fly control.

Use of fly baits outside the plant and spraying outside wall areas at critical points with long lasting insecticides is a good procedure to prevent fly entry into the plant. Should some flies gain entrance into the plant only an approved insecticide may be used in aerosols for killing flies. Spraying should be done after processing for the day is completed but before plant cleanup. For effectiveness of the chemical ventilating fans should be stopped before spraying.

Prevention is the best approach to fly control; however, the use of a double door vestibule into processing areas is recommended. When one enters the vestibule a small sprayer operates automatically fogging the enclosure only sufficiently to prevent fly entry. The sprayer is stopped automatically by a timer control.

Air curtains have proved useful in retarding fly entry. Fan selection and air velocities have been quite well-established for various size door openings. Also see Fig. A.13 and A.14. Some modern air curtains have been developed with blower units whose discharge is through an adjustable nozzle for maximum benefit for a given door opening. The nozzle is quite narrow and usually extends across the top of the door. Deflectors produce a more effective air curtain from the discharge of a propeller type fan.

Roaches

Roaches breed in dark, moist places, and because they do not expose themselves during daylight hours or under well-lighted conditions, their presence is not always apparent. As with flies the first step in control is to eliminate obvious breeding places. Wall cracks, crevices, and small openings should be sealed. Accumulations of waste materials in little-used areas should be avoided by prompt cleaning.

Air curtains are of no value in roach control. Roaches hide in returned cases or boxes and gain entry to a plant. Insecticides must be changed from time to time when the insects are shown to have become resistant to the one in use. Residual oil base insecticides are recommended, since they are a nonconductor and may be used in electrical switch boxes, a favorite hiding place. Insecticidal dusts are not recommended because of their tendency to float in air, a characteristic which could result in food contamination.

Prompt washing of returned cases will help prevent roach entry into the plant. A commercial type vacuum cleaner is a useful tool to achieve good plant sanitation and eliminate breeding places. Dust particles serving as food may be removed with the vacuum cleaner at intervals of 3 to 4 weeks which normally is sufficient as a preventive measure.

Rodents

For effective rodent control in a food plant, the following practices are considered essential.

(1) Rodent-proof the building. (2) Eliminate breeding and harborage places outside the plant. (3) Install weatherproof bait boxes outside the plant for perimeter

baiting. (4) Eliminate hiding places inside the plant. (5) Use a trapping program for any rodents that might enter the plant.

Many items constitute rodentproofing a building. Some of these include the use of steel vertical ladders set away from the wall at docks, tight-fitting doors, adequate screening, protecting down spouts, etc. The perimeter baiting program in approved secured bait boxes using anticoagulant compound is a good preventive program. Design of the baitbox must be such to prevent pets and other animals from feeding. A $3^1/_4$ by $3^1/_2$ in. rectangular opening is usually satisfactory. The box should be equipped with an internal partition having another opening of the same size, but not in line with the outside opening. This contains the bait in the self-feeder area of the box.

Rats do not jump up vertically more than 3 ft. Therefore, storage of garbage containers at least 3 ft above the ground is recommended. Paving or blacktopping the area around the plant to prevent puddles and accumulation of filth is very helpful in eliminating harborage areas for rodents.

Good housekeeping inside the plant and following a trapping program will normally maintain rodent control. The simple snap trap with peanut butter, bacon rind, raw meat, or certain fruit and vegetables as bait is generally satisfactory.

Insect and rodent control requires continuous attention by competent people who conduct frequent careful plant inspections.

Reference

REYNOLDS ELECTRIC CO. Fly chaser fan installation, Bull. *233*. River Grove, Ill.

Cross-reference: *Sanitation.*

FOAM MAT DRYING

The product to be dried is first stabilized. Air is fed to the product in a closed mixer where a porous product is formed. The air-product mixture is extruded onto perforated drying trays. The tray of foam passes over air jets cratering the foam to increase drying surface. The trays then move into and upward in the drying chamber in the same direction as the air moves. Air at 220°F with a velocity of 330 to 400 fpm is used, traveling cocurrently with the tray. At the top section of the drier, after the warm, drying air is emitted, cool air enters to cool the product. The dry product is produced in 1.5 to 15 min and is porous and readily soluble.

One approach consists of placing a foam film up to 40 mil thick on a stainless steel belt. The product is exposed about 1 min and normally does not exceed 170°F. The system can produce 1.0 to 1.5 lb of dry product per hr per sq ft of belt.

Cross-reference: *Foam Spray Dryer.*

FOAM SPRAY DRIER

Common dairy products, including skim milk, whole milk, buttermilk, sweet and sour cream (up to 3:1 fat to SNF), whey, and emulsified cheese slurry can be foam spray dried. Foam spray drying can be accomplished by (1) preparing a mixture of

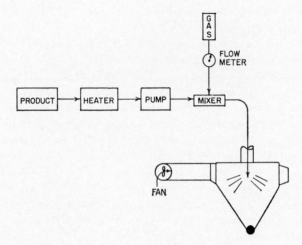

FIG. F-18.   System for foam spray drying

gas and liquid ahead of the pump, or (2) forcing the gas into the liquid after the pump before the atomizing nozzle supplying the drier (Fig. F.18).   It is necessary to maintain a pressure over the mixture to get appreciable incorporation of the gas in the liquid if done ahead of the drier.   An Oakes mixer is commonly used for this purpose. To move gas into the liquid requires that the gas be about 200 psi pressure above the pump pressure which is commonly at 1,000 to 1,800 psi for milk.

Gas

Air is commonly used as the added gas for making foam spray nonfat dry milk. Nitrogen is commonly used for making foam spray-dried whole milk.   The quantity of gas used is from 0.5 to 2.0 std cu ft per gal. of product, for 40 to 60% total solids (NF).

Spray Dryer

Foam spray drying provides a means of using most conventional spray-drying equipment for drying liquids up to a maximum of 60% total solids (ts) as compared

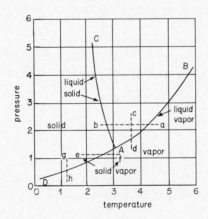

FIG. F-19.   Phase diagram of water

to 50% on a particular drier; for drying special products, such as malted milk and cottage cheese whey; for obtaining an instant type powder, but with characteristics different than the product prepared by agglomerating processes normally used following the spray drier; and provides a procedure for increasing the capacity of conventional equipment.

Properties

Foam spray nonfat dry milk has a bulk density of about 9.35 gm per ml or less (about the same as agglomerated or conventional instantized powder). The foam spray-dried product will withstand considerable handling and can be compressed into smaller volumes without appreciably affecting the dispersibility. The foam spray-dried product will remain on top of water for an extended period and needs to be mechanically mixed to form a solution. A more uniform particle size is obtained with foam spray drying. The capacity of a conventional drier can be increased appreciably by using a higher total solids in the input. By removing the water ahead of the drier, the cost of operation can be decreased. Approximately twice as much product can be handled by the drier with an infeed of 60% ts as compared to 42.5%.

Pretreatment

Providing a liquid milk product at 60% ts requires special consideration for heat exchangers and evaporation. In general, larger heat exchanger surfaces or continuous forced flow of the product through the heat exchanger is required. As the hold time increases, the viscosity increases and makes handling difficult, and dispersibility decreases. By holding the product, however, one can obtain a product with more crystalline lactose. Holding 52% ts condensed nonfat milk at 95°F for 15 min provides 7.7% crystalline lactose in the powder; for 35 min, 17.1%; and for 60 min, 35%. Conventional agglomerated dry milk has from 5 to 25% crystalline lactose. The greater the percentage of crystallized lactose, the less hygroscopic is the dry product.

Cottage Cheese Whey

The principle has been especially valuable for producing dry cottage cheese whey. The product was provided to the drier at 130°F at 1,800 psi, but difficulty has been encountered because of sticking to the drier. A product of low density, excellent flow properties and highly hygroscopic, and rapid solubility is obtained using this method. The gas is injected at room temperature at a rate of 1 to 1.5 cfm with the whey at 45% ts being pumped at a rate of 1 gpm.

For foam spray drying, with an increase in total solids, it is necessary to increase the rate of injection of compressed gas required for drying. By increasing the rate of injection, it was possible to dry up to 60% ts and to substantially increase the drier output.

References

HALL, C. W., and HEDRICK, T. I. 1966. Drying of Milk and Milk Products. Avi Publishing Co., Westport, Conn.

HANRAHAN, F. P., and WEBB, B. H. 1961. USDA develops foam spray drying. Food Eng. *33*, No. 8, 37–38.

Cross-references: *Foam Mat Drying; Spray Driers.*

FORKLIFT TRUCKS

Forklift trucks or forklifts have proved extremely valuable in reducing materials handling costs by greatly increasing the effective work of a man. Fork trucks operate under a variety of conditions and are successful in handling many types of products. There are several types of fork trucks available; therefore, it is a matter of selecting the correct one for a given purpose.

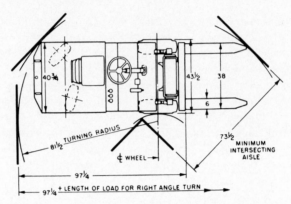

Courtesy of The Baker-Raulang Co.

Fig. F-20.   Specifications for heavy duty fork truck

Principles

Fork trucks are designed into a materials handling system for the purpose of increasing productivity and reducing costs. The entire materials handling operation should be carefully analyzed when selecting a piece of equipment whether it be conveyors, fork trucks or some other kind. With the fork truck operation the material to be handled must be in the form suitable for a forklift. This would include either palletized units or unitized containers. The unitized system eliminates the necessity

TABLE F.14

POWER SPECIFICATIONS FOR 3,000 LB STANDUP ELECTRIC LIFT TRUCK

Capacity	3,000 lb with 48 in. long load
Drive	Electric powered, front wheel drive, rear wheel steer, tiering, tilting, telescoping, end control, standup type. Fork truck
Weight	83 in. high model—6900 lb incl. battery
	68 in. high model—6700 lb incl. battery
Power Unit	Lead acid batteries in steel trays
	16, 15, or 12 cells, 450 to 660 amp hr capacity
	16 cells—450 to 600 amp hr capacity
	Nickel—alkaline batteries in steel cradle
Tires	Drive $17^3/_4 \times 6$ in. cushion; trail 9×5 in. solid
Speeds	Based on 32 volt power supply:

	Full Load	No Load
	Travel 5.5 mph	6.0 mph
	Lift 35 fpm	62.0 fpm
	Lower 65 fpm	60.0 fpm
	Tilt (full load) 15°	

TABLE F.15

SPECIFICATIONS OF FORKLIFT FOR REAR OF TRACTOR

Mounted on tractor with 14 $\times$ 24 rear, 7.50 $\times$ 16 front tires
Capacity—4,000 lb at 24 in. load center, 5000 lb at 15 in. load center

	Lift Height	8 ft 6 in.	10 ft 6 in.	12 ft 6 in.
A.	Ground clearance	$12^{1}/_{2}$ in.	$12^{1}/_{2}$ in.	$12^{1}/_{2}$ in.
B.	Tower height—lowered	$82^{1}/_{2}$ in.	$94^{1}/_{2}$ in.	$106^{1}/_{2}$ in.
C.	Tower height—raised	$134^{1}/_{2}$ in.	$158^{1}/_{2}$ in.	$182^{1}/_{2}$ in.

Overall tractor width	74 in.
Overall length, less attachments	133 in.
Turning circle, with brakes	15 ft 10 in.
Lift speed, with capacity load	40 fpm
Tilt—backward or forward	10°
Forks: optional lengths	30, 36, 42, 48 in.
Construction	$1^{1}/_{2} \times 4$ in. heat treated alloy steel

Weight: Tractor, 10 ft 6 in. fork lift counterweight, reversing transmission   6,600 lb

for a pallet; however, some means must be provided for the tines of a fork truck to be inserted beneath the load.

Fork trucks are useful for storing materials in warehouse, loading and reloading rail cars and trucks, supplying operations such as moving empty containers from storage to fillers, and similar operations.

Specification and Data

Depending upon the application, the type of power used for a forklift may be gasoline engine, liquid petroleum gas engine, or an electric power forklift utilizing batteries. For most operations where the fork truck is exposed to the atmosphere such as unloading rail cars or transferring a product from one storage building to another, the gasoline powered unit is very satisfactory.

Because of exhaust gas fumes, a gasoline engine powered forklift truck is not recommended for use in a closed storage or room. If used, the engine should be well-tuned, the carburetor set properly, approaching a lean air-fuel ratio, but not so lean that the valves are burned. An air-fuel ratio of 15 to 1 is about as lean as can be used, but this ratio may burn valves under heavy load. A poorly-tuned gasoline engine may produce three times as much carbon monoxide as a properly-tuned engine. A catalytic muffler may be used on a gasoline engine to reduce carbon monoxide to low levels. The catalytic muffler is rather ineffective when cold and has little effect on carbon monoxide until the engine is thoroughly warmed. After prolonged use, the catalytic material in these mufflers becomes coated and is ineffective, even when hot. Danger is decreased by converting engines to liquid petroleum gas and using in conjunction with a catalytic muffler.

For operations in tightly enclosed areas, the battery-powered, electric fork truck is the most desirable. Many plants find that charging the batteries overnight works very well.

Some fork trucks are operated with the operator standing on a small platform while in the case of the heavier units, the operator sits on a seat. Some of the design specifications of a standup type fork truck of 3,000 lb capacity are given in Table F.14.

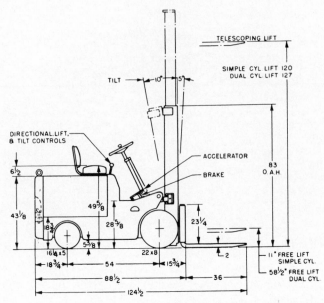

Fig. F-21.   Heavy duty fork lift truck

Heavier models include equipment with a forklift by the rear main drive wheels. These are particularly suitable for heavy-duty outdoor applications. Specifications of a tractor equipped with forklift are in Table F.15.

The standard heavy-duty fork truck with a capacity of 6,000 lb is illustrated by the specifications shown in Fig. F.20.

Various attachments are available for special applications making the versatility of the fork trucks much greater, for example, the vertical handling unit shown in Fig. F.21. Another attachment for handling cartons without a pallet is called the carton clamp. A specially engineered pivot to permit forklift operation in narrow aisles has been designed. This special fork truck has some appeal particularly in cramped quarters where space is at a premium. Instead of requiring almost 12 ft of aisle space this swivel front fork truck with a stabilizing bar can operate efficiently in narrow aisles increasing the usable space about 35%.

Application

Because of its versatility, the fork truck is used for a very wide number of applications in an industry. Some of the heavier units equipped with dual wheels have a capacity of about 20,000 lb. For most food plant operations, a 3,000- to 4,000-lb capacity is adequate. With the wide variety of fork trucks available, the plant operator should select the one which will fulfill the requirement adequately without being greatly undersized or oversized.

Cross-references: *Drum Handling; Materials Handling.*

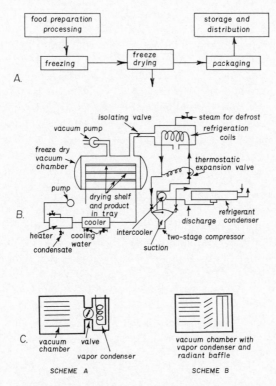

FIG. F-22. Freeze drying relationships: A—the freeze drying cycle; B—process and cycle plant flow diagram; C—arrangement of vacuum freeze drying chamber and condenser

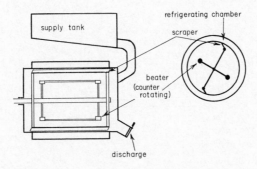

FIG. F-23. Batch type ice cream freezer

FREEZE DRIER

Freeze drying stops or delays bacterial and enzymatic action. Freeze drying removes the moisture in a solid state with the solutes locked in place, so there is no interaction. The product has the same shape as the original, but is lighter and easier to reconstitute than products dehydrated by most other methods. The texture and the flavor are preserved by the low temperatures used. The disadvantages of the process are: higher cost, more difficult processing and packaging, and the product is often brittle and fragile.

Principle

The principle of freeze drying is illustrated by a reference to the phase diagram of water (Fig. F.19). The eutectic point is important. Note at this particular point the product can be either a gas, vapor, or solid. In the operation of the freeze drying process, the product must be completely frozen below its lowest eutectic temperature. This frozen product is then subjected to an extremely high vacuum in a closed container shown in Fig. F.22A, B, C. Heat is slowly added to the frozen product by means of the heated shelves or by radiation; this heat which is carefully kept low enough so that the product does not melt causes sublimation of the ice in the product. This is vaporized off and condensed on cold plates. There are many forms of equipment, some of which have the condenser in the same chamber with the heating shelves; others use a separate chamber.

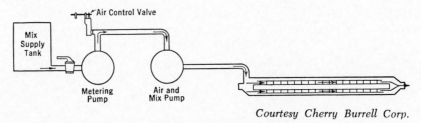

Courtesy Cherry Burrell Corp.

Fig. F-24.   Overrun control system of Vogt continuous freezer

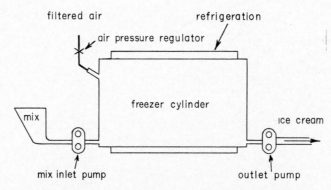

Fig. F-25.   Continuous freezer, C.P. system
Both pumps are synchronized. Outlet pump handles larger volume than inlet,
Overrun controlled by air pressure regulator,

The vapor pressure at the condenser must be lower than that of the ice of the product. For example, the product at $-4°F$ would normally be operated with the condenser at $-40°F$. The rate of sublimation is largely determined by the difference in these temperatures and the resultant vapor pressures.

As the frozen product, e.g., a piece of meat is dehydrated, it begins to dry out on the surface and the frozen undried portion gradually becomes smaller until finally even that in the center of the piece, has been dehydrated. More rapid operation and more uniform results will be obtained if the size of the pieces which are to be dried are kept relatively small and uniform in size.

The drying will take place much faster if heat of sublimation is supplied by a method which will bring the heat easily to the product, keeping in mind that the temperature must never become high enough to cause melting of the ice.

Heat may be supplied by conduction which requires good contact. Heat may be supplied by radiation, or in combination with conduction. Convection is negligible in a high vacuum such as encountered in the sublimation chamber. Dielectric or microwave heating is also used effectively.

The rate of sublimation is

$$W = \frac{q}{x_s}$$

where q = heat transfer
x_s = latent heat of sublimation

The rate of heat transfer is given by the formula

$$q = \frac{k \times (t_s - t_i)}{L}$$

where q = heat transfer per unit surface area, cal per hr per sq cm
k = thermal conductivity, cal per hr °C per cm
L = thickness, cm
t_s = temperature of dried product's surface, °C
t_i = temperature of ice surface, °C

the value of k for porous dried meat = 0.02 Btu per hr per °F per ft at 56°F. Air has a k value of 0.014.

The rate of drying is determined by the temperature relationships. If the ice temperature is as near to the eutectic point as possible, maximum drying rate is obtained. For example, ice at 0°C dries 6 to 7 times faster than ice at $-20°C$. However, the practical limit is the maximum the dried material can withstand without scorching which might be a surface temperature of 100°F. The ice particle temperature in the drying product could be below 0°F.

Stages of Drying

There are two stages of drying. The first stage is as the ice phase recedes and finally disappears. The second stage is involved in the removal of bound (absorbed) water. It is more economical to use microwave heating or a desiccant to remove this water. Desiccants used for this are glycerol or alumina.

Method of Operation

Material which is to be freeze-dried is fully frozen before being placed under the vacuum. A conventional type fast freezing, immersion freezing, or liquid nitrogen freezing system may be used. Some use refrigerated shelves in the freeze drier to accomplish the purpose.

Drying chambers may be rectangular or cylindrical. The shelves may be fixed or movable. The condenser or cold plates may be either external or internal.

The vacuum system, which accounts for 30 to 40% of the equipment cost, consists of a high efficiency, high duty vacuum arrangement such as mechanical pump with refrigerator condenser or a multistage steam ejector. Steam ejectors with refrigerated condensers are also sometimes used.

The heating systems may be conventional, such as a plate shelf with heat transfer liquids such as ethylene glycol. It may be electric using either dielectric heating with a microwave range from 1 to 150 mc. Some difficulty may be noted from ionization of gas and resultant arcing. Microwave heating in the frequency range of 300 to 30,000 mc may be used. One problem with this type of heater is to find a satisfactory temperature-indicating device.

Process variables are important. Extremely quick freezing gives a fine pore structure but reduces the rate of drying and makes the product difficult to rehydrate. Slow freezing gives large ice crystals with faster drying and rehydration, but poor texture due to the rupture of cell walls or denaturing of protein. More rapid operation and greater efficiency are obtained by using small particles rather than large particles.

The product loading density is usually considered to be between 2 to 2.5 lb per sq ft. Melt-back should be avoided. With no refrigeration on the shelf, it is important to evacuate to 2 mm Hg in less than 5 min.

Cost of freeze drying is considered to be in the vicinity of 18 to 26 cents per lb of frozen output in custom freeze drying plants. The freezing cost is usually from $1/3$ to $2/3$¢ per lb to freeze food using a blast with belt or plate freezers. There is a low temperature nitrogen freezing method that is considered to be from 2 to 4¢.

Most freeze drying units are batch or semicontinuous. However work is being done on continuous systems.

References

HARPER, J. C., and ROBERTS, T. E. 1962. Freeze drying of foods. Agr. Eng. *43*, 78–82, 89.
MARICH, F. 1965. Latest design criteria for freeze drying plant. Food Eng. *37*, No. 6, 85–89.
MINER, S. M. 1965. Freeze drying. ASHRAE J. *7*, 92–99.

Cross-references: *Condensers; Dehydro-Freezers; Evaporators.*

FREEZERS, ICE CREAM

The ice cream freezer is a major piece of equipment in the modern food industry. An ice cream freezer can be defined as an apparatus for congealing an ice cream mix by temperature reduction, incorporating air or other gas in the product at a certain predetermined proportion, and for incorporating flavor, fruits, and nuts in the congealed product. The ice cream freezer removes sufficient heat from the product so that it becomes a very viscous or plastic material which can be handled in packages or cans after which the product is fully hardened in the final container.

Principles

Freezers are of two basic types, the batch and continuous freezer. In the batch freezer a definite quantity of the mix, usually 5 gal., is frozen at a time. With the continuous type freezer, the mix is fed into the freezer continuously, and the congealed viscous product is removed from the freezer continuously.

The batch freezer usually consists of a tubular chamber of about 12 gal. capacity fitted with a rotating dasher with scraper. The chamber is surrounded by a refrigerated jacket in which ammonia or other refrigerant is evaporated to provide the cooling effect. Figure F.23 shows a cross section of a typical batch freezer.

In operation, 5 gal. of ice cream mix is dropped into the freezing chamber of a batch unit, the refrigeration turned on and the dasher started. The mix is cooled down to a temperature of about 24°F at which time the refrigerating system is turned off by means of a quick shutoff valve, and the dasher allowed to rotate for 1–2 min to allow the mix to partially congeal. The mix will not absorb much air until a tempera-

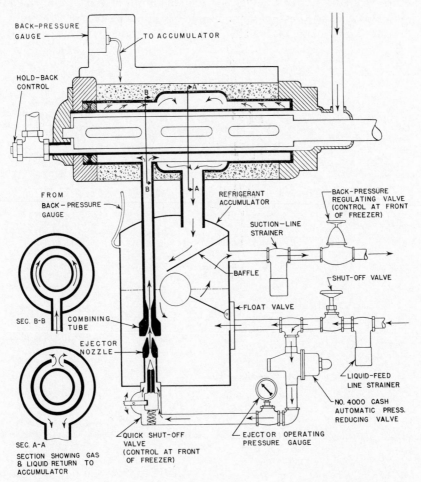

Courtesy of Cherry Burrell Corp.

Fig. F-26.   Jet-type ammonia circulating system used in Vogt freezer (some models)

ture of about 23°F is reached. At this point it will rapidly absorb air up to 100 to 120% of its original volume. Usually, air absorption is stopped at about 100% "over-run" at which point the volume of ice cream derived from 5 gal. of mix is 10 gal. During the whipping period, fruit and nuts may be added to make fancy ice cream. The ice cream is then drawn out of the chamber and into cans or packages which are placed in a −10° or −20°F temperature room for further hardening.

Continuous Ice Cream Freezer

The continuous ice cream freezer was developed in the early 1930's. The principle of operation is very similar to that of a batch freezer, except that the freezing is done under pressure and the air is forced in or drawn into the freezing chamber continuously at a metered rate. The expanded and congealed ice cream is then forced out of the discharge end of the freezer cylinder ready for filling packages and containers. Two types of continuous type freezers are shown in Fig. F.24, F.25, and F.26.

The freezer shown in Fig. F.24 uses two pumps to force the air and the mix into the freezer cylinder, and the frozen product is discharged through a pressure hold-back valve on the discharge end of the freezer. An important part of this freezer is

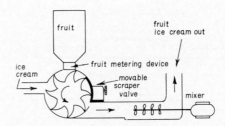

Fig. F-27.   Principle of fruit injector or feeder

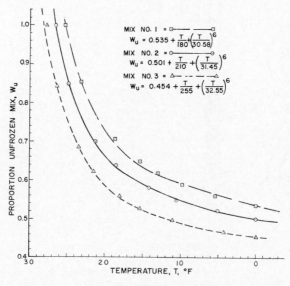

MIX NO. 1 = $W_u = 0.535 + \frac{T}{180} + \left(\frac{T}{30.58}\right)^6$

MIX NO. 2 = $W_u = 0.501 + \frac{T}{210} + \left(\frac{T}{31.45}\right)^6$

MIX NO. 3 = $W_u = 0.454 + \frac{T}{255} + \left(\frac{T}{32.55}\right)^6$

Fig. F-28.   Relation between proportion of unfrozen mix and temperature

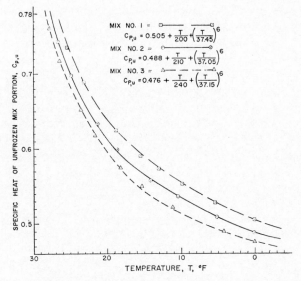

FIG. F-29.   Relationship between specific heat of unfrozen mix and temperature

the overrun control system.   The first pump meters the mix in at specified rate.   The second pump has greater capacity than the first pump, and therefore not only pumps the metered amount of mix, but also draws in a metered amount of air so that the discharge of the second pump contains a metered mixture of mix and air and controls the overrun.

The freezer in Fig. F.25 operates very similar to the freezer shown in Fig. F.24. However, with the former there is a second pump on the discharge of the freezer cylinder, and the air is pumped into the freezer cylinder by an air pump.   The metered amount of mix which enters the cylinder is less than the output of the discharge pump, so the difference between the effective capacity of the outlet pump and the inlet pump provides a metering principle which is used to control the amount of air let into the cylinder and thereby the overrun.   With both types of freezers a simple air adjustment gives accurate control of the amount of air which is allowed to enter the freezing cylinder.

Refrigeration System

The refrigeration system of a continuous ice cream freezer is much more sophisticated than with batch freezers.   First, the rate of refrigeration must be very high per unit area of the heat transfer surface; secondly, very accurate control of the temperature is important for uniform freezing and uniform overrun; third, it is important to be able to stop the refrigeration quickly to prevent freeze-ups, in case something goes wrong with the supply of mix; and fourth, the various refrigeration systems devised for the continuous freezer must have very accurate controls and high thermal efficiency.

Operation

The principal factors in continuous ice cream freezing are as follows.

(1) Ice cream can be frozen much colder in a continuous freezer than in a batch freezer because the freezing is done under pressure. This allows for the incorporation of air at a much lower temperature than is possible in a batch freezer which operates at atmospheric pressure.

(2) Refrigeration systems must be kept clean. Even a small amount of oil from the refrigeration system will greatly reduce the heat transfer efficiency of the freezing cylinder. Important management considerations are: a clean refrigeration system, good oil traps, and a refrigeration system design which does not allow oil to accumulate excessively on the heat transfer surfaces. If the system becomes fouled with oil, it must be drained and the surfaces cleaned with a solvent such as carbon tetrachloride to remove the oil film.

(3) Metering pumps must be kept in good condition to prevent excessive variations in the overrun in the ice cream.

(4) Ice cream mix must be uniform in temperature and composition. This will help obtain uniform results in the finished ice cream. If the mix does not have the proper stability and quality of raw products it will be difficult to incorporate the air uniformly. If difficulty is encountered, inspect the quality of homogenization also. Usually poor homogenization will be evident by excessive deposit of fat on the dasher of the freezer. Also, in severe instances addition of a small amount of egg yolk to the mix will improve the emulsifying power of the mix and remedy the situation.

(5) The average mix will begin to freeze at a temperature of 27°F, and will usually be drawn from the freezer at about 24°F if it is a batch freezer, but from the continuous freezers it is usually removed at a temperature of 22° or 21°F. The lower temperature gives more rapid hardening and therefore a smoother and richer tasting ice cream.

The composition of ice cream mixes varies tremendously depending upon the type of ice cream desired. Sherbets and ices are frozen on ice cream freezers and must be handled somewhat differently than ice creams. Usually they are drawn with a somewhat lower overrun because of the differences in the amounts of sugar and other ingredients.

If the mix contains much corn sugar, the freezing point and stiffness of the mix at a given temperature will be much different. Corn sugar depresses the freezing point more than does cane sugar or beet sugar, and the ice cream must be drawn at a temperature several degrees lower to obtain the same stiffness as in a mix with cane sugar.

Capacities

A 40-qt batch freezer should produce a batch of ice cream about every 4 to 6 min depending upon conditions. Continuous freezers are built in various capacities ranging from about 80 gal. per hr up to 3,000 gal. per hr, at 100% overrun.

Scraper Blades

One of the most important factors in the efficient operation of freezers, particularly continuous freezers, is the condition of the scraper blades. They must be kept sharp or poor heat transfer is encountered. Some plants send the blades back to the manufacturer for sharpening.

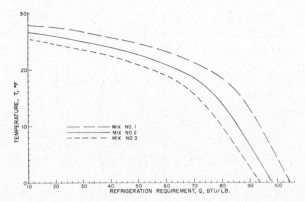

Fig. F-30.   Refrigeration requirements freezing above 0°F

Fruit Feeders

With the continuous freezers the fruit and nuts are added by a special machine called a fruit injector which is placed at the discharge of the freezer. This feeder unit, Fig. F.27, is designed with special adjustments to permit a wide range of capacities for both the ice cream and the fruit feed. The ice cream with fruit which is discharged from the freezer is taken directly to the filling station through sanitary pipes.

Multiflavor and Battery Operation

Continuous freezers are often arranged in batteries to obtain greater capacity and also for the purpose of manufacturing multiflavor ice cream. Three freezer discharges are carried through sanitary pipes to a common filling head. This filling head is fitted with 3 compartments, one for each freezer and, therefore, if each of the freezers is turning out a different flavor of ice cream, a 3 flavor package will result.

In small installations the ice cream is usually filled into cartons directly from the freezing nozzles by hand. One operator can usually fill at least 60 packages per minute. For large operations and specialties, automatic filling machinery is often used. In order for good hand filling, the ice cream must be quite plastic; on the other hand if too stiff, the corners of the packages will not fill. The same comments apply to stiffness required for automatic filling machines. However, softer ice cream will work satisfactorily on most of the automatic fillers.

Most of the ice cream novelties such as ice cream on a stick are made with a setup consisting of a continuous freezer which freezes the ice cream to a relatively soft consistency. This product is fed directly into small metal pockets which serve as a container for each novelty. These containers or pockets are made in gangs and are dropped automatically into a low temperature brine tank where the hardening and freezing of the novelty is accomplished automatically and continuously. The machines insert the sticks, remove the finished hardened novelty from the mold, wash the mold, discharge the novelty, and the mold is returned automatically for a new cycle.

Refrigeration Requirements for Freezing Ice Cream and Similar Mixtures

Refrigeration requirements are expressed as the total heat to be removed in order to reduce the ice cream mix and other products from an unfrozen state to some temperature in the freezing range.

Due to the composition of ice cream, the total heat consists of four parts: (1) sensible heat required to reduce the mix temperature to the initial freezing point, (2) sensible heat required for unfrozen portion of mix at temperatures below the initial freezing point, (3) latent heat requirements, and (4) sensible heat requirements for reducing the temperature of ice.

After reaching the initial freezing point, the last three contributions to total heat occur simultaneously. Since the composition of normal ice cream mix dictates that all three portions of total heat contribute throughout the range of freezing temperatures encountered, predictions of refrigeration requirements must include calculation of each phase.

Theory

The refrigeration requirement or total heat required to accomplish a known degree of ice cream freezing may be written as

$$Q = Q_s + Q_u + Q_l + Q_i \tag{1}$$

where Q_s = sensible heat above initial freezing point
Q_u = sensible heat of unfrozen portion of mix
Q_l = latent heat
Q_i = sensible heat of ice

The sensible heat above the initial freezing point may be calculated in a straight forward manner by a basic heat transfer equation

$$Q_s = WC_{p,s}(T_f - T_s) \tag{2}$$

where W = weight of ice cream mix
$C_{p,s}$ = specific heat of mix above initial freezing point
T_f = initial freezing temperature
T_s = temperature of mix storage

When the freezing process has proceeded to temperatures below the initial freezing point, the calculations become more involved. The composition of ice cream causes definite deviations in the freezing process. The first is a depression in the freezing point to some temperature below $32°F$. During freezing, the water portion of the product starts to crystallize at the initial freezing point. However, the initial crystallization causes concentration of the ice cream components in the unfrozen water, and results in further depression of the freezing point for the unfrozen portion of the mix.

This type of freezing process produces a product which has two portions: frozen ice crystals (W_i), and unfrozen mix (W_u). The proportions of these two parts will change continuously as freezing proceeds to lower temperatures.

The situation which exists during freezing creates definite problems when attempting to calculate the sensible heats of unfrozen and frozen portions (Q_u and Q_l), due to the changing proportions of these parts during freezing. In addition, the specific heat of the unfrozen portion changes as the concentration of mix components increases. Due to these existing problems, the equation for the unfrozen portion must be written as:

$$\Delta Q_u = W_u(T)C_{p,u}(T)\ (T - T_f) \tag{3}$$

where ΔQ_u = sensible heat change for unfrozen mix portion
$W_u(T)$ = weight of unfrozen mix portion at any temperature (T)
$C_{p,u}(T)$ = specific heat of unfrozen mix portion at any temperature (T)
(T) = temperature to which product is frozen
T_f = initial freezing temperature

Equation (3) can be written in differential form

$$dQ_u = W_u(T)C_{p,u}(T)dT \tag{4}$$

By knowing the variation of unfrozen mix weight and specific heat with temperature, the sensible heat would be fully described.

The calculation of the sensible heat (Q_i) for the frozen portion of the ice cream presents a problem similar to the unfrozen portion. However, the specific heat of ice is constant and the equation describing this portion of the freezing process is

$$\Delta Q_I = W_I(T)C_{p,I}(T - T_f) \tag{5}$$

where ΔQ_I = sensible heat change for frozen mix portion
$W_I(T)$ = weight of frozen mix portion at any temperature (T)
$C_{p,I}$ = specific heat of ice
T = temperature to which product is frozen
T_f = initial freezing temperature

$$dQ_I = W_I(T)C_{p,I}dT \tag{6}$$

Knowledge of the variation of weight of ice in the product with temperature describes equation (6) completely.

The latent heat portion of the refrigeration requirement can be calculated from the following expression

$$Q_L = W_I(T)L \tag{7}$$

where L = latent heat of fusion for water.

Knowledge of the proportion of product frozen at the freezing temperature will allow calculation of the latent heat contribution.

The need must be determined for (1) the proportion of unfrozen mix, (2) proportion of frozen product, and (3) specific heat of unfrozen mix portion, as functions of temperature. The method generally used for determining the weights of frozen and unfrozen portions of ice cream mix was presented by Leighton equation (1). This can be accomplished by using the general equation for freezing point depression

$$T = K\frac{G}{M} \tag{8}$$

where K = molar freezing point constant (18.6 for water)
G = parts of solute per 100 parts of solvent
M = molecular weight of solute

The freezing point depression for each ice cream mix component can be calculated. The components which must be accounted for are milk sugar (lactose), added sucrose, corn syrup solids, and milk salt.

In addition to calculation of the initial freezing point of the ice cream mix, the freezing points of ice crystals forming at temperatures below the initial freezing point can be calculated by use of equation (8), and the assumption that certain percentages of the water are frozen.

The specific heat of unfrozen portions of ice cream mix can be predicted from the specific heats as follows:

Component	Specific Heat (Btu per lb °F)
Carbohydrate	0.34
Protein	0.37
Solid fat	0.40
Salt	0.20

The specific heats of unfrozen mix at various temperature can be calculated by knowing the quantities of water frozen at the various temperatures as determined by Leighton's procedures.

Application

Component	Mix No. 1, %	Mix No. 2, %	Mix No. 3, %
Butterfat	10.1	10.1	10.0
Solids-not-fat	11.0	12.0	12.0
Sucrose	10.0	14.0	15.0
Corn syrup solids (CSS)	10.0	3.73	0.0
Stabilizer	0.22	0.22	0.22
Total solids	41.32	40.05	37.22

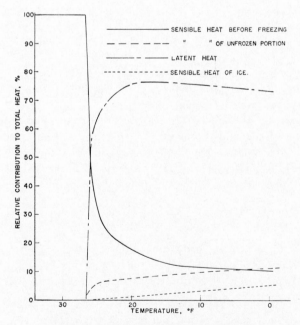

Fig. F-31.   Relative contribution to total refrigeration requirements

The three mix compositions vary primarily on the level of corn syrup solids (CSS) included. The variation is typical of those most frequently encountered and has a significant influence on freezing characteristics.

Calculations are made to determine initial freezing points and temperatures required to attain various levels of ice crystallization. By assuming certain percentages of water frozen, new freezing points can be calculated based on the concentration of sugars and salt in the remaining liquid. From these calculations, the proportions of unfrozen mix and frozen water are obtained at several temperatures in the range from zero to the initial freezing point.

The relationship between the proportion of unfrozen mix and temperature is presented in Fig. F.28. In order to use the relationship in the integration of equation (4),

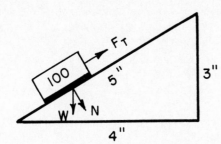

Load = 100 lb.
μ = 0.3
N < W
N = 80 lb.; W = 100 lb.
F = μN = 0.3 x 80 = 24

F_T = 24 + 60 = 84 lb.

Fɪɢ. F-32.   Friction-force diagram

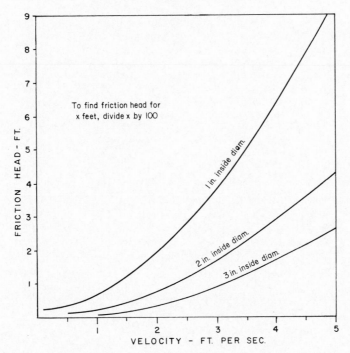

Fɪɢ. F-33.   Friction head for each 100 ft tubing smooth stainless steel tube
(or glass)

a mathematical relationship is required. A curve was fit to the calculated points by using the general form

$$W_u = A + \frac{T}{B} + \left(\frac{T}{C}\right)^n \tag{9}$$

The coefficient (A) was selected as the value of W_u at $T = 0$, and the coefficient (B) was determined from the slope of calculated points between the $0°$ and $10°F$. Using any two values of W_u for temperatures above $10°F$ in two simultaneous forms of equation (9), the coefficient (C) and exponent (n) can be calculated. This procedure is used to determine the equations of the curves as presented in Fig. F.28.

The specific heats of unfrozen portions of ice cream mix are calculated from component specific heats. Since the concentration of components in the unfrozen water increases with decreasing temperature, the specific heat of the unfrozen solution decreases with temperature as illustrated in Fig. F.29.

With the information presented up to this point, it is possible to accurately calculate the various portions of the refrigeration requirement. The sensible heat of the unfrozen mix above the initial freezing point can be calculated directly from equation (2).

Using the developed relationship between the quantity of ice frozen and temperature, equation (7) for latent heat can be written as

$$Q_L = A - \frac{T}{B} - \frac{T^6}{C} L \tag{16}$$

TABLE F.16

GALLONS OF FUMIGANT PER 1,000 BU STEEL BINS

	Wheat, Oats, Soybeans	Grain, Sorghum	Shelled corn	Ear corn[1]
1. Carbon tetrachloride (100%)	3	8	6	6
2. Carbon tetrachloride, carbon disulfide (80%-20%)	2	6	5	5
3. Ethylene dichloride, carbon tetrachloride (75%-25%)	4	8	6	6
4. Carbon tetrachloride, ethylene dichloride, ethylene dibromide (60%-35%-5%)	2	6	5	5
5. Carbon tetrachloride, ethylene dichloride (75%-25%), plus 10% methyl bromide	$1^1/_2$	4	2	2
6. Carbon tetrachloride, carbon disulfide (80%-20%), plus 11% methyl bromide	$1^1/_2$	4	2	2

[1] The dosage for ear corn is per 1,000 cu ft instead of for 1,000 bu. A minimum exposure of 72 hr is required to kill insects.

Note: Increase dosage by 25% if moisture is above 15%.

Note: No. 5 and No. 6 mixtures will likely affect germination.

Source: Dr. Richard T. Cotton, Agr. Res. Serv., Bur. Entomology and Plant Quarantine, U.S. Dept. Agr., Washington, D.C. Courtesy of Butler Manufacturing Co., Kansas City, Mo.

The expressions presented can be used to predict the total heat or refrigeration requirements for freezing ice cream to any temperature in the normal range. The variation in total heat with temperature is illustrated in Fig. F.30 where sensible heat above the initial freezing point is based on an initial mix temperature of 40°F.

Disregarding the contributions of sensible heat of unfrozen and frozen portions would result in predicted refrigeration requirements which are 8 to 10% low when freezing ice cream to the 15° to 20°F range (Fig. F.31).

References

ARBUCKLE, W. S. 1966. Ice Cream. AVI Publishing Co., Westport, Conn.

FARRALL, A. W. 1963. Engineering for Dairy and Food Products, 3rd Edition. John Wiley & Sons, New York.

HELDMAN, D. R. 1966. Predicting refrigeration requirements for freezing ice cream. Mich. Agr. Expt. Sta. Quart. Bull. *49*, No. 2, 144–154.

TRACY, P. H. 1966. Layouts and operating criteria for automation of dairy plants, manufacturing ice cream and ice cream novelties. U.S. Dept. Agr. Marketing Res. Rept. *750*.

FREEZERS, INSTANT

Instant freezers are those which can be used to freeze fruit products in a matter of seconds or at least in a few minutes. Instant freezers are used for products in which slow freezing causes quality deterioration.

Methods

A liquid, air, or gas may be used as a freezing medium in instant freezers. This equipment can be of the continuous type with the product coming in on a moving belt passing through the air blast at −20° to −40°F. This freezer is designed for quick freezing of small loose products such as vegetables, French fries, and fruit, and is also used for freezing packaged and canned products.

In operation, the product is usually washed, dewatered, and distributed by a shaker-spreader from the hopper to a continuous belt. Loose wet product is glazed in the precooler by an updraft of air at about 15°F. Glazing prevents product dehydration, seals in natural flavors, and provides maximum yields. Fluidization eliminates clusters.

Freezing is completed in the freezer sections with low temperature air at high velocity moving evenly through the entire belt area. The frozen product, at 0°F or lower, is discharged from the conveyor in an insulated vestibule.

Another type of instant-freezer is one in which the product is placed in small pockets which are drawn through a low temperature brine solution at −20° to −40°F. This method is often used for freezing ice cream novelties. A third method of instant freezing is by placing the product between extremely cold plates in direct contact with the product. This method is often used for freezing fish and meat products. A fourth method is to immerse the product in liquid nitrogen at a temperature of −320°F, or to spray liquid nitrogen over the product.

Instant freezing is employed because in most cases the product comes out in a more natural state with less protein destabilization; also the moisture particles of the product are much finer. Slow freezing causes large ice crystals with much disruption of the cells in the product, whereas instant freezing causes very little breakage of the cell walls.

Management

Management of quick freezing involves provision to keep excessive moisture away from the product before it is frozen, and also to move the product directly into the freezer storage room through a refrigerated vestibule from the quick freezer as quickly as possible.

The conveyor belt should be kept clean, usually by high velocity air jets or by washing at intervals. The refrigeration system must be kept free from excessive frost buildup, and it is important to keep the ammonia system free from excessive oil. The operating conditions vary so much with different products that performance data should be obtained for a specific product from the freezer manufacturer.

Cross-references: *Immersion Freezing; Nitrogen, Liquid Cooling.*

FREEZERS, SHARP

Sharp freezers are those cold rooms which are normally kept at $-20°$ to $-40°$F. Sharp freezers are used for storing certain highly sensitive food products, and particularly those which are to be stored for a long period of time during which changes in quality might occur.

Sharp freezers are also used for the final freezing stage of certain frozen products such as ice cream.

The rate of freezing can be more than doubled in most instances by using a fan to circulate the air in the room.

Sharp freezers need to be insulated with at least 10 in. of cork board or equivalent. Care should be taken in the design of these low temperature rooms to prevent frost damage due to heaval of the floor. Protection may be obtained with electric heating cables, air ducts, or heating coils installed below the floor. Particular care must be taken to seal all doors and joints tightly to prevent entrance of moisture and air. Special double seal gaskets are used on doors.

Usually, the flooded type of refrigeration system is used. Many new installations use a set of cooling coils fitted with a high velocity fan to increase the heat transfer. The unit is called a cold diffuser. Defrosting of coils is important and should be done when frost has built up sufficiently to cause reduced efficiency. The hot gas line method is most effective.

References

TRESSLER, D. K., VAN ARSDEL, W. B., and COPLEY, M. J.   1968.   The Freezing Preservation of Foods, 4th Edition.   Vol. 1. AVI Publishing Co., Westport, Conn.

RIDEL, L.   1951.   The refrigerating effect required to freeze fruits and vegetables.   Refrig. Eng. *59*, 670–673.

Cross-references: *Freezers, Ice Cream; Freezers, Instant; Immersion Freezers.*

FRICTION

Sliding

A force must be exerted to slide one body over another. The amount of force, pounds, is largely dependent on the characteristics of the contact surfaces. The surface characteristic related to movement or sliding of one body over another is identified by the coefficient of friction, μ (mu). The force required to overcome sliding friction, F, lb is equal to the coefficient of friction, μ, multiplied by the force perpendicular, N, to the plane of motion, or normal to the surface (Fig. F.32) (Table F.17). Thus

$$F = \mu N$$

The force of friction is largely independent of the velocity over the surface. The initial force to initiate movement over the surface is often greater than the force to maintain movement. Lubricants decrease the coefficient of friction and therefore the force of friction.

Rolling Friction

The resistance to movement from rolling friction is small compared to sliding. The coefficient of friction, μ, is used the same as for sliding friction. Representative values of μ are as follows:

Cast iron wheels on rails	0.004
Ball bearings	0.001–0.003
Roller bearings	0.002–0.007

Fluid Friction

The energy required to move a product through a tube increases as the velocity of flow is increased. An increase in velocity requires an increase in energy for the velocity head and for overcoming the friction of the tube (Fig. F.33).

$$\text{Velocity head (ft)} = V^2/2g$$

where V = average velocity, ft per sec, g is acceleration due to gravity, 32 ft per sec^2

$$\text{Friction head (Ft)} = \frac{fLV^2}{D\ 2g},$$

where f = friction factor
D = diameter tube, ft
L = length of tube, ft

For a velocity of 2 ft per sec, through a 50 ft, 1 in. tube, Re = 15,000 and f = 0.026

$$\text{The friction head} = \frac{0.026\ (50)\ (2)^2}{\dfrac{1}{12}\ (2 \times 32)} = 1 \text{ ft}$$

$$\text{The velocity head} = \frac{(2)^2}{2 \times 32} = 0.06 \text{ ft, which is negligible}$$

To find the friction head for 50 ft of 1 in. diam holding tube at a velocity of 2.5 ft per sec, from Fig. F.33 the friction head for 100 ft of tube is 3 ft, thus for 50 ft (50/100) (3 ft) = 1.5 ft head due to friction. This would also be equivalent to a pressure drop through the holding tube of (0.43) $\times$ (1.5) = 0.65 psi.

Cross-references. *Air Movement; Fluid Flow.*

FRYING KETTLES

Frying and heating kettles are widely used in the meat and vegetable processing industries. The same kettles can also be used for blanching and cooking vegetables.

The simplest type of kettle consists essentially of a rounded bottom jacketed chamber supported on legs, and with a cover. Some of the kettles are heated by means of indirect gas flame and some by steam. Those involving the steam jacket should be made to conform to the ASME code for pressure vessels. The usual size of the kettles is from 30- to 150-gal. capacity.

The kettles can be made of stainless steel or of high purity boiler plate. Some are also made of copper. The use of copper, however, is declining, many food products are susceptible to off-flavors after being in contact with copper.

The principle items of concern in operation of the kettles are to check that the safety valve on the kettle is in good working order if it is steam heated, and that the condensate drain or trap is functioning properly. In the case of pressure kettles, the maintenance of the gasket is an important point.

Rendering kettles are usually gas heated. A pressure of 38 psig is correct for rendering of fat. The pop-safety valve should be set to relieve at 40 psig.

A cooking basket can be fitted to some kettles and is used in connection with blanching fruits and vegetables. It is also used when frying potato chips.

FUELS

Coal, fuel oil, and natural and manufactured gas are used for fuels. In some commercial installations, the air is heated by steam formed by one of these fuels. The potential energy output of the fuel is expressed in heating values, Btu per unit weight or volume. The high (gross) heating value, as reported in many references, includes the heat available in the moisture in the products of combustion, and would be utilized only if the combustion products are condensed. The net heating value is more useful because the temperature of exhaust of the heater is far above the original temperature, particularly for the indirect unit (Table E.9). The No. 1, 2, or 4 fuel oil grades are used for portable heaters.

The heating value of the heavy fuel oils is higher than the lighter fuels. Commercial operators can take advantage of this relationship by using a No. 5 or 6 fuel oil, but a method must be provided for preheating the oil in the tank. Storage facilities must be adequate. By installing a large tank, oil may often be secured for a lower price. A carload is 13,000 gal. and a truckload is 3,000 gal. and higher.

The factors which are important in fuel selection, particularly applicable to commercial operations are: (1) energy content, (2) price of fuel, (3) overall efficiency, (4) cost of handling and storage, (5) disposal of refuse, (6) operating labor, and (7) maintenance.

Combustion

Carbon, hydrogen, and sulfur are the components of fuel which can be burned to provide heat and upon complete oxidation in presence of adequate oxygen give carbon dioxide (CO_2), water (H_2O), and sulfur dioxide (SO_2). The presence of carbon monoxide (CO) in the exhaust indicates incomplete combustion. The gross (high heat value) amount of heat produced by burning of fuel is equal to the heat produced from burning the component parts minus the portion of the hydrogen which combines with

TABLE F.17

COEFFICIENT OF FRICTION OF SELECTED MATERIALS

Wood on wood, dry	0.25–0.50
Wood on wood, soapy	0.20
Metals on oak, dry	0.50–0.60
Metals on oak, wet	0.25
Metals on metals, dry	0.15–0.20
Metals on metals, wet	0.30
Smooth surfaces, greased	0.05
Machined and lubricated	0.005

the oxygen to form water. A pound of sulfur produces 4,000 Btu when burned; 1 lb of carbon produces 14,600 Btu; and 1 lb of hydrogen produces 62,000 Btu. The net (low heat value) heating value is more applicable because the products of combustion normally are not cooled to the temperature at which the moisture will condense. The net heating value per pound of fuel, nhv, where the heating value of hydrogen is 52,000 Btu per lb instead of 62,000, is given in the following equation

$$nhv = 14,400C + 52,000\left(H - \frac{O}{8}\right) + 4,500S + 1,100w$$

where C = weight of carbon per pound of fuel
H = weight of hydrogen per pound of fuel
O = weight of oxygen per pound of fuel
S = weight of sulfur per pound of fuel
w = weight of moisture per pound of fuel

The amount of air in excess of the theoretical requirement needed to give complete combustion varies considerably. With stoker-fed coal, the excess air is 30 to 50%; fuel oil, 20 to 30%; and gas, 15 to 20%. The equation applies to complete combustion of fuel.

Obtaining Heat from Fuel

During combustion of a fuel, heat is produced. The quantity is known as the heat of combustion or heating value. Fuels may be classified as gas, liquid, or solid. The heating value of a fuel may be classified as (1) net or low heating value, and (2) gross or high heating value. The net heating value is obtained by subtracting the heat needed to vaporize moisture formed when a fuel burns. Approximately 1,000 Btu are required for each pound of water evaporated from the moisture present in the

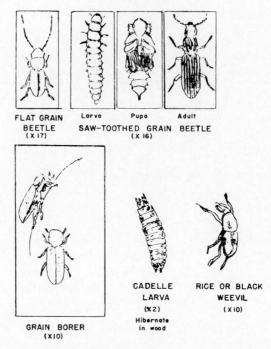

FLAT GRAIN
BEETLE
(X 17)

Larva   Pupa   Adult
SAW-TOOTHED GRAIN BEETLE
(X 16)

CADELLE
LARVA
(X 2)
Hibernate
in wood

RICE OR BLACK
WEEVIL
(X 10)

GRAIN BORER
(X 10)

Fig. F-34.   Principal insects which infest grain

fuel or the moisture formed during combustion.   Water is formed during combustion if hydrogen is present in the fuel.   Equations used to determine the gross heating value in Btu per pound of fuel are as follows

Liquid fuel

$$Q = 13{,}500 \text{ C} + 60{,}890 \text{ H}$$

Solid fuel

$$Q = 14{,}500 \text{ C} + 62{,}000 \left(\text{H} - \frac{\text{O}}{8} \right) + 4{,}500 \text{ S}$$

where Q = Btu/lb heating value
    C = carbon in the fuel, written as a decimal or fraction
    H = hydrogen, written as a decimal or fraction
    O = oxygen, written as a decimal or fraction
    S = sulfur, written as a decimal or fraction

A rule of thumb is to consider that approximately 1 gal. of water is produced per each 1 gal. of fuel oil burned.   The quantity of heat produced can be calculated roughly on the basis of amount of carbon, hydrogen, or sulfur burned.   The total heat produced in oxidizing carbon to carbon monoxide is 4,400 Btu per lb; from carbon to carbon dioxide 14,000 Btu per lb; hydrogen, 62,000 Btu per lb; and sulfur 4,020 Btu per lb.

To provide for the complete oxidation of fuel, it is necessary that the proper amount of oxygen, usually through air supply, be provided. It is the usual practice to provide from 10 to 50% more air than is required to assure complete combustion. However, the addition of more air than is necessary can result in excessive cooling of the flame and low efficiency, and thus should be kept to the absolute minimum.

Fuel Value of Foods

Foods when consumed or oxidized release energy. The fuel values of milk and milk products are presented in Table E.10.

FUMIGANTS

If grain is dry when placed in storage and insects are not present, there is little danger of insect infestation in northern areas. Most insects are dormant below 45°F and are killed at temperatures above 100°F. In the southern areas of the United States there is a much greater problem of controlling insects than in the colder northern climates. Stored grain should be inspected regularly to determine the extent of insect infestation. Infestation usually occurs at the top of the bin where moisture accumulates, and can be noted by an increase in temperature, insect eggs, insects, or damaged kernels of grain. Common insects include the beetle, borer, weevil, and Indian meal moth (Fig. F.34).

Several fumigants are available and new ones are being developed continuously. The recommendations of the manufacturer should be followed implicitly. Standard mixtures and quantities of various fumigants which can be used for small grains are presented in Table F.16. Fumigants are applied as a liquid, gas, or dust over the surface or through the grain. The bin should be sealed so that the fumigant will not be lost. A fan can be used for circulating the fumigant through the bin if a closed recirculating system which prevents loss of the fumigant. An aeration or drying system provides an excellent means of obtaining thorough and uniform fumigation if there are no leaks for loss of the fumigant. A recirculating system is often used.

G

GEARS

Gears are commonly used in food equipment as a means of transmitting power. The tendency is to enclose the gears in a case, where possible, and operate them in oil. This provides excellent lubrication and excludes dust and moisture. Gears are one of the most reliable and satisfactory means of transferring power and changing speeds.

Types

Six types of gears are of most interest to food engineers. (1) The *spur gear* is a very simple design and consists of a series of teeth pointing out radially from center off of a rim. This type of gear if properly designed and lubricated and with antifriction bearings usually gives a mechanical efficiency of 99.5% for each pair of gears. (2) The *bevel gear* which is used to transfer power at a 90° angle is also widely used and is generally about 99% mechanically efficient if properly lubricated and fitted with anti-friction bearings. The old style plain bearing and collar on bevel gears are very seldom used. (3) The *worm gear* is used to transmit power at an angle, and typically at the same time is used to give a large reduction in speed. The efficiency varies greatly. For normal good practice with good antifriction bearings and lubrication, an efficiency of 40 to 90% is obtained. Under conditions of extreme high-speed reduction, the efficiency may be much lower. The worm gear, of which there are many types, is nearly always used where great speed reduction ratios are required. The special type called the hypoid gear is widely used in automotive equipment in the differential drive. This type of drive if used with special high performance lubricant is reasonably efficient and gives long life. (4) The *sun gear* consists of a large gear with a small gear or pinion running on the inside of the rim of the large gear. This is sometimes called a planet gear. (5) The *herringbone gear* has a V-shaped tooth and in reality is a double helical gear. It has the advantage of giving a very smooth operation, is quiet, and eliminates thrust which otherwise might be encountered. (6) The *helical gear* is very similar to a spur gear except that the teeth instead of going straight across the face of the gear parallel to the shaft are set at an angle, so that the gear teeth spiral into each other and give a quieter operation than straight spur gears. A single helical gear generates considerable end thrust which must be taken care of by means of a thrust bearing or washer.

Gear Teeth

Gear teeth are cut in many different configurations for special purposes. The standard full depth gear tooth is cut to give a 14.5° slope of the tooth. A second type is a full depth tooth but with a 20° angle. This tooth is sometimes used where the strains are exceptional. A third type of tooth called the 20° stub tooth is also frequently used for very heavy loads. The short stub shape of the tooth makes it less likely to break than either the standard or the 20° tooth.

One of the most important dimensions of a gear is the so-called diametral pitch. This is the ratio of the number of teeth to the pitch circle diameter. For good operation it is important that the pitch circles of two gears which match, be properly aligned and adjusted with respect to each other. Failure to align gears causes undue wear and noise.

The face of the gear is the width of the tooth surface in a direction parallel to the shaft. Thus, a 4-in. base gear has teeth which are 4 in. long in the direction parallel to the shaft.

Materials

Gears are made from many different materials, including cast iron, cast steel, and steel forged, phenolic-laminated, or special alloy. The least expensive type of gear is usually made of cast iron, cast bronze, or cast steel. The most expensive are those made from steel forged from a solid blank of material or from special alloys.

Phenolic-laminated gears are usually small diameter pinions, and are not made for heavy loads but to bring about quietness.

Cast iron gears are usually for slow speed, not too heavy loads, and are not good for shock loads. Cast steel gears will stand fairly heavy loads, and with some of the improved special centrifugally cast steel gears, extremely good results are obtained.

The gear or pinion made from a steel forged blank has great toughness, will withstand shock, and has excellent wearing quality.

Gears and pinions made from alloys such as steel alloys can be made with extremely high resistance to wear and breakage. They are also quite expensive. The Society of Automotive Engineers has established specifications for alloyed gears. Very frequently the pinion or small gear of a pair is made of alloy steel in order to give it sufficient wearing life and strength to match the larger gear.

For some high-speed applications special bronze gears and pinions are found to be quite satisfactory. These are widely used, particularly in cream separators and special high speed machinery.

For some light power purposes, special gears can be made with pressed and heated powdered metal. These can often be made at much less cost than by regular gear cutting methods.

In small instruments, gears and pinions are frequently punched from a sheet. In this service, noise is not a factor and the movement of the gear train is usually slow.

Care

Several important factors apply to the care of gear systems. (1) The gear must be accurately aligned or it will wear rapidly and is noisy. (2) The gear must be properly lubricated. (3) The recommendation of the manufacturer or an oil company regarding the type of lubricant must be followed. Metal gears should run in a bath of oil or have oil poured over the teeth by a force feed system. (4) The gear should be enclosed in a tight case which will keep water and foreign material out of the system as any solid matter such as grit or powdered material will wear gears very rapidly.

(5) Water must be kept out of gear systems by occasional draining. The natural breathing of the atmosphere into and out of the gear case will bring moisture in and cause it to accumulate. It is often desirable to have a small water trap on the bottom of the gear case so the water may be caught and kept separated from the bulk of the oil and be drained at intervals. (6) Gears must be adapted under load and speed to the conditions in which they are to work. In general, slow speed, heavy gears require the use of heavy lubricants, whereas high speed relatively light load gears require a low viscosity oil. There are special oils available which are resistant to moisture emulsification, and which have a greater clinging or adhesive effect on the gear than most standard oils. In some instances these special oils which may be obtained from a number of oil manufacturers should be investigated if lubrication problems are encountered.

GENERATORS, ELECTRIC

Food processing plants use large amounts of power and heat for processing. The Diesel-driven electric generator is used in many food plants to generate electric energy and may also supply a part of the heat for processing.

The Diesel engine is a heavy-duty type, and can run for long hours with relatively little upkeep. It is relatively clean, and is quite efficient in a processing plant. The best Diesel engines deliver from 35 to 40% of the energy of the fuel as power, and when equipped with a water heating attachment, allow most of the 60% of the heat given off by the engine cooling system to be used for processing heat in the plant.

Many plants maintain a Diesel electric generating system as a standby power unit for use in case of power failure. This is particularly valuable if a plant is located in a remote section away from essential services.

Diesel electric plants are relatively trouble-free. However, periodic maintenance and the supervision of a competent operator are required. The principal servicing of the motor unit involves changing oil at recommended intervals, and replacing filters in the fuel line and in the oil line at required intervals. In addition, some expert maintenance is occasionally needed on the fuel injection system. Good, clean fuel is an essential for trouble-free operation. The cost of electrical power from a diesel unit may be competitive with commercial power. The actual cost can only be determined by a detailed study of the system and setup.

Cross-references: *Electricity; Electric Power; Refrigeration Principles.*

GLASS CONTAINERS

Glass containers are widely used in food and other industries. Advantages available to the processor from the use of glass containers include the following. (1) Glass is comparatively inert to chemical action. (2) Product visibility is important for merchandizing, identification, and use. (3) Package rigidity strengths and product shelf-lives are very good. Shelf-life may be affected by light, however, glass is a complete barrier against vapor and gas transmission. (4) Glass package reclosure is simple and easy; the container is also useful for storage purposes. (5) The container is available in a wide variety of sizes and shapes. Several thousand different glass molds have been made for glass containers. (6) Glass containers are quite economical although heavier for shipment. (7) The Food and Drug Administration has approved glass as a means of packing most all food products. (8) The composition of glass can be varied somewhat by adjusting the type of sand or silica used and some other ingredients.

Specifications

Food processors and glass manufacturers must determine the shape of a glass package to achieve the desired results. The amount of glass in a container will vary considerably depending upon its shape. The surface areas of solids having a volume of 1 cu in. are listed.

	Sq In.
Sphere	4.5
Cube	6.00
Cylinder H = D	5.53
Cylinder H = 2D	5.84
Cylinder H = 3D	6.21
Cylinder H = D/2	5.86
Cylinder H = D/3	6.40

In containers having cylindrical shapes the more the height differs from the diameter, the greater the amount of material required to produce a container of given volume. The additional weight of a container can run 5 to 10% due to shape alone.

Glass may be provided with a variety of coating materials to produce a neater appearance or change the functionality. A comparison of properties of various coating materials for glass is summarized in Table G.1.

TABLE G.1

PROPERTIES OF COATING MATERIALS FOR GLASS

	Sulfur	Metallic Oxides	Non-permanent Wax Type	Semi-permanent Wax Type	Resins	Silicone Oils	Metallic Oxide Plus Polyethylene[2]
Invisible film	No	Iridescent sheen	Yes	Yes	Yes	Yes	Yes[3]
Easily applied—as by spray from water solution, or as a gas	Yes	No	Yes	Yes	Yes	Yes	No
Water insoluble after application (hot and cold water)	No	Yes	No	Yes	Yes	Yes	Yes
Water wettable after application	Yes	Yes	Yes	Yes	Yes	No	Varies
Good lubricity							
Wet	No	Yes	No	Yes	Yes	Yes	Yes
Dry	No	No[1]	Yes	Yes	Yes	Yes	Yes
Puncture strength of film	Low	High	Medium	Medium	Medium	Low	High
Nontoxic	Yes	Yes	Yes	Yes	Yes	Yes	Yes
Easy labeling (hold labels)	Yes	Yes	Yes	Yes	Yes	No	Yes

[1] Depends on surface condensation.
[2] Dual system—tin or titanium oxide applied at hot end of lehr. Polyethylene, as dispersion at cold.
[3] Under some conditions may be iridescent.
Source: Modern Packaging Encyclopedia (1967).

Cross-references: *Bottles and Cartons; Packages.*

GLASS PIPES

Glass pipes (or pipings) possess several fine attributes for handling many food products.   Since glass pipes are lightweight and transparent, they are desirable for the sanitary appearance and visibility of the product being processed.   Most glass pipe is made of borosilicate glass and will operate at temperatures up to 450°F.   It is usually heat shock resistant and will permit quick transition from high to low temperatures.   Glass pipe is corrosion proof with considerable resistance to chemical action.

A wide variety of fittings are available to fabricate a line in many configurations. Gasket materials have been improved and are available in neoprene, gum rubber, Teflon, and silicone rubber.   Some of the joints are flexible; however, they are quite expensive.   Others are specially designed for expansion and contraction.

In making a glass pipe installation the lines must be well-supported with at least 2 hangers for each 10 ft of length for most sizes.   Connections can be made to other types of pipe or tubing with adaptors.   Flange sets of aluminum are commonly employed for making connections, although sets are available in cast iron and stainless steel.   General specifications are given in Table G.2.

Application

Glass pipe in food plants has been found satisfactory for several applications, but should be protected against breakage.   It is obvious that breakage can occur when struck with a hard object.   Glass pipes find major use in long transfer lines for food products such as milk.   These lines may be installed upwards of 7 ft above the floor where they are protected from floor traffic.

Glass pipelines are quite easily cleaned with hot water and circulating detergent solutions normally used in food plants.

TABLE G.2

GENERAL SPECIFICATIONS FOR GLASS PIPE

D	Pipe Size (nominal id), In.	$1/4$	$3/8$	$1/2$	$3/4$	1	$1 1/2$	2	3	4	6
B	Pipe od, In.	0.500	0.625	0.750	1.000	1.313	1.844	2.344	3.406	4.530	6.656
A	Flange od, In.	$23/32$	$24/32$	1	$1 9/32$	$1 9/16$	$2 1/8$	$2 5/8$	$3 24/32$	$5 11/32$	$7 14/32$
C	Pipe wall, In.	0.125	0.125	0.125	0.125	0.156	0.172	0.172	0.203	0.265	0.328
E	Flange angle °, one side	15	15	15	15	12	12	12	12	21	21
L	Pipe length, minimum, In.	2	2	3	3	3	$3 1/2$	4	5	6	6
	Weight, lb per ft	0.10	0.15	0.24	0.40	0.60	1.0	1.13	2.0	3.4	6.3
	Recommended pressure, psi	100	80	70	60	55	55	55	55	35	20

Source: Fischer & Porter Co.

Cross-references: *CIP Systems; Detergents; Piping.*

GRADING

Grading provides a basis for buying and selling. Grade standards are established and enforced by the federal government, federal-state cooperative inspection programs, and associations. The most important grade factors are size, uniformity, color, chemical content, bruises, cut surfaces, spray residues, dust residues, disease, molds, moisture content, color, and soundness (no hollow hearts in potatoes and apples).

Principles Used for Separation of Fruits and Vegetables

Specific Gravity.—The weight per unit volume of fruits and vegetables varies greatly. The specific gravity of a product will vary with varieties, maturity, and soundness. Separation is usually done in a solution with a controlled specific gravity in which the heavier products settle to the bottom and the lighter products rise or remain on top. In some operations the heavier products are preferred, and in others, the lighter. Specific gravity can also be utilized in separation of vegetables in a moving air stream. The heavy materials settle in the air stream, the light ones are carried out. The air stream is also used for separating materials with different surface characteristics such as removing split peas or beans from whole ones and the removal of stems, leaves, and trash.

Size.—Size separation can be made by a screen, chain, holes in belt, cups, roller above a belt, or over a diverging opening, such as made by a roller and spring or two rollers. The screen is normally used for separation of small materials and the other devices are usually used for separation of larger materials. A spool-type separator can be used in which the spools may be spaced different distances depending on the sizes to be separated. The spool separation also accomplishes some cleaning during the process.

Weight.—Weighing devices are used for measuring the weight of the individual product such as fruit, vegetables, or eggs. With these the small or light materials are removed first. Basically, a pocket holding the material rides along with the opposite end on a tripping device which can be adjusted for the weight. For more exact separation, weight methods are used because the weight varies as the cube of the diameter, which makes it a more sensitive means than diameter separation with the usual range of weighing devices. Often a group of several items, such as a dozen, crate, or bushel, is weighed in mass to obtain the total weight to compare the number of items included for that particular grade.

Color.—Electronic or manual means are used for color separation. For manual and visual color separation lighting of the product, the belt, belt background, and the room background are important. It is desirable to use a color which will enhance the product differences, and thus make it easier for the picker to remove the undesirable, damaged, or off-color product. A light should be used which is easy on the eyes and does not cause fatigue of the workers. With the electronic methods, light is directed on the product and reflected. The intensity of reflected light is used as a measure of the quality of the product being checked.

Surface Characteristics.—In addition to using an air stream for separating broken vegetables from whole ones, another principle of surface characteristic for separation, known as froth flotation, can be utilized. Air incorporated on the surface of vegetables inhibits the settling rate in a solution or in water. To enhance the formation of air on the surface, chemicals may be placed into the water. Normally fruit which is damaged or which is of poor quality will stay on the surface because of the air held on the surface.

Chemical Analysis.—A representative sample is removed from the product in question and analyzed for moisture content, percentage sugar, solids content, acidity, and impurities. Impurities might be placed on the product by rodents, spraying, fumigation, etc.

Mechanical Properties.—The firmness of an item can be used as a means of classification. The resistance to loading without damage, the resilience of a material, and the ability to conduct sonic or ultrasonic waves or to absorb various energy sources can be used as a means of separation. Penetrometers or "mechanical thumbs" are available for testing the hardness of some fruits and vegetables. Separation may also be done on the basis of the coefficient of friction of the surface on the material.

Packing House.—Immediately after harvest, apples are moved to the packing house. The packing house should be designed for proper handling, washing and cleaning, grading and sizing, and for packing of the fruit. From 2.5 to 4 sq ft of floor area is needed for the packing house for each bushel of fruit that is to be packed in one 10-hr day. A grower packing 500 bu per day needs a packing house with 1,250 to 2,000 sq ft of floor area (Fig. G.1).

Growers packing less than 10,000 bu of fruit will typically use roller conveyor, hand truck, and dollies for handling. For those packing over 10,000 bu of fruit, a forklift truck is usually economical. Design of the packing house must consider the method of handling.

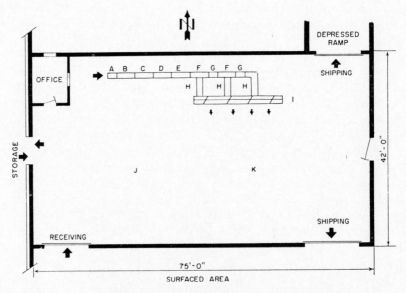

Fig. G-1.   Packing house layout

A—Dumping air.   B—Feed belt.   C—Eliminator.   D—Brusher.   E—Sorting rolls.   F—Sizer.   G—Spacer belt.   H—Crossover belt.   I—Return-flow belt.   J—Ungraded fruit.   K—Packed fruit.

Washing.—Spray residues on the fruit must not exceed a certain amount, often established by government agencies. Arsenic, DDT, and certain other chemicals must be removed. If spraying precedes harvest by 4 or 5 weeks the amount of chemical on the apple usually will not exceed the tolerance of FDA. A cooperative or commercial packing house should be prepared to remove chemicals when the product is received because several growers are involved. A standard cleaning solution for arsenic sprays (i.e., lead arsenate) is made of 1% hydrochloric acid solution. To assist in removal of the residues, heating of the cleaning solution to 100°F or the use of detergents may be necessary. Where spray residues are on the surface, washing the apples in water to remove dirt is usually sufficient. Washers may consist of a tank through which the apples are moved, brush rolls, or high-pressure sprayers. If a strong chemical such as an acid is used for washing the apples, the fruit should be thoroughly rinsed with water following washing. About 3 to 4 gal. of water per bushel of fruit is required for rinsing after acid cleaning. Usually it is not necessary to dry after washing. Excess moisture can be removed with a high speed air stream or an absorbent cloth roll.

Waxing of graded fruit is often carried out to improve appearance and to lengthen the shelf- or storage-life. Waxing is a part of the packing line operation.

Grading and Sizing

Damage to the fruit must be avoided particularly for the fresh market. Dumping aids are available for crates or bulk boxes, so that as the apples are dumped from their containers they feed uniformly onto the belt feeding the grading line. These devices include a spring-loaded lid which permits the product to feed out slowly and uniformly without dropping from the top of the container to the belt. From the dumping station, a belt moves the fruit to an eliminator which removes small fruit, usually less than 2 in. in diameter. These apples might be used for cider. Next, a brushing unit removes dust, spray material, or other foreign matter. Washing of the fruit might be carried out. Thorough visual inspection takes place at the sorting rolls. A sorting area should be well-lighted. The fruit is turned so that the inspector can see all sides. Sizing of the fruit is done with equipment. Most apple sizing is done on the basis of diameter. Size grading is done on perforated belts, link chain belts, or pockets which expand as they move along the grading line. The small fruit are removed first. From the standpoint of quality pack, it would be desirable to remove the large diameter products first to avoid the damage during handling through each grading unit. Large apples can be removed by placing a brush diagonally across the feed belt to move the large apples to one side where they can be removed. For accurate sizing it might be necessary to run these large diameter products through a sizing chain, perforated belt, or expanding pockets.

Weight Separation

Products are placed on a canvas pocket and moved to various weighing stations. At the appropriate station, the pocket tips and the product moves into the appropriate grade. Weight separation of apples is used more in Western States than in other areas.

After sizing, the products may be bagged and placed in baskets or special containers. The apples may be individually wrapped or may be ring-packed for placing in baskets. Padding of surfaces will help decrease or eliminate injury to the fruit.

Speeds of not more than 30 fpm should be used for belts and rollers to avoid damage. Excessive slopes should be avoided. Other sources of damage to apples are: dumping onto belt; poorly designed grader, where the fruit may be banged against the walls or dropped excessive distances from the sizing belt to the accumulation area; overfilling of market containers; forcing lids over filled containers; and rough handling of the products to the truck, on the truck, and in the retail stores or in storage.

Economics and Efficiency

Conventional packing plants in Washington using belt conveyors and hand trucks had the highest labor requirements. Handling with belt conveyors and hand trucks required only 60% of the cost incurred by the use of elevators and hand trucks. The most costly method of handling is by the use of elevators and clamp type two-wheel hand trucks. The most efficient method of handling was with the forklift truck. For loading refrigerator cars the clamp type two-wheel hand truck was the most efficient. For loading of delivery trucks of product wholesalers using belt conveyors, the labor and equipment costs per ton are slightly lower when four-wheel platform trucks are used for performing the operations. For receiving grocery orders the most productive method is the wheel-type gravity conveyor.

Reference

HALL, C. W. 1963. Equipment for Processing Agricultural Products. Edwards Brothers, Ann Arbor, Mich.

Cross-references: *Materials Handling; Refrigerated Storage.*

GRANULATORS

Granulators are designed to divide particles such as nutmeats into smaller pieces or serve a dual purpose of drying while achieving particle separation such as in granulation of sugar. Granulators have been used extensively in the sugar industry where crystals of sugar are separated one from another. White sugar of approximately 1% water moves through the granulator during the final drying operation.

Construction

The granulator is a metal drum about 6 ft in diameter, 25 ft long, and slightly inclined in a horizontal position toward the discharge end. As the drum revolves warm air is driven through the cylinder with an exhaust fan. The heated air removes sugar dust from the granulator as well as moisture. Steam coils are generally used for heating the air entering the granulator. Two granulator drums are usually operated in series with the upper one discharging into the lower drum. Most of the moisture is removed in the upper drum, therefore, only the finishing is required in the lower. The sugar should leave the lower drum below 110°F. Sanitation is an important factor; therefore, filtered and washed air should be used to supply the granulator. Single-pass granulators are also in common use. This system involves only one drum. These drums have a variable angle of tilt which can be increased to increase the capacity of granulation. The capacity may be increased during those times when the sugar is drying exceptionally well, and reduced during times of poor drying conditions. The single-pass system reportedly produces dry, unscratched, and cool sugar. With large-grain sugars the type of granulator used will influence the amount of crystal scratching. The conventional drum granulator tends to produce more scratching than other types of driers, multipass belt driers or small diameter drums, in which the crystals lower in the warm air current without falling.

The conventional type of granulator is shown in Fig. G.2. One commercial unit consists of an outer cylindrical shell about 6 by 18 ft, and an inner shell made of louver plates which are attached to the full length tapering radial plates. This inner shell gradually increases in diameter as it approaches the discharge end. The space between the inner and outer shells is partitioned into hot air passages forcing the air to exit between the louver plates. Wet sugar which is fed at a uniform rate into the inner drum is slowly tilted in the direction of rotation causing it to fall on the top surface of louver plates. In this manner, the sugar travels through a spiral path to the discharge end with a gentle motion.

Nut Granulator

For making confections or other food products comminuting of various kinds of nutmeats, e.g., peanuts, pecans, cashews, and walnut pieces, is desirable. Equipment for this type of granulation is comparatively small. For example, one model utilizes only a $^1/_2$ hp motor to drive a rotary knife which does the comminuting. The other comminutor is equipped with a sorting shaker to meet size requirements of the various granulated nutmeats. Knife assemblies for $^3/_{16}$ in., $^1/_8$ in., or fine $^1/_{16}$ in. size cuts are interchangeable. The standard size cutter assembly is $^1/_8$ in. and also includes a magnetic separator. One model (Bauer Brothers model 365) nut granulator has a capacity of 600 to 800 lb per hr of peanuts with dimensions 34 in. long, 20 in. wide, and 44 in. high. The unit is driven with a $^1/_2$ hp motor. The granulator is shown in Fig. G.3. The magnetic separator serves to remove any iron particles from the product.

Reference

MEADE, G. P. 1963. Cane Sugar Handbook, 9th Edition. John Wiley & Sons, New York.

GRAPHITE

Graphite is a special form of carbon. It comes in three different types. Flake and amorphous graphite are found in nature. A third type or artificial graphite is

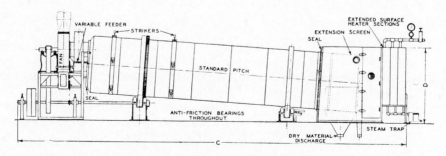

FIG. G-2. Granulator

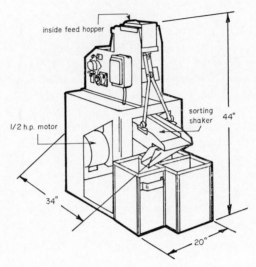

inside feed hopper

1/2 h.p. motor

sorting shaker

44"

34"

20"

FIG. G-3.   Nut granulator

amorphous carbon converted to graphite by a high temperature treatment in an electric furnace. It is a very pure form.

The best natural graphite comes from the island of Ceylon. The state of New York also supplies a large amount of natural graphite.

The specific gravity of natural graphite varies from 2.015 to 2.583. Refined graphite has a specific gravity of 1.802.

The hardness of graphite on the Mohs scale is between 1 and 2.

Two very important characteristics of graphite are that it is a very good lubricant, and a good conductor of heat.

Flake graphite is used in the manufacture of crucibles and refractors. The flake graphite mixes well with clay to form a stiff mixture which can be hardened. Flake graphite is also widely used in paints and in lubricants.

Amorphous graphite is widely used in paint because it is very resistant to acids and alkalies. It is also used in the formation of elastic films. It can be used alone, with water, or with oil.

Amorphous graphite is widely used for electrodes. It is also an excellent lubricant after deflocculation which makes it possible to form a colloidal suspension in oil or water.

GRAVITY

Gravity is the natural phenomenon which causes all objects to be drawn toward the earth. Little is known about the true nature of gravity except that it causes a force which can be definitely measured and predicted and which acts on all types of material and in the same direction.

Gravity is defined as that force which at sea level and latitude 45° north causes an acceleration of 980.665 cm per sec² or 32.1740 ft per sec² on an object which is free-falling in a vacuum. There is a correction of −0.003 ft per sec² for each 1,000 ft of altitude. The force of gravity acts upon an object irrespective of its density.

Gravity is a factor in many types of machines, and in a gravity scale is the basic element which makes the scale function. A gravity-operated scale is less likely to lose its calibration than a spring-operated scale, since gravity for practical purposes never changes.

The center of gravity is an important point on machines or equipment in that a body can be considered as having a point at which all of the weight is concentrated. However, this is not true for objects which are moving rapidly and subject to centrifugal forces.

In a triangle, the center of gravity is at the intersection of lines joining the midpoint of each side drawn to the opposite vertex. The center of gravity is also found to be at a point at $1/3$ of the altitude of a line drawn from the base of the triangle to the opposite vertex. An object which has a high center of gravity is easily tipped over.

Cross-references: *Energy; Friction.*

GRINDERS

There are four general classifications of equipment used for size reduction—burr mill, hammer mill, roller mill, and combination mill. The roller mill as used for crimping has recently come into prominence. The combination mill is a burr mill or hammer mill plus a device for chopping forages. The chopping device may be a cylinder head or a cutter's wheel.

Burr Mill

The burr mill, also called attrition, plate, or disc mill, consists of plates, usually 2, of 4- to 60-in. diam which rub together. These plates might be in a horizontal or vertical plane, usually vertical for agricultural mills. If two burrs are used, one moves on a shaft and the other one is fixed or moves in the opposite direction. If 3 plates are used, the center one has cutting edges on both sides and turns while the 2 outside plates are stationary. Coarse, medium, and fine burrs are available. Burr mills originally consisted of two stones rubbed together in a horizontal position for reducing the size of material. The burr mill is particularly good for coarse grinding and for some medium grinding. The exception is for medium grinding of oats, which is more costly than with the hammer mill. Fine grinding is more costly with a burr mill than with a hammer mill. Running of the mill empty should be avoided unless the pressure on the plates is relieved. These units are usually low speed, operating between 400 and 1,800 rpm. Burr mills have a lower initial cost than hammer mills for the small sizes. In general, the output of a burr mill is about 2 to 3 bu per hour per horsepower. The fineness obtained depends upon the plate or burr being used, the speed of the plate, condition of the plates, pressure on the burr, rate of feeding, grain being ground, and the moisture content of the grain. A device should be provided ahead of the burrs to give positive and controlled feeding. A safety device should be available to permit the plates to separate if an obstruction enters.

For any given modulus of fineness, power required to grind decreases as the speed of the mill increases. Power requirements decrease to a speed of about 2,000 rpm. To grind grain to a modulus of 2.5; 0.6 hp per hr are required per 100 lb, and 0.2 hp per hr for a fineness modulus of 3.9 at 200 rpm. When the speed is increased to 2,000 rpm, about 10 times as much grain can be ground per horsepower-hour.

The burr mill gives a more uniform ground product for coarse and medium than does the hammer mill. The capacity of a particular mill depends upon the fineness, speed of the mill, product, and power available.

Hammer Mill

The hammer mill consists of fixed or swinging hammers mounted on a rotating shaft (Fig. G.4), a screen, and a fan. These hammers are 1 to 3 in. apart and revolve at a speed of 2,500 to 4,000 rpm depending upon the diameter at the tips of the hammers. The tip speed of the hammers is usually between 15,000 and 20,000 fpm. A screen through which the reduced product must pass is mounted below, above, or around the hammers. The product being ground remains in the grinder until it is small enough to go through the holes in the screen. The hammer should not touch the screen. The hammers can be reversed to give four wearing surfaces or often have removable tips which can be replaced after wear. The rate of feeding to the mill is controlled by slide gates or by a positive feeder such as an auger. As the product passes through the screen, it is usually picked up by an air stream supplied by a fan and carried to the feed collector and then to the bin or bag. Not all of the air passes through the screen. Some enters the mill on the opposite side of the grinder from the

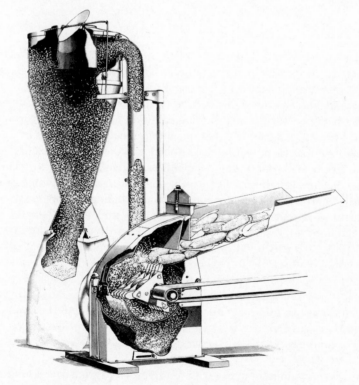

Courtesy of Deere & Co.

Fɪɢ. G-4.   Cross-section of hammer mill

feed collector. Recent work has shown that less power is required for grinding with the screen located above the hammers.

The hammer mill is particularly adaptable for medium and fine grinding. Because of the high speed at which the hammers operate, the hammer mill is excellent for connecting to an electric motor. Running empty is not detrimental. Foreign materials, such as rocks or metal, are not so likely to cause extensive damage as might occur in the burr mill. Less power is required for fine grinding with the hammer mill than with the burr mill. The fineness of grinding depends upon the screen size and the rate of movement of the ground material through the grinder. The capacity of a particular grinder depends upon the grain, the fineness, power available, speed, and moisture content of the product. Normally about 1 hp is required per 1.5 bu, or for 100 lb per hr for medium grinding.

Size reduction occurs because of (1) explosion due to impact of the hammers, (2) cutting by the edge of the hammers, and (3) attrition or rubbing action. The rubbing action is important with cereals, and the impact is important with corn and heavy, brittle materials.

Whereas a burr mill will require 1 to 2 hp when running empty, a hammer mill will require from 4 to 8 hp when running empty (of a unit requiring 35 hp when grinding a full load). Most hammer mills have fans which require considerable power, for moving the ground grain through the screen and to the feed collector (Fig. C.37).

The product may be fed in from the side or into the ends of the hammers. Generally the point of intake is almost directly above the shaft of the rotor, so that if you look at the mill when it is turning clockwise, the intake should be between 1 and 2 o'clock.

Roller Mills

Roller mills are usually sized according to the diameter and length of the roller. A 10- by 18-in. mill refers to one with rollers of 10 in. diam and 18 in. roller face length. The diameters range from 6 to 12 in., with the most popular sizes being 9 to 10 in., whereas the lengths vary from 4 to 42 in.

Roller mills cannot be started with grain on the rollers. The mill must be brought up to speed before the grain is fed to the rollers. Otherwise, belt slippage, motor stalling, or shearing of the safety pin will occur.

There are many different rules used for adjusting roller clearance. The space between the rollers should be adjusted with a postcard or with a feeler gage, with about 0.10 in. for corn and about 0.035 in. for barley. A sample should be rolled and the adjustment may be changed to obtain a coarser or finer material if desired. Capacity is reduced, dust produced, and more power required if the rolls are set too close. A mashed, crimped kernel is recommended for oats and barley, whereas simple cracking and slight crushing of the kernel is sufficient for corn. It is necessary to periodically adjust the roller because of wear.

The rolls must not be fed too rapidly. Roller speeds of 350 to 600 rpm are generally used, and higher speeds of 500 to 600 rpm for wet grains. In some units, one roll operates faster than the other to provide a slight grinding action as the material passes between the rolls. Farm size roller mills are usually equipped with corrugated rollers, usually parallel to the shaft of the roller. The number of grooves per inch to

Table G.3

MODULUS OF FINENESS AND MODULUS OF UNIFORMITY

Sieve (or Screen)	% on Each Sieve		Assigned Number		Product		Sum of % on Sieve		Nearest Whole Number
$^3/_8$	0.0	×	7	=	0.0	⎤			
4	3.5	×	6	=	21.0	⎬—Coarse =	9.5 ÷ 10 =	0.95 = 1	
8	6.0	×	5	=	30.0	⎦			
14	25.0	×	4	=	100.0	⎤—Medium =	67 ÷ 10 =	6.7 = 7	
28	42.0	×	3	=	126.0	⎦			
48	20.5	×	2	=	41.0	⎤			
100	2.0	×	1	=	2.0	⎬—Fine =	23.5 ÷ 10 =	2.35 = 2	
Pan	1.0	×	0	=	0.0	⎦			
Totals	100.0				320.0				

$$\text{Modulus of fineness} = \frac{320}{100} = 3.2 \qquad \text{Modulus of uniformity} = 1:7:2 = \text{coarse:medium:fine}$$

Source: Hall (1963).

Table G.4

ENERGY, COST, AND UNIFORMITY OF GRINDING DIFFERENT GRAINS TO VARIOUS FINENESS (DOCKING 1960)

Kind of Grain	Moisture, % Wb	Grind	Capacity, Bu/Hr	Kw/Hr	Cost (¢)/Hr 2c/Kwh	Cost (¢)/Bu 2c/Kwh	Uniformity Index
Burr mill (Plate Grinder)[1]							
Wheat	13.0	Coarse	17.2	3.93	7.86	0.46	1.8.1
Wheat	13.0	Medium	16.9	4.48	8.96	0.52	0.8.2
Wheat	13.0	Fine	6.2	4.51	9.02	1.44	0.5.5
Barley	15.5	Coarse	15.9	3.7	7.4	0.46	1.8.1
Barley	15.5	Medium	12.6	4.4	8.8	0.7	0.8.2
Barley	15.5	Fine	5.35	5.6	11.2	2.1	0.5.5
Oats	13.2	Coarse	15.9	3.36	6.7	0.42	1.8.1
Oats	13.2	Medium	10.6	3.52	7.0	0.66	0.8.2
Oats	13.2	Fine	6.6	4.0	8.0	1.2	0.5.5
Hammer mill[2]							
Wheat	13.0	$^1/_4$ in. Coarse	34.0	2.62	5.24	0.15	1.8.1
Wheat	13.0	$^3/_{16}$ in. Medium	19.0	2.65	5.3	0.28	1.8.1
Wheat	13.0	$^1/_8$ in. Fine	9.1	2.66	5.3	0.58	0.7.3
Barley	15.5	$^1/_4$ in.	23.0	2.62	5.24	0.22	3.6.1
Barley	15.5	$^3/_{16}$ in.	10.1	2.65	5.3	0.52	1.7.2
Barley	15.5	$^1/_8$ in.	7.2	2.9	5.8	0.8	0.8.2
Oats	13.2	$^1/_4$ in.	27.0	2.54	5.0	0.2	0.8.2
Oats	13.2	$^3/_{16}$ in.	11.4	2.35	4.7	0.41	0.7.3
Oats	13.2	$^1/_8$ in.	11.0	2.54	5.0	0.45	0.6.4
Grain roller[3]							
Wheat	13.0	Coarse crack	17.5	1.48	3.0	0.17	5.5.0
Wheat	13.0	Medium crack	10.0	1.5	3.0	0.3	1.8.1
Wheat	13.0	Fine crimp	5.0	1.68	3.4	0.68	1.7.2
Barley	15.5	Coarse crack	13.3	1.5	3.0	0.23	8.2.0
Barley	15.5	Medium crack	8.0	1.4	2.8	0.35	5.4.1
Barley	15.5	Fine crimp	5.0	1.8	3.6	0.72	2.6.2
Oats	13.2	Coarse crack	18.4	1.3	2.6	0.14	8.2.0
Oats	13.2	Medium crack	10.0	1.4	2.8	0.28	7.3.0
Oats	13.2	Fine crimp	6.2	1.7	3.4	0.55	5.4.1
Oat roller							
Oats	13.2	—	40	1.8	3.6	0.09	

[1] The medium feed auger was used. Considerable dust particularly in the finer grinds. Magnetic trap operated well in catching metallic objects.

[2] Very dusty in all grinds. Barley being tough reduced the capacity of the machine. Oats easily broken by the hammer mill.

[3] Manufacturer recommends 1 or 2 hp motor. Capacity would increase if 2 hp motor used.

Source: Hall (1963).

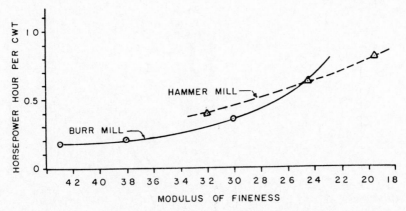

Fɪɢ. G-5.   Effect of fineness on power requirements for shelled corn

use with various sizes of grain is designated by the manufacturer, usually 14, 12, or 10 grooves per inch for small grains, and 8, 6, 5, or 4 grooves for corn or coarse cracking.

The power requirements will vary according to the kind or quality of grain to be rolled, degree of fineness, condition of rollers, moisture content, operating speed, available power, and rate of feed.   In general, however, for a feed rate of 40 bu per hr, these are 1 to 2 hp for small grains and $1/2$ hp for shelled corn, and for 200 bu per hr, 7.5 to 10 hp for small grains and 5 to 7 hp for shelled corn.   A rule of thumb is that 1 kwh (or 1 hp-hr) is required per ton of grain for crimping, and 2 hp-hr for cracking corn.

The roller mill has long been used in the flour industry in which two rolls move in the opposite direction toward each other, with one roll at a speed of 2 to 3 times the other roll.   In the final operation of making flour, smooth rolls are used with one roll operating at a speed 25% faster than the other.

Power Requirement

There is an increase in power requirement for grinding for both the burr mill and the hammer mill, particularly when the moisture content of ear corn and shelled corn increases from 9 to 26%.   From 1.5 to 2 times as much feed can be ground at 10% as 25% moisture.   The increase in power requirement is more for the burr mill than the hammer mill for shelled corn as the moisture content is increased.   The effect of fineness on power requirements of the burr and hammer mill is shown in Fig. G.5 and Tables G.3 and G.4.

During shelled corn grinding, the burr mill shows a lower power consumption for coarse grinding than the hammer mill at the same fineness.   The burr mill will grind shelled corn and wheat to a coarse fineness with less power requirement than the hammer mill.   For fine grinding, the reverse is true.   Grains with a high fiber content like oats show a higher power requirement for fine grinding.   The grinding range of oats is greater when using the hammer mill.

Reference

Hall, C. W. 1963. Processing Equipment for Agricultural Products. Edwards Brothers, Ann Arbor, Mich.

Cross-references: *Cyclone Separator; Size Designation.*

H

HEAT

The transfer of heat for heating and cooling is one of the most important aspects of food processing operations. Heat cannot be measured directly. The quantity of heat present in a body is based on several parameters of the product. A major concern, rather than the quantity of heat present, is the quantity of heat which must be transferred to reach a desired temperature or to attain a desired thermal effect.

Sensible and Latent Heat

Heat may be added to change the temperature of a gas, liquid, or solid. When all of the heat added is used for changing the temperature, that is, for increasing the kinetic energy of the molecules, it is known as sensible heat, which can be sensed with a thermometer. The specific heat is used for calculating sensible heat.

Heat added or removed to change the state is known as latent heat and is expressed in heat units per unit mass and is 970.4 Btu per lb for water or steam, or 540 cal per gm in the atmosphere at sea level. Latent heat is involved in changing the state from solid to liquid to gas by adding heat. Heat is removed to change the state from a gas to liquid to solid. Heat absorbed or given up at a constant temperature during fusion, that is, melting or solidification, is called the latent heat of fusion, and is expressed in heat units per unit mass. For water or ice, the latent heat is 144 Btu per lb or 80 cal per gm (Fig. H.1).

Heat added to change a state is utilized as internal or potential energy of the body. It is effective in changing the distance between molecules, but none of the heat added increases the kinetic energy. The state of matter is dependent upon the distance between molecules. The closer the molecules the more dense the substance. In a solid the molecules are closer together than in a liquid.

For a substance such as ice, which contracts on melting, an increase of pressure lowers the melting point of the substance. Upon melting, ice will contract about 9%.

The freezing point of a solution is lower than that of the pure solvent. As a material which dissolves is added to water, the freezing point becomes lower. The greater the concentration, to a certain limit, the lower the freezing point. One gram molecular weight of substance dissolved in 1,000 gm of water will cause a decrease in the freezing point of $1.86°C$ or $3.35°F$. The addition of water to milk can be very accurately detected by a raising of the freezing point. The unit used for detecting such adulteration is known as a cryoscope.

For very concentrated solutions, the solute will leave the solvent upon freezing, and the solvent will freeze as a pure substance. The temperature at which the freezing point is not lowered by the addition of solute is known as the eutectic. To the right of the eutectic and below the line, saturated liquid exists. To the left of the eutectic

374

below the line, saturated solid exists.   The eutectic is the point at which the freezing temperature is at the lowest and at a particular concentration of solution.

There are two kinds of freezing or fusion.   These are known as crystalline, such as ice, or amorphous.   With crystalline freezing, the change of state takes place at one temperature only.   With amorphous freezing, the viscosity increases as the temperature decreases with freezing.   During the solidification of lactose in dry milk, depending upon the temperature, humidity, and time, either type of structure may be obtained.   The latent heat of an eutectic made up of a salt and water solution is lower than the latent heat of pure water.   The eutectic point is also applicable to a mixture of two metals forming an alloy, where the freezing point or temperature of solidification is lower than the temperature of either individual component.

The quantity of heat involved in changing the state from a liquid to a gas or gas to liquid is identified as the latent heat of vaporization or latent heat of evaporation. The boiling point is that temperature at which there is vaporization throughout the liquid.

The boiling point temperature is increased as solute is added to the solvent.   The effect on the boiling point is important in the change of temperature of vaporization when producing condensed milk.   The magnitude of the increase in the boiling point is related to the molecular weight of the solute to the volume or weight of the solvent. The change in boiling point can be used to determine the molecular weight of a nonvolatile substance.   One gram molecular weight (1 mole) of a substance dissolved in 1,000 gm of water, will increase the boiling point by 0.9°F, or 0.5°C.

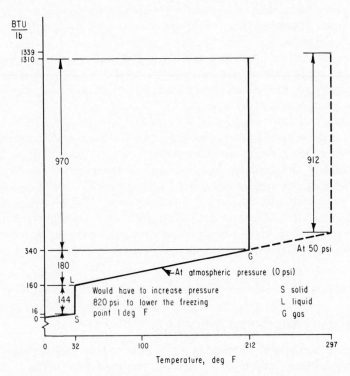

FIG. H-1.   Heat in one pound of water at various temperatures

The increase in temperature above the normal boiling point is proportional to the concentration of the added solute and inversely proportional to the molecular weight of the solute.

The temperature of vaporization can be altered by changing the pressure above the liquid. By increasing the pressure above the liquid, the boiling point increases. As the boiling point increases, the latent heat decreases. The values of boiling point versus pressure and the quantity of latent heat involved are incorporated in steam tables for water. Similar relationships with different values exist for refrigerants and other chemicals involved where a change of state occurs.

The reverse action, the change of state from a gas to a liquid, is known as condensation. The temperatures, pressures, and latent heat values are the same for condensation as for vaporization.

There is considerable increase in volume per pound of product as the liquid changes to a vapor. The volume of water vapor at 100°C (212°F) and at sea level atmospheric pressure is about 1,700 times the volume of the original liquid water. A cubic inch of water when vaporized produces about 1 cu ft of steam.

Distillation is a process involving first vaporization and secondly, condensation. It is used for obtaining distilled water. The liquid to be distilled is heated in a suitable container and the vapor produced is passed through a condenser which can be cooled so that the gas changes to a liquid. The liquid produced is free of the solid matter it originally contained.

Some substances pass from the solid to the vapor state without going through the liquid state. The process is known as sublimation. Dry Ice or carbon dioxide in a solid form is used for cooling or freezing. Dry Ice sublimes or passes directly to the vapor state upon absorbing heat. Pressure can be used to make the product pass through the liquid state.

The latent heat of sublimation is the sum of the heat of fusion and heat of vaporization at the temperature of sublimation. Except for carbon dioxide (Dry Ice), vacuum is usually required to effect sublimation. At the melting point of Dry Ice of −109°F, the latent heat is 241 Btu per lb.

The quantity of heat which must be removed to change fat from a liquid to a solid (as well as other organic compounds) is known as the heat of solidification. The temperature at which milk fat solidifies is from 24.4° to 10°C (76° to 50°F). The solidifying point of the insoluble fatty acids in butterfat is 33° to 39°C. The fat does not solidify at one temperature, but begins to solidify and is considered to be very nearly completely solid at the lower temperature. The heat of solidification of milk fat is approximately 20 cal per gm. The quantity of heat involved in the change of state of organic compounds, where the percentage of material solidifying changes with the temperature, is usually considered as sensible heat and is called apparent specific heat.

Cross-references: *Btu; Dry Ice; Energy; Fuels; Insulation; Refrigerated Storage.*

HEAT AND MASS TRANSFER, DROPLETS

The unit of measure of the heat transfer from the air through the film into the droplet is the *h*-value, known as surface or film coefficient of heat transfer, Btu per hr sq ft °F. The quantity of heat transfer can be obtained by

$$Q = hA\,(\Delta t)$$

where A = area of surface of droplet, sq ft

Δt = difference in temperature between droplet and surrounding air outside of the film, °F

"The drop temperature can be estimated from a psychrometric chart at the point where the adiabatic saturation line drawn through the drying air condition crosses the curve for humidity over a saturated solution of the nonvolatile material."

The film coefficient, h, can be calculated from

$$h = h/D(2.0 + 0.54\,\mathrm{Re}^{1/2})$$

or

$$h = 1.6(1 + 0.3(\mathrm{Pr})^{1/3}\,(\mathrm{Re})^{1/3})$$

where k = conductivity coefficient, Btu ft per hr sq ft °F

D = diameter of drop, ft

Re = Reynolds number = $DV\rho/\mu$

Table H.1

TERMINAL VELOCITY OF PRODUCT WITH SPECIFIC GRAVITY OF 1.0 BASED ON STOKES LAW WITH AIR AT 155°F

Diameter, μ	Terminal Velocity, Ft per Sec
10	0.008
30	0.086
60	0.31
90	0.70
120	1.24

Source: Hall and Hedrick (1967).

Table H.2

VISCOSITY OF AIR AND WATER VAPOR

Temperature, °C	Temperature, °F	Poises
Air		
0	32.0	171×10^{-6}
18	64.4	183×10^{-6}
40	104.0	196×10^{-6}
74	165.2	210×10^{-6}
100	212.0	220×10^{-6}
229	444.2	264×10^{-6}
334	633.2	312×10^{-6}
357	692.6	318×10^{-6}
409	768.2	341×10^{-6}
Water vapor		
0	32.0	90×10^{-6}
100	212.0	132×10^{-6}

Source: Hall and Hedrick (1967).

where V = relative velocity of drop and air, ft per sec (Table H.1)

ρ = density of air, lb per cu ft

μ = viscosity of air, centipoise/1,488 (Table H.2); lb per ft sec

Other dimensionless numbers commonly utilized for expressing relationship in heat transfer are Nu (Nusselt number) and Pr (Prandtl number), which are

$$\text{Nu} = hD/k \text{ (Nusselt number)}$$
$$\text{Pr} = c\mu/k \text{ (Prandtl number)}$$

The relationships of the Nusselt number and the Prandtl number and Reynolds number are given in Fig. H.2. Along the ordinate are plotted values of the Nusselt number from which it is a common practice to calculate h (from hD/k), which can be determined if values for D, V, ρ, c, Nu, and k are known.

Corresponding to heat transfer coefficient is the mass transfer coefficient k_g, which can be utilized for determining the rate of mass transfer, water or vapor, in pounds per hour.

$$R = k_g A (\Delta p)$$

where R = rate of mass transfer, lb per hr

k_g = mass transfer coefficient, lb per hr sq ft unit partial pressure

A = area, sq ft

Δp = dimensionless partial pressure ratio

$p_{vi} - p_a$ = vapor pressure at interface − pressure of diffusing vapor

$p_{vi} - p_s$ = vapor pressure at interface − vapor pressure of drying air

Inasmuch as heat and mass transfer take place simultaneously these values can be plotted as shown in Fig. H.2. However, different dimensionless numbers are used to represent mass transfer, such as Schmidt number, Sc, and modified Nusselt number Nu$'$. Dimensionless values utilized in analyzing mass transfer are as follows

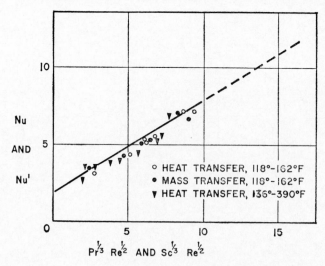

From Ranz and Marshall (1952)

FIG. H-2.   Heat and mass transfer of evaporating water drops

$$Nu' = \frac{k_g MDP_f}{(\text{diff.})(\rho)} \quad \text{(modified Nusselt number)}$$

$$Sc = \frac{\mu}{\rho(\text{diff.})} \quad \text{(Schmidt number)}$$

$$Re = \frac{DV\rho}{\mu} \quad \text{(Reynolds number)}$$

where M = average molecular weight of gas mixture in transfer path

D = diameter of droplet, ft

P_f = average value of pressure difference across transfer path

diff. = diffusivity of vapor in air, at $300°F$, diff. = 1.425 sq ft per hr;   at $32°F$, diff. = 0.853 sq ft per hr

μ = viscosity of air, lb per ft sec.

ρ = density of air, lb per ft sec.

Thus, when using Fig. H.2 for mass transfer, the modified Nusselt number, Nu', versus Sc and Re, and for heat transfer, Nu versus Pr and Re, are used.

The proper quantity of air must be supplied to furnish heat for vaporization and to provide moisture carrying capacity for removing the vapor.   For making preliminary calculations, the following equation may be used

$$wc(t_1 - t_2) = q = Ua(\Delta t_m)V_d$$

where w = mass flow rate of the air, lb per hr

c = specific heat or humid heat capacity, Btu per lb $°F$

t_1 = inlet air temperature of the drier, $°F$

t_2 = outlet air temperature of the drier, $°F$

q = total rate of heat transfer which may be calculated on basis of water to be evaporated, Btu per hr

Ua = volumetric heat transfer coefficient, with values of 9 to 17 Btu per hr cu ft $°F$

Δt_m = mean temperature difference throughout drier, $°F$

V_d = volume of drier, cu ft

The value of U as reported above of 9 to 17 Btu per hr cu ft $°F$ is for a small experimental unit.   The relationships used can be based only on experience, knowing the temperatures involved and quantity of product to be dried.   Also, the quantity of air can be determined from psychrometric calculations.

One pound of air heated to $300°F$ and exhausted at $175°F$ will give up 29.8 Btu and evaporate 0.030 lb of water;   from $500°F$ to $175°F$, 0.078 lb of water will be evaporated.

Reference

HALL, C. W., and HEDRICK, T. I.   1966.   Drying of Milk and Milk Products.   AVI Publishing Co., Westport, Conn.

Cross-references: *Heat Transfer; Spray Dryer.*

HEAT EXCHANGERS

Processing of food products nearly always involves either heating or cooling of the product, thus requiring a heat exchanger. The variation in the viscosity and form of the food product requires the use of many different types of heat exchangers varying from direct steam injection to swept surface type exchangers which are used in connection with products of high viscosity.

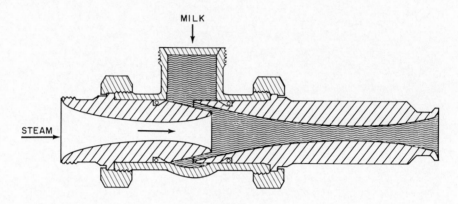

DIRECT STEAM INJECTOR

Fig. H-3. Steam injector

The heat exchangers should be made so that they may be properly sanitized and readily dismantled for cleaning. Heating of food products also involves accurate control of temperatures to prevent damage to the product through overheating of the product film being heated.

Principles

Heat and mass transfer in connection with food products follows general laws of heat transfer and thermodynamics. Heat may be transferred by conduction, convection, or radiation.

The general formula for heat transfer is

$$Q = U \times A \times T_1 - T_2$$

where Q = Btu transferred per hour

$\quad U$ = heat transfer coefficient of the heat transfer surface in Btu per sq ft per °F

$\quad A$ = area of the heat transfer surface, sq ft

$\quad T_1$ = the high temperature side of the wall

$\quad T_2$ = the low temperature side of the wall, °F

Types

The simplest type for heating of liquid products is to inject steam directly into the product. Figure H.3 illustrates a typical steam injection heater. The efficiency of the steam injection heater is practically 100% and the amount of heat transferred, assuming the steam is saturated, is given by the formula

$$Q = W (H_t - H_l)$$

where Q = total Btu transferred

W = weight in pounds of steam injected per hour

H_t = total heat of the steam at the temperature it is applied

H_l = heat of liquid at the temperature of the fluid being heated

Direct injection of steam also adds a certain amount of moisture to the product. In practice this moisture is removed by flashing the product through a vacuum system as shown under flavor control systems.

Steam Infuser

The steam infuser accomplishes the same purpose as the steam injector. However, the action is different as shown by Fig. H.4. In this system the product to be heated is injected into a chamber full of steam under pressure in which there is some-

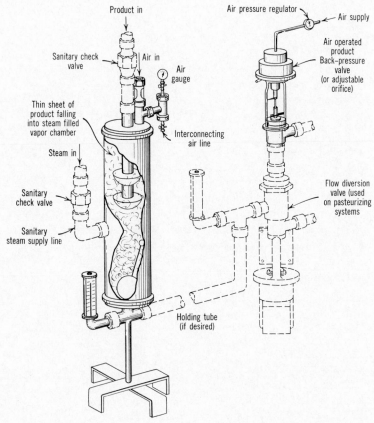

Courtesy of C. P. Div., St. Regis Co.

FIG. H-4.   Infusion type direct-steam heater

what less agitation of the product being heated.   The net effect of the heating system is practically identical to that of the steam injector.   Excess moisture is removed from the product by means of a vacuum flash process similar to that used with the steam injector.

Small Diameter Tube System

The small diameter tube heating system is designed to provide an extremely rapid movement of the product through the heat transfer system, thus giving a very high rate of heat transfer and a short exposure to the temperature.   Figure H.5 shows a heating system of this type.   This system is not widely used on account of the difficulty of cleaning the heat transfer surface, and also because a high pressure of anywhere from 500 to 2,000 psi must be used to force the product through the tubes.

Triple Tube Heater

The triple tube heater is made of three concentric tubes as in Fig. H.6.   The velocity in the heater is quite high and excellent heat transfer rates are obtained. The triple tube arrangement makes possible the use of a regenerative hookup which is efficient and compact.   This system is used on products of reasonably low viscosity. With the proper CIP system cleaning can be readily accomplished.

Plate Heat Exchangers

One of the most popular type of heat exchangers is the plate system in which thin corrugated plates are stacked together to provide passages for the product and for the heating and cooling fluid.   Figure H.7 shows a typical plate heat exchanger.   This type of heater has several important advantages.   (1) The heat transfer surface requires only a small space.   (2) The equipment can be readily cleaned either by opening it up or by CIP methods.   (3) A high rate of heat transfer is obtained due to the configuration of the plate surface.   (4) By means of special heaters it is very simple to build up a heat transfer unit which can be used for heating, cooling, and regeneration in one compact unit.   The U-value with this type of heat exchange equipment is usually in the range of 400 Btu per hr per sq ft per °F difference in temperature.   A complete pasteurizing unit for a large plant can be assembled in one press, plus the addition of the holding tube and the necessary control equipment.

Barrel Heat Exchangers

The barrel type heater is very simply made as shown in Fig. H.8.   It consists of a series of tubes which carry the food product, fastened into a header at each end.

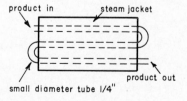

FIG. H-5.   Small tube heat exchanger

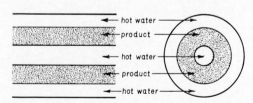

FIG. H-6.   Triple tube heat exchanger

The space which surrounds the tubes is filled with steam or hot water as desired.   This is a relatively inexpensive type of heater, is easily cleaned, and is widely used for "rough" heating of food products of moderate viscosity.

Surface Heat Exchanger

Surface type heaters are a very simple type of heater made up of a series of tubes stacked vertically as shown in Fig. H.9.   This is an inexpensive type heater and one in which there is no back pressure placed on the product.   The product flows down the outside of the heater tubes.   Considerable vapor is lost to the atmosphere.   This exchanger has quite good heat transfer capacity;   usually the U-value is 300 to 350 Btu per hr per sq ft per °F.

Swept Surface

A swept surface heat exchanger consists essentially of a heat jacketed tube in which is operated a scraper very similar to that used in an ice cream freezer.   The product passes through the apparatus in the same manner as in an ice cream freezer. A feature of this apparatus is that it will handle very viscous materials and do it under a closed system with excellent heat transfer characteristics.   Figure H.10 illustrates this type of apparatus.   The motor driven agitator is rotated at a speed to match the viscosity and type of product which passes through.   The heat transfer coefficient

Courtesy of C. P. Div., St. Regis Corp.

FIG. H-7.   Plate heat exchanger

of this type of apparatus is in the neighborhood of 500 Btu per sq ft per °F. The heat transfer surface is usually made of nickel or steel that is chrome-plated. It is important that the scrapers be made of a material which wears well against the cylinder surface.

Radiation

Radiant energy is often used in the food industry particularly for drying materials or in baking. Ordinary heat lamps are very efficient. However, any hot surface can be used as a radiant energy source providing the temperature is correct. Transfer by radiant energy eliminates the need for a contact heat transfer surface. The amount of energy transmitted is proportional to the fourth power of the absolute temperature.

Convection Heating

Convection heating involves the use of thermal circulation or currents, and is important in some types of heating of liquids. The circulation is brought about in the same manner as the old thermosyphon cooling system at one time widely used in

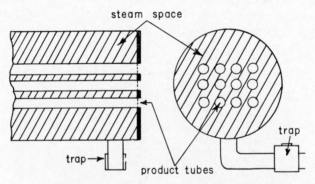

FIG. H-8.   Barrel type heat exchanger

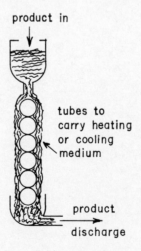

FIG. H-9.   Surface type heat exchanger

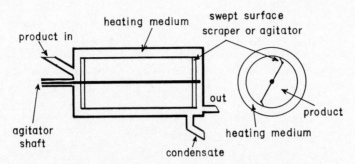

FIG. H-10.   Swept surface type heat exchanger

automobiles.   To take advantage of convection heating the heat should be applied near the bottom of the container.   In modern equipment it is usually necessary to supply agitation by means of a mechanically driven agitator rather than to depend upon convection currents for transferring heat.

Practices

The rate of heat transfer to food products varies tremendously depending upon the characteristics of the product.   A basic principle is that the product film next to a heat transfer surface must move rapidly if good heat transfer is to be maintained, and if overheating of the film is to be prevented.   The basic heat transfer formulas applying to specific conditions are reasonably accurate and the heat transfer can be accurately calculated if all of the conditions are known.   In general, liquids of low viscosity are much more easily heated than those of high viscosity.

The rate of movement of the product across the heat transfer surface which will give turbulent flow in accordance with Reynolds number calculations is usually desirable.

When heating certain heat sensitive products such as milk, best results are usually obtained by having only a few degrees temperature difference between the heating medium and the product being heated to prevent overheating of the milk film which is in direct contact with the heat transfer surface.

Cooling

Most of the heat exchangers mentioned can be used equally well either for cooling or for heating.   The most efficient setup is usually with direct expansion refrigerant. However, brine or other antifreeze solution can sometimes be used.   The heat exchange rate actually obtained from equipment is somewhat higher when heating than when cooling, since the liquid film of the product being heated is more viscous when it is being cooled than when heated.

In the cooling of products such as milk which are susceptible to freezing at a temperature near 32°F, it is customary to use sweet water (plain chilled water) as the cooling medium to prevent freezing of the milk product.

In cooling of viscous products with a swept surface agitator type heat exchanger, it is necessary to provide additional refrigeration to offset the Btu equivalent of the work done in driving the agitator.   This amounts to 2,545 Btu per hp hr.

Falling Film

A very efficient type heat exchanger is that of the falling film type unit which is used in connection with vacuum evaporation.   In this unit the product is dropped in a thin film vertically down the periphery of tubes which are surrounded by the heat source such as steam or vapor.   This unit gives very high rates of heat transfer plus rapid release of vapors.

References

Copson, D. A.   1962.   Microwave Heating.   AVI Publishing Co., Westport, Conn.

Herreid, E. O., and Tobias, J.   1959.   Ultra high temperature short time experimental studies in fluid milk products.   J. Dairy Sci. *41*, No. 9, 702.

Peeples, M. L.   1962.   Forced convection heat transfer characteristics of fluid milk products during cooling.   J. Dairy Sci. *45*, 1456–1462.

Peeples, M. L.   1963.   Forced convection heat transfer coefficients.   J. Dairy Sci. *46*, 359.

Cross-references: *Boilers; Cooling Milk; Heat; Evaporators; Dryers; Heat and Mass Transfer; Refrigeration Principles; UHT equipment.*

HEAT PUMP

The heat pump uses the refrigeration system as a means of transferring heat from one temperature to a higher temperature.   An advantage of heat pumps of this type is that either heating or cooling can be accomplished.   The cooling procedure is discussed under refrigeration.   The heating procedure is usually accomplished by using electricity to drive a motor to operate the system.   The heat output is at the condenser of the system.   The heat delivered divided by the work input gives the

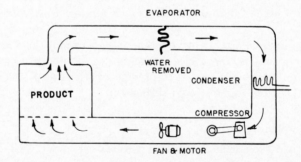

Fig. H-11.   Closed circuit refrigeration heat pump dryer

coefficient of performance.   The coefficient of performance varies from 3 to 7.   The heat flow into the system at the evaporator may come from air or water.   Heat pumps can be used for space heating, humidity control, drying, or cooling.

As a heating installation, the cost of the heat pump installation usually exceeds other methods of space heating.   However, where both heating and cooling are required, the heat pump installation provides economical methods.

The use of a refrigeration cycle circuit heat pump for drying heat sensitive products offers considerable possibility (Fig. H.11).   The cost of energy per bushel for a continuous shelled corn dryer reducing the moisture from 25 to 13.6%, db, for 1,000 lb per hr, with electricity at 2 cents per kwh and oil at 12 cents per gal., gave a cost per hour of operation of 2.7 cents for a closed cycle heat pump, and 3.3 cents for an oil-fired drier. The heating coefficient of performance was 4.3. With a heat pump drier the high temperatures obtained with oil-fired driers are not obtained. The sequence of events for moisture removal for a closed heat pump refrigeration cycle is: (1) fan moves air through the duct system, (2) air moves through grain, (3) air with moisture moves over the evaporator where the moisture is condensed and removed from the system, (4) air moves over the condenser where it is heated, (5) air moves over the compressor and motor where it is heated, and (6) air moves to fan, and cycle is repeated.

HEAT TRANSFER

Three mechanisms are involved in heat transfer: conduction, convection, and radiation. Seldom does a practical application involve only one of these mechanisms. Two or three of these mechanisms may be operating simultaneously in the transfer of heat. The driving force for the transfer of heat is the temperature difference between the hot and cold body.

Conduction

Conduction involves the transfer of heat from molecule to molecule. With an increase in heat there is also a greater molecular vibration, and a greater flow of free electrons, particularly in metals, which pass energy to adjacent molecules in the conducting system.

Convection

Convection involves the transfer of heat due to movement of the mass, caused by the change of density of fluids. The distance between molecules increases as the temperature of the molecules increases, causing the fluid to become lighter and to rise in the gravity field, with heat being carried by molecular transfer. Forcing movement of molecules of a fluid by a pump or fan is also considered a method of convection.

Radiation

Radiation transfer of heat occurs due to electromagnetic radiation of a body because of vibration of the molecules. In radiation, both the hot and cold bodies radiate. All bodies radiate heat in proportion to the fourth power of their absolute temperature, T^4.

Conduction

The ability of a substance to conduct heat is known as the thermal conductivity. A good conductor of heat has a poor resistance (R) to heat transfer. Generally, good electrical conductors, particularly metals, are also good thermal conductors. In metals, energy is transferred by free electrons. Insulation materials have few free electrons, limited molecular activity, and less heat is transferred.

The rate of heat transfer, q, Btu per hr, through or across a body for a steady-state condition, where the temperatures remain constant, can be calculated if the following are known:

(1) The conductivity of the substance, k, which has been determined experimentally for many materials and is available in tabulated values (the conductivity is expressed in Btu per hr sq ft °F per ft of thickness or per in. of thickness, and is sometimes expressed as Btu per hr ft °F);   (2) the area, A, perpendicular to the direction

TABLE H.3A

THERMAL CONDUCTIVITY OF SELECTED MATERIALS AT ROOM TEMPERATURE

Material	Thermal Conductivity, Btu/Hr Sq Ft °F/Ft
Glass wool	0.023
Ammonia	0.013
Air	0.012
Concrete	0.17
Glass	0.45
Ice	1.1
Iron	35.0
Aluminum	118.0
Copper	222.0
Steel	34.0
Water	0.36
25% NaCl brine	0.32
Water vapor	0.01
Wood, pine	0.08
Sandstone	1.06
Sawdust	0.03
Fiber insulating board	0.028
Corkboard	0.025
Steam	0.02

If k in $\dfrac{\text{Btu} - \text{ft}}{\text{hr sq ft °F}}$

Multiply by 12 to obtain Btu/hr sq ft °F/in.
0.00413, cal/sec sq cm °C/cm

Source: International Critical Tables.

of heat transfer, sq ft;   (3) the thickness or length of the path the heat is transferred, x, given either in feet or inches, the same units as used in the k-value (for structural materials, the thickness is often expressed in inches);   and (4) the temperature difference or gradient along the length of the path of heat transfer, Δt, in °F.

These variables may be related in equation form to provide the Btu per hr heat transfer

$$q = \frac{k}{x} A (\Delta t)$$

The thermal conductivity is available for many materials in the International Critical Tables.   A few representative values are given in Table H.3.   Although there are some equations for calculating the thermal conductivity of a few materials, in general the thermal conductivity is determined experimentally, rather than by calculation. The thermal conductivity of some metals, such as brass and aluminum, increases with an increase in temperature; while with others, nickel, steel, cast iron, there is a decrease in conductivity with an increase in temperature, with the exception of superheated steam. Water increases in conductivity with an increase in temperature. With insulation materials, as the density is increased, the thermal conductivity, k, first decreases, and then increases, because of the change in density, and at the higher densities, with the removal of air. In the normal range of temperatures, the variation in thermal conductivity is not very great for different temperatures, so it is customary to use an average value of thermal conductivity based on the average temperature involved in the heat transfer problem.

TABLE H.3B

THERMAL CONDUCTIVITY OF SELECTED PRODUCTS

Material	Moisture Content, % (Wb)	Mean Temperature, °F	k, Btu-in. Ft² Hr °F
Air		32	0.163
Castor oil			1.23
Concrete		32–212	5.28
Corn	13.2	80–88	1.22
Fuels, liquid: gasoline, kerosene		86	1.1
Ice			6.44
Leather			1.22
Lime			8.45
Linen			0.61
Oats	12.7	20–88	0.90
Olive oil			1.15
Sand, dry		68–315	2.5
Sawdust, shavings			0.35
Silk			0.276
Snow, compact			1.48
Soil, dry			0.96
Straw	Air dry, cut		0.70
Turpentine			0.95
Water		32.0	4.04
		68.0	4.15
		86.0	4.65
Wheat	12.5	87.0	0.89
	12.5	97.2	0.95
	14.0	77.7	0.95
	14.0	91.2	0.98
	23.0	79.4	1.04
	23.0	89.6	1.07
	23.0	89.7	1.11
Wood, pine, across grain			1.03
Wool, cotton, 5 lb/cu ft		70	0.29

Conversion relationships:

1 Btu-in./hr ft² °F = 3.447 × 10⁻⁴ Cal − cm/sec cm² °F = 1/12 Btu − ft/hr ft² °F; 1 cal-cm/sec cm² °C = 2,901 Btu-in./hr ft² °F

Conduction through a flat wall can be calculated directly from the equation

$$q = \frac{k}{x} A(\Delta t) \quad \text{or} \quad \frac{k}{x} A_m(\Delta t)$$

where direction of heat transfer is perpendicular to the faces. Special equations are available for calculating the areas for different shapes. Simplified shapes, such as a cylindrical or spherical wall, can be treated by special consideration.

For a cylinder, the inside area, A_i and the outside area, A_o, are different. The log mean area, A_m, of the two areas may be used if the outside area is more than twice the inside area. If not twice as large, the arithmetic mean may be used to calculate A, which is

$$A_m = \frac{A_o + A_i}{2}$$

The logarithmic mean for a cylinder is calculated by

$$A_m = \frac{A_o - A_i}{\ln(A_o/A_i)}$$

For a sphere, the area which is represented by the geometric mean is used.

$$A_m = \sqrt{A_o A_i}$$

The quantity, Q, of heat transferred in Btu over a period of time θ, is equal to $(q)(\theta)$.

Example: What is the rate of heat transfer through a 10 by 8 ft concrete wall 8 in. thick, with an inside surface temperature of $70°F$, and an outside surface temperature of $20°F$? How much heat is transferred in 6 hr?

$$q = \frac{0.17}{8/12}(8)(10)(70 - 20) = 0.255(80)(50) = 1{,}020\,\frac{\text{Btu}}{\text{hr}}$$

$$Q = (q)(\theta) = \left(1{,}020\,\frac{\text{Btu}}{\text{hr}}\right)(6\text{ hr}) = 6{,}120\text{ Btu}$$

Many problems involving heat transfer have more than one material through which heat passes perpendicular to the face. The heat transfer equation written previously may be written as

$$Q = \frac{(A)(\Delta t)}{x/k} = \frac{A\,\Delta t}{R_t}$$

where R_t is the thermal resistance of all materials
for one material $R_t = x/k$
for two materials $R_t = (x_1/k_1) + (x_2/k_1)$

where x_1 represents first material
x_2 represents second material

Tables are available which provide the R-values for different materials of different thicknesses. The R-values can, of course, be calculated if the k-value and the thickness of the material are known. The total resistance to heat transfer is equal to the sum of the individual resistances of the materials.

The applications discussed previously involve a steady rate of heat transfer where the difference in temperature does not vary with time. Unsteady state heat transfer is often encountered and is considerably more difficult to handle. Calculations of unsteady state heat transfer are beyond the limits of this book. The rate of change of the heat content of a product is equal to the product of the thermal capacity times the rate of change of temperature. Unsteady state heat transfer equations are often solved from prepared tables or charts. One component encountered in unsteady state heat transfer is the thermal diffusivity, which is

$$k/c\rho = \alpha \text{ (thermal diffusivity, sq ft per hr)}$$

where k = thermal conductivity, Btu per hr sq ft °F per ft
c = specific heat, Btu per lb °F
ρ = density, lb per cu ft

Convection Heat Transfer

Heat is carried from one position to another by movement of a fluid. In natural convection, a heated fluid expands, rises in the mass of fluid, and sets up a flow known as convection current. A cooled fluid contracts, and falls as it sets up convection currents. To provide maximum heat transfer by gravity or natural convection, heating is done from the bottom, and cooling from the top of a fluid.

Convection heat transfer is particularly applicable in boilers, most heat exchangers, ventilation and refrigeration systems, water, brine, and air heaters and coolers.

Heat moves from the higher temperature heater to a fluid adjacent to the heater. A film or layer of fluid exists between the surface of the heat exchanger and the bulk of the fluid being heated. On the surface of the heat exchanger, the velocity of the fluid is zero. There is a layer or film next to the heat transfer area which is relatively stationary. The heat transfer properties of the film, or the equivalent film, control or limit the rate of heat transfer. Heat moves through this stationary film by conduction. There is an equivalent thickness of a stationary film which would provide the same resistance to heat transfer as that provided by the film under the particular heating conditions.

The film coefficient or surface thermal conductance, h, in Btu per hr sq ft °F is used to calculate the heat transfer by convection where

$$q = hA\Delta t$$

It can be seen that h is equivalent to k/x in the heat transfer equation, from which x, an equivalent thickness for the same rate of heat transfer, can be calculated, and

A = cross-sectional area, sq ft
Δt = temperature difference between bulk of the fluid and surface of the material through which the heat is being passed, °F

Some authors use f instead of h for the film coefficient, which is sometimes referred to as surface thermal conductance.

For a high rate of heat transfer, a high value of h is desired. The film coefficient is affected primarily by (1) conductivity of the fluid, and (2) the thickness of the film, which depends primarily upon the viscosity, velocity, turbulence of flow, and the temperature of the fluid. The opposite effects are desired to provide insulation or low heat transfer properties.

There are many different empirical equations available for calculating the h-value depending upon the conditions and variables involved. In using these equations, the fluid and conditions must be classified under one of the following:

> Forced or free (i.e., gravity)
> Velocity of flow
> Laminar or turbulent flow
> Cooling or heating
> Viscosity range
> Tubes or flat surfaces involved in heat transfer
> Fluid inside or outside of tubes or pipes
> Flow of fluid perpendicular or parallel to surface
> Position of heating surface, vertical, horizontal, inclined
> Gas, vapor or liquid flow involved

For natural convection, the h-value depends primarily on the fluid and the temperature difference. For example, for air, $h = 0.38(\Delta t)^{1/4}$ for a horizontal surface for heating air facing up. For a vertical surface, $h = 0.27(\Delta t)^{1/4}$. More involved equations are available which can be used generally for many different fluids, but for which it is necessary to know many of the thermal and viscous properties of the particular fluid. The film coefficient of water flowing at high velocities inside pipes is given by the equation

$$h = \frac{138}{D^{0.2}}\left(1 + \frac{50}{r}\right)\left(\frac{V}{\mu}\right)^{0.8}$$

where D = inside diameter of the pipe, in.
r = ratio of length of pipe to diameter
V = average water velocity, ft per sec
μ = viscosity of water, at average temperature, centipoise

At normal temperatures, the viscosity of water is one centipoise.

Using the same equation, the h-value for an infinitely long pipe with water would be

$$h = \frac{138}{D^{0.2}}(V)^{0.8}$$

For a pipe 1 in., the equation would simplify to

$$h = 138(V)^{0.8}$$

Values of the film coefficient, h, are often calculated for typical applications. Representative values are given in Table H.4

The so-called radiator used for heating air transfers approximately $1/2$ or more of its heat in convection. The equivalent amount transferred by radiation is often represented by h_r. The combination of heat transfer by radiation and convection may be represented by

$$h_r + h_c \text{ or } h_{r+c}$$

and is used in the same manner as the h mentioned previously for calculating the rate of heat transfer.

Values of the coefficient, h, are given for air having different temperatures and different flow rates, and for water at different velocities and different temperatures, Fig. H.12 and H.13. The overall heat transfer coefficient, U, Btu per hr sq ft °F is commonly used for heat transfer calculations. Overall values are given in Table H.5.

TABLE H.4

REPRESENTATIVE VALUES OF THE FILM COEFFICIENT, h

	Btu/Hr Sq Ft °F
Air inside tubes at 32 ft per sec	8.0
Air perpendicular to tube, $7\frac{1}{2}$ ft per sec	7.5
Water inside tube, 5 ft per sec	1,200
Water perpendicular to tubes	800
Boiling film of water on vertical surface	1,000

TABLE H.5

SOME APPROXIMATE OVERALL HEAT TRANSFER COEFFICIENTS, U

10 in. concrete monolithic wall	62
Windows	1.13
Steam boiler	2–15
Surface steam condenser	200–1000
Water heaters	200–1500
Air heaters; air coolers	1–5
Shell and tube ammonia and Freon condensers	150–300
Shell and tube water cooler	15–25
Shell and tube brine units	90–100
Shell and tube steam heater for water	350–750
Evaporator—to forced air	4–10
Water cooling coils to forced air	5–10
Shell and tube water to water	100–300
Double tube water—brine	150–300
Coil in vat water—water natural	20
Water to water, free convection	25–60
Water to water, forced convection	150–300
Hot water radiator	1–10
Brine cooler, liquid to boiling liquid, forced convection	50–150
Surface cooler, milk to water	175
Coil vat, revolving coil (milk)	200
Gravity pasteurizer	150
Jacketed kettle with stirrer	300
Jacketed kettle evaporating	500
Disc milk cooler	200
Vacuum pan, evaporating	500
Flash pasteurizer	600

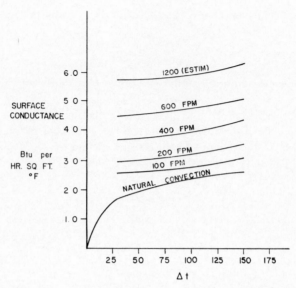

Fɪɢ. H-12. Film coefficient, h_1 surface conductance of air

Using these values it is easy to estimate the area of heat exchange surface required to provide the rate of heat transfer desired. Heat to be transferred, and the fluids on each side of the heat transfer surfaces are known and we have some idea of the temperature involved, so that it is easy to utilize U-values to determine the area required to give the rate of heat transfer desired. The overall value may be based on either the inside or the outside area where the two heat transfer surfaces are of unequal areas, such as in a double tube or shell and tube heat exchanger. Some manufacturers rate their equipment from the inside and some on the outside and some on the hottest side of heat exchanger surfaces.

The overall heat transfer value, U, includes the heat transferred by any of the three mechanisms, however, usually convection and conduction, and has the same units as h.

The U-value can be determined if the film coefficients and thermal properties are known

$$U = \frac{1}{(1/h_i) + (x_1/k_1) + (x_2/k_2) + (1/h_o)}$$

where h_i = inside film
h_o = outside film

This can then be used for a particular application in the equation

$$Q = UA\Delta t \frac{\text{Btu}}{\text{hr}}$$

Heat exchanger surface areas are commonly determined on the basis of the U-values, either calculated or furnished by the manufacturer. The temperature difference, Δt, often cannot be determined directly as is the case for previous problems. Heat exchangers are generally of three types from the standpoint of flow of the me-

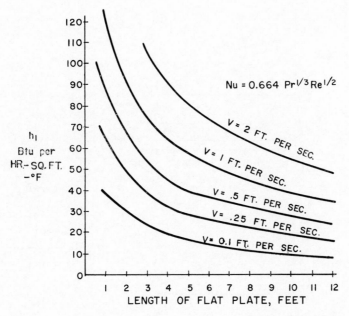

$$Nu = 0.664 \, Pr^{1/3} Re^{1/2}$$

$V = 2$ FT. PER SEC.

$V = 1$ FT. PER SEC.

$V = .5$ FT. PER SEC.

$V = .25$ FT. PER SEC.

$V = 0.1$ FT. PER SEC.

h_1 Btu per HR.-SQ.FT. $-°F$

LENGTH OF FLAT PLATE, FEET

Based on Schenck 1960

FIG. H-13.   Film coefficient, h_1 of water at 70°F on smooth surfaces

diums: parallel flow, counter flow, and cross mixed flow, with a heat exchanger surface between the fluids. Regardless of the type of flow, the temperature difference, Δt, is accurately represented by the log mean temperature, t_m

$$t_m = \frac{Gtd - Ltd}{\ln \, (Gtd/Ltd)}$$

where Gtd = greatest temperature difference of the ends of the heat exchanger
     Ltd = temperature difference of the ends of the heat exchanger
A schematic representation of the temperature along the length of two types of heat exchangers with the representation of the temperature differences is shown in Fig. H.14.

Thermal Radiation

All bodies radiate electromagnetic waves. The waves travel at the speed of light. The wavelength, λ, normally in the range of 20 to 30 μ for thermal energy, decreases as the temperature, T_1, absolute increases. In heat transfer, the rate or quantity of thermal energy exchange is of interest. Equations for heat transfer are used for calculating the increase or decrease in temperature due to the net exchange of energy between two or more bodies.

Electromagnetic waves move through a vacuum without change. Waves which are absorbed are converted to heat. A body which has been heated by radiation then reradiates energy at a lower temperature with energy of longer wavelength. The earth is heated by radiation from the sun which is at 6,150° Kelvin or 10,000° Rankine at the rate of 120 cal per hr sq cm (442 Btu per hr sq ft). Water vapor, carbon dioxide,

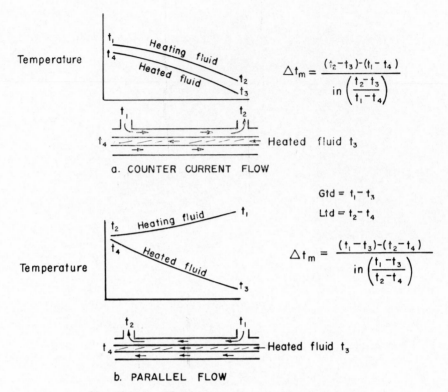

$$\Delta t_m = \frac{(t_2 - t_3) - (t_1 - t_4)}{\ln\left(\frac{t_2 - t_3}{t_1 - t_4}\right)}$$

a. COUNTER CURRENT FLOW

Gtd = $t_1 - t_3$

Ltd = $t_2 - t_4$

$$\Delta t_m = \frac{(t_1 - t_3) - (t_2 - t_4)}{\ln\left(\frac{t_1 - t_3}{t_2 - t_4}\right)}$$

b. PARALLEL FLOW

FIG. H-14.   Fluid temperatures in heat exchangers

dust particles, and other gases in the atmosphere absorb thermal radiation. This accounts for the envelope of warm air around the earth. Oxygen, O_2, and nitrogen, N_2, and other diatomic gases do not absorb applicable radiant energy in the normal temperature ranges. A body at a constant temperature does not stop radiating energy, but is receiving energy as rapidly as it is emitting energy. The earth, even though heated by the sun, is reradiating energy to outer space, day and night. The tendency on the earth is for all bodies to approach equilibrium, which is an example of entropy, a measure of the unavailable energy, which increases with time.

Thermal radiation may be considered as similar in response to that of light. The energy can be absorbed, α, reflected, ρ, or transmitted, τ.

$\alpha + \rho + \tau = 100\%$ of the energy, with the quantity of energy depending upon the area involved. Another term not to be confused with these is the emissivity, ϵ, of a surface. The emission depends upon the material, surface coating (oxide), temperature, surface roughness, etc. In general, the emissivity increases with the temperature of the body and is higher for nonmetals than metals.

The rate of thermal radiation depends upon the surface properties and the temperature of the body. A perfect radiation body is called a black body. It is both a good radiator, or emitter of heat, and a good absorber of heat. Black bodies are identified by a rough surface and black as contrasted to a polished, smooth surface. The rate of thermal absorption by a black body is

$$q = \sigma A T^4 \qquad \text{where } \alpha = 1$$

TABLE H.6

TYPICAL VALUES OF EMISSIVITY AND ABSORPTIVITY OF SURFACES

Surface	Emissivity, ϵ	Absorptivity of Solar Energy, α
Copper, polished, 65°F	0.03	0.26
Copper plate, thick oxide after heating, 77°F	0.78	
Iron, 100°F	0.30	
Oxidized iron, 212°F	0.74	0.74
18-8 Stainless steel, after heated, 400°F	0.44	
Tungsten, filaments, 6,000°F	0.35	
Red brick building, gypsum, 70°F	0.93	0.75
Aluminum foil, 212°F	0.087	
Oil paints, all colors, 212°F	0.93	
Aluminum polished plate, 500°F	0.04	0.26
Water, 32 to 212°F	0.96	0.93
Brick, red (irregular surface)	0.93	0.75

where q = rate of heat transfer, Btu per hr

$\quad$ = Stefan-Boltzmann constant, which is 0.173×10^{-8} (fph system) or 1.36×10^{-12} for q in cal per sec per sq cm (cgs system)

and with the temperature in °Kelvin

$\quad\quad\quad A$ = area, sq ft or sq cm

$\quad\quad\quad T$ = temperature absolute, °R or °K

Likewise, the emission of a black body would give the same rate of heat transfer, and would be

$$q = \sigma A T^4 \quad\quad \text{where } \epsilon = 1.$$

Typical values of the emissivity and absorptivity are given in Table H.6. Although the absorption of thermal energy varies with the wavelength of the energy, it is generally assumed for calculations that absorption is the same for all the wavelengths of energy being received. Such a body is called a gray body. Also, under such conditions, the emissivity, ϵ, may be used as the absorptivity. In such cases, the rate of heat transfer, q, Btu per hr, is

$$q = \sigma A \epsilon (T_1^4 - T_2^4) = 0.173 A \left[\frac{(T_1)^4}{100} - \frac{(T_2)^4}{100} \right]$$

An equivalent h-value is often obtained for radiation heat transfer so that overall values of heat transfer, U, might be calculated. The h-values for radiation, known as h_r may be calculated knowing the amount of radiative heat transfer and substituted appropriately in the equation to determine U and figured in the manner similar to that used for conduction and convection heat transfer.

$$h_r = \frac{q_r}{A(t_1 - t_2)}$$

$$= \frac{0.173 \, \epsilon \, [(0.01 T_1)^4 - (0.01 \, T_2)^4]}{T_1 - T_2}$$

For example, a material with an emissivity of 1 with a radiating surface of 1,000°F and absorbing surface at 200°F will have an $h_r = 9$ Btu per hr sq ft °F.

Standard equations for heat transfer by radiation are as follows:

(1) A body radiating to the atmosphere (either gaining heat during the day or losing heat at night)

$$q = \epsilon \sigma A (T_1^4 - T_2^4)$$

(2) Between parallel plates

$$q = \frac{\epsilon_1 \, \epsilon_2 \sigma A}{\epsilon_1 + \epsilon_2 - \epsilon_1 \epsilon_2} \quad (T_1^4 - T_2^4)$$

(3) Between concentric spheres or cylinders (long)

$$q = \frac{A_1 \sigma (T_1^4 - T_2^4)}{\dfrac{1}{\epsilon_1} + \dfrac{A_1}{A_2}\left(\dfrac{1 - \epsilon_2}{\epsilon_2}\right)}$$

Radiant heating is being applied in the food industry for heating, pasteurizing, sterilizing, or maintaining the temperature of heated foods. Radiant cooling will be applied to a greater extent in the future for cooling dry powder and prepared foods as these leave heating chambers, and where rapid cooling is desired. The same laws govern determination of the cooling rates as for the heating rate.

Cross-references: *Heat; Heat Exchangers; Heat and Mass Transfer; Insulation.*

HEATING SYSTEMS FOR HTST

Heat for the HTST unit may be supplied from hot water, steam, or electricity. The final carrier of the heat is usually hot water which is circulated over the plates. Heating systems may be classified as follows.

(1) *Hot water circulating unit:* Steam is condensed in water, thus heating it. The steam may be discharged between two concentric cones or into the water from nozzles. The water is circulated around the plates for heating the product.

(2) *Enclosed system:* Water is heated as it passes through tubes of a shell and tube heat exchanger. Steam is not added directly to the water, but is added to the shell surrounding the tubes. Indirect heat transfer results. Provisions must be made for removing the condensate from the heat exchanger.

(3) *Combination hot water and cleaning unit:* This unit heats water for pasteurization and provides a solution tank for circulation cleaning. Nozzles mix steam with hot water.

(4) *Vapor:* Steam is placed directly into the water circuit of the plate heat exchanger. Sufficient vacuum is maintained for desired operating conditions.

(5) *Electric heating:* Water is heated with an electric resistance element. The water is circulated over the plates for heating the product. This differs from the direct heating of the product with electricity as discussed previously.

Heating or Preheating Equipment

The tubular and plate heat exchangers are the most commonly used devices to preheat milk before a given process or before pasteurization. The tubular heat exchanger may be (1) barrel or box type (in which water surrounds the tubes through which the product is passed, and the water is heated by steam in the same chamber), or (2) double tube design, with the internal tube used for the product being heated. The heating medium is pumped through the unit around the internal tube and provides more positive control than the barrel or box type. Low pressure steam, as well as hot water, might be used for heating. The tubular heat exchanger of the double tube design is particularly useful for regeneration systems in which the hot product leaving the pasteurizer (usually batch) is placed between the two tubes, with the incoming cold product moved through the internal tube.

Cooling of Milk

Coolers consist of the tubular internal tube type, plate units, or surface tubular coolers. The first two were discussed previously. The surface cooler of the tubular type consists of horizontal heat exchange surfaces of stainless steel or tinned copper over which the product flows. As a thin film passes over the tube, the product is cooled. The cabinet cooler is made up of a series of two or more banks of surface coolers of the tubular type. The cabinet cooler, sometimes called a fan type cooler is commonly used in dairy plants for cooling the product immediately after pasteurization and before bottling. There is less effect on the cream line with the surface cooler as compared with other coolers, but with the surface equipment the product contacts the surrounding atmosphere of the plant and the milk might become contaminated.

Cooling might be done with the incoming cold product, water, sweet water, brine, or refrigeration. In some surface coolers, the top of the cooler does the first part of the cooling with water, with the remainder of the cooling by brine, sweet water, or direct expansion refrigeration. The selection of the method of cooling depends almost entirely on the economics involved, the cost of utilities, refrigeration, water, electricity, and the cost of providing the heat exchanger surface. The water normally flows counter to the direction of the flow of product across the heat exchanger, and, more specifically cross flow results. It is estimated that the film thickness over the surface heat exchanger is 0.01 in.

Double Tube Heat Exchanger

Parallel Flow.—A parallel flow heater of a double tube type consists of a small inner tube or pipe, surrounded by a larger one, with the milk flowing through the inner tube and with hot water on the outside. The temperature of the milk rises while that of the water falls, the tendency being for both to approach the same temperature (Fig. H.14). Since the temperature difference between the two liquids rapidly diminishes, it is obvious that a temperature difference is soon reached where an excessively large heating surface is required for a small transfer of heat. If it is intended to utilize only a relatively small part of the available temperature difference, this arrangement may be used to advantage because less heating surface is required to produce the same results in parallel flow as in some other arrangements. With milk entering at 50°F and leaving 145°F and water entering at 180°F and leaving at 150°F, the mean temperature difference is 38.36°F. The log mean temperature difference is used if the temperature difference at one end of the heat exchanger is more than twice the other end. There is about 5% heat loss from the outside tube, due mainly to radiation.

Counter Flow.—Where double tubes are used the milk is in the inside tube, except for regenerators. More water is circulated than milk. In the counter current type it is possible to economize on hot water to offset the large heating surface required. In the parallel current unit, the greatest temperature difference always occurs at the entrance to the apparatus, and the heating medium must always leave at a temperature higher than the highest temperature of the liquid being heated (Fig. H.14). Therefore it follows that much more heating medium must be used for parallel flow than with counter flow apparatus. The log mean temperature difference is used as before.

Surface Cooler.—An internal velocity of 150 fpm for circulation of brine or cold water gives satisfactory results. There is natural circulation of air over the surface of warm milk and a velocity of 3 fps of milk over the surface by gravity flow.

The surface cooler might be used as a regenerator. Hot milk from the pasteurizer enters the tube at the bottom and passes up through the unit and out at the top. The cold milk flows down and over the outer surface and is caught below. With constant and continuous flow and the quantity over the outer surface and into the tubes equal, a *U*-value of 186 is obtained with the milk inside the tubes moving at 56 fpm and over the other surface at 30 fpm. The total rise in temperature of the milk is from 64° to 162°F. The temperature of the milk inside the tubes drops from 162° to 90°F, and the temperature of the milk passing over the outer surface increases from 64° to 136°F. The total saving in heating and cooling by the use of the regenerative principle for a surface heat exchanger amounts to 65.3%.

Hot Water Heaters.—Large quantities of hot water are needed in the food industry, for washing, and for processing. Many plants have central hot water systems using a large indirect heater (Fig. H.15). This is a very satisfactory system, however care must be taken to occasionally remove scale deposits on the heater tubes.

The principal care of steam injection water heaters is to see that scale deposits do not build up. Also, temperature controllers and steam traps must be properly serviced.

Other plants use a steam and water mixing value to give hot water at the point of use. Figure H.16 shows a valve of this type. Another widely used hot water heater is shown in Fig. H.17. This device uses steam injection into a heating tube in which water is circulated by a pump and the temperature automatically controlled.

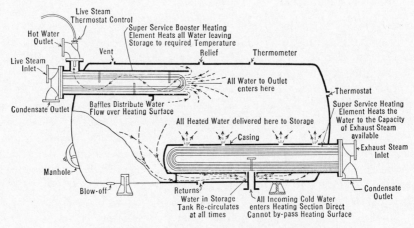

Fig. H-15.   Water heater and storage tank

A steam injection hot water heater similar to Fig. H.17 is used with a high-temperature short-time pasteurizer. This is a very common hookup.

The advantages of direct steam injection are (1) it is quick, (2) there are no heat transfer surfaces to be kept clean, and (3) the unit is relatively inexpensive. In the direct steam injection unit the condensate from steam is mixed with the circulating hot water. Usually a float valve is used to drain the surplus water into the condenser from the system.

To obtain accurate temperature control on steam injection heaters, it is necessary to balance the steam supply pressure and orifice with the amount of heat needed by the system. Excessive steam pressure combined with a large orifice makes temperature control very erratic. In order to obtain water temperatures above 212°F, it is necessary that the hot water system be under sufficient pressure to prevent flashing of steam.

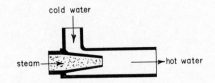

Fɪɢ. H-16.   Steam and water mixing valve

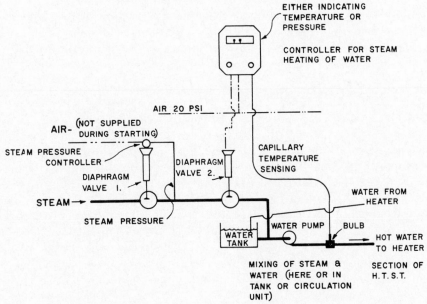

Courtesy of St. Regis Corp.

Diaphragm Valve 1. Air-to-close for maintaining uniform
steam pressure (direct acting)
Diaphragm Valve 2. Air-to-close for supplying steam to
water being pumped to heater

Fɪɢ. H-17.   A pressure tube type pump circulated water heater and mixer

The heating water is usually circulated at a rate of from 2 to 4 times the flow rate of the product heated.

To find the flow and temperature relationship

$$\text{Gpm} = \frac{\text{Btu per min to be transferred}}{8.34 \times (T_1 - T_2) \times \text{efficiency}}$$

where T_1 = high temperature of water (inlet)
    T_2 = low temperature of water (outlet)
efficiency = 90–95%

To find the pounds of steam required

$$\text{Pounds of steam at given pressure} = \frac{\text{total Btu needed (include losses)}}{H(t) - H(L)}$$

where $H(t)$ = total heat of the steam at working pressure
   $H(L)$ = heat of liquid of steam at working pressure

Cross-references: *Controllers; Cooling Milk; Heat Exchangers; HTST Pasteurization; Steam.*

HIGH-TEMPERATURE SHORT-TIME

The forerunner of high-temperature short-time pasteurization was the electrical conductivity method of heating milk for pasteurization. Originally the holder method at 143°F for 30 min predominated. With the electric method, milk could be treated continuously at 160°F for 15 sec. Heating of milk by conduction of electricity was developed in the 1920's. The electric conductivity method is seldom used.

Electric Conduction Pasteurization

The preheated milk is pumped through a heating chamber, then through a holding chamber and then cooled over a surface heat exchanger in the system. The pump is adjusted to provide the proper flow, so the product is in the holding chamber 15 sec or more. Approximately 45 sec is required for product to pass through the whole unit. The heating chamber is rectangular, with the milk passing vertically between two opposite walls of carbon electrodes. The other two walls are made of glass or other insulating material. The heating chamber is heated with alternating current with a noninductive load of 15 kw. A contactor controls the power supply to the electrodes to maintain a temperature above 160° ± ¹/₂°F. If the temperature of the milk drops below 160°F the pump stops, and gravity returns the milk to the supply tank. The temperature can be controlled by (1) keeping flow constant and adjusting the voltage of the plates, (2) keeping voltage constant and varying the milk supply, and (3) a combination of the two.

At the outlet of the holding chamber is a temperature recording instrument giving the temperature of the milk at any time. The milk passes out of the holding chamber into a spreader to be cooled over surface coils. In the final stage of the cooling, brine or refrigeration is used for cooling the product to bottling temperature.

A common unit handling 100 gal. per hr is generally used by dealers selling 1,200 qt per day. A unit occupies a space of 2.5 by 7 ft. A single unit uses approximately

15 kwh for each 100 gal. of milk pasteurized. The electrical efficiency is 95 to 98%. The heating chamber is cooled by water which moves over the outer surfaces. This was sometimes known as the "Electro-pure process."

H.T.S.T. Pasteurizer

The high-temperature short-time (HTST) continuous pasteurizer provides a heat treatment of not less than 161°F for not less than 15 sec, without impairing the quality of product. The equipment encountered in usual order: float tank, cold milk entering regenerator, warm milk leaving regenerator, timing pump, homogenizer, heater, holder, flow diversion valve (FDV), regenerator (pasteurized milk side), and cooler (Fig. H.18). Cooling may be by water, brine, or direct refrigeration. There are many variations in methods of assembling the components.

Plates

The plate heat exchanger is commonly used for high-temperature short-time (HTST) units, especially for temperatures of heating below the boiling point. It is compact, simple, easily cleaned, and easily inspected. Plates may be used for heating, cooling, regeneration, and holding. These plates are supported in a press between a terminal block for each section for heating and cooling. The heat moves from the warm to cold medium through stainless steel plates. The plates are constructed of 18-8 stainless steel often with an electro-polish finish. Type 304 is most commonly used, with some manufacturers using type 316, particularly where corrosion may be severe. A 20 gage thickness is used for medium-sized units. Nearly $1/8$ in. space is maintained between the plates by a nonabsorbent rubber gasket or seal vulcanized to the stainless steel. The vulcanized gasket can be repaired at the factory if necessary. The plates are tightened into place with a jack or screw device on the frame. Plates are normally mounted vertically in banks. The recent trend is to have the long edge of the plate in an up-down position rather than in a horizontal position to save space. The plates are numbered and must be properly assembled. The

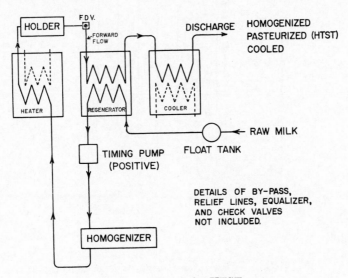

Fig. H-18.   Circuit for HTST system

plates are designed to provide uniform, but not excessive turbulent flow of products and rapid heat transfer. Raised sections in the plate in the form of knobs, diamonds, and channels help provide the turbulent action required. Greater capacity is secured by adding more plates.

Approximately 2.5 to 4 times the quantity of product is circulated for cooling a product from 80° to 40°F using a coolant at 34°F. For heating from 40° to 140°F with 150°F hot water, from 4 to 6 times as much heating fluid is circulated as product. For heating, the inlet hot water is normally only about 2° to 3°F above the highest temperature to which the product is to be heated to avoid burn-on.

For proper operation the plates should (1) be sealed tightly so there is no dripping, (2) be designed so that all of the plate is utilized for heat transfer, (3) allow product to be drained from the heat exchanger plates without opening of the plates, and (4) provide venting so that air is eliminated during startup and operation.

Ports are provided in appropriate top and bottom locations of the plates to permit flow of the product and heating or cooling medium without mixing (Fig. H.19).

Installation of Plate Heat Exchangers

Clearance.—From 18 to 24 in. should be provided around the equipment unit for clearance. Normally five times the floor area of the unit is required for space around the unit and aisle space associated with the particular piece of equipment.

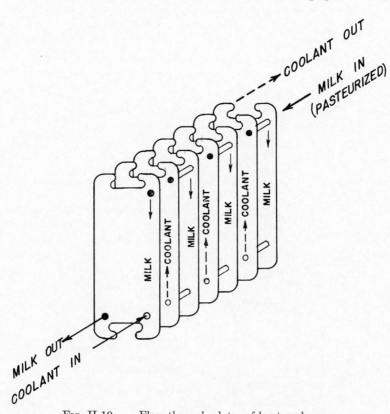

Fɪɢ. H-19.   Flow through plates of heat exchanger

Utilities.—The placement of the unit should consider the proximity of steam, water, electricity, and air supply. A steam strainer should be placed in the line ahead of the manual valve to control the steam supply. The air supply should be clean with provisions for removing condensate. The heating and circulating units should be placed near the plate heat exchanger, so that short connections with low pipe friction will result.

Pressure.—Various plate heat exchangers have been designed for different maximum pressures. Plate heat exchangers for high-temperature short-time pasteurization will normally withstand pressures of up to 200 psi for utilities and products. A pressure relief valve should be supplied with positive pumps to assure that maximum pressure is not exceeded.

Piping.—Connections to the press should be made with flexible piping except those to the fixed head. For sanitary piping, there should be a 90° bend to the unit to provide for expansion and contraction during heating and cooling.

Gaskets.—Before closing the press of plates, the plates should be wetted with cold water, which serves to lubricate the plates and lengthens the life of the gaskets. When not in use the pressure on the plates should be released to relieve the pressure on the gaskets.

Filter

Some HTST units use a filter cloth for removing materials from the milk during its passage through the unit. The filter cloth is placed over a cylindrical sleeve to provide a large surface area for filtration. The pressure on the pump will indicate the extent of clogging. Two filters, one in operation at a time, can be utilized.

Regeneration

The reuse of the heat added for heating is known as heat regeneration. Regeneration is particularly economical for pasteurization equipment. In one type of heat regenerator, the cold incoming product is partially heated with the hot outgoing product. Thus, the incoming product requires less additional heat for the temperature to be raised; and the outgoing product requires less cooling for the temperature to be lowered. The greater the reuse of heat, the greater is both the heating and cooling efficiency. The equipment devoted to this function is known as the heat regenerator.

Heat regeneration is usually done with a plate, surface, or tubular heat exchanger. The primary consideration in the hookup is to be sure the pasteurized product cannot become contaminated. This is done by having (1) pasteurized product at a higher pressure than raw product in case leaks occur in the heat exchanger, and (2) pasteurized product protected from contamination from other sources. Raw milk is pulled through the heat exchanger and pasteurized milk pushed (at a higher pressure) through the heat exchanger to prevent contamination.

The most used high-temperature short-time pasteurization unit is constructed of plate heat exchangers and is particularly well-suited for continuous regeneration.

In using milk at 40°F to be pasteurized at 165°F and then cooled to 40°F, the following temperatures are obtained with 80% regeneration. Thus, $0.80 \times (165° - 40°) + 40° = 140°F$ temperature at the regenerator. Heat must be added to increase the temperature by 25°F to the pasteurization temperature. On the opposite side of the heat exchanger, the milk is cooled from 165° to 65°F with the remainder of the cooling by refrigeration.

The heat regenerators described are of the milk-to-milk type. Although less prominent, another heat transfer fluid can be used in between, such as water in a milk-to-water-to-milk. The heat transfer fluid, water, must be kept at higher pressure than the raw milk. Milk-to-water-to-milk regenerators are less efficient, 65% versus 80%, and more costly than milk-to-milk regenerators.

Milk-to-milk regenerators may be of the following types: (1) both sides closed to the atmosphere, (2) only raw milk open to the atmosphere, (3) only pasteurized milk open to the atmosphere, and (4) both sides open to the atmosphere.

Types (1) and (2) provide acceptable systems whereby the pasteurized product can be maintained at a higher pressure than raw milk. Type (3) regenerators should be installed and operated so that the raw milk side of the regenerator will be at a pressure below atmospheric pressure. Type (4) regenerators may not be used because the pasteurized product cannot be at a greater pressure than the raw milk side.

The *holder* pasteurization method requires a separate piece of equipment (heat exchanger) for heat regeneration. The heat regenerator is 70 to 80% efficient. Only about 1% heat loss occurs by convection and radiation to the atmosphere from the system. Thus, raw milk entering the heat regenerator at 40°F will be heated to about 120°F; the remainder of the heat supply will be furnished by hot water; and pasteurized milk at 143°F will be cooled to 63°F. Because of the 30 min holding period, heat regeneration is best incorporated into the pasteurizing operation if there are at least four holding vats. Thus, as hot milk is removed from one vat, it is used to heat cold milk for the next vat. Whether the use of the heat regenerators is economical depends on the value of utilities saved as compared to the cost of equipment. The economics of each installation must be determined separately.

Holders

The holder ensures that the product is held for a specified time, not less than 15 sec, if heated to 161°F or more. The time of 15 sec measures the most rapidly moving particle passing through the holder, tube, pipe, or plates. For a particular holder, timing is based on the timing pump flow rate. The temperature is determined at the discharge of the holder. The product moves to the flow diversion valve when used, and if up to the required temperature, passes to the regenerator section.

A tube, pipe, or series of plates, as a part of the HTST system located on the plate supports, may be used for the holder. The tube or pipe is not normally insulated and the heat loss causes a drop in product temperature less than 1°F. In some units, the holding tube is located in an air-insulated chamber in the control panel of the HTST unit. The holder may be long with small diameter, or relatively short with a large diameter.

There must be no other passage for the milk except through the holder. The design must be such that all of the sections must be installed before the system will operate. The tube or pipe must slope upward in the direction of milk flow so that it will not trap air.

Holding Time

The holding time of a continuous flow pasteurization system must be checked (1) upon installation; (2) whenever the seal is broken on the pump; (3) after replacement of belt, motor, or pump; (4) quarterly, if a variable speed pump is used (because speedup may occur through wear of belts on the change of speed device); and (5) semiannually, according to the U.S. Public Health Requirements. The design should be such that wear on the belts or parts will cause a slow down in milk flow. If belts do wear and there is an increase in product flow, the wear must be such that an excessive amount of product will not be pumped through the holder tube within the six months required inspection time.

Whether or not auxiliary equipment is operated during the time of checking, the holding time of the unit depends on its effect on the flow rate. The maximum rate of flow that can possibly be obtained with the system is necessary during checking the holding time. If a homogenizer is used, the valves are left open during determination of the holding time. Tests should be made with the pump at the maximum flow rate which can be obtained. The holding time must hold for either forward or diverted flow.

Determining Holding Time

The holding time in a given installation may be determined by injecting a sodium chloride solution of 10 ppm into one end of the holder and determining the time until a set of electrodes at the discharge end of the holder detect the passing of the solution. Commercial testing equipment is available for carrying out this procedure. Tests are normally run with water and converted to milk flow equivalent, on either an equal volume or equal weight basis. Water is pumped into a can or a tank of known volume or known weight and after several readings the values are averaged. The same pumping procedure is used for milk flow.

$$\text{The holding time for milk} = \frac{T \times M_v}{W_v} = \frac{T \times M_w \times 1.032}{W_w}$$
$$\text{(by volume)} \quad \text{(by weight)}$$

where T = average holding time for water, determined by salt

M_v = average time required to deliver a measured volume of milk

M_w = average time required to deliver a weighed quantity of milk

W_v = average time required to deliver an equal volume of water

W_w = average time required to deliver an equal weight of water

If the computed holding time is below the minimum required, the speed at the timing pump should be decreased and the timing test repeated until a satisfactory holding time is obtained (see detailed requirements for assuring proper holding time with auxiliary apparatus, using clarifier, homogenizer, etc.).

A dye, methylene blue, may be injected in the inlet of the holder. Samples are taken at the end of 10, 11, 12, 13, 14, 15, 16, and 17 sec from the outlet of the holder with the holding time determined by the presence of dye in the samples.

The holding time should be determined in diverted flow as well as forward flow. The resistance to flow may be less in diverted flow, thus reducing the holding time for some pumps and arrangements. A resistance orifice in the diverted line is often used.

Cold pasteurized milk can be injected into the inlet of the holder. When the cold milk reaches the outlet of the holder, the flow diversion valve should divert. The holding time can be determined with a stop watch.

Flow of Product Through the Holding Tube

As a fluid moves through a circular cross section, as milk through a holding tube, laminar or turbulent flow occurs. With laminar flow, the product flow throughout the cross section of the tube is along parallel planes. With turbulent flow there is considerable mixing of the product throughout the cross section. In both cases, however, the maximum velocity is in the center of the stream, with a lower velocity of the fluid nearer the wall. The layer of fluid or film next to the tube is practically stationary. The type of flow is determined by Reynold's number, Re, which is equal to $DV\rho,/\mu$ where D is the diameter of the tube, ft; V, the average velocity, ft per sec; ρ the density of the fluid, lb per cu ft; and μ the viscosity, lb per ft sec. If Reynold's number is less than 2,000, the flow is laminar; if above 3,000, turbulent. Between the two values flow is in a transitional zone. The viscosity of milk varies with the temperature and effect of heat on its constituents. The viscosity of milk at 160°F is nearly the same as water at 60°F. As the temperature is lowered, the viscosity increases. At high temperatures, the constituents may clump causing an increase in viscosity.

The viscosity of milk and other products is often given in centipoise. To convert centipoise to lb per ft sec, divide by 1,488. If the volume of flow in gallons per minute is known, the velocity of flow V, ft per sec, is 0.408 gpm/d^2 where d is the inside diameter of the tube in inches.

The average velocity in laminar flow is $1/2$ of the maximum velocity, which occurs at the center. The average velocity in turbulent flow approaches 0.8 of the maximum velocity as the velocity is increased.

A typical installation might have a 2.5 in. diam holding tube with a flow rate of 1,800 gph of milk at 165°F and viscosity of 1 centipoise. Then

$$V = \frac{(0.408)\,(1,800)}{(2.5)^2} = 1.2 \text{ ft per sec}$$

$$Re = \frac{DV\rho}{\mu} = \frac{\left(\dfrac{2.5}{12}\right)(1.2)\,(62.4)}{1/1,488} = 22,000 \text{ (which is turbulent flow)}$$

Holding tubes usually carry milk in turbulent flow.

One method of determining the holding time of a continuous pasteurizer is to inject a salt solution into the holding tube and determine the time for the salt to traverse the tube. As mentioned previously, the product does not move uniformly. The maximum velocity is at the center of the tube. Therefore, to assure proper holding, the holding time is determined on the basis of the maximum velocity. The product around the edge of the tube moves less rapidly through the tube and has a greater holding time. Thus, overholding of a part of the product occurs in the holding tube. As the average velocity approaches the maximum velocity, less overholding will occur. With an increase in Reynold's number, there will be less overholding of the product. The Reynold's number is increased by increasing the velocity of flow in a given tube or by decreasing the diameter of tube (thus increasing velocity) for a particular flow rate. Thus, to minimize overholding the smallest practical holding tube should be used.

Metering Pump (Timing) and Drive

A positive pump is often used as a timing device for a high-temperature short-time unit. The metering pump is normally located so that the milk is heated in the regenerator first, then the milk goes to the pump and then to the other heater, in a system with the milk-to-milk regenerator. A rotary positive pump or a homogenizer is used. The homogenizer may be used as a timing pump (Fig. H.20).

In many European countries the centrifugal pump is used with a flow control device to assure constant output. Two rotary vane wheels made of stainless steel, rubber, or plastic are used for the rotary positive pump to force the product through the pasteurizer at a nearly uniform rate regardless of head. The capacity of a pump decreases at a constant head as the rotary lobes become worn. As the capacity tends to decrease with wear, the holding time will become greater so that the minimum standards for pasteurization are still met. Where the pump is used for two flow rates, and a speed change device utilized, wear of belts may cause an increase in flow rate. The pump is sealed at the proper maximum flow setting, and rechecked at least every 6 months, or every 3 months for a pump with a variable speed drive. The rotary parts are made of hardened stainless steel of the 400 series in order to obtain longer wearing properties, but are easily chipped through handling, and corroded by contact with chlorine solutions. Parts must be handled carefully to avoid damage. During operation, butterfat from the milk lubricates the rotary parts. The pump should not be operated excessively without product or with cleaning solution only.

The operating specifications of a pump include flow rate, depending on capacity, and head in psi or ft, depending on the resistance of flow. A typical 20,000 lb/hr plate high-temperature short-time pasteurizer will have a head of 100 ft. The fluid or theoretical horsepower is equal to

$$\text{Fluid hp} = \frac{(\text{lb per min}) \ (\text{ft of head})}{33,000}$$

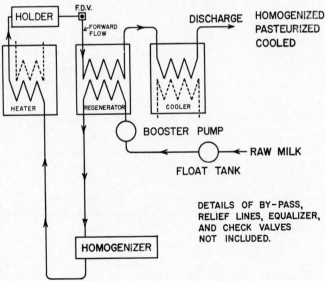

Fig. H-20.   Homogenizer used as a timing pump for HTST pasteurization

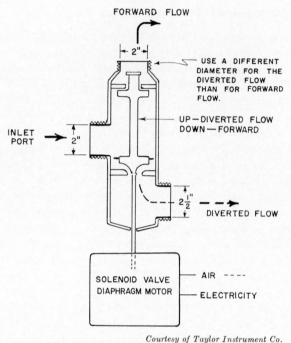

FORWARD FLOW

2"

USE A DIFFERENT
DIAMETER FOR THE
DIVERTED FLOW
THAN FOR FORWARD
FLOW.

UP—DIVERTED FLOW
DOWN—FORWARD

INLET
PORT

2"

$2\frac{1}{2}''$

DIVERTED FLOW

SOLENOID VALVE
DIAPHRAGM MOTOR

AIR ----

ELECTRICITY

Courtesy of Taylor Instrument Co.

Fig. H-21.   Flow diversion valve

The fluid horsepower should be multiplied by 1.5 to 3 to get the motor horsepower for operating the pump.   Induction motors are normally used.

A particular high-temperature short-time pasteurizer may be used for two products such as fluid milk and cream.   A speed change is provided for varying the output of the positive pump.   The speed change commonly used is based on changing the sheave spacing, and thereby the diameter of the pulleys between the motor and the pump.

The pump which produces flow in the unit must be placed ahead or upstream from the holder.   The design of the high-temperature short-time plate unit must be such that the pasteurized milk on one side of the regenerator is at a higher pressure, normally 1 psi, than the milk or water which is not pasteurized on the opposite of the plate.   A device such as a check valve is placed between the pasteurized milk inlet and regenerator to maintain milk between the plates and to keep pressure on the pasteurized product.   A sanitary liquid level switch or a pressure switch can be connected with the metering pump to prevent the pump from starting unless the level of the milk is maintained in the plate.   When the unit is shut down, milk should drain freely back to the raw milk supply tank when the raw milk line is disconnected.

When a flow diversion valve is not used, the pump motor can be connected to a stop-go switch which permits pumping of the product only after it has been heated to the proper temperature.

Centrifugal Pump

Some high-temperature systems use a centrifugal pump to move the product through the plate heat exchanger.   The output of a centrifugal pump decreases with an increase in head. To maintain a uniform head on the centrifugal so that uniform flow is maintained, a flow control valve has been developed. The flow controller is placed on the discharge side of the centrifugal pump which handles raw milk. The flow controller consists of a series of plungers mounted in a vertical tube with valve guides and ports to maintain a uniform flow despite a change in head of the external system (not including the controller).

Booster Pump

The booster pump is usually a centrifugal pump used to reduce the suction (increase the pressure) on the intake side of the metering or timing pump, be it a positive pump or homogenizer (see Fig. H.20). The booster pump is not normally located between the raw milk supply tank and the raw milk inlet to the regenerator, unless it

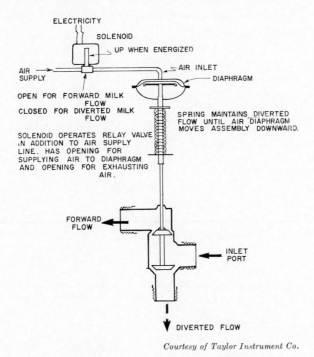

Courtesy of Taylor Instrument Co.

Fig. H-22.   Diversion valve and control

can operate only when milk is flowing through the pasteurized milk side of the regenerator and when the pressure of the pasteurized product is higher than the maximum pressure produced by the pump. This can be accomplished by connecting the electrical wiring so that the booster pump cannot operate unless (1) the metering pump is operating, (2) the flow diversion is in forward flow, and (3) the pressure switch on pasteurized product is 1 psi or more above maximum booster pump pressure.

The booster pump should not operate during either shutdowns or at the beginning of a run. Booster pumps are widely used on the intake side when a homogenizer is used for a timing pump. The purpose of the booster pump is to avoid low suction pressures on the intake of the homogenizer.

Flow Diversion Valve

The flow diversion valve directs the product through the units if pasteurized, or diverts the flow so as to pass through the system again if not pasteurized (Fig. H.21 and H.22). The flow diversion valve is controlled by the safety-thermal-limit recorder. If failure of electrical power, air, or controls occurs, the valve will fail "safe," that is, flow is diverted back to the float or balance tank. If the valve moves too slowly, the air in the valve mechanism within the solenoid should be checked. The milk to the inlet opening of the valve comes from the holder (tube or plate). When the product is not held above the minimum temperature a fluctuation in the flow division recurs. There are several possible causes for the flow fluctuation: (1) not enough margin of temperature, i.e., the temperature may not be enough above the minimum so that small fluctuations cause the temperature to drop below the minimum, (2) air present in water circulation system so that insufficient heat is supplied to maintain the temperature (low water), and (3) air enters the milk stream, thus decreasing the rate of heat transfer to the product.

If the flow diversion valve is improperly assembled, the plug does not seat properly; if the milk is at the proper temperature a signal is sent through the controller to a microswitch which activates an electrical solenoid which directs air to a diaphragm which in turn moves the stem, opening and closing appropriate valves for milk to move in forward flow.

An opening, known as leak detector valve, may be incorporated in the housing of the flow diversion valve between the diverted flow outlet port and the flow diversion valve and seat. This detector may be used to determine if the valve is leaking during forward flow.

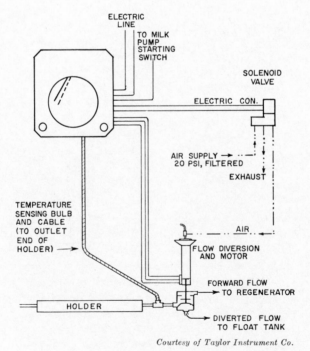

Courtesy of Taylor Instrument Co.

Fɪɢ. H-23.   Safety thermal limit recorder-controller

Milk Pump Stops

The flow diversion valve provides one method of stopping the flow of improperly pasteurized milk. The flow of milk can also be stopped with pump-stops which automatically stop the milk-pump motors if the product temperature drops below the desired level, and starts the pump when the proper temperature is reached.

Safety-Thermal-Limit Recorder-Controller

The safety-thermal-limit recorder-controller (Fig. H.23) is the major development responsible for control of the high-temperature short-time system (Fig. H.26). This part contains a Bourdon-type element for transmitting the pressure of the vapor or liquid in the capillary tube connected to the temperature sensing element. A pen records the corresponding temperature on a chart. Thus, the unit indicates, records, and controls.

The recorder-controller contains a recording thermometer which records the temperature on charts to give the temperature of the milk leaving the holder tube. The charts may be circular or strip type. The recording thermometer should not read higher than the indicating thermometer which must be at the same location or slightly upstream from the bulb of the recording thermometer. A temperature of the indicating thermometer must be written on the chart some time during the daily operation. The time when the milk flow is in forward flow or diverted flow position is also marked on the chart, usually along the edge. The recorder-controller controls the flow diversion valve to forward- or diverted-flow according to the temperature sensed at the discharge of the holder. An electrical signal to a solenoid valve controls the compressed air supply to the air diaphragm motor which directs the flow of the milk. In addition, a signal is sent to a pen to record forward or diverted flow on the chart. The temperature at which the flow is cut-in or cut-out must be determined daily and recorded on the chart. The recorder-controller indicates forward flow by a green light or diverted flow by a red light. It combines proper operation of the flow diversion valve and steam controller for proper heating of the water.

Circular charts should cover a maximum of 12 hr per chart, and should not be used more than once. The chart drive may be electric or spring driven. The temperature ranges are from $100°$ to $200°F$ in $1°F$ intervals from $100°$ to $165°F$. The higher temperature is to the outside of the circular chart where it is easier to read. The chart should contain the appropriate temperatures; operator's notes for checking the temperature; and operation of flow diversion valve. The chart is an official record and is utilized by health and inspection personnel as well as a plant quality control personnel. The chart must be preserved for three months. Strip charts will be used more in the future because of the simplicity and convenience.

The recorder-contoller for the high-temperature short-time unit must operate accurately and rapidly. The accuracy can be checked by immersing the sensing bulb in a milk can along with a test thermometer and heating with steam while comparing the temperature of the two units. Test thermometers are normally of a partial immersion type of about 4 in. and divided into $1/5°$ of $1°$ divisions depending upon the range. The recorder-controller thermometric lag over 63.2% of the range of operation from room temperature to pasteurization temperature must occur in 5 sec or less. The response time, that is the time between cut-out and diverting of flow of the product, should not exceed 1 sec.

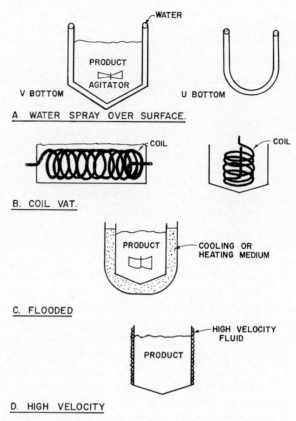

FIG. H-24.   Types of batch pasteurization units

Cooling Section

The final cooling may be done in a section of the HTST unit.   The cooling section may be cooled using cold water, brine, or direct expansion refrigeration.   Final cooling might also be carried out on a surface cooler, often known as a cabinet cooler.   Various coolants may be used for the surface cooler.

Efficiency

The so-called "efficiency" of a high-temperature short-time system is defined as the actual time required for the milk to pass through the holder divided by the theoretical time to pass based on maximum velocity, multiplied by 100%.   It might be more easily visualized as the average velocity divided by the maximum velocity, multiplied by 100%.   A preferred term describing this relationship is effectiveness of the holding tube.

Reference

HALL, C. W., and TROUT, G. M.   1968.   Milk Pasteurization.   AVI Publishing Co., Westport, Conn.

Cross-references: *Clarifiers; Controllers; Fluid Flow; Friction; Heat Exchangers; Heating Systems for HTST; Homogenizers; U.H.T. Systems.*

HOLDING METHODS OF PASTEURIZATION

Batch Holder Pasteurizers

In batch holding systems, heating is done indirectly. The heat moves through a metal wall into the product. The speed of heating or cooling is especially important if an appreciable portion of the heating or cooling is done in the pasteurization vat (Fig. H.24). The pasteurizing vat is often used for pasteurization only or for only a slight amount of heating, so that the vat can be used for a greater capacity during a given time. Agitation must not be so rapid that whipping or churning is caused. The outside of the tank is usually insulated to prevent excessive heat loss. From 3 to 5 tanks may be connected so that continuous processing may occur, although this is seldom used nowadays.

Water Spray Over Wall

In the film heat transfer units, a film of water is sprayed from a perforated pipe over the surface of the tank holding the product. The product is agitated. A rapidly moving continuous film of water provides rapid heat transfer. With a spray unit, milk can be heated from 50° to 143°F in 25 min using hot water at 160°F. Hot water is moved by a $1/4$ hp motor for the pump on a 150 gal. spray vat. Agitation is accomplished by a $1/4$ hp motor on a 150 gal. tank at a speed of 45 to 50 rpm. The main advantage to the water spray method of heat exchange is that quicker control is provided than with most methods which can be controlled either manually or automatically. The U-value of a water spray heat exchanger is approximately $U = 200$ Btu per hr sq ft °F.

Coil Vat

With the coil vat the heating or cooling medium is pumped through a coil which may be in either a horizontal or a vertical position. The coil is turned through the product. The turning coil provides agitation to the product, but additional agitation may be necessary. The coils and walls of the tank may be constructed of tinned copper. However, in recent years, stainless steel has been used. Regardless of the material of construction, the sides and bottom of the outer shell of the tank include 2 to 3 in. of insulation. About 1 hp is required for turning the coil for tank capacities up to 500 gal. A speed of 130 rpm is common for milk, and other speeds are available for other products. Approximately $2/3$ of the vat capacity is required to cover the coil in a horizontal tank. Coils are difficult to clean, and therefore have not been used as much in recent years as in the past. Steam may be used for heating water, and with appropriate piping the steam may be used for circulating the hot water. The heat transfer coefficient is $U = 200$ Btu per hr sq ft °F, with water moving through the coils at about 100 fpm.

Flooded Tank

The heating or cooling medium (water, steam, brine, etc.) is placed around the container holding the product in the flooded tank system. Because of the difficulty of controlling temperature, the method is not in common use. To obtain higher heat transfer rates, the water may be circulated rapidly. For gravity heating, $U = 200$ Btu per hr sq ft °F, and with an agitator, $U = 300$ Btu per hr sq ft °F.

High Velocity Liquid

Channels or pipes surrounding the tank direct the heat exchange medium at high velocity over the outside surface of the tank. The pump horsepower is greater for moving the cooling or heating medium at a high velocity than for agitating the fluid in other types.

Controls on Batch Pasteurizers

A self-acting regulator controls the admission of steam to the heating water to within $\pm \frac{1}{4}$ °F of the desired temperature, to avoid over- or underheating. When the product reaches the desired pasteurization temperature, a control automatically shuts off the motor which drives the hot water pump. A recording thermometer with chart and standard thermometer for a check must also be provided.

Accessories to Vat to Assure Pasteurization

Every particle of product must be uniformly subjected to no less than 143°F for not less than 30 min without damage to the product and without contamination from the outside. It must be considered that the foam is usually colder than the milk during pasteurization. To assure pasteurization, the following accessories are incorporated.

Air Space or Foam Heater.—The space above the product in the vat should be given the same treatment as the product to avoid contamination. An air space thermometer should be provided so that the space is at least 5°F warmer than the milk. Pipes with $\frac{1}{8}$ in. diam openings to release steam are used with traps preceding the outlet. The trap helps avoid excess addition of water. A screen is incorporated to remove particles from the steam. Steam must not contain compounds which damage or affect the product. An electric heater element can also be used for heating the space.

Valves.—Valves at the outlet of the tank should be of the flush-type, fitting closely to the tank preventing a pocket of unpasteurized product. The valve should have a leak protector (or leak detector) which allows the liquid trapped by the plug to drain. Thus, there can be no leakage of unpasteurized milk past the valve into the product. Also, if the plug does not fit properly, dripping will continue after the valve is closed.

Agitator.—The speed of the agitator should be such to assure proper mixing without churning or whipping of the product. The effective agitators normally push the product down and then sweep it across the heat exchanger surface on the bottom of the vat.

Covers and Openings.—The covers and openings of the tank should be designed so that no materials can run into the tank. There is a lip on the edge of the lid and raised edges on other openings. Connections to temperature recorders indicate if the lid has been opened during the heat treatment. The lid should not be opened during the pastuerization, because the product must have a 30 min continuous heat treatment for proper pasteurization.

Piping or Tubing.—Piping or tubing to the pasteurizing vat must slope away from the tank. In some situations the tubing must be disconnected before starting the pasteurization cycle.

Temperature Recorders.—The recorders show the temperature of the product at any time during filling, heating, and cooling in the pasteurization vat. (Self-acting controls are often used on batch systems.)

Pocket and Continuous-Flow Holder Pasteurizers

The batch holding systems previously described are manually operated. These systems may be utilized so that heating, holding, and cooling all take place in the same batch container. In these holding methods, heating and cooling are accomplished in an apparatus separate from the holding container. Only the time-temperature treatment required to assure pasteurization is maintained.

Pocket holders may be of the stationary or moving type. The pocket holds the milk for 30 min after being heated to 145°F with a separate heater used to raise the milk to that temperature. Hot water at the holding temperature surrounds the pocket holders. At the completion of the holding time, the valve on the discharge opens and the pocket holders are emptied.

The continuous-flow holder consists of a series of large tubes so arranged that 30 min are required for the heated milk to pass through the tubes. A timing pump is used to provide proper flow. The holder tubes are maintained at pasteurizing temperature by a jacketed covering. The temperature is lower and the holding time longer than in the conventional high-temperature short-time unit.

In-the-bottle Pasteurization

Pasteurization in-the-bottle provides a method of assuring proper product treatment, preventing any possibility of postpasteurization contamination. Several methods have been attempted but none has been commercially acceptable in the United States. Treatment usually consists of holding at 145°–150°F, for 30 min. In such cases, using higher temperatures for a shorter time has the definite advantage of reducing the space requirements.

Another in-the-bottle process consists of heating the milk to the pasteurization temperature externally and placing the heated milk into heated bottles. After capping, the bottles are moved through a water bath or hot air chamber at the pasteurization temperature. After 30 min, the bottles pass through water sprays of decreasing temperature to cool the product and bottle. By heating the milk previous to capping, some odors may be removed.

The bottles may move through the unit vertically, horizontally, or in batches of bottles in cases in a frame or on a pallet. In the available case methods of handling several bottles, milk is placed cold into the bottles.

Home Pasteurizers

All home pasteurizers operated on the holding method should heat the milk to at least 145°F for not less than 30 min. The milk may be pasteurized in the bottle or in a pan. The capacity of the units is 1 to 2 gal. Many units have a buzzer or bell which sounds at the end of the heating period. The total time for heating, holding, and cooling varies from 60 to 90 min. Cooling is completed in about 20 min using cold water. Electric heating elements range in size from 300 to 1,500 watts.

Cross-reference: *HTST Pasteurization.*

HOMOGENIZERS

A homogenizer is a device which treats an emulsion or mixture of several items, such as butterfat in milk, in such a manner that the components are thoroughly mixed. The particles are separated and made smaller and the emulsion stabilized so that upon standing the various ingredients will not separate for an extended period of time. This process is accomplished by forcing the product at high pressure through extremely small orifices and/or between two smooth but very slightly separated plates, or through a maze of compacted wires.

Homogenization has come to be a very important treatment for food products because the process can often be used to improve the body and texture of ice cream, peanut butter, or fruit juices, and it prevents, to a large extent, the separation of the ingredients of the product in storage or on the shelf. Homogenization also affects the taste and flavor of products, and in the case of homogenized milk, greatly decreases the curd tension. Most of the milk sold in the United States is homogenized. Evaporated sterilized milk when properly homogenized will remain stable and will not separate for several years.

A process somewhat equivalent to homogenization is accomplished by means of a colloid mill. With this device the product is forced at low or practically nil pressure between the rapidly rotating surface of a high speed rotor and a stator. This mill is used on coarser materials and is often a treatment which precedes actual homogenization.

Principle

The principle of homogenization is that a mixture of more than one material is

TABLE H.7

CURD TENSION OF HOMOGENIZED MILK

(Homogenized before pasteurization)[1]

	Grams Curd Tension Homogenization Temperature °F		
Pressure	145	120	90
None	51	59	60
500	47	58	58
1,000	27	40	48
1,500	22	32	39
2,000	20	25	27
2,500	18	26	23
3,000	17	25	23

[1] These data are from a conventional poppet-type homogenizer valve machine. Lower pressures are required when the Creamery Package multiflow valve is used.

Source: P. H. Tracy.

forced through a very fine aperture (1/1,000 in. or less) at extremely high speed and pressure, thereby breaking up the solid materials into extremely fine particles and mixing them with the serum portion of the mixture. In order to have a stable mixture after homogenization, the particles must be fine enough or small enough in diameter that gravity will no longer separate the particles from the serum portion of the mixture. According to Stokes law, particles of 2μ and under in size will not settle out. It is also essential that the solid particles, butterfat for example, must be entirely surrounded with serum. If the solid particles are left to adhere together, clumps or clusters will be formed. Even though the individual particles are small, the product may still be unstable and, in addition, with some mixtures, such as cream, will have high viscosity.

Another result of homogenization, particularly of milk, is that the curd tension of the product is reduced with homogenization. Table H.7 shows a relationship between curd tension and homogenizing pressure for a standard milk product.

Use

The greatest use of homogenization in the food industry is for homogenizing milk. In the year 1940, with the advent of improved sanitary type homogenizers, many milk processors began to produce homogenized milk and today nearly all of the fluid bottled milk is homogenized. The evaporated milk business and the ice cream business would not be practical without homogenization of the product.

The homogenizing system consists essentially of a high pressure pump which forces the product through the homogenizing valve thereby exposing it to the high pressure treatment as described under homogenizing valve.

Pressure

The pressure of homogenization required is dependent on the design of the homogenizing valve, the product being treated, and the desired results. Table H.8 shows the relationship between pressure and fat globule breakup with milk.

The homogenizer pump is usually a 3 to 5 cylinder plunger type pump capable of pressures up to 3,000 psig or higher. A steady pressure is desired and results indicate that a 3 or 5 plunger pump will give more uniform results, and at a lower pressure than

TABLE H.8

RELATIONSHIP OF HOMOGENIZATION PRESSURE ON FAT-GLOBULE BREAKUP

Pressure, Lb	Range of Size of Fat Globules, Microns	Average Size of Fat Globules, Microns
None	1 to 18	3.71
500	1 to 14	2.39
1,000	1 to 7	1.68
1,500	1 to 4	1.40
2,000	1 to 3	1.08
2,500	1 to 3	0.99
3,000	0.5 to 2	0.76

Source: P. H. Tracy.

will a single plunger pump. The triplex pump is normally used for moderate and small-sized homogenizers. In the larger sizes a five cylinder unit is available.

Homogenizer pumps must be built to withstand constant heavy pressure. Homogenizers must be made so that they can be disassembled readily for cleaning. They must be constructed of stainless steel to prevent flavor damage to the product. Gasket construction and material and packing are very important points requiring service and special attention. For gaskets an O-ring using a plastic or rubber material is generally quite satisfactory. The packing is usually a single ring with a cross section shaped like a "C." Some machines use multiple packing rings. The packing ring material is usually a plastic or rubber combination.

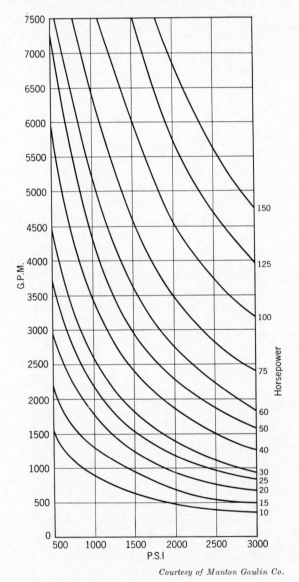

Courtesy of Manton Gaulin Co.

Fig. H-25.   Power requirements of homogenizers

The horsepower required to drive the homogenizer is directly proportional to the pressure as shown in Fig. H.25.

Operation

It is desirable to feed a homogenizer by gravity or pressure, because the slightest air leakage into the suction line will cause knocking and inefficient homogenization. Several satisfactory hookups are used for homogenization of milk. Figure H.26 shows a widely used system. There is positive pressure on the suction side of the homogenizer and a bypass around the homogenizing valve, so that the rate of flow of liquid through the homogenizer is independent of the metering type pump used on the pasteurizer. In some instances the homogenizer can serve as the metering pump on the pasteurizer. Figure H.27 illustrates the use of homogenizer in vat pasteurization.

The temperature at which the product is homogenized is important. For example, if the butterfat globules in milk are cold and solidified, it is more difficult to perform satisfactory homogenization. Normally, a temperature of 100°F or above is desired to avoid undesirable lipase activity. The energy put into the homogenizing pump causes an increase in the temperature of the product of about 6° or 7°F.

Operating Problems of Homogenizer

(1) Lack of capacity—caused by leaky valves, strainer plugged, leaky intake or discharge valves, and air getting into system (homogenizing valve has little to do with lack of capacity)

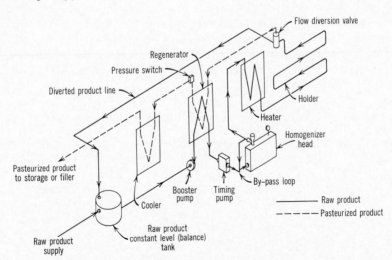

FIG. H-26.   Diagram of HTST pasteurizing system with booster pump, timing pump, and homogenizer

The homogenizer with the bypass loop arrangement must pump more fluid than the maximum delivery of the timing pump. The timing pump regulates the through-put of the system. Notice the pressure switch at the outlet of the pasteurized product from the regenerator. This prevents operation of the booster unless there is at least 1 psi more pressure on the pasteurized than on the raw side of the regenerator. This diagram could serve also for a UHT pasteurizer by shortening the holder.

(2) Gage vibrates badly—caused by leaky pump valves, insufficient supply, leaky plunger packing (perhaps worn plungers)

(3) Pounding of homogenizer—comes from worn pump valves on discharge side of homogenizer, possibly caused by lack of supply or air leak

(4) Pump valves and seats pitted—caused by strainer not fine enough to remove particles, material in ice cream mix (a Brinell difference of 50 between seat and valve)

(5) Pump valves stick—due to constant pounding of pump valves against seat, which upsets metal.

Standards and Efficiency

One method of measuring homogenizing efficiency is to examine the product under a high power microscope.

A second method is to use a Coulter counter which will accurately measure the diameter of all the particles in an homogenized product.

A third method is to measure the number and size of particles within a certain number of fields when examined under a high power microscope, and evaluate them in accordance with a mathematical scale which indicates the amount of product not below the 2 μ size in a given field. This method is called "the Farrall Index." The feature of this method is that it gives a mathematical measure of the product which is not properly homogenized. Also the index can be determined by microscope in a few minutes. It also gives a mathematically comparable rating of the degree of homogenization.

Another method of determining homogenization is by comparison of the color of a homogenized product with a standard. This is a purely empirical determination and can be used for quick determination of approximate degree of homogenization of products in which color changes with degree of homogenization.

The most commonly used method for determination of homogenization efficiency for milk is the U.S. Public Health Service test. This test is made by taking a 100 gm sample from the top of a 1 qt bottle of homogenized milk after the product has set for 48 hr.

The U. S. Public Health Service definition is stated as follows:

"Homogenized milk is milk which has been treated in such a manner as to insure breakup of fat globules to such an extent that after 48 hr quiescent storage, no visible cream separation occurs

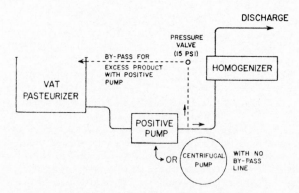

F<small>IG</small>. H-27.   Homogenization after vat pasteurization with homogenizer above vat with positive or centrifugal pump with capacity greater than homogenizer

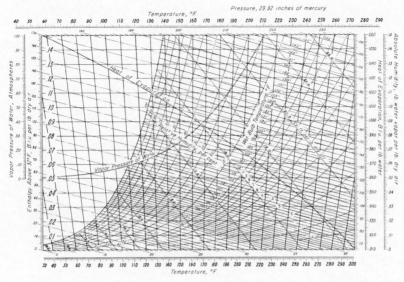

From Van Arsdel (1963)

FIG. H-28. Psychrometric chart

in the milk and the fat percentage of the top 100 ml in a quart volume or of proportionate volumes in containers of other sizes, does not differ by more than 10% of itself from the fat percentage of the remaining milk as determined after thorough mixing."

References

FARRALL, A. W. 1963. Engineering for Dairy and Food Products, 3rd Edition. John Wiley & Sons, New York.
TROUT, G. M. 1953. Homogenized Milk. Michigan State Univ. Press, E. Lansing, Mich.
U.S. PUBLIC HEALTH SERV. 1965. Milk Ordinance and Code, Washington, D.C.

Cross-references: *Brinell Hardness; Colloid Mill; Holding Methods of Pasteurization; HTST Pasteurization; Pumps.*

HORSEPOWER

Horsepower is the term used to give the rate at which work is done. It is equivalent to the work done in lifting 33,000 lb a distance of 1 ft in 1 min. One horsepower is equal to 746 watts or 0.746 kilowatts. The formula for calculating horsepower is

$$\text{hp} = \frac{\text{ft-lb per min}}{33,000}$$

There are several methods of expressing horsepower. The horsepower of an engine or a motor is usually given in brake horsepower, which is determined by the above formula. In some types of prime movers, horsepower is designated as nominal horsepower. This is a more of less arbitrary rating usually about $\frac{1}{3}$ of the actual brake horsepower.

Drawbar horsepower is the horsepower developed in pulling at the drawbar of a tractor or other vehicle. The drawbar horsepower is equal to the pull in pounds times the feet per minute movement divided by 33,000. It is apparent that the rate of forward movement of the vehicle has a great bearing upon the pull in actual pounds for a given horsepower. Thus, a tractor or vehicle pulling with a force of 1,000 lb at the rate of 4 mph will have only $^1/_2$ the actual drawbar horsepower of the vehicle pulling with the same force but at the rate of 8 mph.

Horsepower-hour is the work done by 1 hp working for 1 hr, and 1 hp-hr = 0.746 kwh.

Cross-references: *Belts; Energy.*

HUMIDITY CHART

The humidity or psychrometric chart (Fig. H.28) can be used as a basis for analyzing the drying, wetting, heating and cooling of a product by studying the external factors. The psychrometric chart provides the thermodynamic properties of the air and vapor. By knowing any 2 of the 3 temperatures, dry-bulb, wet-bulb, or dew-point, the physical properties can be described (Fig. H.29).

Definitions

Dry-bulb Temperature: The temperature of the air or product indicated by a thermometer which is not affected by water vapor content of the air.

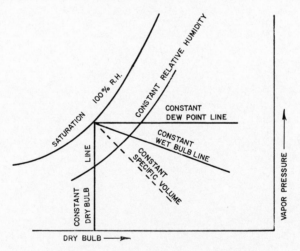

Fig. H-29. Psychrometric relationships

Wet-bulb Temperature: The temperature given by a thermometer with its sensing bulb covered with a thin layer of water and moving through the air until a steady temperature during evaporation is obtained. The difference between the dry-bulb and wet-bulb temperature is called the wet-bulb depression.

Dew-point Temperature: The temperature at which condensation of water vapor begins if a mixture of air and water vapor is cooled.

Humidity (absolute humidity, specific humidity): Weight of water vapor, usually in pounds or grains per pound of dry air (7,000 gr = 1 lb).

Relative Humidity: Ratio of actual partial pressure of the water vapor to the pressure at saturation at the dry-bulb temperature, usually expressed as a percentage.

Humid Heat: The specific heat of the air with water vapor it contains.

The following relationships describe some of the basic humidity relationships.

(1) The dry-bulb, wet-bulb, and dew-point temperatures are equal when the relative humidity is 100%.

(2) The dew-point < wet-bulb < dry-bulb temperature when the relative humidity is less than 100%.

(3) The rate at which heat is transferred from the air to the water is proportional to the wet-bulb depression.

(4) All values are based on a barometric pressure of 1 atm.

(5) The water vapor pressure nearly doubles for each 20°F increase in temperature.

(6) The density of air saturated with vapor is less than the density of dry air at a given temperature.

(7) The difference between the dew-point and dry-bulb temperature is nearly constant for a given relative humidity.

(8) The latent heat of vaporization increases as the temperature of evaporation decreases.

(9) The dew-point of a given air condition is the same regardless of amount of heating of the air.

Reference

Van Arsdel, W. B. 1963. Food Dehydration, Vol. I. The AVI Publishing Co., Westport, Conn.

HYDRAULICS

Hydraulic systems are widely used as a means of converting fluid energy to mechanical power. The hydraulic system is often used where an electric system might not function or might become inoperable or might be dangerous because of moisture conditions. The hydraulic system must include four components: the reservoir to store oil; a pump to push oil through the system; valves to control the oil flow; and pressure and a cylinder (motor) to convert fluid flow to work.

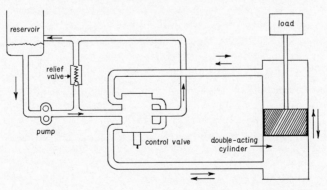

FIG. H-30.   Hydraulic system with relief valve, 4-way control and double acting cylinder

In general, there are two types of systems. One is the open center hydraulic system where the pump runs continuously. This system is simpler, operates at a lower pressure, and has less maintenance than the the closed center hydraulic system where the pump runs intermittently during neutral positions. The closed center system maintains the system pressure, is quicker in response, more often used, and most commonly used where there are several work or control functions to be served.

Operation

Most work systems are now designed with a double-acting cylinder, so that a load can be moved in either of two directions by positioning of a control valve. A relief valve also is required for safety reasons and as a means for maintaining proper pressure on the system (Fig. H.30).

The oil is normally pushed into the pump, not drawn into it. An air vent is necessary in the top of the oil reservoir, so that the oil is forced by the atmosphere from the reservoir. With a small pump and large cylinder, there is a greater force at less speed on the cylinder. With a large pump and small cylinder, there is less force at a greater speed on the cylinder.

Basic Types of Hydraulics

The *hydrodynamics* provides for the use of fluids at high speeds and provides a force on impact to provide power. An example is the torque converter.

Hydrostatics refers to the use of fluids at low speeds but high pressure to supply power. This type of hydraulics is used on systems for control.

Pumps

Gear, vane, and piston pumps are used in hydraulic systems. The capacity, pressure, and speed vary according to the load to be moved (Table H.9). Malfunction of the pump is often due to the human factors of poor maintenance, bad repair, and exceeding the operating limits. One of the major reasons for malfunction is the use of a fluid in the hydraulic system which is dirty or of poor quality.

Low or erratic pressure of the pump can be due to the following: (1) cold fluid, (2) fluid viscosity incorrect, (3) air leak or restriction at air-inlet line, (4) pump speed too slow, (5) internal parts in pump are sticking, and (6) distance between internal parts has increased due to wear or malfunctioning of bearing.

If the pump does not deliver fluid, possible causes are: (1) fluid level in reservoir too low, (2) pump inlet line clogged, (3) air leak in pump inlet line, (4) pump speed too low, (5) sludge or dirt in pump, (6) fluid viscosity too high, (7) variable control mechanism out of adjustment, and (8) broken or worn parts inside the pump.

TABLE H.9

NORMAL CAPACITY RANGE OF HYDRAULIC PUMPS

	Flow, Gpm	Pressure, Psi	Speed, Rpm
Gear	0.2–150	250–2,500	200–3,500
Vane	0.5–250	250–2,500	1,200–4,000
Piston	0.5–450	750–5,000	600–6,000

General Maintenance

The key maintenance problems include insufficient oil in reservoir, clogged or dirty oil filters, loose intake line, and incorrect oil in the system. With respect to the entire system, cleanliness is one of the most important factors in maintaining proper and efficient operation of hydraulic systems. The system should be drained periodically, cleaned and flushed, and refilled with the proper fluid. Another major cause of malfunction is air in the oil. The air may be detected by spongy action of the system, chattering, a noisy pump, or the pump not operating. To keep air out of the system it is important that the oil level in the reservoir be maintained properly, that leaky sections of the suction line be replaced, that connections be kept tight, and that air be bled from the system after refilling with fluid or when attaching remote cylinders. Air vents are located at the highest point in the system to remove incorporated air.

Cross-references: *Hydrostatic Drive; Lubricants.*

HYDROCOOLING

The use of water to remove heat from products is called hydrocooling. Fruit and vegetables are commonly cooled with (1) water from the well, cistern, or fresh water source to remove the field heat, or (2) water which has been cooled by ice or refrigeration to remove the field heat or respiration heat. The quality of fruits and vegetables is greatly enhanced by rapid cooling immediately after harvest, and through maintenance of low temperatures before processing or storage.

Hydrocooling can be combined with other procedures for removing trash, cleaning, and chemical treatment. Handling fruits and vegetables in water provides a method of reducing damage during handling. Possibilities of sorting and grading in water may be developed.

Cross-references: *Refrigeration Principles; Vacuum Cooling.*

HYDROGRAPH

The hydrograph is an instrument, usually of the recording type, used for measuring and recording the flow of a fluid either in an open channel or in a tube. The chart is moved by an electric motor or time clock, and the recording pen is actuated by a calibrated operating device, such as an orifice or a float, which gives the flow rate at a given instant and records the amount on a chart which moves with time. A graph representing volume of flow versus time is produced.

HYDROSTATIC DRIVE

The food industry encounters many situations where an infinitely variable speed drive is desirable. These applications include driving a processing machine, conveyor, forklift truck, or delivery truck.

Hydraulic drive systems have been improved to the point where they are now simple and reliable. The efficiency is usually not quite as high as a gear drive or belt drive; however, with a properly designed system, 40 to 70% efficiencies can be obtained and the other advantages of the hydraulic drive make it worth consideration.

428.   *Hydrostatic Drive*

Basically, the hydraulic transmission consists of a variable capacity pump which furnishes fluid under pressure to a hydraulic motor.

A number of controls are needed, such as a pressure relief valve and check valve. No clutch is required, no gear changing is needed during operation, and a single lever control provides infinitely variable forward and reverse speeds and dynamic braking. Rapid reversals of direction can be made without damage to the drive or to a vehicle or machine.   The speed of the motor can be varied "on the go."

Hydrostatic transmissions usually operate at pressures around 2,000 to 3,000 psig. However, heavy-duty units may be operated up to 5,000 psig.   Hydrostatic units are obtainable in speed ranges as desired, and horsepower ranges from small 10 to 20 hp to 450 hp.

Care of hydraulic drive systems consists principally of maintaining the oil in a clean condition, preventing excessive pressure buildup and preventing leaks in the system.   Normally the amount of maintenance service required is moderate.   Only the highest quality of special oil for the purpose should be used.

Cross-references: *Fluid Flow; Hydraulics.*

I

ICE CREAM HARDENING AND STORAGE

Ice cream mix is frozen to about 21°F in a continuous freezer, and is then hardened in a low-temperature room or by plate contact equipment to about −20°F. The amount of refrigeration required at the ice cream freezer and also in the hardening room will vary with mix composition and overrun. The higher the overrun, the lower will be the refrigeration requirement per gallon of ice cream. As a rule of thumb refrigeration requirements are sometimes roughly estimated by assuming the load to be 500 Btu per gal. at the ice cream freezer, and a hardening load of 500 Btu per gal. This figure assumes various refrigeration losses and packaging, wrapping, and carton materials as part of the refrigeration requirement. For greater accuracy the composition of the ice cream mix, overrun, and other factors must be taken into consideration in computing the requirement for a given product.

Hardening Room Construction

Various methods are used for constructing and insulating ice cream hardening rooms. Some methods are based on erecting a curtain wall and adding the insulating materials. The hardening room is normally held at −20° to −25°F; therefore, 8 in. of insulation is generally required in temperate climates. The ceiling, side walls, and floor are usually insulated equally. One important consideration in constructing a hardening room is to provide a means of preventing frost damage. This has been done with a horizontal pipe network vented to atmosphere or electric heating cables or with warm circulating antifreeze. A subfloor is usually poured of concrete on which insulation is placed. On top of the insulation is then placed the service floor which is usually concrete. The heat transfer through most hardening rooms will average 1 Btu per sq ft of surface per °F temperature difference between inside and outside temperatures. A hardening room should be equipped with can pass doors and vestibule to reduce refrigeration loss to a minimum. Air curtains have also proven satisfactory not only for control of insects and odors, but in reducing refrigeration losses. These losses can be reduced 50 to 60% with air curtains having a velocity of 700 fpm. The capacity of hardening rooms is given in Table I.1.

Tunnels

Ice cream hardening tunnels specifically designed with high air flows around ice cream packages provides quick hardening. The tunnel is placed in a convenient location to serve the ice cream freezers and the storage room. Usually the tunnel is on one side of the palletized ice cream storage room. Two common types of conveying methods are employed in hardening tunnels for the packages. One is a roller bed which slowly conveys packages through the wind tunnel by means of a revolving series of parallel rollers. The rollers revolve slowly to permit adequate exposure of the product to high velocity cooled air. The other type of mechanism consists of a series of shelves conveyed through the air blast by a power chain on each end of the shelf. In both methods, packages load and discharge from the mechanism automatically. In practice, the packages are placed on a pallet as they are discharged from the hardening tunnel and stored in a high ceiling storage room. The pallets are placed in racks 3 or 4 high with a forklift.

Plate Hardeners

Plate type hardeners, which are equipped with automatic load and discharge, are finding wider use in the ice cream industry. The plates exist in 2 different arrangements in 2 of the hardeners available. In the one the plates are in a horizontal position, and in the other machine the contact plates are in a vertical position. With

TABLE I.1

STORAGE CAPACITY OF HARDENING ROOMS AND MILK COOLING ROOMS[1]

Ice Cream Hardening Rooms	Recommended Temperature, $-15°$ to $-25°$F Gallons per Square Foot of Floor Space	
	Maximum	Average for Efficient Handling
Bulk	22 gal.	14 or 16 gal.
Pints and quarts	18	10 to 14
Novelties and cups	15 (50 doz)	8 to 12
Assortment of above: 50% bulk, 25% pkg., 25% misc.	18 gal.	13 to 16 gal.

Recommended: 2 in. between bulk cans and 2 to 3 in. between packaged units—to assure circulation of air and heat removal for fast hardening
Quart package: $8 \times 2^1/_2 \times 3^1/_4$ in. Philadelphia pint: $4 \times 3^1/_8 \times 2^3/_8$ in.
Stick novelty: ($3^1/_2$ doz per gal.) 1 doz box—4 in. $\times$ 8 in. $\times$ 5 ft or 2.75 gal. per cu ft
Heat Removed (approx.)
    Ice cream $+23°$ to $-20°$ = 75 Btu per lb
    Ices $+23°$ to $-20°$ = 110 Btu per lb
Additional hardening on prehardened novelties from $+5°$ to $-20°$:
    Ice cream 20 Btu/lb   25 Btu/doz   86 Btu/gal.
    Ices   30 Btu/lb   50 Btu/doz 250 Btu/gal.

[1] Allowance of 25% of floor area for aisles and 20% stacking space.
Source: Farrall (1963).

horizontal plates, there is a vertical movement of the plates from the load position cycling and returning to the discharge position. The vertical plate hardener utilizes comparatively stationary plates, which accept the ice cream cartons at the top and discharge the hardened packages from the plate section at the bottom. Theoretically, the plate type hardeners are more efficient than cold air convection hardening systems. However, they do not readily handle a variety of packages which may have retarded their acceptance.

Hardening Time

Several investigators have determined that the cooling rate is greatly increased when ice cream packages are exposed to moving air. When ice cream is packaged tightly on a shelf in a hardening room, the hardening time is lengthened considerably. A comparison of hardening rates is shown in Fig. I.1.

Hardening time is affected by package sizes. The hardening time of various size packages is as follows:

Package Size, Gal.	Hardening Time, Hr
1	$5^1/_2$
2	$9^3/_4$
3	$11^1/_5$
5	15

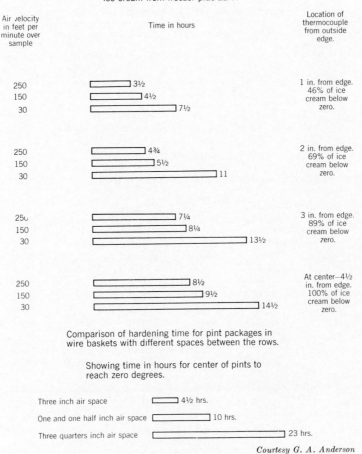

Time required to reach zero degrees at various locations in 2½ gal. samples with different air velocities over the samples.

Room temperature minus 25 F.
Ice cream from freezer plus 22 F.

Air velocity in feet per minute over sample	Time in hours	Location of thermocouple from outside edge.
250	3½	1 in. from edge. 46% of ice cream below zero.
150	4½	
30	7½	
250	4¾	2 in. from edge. 69% of ice cream below zero.
150	5½	
30	11	
250	7¼	3 in. from edge. 89% of ice cream below zero.
150	8¼	
30	13½	
250	8½	At center—4½ in. from edge. 100% of ice cream below zero.
150	9½	
30	14½	

Comparison of hardening time for pint packages in wire baskets with different spaces between the rows.

Showing time in hours for center of pints to reach zero degrees.

Three inch air space		4½ hrs.
One and one half inch air space		10 hrs.
Three quarters inch air space		23 hrs.

Courtesy G. A. Anderson

FIG. I-1.   Hardening rate of ice cream

Air velocity is considered to reduce hardening time approximately 50% as compared with still air.

Coils and Equipment

Hardening room evaporators are either the $1^1/_4$ in. coil or compact blower units. The more recent refrigeration systems employ the compact blower units in preference to the $1^1/_4$ in. pipe shelf coil in order to obtain greater efficiency in heat transfer while achieving air circulation within the hardening room. In palletized ice cream rooms the coils are not useful as shelves and are more bulky as well as being more difficult to defrost. Especially designed blower units utilize electricity, hot gas, hot air, and water spray defrost systems, all of which have proved satisfactory.

In selecting an evaporator for the ice cream hardening room, it is important to realize that fin spacing on the coil greatly affects frost accumulation which impedes airflow. A fin spacing of at least $^3/_8$ in. is recommended. Some engineers prefer to use plain prime surface coils without fins because of the problem of frost removal.

TABLE I.2A

TYPICAL COMPOSITION OF ICE CREAM MIXES[1]

Milk Fat, %	Serum Solids, %	Sugar, %	Stabilizer, %	Water, %	Total Solids, %
4	13	16	0.5	66.5	33.5
12	11	16	0.3	60.7	39.3
18	10	12	0.2	59.8	40.2
0	14	16	0.5	69.5	30.5

[1] There are many variations of composition for special purposes.

TABLE I.2B

COMPOSITION OF ICE CREAM AND RELATED PRODUCTS (BASED ON 100 GM EDIBLE PORTION)

| Product | Ice Cream | | | Ice Milk | Ices | Sherbet |
	10% Fat	12% Fat	16% Fat			
Water, %	63.2	62.1	62.8	66.7	66.9	67.0
Food energy, cal	193.0	207.0	222.0	152.0	78.0	134.0
Protein, gm	4.5	4.0	2.6	4.8	0.4	0.9
Fat, gm	10.6	12.5	16.1	5.1	trace	1.2
Carbohydrate, gm	20.8	20.6	18.0	22.4	32.5	30.8
Ash, gm	0.9	0.8	0.5	1.0	trace	0.1
Calcium, mg	146.0	123.0	78.0	156.0	trace	16.0
Phosphorus, mg	115.0	99.0	61.0	124.0	trace	13.0
Iron, mg	0.1	0.1	trace	0.1	trace	trace
Sodium, mg	63.0	40.0	33.0	68.0	trace	10.0
Potassium, mg	181.0	112.0	95.0	195.0	3.0	22.0
Vitamin A, IU	440.0	520.0	660.0	210.0	0.0	60.0
Thiamin, mg	0.04	0.04	0.02	0.05	trace	0.01
Riboflavin, mg	0.21	0.19	0.11	0.22	trace	0.03
Niacin, mg	0.1	0.1	0.1	0.1	trace	trace
Ascorbic acid, mg	1.0	1.0	1.0	1.0	1.0	2.0

Source: Agriculture Research Service, 1963. Agriculture Handbook 8, U.S. Dept. Agr., Washington, D.C.

When coils are of the flooded type, the heat transfer from pipe coils is about 2.5 Btu per hr per °F per sq ft of surface in still air, and approximately 10 in still brine. Agitation of brine or air movement increases the heat transfer through pipes. In selecting a blower unit for a hardening room, a temperature difference between the air and refrigerant of about 15°F is usually satisfactory. Refrigeration systems in modern plants are controlled automatically and usually are two stage compression systems.

Cross-references: *Air Curtain; Floors; Freezers; Ice Cream, Physical Properties; Refrigeration Principles.*

ICE CREAM PHYSICAL PROPERTIES

Ice cream is a mixture of milk, butterfat, sugar, stabilizer, and flavoring. There are many variations and types of ice cream, ices, and sherbets produced by the industry. The properties of these different mixes vary tremendously and are determined largely by the percentage of overrun, sugar, and solids in the mixture. Tables I.2A and I.2B show the approximate composition of some typical ice cream mixes and sherbets.

The physical properties of the different mixes are closely related to the freezing point, amount of refrigeration required, body, texture of the resulting ice cream product, and stability of the product in storage. There are six principal physical properties of ice cream mixes with which the processor is concerned.

Freezing Point.—The freezing point of the mix depends entirely upon the composition of the mix. The amount and type of sugar has the greatest effect for normal ice cream mix. The usual temperature at which the mix begins to freeze is about 26° to 27°F. The freezing point of a mix can be calculated if the composition is known.

After the mix begins to congeal at about 27°F, it gradually freezes until at a temperature of about −20°F most of the water is frozen, as shown in Fig. I.2. Since the ice cream is drawn from the freezer at about 21° to 22°F, almost half of the refrigeration required for freezing is removed in the hardening process which follows. Corn sugar depresses the freezing point much more than does the cane or beet sugar.

Heat Absorption.—Heat must be removed to freeze the ice cream mix. In practice about $^1/_2$ of the heat is removed in the freezer and $^1/_2$ in the hardening room.

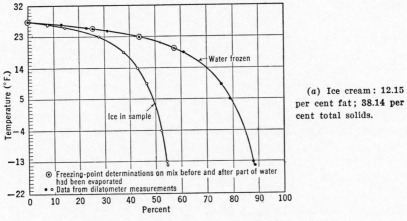

(*a*) Ice cream: 12.15 per cent fat; 38.14 per cent total solids.

Fɪɢ. I-2.   Percent of water frozen in ice cream

The amount of heat that can be removed varies with the mix composition. For a mix of the approximate composition butterfat, 12%; serum solids, 11%; stabilizer, 0.4%; and sugar, 15%, the approximate percentage of water frozen in the freezer is 52%, as shown on the chart. The amount removed in the hardening room is 38%, since about 10% remains unfrozen even in hardened ice cream.

Air Holding.—Ice cream normally has a quantity of air mixed with it in order to give it a certain amount of lightness and improve its eating quality. For example, 5 gal. of ice cream mix when frozen with the equal amount of air gives 10 gal. of ice cream having 100% overrun. The amount of air which is added can be varied and in some high priced ice creams the overrun may be only 60 to 80%. On the other hand ice cream is often sold with an overrun of 110 to 120%, which is common in the soft serve ice cream and frozen dessert industry.

The air holding capacity of a mix is very important because if the air is not properly incorporated, ice cream will shrink upon storage. The ability of the ice cream to hold air is determined largely by the temperature and the composition of the mix. A certain amount of so-called stabilizer which might be gelatin or a gelatin-like material assists in holding the air. If the milk and food products are fresh and of high quality, air will be held better. During some seasons of the year, for example in the spring, milk sometimes is lacking in elements which give a stable emulsion. Usually the addition of a small amount of egg yolk will remedy a situation where the mix does not hold air properly. Normally the ice cream must be frozen down to a temperature of 23° or 24°F before it will hold air well. The freezing of the product under pressure such as is found in a continuous freezer greatly increases the air holding capacity of a mix.

Weight per Gallon.—The density of weight per gallon of ice cream is an important matter. A normal mix weighs about 9 lb per gal. When it is frozen and has an equal amount of air, the ice cream weighs about 4.5 lb per gal. The weight per gallon and overrun relationship is shown as follows

$$\% \text{ overrun} = \frac{\text{wt of gal. of mix} - \text{wt of gal. ice cream}}{\text{wt of gal. of ice cream}} \times 100$$

Uniformity of weight per gallon is very important from the standpoint of quality in ice cream and also for the profitability of the business. A mix which holds air well, usually allows steady and uniform weight control.

Color.—The color of ice cream is important. Artificial coloring materials are often added to the mix at the time of freezing. A uniform coloring is quite important from the standpoint of customer satisfaction for the various flavors.

Viscosity.—Excessive viscosity in ice cream mix makes the incorporation of air difficult. Excessive viscosity also makes cooling and pumping of ice cream mix difficult. Excessive viscosity is usually caused by improper homogenization of the mix. Excessive viscosity can be controlled by using proper homogenization pressure, a second stage of homogenization, or by proper selection of the stabilizer.

Ice cream as it is being frozen develops a plasticity which is dependent upon the composition of the mix and the temperature. Mixes which have corn sugar and are low in stabilizer usually develop much less plasticity than other mixes. In modern production the ice cream is pumped through pipes to the filling apparatus. Excessive viscosity may put excessive strain on the pump and pipelines, and may interfere with the proper incorporation of air. In practice the plasticity is adjusted by means of the freezing temperature. Occasionally a lack of sufficient plasticity makes the product difficult to handle in packaging equipment. In this case either a lower temperature or an adjustment of the composition of the mix is desirable.

Calculation of the Freezing Point of Mixes

The freezing point of an ice cream mix is lowered by the milk sugar, by salts, and by the sucrose (cane sugar), or other substances which are in true solution. The fat has no direct effect on the freezing point; if, however, the fat and the milk protein or other solid content of the mix are increased, there is less water to hold the soluble salts and sugar, and the freezing point will also be depressed.

On the basis of these principles, the freezing point of a given mix is figured as follows.

(1) Assume that 54.5% of the serum solids of the mix is lactose.

(2) Assume that mixtures of sucrose and lactose follow the freezing-point curve for sucrose. Note: Glucose (corn sugar) depresses the freezing point 1.9 times as much as sucrose.

(3) Referring to Table I.3, the lowering of the freezing point caused by the sugars can be found.

(a) Percentage serum solids times 0.545 + percentage sucrose = parts sugars.

(b) Find concentration in percentage of sugars in unfrozen water.

$$\frac{\text{parts sugars} \times 100}{\text{parts sugars} + \text{parts unfrozen water in mix}} = \text{percentage sugars in unfrozen water}$$

(c) Refer answer to (b) in Table I.3 to find freezing-point lowering due to sugars. (Subtract value obtained for table from 32°F to get lowering.)

(4) Find lowering of freezing point due to milk salts by:

$$\frac{\text{percentage serum solids} \times 4.26}{\text{percentage water in mix}} = \text{lowering due to milk salts, °F}$$

(5) Total freezing-point depression = lowering due to sugars + lowering due to milk salts.

TABLE I.3

FREEZING POINT OF SUGAR SOLUTIONS

Sucrose, %	Freezing Point, °F	Sucrose, %	Freezing Point, °F
0	32.0	40	24.1
5	31.25	45	21.75
10	30.5	50	19.4
15	29.9	55	15.0
20	29.3	60	10.6
25	28.25	65	7.1
30	27.20	70	3.6
35	25.55		

Freezing point $= 32°F -$ total freezing-point depression (°F)

In the freezing of an ice cream mix, the freezing point becomes progressively lower since the ice crystallizes out, and the remaining solution, therefore, becomes more concentrated. This process continues until the freezing point of the remaining solution becomes very low, in fact, with most ice cream mixes, there is some unfrozen solution even at 0°F.

Cross-reference: *Freezers, Ice Cream.*

ICE REFRIGERATION

Ice refrigeration has been used for many years to preserve food. Although now largely superseded by mechanical refrigeration, ice is still used for cooling drinks, foods, and for special purposes where refrigeration is needed for a short time.

Ice refrigeration is based upon the principle that ice at 32°F will absorb tremendous amounts of heat. For example, cooling with water, 1 lb of water changing 1°F will absorb 1 Btu; however, 1 lb of ice at 32°F will absorb 144 Btu in changing into water. If the ice is colder than 32°F it will absorb an additional $1/2$ Btu per lb per °F.

The amount of heat absorbed by 1 ton of ice in changing from ice at 32°F into a liquid at 32°F is $2{,}000 \times 144 = 288{,}000$ Btu. This amount of refrigeration is a standard for measuring capacities of refrigeration machines. A 1-ton machine will under standard conditions, remove 288,000 Btu in 24 hr. Many of the newer machines are now rated in a refrigerating capacity of so many Btu per hr.

Ice for Refrigeration

The simplest method of utilizing refrigeration is to pack the crushed ice around the product or place ice in the product to be cooled. A second method is to circulate air over blocks of ice and into the room or area to be cooled. A third method is to circulate water over blocks of ice and through cooling pipes which are in contact with the product to be cooled.

The addition of salt to ice will result in a lowering of the freezing temperature of the ice and the resulting brine, and in this way temperatures as low as 5°F above zero can be obtained. Table I.4 gives the freezing point of the ice and salt mixtures in different proportions. Table I.5 gives the amount of refrigeration available per pound of ice with different percentages of salt.

Corrosion problems are often encountered with salt-water solutions. Heavy galvanized coatings or other special prepared coatings for metal parts are frequently used to minimize corrosion.

If stainless steel is used with brine refrigeration, the equipment should be thoroughly rinsed and cleaned immediately after using to prevent corrosion.

Ice Manufacturing

Large scale commercial manufacture of ice is usually carried out by placing cans of water in a cold brine tank and freezing. The cans are usually of the size that will make 50-, 100-, or 200-lb ice cakes. The brine temperature in such an ice making tank is usually kept at 5°F or lower.

TABLE I.4

TEMPERATURES OBTAINED WITH ICE-AND-SALT MIXTURES (NaCl)

Percentage of Salt in Mixture	Temperature of Mixture, °F	Percentage of Salt in Mixture	Temperature of Mixture, °F
0	32	15	11
5	27	20	1.5
10	20	25	−10

Source: U.S. Dept. Agr. Bull 98.

TABLE I.5

REFRIGERATION AVAILABLE PER POUND OF ICE AND SALT (NaCl)

Salt per 100 Lb Water, Lb	Heat of Solution, Btu	Total Heat of Resulting Solution, Btu	Heat Required Pound of Mixture, Btu	Salt per 100 Lb Water, Lb	Heat of Solution, Btu	Total Heat of Resulting Solution, Btu	Heat Required Pound of Mixture, Btu
1	58.0	14,458	143.0	20	27.0	14,940	124.5
5	49.7	14,668	139.5	25	22.5	14.962	119.5
10	40.5	14,806	134.5	30	19.1	14,973	115.0
15	33.0	14,895	129.5	35	16.4	14,974	111.0

Source: U.S. Dept. Agr. Bull. 98.

Air bubbles which cause a milky appearance of the ice must be eliminated.   This is usually done by bubbling air into the ice cans, so that it will carry out otherwise small residual air bubbles before being frozen into ice.   The ice is removed from the cans by means of an ice dump which has a warm water attachment to loosen the ice from the can after which it slips out and goes to storage.

Flaked Ice

Much of the ice today is used for cooling products by small chunks or flakes of ice. Special machines have been designed to make this type of product directly.   Usually the water is frozen on a drum or in a tube to a thickness of perhaps $1/8$ to $1/4$ in., then the machine cycles and applies a small amount of heat to the tube which causes a shell of ice to be loosened where it can be removed automatically.   Other type machines freeze the ice on a cylinder and chip it off, much as a lathe takes a cut off of a shaft or tube.

The ice crusher is used to make crushed ice from large chunks of ice.   This machine has a rotary drum on which spikes are mounted, and as the drum rotates it chips off chunks from the large block of ice against which it works, and delivers it to the conveyor or where the ice is to be used.

Ice which is used for cooling drinks or food for human consumption should be made from potable water and handled in a sanitary manner.

Reference

FARRALL, A. W. 1963. Engineering for Dairy and Food Products, 3rd Edition. John Wiley & Sons, New York.

TABLE I.6

RECOMMENDED FOOT CANDLES FOR SOME AREAS AND OPERATIONS

Operation or Area	Footcandles (Minimum on the Task at All Times)	Operation or Area	Footcandles (Minimum on the Task at All Times)
Bakeries		Central Station Indoor Locations	
Mixing room	50	Air-conditioning equipment, air preheater and fan floor, ash sluicing	10
Face of shelves (vertical illumination)	30		
Inside of mixing bowl (vertical mixers)	50	Auxiliaries, battery rooms, boiler feed pumps, tanks, compressors, and gage area	20
Fermentation room	30	Boiler platform	10
Make-up room		Burner platform	20
Bread	30	Cable room, circulator or pump bay	10
Sweet yeast raised products	50		
Proofing room	30	Coal conveyor, crusher, feeder, scale areas, pulverizer, fan area, transfer tower	10
Oven room	30		
Fillings and other ingredients	30		
Decorating and icing		Condensers, deaerator floor, evaporator floor and heater floors	10
Mechanical	50		
Hand	100		
Scales and thermometers	50	Control rooms	
Wrapping room	30	Vertical face of switchboards	
Breweries		Simplex or section of duplex facing operator	
Brew house	30	Type A—Large centralized control room 66 in. above floor	50
Boiling and keg washing	30		
Filling (bottles, cans, kegs)	50	Type B—Ordinary control rooms at 66 in. above floor	30
Candy Making			
Box department	50	Section of duplex facing away from operator	30
Chocolate Department			
Husking, winnowing, fat extraction, crushing and refining, feeding	50	Bench boards (horizontal level)	50
		Area inside duplex switchboards	10
		Rear of all switchboard panels (vertical)	10
Bean cleaning and sorting, dipping, packing, wrapping	50	Emergency lighting, all areas	3
Milling	100	Hydrogen and CO_2 manifold	20
Cream making		Chemical laboratories	50
Mixing, cooking, molding	50	Precipitators	10
Gum drops and jellied forms	50	Screen house	20
Hand decorating	100	Soot or slag blower platform	10
Hard candy		Steam headers and throttles	10
Mixing, cooking, and molding	50	Switchgear power	20
Die cutting and sorting	100	Telephone equipment room	20
Kiss making and wrapping	100	Tunnels or galleries, piping	10
Canning and Preserving		Turbine bay sub-basement	20
Initial grading raw material samples	50	Turbine room	30
		Visitors' gallery	20
Tomatoes	100	Water treating area	20
Color grading (cutting rooms)	200[1]	Central Station Outdoor Locations	
Preparation		Catwalks	2.0
Preliminary sorting		Cinder dumps	0.1
Apricots and peaches	50	Coal unloading	
Tomatoes	100	(a) Dock (loading or unloading zone)	5.0
Olives	150		
Cutting and pitting	100	(b) Barge storage area	0.5
Final sorting	100	(c) Car dumper	0.5[1]
Canning		(d) Tipple	5.0
Continuous belt canning	100	Coal storage area	0.1
Sink canning	100	Conveyors	2.0
Hand packing	50	Entrances	
Olives	100	Generating or service building	
Examination of canned samples	200[1]	(a) Main	10.0
Container handling		(b) Secondary	2.0
Inspection	200[1]		
Can unscramblers	70		
Labeling and cartoning	30		

TABLE I.6 (*Continued*)

Operation or Area	Footcandles (Minimum on the Task at All Times)	Operation or Area	Footcandles (Minimum on the Task at All Times)
Gate house		Garages—Automobile and Truck	
(a) Pedestrian entrance	10.0	Service garages	
(b) Conveyor entrance	5.0	Repairs	100
Fence	0.2	Active traffic areas	20
Fuel oil delivery headers	5.0	Parking garages	
Oil storage tanks	1.0	Entrance	50
Open yard	0.2	Traffic lanes	10
Platforms—boiler, turbine deck	5.0	Storage	5
Roadway		Inspection	
(a) Between or along buildings	1.0	Ordinary	50
(b) Not bordered by buildings	0.5	Difficult	100
Substation		Highly difficult	200[1]
(a) General horizontal	2.0	Very difficult	500[1]
(b) Specific vertical (on		Most difficult	1,000[1]
disconnects)	2.0	Machine Shops	
Dairy Products		Rough bench and machine work	50
Fluid milk industry		Medium bench and machine work,	
Boiler room	30	ordinary automatic machines,	
Bottle storage	30	rough grinding, medium	
Bottle sorting	50	buffing, and polishing	100
Bottle washers	[2]	Fine bench and machine work,	
Can washers	30	fine automatic machines,	
Cooling equipment	30	medium grinding, fine buffing,	
Filling inspection	100	and polishing	500[1]
Gages (on face)	50	Extra fine bench and machine	
Laboratories	100	work, grinding—fine work	1,000[1]
Meter panels (on face)	50	Materials Handling	
Pasteurizers	30	Wrapping, packing, labeling	50
Separators	30	Picking stock, classifying	30
Storage refrigerator	30	Loading, trucking	20
Tanks, vats		Inside truck bodies and freight	
Light interiors	20	cars	10
Dark interiors	100	Meat Packing	
Thermometer (on face)	50	Slaughtering	30
Weighing room	30	Cleaning, cutting, cooking,	
Scales	70	grinding, canning, packing	100
Exterior Areas		Storage Rooms or Warehouses	
Entrances		Inactive	5
Active (pedestrian or		Active	
conveyance)	5.0	Rough bulky	10
Inactive (normally locked,		Medium	20
infrequent use)	1.0	Fine	50
Vital locations or structures	5.0	Sugar Refining	
Building surroundings	1.0	Grading	50
Active shipping area surroundings	5.0	Color inspection	200
Storage area—active	20	Testing	
Storage area—inactive	1	General	50
Loading and unloading platforms	20	Extra fine instruments, scales, etc.	200[1]
Flour Mills		Tobacco Products	
Rolling	50	Drying, stripping, general	30
Sifting	50	Grading and sorting	200[1]
Purifying	50	Woodworking	
Packing	30	Rough sawing and bench work	30
Product control	100	Sizing, planing, rough sanding,	
Cleaning screens, manlifts,		medium machine and bench	
aisleways and walkways, bin		work, glueing, veneering,	
checking	30	cooperage	50
		Fine bench and machine work,	
		fine sanding and finishing	100

[1] Obtained with a combination of general lighting plus specialized supplemental lighting.

[2] Special lighting such that (1) the luminous area shall be large enough to cover the surface which is being inspected, and (2) the brightness be within the limits necessary to obtain comfortable contrast conditions.

Source: Illuminating Engineering Society.

Cross-references: *Immersion Freezing; Refrigeration Principles.*

ILLUMINATION FIXTURES

The choice of a lighting system is influenced by the desirable direction and diffusion of light. The design should take into account the horizontal, inclined and vertical surfaces involved in the work areas. After careful study of many areas in a variety of food processing plants, lighting recommendations have been made by the Illuminating Engineering Society, as presented in Table I.6.

Relatively low illumination can be provided over the general area if adequate illumination is available in specific work areas or on pieces of equipment. This can be noted by the values presented in the preceding table.

The plant engineer can choose from a wide selection of light fixtures to provide adequate light. Safety and protection of food products must be considered in choosing fixtures. Enclosed or protected fixtures are recommended in processing and package-filling areas. In cold storage rooms the enclosed incandescent fixture is desirable. The glass globe screws against an asbestos gasket. These fixtures are frequently porcelainized steel reflectors.

Fluorescent lighting offers the advantage of about 2.5 times the operating efficiency obtainable from incandescent lamps. A soft illumination and less glare is obtained from the large light source of the fluorescent tube. The initial cost of fluorescent fixtures is approximately twice that of the incandescent type for a given amount of illumination. The lamp-life is dependent upon the number of starts. If the lamp is started two times per day, it should last approximately 2,500 to 4,000 hr. A wide variety of reflectors are available which may be obtained with several patterns and aperture sizes for illuminating the ceiling, and thus eliminating undesirable contrasts. The mounting height is usually 10 to 12 ft above the floor for overall lighting. Power consumption for typical fluorescent lights is given in Table I.7.

As with other plant equipment, lighting fixtures require proper maintenance. Lamps gradually lose lighting capability and in some cases should be replaced prior to actual burnout. This is particularly true in critical areas where a light failure would interrupt operations. Some operators remove bulbs on a time schedule before failure,

TABLE I.7

POWER CONSUMPTION FOR FLUORESCENT LAMPS

| | Approximate Watts | | | |
| Lamp Type | 2-Lamp | | 3-Lamp | |
	Per Lamp	Total	Per Lamp	Total
Preheat (48 in. 40-W, T-12)	40	92	40	141
Rapid-start (48 in., 40-W, T-12)	40	92	40	141
Rapid-start (48 in., 800 ma., T-12)	60	150	60	230
Rapid-start (96 in., 800 ma., T-12)	105	230	105	360
Slimline (48 in., T-12)	38.5	103	38.5	164
Slimline (96 in., T-12)	73	168	73	266
Preheat (60 in., 90–100-W, T-17)	90	196	No equipment	

Source: Benjamin Electric Mfg. Co.

when illumination has dropped greatly. A clean reflecting surface is needed for maximum illumination and such cleaning should be included in the regular housekeeping program.

References

ALLPHIN, W. 1959. Primer of Lamps and Lighting. The Chilton Co., Philadelphia.

FARRALL, A. W. 1963. Engineering for Dairy and Food Products, 3rd Edition. John Wiley & Sons, New York.

MILK INDUSTRY FOUNDATION. 1967. Manual for Milk Plant Operators, 3rd Edition. Washington, D.C.

Cross-references: *Lighting; Paint.*

IMMERSION AND BLAST FREEZING

Liquid immersion for cooling in brine (Table I.8) or in nitrogen is probably the most rapid means of cooling, but has not been found to be economical on a wide range of products. About twice as long is required to cool in an air blast at $-30°F$ as in liquid immersion at $-10°F$. Much research has been conducted on hardening of ice cream with an air blast. Most air blast tunnel hardeners operate at velocities between 500 and 1,500 fpm over the packages. The velocity of air of 750 fpm seems to be the optimum. By bagging ice cream packages, about 10% more time is required than when packaged only. For a blast tunnel with $-40°F$ air, the hardening time should be 45 min for unwrapped pint containers, 105 min for unwrapped $1/2$ gal., and 180 min for wrapped gallons. It was found that $8^3/_4$ hr were required for hardening the centers to $0°F$ with $-28°F$ air blast at 250 fpm. The plate hardening time for unwrapped cartons is about 110 min for $1/2$ gal., 80 min for a square quart, and 50 min for a flat quart.

It is necessary to maintain low temperature during transportation and to avoid necessity of rehardening. During an increase of temperature and subsequent cooling large ice crystals are formed making an undesirable product. Also, maintenance of overrun is difficult if thawing occurs. Dry Ice, eutectic salt solution frozen in cooling coils, direct expansion refrigeration system using Freon or ammonia, or liquid nitrogen for low temperature may be used to maintain proper temperature during transportation. The freezing point of nitrogen is about $-290°F$.

Cross-references: *Ice Cream Hardening and Storage; Ice Refrigeration; Nitrogen, Liquid, Cooling; Refrigeration Principles.*

TABLE I.8

TIME FOR ICE CREAM HARDENING BY IMMERSION, HOURS FOR CENTER TO COME TO $0°F$

Brine Temperature, °F	Pint	Quart	$1/2$ Gallon	2.5 Gallons
-5	1.5	2.1	3.8	10.0
-10	1.2	1.4	3.2	8.8
-20	0.9	1.3	2.9	7.8
-30	0.8	1.2	2.4	7.3
-40	0.7	1.1	2.2	7.0

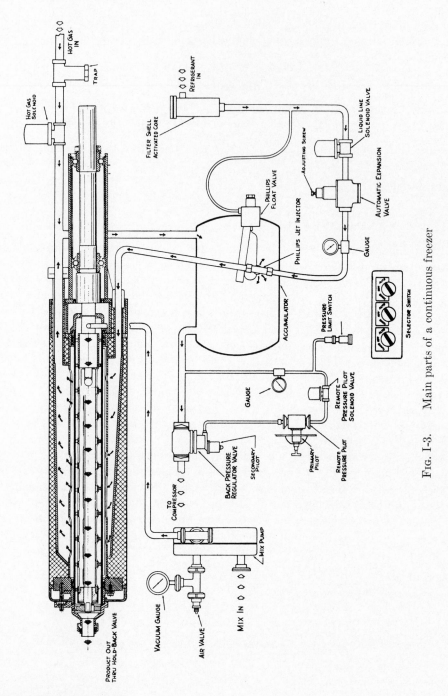

FIG. I-3.   Main parts of a continuous freezer

INDUCTION HEATING

Heating is accomplished by a high ac current with a low voltage.   The frequency of the induction coil varies over a large range, depending on the method of obtaining the effect.   Uniform heating is obtained in the normal frequency range: standard,

480, 960, 3,000, 9,600 cycles per second; spark gap, 20,000 to 40,000 cycles per second and electronic, 450,000 cycles per second. High frequency induction at 100,000 to 500,000 cycles per second gives surface heating.

Cross-reference: *Electricity.*

INSULATION

The purpose of thermal insulation is to reduce the rate of heat transfer through a wall. Insulation may be used to keep a space at a uniform temperature, low or high, at a minimum cost. As more insulation is added, the transfer of heat is reduced. Insulation, its installation, and maintenance cost money. Reduction of heat transfer saves money for energy. Thus, economical insulation means balancing the cost of insulation to the cost of energy saved, be it for heating or cooling. For a given temperature difference, more insulation for cooling or refrigerating can be justified than for heating.

Types

Heat transfer occurs by conduction, radiation, and convection. Still, dry air is a good insulator which minimizes heat transfer by conduction and convection. Poor conductors, good insulators, incorporate small, distinct air cells. Fill, rigid, and flexible materials serve this need. Radiation is reduced with shiny, smooth surfaces. Reflective insulation (film or sheets) serves this need.

Thickness

Fill or rigid insulation is most commonly used to reduce conduction and convection heat transfer. Corkboard or corkboard equivalent is often used as the basis of comparing insulation materials. For a cold storage room the following thicknesses, or equivalent, of corkboard are economical in temperate climates:

°F (Room)	In.
30	3
20	4
10	5
0	6
−10	8

Thicker insulation is needed for warmer external climates, where electrical costs are more expensive, and for critical products. With reflective insulation, which can be used for cold or warm rooms, each shiny surface is equivalent to approximately $1/2$ in. of dry fill or rigid insulation. Air space provides insulation value but if over $3/4$ in., air movement permits excessive heat loss by convection.

Insulation values may decrease if materials are damaged by mechanical abuse or absorb moisture. Proper installation includes (1) protecting insulation against possible injury; (2) covering insulation with a vapor barrier if the material is not a natural vapor barrier; and (3) assuring that all joints are properly sealed.

Vapor Movement

Vapor moves from high-temperature to low-temperature locations.   Vapor would normally move from outside toward the inside of a refrigerated area.   The vapor would normally condense, and possibly freeze, at some location in the insulated wall.   To avoid possible damage to the wall and subsequent reduction in insulation properties, a barrier to vapor flow should be placed on the warm side of the wall.   Vapor barriers commonly used are plastic foil, asphalt, metal, mastics, glass, or insulation materials which are inherent vapor barriers.   Installation practices must make the joints as a vapor barrier.

Terminology

There are certain terms and conceptions that must be understood.   The measure of quantity of heat is the Btu (British thermal unit).   When used in figuring heat loss, it is always accompanied by a definite time factor generally 1 hr and a unit of area generally 1 sq ft.   Heat loss is figured on the basis of the number of Btu lost per °F difference in temperature, the temperature on the warmer side of the wall being

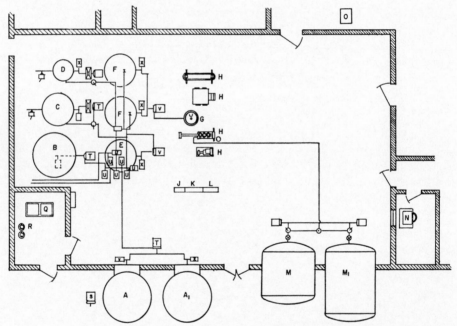

Courtesy o St. Regis Corp.

Fig. I-4.   Floor plan of a completely automatic mix making system
A, A₁, B, C, and D—Ingredient storage tanks. E—Batching tank on load cells. F and F₁—Intermediate surge tanks. G—HTST float tank. H—HTST system. J—Storage tank level indicating and control. K—Auto-flow batch builder control panel. L—HTST control panel. M and M₁—Pasteurized mix storage. N—Plant manager's office with tape printer. O—Auto-flow batch builder computer programmer. P—CIP control panel. Q—CIP system. R—Chemical injection systems. S—Ingredient receiving pump. T—Ingredient feed pumps. U—Ingredient control valves. V—Mix transfer pumps. X—APC air-operated valves.

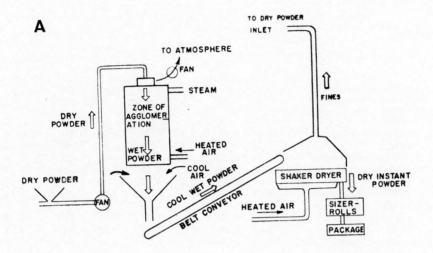

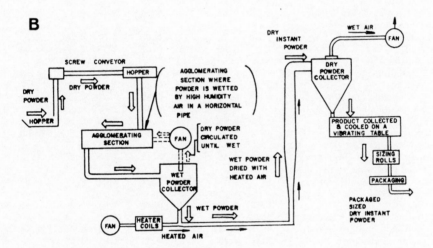

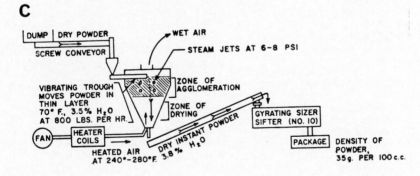

FIG. I-5.   Several processes for instantizing dry milk
A—The Peebles process.   B—The A.R.C.S. system.   C—The Blaw-Knox system.

TABLE I.10

COEFFICIENTS OF TRANSMISSION (U) FOR VARIOUS WALLS

| | | | | | ½-in. Plaster on | | | |
| | | | | | | ³/₄-in. Furring | | |
Wall Construction[1]	Plain Wall, No Plaster		Wall Direct		³/₈-in. Plasterboard		½-in. Rigid Insulation	
Concrete Masonry								
Cores not filled								
8-in. Sand and gravel or limestone	1.89	**0.53**	2.04	**0.49**	3.22	**0.31**	4.46	**0.22**
8-in. Cinder[2]	2.70	**0.37**	2.85	**0.35**	4.03	**0.25**	5.27	**0.19**
8-in. Expanded slag or clay[2]	3.01	**0.33**	3.16	**0.32**	4.34	**0.23**	5.58	**0.18**
12-in. Sand and gravel or limestone	2.06	**0.49**	2.21	**0.45**	3.39	**0.30**	4.63	**0.22**
12-in. Cinder[2]	2.85	**0.35**	3.00	**0.33**	4.18	**0.24**	5.42	**0.18**
12-in. Expanded slag or clay[2]	3.10	**0.32**	3.25	**0.31**	4.43	**0.23**	5.67	**0.18**
Cores filled with cork or equal								
8-in. Sand and gravel or limestone	2.57	**0.39**	2.72	**0.37**	3.90	**0.26**	5.14	**0.19**
8-in. Cinder[2]	4.97	**0.20**	5.12	**0.19**	6.30	**0.16**	7.54	**0.13**
8-in. Expanded slag or clay[2]	5.73	**0.17**	5.88	**0.17**	7.06	**0.14**	8.30	**0.12**
12-in. Sand and gravel or limestone	...	...	...	...	...	...	...	...
12-in. Cinder[2]	5.13	**0.20**	5.28	**0.19**	6.46	**0.15**	7.70	**0.13**
12-in. Expanded slag or clay[2]	6.85	**0.15**	7.00	**0.14**	8.18	**0.12**	9.42	**0.11**
Cast-in-Place Concrete								
6½-in. Wall	1.32	**0.76**	1.47	**0.68**	2.65	**0.38**	3.89	**0.26**
8-in. Wall	1.45	**0.69**	1.60	**0.62**	2.78	**0.36**	4.02	**0.25**
4-in. Face Brick Plus								
4-in. Common brick	2.01	**0.50**	2.16	**0.46**	3.34	**0.30**	4.58	**0.22**
4-in. Clay tile	2.21	**0.45**	2.36	**0.42**	3.54	**0.28**	4.78	**0.21**
4-in. Hollow sand and gravel unit	1.87	**0.53**	2.02	**0.49**	3.20	**0.31**	4.44	**0.23**
4-in. Solid sand and gravel unit	1.54	**0.65**	1.69	**0.59**	2.87	**0.35**	4.11	**0.24**
4-in. Hollow cinder unit	2.21	**0.45**	2.36	**0.42**	3.54	**0.28**	4.78	**0.21**
4-in. Solid cinder unit	2.03	**0.49**	2.18	**0.46**	3.36	**0.30**	4.60	**0.22**
4-in. Hollow expanded clay or slag	2.30	**0.43**	2.45	**0.41**	3.63	**0.27**	4.87	**0.20**
4-in. Solid expanded clay or slag	2.21	**0.45**	2.36	**0.42**	3.54	**0.28**	4.78	**0.21**
1-in. Wood sheathing, paper, 2 × 4 studs (wood lath and plaster)	...	...	3.69	**0.27**	3.71	**0.27**	4.95	**0.20**
4-in. Common Brick Plus								
4-in. Clay tile	2.58	**0.39**	2.73	**0.37**	3.91	**0.26**	5.15	**0.19**
4-in. Hollow sand and gravel unit	2 23	**0.45**	2.38	**0.42**	3.56	**0.28**	4.80	**0.21**
4-in. Solid sand and gravel unit	1 91	**0.52**	2.06	**0.49**	3.24	**0.31**	4.48	**0.22**
4-in. Hollow cinder unit	2.58	**0.39**	2.73	**0.37**	3.91	**0.26**	5.15	**0.19**
4-in. Solid cinder unit	2.40	**0.42**	2.55	**0.39**	3.73	**0.27**	4.97	**0.20**
4-in. Hollow expanded clay or slag	2.67	**0.37**	2.82	**0.35**	4.00	**0.25**	5.24	**0.19**
4-in. Solid expanded clay or slag	2.58	**0.39**	2.73	**0.37**	3.91	**0.26**	5.15	**0.19**
Wood sheathing, paper, 2 × 4 studs (wood lath and plaster)	...	...	4.06	0.25	4.08	**0.25**	5.32	**0.19**
Wood Construction								
Wood siding, 1-in. wood sheathing, 2 × 4 studs (wood lath and plaster)	...	...	4.09	**0.25**	4.11	**0.24**	5.35	**0.19**
Clay Tile Walls								
6-in. No exterior finish	2.35	**0.43**	2.50	**0.40**	3.68	**0.27**	4.92	**0.20**
8-in. No exterior finish	2.45	**0.41**	2.60	**0.38**	3.78	**0.26**	5.02	**0.20**
10-in. No exterior finish	2.50	**0.40**	2.65	**0.38**	3.83	**0.28**	5.07	**0.20**
6-in. Stucco exterior	2.43	**0.41**	2.58	**0.39**	3.76	**0.27**	5.00	**0.20**
8-in. Stucco exterior	2.53	**0.40**	2.68	**0.37**	3.86	**0.26**	5.10	**0.20**
10-in. Stucco exterior	2.58	**0.39**	2.73	**0.37**	3.91	**0.26**	5.15	**0.19**
Cavity Walls[3]								
Built in two units with a 1-in. or larger air space between.								
Cavity not filled								

TABLE I.10 (*Continued*)

Wall Construction[1]	Plain Wall, No Plaster		Wall Direct		¹/₂-in. Plaster on			
					³/₄-in. Furring			
					³/₈-in. Plasterboard		¹/₂-in. Rigid Insulation	
9-in. Wall of two 4-in. sand and gravel or limestone units	2.86	**0.35**	3.01	**0.33**	4.19	**0.24**	5.43	**0.18**
9-in. Wall of two 4-in. lightweight units[4]	3.56	**0.28**	3.71	**0.27**	4.89	**0.20**	6.13	**0.16**
9-in. Wall of 4-in. face brick and 4-in. lightweight unit[4]	3.00	**0.33**	3.15	**0.31**	4.33	**0.22**	5.57	**0.18**
13-in. Wall of 4-in. face brick and 8-in. lightweight unit[4]	3.85	**0.26**	4.00	**0.25**	5.18	**0.19**	6.42	**0.16**
13-in. Wall of 4-in. lightweight unit and 8-in. lightweight unit[4]	4.29	**0.23**	4.44	**0.23**	5.62	**0.18**	6.86	**0.15**

[1] The lightface figures in table are total resistances. Boldface figures are *U*-values.

[2] Resistance of 0.19 for two coats of portland cement paint added for these walls.

[3] Value of 0.78 used for air space due to transfer across ties. This value will vary with type and amount of wall ties used.

[4] Cinder or expanded slag, clay or shale.

insulation is 1.5 in., and for pipes smaller than 4 in., an insulation thickness of 1 in. is used. Piping which is outdoors or exposed to weather is usually insulated to a thickness of ¹/₈ to ¹/₄ in. greater than that used for indoor pipes, and in addition, the outdoor lines are covered with a waterproof jacket.

The thickness of insulation for covering brine piping is given in Table I.13.

Efficient Heat Exchange Surfaces

Wherever steam is used in a plant, more efficiency will result if the heat exchange surface is clean. Rust or scale always reduces the effectiveness of heat exchange surfaces. For this reason, corrosion which builds up within heat exchanger tubes reduces the transfer of heat, therefore, a greater temperature difference between the steam and opposite side of the tube is required.

Reference

Am. Soc. Heating, Ref. Air Cond. Engrs. Heating, Ventilating, Air Conditioning Guide, Ann. Publ., New York.

Cross-references: *Building Materials; Heat Transfer; Piping; Refrigerated Storage; Steam.*

IONIZATION

The flow of electrons in liquids differs considerably from the flow in solids. Such liquids as water, alcohol, and oils are very poor conductors of electricity, but acids, salts, and alkalies dissolved in water divide into electrically charged particles called ions. Salts and alkalies usually contain a metal which forms the positive ion, although ammonia, a nonmetal, also forms positive ions. Hydrogen forms the positive ion in

TABLE I.11

HEAT LOSSES FROM HORIZONTAL BARE STEEL PIPES

Btu per hr per lineal ft per °F diff. with 70° still air

Nominal Pipe Size In.	Hot Water, °F			Steam, °F			
	120	150	180	210	227.1 5 lb	299.7 50 lb	337.9 100 lb
	Temperature Difference, °F						
	50	80	110	140	157.1	227.7	267.9
$1/2$	0.455	0.495	0.546	0.584	0.612	0.706	0.760
$3/4$	0.555	0.605	0.666	0.715	0.748	0.866	0.933
1	0.684	0.743	0.819	0.877	0.919	1.065	1.147
$1^1/_4$	0.847	0.919	1.014	1.086	1.138	1.324	1.425
$1^1/_2$	0.958	1.041	1.148	1.230	1.288	1.492	1.633
2	1.180	1.281	1.412	1.512	1.578	1.840	1.987
$2^1/_2$	1.400	1.532	1.683	1.796	1.883	2.190	2.363
3	1.680	1.825	2.010	2.153	2.260	2.630	2.840
$3^1/_2$	1.900	2.064	2.221	2.433	2.552	2.974	3.215
4	2.118	2.302	2.534	2.717	2.850	3.320	3.590
5	2.580	2.804	3.084	3.303	3.470	4.050	4.385
6	3.036	3.294	3.626	3.886	4.074	4.765	5.160

Reprinted by permission from Heating, Ventilating, Air Conditioning Guide (1956).

TABLE I.12

HEAT LOSS FROM HORIZONTAL TARNISHED COPPER PIPE

Btu per hr per lineal ft per °F diff. with 70°F still air

Nominal Pipe Size (In.)	Hot Water, °F (Type K Copper Tube)			Steam, °F (Standard Pipe Size Pipe)			
	120	150	180	210	227.1 5 lb	297.7 50 lb	337.9 100 lb
	Temperature Difference, °F						
	50	80	110	140	157.1	227.7	267.9
$1/2$	0.250	0.287	0.300	0.321	0.433	0.500	0.530
$3/4$	0.340	0.381	0.409	0.429	0.533	0.543	0.654
1	0.440	0.475	0.509	0.536	0.636	0.746	0.803
$1^1/_4$	0.500	0.559	0.618	0.622	0.764	0.878	0.934
$1^1/_2$	0.580	0.656	0.710	0.750	0.904	1.053	1.120
2	0.730	0.825	0.890	0.957	1.101	1.273	1.364
$2^1/_2$	0.880	1.000	1.091	1.143	1.305	1.490	1.605
3	1.040	1.175	1.272	1.343	1.560	1.800	1.940
$3^1/_2$	1.180	1.350	1.454	1.535	1.750	2.020	2.170
4	1.460	1.500	1.635	1.715	1.941	2.240	2.430

Reprinted by permission from Heating, Ventilating, Air Conditioning Guide (1956).

TABLE I.13

RECOMMENDED THICKNESS OF INSULATION OF MAGNESIA (85%) OR ASBESTOS

Internal Temp., °F	Insulation Thickness, In.			
	Pipe 3 In. Diam and Less	Pipe 3–6 In. Diam	Pipe 6–9 In. Diam	Pipe over 9 In. Diam and Flat Surfaces
Up to 200	1	1	1	1
200 to 300	1	1	1.5	2
300 to 400	1	1.5	2	2.5
400 to 500	1.5	2	2	2.5
500 to 600	1.5	2	2.5	3
600 to 700	2	2	2.5	3
700 to 800	2	2	2.5	3

Source: Lyle (1947).

acids. The negative ions in acids and salts are formed by nonmetals often combined with oxygen, and sometimes they are formed by the oxides of metals acting as a nonmetal of which chromates are an example. Examples of common nonmetals are chlorides, chlorates, nitrates, phosphates, carbonates, sulfates, and silicates. Alkalies have hydroxyl for the negative ion which is a dependent combination of 1 oxygen atom and 1 hydrogen atom. Hydroxyl combines with the hydrogen in acids to form water when an alkali is mixed with an acid, leaving the metal and nonmetal to form a salt in the solution.

The positive ions formed by metals, hydrogen, and ammonia have lost some of their electrons leaving them unbalanced. The lost electrons attach themselves to the nonmetal portion to form the negative ions. When an electric current is passed through an ionized solution, the metallic ions move to the negative terminal where they obtain electrons from those flowing in the current to replace those which have been lost. As soon as the electrons are obtained the potential is neutralized, and the metal goes out of solution in metallic form and plates itself on the terminal or drops to the bottom of the solution as a precipitate. If hydrogen is the positive ion, it bubbles away as a gas.

The nonmetallic ions move to the positive terminal where they release their surplus electrons which flow as electric current in the circuit. The nonmetals bubble away if gas, or precipitate if not. This process is called electrolysis; the terminals are called electrodes; and the solution is an electrolyte.

Some of the metals are more active at forming ions than others and will displace each other in solution. Batteries operate on the displacement principle. Beginning with lithium and following in order of activity are potassium, sodium, barium, calcium, magnesium, aluminum, manganese, zinc, chromium, cadmium, iron, cobalt, nickel, tin, lead, hydrogen, copper, arsenic, mercury, silver, platinum, and gold.

To generate an electric current it is necessary to arrange a cell with connected terminals. If the cell is filled with silver nitrate, and one of the electrodes is composed of any of the metals that precede it, the more active metal will dissolve in the solution and cause the less active metal, which in this case is silver, to precipitate out or deposit on the other terminal. The silver ions in solution will go to the negative electrode to pick up electrons which arrive at that terminal over the wire connecting the two electrodes. The electrons come from the positive electrode where they are released when the nitrate ions give up their surplus electrons. Copper will displace silver, iron will displace copper, and in turn be displaced by zinc, which can be displaced by aluminum or magnesium. Magnesium is the most active metal in common use and will displace all other metals that go into ordinary construction materials. The voltage generated by a battery cell depends upon the relative standing of the two metals. The further apart their standing, the greater the voltage. Larger cells develop larger amounts of current as the exchange of electrons can proceed faster if the surface area of the electrodes is increased and the volume of the solution is large enough to provide numerous ions. Both dry cell and wet cell batteries operate on the displacement principle. Storage batteries are made of materials that can be reversed when current is forced into the cell against the cell potential.

Gases may be ionized by heat, friction, or radiation. Solar radiation falling upon the outer atmosphere ionizes the upper portion of the atmosphere and makes long distance radio possible.

Ionized gases are used commercially in lamps which contain gas or vapor. Ionization of the gas permits it to exchange electrons and to conduct electricity.

A wire gets warm or hot when conducting an overload of electricity, and this principle is applied to tungsten filaments to produce light. The same principle applies to gases which conduct electricity. In vapor lamps the ionized gases of mercury, neon, sodium, or helium are heated until light and ultraviolet are emitted.

The use of negatively ionized air has been proposed as a means of improving the environment for workers, for animals, and as a means of reducing microorganisms in the air. Negative ions have been claimed to be beneficial for improved work productivity, for the relief of respiratory diseases, or for healing. Controversy and contradictory evidence and claims exist with respect to the use of ionized air. The strength of ionized air is designated in ions per cubic centimeter.

Cross-references: *Batteries; Electricity; Electrolytic Corrosion; EMF Series.*

IRRADIATION

Irradiation is done with naturally occurring gamma rays or artificially accelerated high energy electron cathode ray (beta rays). Gamma radiation provides deep penetration up to several inches in a product and its container. Cathode radiation is generally used for surface treatment of products. The penetration of 1 mev (million electron volt) is $1/_5$ in. for material of a density of 1 gm per cc.

Irradiation of products is used (1) to increase the storage or shelf-life through pasteurization or sterilization, (2) to cause mutations in seeds to develop new plants, and (3) to change certain physical and chemical properties of the product. For treatment of food products, the process is often called "cold sterilization."

The quantity of radiation is called dose or dosage and is identified as the energy in roentgens for gamma irradiation, and in rep (roentgens equivalent physical) and rad (about 0.93 × rep, depending on the density) for particle irradiation. A dosage of 1 million rep is equal to 2 cal per gm of energy.

The effect of the irradiation is to ionize or to chemically change the substance, hopefully accomplishing a desirable effect, such as effecting germination, destroying microorganisms, etc. As the level of evolution of plants and animals becomes more

TABLE I.14

APPROXIMATE EFFECTS OF IRRADIATION ON BIOLOGICAL TISSUES

Product	Energy, Rep	Effect
Man	500	To kill
Plants	1,000	To induce mutations
Plants	10,000	To inhibit germination
Insects	10,000	To sterilize
Insects	100,000	To kill; near pasteurization
Nonspore forming bacteria and molds	100,000	To kill; near pasteurization
Spore forming bacteria and molds	1,000,000	To kill; near sterilization
Viruses	3,000,000	To destroy
Enzymes	10,000,000	To destroy

specialized, a lower irradiation dosage is required to cause a damaging effect on the material or organism (Table I.14). Thus, 1 million rep are required to destroy enzymes, and only 10,000 rep to inhibit germination of plants. The cost of electrical energy for a treatment of 10,000 rep with electricity at 2 cents per kwh is approximately 1.52 cents.

Present uses of irradiation which appear feasible for large installations such as terminal markets and elevators are (1) inhibiting sprouting of potatoes—10,000 rep; (2) sterilizing granary weevil and other insects in wheat and other cereals—10,000 rep; (3) killing granary weevil and other insects in wheat or other cereals—100,000 rep; (4) sterilizing some foods, such as ham or other meat in packages.

When sterilizing foods, it is necessary that the product be kept in a sterile condition after sterilization. This requires that sterilization be carried out in a package or container or in an aseptic environment and then packaged.

Irradiation of Milk with Ultraviolet

Ergosterol in milk is converted to Vitamin D through irradiation with light having a wavelength in the region between 2,300 and 3,100 Å, which is in the ultraviolet range of the spectrum. Carbon-arc lamps, mercury-vapor lamp, or special lamps designed for producing this range of wavelengths are used. A 1,000 watt unit is needed for each 2,000 lb per hr of milk. A thin film product is moved over a surface in the irradiation source.

Ultraviolet Irradiation

The ultraviolet portion of the electromagnetic spectrum is in wavelengths between 136 to 4,000 Å. The visible portion of the spectrum is in the 400 to 800 Å wavelength. The shorter wavelengths, less than 1,000 Å, produce X rays; 1,000 to 2,000 Å are ozone forming; 2,000 to 2,950 Å have bactericidal effects; 2,800 to 3,300 Å are used for tanning; and black lights which peak at 3600 Å are used for inspection of surfaces.

Cross-references: *Electricity; Moisture Measurement in Grain.*

J

JACKETED KETTLE

A jacketed kettle has space between the liner holding the product and an outer liner, between which a heating medium is placed. In a jacketed kettle there is a tendency for the steam to pass from the entrance directly to the outlet. Thus, the surface in contact with the pan is not used effectively. To maintain an approximately equal temperature in all parts of the jacket, the steam should be admitted at several points, or a single pipe should pass into and around the jacketed space with suitable openings for discharging steam over the entire heating surface. Not only should the steam be discharged equally over the heating surface, but means should be provided for thorough drainage of the condensate from the jacket. The more rapid the movement of the steam over the heating surface, the greater the transfer of heat from the steam to the liquid.

Cross-references: *Heat Exchangers; Heat Transfer; Holding Methods of Pasteurization; Retorts.*

JOB EFFICIENCY

The term job efficiency usually refers to the efficient utilization of labor in the performance of normal duties associated with production. Considerable effort and study have been devoted to the analysis of jobs performed by workers in an endeavor to achieve maximum efficiency. Most work performed in a food processing plant combines the effort of the worker with the operation of one or more machines.

By employing time and motion study to analyze the steps involved in an operation the efficiency of the worker can frequently be increased. Included in the analysis are methods, materials, tools, and equipment. Four main objectives to be achieved from the study are (1) to determine the most economical methods of doing the work; (2) to standardize the methods, materials, and equipment; (3) to determine accurately the time required to do the task; and (4) to assist in training the worker.

Work simplification to achieve these objectives was begun with the studies made by Frank C. Gilbreth and his wife. The theory of their investigations was to break down a job into fundamental motions of the two hands of the worker. In present day time and motion studies the steps are set forth on a process chart to make a graphical representation. A flow diagram is then made which traces the path of the operator, supplies, or other materials through the plant. An activity chart is then developed which details the operation as plotted against a time scale. After collecting the data on an operation, the analysis is made in an effort to develop an improved method.

Operational steps can sometimes be eliminated or combined resulting in greater economy. The design and utilization of a particular machine can often be improved so as to improve the productivity of the worker, reduce drudgery, or improve safety.

In making time and motion studies the cooperation of the worker is very important. A person who realizes that through an improved method his job may be made easier will usually cooperate in the analysis.

Some of the general principles involved in improving job efficiency for an individual include the following. (1) Both hands should begin and end their motions at the same time. (2) The arms should move in a symmetrical manner usually in opposite directions simultaneously. (3) A person's motions should be as small as possible to reduce fatigue. Motions producing minimum fatigue and maximum economy in order are finger motions; finger and wrist; finger, wrist, and lower arm; finger, wrist, lower arm, and upper arm; finger, wrist, lower arm, upper arm, and body motions. (4) Momentum should be used to assist the worker where possible and reduced to a minimum when it must be checked by muscular effort. (5) Continuous curved motions are more desirable than straight line motions for the worker's arms. (6) Arrangements should be made to develop rhythmic motions.

A method of checking labor utilization is known as the occurrence study technique which is suitable for analyzing the work of people rather than machines. The observer of an operation collects data on an observation sheet noting the job performed by a worker at random times. The various job elements are listed on the observation sheet and noted with a simple mark when being performed at random times. This summary shows which elements of an operation are receiving most of a person's time. The number of observations needed to assure statistical reliability at the 95% level may be computed using the following formula

$$N = \frac{4P\,(1 - P)}{0.0016} = \frac{P\,(1 - P)}{0.0004}$$

where N = number of observations needed

P = % of occurrence

After determining the percent occurrence of a job element, basic and standard performance times for an element can be determined. Basic time adjusts for a person working faster or slower than normal speed in producing a certain number of units, whereas standard time adjusts further to make other time allowances as a rest period. The method helps managers plan production, develop incentive pay rates, and estimate costs.

Job efficiency is closely associated with the arrangement of equipment, the work place, and general plant layout. Supplies must be made readily accessible to reduce lost time. Convenience of controls, valves, adjustments, and the like are very important. The motion study should point up weaknesses in a plant layout, equipment arrangement, and methods. Various techniques are used to make studies: work sampling, photography, stop watch, etc.

References

MORROW, R. L. 1957. Motion Economy and Work Measurement, 2nd Edition. Ronald Press Co., New York.

MUNDEL, M. E. 1955. Motion and Time Study. Prentice Hall, Englewood Cliffs, N.J.

456. *Job Efficiency*

TRACY, P. H., ARMERDING, G. D., and HANNAH, H. W. 1958. Dairy Plant Management. McGraw-Hill Book Co., New York.

Cross-references: *Dairy Plant Layout and Design; Flow Charts; Plant Layout.*

L

LACTOMETER

The lactometer is an instrument for estimating the specific gravity and the solids content of milk. It consists of a cylindrical instrument with a float, so weighted that it floats upright in milk, and is based on the principle that a body floating in a liquid is pushed upward by the liquid with a force equal to the weight of the displaced liquid. There are three types of lactometers: the Quevenne, which is the most common, the New York Board of Health lactometer and the Watson.

The Quevenne lactometer is floated in milk and resembles a large air chamber with a bulb of shot or mercury at the bottom. A scale in lactometer degrees reading from 15 at the top to 40 at the bottom is attached, as is also a thermometer. Because of lack of space on the glass stem which is very small in diameter, the 1.0 reading is omitted and therefore to obtain a full lactometer reading, 1.0 is added to the reading on the stem. If the reading on the stem is 30, the total reading would be 1.030. The reading indicated on the lactometer is correct when the milk is at 60°F. If the milk is between 50° and 70°F, a correction factor is used to give the proper correct reading. This reading is 0.1 of a lactometer degree and is added to the lactometer reading for each degree the temperature is above 60°F, and subtracted for each degree that the milk is below 60°F.

The New York Board of Health lactometer is somewhat similar to the Quevenne lactometer and is used for the same purpose. No thermometer is attached and the scale reads from 0 down to 120. A Watson lactometer is read at 102°F.

The lactometer is used primarily for the purpose of determining whether the milk has been diluted with water. It is essentially a highly accurate hydrometer.

There is also a special test for total solids by use of lactometer which is done at 102°F.

For borderline samples or where great accuracy is required as for court cases, it is suggested that the Mojonnier or a chemical method as recommended by the Association of Official Agricultural Chemists be used. Normal 3.5% fat milk will have a specific gravity of 1.034; 4% fat milk will have a specific gravity of 1.032; 5% fat milk will have a specific gravity of 1.031.

References

FRANDSEN, J. H. 1958. Dairy Handbook & Dictionary. Available from AVI Publishing Co., Westport, Conn.
HENDERSON, J. L. 1971. The Fluid Milk Industry, 3rd Edition. AVI Publishing Co., Westport, Conn.

Cross-references: *Density of Milk; Specific Gravity.*

LAGOON

A lagoon is a shallow body of water of moderate size, which may cover several acres. It is of particular interest to food engineers because of its use for disposal of waste products. If the lagoon is large enough to supply the necessary aeration for oxidation of organic matter, it is quite effective as a means of disposing of milk or cannery waste.

Types

Lagoons are of two types, the aerobic and the anaerobic. Aerobic (odor free) lagoons are made from 3 to 5 ft deep, and there is sufficient oxygen in the water to support fish and marine life. The loading can be from 17 to 20 lb of BOD per acre of surface per day, although some authorities may recommend as high as 40 lb BOD per day per acre. The space required is prohibitive for most urban plants.

The anaerobic lagoon is usually from 15 to 20 ft deep, as the size is determined by volume rather than surface area. The loading would be about 15 times the maximum load per square foot of surface as used in aerobic lagoons. In this type of lagoon, groups of anaerobic microorganisms take over and the process is known as anaerobic stabilization. The anaerobes require oxygen, but it is obtained from the decomposition of organic materials which contain molecular oxygen.

Construction

When constructing a lagoon, care should be taken to avoid pollution of underground water supplies. The local soil conservation engineer and the county sanitarian should be consulted about the type of soil and what is required to adequately seal the lagoon. In gravel or sandy soils, the problems of sealing the lagoon may be so great that other methods of disposal should be considered. Three methods of sealing have been used: (1) the sides and bottom can be lined with about 6 in. of clay if there is a local supply; (2) bentonite (colloidal clay) can be mixed with the top 2 to 3 in. of soil; and (3) the pit can be lined with plastic film (6–8 mil thickness). Problems have been encountered with plastic film, because waste may seep under and bacteria decompose the waste and produce gas which causes the plastic to rise to the surface.

Operation

The first loading of a lagoon should be gradual in the summer months. A truck load of sludge from a septic tank might be helpful in starting a lagoon, but this has not been proved by research. If a lagoon is started in the winter, the loading rate is not as important because decomposition will probably be slight before warmer weather. After the lagoon is full, uniform loading at least twice a week is desired.

Some townships and counties are considering ordinances to restrict the use of lagoons. The main complaint has been from odors. An anaerobic lagoon, will have some objectionable odors at times during the year.

Planning and Construction of Anaerobic Lagoons

Before constructing a lagoon, check with the local sanitarian about ordinances which prohibit or restrict their use.

Location.—Place the lagoon a minimum of $1/4$ mile from a residence. This means that lagoons should not be placed close to roads or property lines. Locate the lagoon downhill from the building it is to serve so gravity will carry the waste.

Size.—Based on volume, allow a minimum of 600 BOD per acre per day.

Depth.—Suggest that the maximum depth be 10 to 12 ft. Check with local Soil Conservation Service office about soil types, methods of sealing, and general construction. The practical minimum depth should be 3 to 5 ft.

Water.—Water from the surrounding watershed should not be allowed to enter the lagoon except during the initial filling period unless approval is obtained to route the overflow to a river or stream. To maintain the water level in large lagoons at the design depth, additional water may have to be supplied during hot weather.

Fence.—The embankments should be fenced to keep out animals and trespassers. Post warning signs and keep gate locked. Maintain mowed, low-growing, spreading grasses on the embankments.

Pipe.—To carry the sewage water mixture to the lagoon a 6 to 8 in. sewer tile or pipe with driven or masonry joints should be used. A slope of approximately 2% is recommended.

Inlets.—A free-loading inlet over the lagoon works well. Rodent entry is discouraged if the opening is 2 ft above the waterline, over deep water, and is covered with a flap gate. Dribbling liquids through a free-loading inlet may freeze in the winter, and solids may plug the line in the summer. Provide a stopper at the building, and drain gutters intermittently.

Outlets.—A trickle tube handles normal discharge. The extension into the lagoon prevents entry of floating material, but may be damaged by ice movement. A sodded spillway is required if surface water is routed to the lagoon.

Lagoon Management.—Two principal problems arise in the operation of a waste disposal lagoon. The first is objectionable odors. This is caused by insufficient surface area of the lagoon in proportion to the quantity of the material fed into the lagoon. The second problem is that of the accumulation of solids. This is a natural result of continued feeding of material of a fibrous and solids nature into the lagoon and eventually filling to the point where it must be cleaned by removing the undigested solids and disposing of them in a land fill or some other suitable place.

Many waste disposal lagoons are in use. However, in many locations there is not sufficient surface area available for the successful operation of a lagoon and therefore another method must be used.

References

Gurnham, F. C. 1965. Industrial Waste Control. Academic Press, New York.
Rudolph, W. 1953. Industrial Wastes. Van Nostrand Reinhold Co., New York.
U.S. Public Health Serv. 1959. An industrial waste guide to the milk processing industry. Publ. *298*.

Cross-reference: *Waste Disposal and Treatment Systems.*

LEVEL MEASUREMENT AND CONTROL

Measurement

Process industries require accurate liquid level measurement on many tanks. The problem is complicated by often difficult sanitary regulations, and by a need for the device to withstand sterilizing temperatures and other operations.

Types

There are several types of measuring devices. The sight glass Fig. L.1 provides direct measurement of the level of the liquid, either by a glass inside of the tank, or through the use of a connecting tube using Archimedes principle. This method is more frequently used on water tanks and other nonsanitary installations. Special safety devices with extra strength glass and with protected glasses are used for extremely high pressures or where there is a danger of breakage. Special check valves can be installed in the lines leading to the sight glass which will shut off the flow in case of breakage of the glass. A float valve with indicating pointer is another simple type of measuring device (Fig. L.2). This system is also used mostly for nonsanitary installations. The indirect measurement of liquid level is done using a column of mercury or other liquid separated from the main body of the liquid by a flexible diaphragm. This system is quite widely used. It can be made sanitary and is accurate to within 1%. This type of level indicator (Fig. L.3) can be remotely connected so that the levels from various tanks can be read on a battery of indicators at one location. The electric contact indicator is a simple device in which electrodes protrude into the liquid product, and cause a current to flow in an indicating circuit to provide appropriate control (Fig. L.4).

An electronic load cell (Fig. L.5) is a widely used instrument for measuring the amount of liquid in a tank which actuates an electronic meter which can be calibrated

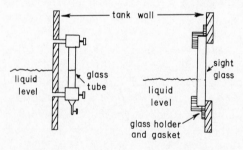

FIG. L-1.   Glass liquid level gauges

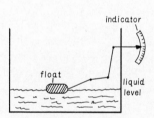

FIG. L-2.   Float type liquid level indicator

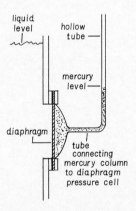

FIG. L-3.   Diaphragm type liquid level gauge
Pressure on inside of tank causes mercury to rise in the tube.

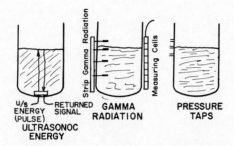

FIG. L-4.   Electrode probes method of level measurement and control

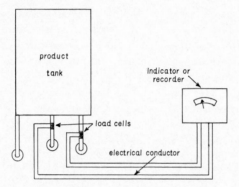

FIG. L-5.   Electronic load cells for weighing product

to read directly in pounds, gallons, feet, or other desired unit.   This method of measurement and control is one of the most sanitary, since there is no contact between the fluid being measured and the measuring instrument.   It is also well-adapted for use on large tanks or vats, and can be used with a totalizing device to show the amount of product added, the amount on hand, and the amount removed.   This type of unit also lends itself to remote control and indication with the recording or indicating instruments located several hundred feet from the tank.

Control

The level controller regulates the product feed to the vacuum pan, or individual level controllers regulate the feed to each effect of a multiple-effect evaporator if the evaporator has natural or forced recirculation.   If the evaporator is of the "single pass" or "straight through" type, and therefore has no recirculation, level controllers if used merely maintain a level on the suction side of the product withdrawal pumps.

Although an operating evaporator exhibits no clear-cut level (because of the frothing condition of the boiling liquid), there is an effective level which can be measured and controlled.

On manually controlled recirculation evaporators, the level is visually observed in a sight glass and the product feed hand valve is throttled to maintain the level.

For automatic level control, numerous approaches have been used.   Some evaporators have built-in level control devices operated by a float or on the basis or differential pressure.   However, the most common means of sensing evaporator level for control purposes is with a differential pressure measuring instrument. One has the differential pressure instrument connected near the bottom of the evaporator body, and the other is connected to the vapor space to provide a reference pressure.

Two types of differential pressure instruments can be used, the "open type" which requires connecting sensing lines between the level taps and the instrument, and the "filled type" which has a sealing metal diaphragm which isolates the product from the instrument proper (Fig. L.4). The open type, such as aneroid manometers, differential bellows, and differential pressure transmitters, require an air or water purge to keep product out of the sensing lines. The "filled type" with a higher initial cost has the advantage of not requiring a purge on the "product side," because the stainless steel diaphragm can generally be mounted directly on the side or bottom of the evaporator body. This also has the advantage of being a more sanitary installation than the open type instrument with its associated purge. A normal range for an evaporator level measuring instrument would be 0 to 100 in. of water. Other devices for level measurement include electrical capacitance, air purged pressure taps, load cells for weighing the products, and aneroid (mercuryless) manometers.

Aneroid manometers are commonly used for evaporator control. Brass bellows are provided for measuring the differential pressure developed by the liquid head which activates the instrument. Aneroid brass bellow manometers which operate in the pressure range from 0 to 150 in. of water are used for evaporators (Fig. L.6).

Cross-references: *Controllers; Flow Measurement; Solids Level Control.*

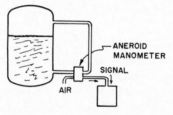

Fɪɢ. L-6.   Aneroid manometer

LIGHTING (ILLUMINATION)

Illumination usually refers to energy radiated in the visible spectrum from 0.38 to 0.70 μ wavelength (3,800 to 7,000 Å wavelength). Illumination is important in the processing plant from the standpoint of visual operation, safety, cleanliness, inspection, and color recognition. Radiation from the spectrum is also important from the standpoint of its effects on biological materials.

The lumen is the amount of light which will give a light intensity of 1 ft-cd over 1 sq ft surface. The foot candle is defined on the basis of a standard candle a distance of 1 ft from the source, whereas the lumen is the light of 1 standard candle over 1 sq ft area at a distance of 1 ft. The foot-lambert is the measure of brightness of illumination and is used for reflected light.

Visible and Near Visible Spectrum

The visible spectrum is made up of the colors red, orange, yellow, green, blue, and violet, from long to short wavelengths. The shorter wavelengths produce ultraviolet;

the longer wavelengths produce infrared radiation.   Ultraviolet radiation may be used for germicidal lamps which peak at 2,500 Å; sun lamps, which peak at 3,000 Å; and black light, which is used for inspection, which peaks at 3,600 Å.

Principles Involved

Light requirements vary with age, background color and light, and amount of detail of the worker for the job.   Older people need more light than younger people, mainly because the size of the pupil decreases with age.   The efficiency and comfort of a worker are decreased because of glare.   Every effort should be made to provide diffused light.   The background effect is produced through the color and smoothness of the surface.   The recommended level of illumination established by the Illuminating Engineering Society of America for different processing operations and location is given in Table I.6; Table L.1 gives their recommendations for various tasks.

Light Intensities and Colors

To fulfill the requirements of proper illumination, light should be well-diffused and constant, that is, nonflickering; to provide proper background the ceiling should have a minimum reflectance of 75% and the side walls from 50 to 60%, and the floor a reflectance of about 20%.   Colors which may reflect too much light and cause glare, and which might otherwise cause image reflections may be used on the ceiling.   The reflectance of the floor, walls, and ceiling with a given light depends upon the roughness and color of the surface.   In many processing plants, because of the smoothness of

TABLE L.1

1958 I.E.S. RECOMMENDED LEVELS OF ILLUMINATION

Offices	Illumination, Foot Candles
Designing, detailed drafting	200
Bookkeeping, auditing, tabulating, rough drafting	150
Regular office work, filing, index references, mail sorting	100
Reading or transcribing handwriting in ink or medium pencil	70
Reading high contrast or well-printed material, not involving prolonged seeing	30
Corridors, elevators, stairways	20

Brightness (422)	Guide Brightness, Foot Lamberts
Most difficult	420 and up
Very difficult	120–420
Difficult	42–120
Ordinary	18–42
Easy	Below 18

	Reflectance	
	60%	6%
Most difficult	700 fc	7000
Very difficult	200–700 fc	2000–7000
Difficult	70–200 fc	700–2000
Ordinary	30–70 fc	300–700
Easy	30 fc and below	300 fc and below

TABLE L.2

LIGHT REFLECTION WITH DIFFERENT COLORS OF PAINT

Color	Reflection, %	Color	Reflection, %
White gloss	84	Light blue	54
Flat white	82	Medium green	52
White, eggshell	81	Maple wood finish	42
Ivory white	79	Medium blue	35
Silver gray	75	Dark gray	30
Yellow	75	Oak wood finish	17
Cream	74	Walnut wood finish	16
Pink	72	Dark red	13
Light buff	70	Mahogany wood finish	12
Ivory tan	67	Dark brown	10
Medium yellow	65	Dark blue	8
Light green	65	Dark green	7
Medium buff	65	Black	5
Medium gray	58		

These values are not intended to represent all paints, but to provide general information of a relative nature regarding paint colors.

surfaces, the color becomes the controlling factor for reflectance and therefore illumination. A dark color will absorb more light, giving a lower reflectance, whereas a light color reflects a large portion of the light. The general reflectance values of different colors are given in Table L.2. Note that different shades of the same color will have different reflectances. Thus, Table L.2 can be used only as an indication of the amount of reflectance.

A blue fluorescent light should be used with blues, blue-greens, greens, and violets; when diffused with orange, a muddy appearance will result. White or soft white fluorescent light should be used with cream, ivory, and tan; when used with green will give a gray appearance.

Light Source

Incandescent or fluorescent light sources can be used. The incandescent has more long-wave radiation, with reds and yellows, than does the fluorescent lighting. Lighting is produced more from the low temperature filament which provides heat as well as light. If it is desirable to have both heat and light, the incandescent light is favored. From the standpoint of light production, the fluorescent tube is about $2^1/_2$ times as efficient as the incandescent. It provides what is known as a cool source because much less heat is given off. If lighting a refrigerated or cool area is desired without increasing refrigeration load, the fluorescent is preferred over the incandescent. However, special tubes must be secured for operations below 40°F. Less glare is provided from most fluorescent lights. The life of the fluorescent tube is based more on the number of times the fixture is turned off and on, but in general is from 2,500 to 4,000 hr. The fluorescent light should not normally be used in a location where there are many-on-off operations; it may be more economical to leave the light on. In general the cost of a fluorescent installation is about 2 to 3 times the incandescent. The power factor, unless the fixture is properly designed and equipped with capacitors, is normally low for the circuit of a fluorescent light. Devices for correcting power can be obtained and should be included, particularly in industrial operations. Instant-start fixtures and tubes are available and now in common use.

To maintain proper illumination, with either incandescent or fluorescent lighting, a regular maintenance program of replacement of bulbs or tubes must be followed. Under prolonged use, the quantity of light output decreases, and can decrease the efficiency of workers, or make their job more dangerous.

Cross-references: *Illumination Fixtures; Irradiation; Paint.*

LINEAR PROGRAMMING

Linear programming is one of the most used mathematical techniques developed for relating and evaluating the relationship of variables for management functions. A typical problem in linear programming will have more unknowns than equations. The unknowns or variables are restricted to positive values. There is some value for which the objective is to minimize or maximize. It is implied that the relationship is linear, i.e., it costs twice as much to handle twice the amount of material. One must be sure that the variables are linear or recognize the limitations if not linear. The two most important procedures of linear programming are the transportation technique and the simplex technique.

Transportation Technique

The problem involves moving materials from surplus areas to deficit areas at a minimum cost. This is sometimes called the distribution method.

Assume that the product is available at 3 different locations, *m:* 1, 2, 3, and is needed at 4 locations, *n:* 1, 2, 3, 4. The distribution matrix is represented by Table L.3.

The cost of moving the product is to be minimized. Thus:

x_{ij} = number of products moved from i the source to jth consumption.
$i = (1, 2, 3, \ldots m)$ at source
$j = (1, 2, 3, 4, \ldots n)$ at consumption
c_{ij} = cost per unit to move from ith source to jth consumption

TABLE L.3

MATRIX WITH QUANTITY AND COST

To → From	1	2	3	n	Supply
1	C_{11} x_{11}	C_{12} x_{12}	C_{13} x_{13}	C_{1n} x_{1n}	S_1
2	C_{21} x_{21}	C_{22} x_{22}	C_{23} x_{23}	C_{2n} x_{2n}	S_2
m	C_{m1} x_{m1}	C_{m2} x_{m2}	C_{m3} x_{m3}	C_{mn} x_{mn}	S_m
Demand	D_1	D_2	D_3	D_n	$\Sigma D = \Sigma S$

$$\sum_{\substack{i=1 \\ j=1}}^{\substack{m \\ n}} C_{ij}\, x_{ij} = \text{minimum}$$

The cost expressed as negative numbers can be imposed on the distribution matrix as shown in Table L.4. Thus

$$0.05x_{11} + 0.03x_{12} + 0.065x_{13} + 0.045x_{14} + 0.055x_{21} +$$
$$0.035x_{22} + 0.06x_{23} + 0.04x_{24} + 0.06x_{31} + 0.03x_{32} +$$
$$0.06x_{33} + 0.035x_{34} = \text{minimum}$$

Subject to storage capacities and utilization as indicated:

Storage	Utilization
$S_1 = 2,000$ cwt	$D_1 = \quad 500$ cwt
$S_2 = 1,200$ cwt	$D_2 = 1,200$ cwt
$S_3 = 1,000$ cwt	$D_2 = 1,500$ cwt
———————	$D_4 = 1,000$ cwt
$S\ \ = 4,200$ cwt	———————
	$D\ \ = 4,2000$ cwt

$$S_1 = x_{11} + x_{12} + x_{13} + x_{14} = 2000$$
$$S_2 = x_{21} + x_{22} + x_{23} + x_{24} = 1200$$
$$S_3 = x_{31} + x_{32} + x_{33} + x_{34} = 1000$$

and

$$D_1 = x_{11} + x_{21} + x_{31} = \quad 500$$
$$D_2 = x_{12} + x_{22} + x_{32} = 1,200$$
$$D_3 = x_{13} + x_{23} + x_{33} = 1,500$$
$$D_4 = x_{13} + x_{24} + x_{24} = 1,000$$

The first feasible solution is obtained by starting at the upper left-hand corner, sometimes called the northwest rule, and filling in the maximum quantities which can be entered depending upon supply and demand. The first feasible solution shows a

TABLE L.4

FIRST FEASIBLE SOLUTION

From \ To →	1	2	3	4	Supply
1	$-.050$	$-.03$	$-.065$	$-.045$	2000
	500	*1200*	*300*		
2	$-.055$	$-.035$	$-.06$	$-.04$	1200
			1200		
3	$-.060$	$-.03$	$-.06$	$-.035$	1000
				1000	
Demand	500	1200	1500	1000	4200

cost of \$187.50. This is a feasible but not necessarily optimum solution. The next step is to determine alternative possibilities and select the optimum arrangement (4, 16). The values in Table L-4 are feasible and, in this case, optimum.

The values used for the cost must be linear to apply in this configuration. Certainly it is difficult to foresee a linear relationship—that is, the same total cost per cwt to handle 100 lb or 1000 lb. The operating costs will be more nearly linear than the total cost.

The operating costs for handling by various methods, c_{mn}'s, can be assessed. The difference in operating costs

$$(x_{mn})(c_{mn} - c_{mn}')$$

using two different methods, can be used to determine the amount of money which can justifiably be invested in one method compared to another method. The c_{mn} value can be used for different methods of handling such as manual, truck, belt conveyor, chain, flight conveyor, auger, portable wagon, or fluidized or pneumatic handling (Table L.5). If it is known that method A costs 5¢ and method B 8¢ per cwt for operating cost for handling 1,000 cwt per yr, \$30.00 more per year could be invested in equipment for method B.

Simplex Method of Linear Programming

The simplex method of linear programming is used to determine an optimum assignment or allocation of materials as contrasted to the schedule which is optimized as covered by the transportation technique. Thus, the simplex method would be useful to solve such problems as the following.

(1) Most profitable mixture of ice cream to sell; optimum use of machine tools.

(2) Optimal program for mixing three grades of nuts.

(3) Planning economical cropping programs.

The restrictions placed on a linear relationship are in the form of linear inequalities. If x is less than or equal to $y (x \leq y)$, and y is 10, x can be any value of 10 or less. By multiplying the inequality by -1, the relationship becomes $-x$ is greater than

TABLE L.5

ESTIMATED COSTS, c_{mn}, FOR ENERGY FOR HANDLING 1 TON A DISTANCE OF 100 FT
BY DIFFERENT METHODS

	Hp-hr per ton	Cost per Ton
Fluid		
Pneumatic	1.3	\$0.026
Pneumatic	0.35	0.0070
Liquid-water-horizontal	0.015	0.0003
Free-flowing or non-free-flowing		
Flight conveyor	0.044	0.00088
Auger conveyor	0.16	0.0032
Belt conveyor	0.02	0.0004
Manual		0.75
Auger	0.42	0.0084
Truck		0.012
Pallet		0.001

$-y(-x \geq -y)$. This relationship is of value to put an equation in comparable form with all the x's or y's on the same side of the equation. The solution to the following system of three inequalities

$$x - y \leq 0, \; y - 1 \geq 0, \; x - 6 \leq 0$$

The simplex method is used to determine a number of solutions to systems made up of inequalities. In an equation as follows

$$0.1x_1 + 0.2x_2 + 0.3x_3 \leq 500$$

it can be changed from an inequality to equality by adding a slack variable, x_4, the prefix of which is identified as P_4.

$$0.1x_1 + 0.2x_2 + 0.3x_3 + p_4\, x_4 = 500$$

The value of P_4, the slack variable, is one. Several equations are expressed as a matrix placing 0's where there are no terms. The slack variables, which have a coefficient of one as associated with column vectors, form a unit matrix with ones along the diagonal P_4 and P_n. The procedure of solving a problem is to progressively select new unknowns to solve the equation until the optimum set is chosen.

The following example illustrates the simplex method of solving mathematical programming. A person needs 1,500 lb per day of product. He may use a small electric motor driven 1-hp (100 lb per hr) continuous mill, g_1, up to 10 hr per day or a large grinder, g_2, driven by a 25-hp tractor (2,000 lb per hr). After grinding, the product can be handled manually—s_1, flight conveyor—s_2, or wagon and trailer—s_3. If processed at the second location, an additional 5¢ per cwt must be added for handling to the feed center (Table L.6). (There is a maximum of 1 hr per day available for manual handling, which can be accumulated to 7 hr per wk.) The P or vertical column represents the time in hours per 100 lb for various methods. Note that some of the spaces are left blank. For example, no manual handling is required for the continuous operation.

Let x_1 = hundred-weight of materials (per day) for process 1 under P_1, so x_n = hundred-weight of feed with various processes. Inequalities governing relationships:

$$
\begin{array}{lllll}
g_1 & 1x_1 \;+\; 1x_2 \;+\; 1x_3 & & \leq 10 \text{ hr per day} \\
g_2 & \qquad\qquad\qquad\qquad 0.05x_1 + 0.05x_5 + 0.05x_6 & \leq\; .8 \text{ hr per day} \\
s_1 & 0.04x_1 \qquad\qquad\qquad + 0.02x_4 & \leq\; 1 \text{ hr per day} \\
s_2 & \qquad 0.002x_2 \qquad\qquad + 0.001x_5 & \leq 10 \text{ hr per day} \\
s_3 & \qquad\qquad 0.03x_3 \qquad\qquad\qquad + 0.01x_6 & \leq\; 1 \text{ hr per day}
\end{array}
$$

TABLE L.6

TIME TO HANDLE 100 LB BY VARIOUS METHODS, IN HOURS

Machines	Continuous Production at Location 1			Production at Location 2		
	P_1	P_2	P_3	P_4	P_5	P_6
g_1	1.0	1.0	1.0			
g_2				0.05	0.05	0.05
s_1	0.04			0.02		
s_2		0.002			0.001	
s_3			0.03			0.01

The first step is to clear the above relationship of factors by multiplying by factors to provide whole numbers throughout.

g_1 $\quad x_1 + x_2 + x_3$ $\qquad\qquad\qquad$ $\leq$ 10 hr per day

g_2 $\qquad\qquad\qquad x_4 + x_5 + x_6$ $\qquad$ $\leq$ 16 hr per day

s_1 $\quad 2x_2 \qquad\qquad +x_4$ $\qquad\qquad$ $\leq$ 50 hr per day

s_2 $\quad 2x_2 \qquad\qquad\qquad + x_5$ $\qquad$ $\leq$ 10,000 hr per day

s_3 $\qquad\qquad 3x_3 \qquad\qquad\qquad + x_6$ $\qquad$ $\leq$ 100 hr per day

Slack variables x_7, x_8, x_9, x_{10}, and x_{11} are then introduced, which denote time not used and which balances the equation

g_1 $\quad x_1 + x_2 + x_3 \qquad\qquad\qquad + x_7$ $\qquad\qquad$ = 10

g_2 $\qquad\qquad\qquad + x_4 + x_5 + x_6 \qquad + x_8$ $\qquad\qquad$ = 16

s_1 $\quad 2x_1 \qquad\qquad + x_4 \qquad\qquad\qquad + x_9$ $\qquad$ = 50

s_2 $\qquad 2x_2 \qquad\qquad + x_5 \qquad\qquad\qquad\qquad + x_{10}$ = 10,000

s_3 $\qquad\qquad 3x_3 \qquad\qquad + x_6 \qquad\qquad\qquad\qquad\qquad + x_{11}$ = 100

These equations can be represented as follows, with P_n representing vectors (ordered set of numbers) for x_n

$$P_1 x_1 + P_2 x_2 + P_3 x_3 + P_4 x_4 + P_5 x_5 + P_6 x_6 + P_7 x_7 + P_8 x_8$$
$$+ P_9 x_9 + P_{10} x_{10} + P_{11} x_{11} = P_0$$

where represents

$$\begin{pmatrix}1\\0\\2\\0\\0\end{pmatrix} x_1 + \begin{pmatrix}1\\0\\0\\2\\0\end{pmatrix} x_2 + \begin{pmatrix}1\\0\\0\\0\\3\end{pmatrix} x_3 + \begin{pmatrix}0\\1\\1\\1\\0\end{pmatrix} x_4 + \begin{pmatrix}0\\1\\0\\1\\0\end{pmatrix} x_5 + \begin{pmatrix}0\\1\\0\\0\\1\end{pmatrix} x_6 +$$

$$\begin{pmatrix}1\\0\\0\\0\\0\end{pmatrix} x_7 + \begin{pmatrix}0\\1\\0\\0\\0\end{pmatrix} x_8 + \begin{pmatrix}0\\0\\1\\0\\0\end{pmatrix} x_9 + \begin{pmatrix}0\\0\\0\\1\\0\end{pmatrix} x_{10} + \begin{pmatrix}0\\0\\0\\0\\1\end{pmatrix} x_{11} = \begin{pmatrix}10\\16\\50\\10,000\\100\end{pmatrix}$$

Rearranging

P_0	P_1	P_2	P_3	P_4	P_5	P_6	P_7	P_8	P_9	P_{10}	P_{11}
10	1	1	1	0	0	0	1	0	0	0	0
16	0	0	0	1	1	1	0	1	0	0	0
50	2	0	0	1	0	0	0	0	1	0	0
10,000	0	2	0	1	1	0	0	0	0	1	0
100	0	0	3	0	0	1	0	0	0	0	1

Note: unit matrix formed by slack vectors.

The values of x_1, x_2, x_3, x_n are determined through a repetitive process to obtain the combination which will accomplish the task in the least time. The example is given to illustrate the approach used in the simplex method. The procedure for solving is too lengthy for presentation here.

References

Churchman, C. W., and Ackoff, R. L. 1957. Introduction to Operation Research. John Wiley & Sons, New York.

Hall, C. W. 1958. Theoretical considerations in materials handling systems. Agr. Eng. *39*, No. 9, 524–529, 539.

LIQUID SUGAR HANDLING

Liquid cane sugar is obtained by stopping the concentration of the mother liquor short of crystallization. Liquid beet sugar is produced through remelting of granulated sugar, which is more expensive than the process for liquid cane sugar. Cane sugar, therefore, has a competitive advantage in certain industries such as bread making, confectionery products, ice cream, and sherbets. In the canning industry corn sugar and corn syrup are gaining in importance. Liquid corn sugar must be heated slightly to prevent excessive viscosity which impairs pumping.

Specifications

Liquid sugars typically possess the characteristics for both sucrose syrup and 50% invert syrup (Table L.7).

The largest volume of syrup for human consumption consists of liquid sugars which range from water-white sucrose of 67° Brix to the white-yellow and light-brown solutions 76° to 77° Brix of sucrose and invert sugar. Some firms ship granulated sugar in bulk to remelting plants where it is filtered and inverted as well as plain liquid sucrose combined to form the desired liquid compound.

The growth of yeast and molds is controlled in liquid sugars by use of ultraviolet light in the storage tank. Some of the yeast which have been discovered in sucrose syrups are *Saccharomyces cerevisiae*. In partially inverted sugar syrups, *Saccharomyces rouxie* has been found at 72° to 76° Brix. *Rhodotorula* and *Candida* have been found in sucrose and partially inverted syrups at 55° Brix in pre-evaporated liquors. In sucrose-corn syrup blends at 68° to 70° Brix *Saccharomyces mellis* has been found.

Handling Procedures

Liquid sugars should be stored in conveniently located large tanks near the point

TABLE L.7

CHARACTERISTICS FOR LIQUID SUGAR

	Sucrose Syrup	50% Invert Syrup
Specific gravity, 68°/68°F	1.328	1.395
Density, °Brix	66.5	77.1
Density, °Baumé (M-145)	35.9	41.0
Color	Same as granulated sugar	Light straw
pH	6.5–7.0	6.5–7.0
Invert, %	0.02	50.0 ± 1.0
Ash, %	0.02	0.06

of use.   Control of microbial growth is achieved by means of filtered air ventilation of the storage tank or by means of ultraviolet light in the air space above the syrup. A combination of proper ventilation and ultraviolet light is often employed.   Good ventilation helps prevent condensation on the sidewalls of the tank which dilutes the syrup and enhances mold growth.   Ultraviolet lights should be installed to avoid contact of the fixture with syrup when the tank is full.   The filtered air should be virtually sterile to prevent contamination of the liquid sugar.   Ultraviolet lights must be kept clean and in good repair for maximum effectiveness.

Liquid syrup will flow by gravity to the point of use.   Therefore, in many installations the storage tanks are elevated in the processing plant.   To justify liquid sugar equipment it has been estimated that a user outside of the refining area should use at least 6,000 to 7,000 cwt per yr of sugar.   Those plants located within range of tank truck delivery from the plant should consume about 3,000 cwt per yr of granulated sugar to make conversion to liquid sugar economical.   All processors using liquid sugar should be equipped to receive at least one shipment per month either by tank truck or tank car on the basis of sound economics.

Certain advantages may be cited in favor of liquid sugars.   There is often an economical advantage since the cost per 100 lb on a dry sugar basis is about 25¢ per cwt lower.   Savings accrue from the elimination of bags and bagging operations, and the reduced handling charges.   There is less heavy manual work involved with liquid sugars.   With proper storage tanks, liquid sugar can be stored and handled with little or no contamination or deterioration.   Perhaps one of the main disadvantages is the cost of transporting the water in liquid sugar.   The food processor must balance the savings in handling liquid sugar within the plant against higher freight costs when long transportation distances are involved.   The relatively high cost of liquid sugar storage equipment is a disadvantage.   Labor savings must again be relied on to make this investment economically feasible.

Smaller processors may split a liquid sugar load with another user in his vicinity. For this type of delivery, many tank trucks are compartmentalized so that more than one kind of sugar can be delivered or delivery may be made to two plants.   One of the large storage tanks is a commercial plant in Detroit which receives liquid sugar from barges.   The tanks in this installation are of 300,000 gal. capacity.   The sugar is then redistributed by tank truck.

Railroad cars have a capacity of 8,000 or 10,000 gal.   Rail cars or tank trucks may be of plain steel for sucrose syrups without damage to the quality.   However, for invert sugar a lining is necessary for plain steel tanks.   Lithcote, amercote, or similar plastic coating material are satisfactory for tank lining.   Before loading a tank car or tank truck with any kind of sugar syrup, it should be thoroughly washed with a suitable cleaner.   A chlorinated cleaner has been found to be very satisfactory in most locations.

For moving liquid sugar in a plant to several locations, a pressure system is advisable.   A controller on each of the discharge lines may be used to regulate the supply pump.   If the pump is filling a comparatively small pressurized tank of about 50 to 100 gal. capacity, the supply lines may be run from this tank.   With the pressure controllers in operation the system can be automatic.

The same general principles of bulk handling are followed for liquid syrup to achieve lower costs and protect product quality.

References

HONIG, P. 1963. Principles of Sugar Technology, Vol. 3. Elsevier Publishing Co., New York.

MATTHEWS, W. J. 1953. Conditions for pumping. Food Eng. *25*, No. 1, 98.

MEADE, G. P. 1963. Cane Sugar Handbook. Spencer-Meade, John Wiley & Sons, New York.

STANFORD UNIV. FOOD RES. INST. 1957. The World's Sugar. Stanford Univ. Press. Stanford, Calif.

Cross-references: *Fluid Flow; Friction; Hydrometer; Specific Gravity.*

LOGARITHMS

Logarithms will be explained by example rather than by definition. The logarithm of a number, with a given base, is the exponent by which the base must be raised so that the result may equal the number.

If $a^x = N$, x is the logarithm to the base a of the number N, which is expressed by

$$x = \log_a N$$

Two values of a are in common use. The common logarithm (Briggs), with $a = 10$, is usually used for calculations, and is represented by $\log_{10} N$, usually abbreviated as $\log N$. The natural logarithm (Napier or hyperbolic) is used, primarily in higher mathematics, and where growth and death or rate of change are involved. For natural logarithms the base is $e = 2.718$. The natural logarithm is represented by $\log_e N$, usually abbreviated $\ln N$. Tables are available which give the logarithms of numbers N for base 10 and base e.

The use of logarithms facilitates multiplication, division, extracting roots and raising to powers, particularly for large numbers. A table of logarithms should be used to provide the desired accuracy in working up data.

The following general rules apply and are used for making computations.

To multiply two or more numbers, the log of each number is added

$$\log (ab) = \log a + \log b$$

To divide two numbers, the log of one number is subtracted from the other

$$\log (a/b) = \log a - \log b$$
$$\log 1/n = -\log n$$
$$\log a^n = n \log a$$
$$\log a = 1$$
$$\log 1 = 0$$

The above rules apply regardless of the base of the logarithm. One can easily change from one base to another, as follows

$$\log_{10} N = 0.4343 \ln_e N$$
$$\ln_e N = 2.3026 \log_{10} N$$

The procedure for using the tables for obtaining the $\log_{10} N$ is different from that used for $\ln_e N$. Values for $\ln_e N$ are read directly from the table. For common logarithms to the base 10, the value of the logarithm is determined in two parts: (1) the decimal part, which is called the mantissa, determined from the table, (Table

TABLE L.8

COMMON LOGARITHMS

N	0	1	2	3	4	5	6	7	8	9
0	...	0000	3010	4771	6021	6990	7782	8451	9031	9542
1	0000	0414	0792	1139	1461	1761	2041	2304	2553	2788
2	3010	3222	3424	3617	3802	3979	4150	4314	4472	4624
3	4771	4914	5051	5185	5315	5441	5563	5682	5798	5911
4	6021	6128	6232	6335	6435	6532	6628	6721	6812	6902
5	6990	7076	7160	7243	7324	7404	7482	7559	7634	7709
6	7782	7853	7924	7993	8062	8129	8195	8261	8325	8388
7	8451	8513	8573	8633	8692	8751	8808	8865	8921	8976
8	9031	9085	9138	9191	9243	9294	9345	9395	9445	9494
9	9542	9590	9638	9685	9731	9777	9823	9868	9912	9956
10	0000	0043	0086	0128	0170	0212	0253	0294	0334	0374
11	0414	0453	0492	0531	0569	0607	0645	0682	0719	0755
12	0792	0828	0864	0899	0934	0969	1004	1038	1072	1106
13	1139	1173	1206	1239	1271	1303	1335	1367	1399	1430
14	1461	1492	1523	1553	1584	1614	1644	1673	1703	1732
15	1761	1790	1818	1847	1875	1903	1931	1959	1987	2014
16	2041	2068	2095	2122	2148	2175	2201	2227	2253	2279
17	2304	2330	2355	2380	2405	2430	2455	2480	2504	2529
18	2553	2577	2601	2625	2648	2672	2695	2718	2742	2765
19	2788	2810	2833	2856	2878	2900	2923	2945	2967	2989
20	3010	3032	3054	3075	3096	3118	3139	3160	3181	3201
21	3222	3243	3263	3284	3304	3324	3345	3365	3385	3404
22	3424	3444	3464	3483	3502	3522	3541	3560	3579	3598
23	3617	3636	3655	3674	3692	3711	3729	3747	3766	3784
24	3802	3820	3838	3856	3874	3892	3909	3927	3945	3962
25	3979	3997	4014	4031	4048	4065	4082	4099	4116	4133
26	4150	4166	4183	4200	4216	4232	4249	4265	4281	4298
27	4314	4330	4346	4362	4378	4393	4409	4425	4440	4456
28	4472	4487	4502	4518	4533	4548	4564	4579	4594	4609
29	4624	4639	4654	4669	4583	4698	4713	4728	4742	4757
30	4771	4786	4800	4814	4829	4843	4857	4871	4886	4900
31	4914	4928	4942	4955	4969	4983	4997	5011	5024	5038
32	5051	5065	5079	5092	5105	5119	5132	5145	5159	5172
33	5185	5198	5211	5224	5237	5250	5263	5276	5289	5302
34	5315	5328	5340	5353	5366	5378	5391	5403	5416	5428
35	5441	5453	5465	5478	5490	5502	5514	5527	5539	5551
36	5563	5575	5587	5599	5611	5623	5635	5647	5658	5670
37	5682	5694	5705	5717	5729	5740	5752	5763	5775	5786
38	5798	5809	5821	5832	5843	5855	5866	5877	5888	5899
39	5911	5922	5933	5944	5955	5966	5977	5988	5999	6010
40	6021	6031	6042	6053	6064	6075	6085	6096	6107	6117
41	6128	6138	6149	6160	6170	6180	6191	6201	6212	6222
42	6232	6243	6253	6263	6274	6284	6294	6304	6314	6325
43	6335	6345	6355	6365	6375	6385	6395	6405	6415	6425
44	6435	6444	6454	6464	6474	6484	6493	6503	6513	6522
45	6532	6542	6551	6561	6571	6580	6590	6599	6609	6618
46	6628	6637	6646	6656	6665	6675	6684	6693	6702	6712
47	6721	6730	6739	6749	6758	6767	6776	6785	6794	6803
48	6812	6821	6830	6839	6848	6857	6866	6875	6884	6893
49	6902	6911	6920	6928	6937	6946	6955	6964	6972	6981
50	6990	6998	7007	7016	7024	7033	7042	7050	7059	7067
N	0	1	2	3	4	5	6	7	8	9

TABLE L.9

NATURAL LOGARITHMS (0–509)

N	0.0	1.0	2.0	3.0	4.0	5.0	6.0	7.0	8.0	9.0
	...	0.0000	0.6931	1.0986	1.3863	1.6094	1.7918	1.9459	2.0794	2.1972
10	2.3026	2.3979	2.4849	2.5649	2.6391	2.7081	2.7726	2.8332	2.8904	2.9444
20	9975	3.0455	3.0910	3.1355	3.1781	3.2189	3.2581	3.2958	3.3322	3.3673
30	3.4012	4340	4657	4965	5264	5553	5835	6109	6376	6636
40	6889	7136	7377	7612	7842	8067	8286	8501	8712	8918
50	9120	9318	9512	9703	9890	4.0073	4.0254	4.0431	4.0604	4.0775
60	4.0943	4.1109	4.1271	4.1431	4.1589	1744	1897	2047	2195	2341
70	2485	2627	2767	2905	3041	3175	3307	3408	3567	3694
80	3820	3944	4067	4188	4308	4427	4543	4659	4773	4886
90	4998	5109	5218	5326	5433	5539	5643	5747	5850	5951
100	6052	6151	6250	6347	6444	6540	6634	6728	6821	6913
110	7005	7095	7185	7274	7362	7449	7536	7622	7707	7791
120	7875	7958	8040	8122	8203	8283	8363	8442	8520	8598
130	8675	8752	8828	8903	8978	9053	9127	9200	9273	9345
140	9416	9488	9558	9628	9698	9767	9836	9904	9972	5.0039
150	5.0106	5.0173	5.0239	5.0304	5.0370	5.0434	5.0499	5.0562	5.0626	0689
160	0752	0814	0876	0938	0999	1059	1120	1180	1240	1299
170	1358	1417	1475	1533	1591	1648	1705	1761	1818	1874
180	1930	1985	2040	2095	2149	2204	2257	2311	2364	2417
190	2470	2523	2575	2627	2679	2730	2781	2832	2883	2933
200	2983	3033	3083	3132	3181	3230	3279	3327	3375	3423
210	3471	3519	3566	3613	3660	3706	3753	3799	3845	3891
220	3936	3982	4027	4072	4116	4161	4205	4250	4293	4337
230	4381	4424	4467	4510	4553	4596	4638	4681	4723	4765
240	4806	4848	4889	4931	4972	5013	5053	5094	5134	5175
250	5215	5255	5294	5334	5373	5413	5452	5491	5530	5568
260	5607	5645	5683	5722	5759	5797	5835	5872	5910	5947
270	5984	6021	6058	6095	6131	6168	6204	6240	6276	6312
280	6348	6384	6419	6454	6490	6525	6560	6595	6630	6664
290	6699	6733	6768	6802	6836	6870	6904	6937	6971	7004
300	7038	7071	7104	7137	7170	7203	7236	7268	7301	7333
310	7366	7398	7430	7462	7494	7526	7557	7589	7621	7652
320	7683	7714	7746	7777	7807	7838	7869	7900	7930	7961
330	7991	8021	8051	8081	8111	8141	8171	8201	8230	8260
340	8289	8319	8348	8377	8406	8435	8464	8493	8522	8551
350	8579	8608	8636	8665	8693	8721	8749	8777	8805	8833
360	8861	8889	8916	8944	8972	8999	9026	9054	9081	9108
370	9135	9162	9189	9216	9243	9269	9296	9322	9349	9375
380	9402	9428	9454	9480	9506	9532	9558	9584	9610	9636
390	9661	9687	9713	9738	9764	9789	9814	9839	9865	9890
400	9915	9940	9965	9989	6.0014	6.0039	6.0064	6.0088	6.0113	6.0137
410	6.0162	6.0186	6.0210	6.0234	0259	0283	0307	0331	0355	0379
420	0403	0426	0450	0474	0497	0521	0544	0568	0591	0615
430	0638	0661	0684	0707	0730	0753	0776	0799	0822	0845
440	0868	0890	0913	0936	0958	0981	1003	1026	1048	1070
450	1092	1115	1137	1159	1181	1203	1225	1247	1269	1291
460	1312	1334	1356	1377	1399	1420	1442	1463	1485	1506
470	1527	1549	1570	1591	1612	1633	1654	1675	1696	1717
480	1738	1759	1779	1800	1821	1841	1862	1883	1903	1924
490	1944	1964	1985	2005	2025	2046	2066	2086	2106	2126
500	2146	2166	2186	2206	2226	2246	2265	2285	2305	2324

L-8), and (2) the whole number or integer part, which is called the characteristic, and is determined by inspection. The characteristic number is negative if the number N is less than 1, is zero if the number is between 1 and 10, is 1 if the number is 10 or more and less than 100, is 2 if the number, N, is 100 or over and less than 1,000, etc. For example.

$$
\begin{aligned}
\log \quad 0.0052 &= 0.716 - 3 \text{ or } \overline{3}.716 \\
\log \quad 0.052 &= 0.716 - 2 \text{ or } \overline{2}.716 \\
\log \quad 0.520 &= 0.716 - 1 \text{ or } \overline{1}.716 \\
\log \quad 5.200 &= 0.716 \\
\log \quad 52.00 &= 1.716 \\
\log \quad 520.00 &= 2.716 \\
\log \quad 5,200.00 &= 3.716 \\
\log 52,000.0 &= 4.716
\end{aligned}
$$

To multiply 5.2×5.2, add $0.716 + 0.716 = 1.432$ which now is located in the logarithm table, and is 27.04.

The natural logarithm tables ($\ln N$) (Table L-9) are easily read above 2.0. Thus

$$
\begin{aligned}
\ln \quad 5.2 &= 1.7 \\
\ln \quad 52 &= 3.95 \\
\ln \quad 520 &= 6.25 \\
\ln \quad 0.52 &= \ln 5.2 - \ln 10 = 1.7 - 2.3 = -0.6 \\
\ln \quad 0.052 &= \ln 5.2 - \ln 100 = 1.7 - 4.6 = -2.9 \\
\ln 5,200 &= \ln 520 + \ln 10 = 6.25 + 2.3 = 8.55
\end{aligned}
$$

Slide Rule

The slide rule is essentially a graphical representation of logarithm tables. Multiplication is carried out by adding lengths of the C-D scales, which represent logarithms to the base 10, to get the value of the product. Likewise, divisons are carried out by substracting lengths of the slide rule representing the $\log_{10}$ of the numbers involved. The logarithm of a number can be obtained by setting the runner on the number on the D-scale and reading the log on the L-scale, to which is added the characteristic of the log.

For detailed tables on logarithms, see Handbook of Chemistry and Physics, published by the Chemical Rubber Publishing Co. A special book on mathematical tables is also published by the same company.

LUBRICANTS

Lubricants are a necessity where there are moving surfaces on equipment. Lubricants are of particular significance and importance in connection with food processing equipment, because of the presence of heat, vibration, moisture, chemicals, and often dust, which may get into bearings and moving surfaces and cause rapid wear.

A particular kind of moving part, whether bearing or hydraulic system, operates under the same general principles regardless of the application. The basic requirements of the oil are the same. For example, a hydraulic fluid must be able to lubricate the pump, as well as transmit force and power.

Normally, a hydraulic oil is expected to stay in service for long periods of time, so the oil must have excellent stability. Frequently, water will find its way into a hydraulic system by way of leaking coolers or condensation, therefore the oil should have anticorrosive properties. The oil should also resist emulsifying to facilitate removal of water from the system. Hydraulic oil should have antifoam properties. If there is a tendency to subject hydraulic systems to overload, one of the new anti-wear oils should be used.

In the case of gears, shafts, and spindles, the primary function of a lubricant is to prevent metal-to-metal contact. The friction which then occurs is fluid friction, and is far less destructive and less power consuming than dry or solid friction. The more effective the oil film, the greater the reduction of friction. Formation and maintenance of an oil film is complex, involving a number of variables, some of which are imperfectly understood and difficult to measure accurately.

In the case of gear lubrication, the contours of the teeth, load, and the speed of operation directly affect the formation of the oil film. During the period that the gear teeth are in contact, considerable pressure is produced in a relatively small area, which the lubricating film must successfully withstand.

When speeds are high, loads are heavy, but duration of contact is often short. A lubricating oil of comparatively light body can be used under such conditions. With low speeds and heavy loads, the contact is usually longer and a heavier oil should be used. When the ambient temperature is between 0° and 70°F a gear drive should be lubricated with an oil of lower viscosity than when the surrounding temperature is higher.

Types of Lubricants

There are many types of lubricants and numerous lubricating systems available to the food processing plant operator. The flooded type of system is the most trouble-free in which the gears and bearings operate in a bath of oil. The system should be examined periodically. Water which has collected in the oil from condensation of moisture from the air should be removed. Many machines have a sight glass which will show when oil is contaminated with water; however, in many machines it is necessary for the operator to check occasionally by means of a drain cock or plug.

Another very important system provides pressure lubrication from a pump to bearings. Another is the zerk system in which grease under pressure is forced into a bearing through a special fitting. In another important system, the so called self-lubricating bearing, the bearing is packed with grease at the factory and does not need further lubrication. This is particularly true of certain types of so-called anti-friction bearings.

Lubrication may be accomplished by incorporating a lubricating material such as graphite and oil in the material of the bearing itself. These self-lubricating bearings are usually used only on light or intermittent loads.

A lubrication system using a soap solution is widely used in the lubrication of conveyors.

Selection

Many types of lubricants are available from many different manufacturers. It is impractical in this publication to give a complete and accurate listing of the different lubricants and their uses. Table L.10 shows the characteristics of some greases. Contact should be made with reliable grease and oil manufacturers for specific recommendations for a given type of service. The recommendations of reliable equipment and lubrication manufacturers should be followed. The particular conditions which determine the type of grease or oil to be used depend principally on the temperature at which the product is to be used, moisture conditions, type of bearing, and loading on the bearing. In general, low temperature conditions require special oils, and ex-

TABLE L.10

CHARACTERISTICS OF GREASE

Class	Type	Kind of Soap	Approximate Dropping Point, °F[1]	Characteristics
Conventional lime soap	Cup	Lime fat	190	Smooth; water resistant; separates on boiling out water content; limited consistency loss on working
	Axle	Lime rosin	170	Smooth; sticky; water resistant; separates on boiling out water content; great consistency loss on working
Soda soap	Fiber and sponge	Soda fat	375	Fibrous; not water resistant; does not separate at elevated temperatures; variable consistency loss on working
	Medium and short, fiber or smooth	Soda fat	375	Semismooth to smooth; not water resistant; does not separate at elevated temperatures; variable consistency loss on working
	Block, brick	Soda fat (variable soda-rosin content)	400	Smooth; hard; not water resistant; does not separate at elevated temperatures
Aluminum soap		Aluminum fat	230	Smooth, transparent, gel-like or stringy; water resistant; becomes fluid at elevated temperatures; limited consistency loss on working
Lithium soap	Multi-purpose	Lithium fat	375	Smooth; water and heat resistant; does not separate at elevated temperatures; limited consistency loss on working
Mixed base		Combination of two or more	Variable (depending on composition)	Variable (depending on composition)
Compounds	Residuum	Usually none (not a true grease)		Smooth; black; adhesive; excellent pressure and water resistance

[1] Maximum usable temperature is considerably below the dropping point because of oxidation and evaporation which occurs at elevated temperatures.

Source: Standard Oil Co.

cessively high temperature operations require special oils. Large bearings require heavier grease than those with light loads and small bearings. Some oils and greases are designed particularly to resist emulsification with water, and are particularly valuable for use in conditions of extreme high moisture.

Refrigeration oil is specially treated so that it will remain fluid even at temperatures as low as 20° to 30°F below zero. This is an important characteristic as otherwise the oil will tend to accumulate in the coils and not return to the compressor. Refrigeration oil is also specially designed to resist high temperature vaporization and deterioration.

Pressure lubrication systems are frequently used in processing machines to provide a more positive method of lubrication. Such a system can be used whereby the operator can lubricate a number of bearings by the simple pushing of a lever. A multiple line unit which meters the lubricant at the pump has separate lines connecting each bearing with the openings in the walls of the lubrication pump cylinder. No extra metering valves are needed with the system.

A single line unit meter system, on the pressure stroke of the pump, forces lubricant from the valve into the bearing. A wide range of metering valve sizes can be used. The single line unit has the following advantages.

(1) Only one pump is required regardless of the number of bearings lubricated. (2) Broken lines (but not stopped lines) are detected readily because the system will lose pressure. (3) A wide range of metering valve sizes can be used to accommodate widely varying lubricant requirements among the different bearings served by the system. (4) The use of quick-disconnect couplings enables a variety of bearings with lines and valves installed to be connected into the central system.

There are several very important points in the management of lubrication, as indicated by the following preventive maintenance program:

(1) Survey every machine in the plant for lubrication needs.

(2) Specify the minimum number of lubricant types that will adequately serve all equipment items.

(3) Prepare lubrication charts and cards for each machine indicating the type of lubricant to be applied at each point, also the frequency and method of application.

(4) Mark all machine lubrication points in a way that ensures application of the right lubricant.

(5) Plan routes and schedules for lubrication servicemen and machine inspection.

(6) Schedule machine downtime.

(7) Set up efficient, economical facilities and methods for storing, handling, and dispensing lubricants.

(8) Keep records to check on the efficiency of the program, and to note program savings as they become evident.

(9) Train plant personnel in the theory and practice of planned lubrication.

(10) Standardize lubrication devices and fittings on plant equipment, and check to ensure that newly purchased equipment is designed in line with these standards.

(11) Set up a program to analyze and test new lubricants as well as those in regular service.

(12) Keep all lubricants and bearing surfaces clean and free from grit or foreign matter.

References

ANON. 1967. Investigate lubrication program to uncover hidden costs. Plant Eng. *21*, No. 10, 198.

RABINOWICZ, E., 1965. Friction and Wear of Materials. John Wiley & Sons, New York.

Cross-references: *Hydraulics; Conveyors; Freezers, Ice Cream; Refrigeration Principles.*

M

MAINTENANCE

Maintenance assumes major importance in modern food plants which are usually highly automated and involve expensive equipment, relatively few people, and often expensive and perishable product. Improved sanitary regulations often require rigorous cleaning methods and materials which further complicate the problem. Processing equipment, particularly in large continuous operations must be maintained so that interruptions of service do not occur or are rare. The maintenance of the building is important from the standpoint of product quality, worker satisfaction and health, and cost.

Building Maintenance

The building should be constructed of sturdy and suitable materials so that maintenance can be kept to a minimum. The use of concrete and tile as basic structural materials, with liberal use of stainless steel or similar noncorrosive types of materials, and moisture- and chemical-resistant tile for floors is desirable.

Proper ventilation and in many cases air conditioning to keep the temperature moderate and to reduce excessive moisture are good methods of preventing excessive maintenance costs in buildings where water and other fluids are handled.

For dry storages, concrete construction is also very desirable. Floors may be reinforced by metal plates or metal grids to prevent serious wear.

A hard tile surface gives practically no maintenance problems even in a room subjected to high moisture; however, there are special moisture-resistant paints which can be obtained for plaster or wood surfaces. Some of the new epoxy enamels are excellent. Drainage is very important and floors on which water is splashed should have a slope of about $1/4$ in. per ft to provide proper drainage. Special drains are available for handling wastes from industrial plants and floors.

In buildings it is essential to have a regular inspection system which can be used to locate cracks, crevices, need for paint, etc. Usually a weekly check of these items is desirable.

Equipment Maintenance

To prevent expensive maintenance on equipment, it is necessary to use a preventive maintenance system which will anticipate as many of the impending breakdowns as possible. An inspection system should be combined with an efficient system for making repairs effectively and quickly.

There are four principal problems in maintenance: (1) lack of proper lubrication,

(2) breakage due to the operator not handling the machine according to instruction, (3) corrosion due to improper washing and cleaning methods, and (4) natural wear and tear.

Lubrication problems can best be solved by having a regular lubrication schedule and chart for each machine setting up frequency of lubrication, type of lubrication needed, and places to be lubricated. The assistance of a lubrication engineer is usually available from a lubrication company to advise on this subject. In some case, over-lubrication can cause overheating of small motors and waste of lubricant. Under-lubrication can result in excessive wear, overheating due to friction, and reduced bearing life.

In most plants the basis of economical maintenance is to train individual equipment operators to handle the equipment as if it were their own, and to provide a continual inspection for troubles. Many inspection checks are sensual, such as an operator knowing the sound of the machine when it is operating correctly.

In small plants it is often best to have the operator make minor adjustment unless the machine is very sophisticated. In large plants, it is customary to have a regular maintenance crew which will take care of all service calls.

Much of the service required on equipment is caused by the operator not being familiar with the manufacturer's instructions for operating the machine. Before operating a machine the operator should thoroughly study the instruction book and understand the operation of the machine. The instruction book should be located at a convenient place for the operator's reference. The plant superintendent should have available an additional copy.

Corrosion

In general, corrosion is caused by an electrochemical action which occurs in the presence of moisture and causes the surface to pit or rust. Ordinarily, the best protection for exterior surfaces of food equipment is to keep them well painted with a good quality moisture- and heat-resistant paint or to use rustproof metallic surfaces such as stainless steel, galvanizing, or chrome plating. Stray electric currents from ungrounded motors can cause undue corrosion. Corrosion can be often prevented by proper ventilation and keeping the surface dry.

Packing

Stuffing boxes and rotary seals are best kept in shape by regular service to keep the surfaces smooth and to repack old hardened packing occasionally. The packing must be adapted to the product and service in order to have a good life.

References

ANON. 1967. Top grade maintenance is vital to automations project picture. Plant Eng. *21*, No. 6, 108–112.
DRYDEN, L. S. 1967. Computer keeps careful check on vehicle maintenance costs. Plant Eng. *21*, No. 8, 123-125.
GREGORY, S. O. 1967. Trouble shooting industrial containers. Plant Eng. *21*, No. 5, 147–150.
SISLER, C. W. 1967. Company specialist evaluates protective coatings. Corrosion Spec. Monsanto Co., St. Louis. Plant Eng. *21*, No. 3, 168.

Cross-references: *Building Materials; Corrosion; Floors; Lubrication; Stainless Steel; Tools and Service.*

MANOMETERS

A manometer is a device in which the difference in elevation of the liquid in the tube can be measured to determine the pressure developed. A convenient material to use for the liquid in the manometer is water, although liquids of lower density might be used for greater accuracy. Manometer fluids are selected on basis of density, freezing point, boiling point, etc. When material of lower density is used the amount of change of liquid level is greater for a given pressure, thus providing greater ac-

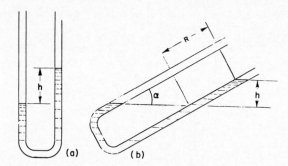

FIG. M-1.   Manometers: A—U-tube; B—inclined U-tube

curacy in reading (Fig. M.1). For small changes in pressure the U-tube may be inclined and the reading of the change in elevation of the fluid taken along the U-tube at R. The static pressure h may be obtained by making a substitution in the following equation.

$$h = \Delta P = R \sin\alpha$$

It is advisable to calibrate the gage because of possible variations in the diameter of the tube and inclination of the two legs.

The draft gage is commonly used for low pressure heads of gases and consists of a U-tube arrangement in which one leg of the tube is a reservoir of large diameter as compared to the diameter of the tube that forms the inclined leg (Fig. M.2). Small variations in the level of the inclined tube produce very little change in the level in the reservoir of large diameter. Commercial draft gages are usually provided with a liquid other than water.

For very precise measurements a micromanometer is used. Basically, it operates on the same principle as a regular manometer, but is provided with an accurate method of reading.

A swinging vane meter may be used in which the impact of the moving air hits an air vane which is connected to a calibrated static pressure scale. These are quite useful for field work and should be calibrated against manometer readings for research work.

Cross-references: *Air Movement; Orifices.*

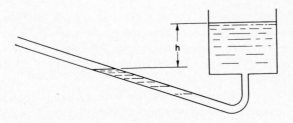

Fig. M-2.   Draft gage

MATERIALS HANDLING

Materials handling is movement of materials from one place to another. In practice it involves the lifting, movement, lowering and storage of materials. Materials handling is one of the basic factors involved in the smooth operation of any food processing plant and can greatly affect both the quality of the material which is handled and the cost or profitability of the operation.

The systems approach is involved in analyzing materials handling operations. A system is an organized group of individual objects which operate together to accomplish a purpose. The parts of a system are (1) the individual units, and (2) the subsystems. The efficient operation of a system requires that all parts of the system be matched in size and capacity so that they function together economically.

Several of the objectives of a materials handling system are (1) lower unit cost of operation, (2) reduce production time (3) conserve storage space, (4) reduce overhead, (5) prevent worker strain and accidents, (6) improve working conditions, and (7) maintain or improve the quality of the product.

Requirements

Some of the methods of obtaining efficiency in materials handling are to (1) minimize movement, i.e., use as short transfer lines as possible or do not move at all unless necessary, (2) handle in bulk or unit load, (3) concentrate the products so that the least possible material need be moved, (4) change the form of the product for easy handling, i.e., by package, sizing, etc., (5) make the operation continuous, and (6) automate the operation if possible.

In analyzing the system the operator should ask: (1) is the operation necessary, (2) is the cost reasonable, (3) are the units properly sized, (4) is the quality of the end product acceptable, (5) is there a better way to do the job, (6) is there unnecessary handling, (7) is there a congestion point, (8) is the time satisfactory, (9) is the work done mechanically rather than manually, and (10) can the system be made automatic?

A basic principle of materials handling is that wherever possible mechanical handling should be used in place of manpower. One man working continuously can generate $1/10$ hp. Assuming that the rate of pay is $3.00 per hr, this means that 1 hp-hr of work done by hand would cost $30. The human should use his mental capabilities, since this is where the potential is greatest for accomplishing what machines cannot do.

In setting up any food plant operation, and particularly when designing materials handling systems, it is essential that an analysis be made of the entire plant product flow. This analysis should show the raw product, major product movement, the specialized or branch movements, the processes, the storages for the various products, and the out movements. It is particularly important to note the areas where high density traffic is found. The sequence of movement should provide for smooth operation of the entire operation.

The effect on food quality is an important item in design of systems for handling food products. If the product is subjected to contamination, excessive temperature change, or severe vibration, severe damage may be done. Simplicity of design is an important factor in dependability. Such matters as ease of lubrication, corrosion resistance, and low maintenance cost are essential. The use of automatic stopping and starting controls, speed regulators, switches, and overload safety devices are all important.

Methods

There are certain methods of handling which are basic to a good materials handling system.

Handling by hydraulic flow is one of the most efficient ways to move many types of products. Improved pumps will handle viscous materials and materials incorporating food or fibrous matter.

Pneumatic or air flotation methods are also quite efficient and widely adaptable.

The conveyor is used in many materials handling systems. Power conveyors are available in many sizes and types and can be fitted with automatic controls, switches, stops, speed changers, and many specialized devices to assist in the efficient flow of material. Figure C.14 shows a typical type of power driven conveyor of the chain type. Belts, either of metallic or rubber composition, are also readily available.

Layout Principles

Some suggestions on designing layouts and locating drive units are as follows: (1) Keep the systems simple and do not use more conveyors than are needed to do the job adequately. (2) Keep the chain speed as low as practical, under 20 fpm if possible. Usually a chain speed of between 25 and 40 fpm is most suitable. (3) Keep the number of power units to the minimum. This can be done by locating power units in the system for the least chain pull by using the slowest possible chain speed. (4) When curves are in the system, locate a bottom chain pull drive as close to the first curve as possible, and locate a top chain pull drive as far away from the first curve as possible. (5) Overlap of the drive units in the center of the conveyor can be effectively used when curves are in the system to minimize the horsepower requirements. Figure M.3 shows a system of this type.

Horsepower to Drive Conveyors

The horsepower required to operate a conveyor is

$$Hp = \frac{\text{chain load (lb)} \times 0.33 \times \text{chain speed (fpm)}}{33,000}$$

Using the conveyor system shown in Fig. M.3, and assuming a chain speed of 30 ft per min, the horsepower requirement is calculated as follows

A to B = top chain pull
C to F = bottom chain pull

A to B = 7 × 60 =   420
B to A = (83 + 7) × 60 = 5,400
                  5,820 5,820

C to D = (83 + 7) × 5 =   450
D to E = 50% × 450 =   225
E to F = (83 + 7) × 10 =   900
F to E = 7 × 10 =   70
                 1,645 1,645

E to D = 50% × 1645 =   822
D to C = 7 × 5 =   35
               857   857

$$\text{Hp} = \frac{8{,}322 \times 0.33 \times 30}{33{,}000} = 2.52 \qquad \begin{array}{l} 8{,}322 \text{ lb total chain} \\ \text{pull} \end{array}$$

Many special attachments, such as automatic diverters or traffic controls, are available for attachment to a materials handling system. Lubrication of chain conveyors is important. Most chain lubricants are of a water-soluble type which washes as well as lubricates. Soap solution can be applied by any one of several types of lubricators as follows: (1) the drip-dry type; (2) the dip-type where the chain is allowed to run through a pan usually located under the drive unit sprocket; (3) a bar soap type where a solid bar lubricant is held against the chain and water is dripped over the bar which permits the chain running against the bar to pick up the soap solution; and (4) some plants use a central control pressure lubricating system which is fed to the various lubrication points on the conveyor systsm.

Belt Conveyors

Belt conveyors are used for carrying cases between floors in multistory plants or up steep inclines between sections of chain conveyors. Belt conveyors are used principally in dry storage warehouses and for unloading warehouse items from delivery

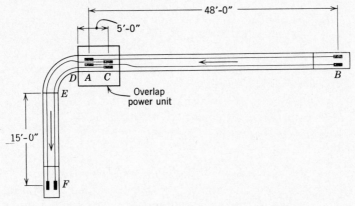

FIG. M-3.   Center pull chain conveyor system

trucks. Belt conveyors are generally used for handling cases and cans where the flow is continuous. The chain conveyor is used where the chain can continue to run under the cases with very little damage to either the case or the chain. With belt conveyors when the cases are blocked on the belt, excessive pressure usually builds up and wears excessively or requires excessive horsepower. Controls, however, can be used with any belt conveyor system to prevent blocked passages from accumulating on the belt. Belts are usually available in standard widths from 6 to 36 in. See Conveyors, Belt for detailed information.

Gravity Roller and Wheel Conveyors

Gravity roller conveyors and wheel conveyors are used to a limited extent in small plants and in short conveying systems. Wheel conveyors which are light-weight, portable, and easily moved are ideal for warehousing.

With the increase of automatic bottle fillers and the high-speed bottle washers, the need for the various types of bottle conveyors has increased. The two types of bottle conveyor chains most commonly used are the flat link and the lateral curve. Both have smooth level surfaces and can be used for either glass bottles or paper containers. The bottle conveyor is the type of chain conveyor using chains which have a 1 to 4 in. pitch. The chain runs on a frame between rails.

Flat Link Conveyor Chain

The flat link conveyor chain can bend only in the vertical plane. Turns at $30°$ to $180°$ are accomplished by transfer discs between the straight sections. Discs are geared to drive sprocket and the straight section so that the disc rotates in synchronism with the speed of the straight section. Standard chains with flat link conveyor systems are from $3^1/_4$ to 7 in. wide.

The same horsepower calculation is made for bottle conveyors as is used for other types of chain conveyors.

A practical rule of thumb for figuring chain speed on bottle conveyors is to use $^2/_3$ fpm for each bottle per minute. For example, a rate of 60 bottles per minute requires a 40 fpm chain speed.

Stackers

Automatic case stacking equipment and case unstacking equipment are widely used in industry. Most stackers will stack up to 15 cases per minute with high stacks 6 high.

The unstacker which is operated either hydraulically of by air will unstack cases at speeds up to 30 cases per minute or more.

Automatic bottle casers are available. A semiautomatic casing setup enables 1 operator to easily hand case up to about 40 bottles per minute.

Pallet System

In many operations, it is more efficient and much more flexible to use the so-called pallet system combined with lift trucks. A pallet is a small frame usually 3 or 4 ft wide by 5 or 6 ft long on which packages or materials are stored, and the packages of product are lifted as a group by means of a lift truck and carried to the desired location and stacked. Pallets can be stacked 4 or 5 high. Each pallet is loaded to approximately 4 to 6 ft high.

Pallets are usually constructed of wood or metal. Pallets usually consist of the platform with the two girders underneath which hold the platform a short distance off the floor, thus enabling the fork of the forklift to get under the pallet for lifting.

Forklift trucks come in various sizes of 2,000 to 10,000 lb capacities or larger. Forklift trucks may be operated by means of a gasoline engine, a propane engine, or electric storage batteries.

Electric storage batteries are gaining rapidly with improvements in batteries, and the use of SCR speed control system which gives approximately 40% greater hours of operation from a given battery charge. The advantages of the electric truck are (1) there is no odor which can be absorbed by food products, and (2) quietness.

One of the important aspects of materials handling deals with highway transportation. Here again there is a great opportunity for increased efficiency through the use of specially designed truck bodies.

The plant owner should also investigate the possibility of the use of leased trucks, as often considerable savings can be made. A good maintenance system for truck life and a good route schedule system are essential for efficient operation.

Cross-references: *Bulk Bins; Case Combiners, Stackers, Destackers; Conveyors; Drum Handling; Forklift Trucks; Grading; Refrigerated Storage; Shipping Docks.*

MILK FAT, RAPID TESTING

Two methods are used for rapid determination of fat in cow's milk, cream, and skim milk; namely, a colorimeteric method, and light absorption. Both methods are gradually gaining acceptance. The colorimetric method is the one most commonly used in the United States.

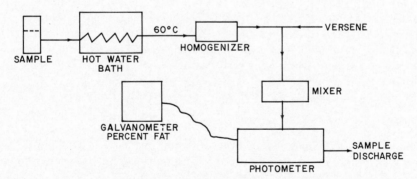

Fig. M-4. Schematic of milk tester
1—Push button for mixing funnel. 2—Push button for versene dispenser. 3—Main outlet. 4—Outlet for photometer. 5—Versene intake. 6—Galvanometer. 7—Sample bottle. 8—Intake tube. 9—Photometer. 10—Cuvette. 11—Photocell. 12—Milk pipette. 13—4-Stage homogenizer. 14—Heating coil. 15—Intake valve. 16—Heating coil. 17—Mixing funnel. 18—Stirring arrangement. 19—Versene dispenser.

Colorimetric Method

The colorimetric method is employed by the commercial Milko-tester. The costs of chemicals and labor are considered to be about 50% lower than for conventional methods of fat determination. The rapidity at which tests can be run is the main advantage. A trained technician can test approximately 100 samples per hour and between 500 and 700 samples per day. The time required to run 1 sample and record the result in only 30 to 33 sec.

The principle of operation of the Milko-tester consists of heating the sample to 60°C followed by homogenization with a 4-stage homogenizer. The sample is then diluted with a Versene solution. The liquid mixture is then subjected to light transmission which is measured by a photo electric cell which acts on a galvanometer. The colorimetric measurement indicates the concentration of milk fat globules and the colorimeter is made for transmission measurements. The flow of product through the instrument is illustrated in Fig. M.4.

Some investigations of the accuracy of the Milko-tester have indicated it to be sufficiently accurate for product standardization for most operations. An analysis of 100 samples of producer milk have revealed a standard deviation of ±0.06% for results obtained by the "Milko-tester" in comparison to those obtained with the Mojonnier tester. Of the samples, 64.6% were within differences of 0.06%, and 3.3% deviated in excess of 0.12%. When samples contained 6% butterfat or more, the agreement between the two methods of testing varied considerably. On the average, duplicate determinations with the Milko-tester agreed within ±0.015% for samples containing 6% fat or less, and within ±0.04% for samples having 6.1 to 8% milk fat.

Some of the limitations set for the Milko-tester by investigators are as follows. (1) Milk composition affects the results. Soluble milk components do not cause inaccuracies; however, milk proteins do and must be solubilized. Seasonal variations produce slight variations in the results, possibly due to the amount of unsaturated fatty acids in the milk fat. (2) Sour milk possessing relatively high acidity should be neutralized with ammonia before testing or the milk may coagulate in the heating unit. (3) High-fat products must be diluted with a known amount of skim milk to result in a fat content between 2 and 6% to achieve accuracy in testing. A small error in dilution in testing a high fat product is magnified by multiplication of the dilution factor. (4) Homogenization other than that provided by the homogenizer in the Milko-tester adversely affects the accuracy of the test. If the apparatus is calibrated for homogenized products, the accuracy can be improved.

Application

Many dairy plants find that the Milko-tester is a valuable instrument for assisting the operator. More frequent tests are run during processing and more samples can be checked to better control fat losses. The instrument is practical for standardization and is generally satisfactory when carefully operated.

Reference

OHIO STATE UNIV. 1966. Res. Dig. Dairy Technol. Dept.

MILK PROPERTIES

Flavor and Odor

The flavor and odor of milk are not affected greatly by the milk being close to cows or to feed fed to cows. Milk does not absorb normal feed and animal flavors through the air or by immediate proximity to these items. In former years the milk-house and various feed rooms were required to be some distance from the barn or from the milk. It has since been established that off-odors and off-flavors get into milk through the blood-stream and respiratory system of the animal. Thus, a feed flavor in the milk is produced by the cow breathing feed odors up to 2 hr before milking. Likewise, the flavor of manure from the barn is absorbed. To avoid these off-flavors and off-odors, it is necessary to make sure that the animals are in a clean area and do not eat silage or other off-flavor producing feeds within a 2-hr period before milking. Vacuum treatment of milk in the processing plant is often done to remove undesirable flavor and odor components.

Enzymes

Several enzymes in milk affect the rate of a chemical reaction, but do not become part of the substances formed. Lipase and phosphatase are two common enzymes that are inactivated when heated sufficiently. If lipase were not inactivated, the milk would become rancid because the lipase assists in breaking down the milk fat. Lipase is normally inactivated by heating to 115°F. Phosphatase is used as a measure of the effectiveness of pasteurization of milk, because it has been found that practically all of the phosphatase will be destroyed if proper pasteurization takes place. Reductase is an enzyme produced as a result of bacterial growth in milk, and is often used as a measure of the bacterial count of the milk.

Physical Properties

Milk at 3.5% butterfat will have 8.6% solids not fat—casein, albumin, sugar, and ash—making a total of 12.1% total solids with a specific gravity of 1.033 or 8.6 lb per gal. The heating value is 315 cal (1.25 Btu) per lb of whole milk. Whole milk has a specific heat of 0.93. The freezing point of whole milk is 31.1°F, and the boiling point is 213°F. Air incorporation in milk at 95°F will induce rancidity in the milk. Rapid agitation will cause clumping of the butterfat resulting in flakes of butterfat on churning. High temperatures cause burn-on of the milk solids on the heat transfer surface. Normal milk has a viscosity of 1.370 centipoises at 25°C.

Cross-references: *Cooling Milk; Cryogenics; Density; Specific Gravity; Specific Heat.*

MILKING MACHINES AND ASSOCIATED EQUIPMENT

A strip cup should be used before milking to check the condition of the milk. Stringy milk, usually the result of mastitis, and bloody milk should be discarded. A small opening on the milk pail to minimize dirt getting into the pail is required in most areas.

Animal Response

Milking machines are now generally accepted, although in some parts of the world, as formerly in the United States, it was felt that they severely damaged the animals. Proper adjustment in the use of the milking machine is necessary to avoid injury. Hand milking requires from 12 to 20 min per cow, whereas the actual time the milking machines should be used on a cow is about $3\frac{1}{2}$ min, although the entire time of milking, including preparation of the cow, removal of equipment, etc., averages about 6 min per cow.

Cows that are groomed, have clipped udders, are kept on clean bedding with manure cleaned regularly, and have udders washed before milking produce a product with much lower bacteria count. A principal requirement is that cows be milked regularly if they are high-producing cows. The regularity of milking is not so important for low-producing animals. Most cows are now milked twice a day because labor costs do not justify the 15 to 20% increase in production obtained from milking 3 times a day. Milking 4 times a day provides only about 5% more milk than 3 times a day.

Components

A milking machine consists basically of a unit for providing (1) a vacuum with a power unit, usually electric, (2) pipes or hoses to the animal, (3) a device for giving pulsations, and (4) a container for collecting the product (Fig. M.5).

Pumps.—Either piston or vane type vacuum pumps are used to exert a vacuum of 10 to 15 in. Hg. A vacuum regulator is provided for maintaining the desired vacuum. A vacuum gage should be installed so that vacuum can be checked periodically, even

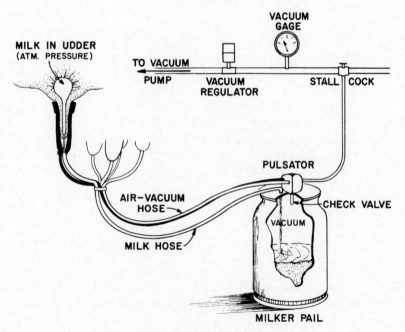

FIG. M-5.   Milking machine system

though the gage has a tendency to be in error after use and should be calibrated periodically. A 3 to 4 gal. tank is usually provided next to the outlet of the vacuum pump to reduce the fluctuations of the piston.

Pipeline.—The cost of electricity used for a pipeline milker is about 2 to 3 kwh per month for a cow. If the vacuum unit is more than 30 ft from the barn, a larger size pipe should be used. Normally, a 1 in. galvanized or black pipe is used for the air line. The air line supports a vacuum gage, vacuum regulator, and stall cock. The pipeline can become a source of contamination to the product, particularly if a milker pail has run over and some milk has gone into the line. Also, milk odors are pulled into the line constantly during milking. The line should be constructed or installed at a slope and should be washed periodically by drawing a cleaning solution and disinfectant into the line at each of the stall cocks. The stall cocks should be opened after cleaning to drain.

Pulsator.—The purpose of the pulsator is to provide fluctuations and squeezing actions of 48 to 54 pulsations per minute for dairy cows or 65 to 75 pulsations per minute for goats. These may be designed to move all 4 of the teat cups together, or move the 2 front, then the 2 rear. The pulsator permits the vacuum to be exerted, then cuts off the vacuum, permitting atmospheric pressure to act on the teat cups.

Hoses.—Two hoses go to the teat cup units: one hose, called the air hose, extends from the pulsator which alternately provides air at atmospheric pressure and vacuum to the teat cups; the other is the milk hose which is under vacuum and moves the milk from the teat cups to the milker pail, or to the pipeline for a pipeline milking machine. Milk is caused to flow from the udder at atmospheric pressure to the teat cups through the milk hose to the milker pail, which is under vacuum (low pressure). The rubber inflation surrounds the teat and provides the massaging action for milking by the air-vacuum relationship set up by the pulsator. The rubber inflation sets in the metal cup and the space between the inflation and the metal cup is alternately connected to air and vacuum thus giving the massaging action. However, the space inside the inflation is always under a vacuum when on the cow. The uniform vacuum on the inside of the inflation holds the teat cups in place. If the front quarters and rear quarters are milked separately a duplex air-vacuum hose is used to alternately supply the pulsations to the quarters.

The operator must exercise caution so that damage to the udder is avoided. It is particularly important that the unit be removed as soon as the cow is milked.

Cleaning

The use of rubber or synthetic inflations presents another consideration for cleaning of dairy equipment. Lye solutions have generally been used for the removal of fat absorbed in the cells of the inflation. Some recommendations in the past have called for boiling the inflations in a strong lye solution to remove these fat particles. However, recent work indicates that it is better to use a lye solution of about 5 to 10% at room temperature over a 7-day period to remove the greatest amount of fat absorbed by the inflations. The higher temperatures tend to drive the fat into the inflation rather than remove it. Inflations are available in latex, synthetic rubber, rubber, and neoprene.

The milker should be properly cleaned after use—the first step being to flush it with tepid water using about 2 gal. per teat cup unit, followed by a washing solution of

140° to 160°F, after which it is again rinsed and the parts permitted to drain. These inflations may be dismantled daily or supported on a rack in a chemical or, as in some areas, sterilized by steam. Prior to milking the units should be sanitized with a chlorine solution of about 200 ppm.

Milk Pipeline Milker

With the advent of bulk handling there has been more use of the milk pipeline to convey the milk from cow to the milkroom. The system is essentially the same as that discussed previously and as presented in Fig. M.6. However, the pail is replaced by a milk line from the cow to the milkroom.

The milk pipeline is constructed of glass piping or stainless steel tubing. If a vacuum bulk milk tank is used, it merely replaces the milker pail, and vacuum on the bulk tank pulls the milk into it. However, many of the bulk milk tanks are atmospheric tanks. For these tanks it is necessary to provide a means of permitting the milk to leave the milk line, which is under vacuum, to go into the bulk tank, which is under atmospheric pressure, through a device called a vacuum releaser. The milk may be collected at the cow in a milk pail and all of it released to the pipeline after milking the cow. The milk moves to the bulk tank in a large volume. Or the milk may be pulled continuously from the cow and moved to the bulk tank. Collecting the milk in the pail at the cow is desirable if the milk is to be weighed. Otherwise, a metering device might be used in the line to measure the quantity of milk produced by the cow.

Milk Pipeline

Activation rancidity which may be caused by adding warm milk to cold milk, by too much stirring, or foaming of warm milk may occur in pipelines for milk. Originally the bulk tanks were blamed for the formation of rancid milk, but it has been found that most of the rancidity is associated with pipeline systems particularly if improperly installed. The damage due to rancidity can usually be attributed to one of the following: (1) too much air intake, (2) air leaks in the milk line, (3) too many or too high risers, and (4) too long a pipeline. Lines of 200-ft length with moderate riser heights may be used without causing rancid flavor, providing the air inlet and milk flow are properly regulated. Air leaks may occur at the valves and at joints

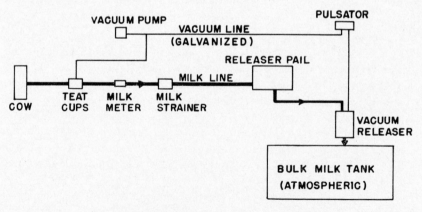

FIG. M-6.   Vacuum milk pipeline system for atmospheric bulk milk tank

between the sections of pipeline which often become loosened due to vibration. If foamy warm milk and turbulence can be witnessed in the line, rancidity will likely result. The number of vertical risers and distance of vertical risers in the pipeline for various lengths have not been established. For washing the milk pipeline, continuous circulation requiring from 12 to 30 gal. is required, and can be estimated on the basis of 1 gal. per 12 ft of line plus the capacity of the pump and weigh jar. Either the vacuum or a pump can be used for circulating a fluid which should continue for 15 min or more.

Cross-references: *Bulk Tankers; Cooling Milk.*

MOISTURE CONTENT REPRESENTATION

The moisture content can be represented on a wet or dry basis. The amount of water removed by drying can be calculated by:

Method A (Using Moisture Content, Wet Basis)

$$0.25 \times 2,000 = 500 \text{ lb of water in product initially}$$

The final weight of the product with 14% moisture is the weight of dry matter multiplied by the pounds of moist material per pound of dry matter which is

$$1,500 \times \frac{100}{100 - 14} = 1,744 \text{ lb final weight of product}$$

Thus, $2,000 - 1,744 = 256$ lb H_2O removed

Method B (Using Moisture Content, Dry Basis)

First, change 25 and 14%, wet basis to 33.33 and 16.28%, dry basis. The amount of moisture removed is equal to dry matter multiplied by the change in dry basis moisture content, or

$$1,500 \times \frac{(33.33 - 16.28)}{100} = 256 \text{ lb } H_2O \text{ removed}$$

Reference

HALL, C. W. 1957. Drying of Farm Crops. Edwards Brothers, Ann Arbor, Mich.

Cross-references: *Equilibrium Moisture Content; Moisture Measurement.*

MOISTURE MEASUREMENT (FOOD)

An analysis of moisture content is necessary for quality control of dry food products. Moisture is of prime importance in determining the storage stability of dry milk, the moisture limit being normally below 5%. The moisture content of dry milk is usually designated on a wet basis; that is, for 5% moisture content, there would be 5 gm of moisture in a 100 gm wet sample.

Although the term, moisture content, is quite often used, there is no agreement as to what is included as moisture. Water exists in the dry milk product in several forms. Water may be adsorbed on the surface of the particles of powder; water may be bound in the crystals of lactose; and water may be imbibed into the colloidal milk protein. Various methods of determining the moisture give different values, primarily because all or part of the water contained in the product may be measured. One can argue that all water in the product should be included in the moisture content. On the other hand, the keeping quality is influenced greatly by the surface moisture. Inasmuch as the time required to make the determination is often critical from the standpoint of processing operations, it seems logical to use a quick method which is reproducible. Such a method will probably be based on the surface moisture content.

The values obtained can be adjusted slightly if the total moisture content is desired for a purpose other than storage. The alpha-lactose hydrate contains about 5% water of crystallization which is not measured by some methods of moisture determination such as the toluol method.

Determining Moisture Content

Direct Method.—The moisture content is usually determined by a direct method in which the vapor pressure of the moisture in the product is greater than the surrounding vapor pressure, thus causing moisture to be removed. The loss in weight of the product of the moisture removed can be weighed to determine the percentage moisture. The vapor pressure of the product is normally increased by using heat, either from air, radiation, or from a warm oil which will absorb moisture.

Toluol Distillation.—The toluol distillation method is recommended by the U.S. Dept. of Agr., and the American Dry Milk Institute (ADMI). The toluol distillation method has four characteristics: (1) enables use of large sizes of samples; (2) each determination can be completed in 1 hr; (3) method is readily adapted for plant control work; and (4) method is as accurate as the vacuum oven method.

Toluol ($C_6H_5CH_3$) is a chemical which has a boiling point of 233°F. Heat is supplied to the toluol, adjusting the amount of heat so that the rate of moisture removal does not exceed four drops per second. The vapor leaving is condensed and collected in a graduated trap. A 50-gm sample is placed in a 300-ml Erlenmeyer flask and heated with about 100 ml of toluol. After 45 min, the quantity of water collected is measured, and then checked again at 60 min, and if the 2 readings agree within 0.05 ml, the distillation is discontinued and the moisture percentage determined. If, however, the reading is greater than 0.05 ml, heating is continued for another 15 min, and repeated until readings are within the desired limits. The milliliters to the nearest 0.05 of water collected, multiplied by 2 equals the percentage of moisture in the sample.

To eliminate some of the difficulties encountered in using the standard toluol method described above, the following recommendations have been made: (1) use standard taper ground joints—24/40 to avoid possibility of toluol leakage; (2) use a 500-ml round bottom boiling flask instead of the flat Erlenmeyer flask; and (3) use a heating mantle and a variable transformer to control the heat to obtain uniform heating.

The toluol method is rejected by some as too expensive and dangerous.

Karl Fischer.—The Karl Fischer method utilizes a chemical means for determining the moisture content. Chemical solvents are used which penetrate the cells and aid in quickly removing water from the material. The material must be finely ground. The moisture is extracted with anhydrous methyl alcohol. The Karl Fischer method removes much of the water of hydration. If 50% of the powder was α-lactose, the Karl Fischer method would give a moisture content 2.5% higher than by using heating. See Official Methods of Analysis for more details.

Air Oven.—An air oven is often used for determining moisture content. One gram of a sample is weighed into a flat bottom metal dish, 5 cm in diameter and placed in a vacuum oven at 212°F with a pressure not above 100 mm Abs of Hg. Up to 5 hr heating may be required until the sample reaches a constant weight. British technologists recommend 214° to 215°F.

To eliminate the variations when drying with an air oven, because of fluctuations in temperature, air velocity, location of the sample, and to obtain quicker results, the Meihuizen method has been used in the Netherlands. The Meihuizen method uses predried air to avoid some of the variation due to the difference in ovens. Air at 210° ± 2°F which has been passed through silica gel to reduce the moisture content is utilized. The sample is dried in about 2 hr.

Rapid Methods.—Quicker methods are often used in the plant to get a check of the moisture. These determinations should be compared periodically with one of the standard methods mentioned above. The air vacuum oven is often utilized to get more rapid drying with a minimum of oxidation to the product. Heating the sample with an infrared lamp for a specific time, usually 20 min, is one method commonly used. Instant powders appear to present further problems in moisture determinations because of the variation in moisture held by lactose.

Standard Error.—The standard error obtained by various methods over the range of from 2 to 5% moisture content are as follows: the Karl Fischer method ±0.037%; Meihuizen ±0.039%; Pregl ±0.042%; and drying ovens ±0.07%.

Selection.—The main two criteria for selecting a method for determining moisture content are: (1) time for making determination and (2) accuracy required. There are no new rapid methods for moisture content determinations which are as accurate as those methods which require more time. An inexpensive, accurate method which would provide the moisture content in a few minutes is needed.

Cross-references: *Equilibrium Moisture Content; Moisture Content; Moisture Measurement (Grain).*

MOISTURE MEASUREMENT (GRAIN)

Regardless of moisture content, there are possibilities for errors in selecting a sample which is representative of the entire lot of material. To reduce the possibilities of error, several samples should be obtained from different locations in the storage bin. Usually a large sample is obtained which is taken to the laboratory for determining the moisture content. If the sample which is taken to the laboratory is not properly divided, errors may again occur. The sample can be divided equally into two parts with the Boerner sampler. These can be further subdivided for more samples.

The standard deviation of the moisture content of individual kernels in a sample taken from a bin of grain of uniform moisture content is about ±0.2%. Under the best conditions in the laboratory, a standard error of sampling of ±0.11% for replicate samples of wheat has been obtained.

The moisture content of the product must be maintained from the time the sample is obtained until the determination is made. Standard metal containers and film bags are available for holding the sample. The familiar cardboard type container will permit considerable moisture loss. For some methods of moisture determination, it is necessary to grind the sample. Grinding is normally done when the moisture content is near equilibrium with the atmosphere so that the moisture change will be kept at a minimum.

Direct Methods

Oven Methods.—Several different oven procedures are available for moisture determination of different materials. The usual procedure is to remove the moisture from the product in an air oven. When warm or hot water is circulated around the walls to heat the oven by the circulating water, it is called a water oven. This method maintains a more uniform temperature than the air oven. Two general procedures are available: (1) grind the grain and dry in the oven from 1 to 2 hr at 266°F, and (2) place the whole grain in the oven at a temperature of 212°F for 72 to 96 hr.

The usual oven methods for moisture determination of grain are as follows.

Air-oven Method, 266°F

(1) *One-stage*, for grain under 13% moisture. Grind duplicate samples of 2 to 3 gm each. Heat 1 hr at 266°F. Place in desiccator; then weigh. Samples should check within 0.1% moisture.

(2) *Two-stage*, for grain above 13% moisture. Remove moisture until 25 to 30 gm sample is below 13% (usually about 14 to 16 hr are required). Continue as discussed under (1) above.

Water-oven or Air-oven Method, 212°F

Place duplicate 25- to 30-gm samples in oven, heated to 211°–212°F for 72 to 96 hr. Place in desiccator; then weigh. Samples should check within 0.1% moisture.

The AOAC has set up slightly different requirements which give a slightly higher value for moisture determination of grain and stock feeds. The material is ground and heated at 275°F for 2 hr. The recommended procedure for determining moisture content of different products should be consulted.

To remove the moisture from a high moisture sample, the two-stage drying method is advocated. With this method, a sample of whole grain is first dried in an oven; the sample is ground and further dried in an oven. The moisture content is determined on the basis of water loss.

The sample should remain in the oven until weight loss stops. It is practically impossible to remove all the moisture from a sample without deterioration of the product. If the sample is in the oven too long, the organic material will be reduced and a loss of weight occurs, which will appear as moisture loss and give an inaccurate value. For most grains, it is considered that the deterioration of dry matter occurs quite extensively after 96 hr in an oven at 212°F. For some air-oven determinations, at 212°F, it is specified that the sample be kept in the oven a minimum of 72 hr. The oven may be heated with electric resistance heaters, infrared lamps, steam, or a high frequency electric field.

The vacuum oven method is used for determining moisture content. For grain, the product is ground and placed in the oven at approximately 212°F, and the oven maintained at 40 mm of vacuum for about 5 hr. By using a lower temperature or a shorter time, there is less possibility of a loss of weight due to deterioration of the dry matter. This is particularly important for fruits and vegetables.

For accurate moisture content determinations it is necessary to prevent the sample from absorbing moisture after the moisture has been removed from the sample. Moisture absorption can be prevented by placing a glass cover plate over the sample and the weight taken after the sample and container have cooled.

Distillation Methods

With the distillation methods, moisture is removed by heating the grain in oil and determining the volume or weight of water removed from the grain in condensed vapor or from the loss of weight of the sample.

The Brown-Duvel distillation method was one of the early accepted methods for determining moisture content of grain. The whole grain is heated in oil, the weighed sample heated, and the vaporized moisture condensed and measured in a graduated cylinder. The procedure for different grains varies, and it is necessary to follow the recommended procedures for different grains. A sample of 100 gm is heated in a flask with 150 ml of oil. About 1 hr is required to determine the moisture content. The equipment is rather simple, and accurate results can be obtained without expensive equipment such as balances. Proper calibration assures accurate results.

The official toluol (methyl benzene, $C_6H_5CH_3$) distillation method for grain requires heating finely ground grain in an apparatus that collects the condensed water. The toluol boils at 233°F, and thus all of the water and other substances are evaporated which have a boiling point below this temperature. Boiling is continued as long as water accumulates in the graduated tube. Usually about 25 gm of material are boiled in the flask with 75 ml of toluol.

With the modified Brown-Duvel method the product is placed in a vegetable oil bath and heated to a predetermined temperature. This process takes only 15 to 20 min. The use of oil permits rapid evaporation by application of large quantities of heat without scorching or burning the product. Starting from room temperature, the oil is heated to 374°F for grains. As soon as this temperature has been reached, the moisture has been driven off, and the dry weight of the product remains. The oil and 100 gm of product in the oil are balanced before heating, and the loss of weight of the product after heating determined. The change of weight is used to calculate the moisture content of the original product.

Drying with Desiccants

The moisture content of a product is determined by placing the sample near an efficient drying agent in a closed container. The material should be finely ground to give rapid response. The desiccant maintains a very low vapor pressure within the container. The vapor pressure of the material is higher than that of the desiccant, and the moisture moves from the material to the drying agent. One standard procedure is to place the sample in a vacuum oven with anhydrous sulfuric acid until constant weight is obtained. This method is particularly useful for materials where dry matter decomposition would be great when the product is heated. With some products, however, the product may decompose before the equilibrium vapor pressure is reached, because of the mold and bacteria growth.

Indirect Methods

Indirect methods involve the measurement of a property of the material which depends upon the moisture content. A direct means is required to calibrate the indirect method. The moisture content is usually expressed on a wet basis for the indirect methods.

Electrical Resistance Methods

The electrical resistance or conductivity of a material depends upon its moisture content. This principle is used as a basis for a number of moisture meters. In wheat it has been found that there is a linear relationship between the moisture content and the logarithm of its electrical resistance from approximately 11 to 16% moisture. These meters must be calibrated for each grain against a standard method. Inasmuch as temperature affects the electrical resistance of a material, corrections for variations in temperature must be made for tests conducted at temperatures other than those at which the calibration is reported. The electrical resistance units are rather simple in design and require a minute or less for making a moisture determination.

The resistance of grain is measured as it is fed between two steel rolls which serve as electrodes, one of which is motor driven. The Tag-Heppenstall moisture meter has been approved for grain inspection by the U.S. Dept. of Agr. A different spacing of rolls or a different roll can be used for various products such as grain, peanuts, walnuts, wood, etc. The standard error of estimation in testing hard spring wheat is about ±0.23%. One of the problems with the meter is the difficulty of maintaining calibration because wear of the bearings and rolls changes the spacing between the rolls and gives a lower moisture content. By proper maintenance, however, this can be prevented.

The pressure exerted on the sample with the electrical resistance method affects the resistance of the product. The relationships of moisture content, pressure on sample, and resistance of various materials are available. The Universal moisture tester presses a sample of grain to a specified thickness in order to get the same pressure each time. The unit incorporates its own power source, thus eliminating the necessity for electrical outlets or batteries. Units are made to cover various ranges of moisture content. A straight line must result when Universal moisture content determinations are plotted against oven determinations, so calibration consists only of determining the compression data which will give a straight line on a 45° slope. This principle is covered by patents of the company. The Marconi moisture meter consists of a test cell in which great pressure is applied to the specimen. The circuit is powered by dry cells or alternating current.

The electrical resistance of grain decreases when the pressure is increased. For 15.2% shelled corn, with a pressure of 100 psi, the dc resistance is 1.0 megohms.

Above 17% moisture content, there is a parabolic relationship between the moisture content and the logarithm of the electrical resistance. Most meters do not give change in readings below 7% moisture, because there is very little change in the electrical conductivity. Grain that has been recently dried with heated air gives lower readings than the actual moisture content of the product. This occurs because the tendency of these meters is to measure to resistance on the surface of the grain. If moisture has been added to the grain, the readings are higher than the average moisture content of the product.

Dielectric Methods

The dielectric properties of products depend on the moisture content. The capacity of a condenser is affected by the dielectric properties of the material placed between the condenser plates. Wet materials have a high dielectric constant, and dry materials have a low dielectric constant. Water has a dielectric constant of 80 at 68°F. Most grains and hay have a value less than 5, and air in a vacuum has a value of 1. The capacitance, an indirect measurement of the moisture content is obtained.

The Steinlite meter is used for grain. A sample of 150 gm is placed into a grain chamber. The grain is then moved to a chamber formed by two plates of a condenser. A standard error of estimate for the Steinlite meter when compared to the vacuum oven is ±0.4%. Meters of this type are less subject than resistance meters to any errors which might result from uneven moisture distribution due to drying or wetting of the kernels of the grain being tested.

Chemical Methods

Water is removed by adding a chemical which decomposes or combines with the water. From the chemical reaction a gas is produced which can be measured volumetrically or which decreases the original weight of the sample. After suitable calibration curves are established the moisture content can be determined.

Calcium carbide reacts with water to form calcium hydroxide and acetylene gas.

$$CaC_2 + 2H_2O \rightarrow Ca(OH)_2 + C_2H_2$$

Calcium hydride has been proposed for the above reaction in place of calcium carbide as follows.

$$CaH_2 + 2H_2O \rightarrow Ca(OH)_2 + 2H_2$$

The chemical method can be used to determine the moisture content by the gas pressure exerted. The higher the gas pressure exerted in a closed container, the higher the moisture content. Or, the volume of gas at a constant pressure would indicate indirectly the amount of moisture in the sample. This method utilizes a receptacle with a gage and a safety valve and is recommended for use by farmers on hay and grain. A reading can be made in about 3 min when grain samples are ground. Note that when calcium hydride is used instead of calcium carbide, twice the volume of hydrogen as compared to the volume of acetylene is produced.

The Fischer method offers considerable possibility for determining the moisture content by chemical means. The method utilizes chemical solvents which penetrate the organic tissues and aid in quickly removing water from the material. The material must be finely ground, and the moisture is extracted with anhydrous methyl alcohol.

Hygrometic Methods

Grain in a closed container comes to equilibrium with the air at a certain relative humidity, dependent upon the moisture content and temperature. The relative humidity of the air in equilibrium with the material is used as a measure of the moisture content.

Certain salts have the property of changing color when exposed to various humidities which can be used to indicate the moisture content of the product. A method has been developed in which a mixture of ferric ammonium sulfate and potassium ferrocyanide is used in a carrier of sodium chloride as colorimetric indicator of humidity. In the dry state the mixture is blue, but in the presence of water it turns red. When used in a range of 8 to 12% for wheat, it is accurate to within 1%.

Even though the hygrometric method may not give quite as accurate values of moisture content of products as some of the other indirect methods, it may actually give a better indication of the storage quality of the product than an accurate moisture content. The growth of microorganisms on the surface of the grain or hay is influenced by the relative humidity and temperature of the surrounding atmosphere. The hygrometric method gives an accurate value of the environment in which these microorganisms would grow, and hence a more accurate indication of the storage quality of the product. It is generally considered that mold growth occurs on grain when the relative humidity surrounding a product is above 75%.

A very simple method of determining whether hay or grain crops will keep in storage has been developed using a salt. Common salt (noniodized), sodium chloride, has an equilibrium relative humidity of about 75% when saturated with water. Common salt is mixed with the sample. If the sample is too wet for safe storage, that is above 75% equilibrium relative humidity, salt crystals will lump together because they become saturated. If the sample is dry enough for storage, the salt will not lump, because the equilibrium relative humidity is below 75%. All that is needed to determine whether a product will keep in storage is a small test tube, a cover of cloth to prevent heat from the hand or exterior getting to the sample while the test is being run, and common salt. The test is run by merely shaking the salt through the product sample.

One of the problems in grain storage is that of determining the moisture content of the product at various locations without disturbing the material in storage. One approach, using the hygrometric method which is based on relative humidity measurement, is to place a device for determining the relative humidity at various places in the bin along with a thermocouple which will give the temperature reading at that location. Thus, by measuring the relative humidity and temperature of the

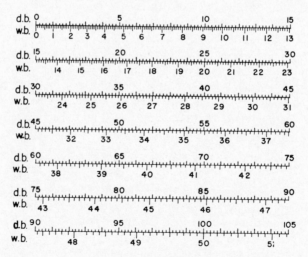

Fig. M-7.   Conversion scale for moisture content representation

air surrounding the product at various locations, the moisture content of the product may be determined during storage or drying. For a ventilated bin, it is necessary to turn off the fan from 1 to 2 hr before the readings are taken so that the relative humidity of the air is at equilibrium with the grain. It appears that an accuracy of within 0.5% can be obtained.

Other Methods

With the advent of the use of radiation sources, new methods have been proposed and used to indicate the moisture content, particularly for soils. In one of these methods, the presence of hydrogen nuclei of water in the product is used as an index of moisture content. Two methods are used for measuring the presence of hydrogen nuclei: (1) the neutron scattering method, and (2) the nuclear resonance absorption method.

In the neutron scattering method, neutrons emitted from a radioactive source are directed into the product being tested. In passing through the material, the atomic nuclei of the material are bombarded by the neutrons. When a neutron collides with a heavy nuclei of a solid, less energy is transferred from the neutron than if it hits a light nuclei as that of the hydrogen in water. When more hydrogen nuclei are present in the material, a greater number of the slow neutrons will be scattered back to the vicinity of the source which can be measured by a sensitive radiation counter. An accuracy within 1% has been obtained in soils.

The nuclear resonance absorption method utilizes a double electrical field; one a magnetic field, the second a radio-frequency field. The maximum absorption of energy occurs when resonance occurs which is shown by an increased flow of current through the coil producing the field. The greater the amount of water present, the greater is the energy absorption from the field.

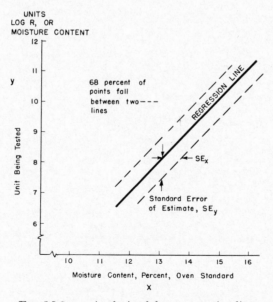

FIG. M-8.   Analysis of data, regression line

Standard Error of Estimate

A regression, or least squares, line can be obtained relating the moisture content to the measured variable (Fig. M.8). For the resistance moisture meter, the measured variable is the resistance, R, which gives a straight line when log R is plotted against the moisture content, MC, obtained by standard oven methods. A straight line is represented by

$$y = mx + b$$

where y = the ordinate, log R
m = the slope of the line
x = the abscissa, MC, moisture content (wb or db)
b = the intercept on y-axis

so the regression line is defined by

$$\log R = m\, MC + b$$

where

$$m = \frac{\Sigma xy - \dfrac{\Sigma x \Sigma y}{n}}{\Sigma x^2 - \dfrac{(\Sigma x)^2}{n}}$$

$$b = \frac{\Sigma y}{n} - m\frac{\Sigma x}{n}$$

n = number of values

Thence, the standard error of estimate, SE, in the y-direction is

$$SE_y = \pm \sqrt{\frac{\Sigma y^2 - \dfrac{(\Sigma y)^2}{n} - m\left[\Sigma xy - \dfrac{\Sigma x \Sigma y}{n}\right]}{n-2}}$$

and

$$SE_x = \pm \frac{1}{m}\,|SE_y|$$

Reference

HALL, C. W. 1957. Drying of Farm Crops. Edwards Brothers, Ann Arbor, Mich.

Cross-references: *Equilibrium Moisture Content; Moisture Content; Moisture Measurement (Food).*

N

NITROGEN

Nitrogen, is a colorless, odorless gas; it is normally noninflammable and nonexplosive. Density at normal temperature and atmospheric pressure is 0.96737. Atomic weight is 14.01; critical pressure is 35 atm. Critical temperature is $-231.25°F$. Melting point of solid nitrogen is $-346.90°F$; boiling point of liquid nitrogen is $-319.9°F$, nitrogen makes up 79% of air by volume, or 77% by weight.

Cross-reference: *Nitrogen, Liquid Cooling.*

NITROGEN, LIQUID, COOLING AND FREEZING

Liquid nitrogen has recently become an important chemical in the refrigeration and handling of certain food products. As a by-product of the production of oxygen used in many modern steel manufacturing mills, liquid nitrogen has recently become available at a more reasonable price. The attractive features of liquid nitrogen include the following: (1) an inert gas, (2) does not affect the flavor, (3) can be used to obtain extremely fast freezing and at low temperatures, and (4) clean and there is no moisture problem.

The principle of liquid nitrogen cooling is simple. Liquid nitrogen is stored in an insulated tank which is open to the atmosphere through a pressure relief valve. An extremely heavy tank would be required to hold the full pressure of the liquid nitrogen at atmospheric temperature. By allowing a small amount of the liquid nitrogen to continually evaporate, the temperature of the product is reduced to the point where its pressure is only a few pounds.

The boiling point of liquid nitrogen at atmospheric pressure is $-320°F$; when changed to a vapor at $0°F$, it has a latent heat of 165.7 Btu per lb. The heat of vaporization is 85.7 Btu per lb and the heat of liquid is 80 Btu per lb. The temperature of the refrigerated space is controlled by the amount of liquid nitrogen permitted to escape.

Cooling Systems

In the food industry, liquid nitrogen is used for freezing food, fish, and bakery and similar products. One method of cooling fish or fruit is to submerge the product in liquid nitrogen. Rapid cooling may cause cracking of the surface. Precooling of the product by a less drastic and rapid method will prevent cracking.

A second method of cooling is to spray liquid nitrogen over the product as it passes through a chamber on a continuously moving belt. A diagram of one type of commercial liquid cooling system which utilizes the liquid nitrogen spray system is given in Fig. N.1.

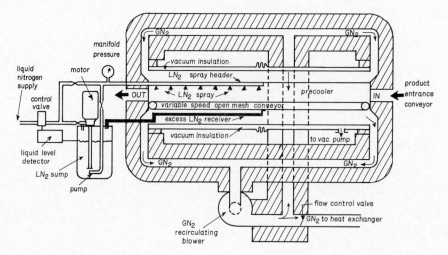

Fɪɢ. N-1.   Nitrogen flash freezer

Working Principles

The basic arrangement of the machine consists of a product conveyor mounted within a double wall, vacuum insulated open ended cylinder.   A liquid nitrogen spray zone is located in a section at the exit end of the unit, and includes spray nozzles above and sometimes below the product.   Blower fans mounted at the other end of the main chamber circulate cold gas which is directed to nozzles and suction parts within the freezer chamber.   The gas nozzles are positioned to direct high velocity cold gas over the surface of the product.   The gas recirculating zones are located between the entrance end and spray zone of the chamber occupying the greater portion of the length of the unit.

Entrance and exit conveyors are synchronized with the main conveyor moving the product into and out of the cryogenic atmosphere.   The conveyor speed is adjustable in order to vary the exposure time of the product within the freezer.   Heads at either end of the vacuum insulated cylinder have openings just large enough to allow the product to move through.   The infiltration of atmospheric air is restricted by directing a curtain of high velocity nitrogen gas across the face of each of these openings.   The liquid nitrogen from the supply tank flows directly into an external vacuum insulated nitrogen storage tank or reservoir.

Liquid nitrogen is added to the system from the supply tank by means of a liquid level controller in the external reservoir activating an on-off solenoid valve in the reservoir at the exit end of the freezer.

A centrifugal pump in the external reservoir pressurizes the liquid nitrogen (now at −320°F and atmospheric pressure) to 5 to 7 psig, and pumps the liquid into spray headers above and below the product.   Most of the liquid flashes to gas when it comes in contact with the product, and liquid which does not contact the product is recollected in the collector pan and flows back out to the external reservoir for recirculation.

The subcooled liquid nitrogen pumped through the spray headers within the chamber keeps the surface of the food product enveloped with liquid nitrogen droplets resulting in rapid heat transfer.

The whole process becomes quite economical by recirculating the $-320°$ F nitrogen gas which is generated in the liquid spray zone of the freezer at high velocity over the surface of the product as it progresses through the freezer, it encounters colder gas temperatures until finally it passes through the spray environmental zone maintainer at $-320°$ F. This is analogous to a counter flow heat exchange which is thermally more efficient than parallel flow. The amount of gaseous nitrogen discharged from the system is dependent on the product flow rate, the final exhaust gas temperature, and the overall machine efficiency.

Vacuum jacket chamber insulation has been one of the major factors in minimizing the heat gain from its surroundings. For the same efficiency, polystyrene (having $k = 0.23$ Btu per hr ft^2°F) covered unit of the equal size would require about 4 times thicker insulation.

Liquid nitrogen may be utilized for cooling refrigerated trucks or boxes. Figure N.2 shows a refrigerated truck body employing liquid nitrogen refrigeration. This method of refrigeration is quite trouble free, has lower initial cost, and is considerably lighter in weight than mechanical refrigeration systems.

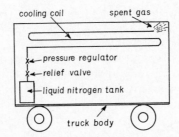

Fig. N-2. Liquid nitrogen truck body refrigeration system

Nitrogen gas is also used to provide an oxygen free atmosphere in packaged food products. This gas can be obtained in gaseous form in high pressure cylinders or from liquid nitrogen which is permitted to vaporize.

Perhaps the most important feature of the liquid nitrogen freezing is that it allows food products to be frozen so quickly that in most instances there is a maintenance or improvement in texture, appearance, and character of the frozen product. Products such as sliced tomatoes, avocados, sliced peaches, and sliced pears can be frozen by this method. Fish fillets, whole kernel corn, asparagus, cherries, raspberries, mushrooms, and many bakery products can be frozen with liquid nitrogen. Breakage and discoloration of the product is minimized and it is claimed that there is less loss of vitamins.

References

ANON. 1967. Food processors go super cold with liquid nitrogen. Food Technol. *21*, No. 1, 21, 23.

TRUSLOW, J. D. 1968. Liquid nitrogen saves plant space. Plant Eng. *22*, No. 9, 120–121.

Cross-references: *Immersion Freezing; Vegetable Freezers.*

NOISE

Noise is important in a food plant primarily from the standpoint of the welfare of personnel. Excessive noise causes fatigue in personnel and is likely to cause errors due to misunderstanding of communication.

Noise in the range of ultrasonics is also used to some extent for agitation in industrial processes, such as, agglomeration of aerosols, production of emulsions, suspensions of insoluble materials, and for nondestructive testing.

Noise as such is merely a vibration in the atmosphere causing audible sounds of such loudness, pitch or quality that it is usually unpleasant. The intensity may vary greatly.

The intensity of noise is measured by the decibel. The decibel is a logarithmic scale unit for expressing relative magnitude of sound. The magnitude of sound is specified by its sound pressure in decibels, which is defined at 20 times the log to base 10 of the ratio of the sound pressure to a standard reference of sound pressure. The standard reference of sound pressure normally used is 0.0002 microbar. Some engineers use 1 microbar as the standard. A level of 0.0002 microbar corresponds to the stimulus which is barely audible to persons having acute hearing.

Sound waves between 16 and 20,000 cps (cycles per second) are perceived as sound. Frequencies below this range are in infrasonic range, and those above are ultrasonic.

Within the audible frequency range the ear is responsive to a wide range of frequencies. The most sensitive range is 500 to 5,000 cps. The minimum detection tolerance varies with the frequency. At 50 cps a sound must be 10^6 times as strong as at 3,000 cps, in order to be detected. Continuous noise levels above 90 decibels will cause gradual loss of hearing.

TABLE N.1

SOUND LEVELS

	Decibels	Decibels
	120 Threshold of feeling	60 Noisy home
	120 Thunder, artillery	50 Average office
Deafening	110 Elevated train	
	100 Boiler factory	40 Quiet radio
Very loud	90 Truck, unmuffled	
	80 Noisy office	30 Quiet conversation
Loud	70 Average street noise	20 Whisper
	70 Average radio	10 Threshold of audibility

TABLE N.2

SOUND TRANSMISSION LOSS IN WALLS (125–400 CPS)

Wall	Transmission Loss, Db
Wood 0.2 in. thick	18.5
Plate glass $1/4$ in. thick	27.0
Hollow gypsum tile unplastered	27.2
Brick wall plastered	43.0

Source: Sabine, Paul E., *Acoustics and Architecture*, McGraw-Hill Co.

Measurements can be made by a sound level meter either of the indicating or recording type. The sound level in decibels is given in a reading which conforms to the American standard or sound level meters. Table N.1 lists sound levels of different noise conditions.

The noise level can be kept low by several procedures. Among these are: (1) use of sound deadening insulation, (2) use of projections to break up large expanses of flat surfaces, (3) keep machinery and equipment properly adjusted so that there are no loose or noisy bearings, (4) eliminate leaking steam or air jets, (5) mount equipment on sound deadening bases, (6) separate the noisy object by a room wall or petition, and (7) maintain low air velocities through ducts and outlets.

Table N.2 shows the sound loss through walls of various types.

If it is necessary to expose workers to excessive noise levels, protective devices should be furnished and worn to keep noise within acceptable limits.

References

BERANEK, L. L. 1954. Acoustics. McGraw-Hill Book Co., New York.
HARRIS, C. M. 1957. Handbook of Noise Control. McGraw-Hill Book Co., New York.

O

OPERATIONS RESEARCH

The tentative working definition of operations research is the application of scientific methods, techniques, and tools to problems involving the operation of a system so as to provide those in control of the system with optimum solutions to the problems. The approach is particularly applicable to a study of materials handling systems and many other management decisions.

Operations research is a procedure for helping management make proper decisions. Application of rigorous methods of analysis to an entire system, rather than to just one operation to obtain an optimum solution, might be called operations research or systems engineering. Operations research, pioneered by the British, has been used extensively by government and industry during and since World War II. Operations research has been used to determine: (1) load and flight patterns during the Berlin airlift after World War II, (2) quantity and variety of products to be merchandized, (3) warehouse and building placement, (4) size of flight for bombing missions during World War II, (5) machine replacement, and (6) cropping programs.

A large vegetable crop producing farm on the East Coast using operations research found the most economical time to harvest to obtain maximum returns. As a result of the studies, a device was developed to aid management in making decisions regarding harvest. In surface mining operations, recommendations developed by operations research resulted in an increase of nearly 70% in operating efficiency.

Operations research or systems engineering is usually carried out as follows: (1) set up the problem, (2) make a mathematical model, (3) derive a solution from model, (4) test model, (5) set up controls, and (6) put solution to use.

After the problem is established, the major task is establishing and evaluating mathematically the many possibilities. Engineers are particularly well-qualified to apply these relationships in the form of mathematical models which represent in part the actual situation. The results obtained must be applied wisely. Symbolic models are developed using mathematical terminology. Various numbers are substituted in the model to obtain the optimum value. By trial and error, called iteration, a solution or solutions which give an optimum solution are obtained. There may be several feasible or several acceptable solutions. A discussion and development of the various mathematical models is beyond the objective of this book. Several books, publications, and journals are devoted to the subject. Among the well-known mathematical models are the following: (1) inventory models—elementary, with price breaks, with restrictions; (2) allocation models—linear programming, resource assignment; (3) waiting time models—queuing, traffic delays, sequencing; (4) replacement—cost, mortality, probability of failure; and (5) competitive—games, bidding.

Reference

CHURCHMAN, C. W., and ACKOFF, R. L. 1957. Introduction to Operations Research. John Wiley & Sons, New York.

Cross-reference: *Linear Programming.*

ORIFICES

An orifice is an opening, usually round, in a pipe, conduit, tubing, or at a discharge through which a fluid, gas, or liquid flows. The orifice is used as a means of measuring or regulating flow. For a particular fluid, the quantity of flow depends on the size and shape of the orifice and the head of the fluid over the orifice. Orifices are easy to construct and install and are usually inexpensive. Considerable design data are available for orifices making them easy to utilize.

The quantity of flow, Q, cfs, for a liquid is

$$Q = CA(2gh)^{1/2}$$

where Q = the discharge quantity, cfs
C = the coefficient of discharge, approximately 0.6
A = the cross-sectional area of orifice opening, sq ft
g = the acceleration due to gravity, 32.2 ft per sec^2
h = the head of fluid above the center of the orifice, ft

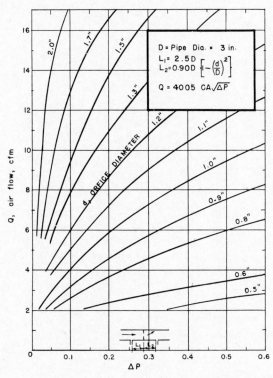

FIG. O-1.   Pressure drop through 3-in. orifice for determining airflow

The flow of air through an orifice is more difficult to determine. The size of orifice, size of pipe, and method of measuring the pressure drop (Fig. A.10) have considerable influence on the results. Pressure taps to determine the pressure before and after the orifice may be placed in various locations. A common procedure involves placing the tap 1 diam of the pipe upstream and $1/2$ diam downstream.

The C-values presented are for general use (Tables O.1 and O.2). For precise and accurate research data considerable study may be needed to design and calibrate orifices.

Cross-reference: *Air.*

O-RINGS

One of the most significant developments in the past few years has been the O-ring. This ring is made to fit in a groove, usually rectangular, of one part of a system to be

TABLE O.1

FLOW COEFFICIENTS, C, FOR AIRFLOW THROUGH AN ORIFICE, REYNOLDS NO. OF 105,000

Diam Ratio $\dfrac{\text{Orifice}}{\text{Pipe}}$	Diameter of Pipe	
	2 In.	16 In.
0.30	0.60	0.60
0.40	0.61	0.61
0.50	0.625	0.63
0.60	0.65	0.66
0.70	0.705	0.71

Only slight decrease in Q as Reynolds No. decreased, $Q = CA\sqrt{2gh}$.

TABLE O.2

ORIFICE COEFFICIENTS
Coefficients of discharge (c) for circular orifices, for water[1]

Head from Center of Orifice in Feet	Diameters in Feet					
	0.02	0.05	0.1	0.2	0.6	1.0
0.5	. . .	0.627	0.615	0.600	0.592	. . .
0.8	0.648	0.620	0.610	0.601	0.594	0.591
1.0	0.644	0.617	0.608	0.600	0.595	0.591
1.5	0.637	0.613	0.605	0.600	0.596	0.593
2.0	0.632	0.610	0.604	0.599	0.597	0.595
2.5	0.629	0.608	0.603	0.599	0.598	0.596
3.0	0.627	0.606	0.603	0.599	0.598	0.597
3.5	0.625	0.606	0.602	0.599	0.598	0.596
4.0	0.623	0.605	0.602	0.599	0.597	0.596
6.0	0.618	0.604	0.600	0.598	0.597	0.596
8.0	0.614	0.603	0.600	0.598	0.596	0.596
10.0	0.611	0.601	0.598	0.597	0.596	0.595
20.0	0.601	0.598	0.596	0.596	0.596	0.594
50.0	0.596	0.595	0.594	0.594	0.594	0.593
100.0	0.593	0.592	0.592	0.592	0.592	0.592

[1] Approximately 0.005 higher for square orifices.

Fɪɢ. O-2.   Sanitary ell for O-ring gasket and clamp connector

sealed as it slides on the other part.   A good example of this type of seal is in the sanitary fitting joint (Fig. O.2).

The important feature of this seal is that the greater the pressure usually the greater the tightness with which the joint holds.   At the same time when the pressure is eliminated, the joint loosens and can be readily disassembled.

O-rings can be used on flat surfaces as well as over shafts or tubing.   They can also be used either on the movable or on a stationery part of the joint.   An important feature of this type of joint is to have smooth surfaces and reasonably accurate clearances. The clearances need to be in proportion to the size of the joint.   Another important feature is the composition of the elastic ring.   For most purposes a fat or oil resistant ring of neoprene or similar material is used.

O-ring gaskets are commonly made of neoprene, Teflon, and silicon rubber compounds.

Cross-reference: *Stuffing Boxes.*

OVERRUN

Overrun is the extra volume of a product obtained as compared to the volume of the original ingredients of the product.   In the manufacture of ice cream, the usual practice is to adjust the operation so that for every 5 gal. of ice cream mix which is frozen, there will be approximately 10 gal. of ice cream produced.   The additional 5 gal. of ice cream over the volume of the mix is called the overrun.   This is important not only from the economic standpoint, but also for the quality of the product.   Overrun on ice cream normally is from 80 to 120%.

The general formula for overrun calculation of ice cream for example is

$$\% \text{ overrun} = \frac{\text{weight (per gal. of original mix)} - \text{weight (per gal. of ice cream)}}{\text{weight (per gal. of ice cream)}} \times 100$$

The overrun could be figured on either a weight or volume basis.

In connection with the manufacture of butter, a somewhat similar procedure is used.   For example, in a pound of butter, there is usually only 80% of a pound of butterfat. This means that for every 80 lb of butterfat the manufacturer will recover approximately 100 lb of salable butter. The official standard for butter recognizes this point and gives the following as the minimum standard for commercial butter manufacture.

The formula for figuring overrun is

$$\frac{\text{wt of butter } - \text{ wt of fat}}{\text{wt of fat}} \times 100 = \% \text{ overrun}$$

References

Hunziker, O. F. 1940. The Butter Industry, 3rd Edition. Published by the author. La-Grange, Ill.

Wilster, G. H. 1957. Practical Buttermaking, 8th Edition. Oregon State Cooperative Assoc., Corvallis, Ore.

Cross-references: *Butter Churns; Butter, Physical Properties; Freezers, Ice Cream.*

OXYGEN—EFFECT ON FOODS

Many food flavors are adversely affected by oxygen. The deleterious effects of oxygen are increased by exposure to higher temperatures, contact time, concentration of the oxygen in contact, moisture content of the food, and light quality and intensity. In addition, the presence of certain metallic ions, such as copper, will often catalyze fat oxidation. The catalytic metal need be present in only trace amounts to promote oxidation.

Fat

Foods containing fats are usually most adversely affected by oxygen. The presence of sugar has been shown to increase the shelf-life of some foods by delaying oxidation and development of off-flavors. Salt in nuts has been observed to produce off-flavor development more rapidly. In general animal fats appear to be more subject to oxidative changes than vegetable fats.

Favorable Effects

Oxygen produces favorable effects on certain food products. For example, the development of bright red color in fresh meat is brought about by the oxygenation of the myoglobin. The color changes from a light purple to red. Foods requiring mold growth must have oxygen; examples of these are Roquefort and Camembert cheese. For certain processes the need for oxygen to support the growth of yeast is also a necessity. Whether an environment is anaerobic or aerobic will determine to a large extent the type of fermentation caused by microorganisms.

Responses from Oxygen

The behavior of microorganisms in food is determined to a large extent by the amount of oxygen present. In the presence of atmospheric oxygen, most foods are quite completely though slowly oxidized. When sugar is oxidized, the end products are carbon dioxide and water. When amino acids are oxidized, carbon dioxide, ammonia and water are formed. Whether oxidation results in the formation of fatty acids, carbon dioxide, and water, the end products resulting from microbial action will be determined not only by the substrate, but by the amount of oxygen (oxygen tension) present. As the oxygen tension is lowered, intermediate products such as alcohol, lactic acid, acetic acid, hydrogen sulfide, sulfites, glycerol, and various other compounds may be formed. The conversion of sugar to alcohol by yeast requires a small amount of oxygen. In the production of yeast, large amounts of oxygen must be supplied.

The breakdown of fats through contact with oxygen gives the food industry some of its major problems through the development of stale and other off-flavors. Many rancid flavors are the result of oxidative activity. Some fats and oils develop off-flavors before the development of rancidity. This change is called reversion. Fats and oils which exhibit oxygen uptake have a period of time before a rancid flavor is detected. This time is called the induction period which is followed by more rapid oxygen uptake. Eventually the rate of oxidation of a fat tapers off. The length of each phase is affected by the type of fat involved, and the chain of oxidative chemical reactions. Temperature, moisture, amount of air present, light, ultraviolet light, and the presence of antioxidants influence the reaction rate. Some natural fats contain antioxidants while others contain prooxidants which accelerate rancidity.

Unsaturated fats tend to be more susceptible to the adverse affect of oxygen than saturated fats. Natural fats vary in the amount of antioxidants they contain. Therefore, it is not surprising to find conflicting reports regarding the effect of oxygen. The oxidation of an unsaturated fat is usually a simple oxidation of the double bond. Upon analyzing the volatile compounds produced in rancid fatty material, it has been shown that a complex mixture of compounds are formed. The most commonly isolated compound evolved from rancid fats is heptyl aldehyde. Other short chain compounds isolated include aldehydes, ketones, keto acids, hydroxy acids, and other acids.

The induction period of chemical change produces products normally referred to as peroxides. There is some question as to whether or not the products are chemically true peroxides because the reaction with potassium iodide is very nonspecific. The entire course of oxidation of fats is a rather complicated series of chemical reactions. Some compounds formed initiate other changes which tend to propagate the oxidation.

Antioxidants

Manufacturers have made available synthetic antioxidants for use in the food industry. Some of these are used singly, whereas, others are combined to obtain a synergistic effect. An example of a combination for the protection of nuts is composed of 14% butylated hydroxyanisole, 6% propyl gallate, and 3% citric acid in ethyl alcohol The antioxidants tocopherols commonly occur in nature. A wide variety of products have been used experimentally for the protection of foods against oxidation. One approach to control the oxidative changes is to lower the oxygen content inside a package of food by using a catalyst (palladium) in the presence of hydrogen. In this case, the hydrogen combines with the free oxygen to form a molecule of water.

Vacuum packaging and nitrogen flushing assist in protecting many foods against the damaging effect of oxygen. Package material must be selected with oxygen permeability as one of the considerations. Oxygen permeability is important for films or other material used in packaging fresh red meat. Low oxygen permeability is important for most packaging requirements.

References

HALL, C. W., and HEDRICK, T. I. 1966. Drying Milk and Milk Products. AVI Publishing Co., Westport, Conn.

JOSLYN, M. A., and HEID, J. L. 1963. Food Processing Operations, Vol. 2. AVI Publishing Co., Westport, Conn.

JOSLYN, M. A., and HEID, J. L. 1964. Food Processing Operations, Vol. 3. AVI Publishing Co., Westport, Conn.

MEYER, L. H., 1960. Food Chemistry. Reinhold Publishing Corp., New York.

WEISER, H. H. 1971. Practical Food Microbiology and Technology, 2nd Edition. AVI Publishing Co., Westport, Conn.

Cross-references: *Antioxidants; Bottles and Cartons; Canning; Carton Forming and Filling; Packages; Packaging; Vacuum Packaging.*

P

PACKAGES

Most foods require some kind of package, particularly at the retail level, for handling of the product as well as for identification and protection. Some raw products such as fruit and vegetables are sometimes retailed without a package other than a simple paper sack. However, the majority of products require some kind of protection and the package must meet legal standards. With the large variety of food products produced and with the variations in requirements, a great many packaging materials must be used.

Requirements for Legally Accepted Packages

The package manufacturer or food processor must satisfy several requirements as stipulated by government agencies. A partial check list of the requirements are: (1) avoid deceptive construction such as false bottoms, hollow dividers, fillers, excessively thick sidewalls, and deceptive covers; (2) the package or label in contact with with food must be free of any substance which could be a health hazard; (3) if required, have the package clearance by FDA; (4) the name of the product should appear in a prominent position as set forth in governmental standards of identity; the name should accurately describe the product if no standardized name applies; the name given the product must be sufficiently descriptive; (5) avoid all words in a product name which may be deceptively misleading; (6) have all words in a product name carry the same letter size, style, type, color, on the same background and of equal prominence; and (7) packages must be labeled in accordance with the requirements of the Fair Packaging and Label Act.

Labeling

The package of a food product must not only have a descriptive name but provide the consumer with required information. Some requirements on packaging are as follows. (1) Only optional ingredients which are used must be declared on the label as required by standards of identity. (2) The name and address of the manufacturer, packer, or distributor must appear in accordance with regulations by FDA, Meat Inspection Act, Poultry Inspection Act, and the Fair Packaging and Labeling Act. (3) The work "imitation" should appear where applicable. (4) Where applicable, adequate descriptions and necessary warning labels must appear on the package. (5) If a product is subject to deterioration, suggested storage conditions are recommended to retard spoilage. (6) The quantity of contents in a package must be declared on the label. This can appear in a variety of sizes depending upon the type of product. In

515

some cases weight is stated or if the product is liquid, a standard unit of measure is suitable. The unit bushel, peck, dry quart, or dry pint whatever the case may be is acceptable for certain products. (7) The weight declaration must be expressed in the number of the largest unit. For example, a package containing 32 oz must declare contents as 2 lb rather than 32 oz. (8) The label should declare whether the contents are minimum or average net weight. Reasonable tolerances are permitted under average weights but no shortages are permitted under the minimum weight statement. (9) The processor should determine the tolerances and exemptions allowed for a given product. Certain allowable tolerances are related to bulk shipments, packages handling $1/2$ fluid or avoirdupois ounce, or less, and packages containing less than 6 units which can be easily seen and counted through a transparent wrapping.

Copyrights

The processor should protect his label against unauthorized copying by means of a copyright. To be protected by copyright the new and original package and label must bear the word "copyright" or the abbreviation of "copr." or the symbol © followed by the name, initial, or mark of the individual claiming the copyright. If copyright protection is desired internationally under the Universal Copyright Convention, the symbol © and the year of publication should be included in the copyright notice. To obtain a copyright, the manufacturer should publish the necessary information pertaining to the name. Promptly after publication two complete copies with a properly executed application and the required fee should be submitted to the Register of Copyright, Library of Congress, Washington, D.C. A copyright when claimed remains in effect for 28 yr and is renewable 1 yr before the date of expiration for an additional 28 yr.

Trademarks

Trademarks consist of a name, portrait, or signature of a living person. It is a surname, description, or nondescript of the goods covered. After a newly created trademark has been used in interstate commerce, the application for registering the trademark may be submitted. Action on the application is taken in the United States Patent Office. A trademark notice can then be used: "Registered in United States Patent Office," or "Reg. U.S. Pat. Off.," or ®.

Design

The characteristics of the product and method of merchandizing will dictate to a large measure the type of package which may be used. A package must be functional as well as meet the necessary labeling and merchandizing requirements. A package with consumer appeal is very important for increasing sales. Cost is an important factor in designing a package. The expected shelf-life of a product will also influence the type of package which may be acceptable. To obtain a slightly greater shelf-life, packaging costs may be increased more than the benefit derived.

Coding

Most food containers carry a code applied by the manufacturer. Some legal requirements necessitate coding (Table P.1).

TABLE P.1

CODING OF PACKAGES

Short Product Life		Intermediate Product Life		Long-term Product Life	
Procedure	Example	Procedure	Example	Procedure	Example
Under One Week		Under Six Months		Over Six Months	
Number days; rearrange	Wed = 1 Thurs = 2	Designate day, month in numbers. Reverse order. Use 0 before single digits	Dec. 1 = 12-01 = 10-21 Jan. 2 = 01-02 = 20-10	Convert month, day, year to usual numbers. Divide month number into nearest equal digits. Place digits in position 1 and 6. Day and year are positions 2 to 5. Use 0 with single digits	Mar. 9, 1968 = 3-9-68 = $(1 + 2) + 09 + 68$ = $1 + 09 + 68 + 2$ = 109682 May 12, 1968 = 5-12-68 $(2 + 3) + 12 + 68$ = $2 + 12 + 68 + 3$ = 212683
Use word with no duplicate letters	Newark = 6-day week Sun = N Mon = E	Designate months A to M. (Omit I.) Days in numbers	Jan. 21 = A21 Nov. 1 = L1		
Under One Month		Use A to Z for 2-week periods. Number days for 5-day work week	Jan. 1 to 12 = A1 to A10 Jan. 15 to 26 = B1 to B10	Use key words for numbers 1 to 12. Convert usual number sequence to letters	A pure cows m i l k 0 1234 5678 9 10 11 12
Start any date. Advance 1 number monthly	Jan 15 = 1 Jan 16 = 2 Feb 16 = 1 Feb 17 = 2				
Use 10 non-repeating letters	Nourish eat 1234567 890 on = 21 ne = 18	Use words—no recurring letters—for numbers to 12	Black or wh i t e 12345 67 89 10 11 12 Jan. 1 = 1-1 = BB	Show date as a number of the year—1 to 365. Place year first, using last 2 digits. This gives ascending number; allows first-in-and-out method. Add 0 after year as needed	Jan. 12, 68 = 12th day, 68 = $68 + 0 + 12$ = 68012 Dec. 31, 68 = 365th day, 68 = $68 + 365$ = 68365
Number days: reverse. Add 0 to single numbers	01 = 10 10 = 01 18 = 81	Day and month in usual numbers. Divide month number into nearest equal digits and place in positions 1 and 4; numbers for days in positions 2 and 3. Use 0 with single digits	Jan. 22 = 1-22 = $(1 + 0) + 22$ = 1220 Feb. 15 = 2-15 = $(1 + 1) + 15$ = 1151 Nov. 27 = 11-27 = $(5 + 6) + 27$ = 5276		

Source: Modern Packaging Encyclopedia (1967).

TABLE P.2

TESTS AND SPECIFICATIONS FOR PACKAGING MATERIALS AND CONTAINERS

Films and foils also use many of these tests with appropriate modifications

	ASTM[1]	PI[1]	Tappi[1]	Federal Test Method Standard No. 101a[1]
Paper and Paperboard				
General				
Basis weight	D 646	T 3603	T 410	204
Brightness	D 985	T 3612	T 452	
Gloss: 75.0°	D 1223	T 3633	T 480	272, 281
Odor			T 483	220
Opacity	D 589	T 3613	T 425	263
Paraffin	D 590	T 3631	T 405	232
Thickness and density	D 645	T 3604	T 411	301
Mechanical				
Air resistance	D 726	T 3625	T 460	
Bending quality		T 3619	T 474	244, 326
Bursting strength	D 774	T 3606	T 403	250
Compression (ring crush test)	D 1164	T 3618	T 472	
Conditioning for testing	D 685	T 3602	T 402	298
Edge tearing resistance	D 827	T 3614	T 470	
Flexural resistance, deflection			T 469	309
Folding endurance	D 643	T 3616	T 423	242
Internal tearing resistance	D 689	T 3607	T 414	327
Moldability (crease retention)	D 920	T 3627	T 446	234
Pinholes in glassine, greaseproof papers	D 1221-64		T 485	
Puncture, containerboard	D 781	T 3635	T 803	321
Stiffness, rigidity, softness[2]	D 781	T 3610	T 451, 489	321
Stretch	D 987	T 3609	T 457	246
Surface strength (wax pick test)			T 459	
Tensile breaking strength (dry)	D 828	T 3608	T 404	246
Tensile breaking strength (wet)	D 829	T 3615	T 456	246
Chemical and Performance				
Asphalted, bleeding resistance		T 3630	T 475	1401
Creasing of paper for WVP	D 1027	T 3624	T 465	
Grease resistance (Turp. test)	D 722	T 3626	T 454	262
Insect resistance			T 473	
Mildew (fungus) resistance	D 2020		T 487	233
Smoothness		T 3632	T 490, 479	
Water resistance of paper	D 779	T 3620	T 433	264, 266, 4270
WVP at high temperature and humidity	E 96	T 3623	T 464	286
WVP at normal atmospheric conditions			T 448	286
Use Characteristics				
Blocking resistance	D 918	T 3629	T 477	223
Flammability	D 777		T 461	
Moisture content	D 644	T 3605	T 412, 484	205
Films, Foils, Plastics, Printing				
Films and Foil				
Accelerated aging	D 756	T 3404		298
Blocking		T 3405		223
Conditioning plastics films for testing	D 618	T 3401		298

Table P.2 *(Continued)*

	ASTM	PI	Tappi	Fed. Std. 101a
Folding endurance[2]	D 643	T 3402		242
Gas transmission of plastics films	D 1434			
Internal tearing resistance	D 689	T 3403		327
Transparencies of plastics sheeting	D 1746			
Stretch	D 882			245
Tensile strength	D 882			245
Tear strength	D 1922			
WV transmission	E 96			286
Heat sealed seam test				259
Printing				
Block point, flexible films	D 1146	T 1005		
Dry rub resistance		T 1004		
Effect of alkali		T 1001		
Fadeometer	E 42	T 1002		
Resistance to fats and oils		T 1003		

Packages and Components

	ASTM	PI	Tappi	Fed. Std. 101a
Packages				
Bursting strength of paperboard and liner board			T 807	250
Compression test	D 642	T 3805	T 804	295
Conditioning paperboard	D 641	T 3801		298
Cushioning materials, dynamic properties	D 1372			
	D 1596			
	D 2221			
Drop test	D 775	T 3804	T 802	216
Drop test for bags	D 959			216
Drop test (cylindrical)	D 997			216
Flat crush of corrugated	D 1225		T 808	
Incline impact test	D 880	T 3803	T 801	211
Puncture, stiffness: paperboard, corrugated, solid fibre	D 781	T 3807	T 803	321
Revolving drum test	D 782	T 3802	T 800	243
Static bending, corrugated	D 1098			309
Vibration	D 999	T 3806		278, 279
Water resistance, spray method	D 951		T 805	
WVP of packages	D 895			
	D 1251			252
WVP of shipping containers	D 1008			252
Adhesives				
Adhesiveness: seals, closures			T 806	
Bonding of labels to bottles	D 1581			
Liquid, total solids content of	D 1489-90	T 3003		
Closures				
Comparing rubber closures		T 3203		
Compatibility, rubber closures		T 3204		341
Measuring torque		T 3205		1151, 218
Screw cap, WVT in lining		T 3201		
Screw cap liner, compatibility		T 3202		339, 341
Sizes and gages		O 2		

TABLE P.2 (*Continued*)

	ASTM	PI	Tappi	Fed. Std. 101a

Federal and Military Specifications

Adhesives
    Methods of testing   Fed. Test Meth. Std.-175
    Paper label, water-resistant   MIL-A-3941
    Paper label, water-resistant, water emulsion type   MMM-A-179
    Water-resistant, for sealing fibreboard boxes   MMM-A-250
    Water-resistant, waterproof barrier material   MMM-A-260

Bags
    Bags and envelopes, cellophane   PPP-B-15
    Bags, sacks, for subsistence items   MIL-B-137
    Envelopes: packaging, water-vaporproof, flexible   MIL-E-6060
    Interior packaging   MIL-B-117
    Plastic, polyethylene (general purpose)   PPP-B-0026
    Sacks, shipping, paper   UU-S-48
    Transparent, flexible, heat sealable   MIL-B-22205

Barrier materials
    Greaseproofed, flexible (waterproof)   MIL-B-121
    Water-vaporproof, flexible   MIL-B-131
    Waterproofed, flexible, all-temperature   MIL-B-13239
    Wrapping, laminated and creped   MIL-P-130
    Wrapping, waterproofed, kraft   UU-P-271

Boxes, Folding, Set-up
    Folding, paperboard   PPP-B-566
    Set-up, paperboard   PPP-B-676
    Water-resistant paperboard, folding   MIL-B-43014

Boxes, Shipping
    Corrugated, triple-wall   PPP-B-640
    Fibreboard   PPP-B-636
    Wood, wirebound   PPP-B-585

Cans
    Fibre, paperboard (paper or metal ends)   PPP-C-55
    Metal, 28-gage and lighter   PPP-C-96

Drums
    Fibre   PPP-D-723
    Metal, shipping & storage   MIL-D-6054
    Metal, 55 gal.   PPP-D-729

Paper and Paperboard
    Fibreboard, corrugated and solid   PPP-F-320
    General specs and methods of testing   UU-P-31
    Kraft, untreated, wrapping   UU-P-268
    Paperboard, wrapping, cushioning   PPP-P-291
    Wrapping, chemically neutral, noncorrosive   MIL-P-17667
    Wrapping, tissue   UU-P-553

Plastics
    Cellulose acetate, sheets and film   L-P-504
    Films, flexible, vinyl chloride   L-P-375
    Films, polyvinyl and vinyl copolymer   L-P-00370
    Films, polyethylene, thin gage   L-P-378

TABLE P.2 (*Continued*)

	ASTM	PI	Tappi	Fed. Std. 101a
Films, transparent, flexible, heat sealable			MIL-F-22191	
Films, transparent, flexible, heat sealable, VCI treated			MIL-F-22019	
Methods of testing			Fed. Test Meth. Std.-406	
Preservation, Packaging, Packing				
Methods of preservation			MIL-P-116	
Tubes				
Collapsible, 8-oz.			MIL-T-3689	

[1] Complete designations include year of issue and of latest revision, plus indication of when a standard is tentative. Users are advised to seek current test in each instance.

[2] Federal specification UU-P-556 contains Handle-O-Meter stiffness test.

For Federal specifications, see "Index of Federal Specifications and Standards," published by General Services Adm. For military specifications see "Dept. of Defense Index of Specifications and Standards," comprised of Part 1, an alphabetical listing, and Part II, a numerical listing. Copies of these publications are sold by Supt. of Documents, U.S. Govt. Printing Office, Washington, D.C.

TABLE P.3

FEDERAL PACKAGING REGULATIONS AND THE AGENCIES THAT ENFORCE THEM

Federal Enforcement Agencies	Foods Including Meat, Poultry, and Soft Drinks	Alcoholic Products and Tobacco	Chemicals and Related Products	Title No.	Federal Register Act and Date
Dept. of Agriculture	Meat, meat products			9	Inspection Act, 1906
Consumer and Marketing Service	Poultry, poultry products			7	Poultry, Products Insp., 1957; Standard Container Acts, 1916, 1928
Dept. Health, Education and Welfare	Foods incl. pet unless otherwise stated	Alcohol in drug products	Food additives	21	Food, Drug, Cosmetic Act, 1938 with including Food Additives Amendment, 1958
Food and Drug Administration	Enforces regulations designed to prevent deceptive and unfair trade practices; including deceptive packaging and labeling Hazardous Substances				Fair Packaging and Labeling Act 1966
				21	Hazardous Substances Labeling Act, 1960; Caustic Poison Act, 1921; Child Protection Act, 1966
Treasury Dept., Alcohol and Tobacco Tax		Alcoholic beverages Industrial spirits		26 27	Internal Revenue Code Alcohol Administration Act
		Products with denatured spirits		26	Internal Revenue Code
Bureau of Customs	Enforces regulations regarding imports			19	Tariff Act 1930 (amended)
Federal Trade Commission	Enforces regulations designed to prevent deceptive and unfair trade practices, including deceptive packaging and labeling			16	FTC Act, 1914; Wool Products Labeling Act 1939; Textile Fibre Products Ident. Act, 1951; Fur Fair Packaging and Labeling Act, 1966

Specifications

Table P.2 itemizes the tests and specifications for packaging materials and containers, and Table P.3 lists federal packaging regulations.

Reference

MODERN PACKAGING ENCYCLOPEDIA. 1967. McGraw-Hill Book Co., New York.

Cross-references: *Antioxidants; Bottles and Cartons; Conversion Values; Dehydrating Agents; Packaging; Vacuum Packaging.*

PACKAGING

Gas Packaging

To obtain a low level of headspace oxygen in dry whole milk, a double gassing technique is applied. The customary procedure is the collection of filled cans on trays to be conveyed into the vacuum chamber. The air is removed rapidly (60 sec) with the gage indicator decreasing to 29+ in. Hg of vacuum. After a 2 to 5 min hold, the pressure is restored with nitrogen to 0.5 to 1.0 psi above atmospheric pressure. Nitrogen may be replaced with a mixture of nitrogen and carbon dioxide, the latter being restricted to 5 to 20%. After removal from the chamber, the containers are sealed by soldering the 1- to 2-mm hole in the lid or crimping on the lid. The containers are held for oxygen desorption. When an oxygen equilibrium has been attained in the headspace, usually within a week but at the most ten days, the cans are punctured and vacuum treated, repressurized with nitrogen, and the sealing steps are repeated.

Gas packaging of dry whole milk should not be delayed after drying. Otherwise quality deteriorates during the holding period. Warm powder directly from the drier tends to have a more rapid rate of oxygen desorption under vacuum. If the production is not large, dry whole milk may be placed into metal drums and the air exhausted. By holding the product under partial vacuum for oxygen desorption the first gassing step in the package may be eliminated, while achieving a final maximum of 2% oxygen.

Oxygen Limits

A good commercial operation using continuous gassing equipment can reduce the oxygen level to approximately 2.5% with a single gassing. This may be satisfactory for many storage conditions, but not if the storage temperature will be 90°F or above. A maximum limit of 3.0 to 3.5% oxygen in the headspace of the can is required for a noticeable delay of oxidation. United States Standards for grading permit a 2% maximum in Premium and 3% for U.S. Extra Grade dry whole milk.

Oil Impurity

Water pumped nitrogen (not oil pumped) may be purchased in high pressure drums. It can be prepared at the plant by burning propane gas with controlled conditions. Oxygen impurity is removed by exposure to hot iron shavings.

Oxygen Removal by Reaction

Another procedure consists of the addition of 5% hydrogen to the nitrogen in the package to restore atmospheric pressure after deaeration. A packet containing a catalyst is added to the container after filling with the dry milk. The catalyst may be palladium or platinum. Each of these causes the oxygen to react with the hydrogen forming water, thus effectively removing the oxygen available for oxidative reactions.

Commercial usage and tests have demonstrated that flexible packages as well as metal cans are satisfactory for gas packaging of dry milks containing fat. The flexible packages are more easily damaged by rough handling, but this should not prove a limiting factor in domestic outlets.

Recently an interesting modification of the flexible package has been developed. The oxygen scavenger is placed between the layers of the pouch package. Oxygen passes through the wall of the pouch, contacting the scavenger and forming water, which cannot pass back through the pouch liner into the dry product.

Retail Carton

Retail cartons of fiberboard foil and plastics are widely used. Because of the hygroscopic nature of dry milk, the packaging materials must provide a good vapor barrier. Of several types in use, one is a fiberboard carton with an overwrap of foil laminated to paper. Another consists of a fiberboard carton with an inner liner of foil laminated to paper. A polyethylene bag inside the fiberboard carton is also used. Other combinations of layers of polyethylene, foil, and paper either in liner or overwrap are available for packaging.

Fillers for rapid speed operation are on the market. Common size packages range from individual use packets of 3.2 oz. (intended for 1 qt of reconstituted skim-milk) to packages of 9.6 oz to 5 lb or larger.

Packaging of nonfat dry milk and other dry food products is quite routine. Principal considerations involve keeping machine downtime to a minimum, maintaining the correct net weight within narrow limits, and providing a good seal. The packages are packed in cardboard cases for storage and/or shipment. Coding of each package provides a means of identification for quality control.

Packaging of Nonfat Dry Milk

A suitable container for dry milk should be: impervious to moisture, light, gases, and insects; durable for handling; resistant to corrosion; of low cost; and relatively easy to fill, seal, handle, and empty. The retail package should have a reclosable opening.

Nonfat dry milk for industrial use and storage may be packaged in barrels, drums, and bags or for retail purposes in metal cans, glass jars, or cartons. Except for the retail market, most of the yearly production goes into 100- or 50-lb bags. Government purchase under the support program requires a minimum polyethylene liner, 3 mm thick inside a 6-ply kraft paper bag. In 1963, the government issued standards for the purchase of nonfat dry milk in bags having tape over the top seal; and offered a premium price for nonfat dry milk in this bag (Type G). In 1966, this type became mandatory. The purpose of this type bag is to prevent insect infestation of the product after packaging.

Nonfat dry milk in domestic commercial trade is commonly packaged in a 2-mil polyethylene bag inside a 4-ply kraft paper bag.   The outside layer is usually plain, but a crinkled type is available.   Freezing, high temperature, and low humidity during storage of bags cause them to become brittle, and thus susceptible to damage in handling.

Manual filling of the bags is most commonly completed by means of a simple device attached to the sifter.   Automatic bagging equipment is readily available to dispense the correct weight of powder in one bag before shifting the product flow into the next bag.   Bags are sewn 3 to $3^1/_2$ stitches per inch automatically or by a manually operated sewing machine suspended and counterbalanced within easy reach of the filling area.   Type G bags require special heat sealing equipment for the protective tape.   After closing, the bags are usually stacked on pallets.   The bag overhang from the pallet should not be more than 2 in.

Many of these principles apply to most other dry food products.

Reference

HALL, C. W., and HEDRICK, T. I.   1966.   Drying of Milk and Milk Products.   AVI Publishing Co., Westport, Conn.

Cross-references: *Antioxidants; Bag Fillers; Bottles and Cartons; Carton Forming and Filling; Dry Milk; Packages; Poultry Processing; Vacuum Packaging.*

PAINT

Paint Constituents

The colors are supplied by painting over the building material or as a part of the building material itself.   Although an important item, the color is far from the most important factor to consider in paint selection.

Paint is a mixture consisting of a pigment made up of a finely divided substance held in suspension in a liquid called a vehicle.   The pigment is made up of finely divided particles which impart the color to the paint.   Generally, the quality of the paint is increased with an increase in the percentage of pigment.

In addition to the vehicle, thinners or solvents and driers are often used in various proportions.   Additives can be purchased and added to the oil base paint to prevent fungus growth, as well as being incorporated in the paint.

Linseed, tung (wood), and fish oil are vehicles commonly used for paints with the latter two recommended for water resistant paints.   Tung oil dries to a hard smooth film with a heavy gloss.   Tung oil is more water resistant than linseed oil, less durable, and faster drying, as it takes about $^1/_3$ as long to dry as for linseed oil.   A large amount of thinner, usually turpentine, is added to the first coat to obtain penetration, and more vehicle, e.g., linseed oil, is used in the following coats.   Generally, cold water paints are cheaper and will not give as good service as oil paints.   The addition of a drier, such as Japan's makes a paint less durable.   Fish (menhaden) oil will withstand heat and will maintain good elasticity, which is usually used in conjunction with other paint vehicles.

Latex

Many advances have been made in paint technology in providing protective and attractive surface coatings, but probably one of the more important developments has been the formulation of water-thinned latex paints.

The principal difference between oil-base and latex paints is in the vehicle or liquid which carries the pigment onto the surface being painted. An oil-based paint vehicle may be composed of drying oils, resins, and solvents (or volatiles), while the vehicle in latex paint is an emulsion of binder and water. Oil paints are relatively slow drying because the process takes place by oxidation, solvent evaporation, and polymerization. Emulsion paints dry by evaporation of water.

Several advantages of the latex emulsions over oil-type paints can be cited. Among these are water-thinning, little or no painty odor, rapid drying, ease of spreading, and water cleaning of equipment. The importance of water thinning is greater than sometimes realized in that surfaces being painted do not have to be dry (as with oil-based paints), but only free of surface water. In other words, latex paints can be applied soon after rains and earlier in the morning with little regard for dew. Quick drying results in less dust and insect collection on the surface, and usually is rapid enough to allow the application of a second coat the same day.

Latex coatings contain no oils for mildew to feed upon, but their "breathing-film" qualities may allow fungi to reach the oil in the prime coat. Consequently, fungicides

TABLE P.4

QUALITIES OF LATEX EMULSIONS

Type of Emulsion	Latex Paint Characteristics
Vinyl	Interior Use
	1. Easy application with brush or roller
	2. Absence of paint odor
	3. Self-sealing
	4. Excellent alkali resistance
	5. Exceptionally uniform flat appearance
	Exterior Use
	1. Excellent adhesion on properly prepared surfaces
	2. Nonfading
	3. Good alkali resistance
	4. Blister-resistant on properly prepared surfaces
Acrylic	1. Very good water resistance
	2. Very elastic, flexible film (highly desirable for exterior applications)
	In Comparison with Vinyl Emulsions
	1. More disagreeable odor
	2. Tendency to bubble with roller application
	3. Shorter wet edge time
	4. Lacks uniform finish features
	5. Tendency to pick up dirt in exterior use
	6. Less fade resistance on exterior surfaces
Rubber	1. Inferior sheen uniformity
(Butadiene-	2. Disagreeable odor
styrene)	3. Requires 30 days to develop hardness and washability
	Special Formulations
	1. Good alkali and water resistance when completely dry (desirable in porch and floor paints)

should be added to the primer in a latex-paint program if mildew is considered likely to be a problem.

The covering power of latex paints is less than that of comparable quality oil-base coatings. In certain instances, it may be necessary to use two coats of latex paint to cover a surface where a single coating of oil-base paint would be satisfactory.

Three latex emulsions are made commercially under the names of vinyl latex (a polyvinyl acetate), acrylic latex, and rubber latex (styrene-butadiene). All three types of emulsions are suspended in water. Qualities to consider in application are listed in Table P.4. Uses of latex emulsion are listed in Table P.5.

Application

Water resistance, paint hardness, light reflection, surface to be covered, the effect of milk acid, and color should be considered in paint selection. The pigment and vehicle are varied according to the application. Because of the difficulty of knowing the specific characteristics of a paint, the reputation of the manufacturer must be considered. Because of the many variations in the method of applying paint, the manufacturer's recommendations must be followed.

If the reflective qualities of the paint are to be maintained the paint must be properly selected and applied. A solution of 1 lb of lye and 5 pt of water will usually dissolve old paint. One gallon of paint will usually cover 600 sq ft. Paint should not normally be applied when the temperature is below 40°F. Some types of paint, such as weather coatings and weather proofings may cover only 150 sq ft per gal.

Concrete and Plaster.—Several types of paint have proved satisfactory for concrete (often called cement). Unless the concrete has weathered over 6 months, the surface must be treated by scrubbing with a 20% solution of muriatic (hydrochloric) acid, followed by a thorough rinsing of water.

Portland cement paint, manufactured by many different companies, is obtainable in a large number of colors and has proved satisfactory for concrete walls, but should not be used on wood, metal, enamel, brick, glazed brick or tile, over old paint, or on floors. This material must be placed on wet surfaces which are free of oil or grease, or can be put on fresh concrete after 24 hr. Chlorinated rubber paints are also satisfactory for concrete.

Plaster should be treated with a zinc sulfate solution if the plaster is to be painted before it is cured. After treatment, the dry surface should be covered with a sizing before it is painted.

TABLE P.5

LATEX PAINTS AND THEIR USES

Paint Type	Areas of Use
Interior Use	
Latex flat	Plaster, gypsum board, masonry walls, wood doors, windows, and trim
Latex semigloss	Wood trim
Latex floor	Concrete floors, resilient tile floors
Exterior Use	
Latex house	Wood siding, shingles, and shakes; asbestos shingles; stucco, brick, or concrete; wood doors, windows and trim; wood fences
Latex floor	Concrete patio floors
Latex masonry	Asbestos shingles; stucco, brick, and concrete

Paints for a concrete floor in a processing plant must withstand considerable abrasion and wear. Paints with a phenol resin base and rubber base have proved satisfactory if 2 or 3 coats are used. These paints require a dry floor and may present a problem where moisture comes up through the floor. Rubber coat enamels can be painted over wet concrete or plaster.

Machinery and Metal Work.—Priming the surface is the most important step in painting all metal work, for which special primers are available. A metal top coat which has great endurance qualities is a graphite paint.

Asphalt paints have good resistance to acids, alkalis, brine, etc., but will crack under much expansion of the surface. A primer must be applied on steel before asphalt paint. Overcoating asphalt of a different type of paint should not be used because the asphalt will bleed through the paint.

Paint for hot water pipes may be applied when the pipe is warm to bake the paint on, but should not be applied when the pipe is hot to avoid blistering. If the water pipe is galvanized a special treatment should be given the pipe. A wash coat of copper sulfate solution of about 1 lb of copper sulfate dissolved in 1 gal of water may be used. After rinsing, the surface should be primed and painted according to the instructions of the manufacturer. Special treated tung oil is often used as a vehicle for machinery paints.

Tanks.—The inside of tanks and vats for raw fruit and vegetable products unless constructed of stainless steel or aluminum, should be coated to prevent rusting or corrosion, or off-flavors to the product. A galvanized coating is preferred, which if properly done, will last 5 to 10 yr. If painted, a new coat must be applied every 2 to 3 yr. Painting with aluminum, Rustoleum (trade name) red, or lead free white enamel makes an acceptable finish if maintained.

Wood

Turpentine is usually used as a thinner for a wood paint because it increases the penetrative power by dissolving the pitch in the wood. The surfaces should be dry and sufficient time should be allowed for drying between coats of paint. It is important to follow the instructions of the manufacturer for thinning the paint because different thinners and vehicles might have a tendency to react with each other if improperly selected. Special clear protective coatings are available for various wood, concrete, and metal surfaces.

It is important to consider the use of color coats for identifying pipelines and outlining safety areas for the protection and efficiency of the workers. Benefits far in excess of the paint cost might be realized from proper coating. The painting and lighting must be planned together. The paint should approximately reflect the light according to the specifications set by the Illuminating Engineering Society. The color is just one factor in paint selection. If the paint is to hold up and maintain its original qualities, the surfaces must be properly cleaned and prepared, and the paint must be properly selected and applied. There is no universal paint—that is, a paint that can be applied to all surfaces, regardless of exposure, surface, and wear.

Additives

Chemicals may be used to provide protection of the paint and structure against mildew and fungus. About 0.01% bichloride of mercury and phenyl mercury acetate are compounds used to prevent mildew. Mildew develops rapidly in food plants where there is a high humidity and little ventilation. Borax (at least 25%) may be added to paint to provide fire-retardant properties.

Cross-references: *Lighting; Piping; Safety.*

PASTEURIZATION

The primary purpose of pasteurization is to kill the pathogenic organisms in a product—liquid, solid, or gas. Certain favorable chemical reactions occur, such as

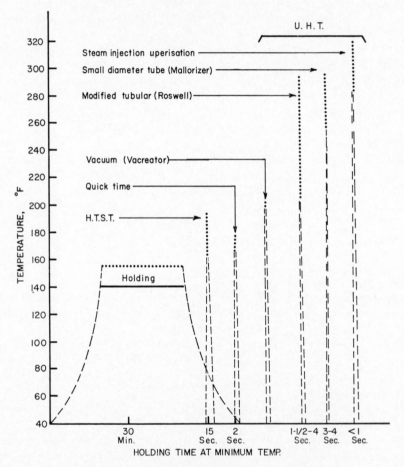

FIG. P-1.   Pasteurization by various methods

inactivation of enzymes so that the pasteurized product has a longer storage life or better keeping quality. The pasteurization process must also be carried out without excessively damaging the product.

Milk and milk products are those most commonly pasteurized. Standards developed for milk are used as a basis for other food products. Heat has been the most widely used source of energy for pasteurization. Radiation offers possibilities for pasteurization. In the United States, the heat treatment for the holding method of pasteurization requires at least 145°F for no less than 30 min, and for the continuous method at least 161°F for no less than 15 sec. Milk products which have added fat or sweeteners must be heated to at least 150° and 166°F, respectively, for the holding and continuous methods. Temperatures up to 300°F have been used, with those above 200°F often identified as UHT, ultrahigh temperature systems, where exposure times of less than 1 sec are often involved (Fig. P.1).

A comparison of the name given to various methods of pasteurization by heat treatment and the time-temperature relationship are given in the attached figure.

The pasteurization unit, PU, relating time-temperature (with the slope of the semilog curve as z = 18°F) is represented in Fig. P.2.

The effects of heat treatment on the various constituents of milk are well-known (Figs. P.3–P.6).

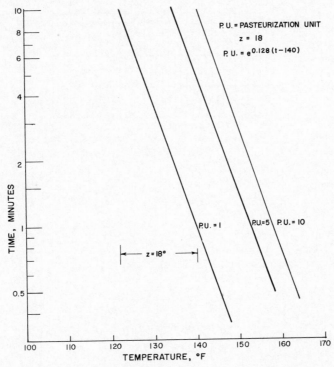

FIG. P-2.   Representation of P.U. (pasteurization unit)

References

HALL, C. W., and TROUT, G. M.   1968.   Milk Pasteurization.   AVI Publishing Co., Westport, Conn.

Cross-references: *Heat Exchangers; Heating Systems for HTST; HTST Pasteurization; Holding Methods of Pasteurization; UHT Equipment.*

PELLETING

A pellet is described as a small quantity of material which is held together in a compact form which will retain its shape under normal handling conditions.

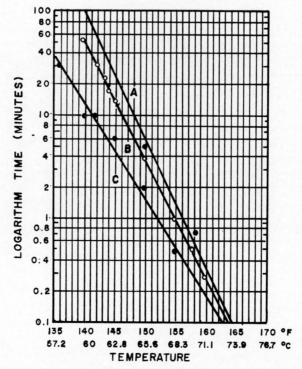

FIG. P-3.   Scale of time-temperature values for milk pasteurization
A—Cream layers reduced.   B—Standard for pasteurization.   C—Thermal death
points.

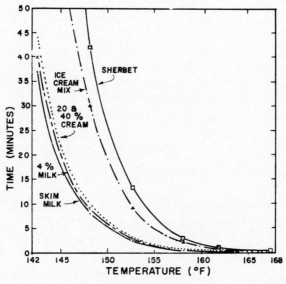

FIG. P-4.   Times and temperatures of heating required to reduce phosphatase

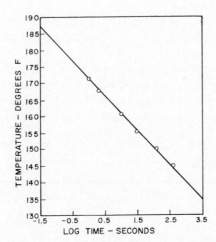

Fɪɢ. P-5.   Time and temperature relationship for the inactivation of the lipase
enzyme in milk

The pharmaceutical industry makes great use of pellets in the form of pills in which the various ingredients are compressed into a rather stable and compact form.   The food industry also makes use of the pellet particularly for use in pet feed and for certain special purposes.

The usual method of making pellets is to combine a mixture of ingredients in the proper proportion and by being forced through a high pressure die machine, the ingredients are pressed into a solid shape retaining form.   Automatic machines of large capacity are used to make these pellets.

The basic principle of the standard pelleting machine is applying heavy pressure, 1,000 to 3,000 psi, to the material in a die to compress, and then force the pellet out.

Satisfactory pelleting of materials requires strict attention to the moisture content.   Usually material exceeding 25% moisture does not pellet satisfactory and material of less than 15% does not give a stable pellet.   There is a great difference in the ease with which various mixtures and types of material will pellet and it is important that the material be tested in a machine before purchasing equipment. Figure P.7 shows the basic principle of the pressure type pelleter.

Care should be taken in pelleting of any material, to avoid exceeding the temperature or pressure beyond which destabilization of the ingredients of the product is encountered.

PIPING

The terms piping and tubing are often used interchangeably.   However, piping is usually a thicker-walled material in which the size is given by a nominal inside diameter.   Thus, a 1-in. diam pipe might have an inside diameter slightly larger or slightly less than 1 in. depending on the wall thickness.   A pipe may in general be identified as light, medium, strong, or extra strong; or more specifically, according to schedule numbers from 10 to 160.

Tubing size is identified by the outside diameter, which is given in exact dimensions.   A 1-in. diam tube will have an outside diameter of 1 in., and as the thickness of tube increases, a smaller inside diameter.   Both piping and tubing have fixed out-side diameters.   Fittings for a given size pipe are interchangeable as far as size is concerned.

Designation and utilization of piping and tubing depend on material, method of manufacture, and industrial practices.   Cast iron is normally made into piping, stain-less steel into tubing, and plastic and glass into either piping or tubing.

A wide range of pipe and tubing materials are available for pumping various fluids (Table P.6).

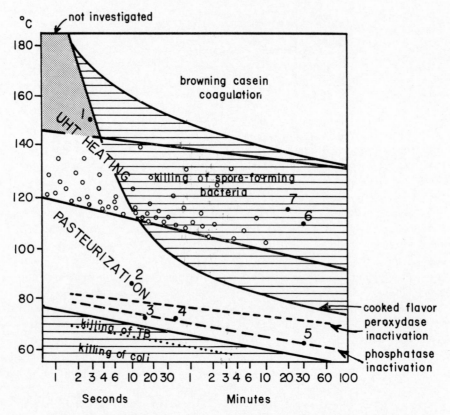

Fig. P-6.   Influence of heat treatment on milk characteristics
1—Uperization. 2—Flash pasteurization. 3—HTST process. 4—Short time pasteurization. 5—Holder process. 6—Pasteur 1860. 7—Sterilization in bottles.

The wall thickness of piping and tubing must be sufficient to withstand the forces exerted; the material must resist excessive corrosion without damaging the product; the internal diameter must be sufficient to avoid excessive costs of pumping the fluid.

Piping and tubing expand or contract as the temperature changes.   Brass and copper expand considerably more than cast iron and steel (Table P.7).   An installation must provide space for expansion of piping and tubing without damage to the piping and tubing, the equipment, or the supporting structure.   To provide expansion of piping and tubing: (1) slip joints can be used with piston rings and packing; (2) packless slip joints can be used; and (3) L-, Z-, or U-bend arrangements can be used.

Fittings

Fittings are used for change in the direction of the lines or for making attachments to equipment or other lines. The fittings can be constructed of stainless steel, or other alloys known as white metals, dairy metals (copper alloys should be avoided particularly for hot milk), chrome-plated brass, or stainless steel. Connections should be made using an expanded attachment which expands the tubing into the fitting. All connections should be made so that there are no seats or pockets in which food

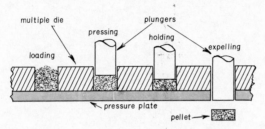

Fig. P-7.　Steps in making a pellet

particles can accumulate. Fittings may also be made of tinned bronze. Threads used on fittings for conveying of milk and other food products should be of the Acme type and not V-cut 60° threads. The sealing of the joint is on the seats between the thread connectors and not between the thread and the piping, as for V-cut threads.

Glass

Glass pipeline is finding acceptance in food plants with the development and use of cleaning-in-place systems. The lines can be inspected in place without disassembly. The joints must be properly assembled and the pipeline properly supported so that the line will function properly without sagging or forming pockets. Pipe made of glass is designated by the nominal inside diameter, where $1^1/_2$-in. pipeline would be approximately $1^1/_2$ in. on the inside. The capacity of a glass pipeline is about 10% greater than that of the tubing which is designated by the outside diameter.

Reference

PERRY, J. H.　1964.　Chemical Engineers' Handbook.　McGraw-Hill Book Co., New York.

Cross-references: *Friction; Glass Pipe; Hydraulics; Refrigeration Principles; Safety; Steam; Valves.*

PLANT LAYOUT

The efficiency of a food processing plant can be greatly affected by the plant layout. There are certain basic factors which must be considered in any food plant; however, the prospective builder is advised to visit a number of good, well-designed, and efficient plants in order to obtain ideas, and to employ a competent architect and engineer to prepare preliminary specifications and plans for a proposed plant.

Principles

The details of the operation will vary tremendously; however, certain basic principles can be applied to practically any food processing plant. Some of these principles are as follows.

(1) Make the plan flexible so that future changes can be made without costly alteration work.

(2) Size the processing areas large enough to handle ample future volume without adding to the original space.

TABLE P.6

MATERIALS USED IN PUMPING LIQUIDS

Liquid	Specific Gravity	Materials Commonly Used (See Key)
Alcohols		AB, AA, 10
Ammonia, aqua		AI
Beer		AB, 4
Beet juice		AB, 4
Beet pulp		AB, SF, AA
Blood		SF, AB
Calcium chloride brine, pH above 8		AI
Calcium chloride brine, pH below 8		AB, 6, 7, 9, 10
Cane juice		SF, AB, 9
Catsup		AB, AA
Citric acid		AB, AA, 8
Coconut oil	0.905	AI, SF, AB, AA, 10
Copper sulfate, blue vitrol		AA, 8, 11
Fatty acid (oleic, palmitic, stearic)		AB, AA
Fruit juices		AB, AA, 10
Gasoline	0.68	AI, SF
Glucose		SF, AB
Lactic acid		AB, AA, 8
Lard, hot		AI, SF
Linseed	0.94	AI, SF, AB, AA, 10
Milk	1.028–1.035	4
Molasses		SF, AB
Olive oil	0.90	AI, SF
Palm oil	0.895	AI, SF, AB, AA, 10
Paraffin, hot		AI, SF
Rapeseed oil	0.92	AB, AA, 10
Slop, brewery		AI, SF, AB
Soybean oil		AI, SF, AB, AA, 10
Starch		SF, AB
Sugar, aqueous solution		AB, AA, 9
Turpentine	0.87	AI, SF
Vegetable juices		AB, AA, 10
Water, distilled		AB, 4
Whiskey		AB, 4
Wine		AB, 4
Yeast		SF, AB

Key: SF, Standard fitted; AB, All bronze; AI, All iron; AA, Types 4, 5, 6, 7, 4, 5, 18-8, Chromium-nickel stainless steel; 6, 15-28% Chromium, 22-36% nickel; 7, Series of nonferrous alloy with less than 20% iron; 8, High silicon iron; 9, Austenitic cast iron with more than 22% nickel-copper-chromium content; 10, Monel metal; 11, Lead; 12, Nonmetallic.

Source: Hydraulic Institute.

(3) Build the cold storage area sufficiently large for the initial volume plus at least moderate expansion, but locate it so that further additions can be made.

(4) Apply the same principle as (3) to the dry storage areas and office facilities.

(5) Arrange the plant so that processing rooms do not become corridors for circulating personnel and visitors to the plant.

(6) Study truck traffic, loading, unloading, and parking to eliminate high automotive costs and inefficient traffic congestion in the building.

(7) Centralize the plant manager's office and laboratory for proper supervision and quality control.

TABLE P.7

EXPANSION OF PIPE DUE TO HEATING (CONTRACTION DUE TO COOLING) IN IN. PER 100 FT, ABOVE 0°F

Temperature, °F	Cast Iron	Steel	Brass and Copper
0	0	0	0
50	0.36	0.38	0.57
100	0.72	0.76	1.14
125	0.88	0.92	1.40
150	1.10	1.15	1.75
200	1.50	1.57	2.38
250	1.90	1.99	3.02
300	2.35	2.47	3.74
350	2.80	2.94	4.45
400	3.30	3.46	5.24
450	3.89	4.08	6.18
500	4.45	4.67	7.06

Example: The expansion of 500 ft of steel pipe, heating from 50° to 250°F = $(1.99 - 0.38) \times 5$ is 8.05 in.

The coefficient of expansion for: Cast iron is $5.8 \times 10^{-6}/°F$; Steel is $7.1 \times 10^{-6}/°F$; Brass is $10.5 \times 10^{-6}/°F$; Copper is $9.3 \times 10^{-6}/°F$.

Source: Perry (1964).

(8) Arrange food equipment for cleaning-in-place treatment where possible. In small plants, processing should be done on one floor. In large plants, multifloor operations are often economical.

(9) Utility lines should be laid out for short length but provide flexibility.

(10) Dry storage rooms should be on the same floor near the center of processing operations.

(11) By-products and minor operations should be adjacent to rather than an integral part of the main plant operation.

(12) Secondary equipment, such as boilers and refrigeration machines, should be centrally located in all plants; however, in large plants, boilers and refrigeration machines may be situated in a separate power plant building.

(13) At least 2 to 3 ft of unobstructed space should be provided around pieces of equipment so that they can be readily cleaned, inspected, and maintained.

(14) Processing equipment should not occupy more than 25% of the floor area alloted to production.

It is important to check with local health authorities concerning the plant layout. These people are familiar with regulations regarding materials, space, clearances, and required arrangements.

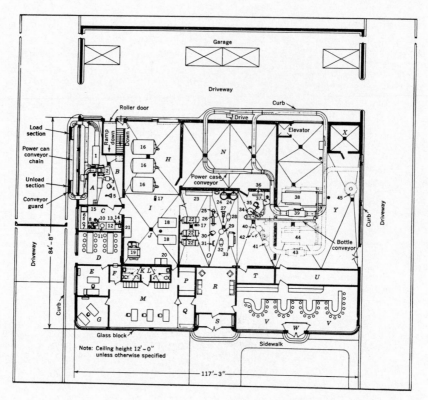

Courtesy of Cherry-Burrell Corp.

Fig. P-8.   Milk plant for 3500 gal. per day

Major equipment: 1. 6-can-per-min can washer, 4. clarifier, 5. plate raw-milk cooler, 16. 1,500-gal. storage tank, 17. pump, 18. cheese vats, 19. butter churn, 20. wash tank, 22. 300-gal. pasteurizer, 24. 100-gal surge tanks, 25. 8,500 lb per hr holder tube, 27. 8,500 lb per hr HTST pasteurizer, 28. timing pump, 29. 150-gal. surge tank, 30. separator, 31. cream surface cooler, 32. pump, 33. homogenizer, 33. bottle filler, 35. bottle hooder, 38. 8-wide bottle washer, 39. case washer, 40–45 for future equipment.

Layout

The layout of the food processing plant should be coordinated with a study of the materials handling system for the plant, as the system will largely determine the relative locations of equipment rooms and facilities.

The arrangement for bringing utilities to the equipment is an important item in plant layout.   It has been found that a utility corridor either at the side, above the ceiling, or in the basement is a very efficient and flexible means of bringing mechanical and electrical services to operating areas.   Access to this corridor may be by door or by the removal of panels such as are frequently used in construction of ceilings of modern processing plants.

Figure P.8 shows a layout for a small dairy plant.   Figure P.9 shows a typical layout for a meat processing plant.   The relative location of the service or satellite room to the main processing room, and the direct movement and short lines for conveyors in the system are of particular interest.   The produce storage room for both raw and finished materials should be located as closely as possible to the main processing room. The size of the finished product storage rooms can be kept reasonably small by the use of delivery trucks to store the product during a portion of the processing cycle; for example, milk after bottling can be stored in the refrigerated milk trucks.

Many companies use a satellite storage plant both for materials to be processed and for finished goods. This has the advantage of eliminating the need for extensive storage in an expensive area where the main plant is located.

Site Selection

Location of the food plant affects the plant layout and is often an important factor in the efficiency of a processing plant. The contour of the land can either assist or hinder the plant operation. The location may also determine the advisability of having a retail store auxiliary and it greatly affects the transportation of products to and from the plant. The following factors should be considered in determining the location.

(1) The availability of satisfactory labor in the area.

(2) The availability of electric power and other utilities, including waste disposal.

(3) The availability of raw materials.

(4) The availability of good transportation to and from the location.

(5) Is the area well-drained?

(6) Is the area subject to floods, or other natural hazards?

(7) Is there room for expansion?

(8) Can a profitable retail sales outlet be built?

(9) Is the land suitable for providing a stable building foundation?

(10) Is the contour of the land such that an efficient plant can be built on the site?

(11) Are the taxes in the area reasonable?

(12) Is the area in a safe and desirable neighborhood?

(13) Is the future status of the area likely to change and if so, how will it affect the plant?

Cross-references: *Dairy Plant Layout and Design; HTST Pasteurization; Materials Handling; Poultry Processing; Refrigerated Storage; Shipping Docks; Slaughter House.*

PNEUMATIC CONVEYING

The food industry has found the pneumatic conveying of materials is often the most efficient and satisfactory method of handling powdered or granular material. One of the most widely used systems is to merely blow the material, such as dry food products, through a tube system and collector. In addition, however, a so-called fluidized system is used for handling cracked ice, cocoa beans, granulated sugar, or dry milk.

Principle of Operation

A simple pneumatic blower system (Fig. P.10) requires a collector or storage bin, feed valve, conductor tube, powder collector, blower, and return line. The velocity of the air in the conductor system must be sufficient to carry the powdered product in suspension, and the higher the velocity, the greater the capacity. Velocities below

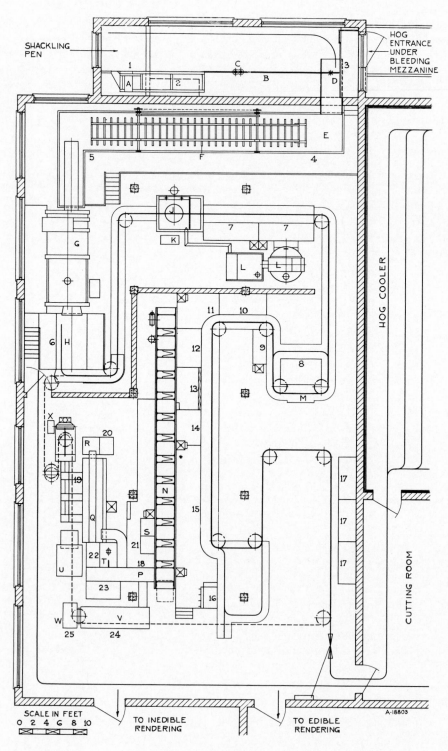

Courtesy of Albrecht Nell Co.

Fig. P-9.   Hog slaughtering and dressing layout

Operations Table: 1—Hog sackling. 2—Sticking. 3—Dropping. 4—Feeding of scalding device. 5—Feeding of conveyor to dehairer. 6—Gambreling. 7—Rosin stripping. 8—Recleaning. 9—Head dropping. 10—Opening. 11—Removing head and placing in pan. 12—Eviscerating. 13—Splitting. 14—Enucleating kidneys; removing spermatic cord. 15—U. S. government inspection. 16—Final inspection. 17—Ham facing; pulling and scraping leaf lard; washing necks. 18—Removing heads and viscera. 19—Viscera separating. 20—Washing fats. 21—Removing infected mesenteric glands; cleaning cut sets of viscera. 22—Opening and washing stomachs. 23—Trimming plucks. 24—Working up heads. 25—Splitting heads; removing brains. Equipment Table: A—Hog hoist with sticking conveyor. B—Hog bleeding rail. C—Blood and water floor drain. D—Power driven hog dropper. E—Cast iron scalding tub. F—Hog scalding device. G—Oneway hot dehairer. H—Stationary gambreling table. J—Automatic rail dropper depilator. K—Adhesive pump. L—Rosin remelting and reclaiming unit. M—Automatic hog rail washer. N—Combination hog head and viscera inspection table. P—Preliminary viscera separating table. Q—Viscera separating table. R—Fat washing box. S—Pans for removing infected mesenteric glands and cleaning cut sets of viscera. T—Stomach opening table. U—Stomach scalder and scraper. V—Hog head work-up table. W—Hog head splitter. X—Casing stripper.

100 fps are not very effective for most products. The product should be metered into the conductor line so that clogging due to overloading is avoided. For food products the conducting air should be taken from a clean environment, and should be filtered. This type system is simple and effective for all types of powdered products and can be cleaned very easily by cleaned-in-place (CIP) methods. For food plants the tubes, collectors, valves, and blower are usually made of stainless steel. Conductor tube sizes are usually 4 in. diam or larger.

The fluidized system is different from the pneumatic system in that it operates at several pounds pressure or vacuum and uses small tubes. For example, 5,000 lb per hr of dry milk can be readily handled through a 2.5 or 3-in. diameter tube system. The principle of the fluidizer is that the product, which may be powder or small chunks like chopped ice, is mixed with sufficient air to make it flow, i.e., it performs like a fluid. This "fluid" can then be pumped, by means of suitable equipment to distances of 500 ft or more. The product can be distributed to several outlets simultaneously.

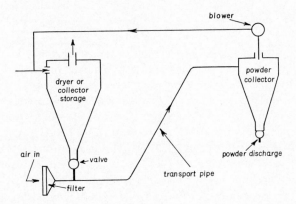

Fig. P-10.   Pneumatic conveyor system for a spray drier

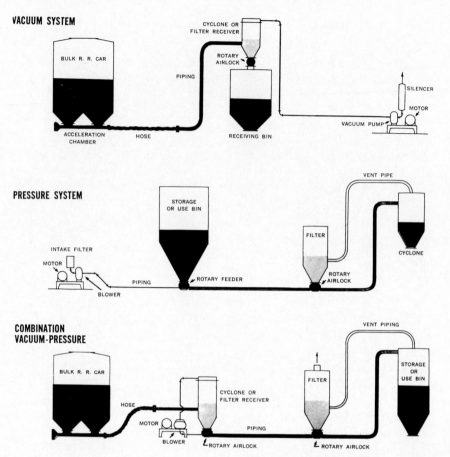

VACUUM SYSTEM

PRESSURE SYSTEM

COMBINATION
VACUUM-PRESSURE

Courtesy of Industrial Products Div., Farmhand, Inc.

FIG. P-11.   Three basic fluidizing conveying devices

There are three types of primary fluidizing systems as shown in Fig. P.11 A, B, and C: vacuum system, the pressure system, and the combination vacuum-pressure system. Each of these has special applications. The *vacuum system* (Fig. P.11A) is especially effective in picking up material from many points and delivering it to one remotely located process or storage area. One power unit serves multiple pickup points. Hookup and start of system are quickly and easily done.

The pressure system (Fig. P.11B) is an economical, compact system particularly applicable for picking up product from one area and delivering to many points—frequently at considerable distances. The system is extremely flexible and can be adapted to specific needs for unloading, in-plant transfer, recirculation, etc.

The combination vacuum-pressure system (Fig. P.11C) is considerably more sophisticated, and combines features of both types described above to expand the range of usage and meet multiple needs. Thus, it can be either stationary or portable. It can unload cars simultaneously from various sidings and can deliver simultaneously to many points—all under push-button control—at high volume, low-cost, and without contamination.

With the fluidizing systems, several important units must be matched to the system. The pressure pump or vacuum pump must be specifically designed for the job and arranged to operate long hours. Lubrication can be a problem, and oil-free pumps and blowers must be used for handling pressure type systems. The rotary feeder is an important item in controlling the product flow. A factor in some systems is that valves have various degrees of tightness. Intake filters for air lines and silencers for vacuum pumps are usually required. The construction and shape of cyclones and receiving or storage bins are also important. In some installations, a final filter or powder collector to prevent dust being discharged to the atmosphere is used. In any system used for handling food products, it is very important to build the system of noncorrosive nonflavor contributing metals. The most satisfactory metal is stainless steel. The system should be designed so that it can be automatically sanitized by means of modern CIP methods.

Cross-references: *Air; Powder Handling Equipment.*

PNEUMATIC LIFTER

Pneumatic lifters are widely used in the food industry for picking up packages, can lids, and many small objects. The lifters are usually a part of an automatic system and can be operated very successfully by electric controls.

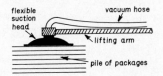

Fɪɢ. P-12.   Principle of pneumatic lifting device

The basic hookup for a pneumatic lifting system is shown in Fig. P.12. The lifting effect of a pneumatic lifter is determined by the area of the vacuum enclosed part of the lifting element and the degree of vacuum. With a perfect vacuum each square inch of lifting surface will theoretically lift 14.7 lb. In actual practice the vacuum employed may be from a few inches of vacuum water pressure to a few pounds per square inch. An important part of the lifting arrangement is a rubber or otherwise flexible lifting head which will effectively seal the vacuum chamber to the surface being lifted.

POSITIVE PUMP

Many pumping situations require a pump which is positive in action, so that for every stroke or revolution of the pump, a definite quantity of fluid is forced through the line, irrespective of the pressure. The so-called positive pump was developed to meet this need. Such pumps are used for metering fluids, for forcing water into a high pressure boiler, or similar uses. Positive pumps are theoretically self-priming, for which a pump must be in good condition for high lifts.

Principle of Operation

The positive pump may be constructed in several different forms. Such pumps operate on the positive displacement principle such as illustrated by the piston pump. A cylinder is filled with liquid and a piston removes the liquid. Each stroke of the pump forces a cylinder full of fluid out through a discharge valve and into the line. The return stroke of the piston draws a vacuum on the cylinder and causes the cylinder to refill through the suction valve after which the pressure stroke forces the fluid out again. A measured amount of fluid is handled at each stroke, and as the fluid is discharged it is positively ejected against the pressure in the line, assuming that the piston is driven by sufficient force to overcome the head pressure in the discharge line.

The capacity of a piston or plunger type pump is given by the formula

$$\text{Gpm} = \frac{(\text{Diam cylinder, in.})^2 \times 0.7854 \times \text{stroke (in.)} \times \text{strokes/min}}{231}$$

where
$$\text{Gpm} = \text{gallons per minute}$$
$$\text{Strokes/min} = \text{pumping strokes per min}$$
$$231 = \text{cu in. in a gallon}$$

Rotary Positive Pump

The rotary positive pump is widely used in the food industry because it has no valves as such. It employs gears, blades, or a double screw arrangement which as they are rotated provide a positive displacement action similar to that of a piston pump; however, it does not need separate intake and discharge valves, because as it rotates, the valve action is provided by the blades or gear teeth as they pass the intake and discharge ports of the pump housing. Theoretically, each revolution of the pump forces a definite quantity of fluid through the line.

Rotary positive pumps depend upon very close mechanical fits between the blades or gears, and the pump casing. They are not adapted to high pressures, i.e., over 100 psig, except for use in oil hydraulic systems. The output of a rotary pump is theoretically equal to the displacement of the pump. However, due to some slippage of fluid past the gear teeth, the rotary pump is only approximately positive in performance.

Positive pumps can be obtained in large or small capacities and of stainless steel construction when needed for pumping food products. They can be obtained in steel, iron, or bronze for other purposes.

Care and Maintenance

Care of plunger type pumps such as are used in homogenizers, consists mainly of keeping the valves properly ground, and in maintaining the packing on the plungers in good condition. Worn plungers cause quick failure of packing. With good valves, good packing, and unworn plungers, the capacity of this type pump will remain fixed throughout its life.

Care of the rotary pumps consists principally of maintaining proper clearance between all parts. The pump cover gasket must be of a certain thickness. A gasket which is too thick will greatly reduce the capacity of the pump. Wear of the teeth or blades also causes a decrease in capacity. To prevent undue wear, never run the pump without fluid. A fluid containing gritty or undissolved solids should not be passed through the pump. In spite of all precautions, this type pump is relatively short-lived, because of the natural wear and consequent enlargement of clearances.

Thousands of these pumps are used, however, because of their simplicity, low cost, compactness and extended trouble-free operation. These pumps are also widely used for pumping fluids containing fruits and other soft solids in the food industry.

The discharge line from a positive pump must have a relief valve if there is any chance of the line ever being blocked, otherwise the pressure may expand and burst the line, or pump, or overload the motor.

Cross-references: *Homogenizers; Pumps, Nonclogging.*

POULTRY PROCESSING

The value of dressed poultry depends, to a large extent, upon the methods and skill exercised in killing, bleeding, and scalding, and the completeness and neatness of the removal of the feathers.

The following practices should be followed to provide a well-prepared bird for market: (1) remove all feed for 12 hr before killing but give water; (2) bleed thoroughly using a sharp instrument; (3) chill as quickly as possible, using ice if necessary; and (4) grade as to size and quality. Box packing will improve the attractiveness of the birds offered for sale (Fig. P.13).

The U.S. Dept of Agr. requires that the following specifications in general be met for standards of quality for individual carcasses of dressed and ready-to-cook chickens. These may be graded A, B, or C quality. For an A-quality, the confirmation, breast bone, back, legs, and wings must be normal, and birds must be well-fleshed and possess adequate fat covering with a breast bone that is not prominent. Dressed birds must be practically free of pin feathers. The birds must be free of cuts and tears with no more than $1/2$ in. flesh bruises, $3/4$ in. skin bruises, and no more than $1\frac{1}{2}$ in. for all

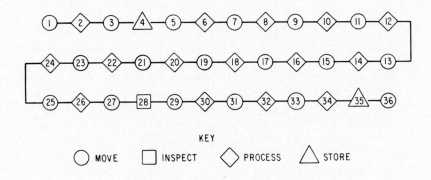

KEY

◯ MOVE　▢ INSPECT　◇ PROCESS　△ STORE

Fig. P-13. Poultry dressing and eviscerating flow chart
1—Ship into plant. 2—Receive and grade. 3—Transfer. 4—Fatten and hold. 5—Transfer. 6—Kill and blood trough. 7—Transfer. 8—Scalding machine. 9—Transfer. 10—Picking machine. 11—Transfer. 12—Dry. 13—Transfer. 14—Wax dipper. 15—Transfer. 16—Spray chamber. 17—Transfer. 18—Wax conveyor. 19—Transfer. 20—Cooling rack. 21—Transfer. 22—Shock cooling cabinets. 23—Transfer. 24—Singe machine. 25—Transfer. 26—Eviscerating table. 27—Transfer. 28—Inspect and wash. 29—Transfer. 30—Giblet table. 31—Transfer. 32—Cutting, wrapping, packing table. 33—Transfer. 34—Freeze. 35—Refrigerated storage. 36—Move out of plant.

discolorations. A few small $^1/_8$ in. diam pock marks as freezer burns may show. Handling of the birds, before, through, and after processing should be such as to maintain the bird in a grade A quality.

Marketed chickens are classified on the basis of live weight as broilers, up to 2.5 lb; fryers, $2^1/_4$ to 4 lb; and roasters, over 4 lb.

Killing and Bleeding

There are several methods of killing and bleeding poultry. One is by cutting the jugular vein inside the throat; another, by cutting the vein from the outside by slashing the throat behind the mandibles, as in Kosher killing; or by inserting a knife at the side of the neck, leaving a small hole on either side. Perhaps the most common method of killing chickens is the so-called "Kosher" method. Another step used in the killing of poultry, especially turkeys or where dry picking is desirable, is a process called braining. This consists of destroying the portion of the brain known as the medulla oblongata which connects the brain with the spinal column. This portion of the brain is located at the rear of the skull. Destroying this portion of the brain destroys the nerve connections to the muscles holding the feathers. This causes the feathers to loosen immediately and ruffle.

The windpipe or the spinal column should not be cut. If the windpipe is severed poor bleeding results. If the spinal column is injured, there is a tendency to set the feathers which makes picking difficult and costly.

Evidences of poor bleeding are (1) external sign of blood in veins and capillaries; (2) discoloration of bones and skin due to poor bleeding will show after birds have been in a freezer for a considerable period; (3) poor shelf-life; (4) undesirable flavors; and (5) blood spots in the follicles and over hips and thighs.

Scalding

After the birds have been thoroughly bled, they are ready to be prepared for picking. In order for picking to work properly, it is necessary to relax or expand the muscles around the base of the feathers so that they may be easily and completely removed without damage to the skin. The purpose of scalding is to loosen the feathers. The temperature of the scald is governed by the age and size of the birds, the length of time in the scald water and the type of scalding process used. Generally, the longer in the scald water and the lower the temperature (within limits), the easier the birds will pick and the better the finished product will appear.

Semiscald.—The semiscald procedure is the most commonly used method in commercial dressing operations. The birds are subjected to scald water at a temperature of 126° to 130°F for a length of time that permits easy and complete removal of feathers without removal of the epidermal layer of skin. These birds retain the original color and "bloom." As a rule, they have more "eye appeal" and longer shelf-life than those scalded at higher temperatures. This is particularly true in poultry shipped as fresh, whole birds.

Subscald.—In this method of dressing poultry the temperature of the scald water is raised to 138° to 140°F. The higher temperature removes all of the epidermal layer of skin. Birds so scalded have a somewhat pink, glossy appearance, and are sticky to the touch after exposure to the air for a few minutes. The birds become darker in color upon long exposure. This method is quite widely used on poultry that is to be tightly wrapped to limit the amount of air in contact with the skin of the bird which is followed by freezing.

Picking

There are two methods of commercially picking poultry: mechanical pickers with pinners, and mechanical picker with a wax dip. The pickers are used after the birds have been scalded. These machines consist of revolving drums with rubber fingers protruding. The drums revolve in opposite directions and as the birds pass through, the rubber fingers remove most of the feathers. Usually two machines are used. Between the two machines are stationed side finishers which operate on the same principle of operation as the mechanical pickers. The purpose of the side finishers is to remove the quills from wings and rump. The birds are turned end-for-end and pass through the second machine with the feet hanging down. This procedure gets more of the feathers which are difficult to remove from around the neck and legs. Manual operators, called pinners, are stationed after the mechanical pickers to remove the pin feathers with dull, short-bladed knives.

The mechanical picker and wax-dip method generally uses one mechanical picker of the type previously described to remove the bulk of the feathers in conjunction with a wax dip. Two separate dip tanks with different temperatures of wax are generally used. Wax in the first tank is carried at a temperature as high as 160°F, and the birds pass through in less than 3 sec with no apparent effect on the skin. The wax is thin and penetrates thoroughly the remaining feathers and around the base of the pin feathers, so that a firmly attached prime coat is formed to which a second coat will adhere strongly. The two wax dipping tanks are spaced far enough apart to allow plenty of time for cooling of the prime coat before the second coat is applied. The wax in the second dip tank is carried as cool as possible, near the solidification point of the wax, 128° to 138°F. The second coat of cooler wax provides a thick firm stripping coat that can be removed from the birds more easily than a thin coat. After the second dip in wax the birds pass to the stripping table where the wax is removed, carrying with it most of the remaining feathers and pins. After the wax is removed, pinners remove remaining feathers and pins.

Singeing

After the bird is completely picked there remains some small fuzzy feathers. For a top quality bird it is necessary to remove these feathers which can be removed by a singer. The machine consists of gas-fired jets. As the birds pass through the machine, they are enveloped in flames from the jets, which burn the remaining feathers.

Cooling

It is essential that the body temperature of dressed poultry be reduced to 35°F or lower as soon as possible after killing. If this cooling is done slowly, bacteria will develop and cause decomposition, thus injuring the flavor and appearance of the bird by the time it reaches the retail market.

One method of cooling is to put the birds into an ice water bath, or to hang them on racks for "shock cooling" in cabinets equipped with brine showers at 24° and 30°F.

Still another way is by direct freezing. For direct freezing, poultry is packed warm from the dressing room in boxes and frozen quickly in a sharp freezer in circulating air at −20°F or lower. Whichever method is used, it should reduce the temperature of the slowest cooling part of the bird (thoracic and abdominal region) to 34°F in from 3 to 4 hr.

For rapid cooling in air the birds should be hung independently so that the air can circulate over them. A fan should be used on the evaporator to obtain rapid cooling.

Evisceration and Inspection

In some operations the bird is cooled and then the viscera is removed. In most operations today cooling follows evisceration. The initial incision is made and the viscera is pulled from the bird. It can be completely removed from the bird and put into a tray which follows with the bird to the inspection station or it can be left protruding from the body until it passes the inspector. As it passes the inspector, he notes if the birds are diseased and determines if the carcass is fit for human consumption. If not, birds are removed from the line and destroyed. The drawing procedure is continued on the remaining birds.

The giblets (heart, crop, and gizzard) are separated from the viscera and pass through a different process, consisting of cleaning, washing, packaging, and freezing.

After the eviscerating process is completed, the birds are washed and cooled. If shipped as whole birds, they are removed from the conveyor and packaged. If not, they continue down the line and are cut up into the various cuts.

Packaging

There are many different ways of packaging poultry. Frozen birds should be carefully wrapped to stop freezer burn which is a bleaching of the skin caused by dehydration. There are several materials available for wrapping such as aluminum foil, cellophane, Pliofilm, or Cry-o-vac. With Cry-o-vac the bird is placed in a plastic sack and air exhausted by a vacuum pump. The sacked bird is then immersed in warm water which shrinks the bag tightly to the bird and exhausts nearly all remaining air. Due to its shrinking, air is exhausted and rancidity largely eliminated. Whole birds, individual cutup birds, or individual parts may be wrapped in this manner.

Markets using frozen poultry are specific in the style of packing and types of packaging materials they want. They may want 6, 12, or 24 head packages, or, frequently, with turkeys, individual bird packages. They may want parchment or moisture-proof loose wraps; vacuumized and sealed and wrapped; breast-up or side packed; or fiber or wood boxes.

Storage

For the preservation of poultry in its natural form, freezing is being employed more and more extensively in the handling of dressed poultry. Formerly, artificial refrigeration was used simply to cool the poultry to an internal temperature of approximately 30° to 35°F. The poultry was then packed and shipped under refrigeration, arriving at markets or refrigerated warehouses in a soft condition. Experiments have proved that prompt hard freezing at low temperatures at the packing plant with shipment and delivery to the retail stores in the frozen condition is a more satisfactory method for preserving original freshness and flavor.

Since the cost of refrigeration increases greatly as the temperature is lowered, plants naturally desire to operate at the highest possible temperature at which the product may be carried satisfactorily. Formerly, it was thought that so long as poultry was hard frozen it could be carried without deterioration. Hence, poultry might be frozen at 0°F and carried at around 15°F, little attention being paid to the fluctuations provided they did not become too great. It was also thought that too low temperatures would dry out flesh and break down cell and muscle structure. However investigations have shown that freezing poultry as quickly as possible and maintaining a low uniform temperature results in a superior product. Owing to the saline content and colloidal structure of the body cells, low temperatures must be reached before the carcass becomes completely frozen. Hence, uniform temperatures in storage of as low as −20°F are not uncommon.

There are many ways of offering poultry for sale other than as live birds. One method is New York dressed which consists of removing the blood and feathers. The other classification is eviscerated or ready-to-eat. For dressing a live bird, 13% of the live body weight is lost and to prepare a bird ready-to-cook, 28 to 33% live weight is lost. An average dressing time of 7 min is required per bird and the cost of supplies, depreciation, interest, repairs, and taxes will be approximately equal to the labor cost.

The equipment, procedures, and standards for processing of rabbits, ducks, geese, turkeys, and other fowls come under the same categories as those described for poultry. There are many types of equipment available with the newer larger systems being almost completely automatic from beginning to end in which birds are handled on conveyors automatically through the various processing machines. These rapid methods of handling provide a finished product of high quality. Poultry may be cut up into sticks, prepared precooked, frozen, canned, or smoked.

Manual operations for dressing of poultry normally may be as high as 200 birds per hour; for dressing and drawing, 100 head per hour. Continuous conveyorized dressing systems for fresh broilers will operate at a rate of about 4,800 birds per hour per line.

Reference

HALL, C. W. 1963. Processing Equipment for Agricultural Products. Edwards Brothers, Ann Arbor, Mich.

Cross-references: *Materials Handling; Refrigeration Principles.*

POWDER HANDLING EQUIPMENT

Major considerations in handling dry, finely divided foods such as flour and non-fat dry milk include the control of dusty conditions which in turn has an influence on sanitation. With the incidence of *Salmonella* contamination of certain dry food products, the importance of sanitation has been reemphasized. Powder handling equipment must be smooth in construction and cleanable preferably with automated washing systems. Dryers including cyclones and sifters are now available in stainless steel of welded construction to permit cleaning-in-place. The use of a vacuum brush assists the operator in removing loose dust particles around equipment especially hopper openings, conveyors, and the like.

Powdered foods may be transferred from one location to another with various types of conveyors including bucket, ribbed belt, flight, or augers. Vibrating screens or panels are also effective in transferring powder where long distances are not involved. The pneumatic conveyor is being utilized to a greater extent in modern plants because of the economy which can be achieved. This system is effective in controlling dusting and permits one person to unload large bulk bins very easily. Large size portable bins can be used effectively with pneumatic conveyors. However, the powder should be well-cooled before it enters the large container.

Blending

The blending of dry ingredients constitutes a handling problem in many plants. Blenders are now available which accomplish blending under vacuum, atmospheric conditions, or in inert or sterilizing gas. These units are also equipped with a jacket which will permit dry blending up to 220°F or at lower temperatures by circulating cooling water through the jacket. The "solids processor" is illustrated in Fig. P.14.

Courtesy of Patterson Kelley Co.

Fig. P-14.   Blender for dry materials

Bulk Bins

In processing nonfat dry milk, a bin or hopper installed between the dryer and packaging equipment greatly reduces the necessity for closely synchronizing the capacity of production with filling. A well-designed stainless steel hopper that can be cleaned-in-place with circulating detergent solutions is beneficial in improving operational efficiency of the plant in many cases. A hopper may be designed with an auger unloading system. Others may utilize some other type of unloading device but the slope of the sidewall should be such to prevent product bridging.

Bulk bins are satisfactory for handling nonfat dry milk between the dryer and packaging equipment. The "tote bins" may be as large as 74 cu ft with a capacity of 3,000 lb. They are made of aluminum and transported around the plant with a fork-lift truck. A product removal door is located at the base to permit dumping into hoppers feeding the fillers. The "tote bins" may be designed with spray cleaning equipment to permit effective CIP applications.

Collectors

To assist in control of product dusting, collectors are used with certain equipment such as blenders.. Effective utilization of a collector has been demonstrated to reduce environmental product losses.

Sifters of modern design include those constructed of stainless steel. These are easily disassembled for cleaning and could be equipped with special spray devices for cleaning-in-place. At the present time most sifters are hand cleaned but it is important that only a minimum effort be required.

Cooling

Powder handling equipment sometimes cools the product while conveying. This is especially important in the case of dry milk. Introduction of cool dehumidified air into the conveying system is an effective means of reducing temperature. Cooling must be done quickly to minimize the deleterious effect of heat on flavor. In large bulk containers, warm powder will hold the heat for considerable time. The thermal conductivity (k-value) is about 0.15 to 0.25 Btu per hr sq ft °F per ft. Powder is usually cooled by conduction or convection. Radiation cooling is a possibility but not extensively used.

Fillers

A wide variety of fillers have been manufactured to handle dry powders or granules. They operate on the principle of gross weight, net weight, or volumetric filling. The types of containers filled include packages of glass, paperboard, metal, or plastic. A range of capacities can be obtained from less than 1 lb to 200 lb packages or larger.

Sanitation

Careful attention should be given the sanitary aspects of all powder handling equipment and methods adopted. Enclosed systems and reduction of dusting must be given special attention. Package filling in extremely sanitary rooms is essential. Special attention should be given air filtration as it enters filling rooms, cyclone separators, dryers, or pneumatic conveying systems. In connection with all these functions the ease of cleaning powder handling equipment must be given special consideration.

References

ANON. 1965A. Blend-fill dusty food ingredients without dustiness. Food Process. *26*, No. 1, 136–138.

ANON. 1965B. Sanitary handling of dry solids, Food Process. *26*, No. 7, 160.
ANON. 1967. Modern Packaging Encyclopedia. McGraw-Hill, New York.
HALL, C. W., and HEDRICK, T. I. 1966. Drying Milk and Milk Products. AVI Publishing Co., Westport, Conn.

Cross-references: *Bag Fillers; Blenders, Centrifugal Separators; Cooling Powder; Pneumatic Conveying.*

PRESSURE ELEMENT

The pressure element and controller for steam on the heating side of the coils are provided to ensure an adequate quantity of steam to carry out the process. A Bourdon tube or spiral element is used for sensing steam pressure. The signal from the element may be used for indicating, or for controlling the pressure by throttling the steam supply valve. A pressure reducing valve from the main steam line to the heating side of the pan or evaporator may also be used. Elements are normally used in the pressure range from 10 to 35 psig for vacuum pans and evaporators.

PRESSURE VESSELS, UNFIRED

Retorts and kettles are pressure vessels in which heat may be added for cooking or processing. These vessels are discussed under those headings. Those pressure vessels in which heat is not supplied from the outside are classified as "unfired pressure vessels," although the product contained may be at a high temperature. Typical unfired pressure vessels are for storage of LP-gas, such as propane; storage, holding, and receiver tanks for refrigerants; compressed air tanks; and pressure water and steam tanks.

Maximum allowable design stresses have been established by ASME for various metals under different applications. The allowable stress decreases as the temperature increases. The methods of heat treatment of the material, and procedures for machining, welding, and riveting different materials are also specified. Additional consideration must be given to the effect of the food product, refrigerant, or other contained substance on the metal, such as corrosion, pitting, or scaling.

Manufacture is followed by inspection of joints, such as by X-ray. Welds and adjacent metal areas may be stress relieved with a heat treatment.

Of special concern on pressure vessels are the fittings and connections. Appropriate high pressure valves, caps, and connections must also be used.

Cross-references: *Boilers; Jacketed Kettle; Retorts.*

PULLEY SPEED CONTROLS

Many machines and conveyor systems in the food industry require that the speed of the equipment be varied from time to time while in operation, or that the speed be matched exactly to a certain rate of movement or travel.

A simple method of speed control is by the use of the Reeves drive (see Fig. P.15). This system uses a double pulley arrangement in which at least one of the pulleys and many times both are made adjustable to give a certain effective diameter. A spring maintains the proper tension on the tapered belt or chain.

Courtesy of Reeves Pulley Co.

Fig. P-15.   Sectional view of Reeves variable speed drive

Other types of variable speed drives such as electrical, and hydraulic are widely used, and are applicable for wide ranges of speed control. A governor or other modulating control can be connected to most of variable speed drives to automatically control the speed.

Cross-reference: *Belts.*

PUMPS, NONCLOGGING

The food industry encounters many situations in which course materials such as cherries, beans, olives, sugar cane, or beans must be pumped. This requires a special type of pump which will not clog. To meet this need the so-called nonclogging pump is used. The particular feature of this pump is that the vanes on the rotor are cast in such a way as to give a very open structure. There are no close tolerances internally to cause binding or excessive wear. Suction intake, pumping chamber, and discharge port are one continuous open passage. The open faced impeller is recessed and seldom contacts the material being pumped. Any particle which will come into the pump can come out easily. The recessed impeller creates a swirling liquid vortex which draws the material into the pump where it can be subjected to the centrifugal action and readily discharged.

Continuous Screw Press

This widely used machine is designed to operate as a continuous low pressure dewatering device for fibrous foods. It can be provided to give 2 or 3 stages of pressing with intermediate mixing, and the material can be rinsed in the system.

Volume reductions as high as 8 to 1 can be achieved in some applications.

Method of Operation

Wet product enters the unit through an offset intake hopper. The combination of a uniformly decreasing pitch and chemical shaft provides a gradual increasing pressure to the product as it passes through the press. Extracted liquid is constantly drained away from the perforated screw cylinder which surrounds the screw. The dewatered press cake is continuously discharged from the end of the machine.

The equipment can be constructed of stainless steel and all major parts can be readily opened up for easy cleaning.

Cross-references: *Centrifugal Pump; Fluid Flow; Hydraulics; Positive Pump.*

PURIFIER

A purifier is equipment that removes impurities from a substance. In a general sense a separator, clarifier, or filter could be regarded as a purifier. An air purger on a refrigeration system might also be considered to perform a purification function. Usually, however, a purifier is involved in the final stage of impurity removal. A typical use of a purifier is found in producing culinary steam.

Steam

In the production of pure steam, a water tube boiler utilizes a separator together with steam drying and sometimes steam washing devices. The principles of change in direction, caused by baffles; centrifugal force action; or gravity separation are used. Approximately 98% of circulating water is removed with the steam separator. Washing of steam for removal of some of the volatile silica is optional, however, some engineers feel that a desirable benefit is obtained. In the steam washing process, feedwater is mixed with the steam and dispersed as a spray. Removal of residual water in steam may be regarded as the purifying or drying process. Low pressure steam passes through the dryers at a velocity of 8 to 10 fps. In high pressure systems, steam velocity through the dryer is reduced to 2 to 3 fps. An effective separator, such as the centrifugal action unit, will reduce the water content of steam to less than 1%. Most dryers are overloaded and do not work efficiently if the entering steam contains more than 10% water. Dryers designed with bent plates or closely spaced screens are effective in reducing the water content of steam to very low levels. Failure to obtain steam with extremely low water content when a dryer is used is usually due to foaming, poor design of boiler internals, operation above design capacity, or sludge interference.

Culinary Steam

The United States Public Health Service suggests for the production of culinary steam for direct injection into milk, a purification system involving a separator, carbon filter, and stationary vane purifier. In this system the principles of change of direction and centrifugal force action are employed with the filtration. Water is quite effectively removed from the steam, as well as, any extraneous matter. Gases such as ammonia or carbon dioxide are usually not effectively removed.

Air

The removal of dust particles, vapors, and odors from air constitute purification. In a compressed air system after coolers are commonly employed to remove moisture. For further information concerning air filtration see the discussion on "Air."

References

KENT'S MECHANICAL ENGINEERS' HANDBOOK. 1954. Power Volume, 12th Edition. John Wiley & Sons, New York.

WEBB, F. C. 1954. Biochemical Engineering, D. Van Nostrand Co., London.

Cross-references: *Air; Boilers; Filters; Steam.*

R

REFRACTOMETER

The refractometer is an important tool or instrument for use in controlling the analysis of commercial products and in identifying unknown substances; it can be used for distinguishing substances of the same boiling point and compounds of similar nature.

Principle

The refractometer is based upon the property exhibited when a ray of light passes obliquely from one medium to another of a different density, and the direction the light is changed as it passes to the surface. This property of refraction is the basis of the instrument. The angle between the ray in the first medium and that perpendicular to the dividing surface is called the angle of incidence, i. The corresponding angle in the second medium is called the angle of refraction, r. The sine of i and the sine of r are directly proportional to the velocities of light in the two media. The sine ratio, $\sin i/\sin r$ is called the index of refraction, N. If the incident ray is in the more dense medium, N will be less than 1; if it is less dense, N will be greater than 1.

The index of refraction for two given materials varies with the temperature and wavelength of the light. It also varies with the pressure if the medium is gas.

Under test conditions, the index of refraction is a characteristic constant for a particular medium and is used to identify or determine the purity of a substance, and to determine the composition of binary mixtures of known constituents.

Specific refraction depends on the nature of the substance. If the specific refraction of a substance is multiplied by the molecular weight, the molecular refraction is exhibited and is approximately the additive property of the groups or elements of which the product is composed.

Use

The refractometer can be used for the identification of a substance, if its nature is known. Identification can be confirmed by relation of its specific refraction to that of similar compounds.

Types

Three general types of refractometers are made: the Abbe, the immersion or dipping type, and the Pulfrich. Pulfrich instruments use monochromatic light, and require a larger sample than the Abbe, which requires only a drop of the liquid. The Abbe refractometer has a range of 1.3000 to 1.7000. The maximum precision obtainable is 0.0001. In the use of a refractometer, temperature should be controlled within ±0.2°C. Usually a small circulating pump is used to pass thermostatically controlled water through the prism casing. The immersion refractometer requires from 10 to 15 ml of sample and is the simplest type. It must be kept at a constant temperature within ±0.05°C.

The refractometer measures concentration more accurately than can be done by ordinary density measurements with a hydrometer. Refractometers can be installed in food lines such as condensed milk to give a continuous reading of the density of the product. The food industry has many uses for the refractometer in the analysis and control of food processing operations.

References

HOLZBOCK, W. G. 1955. Instruments for Measurement and Control. Van Nostrand Reinhold, New York.

UNITED TRADE PRESS LIMITED. 1953. The Instrument Manual. London.

Cross-references: *Density Control; Specific Gravity.*

REFRIGERATED STORAGE OF FRUITS AND VEGETABLES

Refrigerated storage of fruits and vegetables increases the storage life and provides a more optimum time for marketing the product. Refrigerated storage may be carried out on the farm or as an industrial enterprise. Refrigerated storage above freezing of the product is known as cooler or cold storage, whereas if the product is frozen, it is known as freezer or frozen storage. Controlled atmospheres of carbon dioxide or other inert gas around the product, appropriate humidity control, in combination with refrigerated storage may give a longer life to a product.

A refrigerated cold storage should provide the following.

Optimum temperature so that the respiration rate of the product is low, and that decay due to associated microorganisms is minimized and damage to the product through freezing is avoided. Most fruit and vegetable products freeze at approximately 29°F. Cold injury may damage some products without freezing (Tables R.1 and R.2).

Optimum humidity is also important in avoiding decay of the product due to the associated microorganisms. The humidity must be high enough to avoid excessive moisture loss from the product. In general, the relative humidity in the storage should be 85 to 90% for fruits, 90 to 95% for leafy vegetables and root crops, and about 85 to 90% for other vegetables (Tables R.1 and R.2). A high humidity in a storage with respiring products is attained by keeping the evaporator at a relatively high temperature.

Optimum air movement and proper air distribution are necessary to maintain a uniform temperature throughout the storage to prevent stratification of heat and moisture, and for controlled atmospheres, to provide a uniform atmosphere around the product. Ventilation by bringing in outside air is held to a minimum. It is difficult to maintain a high relative humidity in the storage with large amounts of ventilation. It usually does not pay to refrigerate or cool the product by using outside cold air because the outside temperature is below storage temperature for a short time, and resulting savings are negligible.

Sanitation procedures must ensure the storage will be cleaned between use with a soap solution and properly rinsed and often fumigated. Ventilation systems may be used to assist in chemical treatments. With some fruits and vegetables, oxidizing gases such as ozone are utilized to reduce the growth of microorganisms. Rodents must be prevented from entering the storage through proper use of metal, screen, etc. The storage requirements for fresh fruits and vegetables vary considerably (Tables R.1 and R.2).

Precooling

Cooling the product before storage will increase the quality and life of the product

TABLE R.1

STORAGE REQUIREMENTS FOR FRESH FRUITS

Product	Temperature, °F	RH %	Storage Life
Apples			
Most varieties	30–32	89–90	To 5 months
Yellow Newton, McIntosh,			
and Rhode Island Greening	36–38		
Jonathan	34–36		
Apricots	31–32	85–90	1–2 weeks
Avocados			
Most varieties	45	85–90	To 4 weeks
Some West Indian varieties	55	85–90	
Bananas			
Ripening	62–70	90–95	
Holding	56–70	85–90	7–10 days
Blackberries, raspberries	31–32	85–90	5–7 days
Cherries	31–32	85–90	10–14 days
Cranberries	36–40	85–90	1–3 months
Figs	31–32	85–90	10 days
Grapefruit			
If stem rot by Diplodia	45–55	85–90	4–6 weeks
If stem rot by Phomopsis	32	85–90	
Grapes	30–32	85–90	1–6 months
Lemons	50–58	85–90	1–4 months
Limes	48–50	85–90	6–8 weeks
Mangoes	50	85–90	15–20 days
Olives, fresh	45–50	85–90	4–6 weeks
Oranges			
Florida	30–32	85–90	8–12 weeks
California	35–37	85–90	5–8 weeks
Papayas, firm ripe	45	85–90	7–21 days
Peaches	31–32	85–90	2–4 weeks
Pears	30–31	90–95	To 3 months
Persimmons, Japanese	30	85–90	To 2 months
Pineapples			
Mature green	50–60	85–90	2–3 weeks
Ripe	40–45	85–90	2–4 weeks
Plums, including prunes	31–32	85–90	3–4 weeks
Strawberries	31–32	85–90	7–10 days
Tangerines	31–38	90–95	2–4 weeks

Source: Based mostly on U.S. Dept. Agr. Handbook *66*.

by removing heat, and will reduce the refrigeration load on the storage system. The product may be cooled by forcing air through the product to remove the field heat and respiration heat; by moving the product through a chilling or cooling tunnel equipped with a refrigeration system; by water cooling of fruits, such as is done for cherries, apples, etc., known as hydrocooling; by vacuum cooling where a high vacuum is pulled on a product such as lettuce and the evaporation of water provides a cooling effect on the product; by use of icing, or icing plus brine, in which air is moved through the ice and then over the product for cooling.

TABLE R.2

STORAGE REQUIREMENTS FOR FRESH VEGETABLES

Product	Temperature, °F	RH %	Storage Life
Artichokes, globe	31–32	90–95	30 days
Asparagus	32	85–90	3–4 weeks
Beans			
Green or snap	45–50	85–90	8–10 days
Lima	32	85–90	15 days
Beets, topped	32	85–90	1–3 months
Broccoli	32	90–95	7–10 days
Brussels sprouts	32	90–95	3–4 weeks
Cabbage, early	32	90–95	3–6 weeks
Carrots, topped	32	90–95	4–5 months
Cauliflower	32	85–90	2–3 weeks
Celery	31–32	90–95	2–4 weeks
Corn, sweet	31–32	85–90	
Cucumbers	45–50	85–95	2–3 weeks
Eggplants	45–50	85–90	10 days
Garlic, dry	32	70–75	6–8 months
Lettuce	32	90–95	2–3 weeks
Melons			
Watermelon	36–40	85–90	2–3 weeks
Cantaloupes	40–45	85–90	1–2 weeks
Onions	32	70–75	6–8 months
Peas, green	32	85–90	1–2 weeks
Potatoes			
Early crop	50	85–90	
Late crop	40	85–90	5–8 months
Before chipping	50–55	70–75	2–6 months
Pumpkins	50–55	70–75	2–6 months
Radishes, rutabagas, spinach	32	90–95	10–14 days
Rhubarb	32	90–95	2–3 weeks
Squash			
Summer	32–40	85–90	10–14 days
Winter	50–55	50–55	4–6 months
Sweet potatoes	55–60	85–90	4–6 months
Tomatoes			
Ripe	50	85–90	8–12 days
Mature, green	55–70	85–90	2–6 weeks
Turnips	32	90–95	4–5 months
Dried vegetables		70	1 year

Source: Based mostly on U.S. Dept. Agr. Handbook *66*.

Handling

The method and equipment used for handling the product from the orchard or field to the storage are very important from the standpoint of maintaining quality and providing an economical operation.   Rapid handling helps preserve quality.   If rapid handling with precooling can be utilized, better quality is maintained.   Handling must also be done without damage, or within minimum damage, to the product.   A method of handling whereby the product need not be transferred from different containers in the field to other containers for storage and for later removal from storage is desired to reduce damage to the product.

Storage Location, Layout, and Management

The location of the storage will depend greatly upon the type of marketing operation and the location of the orchard or field.   On the one hand, it is desirable to have the storage as close to the production area as possible, while on the other hand, an attractive storage would be of considerable value in making roadside fresh retail sales.

The layout determines to a large extent the efficiency to which the storage can be utilized.   The system for handling the product from the field to the storage and to the retail-wholesale outlet should be studied carefully, and then a layout planned to facilitate the handling procedure.   Decisions must be made with respect to grading, packing, and merchandizing the product.   The packing room should have a minimum of 3 to 4 sq ft of floor space for each bushel that is to be packed in a 10-hr day.   Most farm owners have a one-room storage with the packing room adjacent to the storage. Storage must also be provided for empty crates.   Ground level storage space is usually used for empty crates.   The refrigeration equipment should be in a separate room.

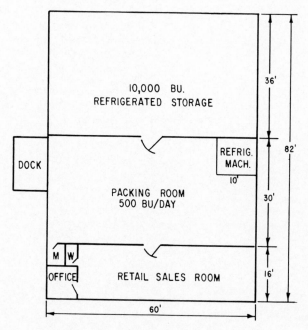

Fig. R-1.   Refrigerated storage layout for wholesale and retail sales

An arrangement for storage, packing, and sales room for a 10,000 bu storage is shown in Fig. R.1. Approximately 2.5 to 2.8 cu ft per bu is required for the storage if no pallets are used, and up to 3.0 cu ft per bu if the crates or baskets are placed on pallets.

The cost per bushel of capacity of storage decreases as the size of storage increases. In general, a 20,000 bu storage would cost from $1.00 to $1.25 per bu (based on 1965 prices). Of this, approximately $1/4$ to $1/3$ of the cost would be for refrigeration equipment. The annual overhead costs based on the original investment are as follows:

refrigeration equipment—10%
storage structure—$3^1/_3$%
interest—4 to 5%
taxes and insurance—2%

Thus, about $1/5$ of the original cost must be planned for fixed or overhead costs per year.

The total cost per crate per year of owning and operating a storage will be about 20% of the original cost, of which about $1/2$ is for the overhead and the remainder for operating the unit, including electricity, labor and handling, and maintenance of equipment.

Heat Load for Refrigeration Storage

The amount of heat to be carried away by the refrigeration system must be known in order to properly size the refrigeration system. A rule of thumb is that approximately 1 ton of refrigeration (12,000 Btu per hr) is required for each 1,000 bu of product, e.g., apples, to be cooled to 30° to 40°F with a daily loading of $1/_{10}$ of storage capacity. Thus, a 10,000 bu storage would have a minimum of 10 ton refrigeration for storing and cooling approximately 1,000 bu per day. If the compressor is driven by an electric motor to cool to the 30° to 40°F temperature range, approximately 1 hp is needed for each 1 ton of refrigeration. In the example given, 10 hp would be required.

The heat load for the refrigeration system can be considered in three categories: (1) wall losses, (2) product heat production, and (3) miscellaneous heat load due to motors, workers, lights, etc. in the storage.

Wall Heat Losses

The heat entering the storage through the wall from the outside must be removed by the refrigeration equipment. A rule of thumb is that approximately 0.13 tons of refrigeration must be provided per 1,000 bu storage capacity for heat load through the wall, ceiling, and floor. The amount of heat load can be calculated on the basis of the material, the area of the wall, and the temperature difference across the wall, floor, and ceiling.

Product Heat

Product heat for cooler storage consists of the sensible heat which must be removed in cooling the product from field to storage temperature and the heat of respiration (often called heat of evolution) of the product.

TABLE R.3

SPECIFIC HEAT AND LATENT HEAT DATA FOR FOODS

Product	Specific Heat Above Freezing	Specific Heat Below Freezing	Latent Heat of Fusion, Btu per Lb	Average Freezing Temperature, °F
Vegetables				
Artichokes	0.90	0.46	115	29.1
Asparagus	0.95	0.43	134	29.8
Broccoli	0.91	0.47	130	29.2
Brussel sprouts	0.90	0.46	122	29.2
Cabbage	0.93	0.43	129	31.2
Corn, green	0.80	0.43	108	28.9
Irish potatoes	0.78	0.48	105	28.9
Lettuce	0.95	0.48	135	31.2
Lima beans	0.89	0.41	100	30.1
Peas, green	0.80	0.42	108	30.0
String beans	0.92	0.47	128	29.7
Sweet potatoes	0.75	0.41	99	28.4
Tomatoes	0.95	0.48	135	30.4
Meats, Milk, Eggs				
Fresh lean beef	0.77	0.40	100	28.0
Butter	0.64	0.24	19	31.0
Eggs	0.76	0.40	100	31.0
Fresh hams	0.67	0.42	66	30.2
Milk, fresh	0.90	0.47	127	31.0
Poultry, dressed	0.80	0.42	101	28.0
Water	1.00	0.51	144	32.0
Fruit				
Apples	0.86	0.45	120	28.5
Apricots	0.92	0.46	122	
Avocado	0.90			27.2
Bananas	0.81	0.43	108	30.0
Blackberries	0.89	0.46	124	29.1
Cantaloupes	0.92	0.34	128	28.8
Cherries	0.86	0.45	118	24.7–27.8
Dates	0.83	0.44	104	−4.1
Fruit, dried	0.47	0.32	43	
Grapefruit	0.92	0.47	128	28.4
Grapes	0.92	0.38	84	28.2
Lemons	0.90	0.39	126	28.1
Melons	0.90	0.47	115	
Oranges	0.92	0.39	125	28.0
Pears	0.86	0.45	120	28.5
Pineapple	0.90	0.46	127	29.9
Plums	0.87	0.45	121	28.0
Raspberries	0.89	0.46	124	29.0
Strawberries	0.92	0.47	130	29.9

Source: Data Book, ASRE (1949).

The field heat is calculated by multiplying the specific heat by the weight in pounds times the temperature difference. The specific heats of various fruits and vegetables are listed in Table R.3. For apples, including crates, the heat removed in cooling from

80° to 40°F is 0.86×55 lb per bu $\times$ 40°F = 1,892 Btu per bu,
or 1,892,000 Btu for 1,000 bu

Over a 24-hr period, the rate of cooling for this latter case would be 78,800 Btu per hr. If the unit is designed to refrigerate $1/10$ of the storage capacity, 7,880 Btu per hr of heat must be removed for each 1,000 bu. This is equivalent to approximately 0.6 tons of refrigeration capacity for each 1,000 bu storage capacity, and $1/10$ loading of the storage capacity for cooling of product only.

The heat of respiration depends upon the temperature. It is assumed that the first day's loading is down to the storage temperature of 32° to 40°F at the end of 24 hr. The refrigeration system must be designed to take the peak heat of respiration, which would be the last day of storage when the last $1/10$ of the storage capacity might be placed into the storage. The refrigeration system must be large enough to remove the heat evolved from the 90% loading previously placed in the storage, respiring at the rate corresponding to 32° to 40°F, plus the higher rate of respiration of the newly placed product in storage. To cool apples to about 32° to 33°F when the heat of respiration is about 700 Btu per ton, in 24 hr, the rule of thumb for the heat of respiration is 0.1 ton per 1,000 bu for 10% loading.

Miscellaneous Heat Load

The miscellaneous heat loads include heat added to the refrigerated storage from workers, electric motors, lights, and additional leaks around the doors. This is normally considered as a service load and accounts for 10% in addition to the loads mentioned above. Some designers use 15% for this value.

Any refrigerated storage which is not constructed according to a standard design should be calculated for refrigeration requirements to assure that adequate refrigeration capacity is available. The rate of loading will vary considerably the refrigeration requirements. If the loading is 5% of storage capacity, about $2/3$ of a ton of refrigeration is required per 1000 bu storage capacity, whereas for 20% loading or $1/5$ of the capacity in a 24-hr period, approximately $1^{1}/_{3}$ tons of refrigeration per 1,000 bu storage are required.

In addition to the heat load due to miscellaneous causes, the use of incandescent rather than fluorescent lighting, motors inside the storage instead of outside, and people working in the storage affect the refrigeration requirements. The values presented are guides for evaluating present systems and for checking designs. A unit designed to cool $1/10$ of the product load in a 24-hr period will be capable of maintaining in the storage approximately 10 times that amount of product. For example, a unit which will cool 1,000 bu per day from the field to storage temperature will maintain about 10,000 bu in storage after the products have reached storage temperature.

Controlled Atmosphere (CA) Storage

In a controlled atmosphere storage, the oxygen level is reduced and the carbon dioxide increased. Lower respiration occurs, thus extending the life of some products to as much as twice the normal refrigerated life. It is important to maintain the proper relationship of oxygen and carbon dioxide depending on the product and the temperature of storage. Considerable research is being devoted to application of CA storage to different products. Apples are the primary product stored under these conditions today.

Sealed storage rooms with a capacity of 10,000 bu are usually used for apples. To get rapid production of carbon dioxide around the product, the storage should be filled with the product within a week. Commercial units are available for placing carbon dioxide into storage upon sealing to rapidly reduce respiration. Doors, joints of construction, and all construction should be nearly gastight. To reduce the diffusion through the walls, a plastic lung can be installed so that as the atmosphere inside the box expands during warming, the gases can move into the lung instead of through the walls.

Evaporators for Refrigerated Storage

The cold diffuser type evaporator is most commonly used for refrigerated storage today. These may be mounted on the floor or from the ceiling. Forced ventilation is used to provide rapid movement of the air and to maintain uniform air temperature throughout the storage. Few storages provide means of maintaining a high relative humidity other than through the moisture produced by the product and by proper refrigeration design. It is desirable to have as large an evaporator as is economical so a high relative humidity can be maintained. With a small size evaporator, the temperature of the evaporator is reduced, thus the moisture is condensed out of the air onto the evaporator, reducing the relative humidity of the air (Fig. R.2).

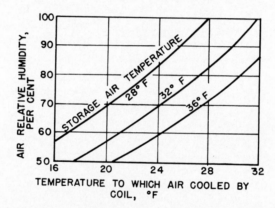

Fɪɢ. R-2.   Evaporator coil surface temperature as related to relative humidity
of storage air

Freezing

For extended storage of fruits and vegetables, freezing is often practiced. The product should be cooled and frozen as quickly as possible. Slow freezing causes formation of large water crystals which damage the tissues and decrease the quality of the product.

Both sensible and latent heat must be removed during freezing. The process of freezing consists of (1) removing the sensible heat above freezing; (2) removing the latent heat at the temperature of freezing, usually between 28° and 31°F for fruits and vegetables; and (3) removing the sensible heat below freezing. The latent heat and specific heat values of various products are given in Table R.3. To freeze 1 lb of peaches from 69.4° to 0.4°F requires that heat be removed as follows

TABLE R.4

APPROXIMATE AVERAGE HEAT OF RESPIRATION BY CERTAIN FRESH FRUITS AND VEGETABLES

Product	Temperature, °F	Btu per Ton per 24 Hr	Product	Temperature, °F	Btu per Ton per 24 Hr
Apples, Jonathan	32	750	Lettuce	32	11,320
	40	830		40	15,990
	60	3,000		60	45,980
Bananas, green	54	3,300	Onions, dry,	32	880
Green	68	8,360	Yellow Globe	50	1,870
Turning	68	9,240		70	3,630
Ripe	68	8,360	Oranges, Florida	32	725
Beans, lima	32	3,160		40	1,430
	40	6,100		50	3,610
	60	27,410		60	4,410
	70	37,120		90	7,330
Beets, topped	32	2,650	Peaches	32	1,110
	40	4,060		40	1,735
	60	7,240		60	8,285
Broccoli	32	7,450		80	20,195
	40	13,800	Pears, Bartlett	32	770
	60	41,900		60	11,000
	70	73,600	Peas	32	8,260
Cabbage	32	1,200		40	14,620
	40	1,670		60	41,880
	60	4,080		80	79,210
	70	6,120	Potatoes, Irish	32	660
Cantaloupe	32	1,320		40	1,430
	60	8,500		70	2,860
Carrots, topped	32	2,130	Raspberries	32	4,670
	60	8,080		40	7,610
Celery	32	1,620		60	20,165
	40	2,420	Spinach	32	4,240
	60	8,220		50	17,940
Cherries	31	1,249		60	38,000
Sweet	36	1,459	Strawberries	32	3,265
	45	2,811		40	5,180
Sour	32	1,590		50	11,285
	60	11,600		60	17,960
Corn, sweet	32	6,560		70	26,325
(unhusked)	40	9,390		80	41,830
	60	38,410	Sweet potatoes	40	3,350
Cucumbers	32	1,690	Not cured	60	6,300
	40	2,550	Cured	40	1,710
	60	10,460		60	4,280
Grapefruit, Florida	32	660	Tomatoes	32	580
	40	1,012	Mature-green	40	1,070
	50	1,735		60	6,230
	60	3,090	Ripe	32	1,020
	70	4.180		40	1,260
Grapes, Concord	32	602		60	5,640
	40	1,170	Turnips, topped	32	1,940
	60	3,487		40	2,150
	80	8,481		60	5,280

TABLE R.4 (*Continued*)

Product	Tempera- ture, °F	Btu per Ton per 24 Hr
Lemons, Eureka	32	690
	40	1,245
	60	3,630
	80	5,000

sensible heat, from 69.4° to 29.4°F = 40 × 0.9 = 36 Btu per lb
at 29.4°F, latent heat = 125 Btu per lb
sensible heat, from 29.4° to 0.4°F = 29 × 0.46 = 13 Btu per lb
a total of 36 + 125 + 13 = 174 Btu per lb

The sensible heat below freezing is approximately $^1/_2$ the value of the sensible heat above freezing for most fruits and vegetables. The specific heat above freezing can be estimated by

$$SH = 0.008 \times MC + 0.20$$

where SH = the specific heat, Btu per lb °F
MC = the moisture content, %, wet basis

At freezing and below, the respiration heat is nil. If considerable time is required in the freezing process above freezing, it is necessary to add an additional heat load due to the heat of respiration of the product (Table R.4). Most frozen products are stored at 0° to −20°F with the lower temperature desired for long-term storage over 6 months. Many freezing chambers and home freezers are provided with sections where the product can be frozen rapidly; then the product can be moved to the storage compartment. Important considerations in freezing are: (1) to utilize a high quality product that is worth the work and expense of freezing, and to properly prepare the material, and (2) to properly package the product to keep moisture loss to a minimum.

Special Considerations

Some products, *e.g.*, bananas, must be handled when green, and ripened close to the market. Ripening consists of holding the product at a higher temperature than normal and may include the use of ethylene to provide a uniform color of the product. Other products, e.g., oranges, lemons, and limes, may be treated with a gas to provide uniform color throughout. Products treated in this manner must be so identified according to the FDA.

Tomatoes are normally in the near mature or mature green state when shipped, and are repacked after ripening for consumption. The rate of ripening can be controlled by the temperature of storage in the range from 55° to 70°F. However, by keeping tomatoes in the 60° to 65°F range at 85 to 90% RH, a better quality product which is firmer and with less decay is obtained.

Potatoes which are to be used for chipping provide better quality chips if held at higher temperatures (60° to 70°F) before processing. The dormancy of onions can be broken if cold onions are ventilated with warm air at the appropriate time. Before storing a particular product, careful study should be given to the physiological properties of the product, and the relationships of temperature, heat, humidity, and associated microorganisms in the response of the product. Many fresh products have such a short storage life, *e.g.*, strawberries, it is necessary to freeze them for extended storage. Otherwise, canning, preserving, drying, or another method of preservation must be utilized.

References

AM. Soc. REFRIG. ENG. 1956. Refrigerating Data Book. New York.
GASTON, H. P., and LEVIN, J. H. 1954. On the farm refrigerated fruit storage. Mich. Agr. Expt. Sta., Bull. *389*.
WRIGHT, R. C., ROSE, D. H. and WHITMAN, T. M. 1954. The commercial storage of fruits, vegetables, and florist and nursery stocks. U.S. Dept. Agr. Handbook *66*.

Cross-references: *Forklift Trucks; Materials Handling; Poultry Processing; Refrigeration Principles; Ventilation.*

REFRIGERATION PRINCIPLES

A mechanical refrigeration system provides a means of removing heat from a product. It is a means of moving heat from a low temperature environment to a higher temperature environment. This does not mean that the principle of flow of heat from the high temperature body to the low temperature body is violated. To accomplish the transfer of heat in a mechanical refrigeration system, energy must be added externally, either as power—electric motor, diesel engine, gasoline engine, or steam engine,—or with heat—gas, electricity, coal or wood. The former are known as compression systems and the latter as absorption systems of refrigeration.

The unit of measurement representing the amount of heat is known as the British thermal unit (Btu). The Btu is the amount of heat required to raise the temperature of 1 lb of water 1°F. The calorie is often used, which is the amount of heat required to raise the temperature of 1 gm of water 1°C. The large calorie, designated Calorie, is the amount of heat required to raise the temperature of 1,000 gm of water 1°C. Inasmuch as the amount of heat required to change the temperature of 1 lb or 1 gm of water varies at various temperatures, the Btu is normally defined as the amount required to heat the water 1°, from 63° to 64°F. The energy equivalent to 1 Btu is given in Table R.5.

Change of State

To understand the principle of operation of a refrigeration system, it is helpful to know the relationships involved as heat is added to a material. Matter exists in the

TABLE R.5

BTU EQUIVALENTS

778 ft-lb
0.000393 hp-hr
1,055 watt-seconds
252 calories
0.252 Calories (kilogram-calories)
1 Btu

three states of solid, liquid, and gas. As heat is added, the molecules become more active. The molecules move very slowly in solids and much more rapidly and over a larger area in gases. Evidence of increased molecular activity in a solid with an increase in temperature can be demonstrated by the phenomena of expansion of materials upon being heated. Theoretically, there is no molecular activity at absolute zero temperature, which has been closely approached but never reached. Absolute zero temperature is $-460°$ on the Fahrenheit scale and $-273°$ on the Centigrade scale.

Using water as a material the following change in temperature occurs as heat is added. As 1 Btu is added to 1 lb of ice, the temperature will not increase 1°F as in the case of water explained above, but will increase about 2.0°F per Btu added. Therefore, the specific heat of ice is 0.5. As heat is added, the temperature approaches 32°F. At 32°F the ice changes state to the liquid form. Considerable heat can be added before the temperature goes above 32°F. The amount of heat added is known as the latent heat (hidden heat) of fusion, which is 144 Btu per lb or 80 cal per gm at 32°F. The latent heat is the same for melting or freezing at 32°F. As more heat is added, the temperature of the water increases approximately 1°F for each Btu added to each pound until 212°F is reached. Again, considerable heat must be added without a change of temperature to increase the molecular activity to the extent that a change of state occurs from liquid to vapor. The amount of heat required is known as the latent heat of vaporization and is 970 Btu per lb or 539 cal per gm for water at normal atmospheric pressure. If additional heat is added it takes approximately 0.48 Btu per lb to increase the temperature of 1 lb by 1°F, which now occupies considerably more volume of vapor. The latent heat involved in vaporization or in condensation, that is, changing from vapor to liquid, is the same. The sensible heat involving a change in temperature is

$$Q = SH \times lb \times \Delta t$$

Ice Refrigeration Systems

The essential parts of an ice refrigeration system are a closed container, ice, and a method of water removal. Heat moves to the ice from the warmer surrounding product and air. The ice is warmed and melts and heat is carried away in the water. The ice must be replenished. The ice might be considered as the refrigerant, the cooling agent, which carries the Btu's from the closed container to the outside. The heat flow provides the change of state from a solid to a liquid. The ice system can cool only to 32°F in a normal atmospheric system and is only very slightly affected by large increases in pressure.

Many systems incorporate the use of ice, which is made with a mechanical refrigeration system. The ice is chopped or flaked into the storage for cooling to 32°F. Ice is often placed over products for transport or placed in separate chambers through which air is cooled to maintain low temperatures during transport and storage.

Mechanical Refrigeration Systems

The essential components of a mechanical refrigeration system are the refrigerant, evaporator, compressor, condenser, and appropriate controls (Fig. R.3).

Refrigerant.—The refrigerant carries the heat from the cold room to the outside. The refrigerants operate between the liquid and gaseous state, as contrasted to ice

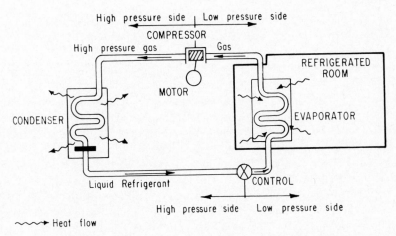

High pressure side | Low pressure side

COMPRESSOR

High pressure gas ... Gas

MOTOR

REFRIGERATED ROOM

CONDENSER

EVAPORATOR

Liquid Refrigerant ... CONTROL

High pressure side ... Low pressure side

∿→ Heat flow

FIG. R-3.   Mechanical compression refrigeration system

systems which involve the solid-liquid state. The refrigerant, however, moves through the system in closed piping, and is used over and over. It is necessary to replace the refrigerant only if leaks occur in the system. Desirable properties of refrigerants are low boiling point, safe, nontoxic, high latent heat, operate on positive pressure, noncorrosive, mix with oil, and from which water can be removed (Table R.6). Refrigerants commonly used are ammonia, Freon, methyl chloride, ethyl chloride, sulfur dioxide, and carbon dioxide. Ammonia is normally used in large commercial installations because of its economy, and the amount of heat carried away per pound of ammonia evaporated is quite high. However, for small household systems and movable units, and for many installations for food, Freon is used because it is inert and operates at a lower pressure difference within the system, so that maintenance problems are minimized. Freon is also more safe. Steel is used for ammonia systems and copper for Freon systems.

Evaporator.—The evaporator, or cooling or freezing coils, is located in the refrigerated room. Heat moves from the products being cooled to the air surrounding the

TABLE R.6

CHARACTERISTICS OF REFRIGERANTS

Refrigerant	Latent Heat Vaporization at 0°F, Btu/Lb	Condensing Pressure at 86°F, Psi[1]	Evaporating Pressure at 5°F, Psi[1]	Boiling Point Atmospheric Pressure, °F	Hp per Ton at 86°F, 5°F[2]
Ammonia (NH_3)	572	155	19.6	−28.0	0.98
Methyl chloride (CH_3Cl)	176	80	6.5	−10.5	1.02
Ethyl chloride	173			54.0	
Sulfur dioxide (SO_2)	172			14.0	
Carbon dioxide (CO_2)	118	1,028	317.0	−108.4	1.83
Freon −12 (CCl_2F_2)	76	93	11.8	−21.6	1.01
Freon −22 ($CHClF_2$)		160	28.3	−41.4	1.02
Propane (C_3H_8)		141	27.2	−44.2	1.03

[1] Standard Oil Co., Engineering Bull. *R-216* (1958).
[2] Condenser-evaporator temperatures.   Courtesy American Oil Co., Chicago, Ill.

product and the air moves either by natural or forced convection to the surface of the evaporator. Heat moves from the warmer air to the cooler refrigerant inside the evaporator coils.

Evaporator coils might be classified as dry or flooded. There is predominantly a vapor in dry coils. Refrigerants exist predominantly in a liquid state in flooded evaporated coils. Most systems are the dry type. As heat is added to the refrigerant, the change of state from liquid to gas for both the dry and flooded types takes place. The change of state compares to the boiling, or evaporation, of water, thus the name evaporator. The temperature of vaporization depends upon the particular refrigerant and the pressure of the system. An ammonia system at 0 psi pressure would boil at −28°F. If it were desirable to cool to a lower temperature, it would be necessary to decrease the pressure inside the evaporator coils. The gas formed in the evaporator moves out, carrying with it the heat (predominantly latent heat) and for ammonia at 0 psi would be approximately 572 Btu per lb of ammonia (Table R.6).

Where the evaporator is adjacent to the material being cooled, it is known as a direct expansion (DX) system. If brine, water, glycol, or other solutions are cooled and these solutions are used for cooling the product, these are designated as indirect systems of refrigeration. The cooling coil or cooler for the brine to cool the product is placed in the refrigerated room and the evaporator is external to the refrigerated room.

Compressor.—The compressor is a pump for moving the refrigerant through the system. The compressor may be a positive piston or rotary or centrifugal type. Inasmuch as many refrigeration systems use an electric motor for driving the compressor, they have come to be known as electric refrigeration systems. However, this is a misnomer, because the compressor can be driven by any type of power. The compression system of refrigeration is a more appropriate classification.

The compressor takes the gas from the evaporator at the suction pressure and increases the pressure to the discharge pressure. In the process of compressing, the temperature is increased so that the gas will be at the temperature of condensation desired in the condenser. At the compressor, heat is added, the pressure is increased, but there is no change of state. This is the heart of the refrigeration system and it is the place where energy is added to provide for a means of moving heat from the low temperature inside a refrigerated room to a higher temperature outside the room.

Where large changes in pressure must be provided in the compressor, more than

TABLE R.7

SIZE OF PIPING CONNECTIONS FOR AMMONIA SYSTEMS

Pipe Diam., In.	Suction Line		Liquid Line	
	Capacity, Tons	Velocity, Ft/Min	Capacity, Tons	Velocity, Ft/Min
$^1/_2$	0.47	1,000	17.7	120
1	3.90	2,000	54.7	120
$1^1/_2$	10.72	3,000	135.0	120
2	22.40	3,750	228.0	120
3	63.50	4,750		
4	117.00	5,000		
5	185.00	5,000		
6	265.00	5,000		

one unit might be used to provide multistage compression. An additional unit is often called a booster compressor. Most units are single stage, but where there is more than a 10 to 1 change in refrigerant pressure, 2 or 3 stages might be used such as for very low temperature refrigeration.

Piping systems must be of appropriate size to provide flow without undue restriction (Table R.7).

Condenser.—The function of the condenser is to transfer heat away from the high temperature gaseous refrigerant entering and to provide a liquid refrigerant leaving. Thus, the second step in the cycle, the change of state from gas to liquid, is accomplished here. Gaseous ammonia at about 180° to 190°F enters the condenser from the compressor. The condenser cools the gas to 80°–90°F and the gas changes to a liquid. The heat moves out of the condenser because there is a higher temperature inside than outside. The heat is carried away by air, water, or other fluid, external to the condenser coils. The fluid may be forced or moved by gravity over the condenser coils. Some refrigeration condensers use water for cooling during the summer and air during the winter.

Many different types of heat exchangers are used for condensers: shell and tube, plate, or double tube units. The external cooling may be done with the convection cooling, or with evaporative cooling of water sprayed over the surface. Because of the cost of water, evaporative cooling or cooling towers are often utilized to reduce cost. The cooling tower water picks up heat from the condenser, and the water is moved over a tower external to the system where the water is cooled and reused. Makeup water must be added to replace the water evaporated. The difference in temperature between the condensation temperature inside the coil and the fluid temperature outside is from 15° to 20°F. If the heat is not carried away rapidly enough, the pressure and temperature of condensation inside the condenser coils will also increase. A rule of thumb is that 2 gpm of water or 500 cfm of air are required per ton of refrigeration.

A receiver is usually used in connection with the condenser. The liquid refrigerant is stored in the receiver when the system is shut down. The refrigerant normally moves from the condenser to the receiver before it is recirculated through the system. The receiver is a storage for the refrigerant, and can supply varying amounts to the system depending upon the cooling load. The receiver is often a part of the condenser or it can be a separate unit.

Controls.—The function of the controls is to maintain proper rate and temperature of refrigeration effect or cooling. The principal method of control is to use an expansion valve, which may be manually or automatically operated. The expansion valve is placed in the liquid line entering the evaporator. As additional cooling is required, more refrigerant is admitted to take away the heat. A thermostatic control can be automatically operated from a thermal sensing bulb on the outlet side fastened on the exterior surface of the evaporator. As the temperature increases, the expansion valve is opened further to admit more refrigerant while maintaining a uniform pressure on the evaporator. The temperature of vaporization, thus the temperature of cooling in the evaporator, is controlled from the expansion valve for a balanced system. The temperature in the condenser is controlled by the rate of cooling of the condenser. If heat is not removed, the temperature and pressure increase in the condenser.

Different controls are used for the flooded system where an accumulator and a float are involved with the float maintaining the height of liquid in the evaporator. The evaporator temperature maintains itself according to the heat load imposed upon the unit, with the float functioning only to maintain a uniform supply of refrigerant to the evaporator and not for maintaining the pressure in the unit as with the dry system.

Capillary tubes with a small inside diameter and of a specific length are often used in small systems to provide a pressure drop in place of an expansion valve. The motor operates according to pressure switches. The temperature is maintained by the pressure setting controlling the motor operation.

The refrigerant is under high pressure from the compressor to the control device. This is known as the high side of the system. The remainder is called the low side.

Rating

A refrigeration system is rated by the quantity of heat which can be removed from a product and surroundings by the system, not the amount of heat rejected at the condenser. The common ratings is a ton of refrigeration, which is the quantity of heat required to change 1 ton of water to 1 ton of ice at 32°F. For mechanical refrigeration systems, the heat is removed in 24 hr. Thus, a 1-ton unit will remove 288,000 Btu per 24 hr or 12,000 Btu per hr. The amount of heat rejected at the condenser is greater than this amount because of heat added by the compressor.

Units are normally rated at some standard inlet and discharge pressure, such as 20 psi suction and 120 psi head for ammonia. There is a definite relationship between power requirement and tons of refrigeration. As the suction pressure is increased, the power required is decreased, and as the head pressure is increased, the power requirement is increased. This is similar to the operation of the pump. To get minimum power requirements, it is desirable to have the inlet or suction pressure as high as possible and the outlet or discharge pressure as low as possible (Fig. R.4). For ammonia, 1 hp-hr per ton of refrigeration is required when operating at 20 psi suction pressure, as compared to 2 hp-hr when operating at 3 in. of mercury suction. As the head pressure is increased from 150 to 200 psi, the power requirements are increased approximately 17%.

Efficient Operation

Efficient operation of a refrigeration system consists of (1) keeping the evaporator clean on both sides by defrosting on the outside and removal of oil from the inside; (2) keeping the condenser clean on both sides by removing scale from the exterior for

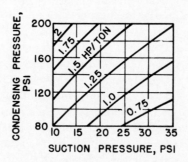

Fig. R-4.   Effect of suction and condensing pressure on power requirements for a typical ammonia compressor

water-cooled systems, or dust and dirt for air-cooled systems, and by removing water which might accumulate in refrigerant through condensation; (3) maintaining low pressure differences between low and high side so that costs of operating the compressor

TABLE R.8

COMPRESSION REFRIGERATOR COMPLAINT DIAGNOSIS CHART

Complaint	Cause	Remedy
System operates too long or continuously	A. Control not cutting out	A. Adjust, repair or replace control
	B. Refrigerant loss	B. Locate leak and correct charge
	C. Unit not ventilated	C. Relocate unit with proper air circulation over condenser
	D. Inefficient compressor	D. Test compressor and make repairs
	E. Too low compressor speed	E. Check current used with current specified on motor. Ensure constant line voltage
	F. Air in system	F. Purge air
	G. Other causes Poor door seal Restricted circulation in floor compartment	G. Check cabinet on user's premises and repair
System operates on short cycles	A. Control not adjusted or defective	A. Adjust, repair or replace control
	B. High pressure gas leaking into low side due to leaking discharge valve	B. Retest and repair discharge valves
Not sufficient refrigeration (Refrigerator temperature too high)	A. Control set too warm	A. Adjust control
	B. Control will not cut in	B. Readjust, repair or replace control
	C. Insufficient refrigerant	C. Locate leak and recharge
	D. Inefficient compressor	D. Test compressor efficiency
	E. Fuse blown, feed line switch open	E. Replace burned fuses or check current supply line
	F. Other causes Poor door seal, and heavily frosted evaporator	F. Check cabinet on user's premises and repair or defrost
Noisy condensing unit	A. Poor location resulting in transmission of noise	A. Relocate and if necessary apply sound insulation
	B. Improper mounting	B. Check mounting and ensure base being free from adjacent parts
	C. Seal squeak	C. Check and correct
	D. Lack of oil	D. Check oil, ensure correct charge and also ensure correct motor rotation
	E. Condenser, motor or compressor loose	E. Tighten loose parts
	F. Worn compressor or motor bearings	F. Replace worn part or contact motor service station
	G. Compressor pumps oil	G. Check and correct oil charge
	H. Too high head pressure	H. Excess air or refrigerant purge
	I. Motor pulley not lined up with flywheel or loose	I. Align and tighten motor pulley
	J. Belt split or frayed	J. Replace belt
	K. Loose flywheel	K. Tighten flywheel bolt

Source: Refrigeration Service Manual—Chieftain. Tecumseh Products Co., Tecumseh, Mich.

are at a minimum, and by keeping the head pressure low and the suction pressure as high as possible; (4) keeping refrigerant clean; (5) removing lubricants from ammonia systems and use of the proper lubricant in any system; and (6) removing moisture in the form of vapor or liquid.   Table R.8 lists remedies for malfunctions.

The lubricant must not vaporize at the higher temperatures, and not congeal or solidify at the low temperatures.   These characteristics are identified by the pour point and flash point.   Oil may be purged from the system at low positions, such as bottom of evaporator, by using the higher pressure of the system when above atmospheric pressure to force the lubricant out.   Water may be removed through driers, materials placed in the line to absorb the water.   Noncondensables are particularly troublesome when refrigeration systems are operated below atmospheric pressure.   Nitrogen, hydrogen, and other noncondensable gases may get into the system and decrease the effectiveness of the heat transfer surface.   These noncondensables are normally removed from a high point of the system, where the system can be vented and the gas removed.

Absorption System of Refrigeration

The absorption system is often referred to as the gas refrigeration system because it was developed for burning gas to provide the external energy for moving heat from a low temperature room to an external high temperature volume.   The heat can also

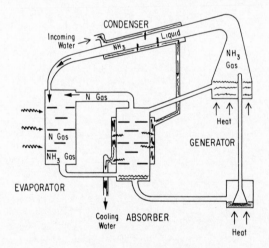

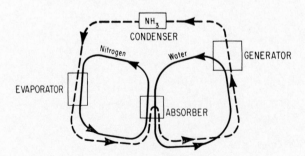

Fig. R-5.   Absorption system of refrigeration

be provided with coal, fuel oil, electricity, or solar heating. The system consists of a generator, evaporator, absorber, absorbent, and condenser, all connected in a closed system (Fig. R.5). There are no moving parts. Cooling water is required to carry heat away from the system. The system operates in the liquid-gas states, as does the compression system. The pressure is the same throughout all sections of the unit. Heat is applied to provide energy for moving the vapor and heat.

Absorbent.—An absorbent is used to carry heat from the system. Ammonia-water, where ammonia is the refrigerant and water is the absorbent, or water-salt, where water is the refrigerant and a salt such as lithium chloride is the absorbent, flow through the system. In ammonia-water systems, as water is heated, ammonia is given off, with nearly all of the ammonia released at the boiling point of water. A cooling effect is provided by evaporation just as when alcohol is evaporated from the skin. When the water cools, ammonia gas is absorbed.

Generator.—The generator contains ammonia dissolved in water. Heat provided from an external source drives off the ammonia vapor and returns the solution to the generator from the absorber. The generator serves the same function in the absorption system as does the compressor in the compression system.

Condenser.—The condenser receives the ammonia vapor driven off from the generator and ammonia is condensed to a liquid. Water is furnished externally to carry heat from the gas, as water is supplied for the condenser of a compression system. The water then goes to the external surface of the absorber for removing additional heat.

Evaporator.—The ammonia liquid enters the evaporator or cooling coils. Hydrogen from the absorber also enters the evaporator. Upon vaporizing, a cooling effect is produced. The liquid ammonia changes to gas and moves to the absorber. A high pressure exists in the evaporator, due to the presence of large quantities of hydrogen. There is only a small pressure due to the ammonia, but the pressure is low enough to provide a low temperature in the evaporator by low vapor pressure ammonia.

Absorber.—In the absorber, ammonia gas moving in from the evaporator and nitrogen rise as water falling down from the top of the absorber dissolves the ammonia. The ammonia solution is returned to the generator and the process repeated. The hydrogen is confined to the evaporator and absorber, causing a high pressure, particularly in the evaporator.

Considering the three basic components of the absorption system, ammonia moves from the generator to the evaporator, to the absorber, and back to the generator. Water moves from the generator to the absorber and back to the generator. Nitrogen moves from the absorber to the evaporator and back to the absorber. There are three gas cycles imposed upon each other to furnish the desirable heat transfer.

Control.—Control of the unit is either manual or by a thermostat which automatically controls the gas valve. Minimum gas input is adjusted by a set screw on the thermostat. Low refrigeration temperature may be caused by improper thermostat adjustment, low room temperature, or too large a flame at the minimum settings. Conversely, the refrigeration may be too warm due to insufficient or warm water for cooling, insufficient gas, improper combustion of gas, or improper distribution of gas flame over the heating surface.

An ammonia absorption machine, operating at 180 psi condenser and 25 psi absorber, requires 35,000 Btu per hr per ton of refrigeration. The unit requires $9^{1}/_{2}$ gpm of water with a 10°F rise in temperature for cooling per ton of refrigeration.

Reference

HALL, C. W. 1963. Processing Equipment for Agricultural Products. Edwards Brothers, Ann Arbor, Mich.

Cross-references: *Btu; Latent Heat; Lubrication; Refrigerated Storage; Sensible and Latent Heat.*

RETORTS

Retorts or so-called process kettles are designed for the processing of all types of canned products that require cooking under pressure (Table R.9). They can be used

TABLE R.9

PROCESSING TIMES (MINUTES) FOR VEGETABLES AT 240°F (10 PSI) AND MEATS AT 250°F (PSI)

Food	No. 2 Can	No. 3 Can	Pt Glass	Qt Glass
Asparagus	30		30	35
Beans				
Dried kidney	70	85	80	90
Lima	40	50	50	55
Snap	25	30	30	35
Beets, baby	30	30	30	35
Carrots	30	30	30	35
Corn, whole				
kernel	50	65	60	70
Peas				
Black-eyed	40	50	50	55
Green	40		45	
Sweet potatoes	95	115	95	120
Tomatoes	25	30	25	35
Vegetable soup	50	65	60	70
Beef				
Fresh	85	120	85	120
Ground				
(Hamburg)	90	120	90	120
Lamb, mutton	85	120	85	120
Pork				
Fresh	85	120	85	120
Sausage	90	120	90	120

a) Add 1 psi pressure for each 2000 ft altitude over 2000 ft.
b) Cool tin cans immediately after processing.
Source: U.S. Dept. Agr. Farmers Bull. *1762.*

for the commercial sterilization of all types of food products in glass or metal containers.

Pressure cooking calls for a temperature of 250°F at a maximum of 15 psig. Special retorts can be obtained for higher pressure operation normally up to 60 psig operating pressure. The high pressure retorts are made under ASME specifications, inspection, and approval. They usually hold 3 standard 4-tier crates.

Retorts can be obtained in either the vertical or horizontal types (Fig. R.6). For large scale operation a continuous cooker is often preferable to a battery of individual retorts.

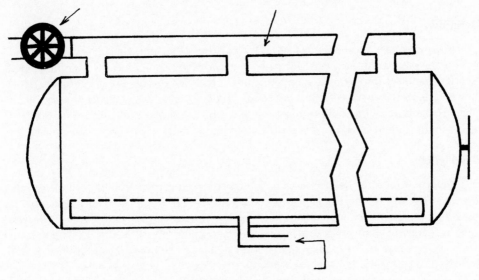

FIG. R-6.   Retort

In operation the rate of heating of products which are being sterilized or heated depends very much upon the product. Manufacturers usually are able to furnish a heating and cooling curve which is approximately correct for a given size can with a particular product and at a certain temperature of heating.

Retorts are supplied with multiple fasteners and hinged covers. The horizontal type retort may be supplied with a door on each end so that cars of loaded product may be handled on a straight through operation. Retorts may be provided with an inside overhead water spray pipe line for can cooling.

Reference

GOLDBLITH, S. A., JOSLYN, M. A., and NICKERSON, J. T. R. 1966. Introduction to Thermal Processing of Foods. AVI Publishing Co., Westport, Conn.

Cross-reference: *Jacketed Kettle.*

RHEOLOGY

Rheology is the branch of physics dealing with flow and deformation of matter. Food rheology is becoming increasingly important for several reasons. First is the ever growing application of mechanical harvesting of many agricultural commodities.

This method subjects the product to mechanical forces which if excessive may lead to damage. Second is the extensive mechanical handling and treatment during processing. A majority of our foods now belong to the class of "fabricated foods," and processing may include such operations as cutting, pulping, extrusion, mixing, pumping, and emulsifying. All of these operations influence the original and final rheological properties of the product. Third is the awareness of consumers of the textural characteristics of foods when consumed. Eating involves chewing, which is fundamentally a rheological process and much importance is now attributed to the textural characteristics of foods.

Definition

Food rheology is mainly concerned with forces and deformations. In addition, time is an important factor since many rheological phenomena are time dependent. Another factor of importance is temperature. Rheology is mostly concerned with the flow and deformation of cohesive bodies or liquids. Also, normally comprised in rheology is the flow of particulate matter and the breakup or rupture of solids into fragments and of liquid into drops, as well as the phenomena of adhesion (stickiness).

Description

Deformation may be of one or both of two types, irreversible deformation called flow, and reversible deformation called elasticity. The work used in irreversible deformation is dissipated as heat and the body is permanently deformed. The work used in reversible deformation is recovered when upon release of the deforming stress, the body recovers its original shape. Irreversible, or viscous deformation is usually expressed in terms of *rate of shear* which is the change in velocity of flow measured at right angles to the direction of flow. Reversible or elastic deformation is expressed as *strain*, or relative deformation.

Elastic

Elastic deformations follow Hooke's law indicating that stress is proportional to the strain according to the following relationship:

$$\frac{\Delta l}{l} = \frac{\sigma}{E}$$

where l = the length,

σ = the tension

E = the *modulus of elasticity* or *Young's modulus*

Beyond a certain value of stress, materials may cease to be elastic and flow or rupture may occur. This tension is called *yield stress* or *yield value*. When deformation occurs volume contraction may take place. This is described by Poisson's ratio μ under conditions of unidirectional stress

$$\mu = \frac{\text{relative lateral contraction}}{\text{relative longitudinal strain}}$$

Poisson's ratio is a measure of the volume contraction on deformation and is equal to

0.5 when no contraction occurs; μ ranges down from 0.5 for aqueous products, such as gelatin gels.

Plastic

Plastic deformations occur when the tension is greater than the yield value, and recovery is not complete after removal of the stress.

Viscous

Liquids without a yield value are called *Newtonian liquids, pure viscous liquids,* or *simple liquids.* For laminar flow, the following expression applies

$$D = \frac{dv}{dy} = \phi T = \frac{1}{\eta}\tau$$

where $(D = dv/dy) =$ the velocity gradient
$\tau =$ the shearing force per unit area
$\phi =$ a constant

The reciprocal of ϕ is η or the coefficient of viscosity.

Graphical Representation

The relationship between stress and deformation or velocity gradient of Newtonian liquids is represented in Fig. R.7 and $D = \tau/\eta$. Only liquids of relatively low molecular weight are Newtonian in character (see section on Viscosity). For purely plastic flow, the curve has the form presented in Fig. R.8 where f is the yield value and $D = (\tau - f)/n$. Other types of flow are pseudoviscous flow (Fig. R.9) where $D = \tau^n/\eta$, where n may be greater than or smaller than 1, and pseudo plastic flow (Fig. R.10) where $D = (\tau - f)^n/\eta$. In those cases where $n \neq 1$ the coefficient η is not identical with the coefficient of viscosity and is sometimes named apparent viscosity. In many cases plastic flow is of the nature represented in Fig. R.11, where the curved part of the line represents pseudoplastic flow and the straight part purely plastic flow. We

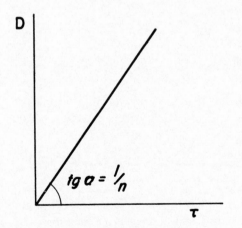

FIG. R-7.   Purely viscous flow

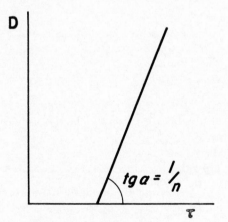

FIG. R-8.   Purely plastic flow

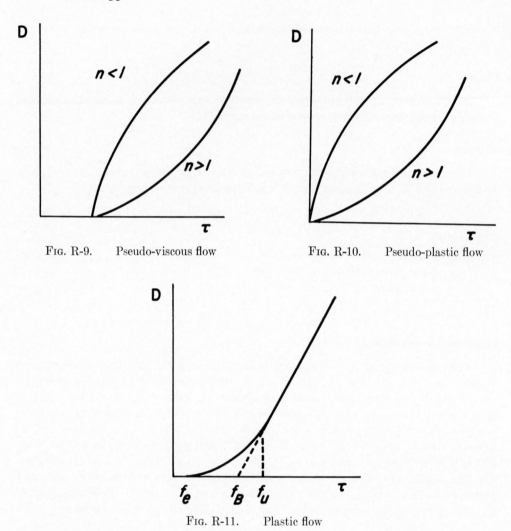

Fig. R-9.   Pseudo-viscous flow   Fig. R-10.   Pseudo-plastic flow

Fig. R-11.   Plastic flow

can distinguish three different yield values, the upper yield value f_u, the lower yield value f_e, and the Bingham yield value f_B.

Creep

Deformation resulting from instantaneous loading and observation as a function of time is called *creep*. The recovery resulting from removal of the load is *creep relaxation*.

Thixotropy

Many biological and food materials are disperse systems or are cellular or fibrous in nature. All of these are non-Newtonian and in addition frequently exhibit the phenomenon of thixotropy. This results from disturbance of weak bonding forces by applied stress and leading to a decrease in apparent viscosity. Thixotropy is an isothermal sol/gel transformation resulting from application of a shearing stress. Thixotropy is pronounced in products such as butter, margarine, potato paste, mayonnaise, and many others.

Instruments

Obtaining knowledge of the rheological properties of a material would require determination of the shearing stress rate of shear curve. This involves determination of the relation between shearing stress and rate of shear over a wide range of values which is not always possible nor desirable. Either time may not permit this or the instrument used may be designed for measurement at only one single rate of shear. Such one point measurements should be treated with caution. In many cases only the presence and magnitude of a yield value is measured. Many instruments that have been used for particular products for long periods yield results which are not amenable to interpretation in objective rheological terms. Such instruments which give readings in arbitrary values are only of use in comparing products. Values thus obtained cannot easily be related to results obtained with different instruments and methods. Food scientists and agricultural engineers are now endeavoring to design instruments based on sound rheological principles.

The various instruments used for measuring rheological properties of foods can be divided into several groups depending on the way the sample is deformed: compression, extension, penetration, shear and flow, or a combination of these.

Compression testing can be done with universal testing machines of the Instron type. The sample can be compressed between plates and force and deformation are recorded simultaneously on the recorder chart.

Extension testing is not common for food products but has been done on meat fibers, etc., and a universal testing machine is the instrument of choice for this application.

Penetration testing is commonly used with foods. It may involve a simple hand held pressure tester (Magnus-Taylor fruit maturity tester) in which a plunger is pushed into the product for a predetermined distance and the force is read from a spring-operated scale. Another penetration test is the consistency measurement of plastic fats with a cone penetrometer. A cone of specified dimensions and weight is allowed to penetrate into the sample under the influence of its own weight, and the depth of penetration recorded. A great variety of penetration tests are in use.

Shear measurements involve the movement or actual separation of different layers of the sample. Such measurements are popular for fruits and vegetables, meats, and other solid products. Examples of instruments are the pea tenderometer for measuring maturity of peas; the Kramer shear press in which the sample is contained in the shear cell and a set of 10 blades forced through the sample and through slots in the bottom of the cell, the sample is compressed and sheared and the force can be read from a gauge or recorded on a strip chart; another example is the Warner-Bratzler shear instrument designed for measuring tenderness of meat.

Flow measurements can be made with a variety of viscometers, including the capillary type of which several varieties exist, rotational viscometers such as the Brookfield and the Stormer viscometer, and the falling ball type viscometer.

In addition to the aforementioned instruments, many specially designed instruments exist for rheological measurements on a variety of foods. Examples are the

Farinograph for measuring and recording dough strength, the Amylograph for measuring and recording the gelling characteristics of starch pastes, the Bloom gelometer for measurement of gel strength, and the Bostwick consistometer for measurement of consistency of pastes.   Prepared by J. M. deMan

Cross-references: *Butter, Physical Properties; Viscosity.*

ROASTERS

Roasters are a class of processing machines and equipment widely used in food processing, particularly for roasting of coffee, peanuts, and similar types of food products.

Roasters are of both batch- and continuous-types. Formerly most roasters were of the batch-type. In the past few years, the continuous roaster is being used much more widely because of the greater uniformity of treatment and the large labor saving possible.

Batch-type roasters consist essentially of a large heated chamber in which the product is placed and agitated under controlled time and temperature conditions.

In addition to precise time and temperature control, other important aspects are the means for loading, unloading, and cooling the product.

With the continuous roaster, an endless conveyor carries the unroasted product through a heated chamber where it is subjected to a specified temperature for a certain time and then discharged and cooled.

Most roasters are heated by means of natural gas which is not only an efficient heating medium, but reduces the oxygen concentration of the atmosphere to which the roasted product is subjected.

The pretreatment of products which are to be roasted is important. The product must be clean, free from foreign material, and of good quality.

Reference

Sivetz, M., and Foote, H. E. 1963. Coffee Processing Technology, Vols. 1 and 2. AVI Publishing Co., Westport, Conn.

ROTARY SEAL

The rotary seal is a device to take the place of a packed shaft. It is widely used in refrigeration equipment and also in food machinery where sanitation is important. In fact, 3A Standards require rotary seals on all shafts having bearings which come in contact with dairy products.

The rotary seal (Fig. C.13) consists essentially of two parts made of dissimilar material so that they may rub against each other without causing undue abrasion. One of the plates is stationary; the other is attached to the rotating shaft. The seal is held against the stationary plate with a spring pressure. The seal is held against the shaft with a synthetic rubber ring, which allows the rotating part to move endwise on the shaft as necessary to maintain good contact with the stationary part.

Rotary seals are made in two general types: the inside, and the outside. With the inside type, the rotating member, the spring, and rotary seal are on the inside of the vat or chamber and are in contact with the product. With the outside type, the spring and rotating part are outside of the product area.

An important feature of the rotary seal is that it can be readily separated thus allowing easy cleaning.

In the selection of rotary seals, it is essential that the seal parts be made of material which is suitable for use in contact with the medium, which it is to seal. For example, if in contact with milk, the seal should be made of hardened stainless steel. If the seal is for a refrigeration machine, it is usually made of hardened alloy steel.

The maintaining of rotary seals involves making certain that they do not become nicked or rough on the sealing surfaces, and that the rubber ring which seals the movable member be kept in a soft, pliable condition. The rotary seal must have a slight amount of lubrication. Otherwise, it will gall and become rough. There is sufficient lubrication in most food products to provide the necessary lubrication, and in refrigeration compressors and in most fluid pumping operations, there is sufficient lubrication from the fluid to allow the unit to operate satisfactorily if the materials in the seal are properly selected.

Reference

FARRALL, A. W. 1963. Engineering for Dairy and Food Products, 3rd Edition. John Wiley & Sons, New York.

Cross-references: *Centrifugal Pumps; O-ring; Positive Pumps; Stuffing Boxes.*

S

SAFETY

The importance of safety in the operations of an industrial processing plant cannot be overemphasized. One or more people should have specific responsibility for plant and product safety as related to workers in the plant and consumers of the product.

The National Safety Council, 425 N. Michigan Ave., Chicago, Ill., has for sale many industrial safety sheets on several subjects. Those of direct interest to processing plants by title and data sheet number are:

Accident Records and Analysis, Work	527	Electric Equipment, Grounding	299
Acetylene	494	Electric Motors for Hazardous Location, Main	546
Air Compressors and Air Receivers, Cleaning	379	Electroplating	302
Air Powered Hand Tools	392	Epoxy Resin	533
Ammonia (Anhydrous)	251	Exhaust Systems	428
Asphalt Roofing Manufacture	582	Exhaust Ventilation Systems	431
Atmospheres in Sewers	550	Falls on Floors	495
Bottles and Broken Glass	355	Floors, Slippery	286
Brazing, Hand Soldering and	445	Food Bins and Tanks	524
Burns, Chemical	523	Grain, Unloading Bulk from Box Cars	521
Capacitors	404	Hand Trucks, Powered	317
Carbon Dioxide (Dry Ice)	397	Heat Control, Radiant	381
Centrifuges	591	Lighting, Emergency	248
Chlorates	371	Lining Tanks and Vessels with Rubber	492
Chlorine	207	L.P. Gas for Industrial Trucks	479
Cleaning Machinery and Electric Motors	285	Management Policies for Occupational Safety	585
Cleaning with Hot Water and Steam	238	Mercury	203
Color in Industry	219	Radiant Heat Control	381
Conveyors, Belt (Equipment)	569	Sewer Pipe Cleaning	577
Conveyors, Belt (Operation)	570	Slings, Wire Rope, Recommended Loads	380
Conveyors, Roller	528	Snow and Ice Removal in Industry	402
Dichloromethane (Methylone Chloride)	474	Static Electricity	547
Dusts, Fumes, and Mists in Industry	531	Trench Excavation	254

For proper management and safety, piping should be coded by name and color identifying the substance being transported. Suggested color schemes are as follows:

Fire protection	Red
Sprinklers	Maroon
Dangerous (high pressure steam)	Orange
Dangerous (low pressure steam)	Deep yellow
Compressed air	Light yellow
Safe materials (cold water)	Green
Safe materials (hot water)	Brown
Extra valuable materials (such as refrigerant- distinguish between liquid and gas lines)	Deep purple

High visibility yellow should be used on curbs, aisles, low beams, changes in floor elevations, etc. Alert orange should be used for interior surfaces of switch boxes, fuse boxes, and equipment guards. Safety green should be used to identify first aid rooms, stretchers, and gas masks. Fire protection red should be used for all fire equipment. Precaution blue should be used to identify equipment and apparatus which should not be moved. Traffic white, including black, gray, and yellow, may be used to identify traffic lanes.

Training programs for the workers should stress the importance of recognizing the various colors used for safety.

Cross-references: *Dust Explosion; Explosion; Floors; Paint; Toxicity; Welding.*

SANITATION

Sanitation is of paramount importance in the production of food and dairy products on the farm and in processing plants. The surface buildup of milk solids called milkstone should be avoided or if present—should be removed. Similar materials may accumulate from other products. The principles involved apply to many food products, but the examples which follow apply to milk. Whether cleaned manually or automatically with CIP the basic fundamental principles are the same. First the surface should be cleaned thoroughly and all solids removed. If solids are on the surface to be cleaned, it is usually necessary to remove these before proceeding with the cleaning. Surfaces should be rinsed with warm water at about 100°F. The surface is washed with a detergent solution at 145°F. Some dairymen use acid solutions and others use alkaline detergent solutions. A typical procedure is to use alternately these solutions or to use 1 solution for 5 days followed by the other solution for 2 days before repeating. After washing, all utensils or surfaces should be immediately rinsed to remove the washing solutions. The surface is then left to dry. For stainless steel, it is important that surfaces be exposed to dry air so that a protective layer, called a passive layer, can form to protect the stainless steel. The procedure of placing hypochlorite solution of about 200 ppm over the surface is known as sanitizing (note: not sterilizing). Sanitization should be done shortly before equipment is used rather than immediately after cleaning. If sanitization is done immediately after cleaning, the solution may cause corrosion and pitting of the stainless steel surfaces if permitted to remain on surfaces for more than 2 hr. Therefore, it is very important that sanitizing be done just before use rather than after cleaning. The manufacturers instructions should be followed closely in using cleaning and sanitizing solutions. Many manufacturers have established recommendations for cleaning various pieces of equipment such as milking machines, pipelines, vacuum lines, and processing equipment in the plant.   Another reason for sanitizing before use is that the surface will be free of contamination upon use.

Standards for the construction and use of various pieces of dairy equipment such as bulk tanks, tankers, homogenizers, pasteurizers, and other processing equipment have been established by a group known as the 3-A organization which represents three associations: U.S. Public Health, the National Association of Milk and Food Sanitarians, and the Dairy Industries Committee.   3-A Standards were originally developed primarily for milk equipment, but are now widely used for food processing equipment.   It is recommended that equipment be selected which meets the 3-A Standards.

Cross-references: *Chlorination; CIP Systems; Cleaning of Equipment; Standards 3-A; Stainless Steel.*

SAUSAGE GRINDER

Several types of sausage grinders or cutters are available.   One type consists of a metal cylindrical body in which a feed screw operates.   The feed screw and body are cylindrical.   The auger has a decreasing diameter toward the outlet, which causes the product to build up pressure which will force it through a perforated plate at the discharge end of the cylinder.   The material is cut off by a rotary knife which chops the material as it is forced through the perforations in the plate.   The meat material is taken from the inlet, picked up by the screw, and forced through in a continuous manner.   Equipment of this type can be obtained with capacities up to 10,000 lb per hr of meat.   The power requirement is from 25 to 40 hp depending upon the size and capacity.

The diameter of the cut plate on the large size machine is 8 in.   The auger is made of heavily tinned iron.   The fineness of the grind is determined by the size of the perforations in the cut plate, and the number of rotations of cutters per minute.   A second type of grinder or cutter, utilizes a twin screw feed.

A third type of cutter used to make sausage, chopped beef, etc., consists of a flat metal table on which a rotating cutter operates at such a manner as to continually work through the meat and chop it or cut it into small pieces.   Machines of this type are said to cause less bruising of the meat and give more of a cut sharp appearance to the meat particles than that obtained from the squeezing type of cutter which forces the meat through a perforated plate and then cuts it off.

The rotating cutter type of machine can be obtained in capacities from 300 to 9,000 lb per hr.

A similar type of machine called the dicer is also used.   This operates on fresh or chilled meat and works best at about 29°F.   A ram drives the material down through a coarse opening or series of openings, and a rotating cutter cuts the particles off into pieces of a certain size.

Stuffer Equipment

A popular type of stuffer is a twin screw machine, (Fig. S.1) which receives the ground material and forces it through a die and into a tube onto which the sausage cover is fastened.

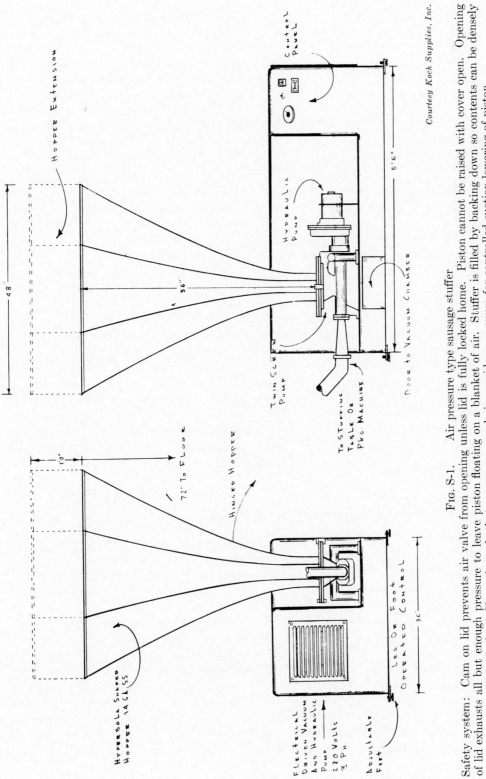

Courtesy Koch Supplies, Inc.

Fig. S-1.   Air pressure type sausage stuffer

Safety system: Cam on lid prevents air valve from opening unless lid is fully locked home.   Piston cannot be raised with cover open.   Opening of lid exhausts all but enough pressure to leave piston floating on a blanket of air.   Stuffer is filled by backing down so contents can be densely packed.   A Venturi nozzle that uses compressed air provides a vacuum for controlled suction lowering of piston.

Another type of stuffer widely used is an air-operated piston operating in a cylinder. The procedure is as follows: (1) the ground meat is placed in the cylinder, (2) the air pressure engaged, and (3) the piston forces the material out through one or more tubes onto which the sausage casing has been fastened. Usually the piston is operated by air at 175 psi. Equipment is available for automatically making the sausages in links.

Cross-reference: *Slaughter House Design and Facilities.*

SCRAPED SURFACE HEAT EXCHANGER

The scraped surface heat exchanger is a special type of heat exchanger and mixer that can be used for either heating or cooling and at the same time agitating or mixing a product.

The unit consists essentially of a tubular heat exchanger which is jacketed for either cooling or heating in which a rotator or scraper agitator operates. The product to be treated is pumped into one end of the tube and is discharged at the opposite end. The heat exchanger tubes may be used singly or in stacks thereby increasing the capacity.

The rate of heat exchange is very high due to the excellent agitation and mixing of the product. The unit is used primarily for heating viscous materials which could not ordinarily be heated or cooled readily in a regular tubular heater.

The capacity of the equipment varies considerably depending upon the viscosity of the product being treated and upon the temperature difference between the heating or cooling medium and the product being treated. Complete performance tables are available from the manufacturer. This equipment is widely used in the cooling of margarine and similar types of materials. The equipment can be used to incorporate a gas or vapor with the product in a continuous manner.

Cross-references: *Evaporators; Heat Exchangers.*

SEED AND GRAIN CLEANING AND GRADING

Cleaning and grading are two extremely important steps in the production of high-quality seed crops and grain. The quality of flour, bread, beans, or macaroni is affected by the purity and the cleanliness of the seeds which go into these products. Wheat with impurities makes poor flour. Off-color pea beans are not acceptable to the housewife. Uniform color of coffee beans is often desirable.

Orderly marketing and purchasing of grain and seeds has been enhanced by established cleaning and grading procedures. Some of the cleaning and grading can be done by the farmer or by commercial concerns. The economics involved determines where the processing is done. Cleaning is often done on the farm and grading off the farm.

Seed which is to be planted should be free of other crop seeds, straw and chaff, sand, dust, smut kernels, and diseased or damaged seeds. State seed laws prohibit the sale of seeds which contain certain undesirable weeds. Since most harvested crops as obtained by the farmer include impurities, cleaning of the grain and seed crops is required before they are used for seeds or processed into food products.

Terminology

Screening refers to the separation of material into two or more size fractions. When only a few large particles are removed in an initial process, the process is known as scalping. Cleaning is the removal of foreign or dissimilar material, and might include washing. Grading is the sorting of products into various quality fractions

TABLE S.1

SCREENS FOR SOME AGRICULTURAL PRODUCTS—FOR TWO-SCREEN CLEANERS

Product	Upper Screen	Lower Screen
Alfalfa	$1/14$ or $1/15$	6×24
Barley	22, 21, or 20	$1/13 \times 1/2$
Beans		
Lima	48	20
Baby lima	30	19
White pea (navy)	20	$11/64 \times 3/4$
Yellow large soy	20	$11/64 \times 3/4$
Small black soy	18	$7/64 \times 3/4$
Great Northern	24	$11/64 \times 3/4$
Beet seed	22 or 20	8
Brome grass	$1/13$ or $1/2$	6×24 or 9 TRI
Bluegrass, Kentucky	26×26	6×40
Cane seed	10	$1/13 \times 1/2$
Clover		
Alsike	$1/19$	6×32
Ladino	$1/20$	6×32
Crimson	$1/13$	6×22
Red	$1/15$	6×22 or 6×24
Sweet	$1/14$	6×24
Corn, cleaning	28, 30	16
Cotton seed, acid delinted	36	$13/64 \times 3/4$
Flax, golden	$1/14 \times 1/4$	6
Kaffir corn	12	$1/12 \times 1/2$
Lespedeza, Korean	6×15	$1/16$
Melon		
Water	24	16
Mush	16	9
Oats	$11/64 \times 3/4$	$1/14 \times 1/2$ or 11 TRI
Orchard grass	$1/22 \times 1/2$	6×32 or .5 TRI
Peas		
Blackeye	22	$10/64 \times 3/4$
Cow	21	$11/64 \times 3/4$
Popcorn, pearl	20	11
Rice		
Paddy	20 or 21	$1/14 \times 1/2$, 6 or 7
Hulled	12	14×14
Rye grass	$3/64 \times 5/16$	$6 \times 32 \times 5$ TRI
Rye	12	$1/16 \times 1/4$ or $1/14 \times 1/2$
Sunflower seed	24 to 32	11
Timothy	$1/19$ or $1/20$	6×34 or 6×32
Tobacco seed	32×32	40×40, 50×50
Tomato seed	10	$1/12$
Wheat	14	$1/13 \times 1/2$, 10 TRI

under a recognized, standard classification on the basis of commercial value and usage, and depends on more factors than size.   Grading standards might be established by governments, association, or individual growers.

Methods

The size of particles is probably the characteristic most commonly used in separating solid materials into grades.   Many grades are based primarily on size with additional consideration given to quality factors.   Quality factors would include color, plumpness of kernel, test weight, moisture content, germination, mold growth, and conformity to the shape normally expected for the product.

The size of various grades of agricultural products may be based on diameter, length, width, thickness, minimum diameter, or maximum diameter.

The density, or specific gravity, of particles in a mixture is also a commonly used factor in separating materials, particularly for cleaning.   When using air for separation, some of the light kernels of acceptable size are removed.   A combination of screens and air is often used to separate or classify seeds (Table S.1).

Screens

Screens are normally available in perforated or wire cloth with round holes, oblong holes, or triangular holes.   The size of the perforation is designed in fractions of an inch, as $1/16$ in., $1/18$ in., $1/20$ in., or a hole number representing the number of $1/64$ in., i.e., 22, which represents twenty-two $1/64$ in.   An oblong opening might be represented as 16 by $3/4$ where the hole is $16/64$ in. wide and $3/4$ in. long.   The triangular hole is normally designated in $1/64$ in. dimensions.

Pneumatic Separation

Air is used for pneumatic separation of products according to differences in size, shape, density, and surface air resistance characteristics.   Air is supplied by a centrifugal fan with an adjustable inlet for controlling the flow.

Air is moved vertically through a chamber into which the product to be cleaned or separated is admitted.   Material not carried by the air screen drops on a tray and is removed.   The other material which can be carried by the air stream is lifted to an air separator from which it is removed from the system.   This unit can be used for separa-

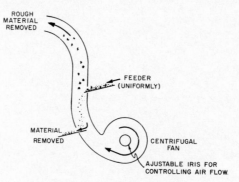

FIG. S-2.   Pneumatic separator

tion of dry or wet materials. Successful operation depends upon proper adjustment of airflow and uniform feeding of the product into the air stream. Stainless steel units are available for handling human food products (Fig. S.2).

Specific Gravity Separators

Specific gravity separators are designed to separate materials by taking advantage of the differences in specific weights of the components of the mixture. The process consists of floating the lighter chaff and seeds on a film of air, aided by mechanical agitation. The machine consists of a triangular, tilted table with a deck through which air can pass. Air is blown through the cloth or perforated metal surface of the table at a controlled rate. The deck acts as a vibrating conveyor (Fig. S.3).

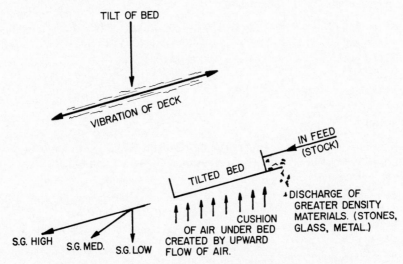

FIG. S-3.   Separating dry commodities by specific gravity

The material is fed in at one corner of the deck. The air moving up stratifies the material according to density. The light materials float to the lower end of the table and the heavier materials sink to the deck and are bounced forward to the upper end of the deck. Gravity separators are used primarily for removing certain weed seeds and other legume seeds and for cleaning and grading of beans. Stones, glass, metal, and similar items are discharged at the upper end bottom of the deck, because of their greater density. Channels are provided for removing low-, medium-, and high-specific gravity materials from one side of the inclined bed.

Operation of Gravity Separator

Some operators clean grains ahead of the gravity table, so the gravity unit can be used for closer separation or grading. The operator can control the airflow, tilting of the table, and vibration of the table. All of these are very critical and must be checked periodically as slight changes in the seed or its moisture content will cause a change in the separation.

Aspirator

An aspirator is used to remove hulls, bees wings, dust, and light screenings. A suction fan draws air through thin streams of grain. Separation of the light materials from the heavier grain kernels is made by the upward moving air stream, which, in effect, weighs the light and heavy material, removing the light. The lighter portions are carried upward to a chamber where the air is slowed down and removed and the lighter portions settle out and fall into an auger conveyor for removal. The volume of airflow is regulated to secure the desired separation. Aspirators are adopted to high volume cleaning when light materials are the principal impurities and work on the same principle as blowing air from the bottom up through the material, but are named differently because of the method of moving the air.

Separation Based on Shape of Particle

Seeds or other materials may be separated on the basis of shape differences. Round seeds tend to roll and may be separated from long or irregularly shaped seeds by gravity or centrifugal force. The round seeds roll away from the regular seeds and may be drawn off into separate containers. In other devices short seeds may be lifted from long seeds in pockets which will take only the short seeds.

Disc Separator

Many grains and seeds are almost the same dimension in width and thickness and are difficult to separate on screen-type equipment; however, these seeds are often of different lengths. Oat, for example, is longer than wheat. Corn cockle, on the other hand, is shorter than wheat. By taking advantage of these differences in length, separation can be made by a disc type or cylinder separator (Fig. S.4).

The cylinder separator consists of a revolving drum with indentations or pockets which are used for collecting the short seed. The short seeds are carried to the top of the cylinder and dropped into an auger for removal.

A disc separator operates on the same principle as a cylinder separator. It consists primarily of a series of discs mounted on a horizontal shaft. Each disc contains hundreds of small pockets which select or reject grain according to length. The material to be separated is fed into the head end of the machine. The shorter materials are lifted out of the mass of grain by the small pockets in the rotating discs. The pockets are designed so that the particles will be dropped out into a spout before the pocket completes its revolution and dips into the grain. In this manner the small particles are removed and the larger particles moved on through the machine by angled flights on the spokes of the discs or by a helical ribbon conveyor. Separation into three sized classes is possible by arranging the disc size, so that a small disc pocket is used at the first half of the separator, followed by discs with larger pockets. An arrangement for wheat could take out cockle at the small pocket discs, wheat at the large pocket discs, and discharge oats and barley at the tailings end.

The cylinder separator consists of a horizontal cylinder with pockets on the inside. Material is fed into the bottom of the cylinder, which rotates and will take the short seeds, leaving the long seeds, moving the short ones around the periphery of the circle subscribed by the cylinder. The small ones are dropped near the top of the path into an auger or flight conveyor for removal.

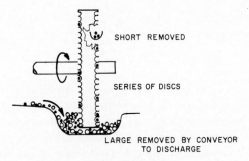

SHORT REMOVED

SERIES OF DISCS

LARGE REMOVED BY CONVEYOR
TO DISCHARGE

A. DISC SEPARATOR

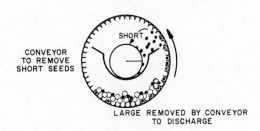

CONVEYOR
TO REMOVE
SHORT SEEDS

SHORT

LARGE REMOVED BY CONVEYOR
TO DISCHARGE

B. CYLINDER SEPARATOR

FIG. S-4.   Length separator

Round seeds can be separated from irregular seeds or from flat seeds with special equipment, such as the spiral separator.

The inclined belt separator, sometimes called the Draper machine, is used for separation of flat and round seeds. Material is fed from above on a belt at an appropriate angle so that round seeds will not stay on the belt, but roll back into a separate container, and flat seeds remaining on the belt are carried up the belt and over the end. The speed of the belt and angle can be changed to obtain the desirable separation (Fig. S.5).

A bumper machine is used for separation of round and flat seeds. The material is set onto a plate which bumps against a side wall. During bumping, the round material rolls off and the flat material is removed from the plate into a separate hopper.

Surface Characteristics

Materials used for surface separation include muslin, velvet, velveteen, and flannel.

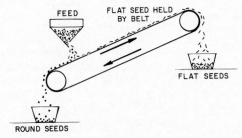

FEED

FLAT SEED HELD
BY BELT

FLAT SEEDS

ROUND SEEDS

FIG. S-5.   Inclined belt separator-draper machine

Another surface characteristic which is often helpful for separation is a surface or seed coat which becomes sticky when wet.

Color Sorting

Color is used as a basis for separating products for which a premium is placed on color uniformity. White navy pea beans, coffee beans, and certain nuts are examples. Top quality beans do not contain any dark colored beans or discolored beans. Since beans are often damaged and discolored by unfavorable weather in the field, it is necessary to pick the off-color beans. Previously this was done by hand, but recently mechanical bean sorters have been developed which utilize the electric eye to differentiate between acceptable and off-color beans.

The electronic sorting machines are normally preceded by pneumatic separators and gravity tables to remove stems, leaves, and irregular shaped beans. Photoelectric sorting may be used for separating on the basis of hue (color), such as the removal of green from yellow products, and relative brightness, which is the removal of white from grey materials, or bright green from dull green materials. Such separation may be used for beans, green coffee, peas, peanuts, or lemons.

The sorting machine consists of: (1) a device to feed the material at a uniform rate, (2) the object to be viewed, (3) the response to be amplified, remembered and transmitted, and (4) a device for ejecting undesirable (or desirable) materials.

One machine consists of a rotating disc with about 60 vacuum nozzles around the edge which pick up the individual beans from a hopper. The disc rotates past a photoelectric cell which is tuned to respond to various colors. When an off-color product passes the photoelectric cell a plunger or air jet is activated to remove the defective bean from the vacuum nozzle into a trough. The acceptable products are

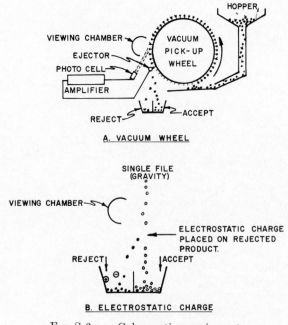

Fig. S-6.   Color sorting equipment

thrown off the discs by centrifugal force at a certain point where the vacuum is also shut off.

Conventional electronic sorting machines have been modified to sort wet beans. Even though beans were sorted prior to soaking it was necessary to sort again after soaking and blanching to remove damaged and discolored beans which hadn't appeared earlier.

Another electric sorting device will view individual beans as they are dropped from a belt in front of or past an electric eye. After being viewed, if the product is unacceptable, it is given a charge through a 18,000-volt source. The charged products are then pulled to one side as they pass an oppositely charged plate, and the acceptable and rejects fall into separate containers (Fig. S.6).

Debearding

To remove the beards from barley, or the tails from oats and similar products, rotating beater arms are used for rubbing the commodity against a stationary arm or bar or screen. A standard hammer mill operated at a speed lower than that used for grinding will often accomplish this objective. This equipment is also used for hulling some seeds.

Polisher

A cleaning agent, such as sawdust, bran, or middlings, is used for cleaning products like white pea beans. The beans are forced through the cleaning agent, at which time the surface is brightened, considerable mold is removed, and dirt and discoloration is removed.

X ray

X-ray techniques may be used to detect rodent urine in grain.

Reference

HALL, C. W. 1963. Processing Equipment for Agricultural Products. Edwards Brothers, Ann Arbor, Mich.

Cross-reference: *Sifters.*

SENSIBLE AND LATENT HEAT

Heat may be added to change the temperature of a gas, liquid, or solid. All of the heat added that is used for changing the temperature, that is, for increasing the kinetic energy of the molecules, is known as sensible heat because it can be sensed with the thermometer. The specific heat value is used for calculating this sensible heat.

Heat added or subtracted to change the state is known as latent heat. Latent heat is involved in changing state from solid to liquid to gas, with heat being added. Heat is removed to change states from a gas to liquid to solid. Heat absorbed or given up at a constant temperature during fusion, that is, melting, or solidification is called the latent heat of fusion, and is expressed in heat units per unit mass. For water or ice, the latent heat is 144 Btu per lb or 89 cal per gm.

The heat added to change a state is involved as internal or potential energy of the body, and is effective in changing the distance between molecules, but none of the heat added increases the kinetic energy. The state of matter is dependent upon the distance between molecules. The closer the molecules the more dense.

For a substance which contracts on melting, as ice, an increase of pressure lowers the melting point of the substance. Upon melting, ice will contract about 9%.

Freezing Point

The freezing point of a solution is lower than that of the pure solvent. As a soluble material is added to water, the freezing point becomes lower. The greater the concentration (to a certain point) the lower the freezing point. One gram molecular weight of substance dissolved in 1,000 gm of water will cause a decrease in the freezing point of 1.86°C (3.35°F). The addition of water to milk can be very accurately detected by a raising of the freezing point of the product. The unit used for detecting such adulteration is known as a cryoscope.

For very concentrated solutions, the solute will leave the solvent upon freezing, and the solvent will freeze as a pure substance. The temperature at which the freezing point is not lowered by the addition of solute is known as the eutectic (Fig. F.24). To the right of the eutectic and below the line, saturated liquid exists, and to the left of the eutectic below the line, saturated solid. The eutectic is the point at which the freezing point is the lowest at a particular concentration of solution.

There are two kinds of freezing or fusion. These are known as crystalline, e.g., ice, or amorphous. With crystalline freezing, the change of state takes place at one temperature only. With amorphous freezing, the viscosity increases as the temperature decreases with freezing. During the solidification of lactose in dry milk, depending upon the temperature, humidity, and time, either type of structure may be obtained.

Latent Heat

The latent heat of a eutectic made up of a salt and water solution is of a lower value than the latent heat of pure water. The eutectic point is also applied to a mixture of two metals forming an alloy, where the freezing point or temperature of solidification is lower than the temperature of either individual component.

The quantity of heat involved in changing the state from a liquid to a gas or gas to liquid, identified as the latent heat of vaporization or latent heat of evaporation, when going from liquid to gas for water is 970 Btu per lb or 540 cal per gm, at 0 psig. The boiling point is identified as that temperature at which there is vaporization throughout the liquid. The boiling point is increased as a solute is added to the solvent.

Vaporization and Condensation

The effect on the boiling point is important in the change of temperature of vaporization when producing condensed products. The magnitude of the increase in the boiling point is related to the molecular weight of the solute to the volume or weight of the solvent. Thus, the change in boiling point can also be used as a means of determining the molecular weight of a nonvolatile substance. One gram molecular weight

(1 mole) of a substance dissolved in 1,000 gm of water, will cause an increase in the boiling point of 0.9°F, or 0.5°C.

The temperature of vaporization can be changed by changing the pressure above the liquid. By increasing the pressure above the liquid, the boiling point increases, and the latent heat decreases. The values of boiling point versus pressure and the quantity of latent heat involved are incorporated in steam tables for water. Similar relationships with different values exist for refrigerants and other chemicals involved in a change of state.

The reverse effect, the change of state from a gas to a liquid, is known as condensation. The temperatures, pressures, and latent heat values are exactly the same for condensation as for vaporization.

There is considerable increase in volume per pound of product as the liquid changes to a vapor. The volume of water vapor at 100°C (212°F) and at sea level atmospheric pressure is about 1,700 times the volume of the original liquid water. A cubic inch of water when vaporized produces about a cubic foot of steam.

The increase in temperature above the normal boiling point is proportional to the concentration of the added solute and inversely proportional to the molecular weight of the solute.

Distillation

Distillation is a process involving first vaporization followed by condensation. The liquid to be distilled is heated in a suitable container and the vapor produced is passed through a condenser which can be cooled so that the gas changes to a liquid. The liquid produced is free from the solid matter it originally contained. Distilled water is obtained by this process.

Sublimation

Some substances pass from the solid to the vapor state without going through the liquid state. The process is known as sublimation. Dry Ice or carbon dioxide in a solid form is used for cooling or freezing. The Dry Ice sublimes or passes directly to the vapor state upon absorbing heat. Pressure can be used to make the product pass through the liquid state.

Solidification

The quantity of heat which must be removed to change fat from a liquid to a solid (as well as other organic compounds) is known as the heat of solidification. The temperature at which milk solidifies is from 24.5° to 19°C. The fat does not solidify at one temperature, but begins to solidify and is considered to be very nearly solid at the lower temperature.

Melting Point

The Handbook of Chemistry and Physics (1968) gives the melting point for the insoluble fatty acids in butterfat as 38° to 41°C. The heat of solidification of fat in milk is 20 cal per gm. The quantity of heat involved in the change of state of organic compounds where the percent of material solidifying changes with the temperature is often incorporated as a part of the sensible heat and called apparent specific heat.

Reference

THE CHEMICAL RUBBER PUBLISHING CO. 1968. Handbook of Chemistry and Physics. Cleveland, Ohio.

Cross-references: *Cryoscope; Specific Heat; Steam.*

SEPARATORS

The usual practice for separation of cream from milk has been to heat the milk to at least 90°F and as high as 160°F. As the temperature is increased, the viscosity is less and more efficient separation is obtained. Recently developed separators are designed for cold milk separation. Such separators eliminate the necessity of heating milk before separation.

The separator may be used before or after the milk is placed in the vat pasteurizer. The product may be preheated to approximately 145°F, followed by separation, then pasteurization in the vat. Another procedure is to separate the pasteurized product before cooling.

In a high-temperature short-time unit it is common to place the separator after the flow diversion valve. When in forward flow the product moves through the flow diversion valve, through an orifice to a surge tank, to the separator feed pump, and then to the separator. The purpose of the orifice is to restrict the flow from the holding tube and flow diversion device when the separator feed pump is operating, so that the holding time is not affected. Two paths are possible for the skim and cream leaving the separator. The warm pasteurized cream or skim milk may be sent to a cooler. Or the warm pasteurized cream or skim milk may be sent to the regenerator and cooler from which it can go to bottling or other storage. Both of these products cannot take the same route. If the warm pasteurized cream goes to the cooler then the common procedure would be to direct the warm pasteurized skim milk through the regenerator and the cooler of the HTST unit.

There are two basic types of centrifugal separators: in one type the flow is controlled by gravity flow of the product, and in the other the rate of flow is controlled by a pump. The airtight separator utilizes a hermetically sealed unit providing a sanitary system which, in addition, permits very little air incorporation into the product. It is important that the proper size pump be used with the separator to avoid excess fat losses or excessive cost of operation.

The control of the separator in a high-temperature short-time system should receive special attention. A separator may continue to operate if the timing pump stops, since the flow through the separator is controlled by the separator pump. It is advisable to electrically connect the separator to the timing pump so that the timing pump will stop if the separator stops. If the separator does not require a feed pump (other than the timing pump) and does not have a vacuum at the inlet of the separator when the separator is running, and the timing pump is stopped, a break to atmosphere such as surge tank or separator pump is not required between the HTST pasteurizer and the separator. When a surge tank is used, an orifice or other fixed flow control should be placed in the line ahead of the surge tank. A control device should also be used upstream from the separator when used without a surge tank and pump to maintain the legal holding time, when the separator is being used. The separator should be placed in the system so that its omission will not require disassembling of the system.

Cross-references: *Centrifugal Separators; Clarifiers; HTST Pasteurization Systems; Ultracentrifuge.*

SHAFTS

In the food processing industry line shafting has practically disappeared in favor of direct drive. However, there are many places where short shafting is still used. Cold rolled line shafting is widely used. Alloy shafting of greatly increased strength and fatigue value may be obtained for special purposes. It is important that the deflection of shafting be limited to about 0.01 in. per ft length. Also shafting should have bearings not more than 8 ft apart, and pulley or gears should be close to the bearings. For shafts subjected to shocks and bending action of pulleys and gears, additional factors of safety should be provided. Table S.2 shows accepted standards of design.

SHIPPING DOCKS

Shipping docks are important in the materials handling system of food processing plants, since the average processing plant must receive thousands of pounds of raw material each day and in turn ship it out after processing.

Use

The shipping docks in small plants are often used for both receiving and loading, however, in most large plants there is a receiving dock on one side or end of the building and the ship-out dock may be on the opposite side. The respective locations must be coordinated with the general plant materials handling system.

Materials Handling

The materials handling flow in a milk plant starts at the unload area where empties are taken from the truck. From here the flow is through the bottle-washing and case-storage area to the filling and casing area where the product meets the package. The filled bottles are cased and the cases then are moved to the refrigerated storage area and then out to the load-out area to the distribution trucks. This flow pattern is followed in every milk plant regardless of the size of the plant. It is within

TABLE S.2

CAPACITY OF COLD ROLLED STEEL SHAFTING, WELL-SUPPORTED AND WITH PULLEYS NEXT TO BEARINGS, HORSEPOWER

Diam of Shaft, In.	Rpm					
	100	200	300	400	500	600
1.5	3.7	7	11	15	18	22
2.0	8.9	17	27	35	44	53
2.5	17.0	35	52	69	87	104
2.75	23.0	46	69	92	115	138
3.00	30.0	60	90	120	150	180

this materials handling flow pattern that the greatest share of labor hours is expended in most food plant operations. It is within this system also that the planned application and installation of conveyors and case and bottle handling equipment can do much to reduce labor costs and thereby contribute to a substantial increase in overall plant efficiency. Much of the flow of cases, cans, and containers is done by conveyors.

Design

The actual design of the shipping dock must depend upon the type of equipment to be loaded or unloaded. For example in a plant which receives its product in bulk liquid, the receiving room is principally, an open space, where tank trucks can be driven in and unloaded by means of a flexible sanitary hose. The floor must be on a slope so that the truck will drain thoroughly.

Facilities may be needed to wash and sanitize the trucks. The room itself must be of sanitary design to meet health department requirements.

In some plants the product may be received in tank cars. The procedure is much the same as for tank trucks, except that facilities are larger.

Important parts of the receiving docks are the pumping or the conveying system, the storage facilities, and methods of weighing and testing the product as it is received.

For standard receiving rooms the dock height is usually 42 to 46 in. so that when trucks back up to unload, the bottom of the truck body is approximately level with the dock height. Some shipping rooms use a floating dock which is adjustable to the height of the truck body.

There are many special receiving arrangements, as for example in handling fruits and vegetables, in lugs, boxes, crates, or in bulk. Each must be designed for the purpose to unload the product quickly, without damage to the material and with minimum labor.

The use of pallets or tote bins is another example of special handling which is finding wide acceptance in industry.

Load-out Docks

Shipping out is an operation which also covers many variables depending upon the product, the package, and the size of plant. Here, one of the problems is how to prevent congestion and to quickly load out, often to trucks which will carry a considerable assortment of products.

Two typical examples of load-out docks are the "Hollywood—or Island Cooler" system, and the "Long Dock" system. Both are widely used in the dairy business but can be readily adapted to other products. A description of each follows:

The Hollywood—or "Island Cooler" Storage Box

This style of box was developed a few years ago on the West Coast, and it has now become relatively popular in other areas of the country. This type of refrigerated storage box is designed long and narrow, usually less than 40 ft wide. An in-floor conveyor is placed down the center of the box with embossed metal flooring covering the floor. Along each wall of the box, load-out doors are placed on about 10-ft centers. Route loads are made up during the day from load sheets prepared one day in advance.

These loads are prepared during the production period and stacked behind each door. There are usually 3 to 6 loads per door. The distribution truck then loads directly from each assigned door with the driver doing the loading of the truck without anyone in the refrigerated storage area directly assisting with the loading. By loading 3 to 6 loads per door in this manner it is possible to load out a great many trucks with only a one-man load-out crew and in a short period of time with a minor amount of truck congestion in the load-out area. During the load-out time the one-man load-out crew in the box handles additions and deletions to the driver's load that may be required because of changes in his load schedule from the day before.

This is an ideal way to handle load-out for large and medium-sized plants with a high percentage of retail distribution. Smaller wholesale trucks could also be handled in this type of refrigerated cooler, although generally wholesale trucks and semitrailer transports are loaded using the long-dock method.

The "Long Dock" Method

This method features the use of an in-floor conveyor running from the refrigerated storage area along a dock outside the plant. The dock may or may not be covered. The dock may be parallel to the plant or extended directly out from the plant. Most long-dock systems follow the procedure of preparing the loads in advance in the refrigerated storage area. When the truck returns from the delivery route, empties are then unloaded usually on the same dock. If the plant is using a self-contained refrigerated delivery truck, then the trucks could be loaded immediately after they have discharged their empties by sending the loads directly out to the truck in stacks. If a truck is not refrigerated self-contained, it will be loaded in the morning by sending the loads in stacks down the dock for loading. Several trucks can receive their loads quickly in about the same period of time. The in-floor conveyor is usually placed 3 to 4 ft from the edge of the dock so that retail and wholesale drivers can pull their loads off the conveyor for loading and permit following loads to go on down the dock to other load positions. The Hollywood-style box is usually more expensive to install and put in operation owing to the great number of doors required for the box. The primary advantages of both the Hollywood and long-dock methods of loading are rapid load-out of all trucks with minimum manpower and case handling in the refrigerated case storage area during the load-out period.

Both the Hollywood box and long-dock methods may be used in a plant. This is common practice in most modern plants, because it enables the plants to take full advantage of labor saving resulting from stack handling techniques in the three areas of load-out, unload, and empty case storage. While the Hollywood-box method has the advantage of less labor cost, its disadvantage is that it has a higher building equipment and electricity cost.

Distribution Stations

Plants located in large metropolitan areas are beginning to find it relatively uneconomical to distribute with the standard retail and/or wholesale truck to the suburban areas which may be located 30 to 50 miles away from the mother plant.

In addition the increase in capacity of food-plant processing and package-handling equipment has made it possible for large plants in metropolitan areas to produce a large volume of product easily in one plant. These high-volume plants have found it more economical to distribute to the outlying areas and smaller towns that they serve through remote distribution points which are commonly called "satellite docks." These satellite docks may be located as much as 250 to 300 miles away from the mother plant. Product is hauled out to these distribution areas or docks by over-the-road transport trailers. The retail and wholesale trucks based at the satellite docks receive the daily supply of product at the satellite dock from the daily delivery by transport.

The larger plants have found that the volume of retail businesses at great distances from the mother plant can be increased by offering better service to the consumer, and further cut their truck-operating costs by running one truck between the mother plant and the satellite dock rather than having several trucks going approximately the same distance. This method of handling increased the marketing area for any one plant.

Satellite docks usually consist of a dock 20 to 100 ft long with an in-floor conveyor running down the center of the dock. There may be a small refrigerated storage box at one end of the dock. The transport will pull out that one end of the dock and discharge stacks on to the in-floor conveyor which will carry the stacks down to the several retail and wholesale trucks located along either side of the dock. Usually 20 to 30 retail and wholesale trucks combined can be accommodated at one satellite dock efficiently and economically.

When used, the satellite dock is usually long and narrow. Other shapes may be used depending upon the available area, the style and type of distribution, and the types of semitrailer trucks. Satellite docks are usually operated by one sales manager with facilities for service for the truck such as a gas pump, a garage area for minor repairs, and a truck-washing area. The semitrailer hauling to the dock will pick up the empty cases and return them to the main plant each day. Empty cases are stored on the dock until pickup occurs.

References

Botz, H. A., and Hagemann, G. E. (Editors). 1958. Materials Handling Handbook. The Ronald Press Co., New York.

Carliss, O. S. 1962. Modern Materials Handling Concepts. Proc. 1st Natl. Food Eng. Conf., East Lansing, Mich.

Heyman, H. W. 1959. Economic Considerations in the Design and Operation of Milk Delivery Transport. Intern. Dairy Congr. 15th, London, *1*.

Cross-references: *Forklift Trucks; Materials Handling.*

SIFTERS

Sifting is a separation of material by particle size and plays a very important role in industrial processing. A sifter or screen separator is referred to by several terms including screening, bolting, rebolting, classifying, scalping, separating, or grading. The term used varies with the particular process and industry.

Capacity

The capacity of a sifter is determined in part by the penetration rate of a product through the separating screen. An objective of a sifter is to expose each particle of product to as many screen openings as possible. Some variations are found in the motion of a separating screen. If the separating screen can achieve a stratifying action which causes the larger particles to rise to the top of the mass very quickly, the capacity is increased. Without stratification, complete particle size separation is difficult to achieve except through the use of excessive screen area. Figure S.7 illustrates the movement of material with three common types of sifting screen motions.

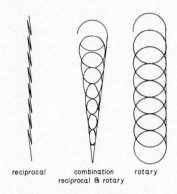

reciprocal   combination   rotary
reciprocal & rotary

FIG. S-7.   Motion of sifting screens

Motion

With reciprocal action the material flows essentially in a straight line across the screen. On a screen which combines rotary and reciprocal action, the product assumes more rotary patterns near the discharge edge of the screen. Rotary sifters develop a circular motion for the product in its travel across the sieve. It is important to avoid overloading a sifter to obtain good particle separation. Sifters may be equipped with a wide variety of sieves to obtain the desired separations.

Flow

Sifting can vary from very simple flow arrangements involving a single separation to one having several separations and discharging of a number of product sizes. Some of these flow arrangements are shown graphically in Fig. S.8.

Size

The type of motion of a sifter, as well as size, shape, and design, varies considerably. Some rather small stainless steel single separation sifters are now available with high capacities. One of these is illustrated in Fig. S.9.

The 34-in. size sifter of this design has a rated capacity of 16,000 lb nonfat dry milk per hour with a 34 mesh U.S. Standard Screen. This unit operating on hard wheat flour has a rated capacity of 12,000 lb per hour with the 34 mesh U.S. Standard Screen.

Selecting the proper screen mesh is necessary for satisfactory results. Once the desired Y separations have been determined, deviation should be approached with caution. A comparison of screen mesh specifications is presented in Table S.3.

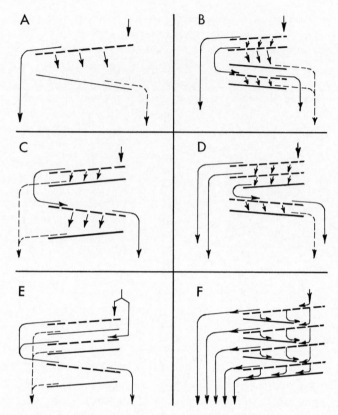

FIG. S-8. Product flow arrangements through typical sifter
A—Simple flow for making a single separation. B—Common flow for 2 separations and 3 product sizes. C—A single separation flow utilizing two sieves of the same mesh. D—Typical flow for 3 separations and 4 product sizes. E—A common single separation flow. F—This flow makes 4 separations for 5 product sizes.

Sanitation

Sanitation in the design of sifters is one major criterion to consider. With emphasis on the prevention of microbial contamination, the sanitary aspects and cleanability of this kind of equipment becomes extremely important. The purchaser of a new sifter should examine the cleaning procedures required to keep the equipment in satisfactory condition.

References

BLAW-KNOX CO., BURNS GUMP DIV. Bull. *505*, Rotary Sifters. Chicago, Ill.
SPROUT-WALDRON CO. Bull. *246-C*, Sanisift. Muncy, Pa.

SIZE DESIGNATION

Size Designation of Droplet

Little information is available, particularly for milk and food products, designating the droplet size specification for spray drying. Data on changes of the droplet as

Fig. S-9.   Stainless steel sifter

it proceeds from the nozzle to the dried particles are practically nonexistent.   A whole new field of investigation awaits the researcher who will develop means of obtaining data on droplet distribution, amalgamation, size, area, temperature, and volume as these variables change with time and as the droplet proceeds from the atomizer as a liquid until the powder is formed.

A frequency distribution curve relates the number or percentage of drops of various diameters, surface areas, volumes, or weights.   A normal distribution would provide a standard bell-shaped curve (Fig. S.10).   The cumulative distribution representation is also used considerably (Fig. S.11).   One hundred percent of the

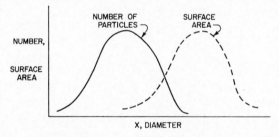

Fig. S-10.   Frequency distribution curves, particles

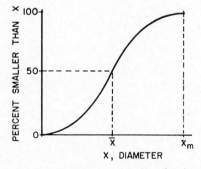

Fig. S-11.   Cumulative size distribution curve

TABLE S.3

SCREEN SPECIFICATION MESH COMPARISONS

U.S. Std.	Tyler Std.	Aper-ture	Mill Screen (Tinned or S.S.)	Durloy or S.S. Bolting Cloth	Tuf-tex	Silk Bolting Cloth				Grit Gauze	
						Std. Silk	X Silk	XX Silk	XXX Silk	G.G.	XXX G.G.
5		.157									
6		.132									
7		.111									
8		.0937									
		.0800	10								
10		.0787									
	9	.0780									
		.0689								14	
12		.0661									
	10	.0650	12								14
		.0620		14							
		.0600									16
		.0582								16	
14		.0555									
	12	.0550									
		.0540	14								
		.0535		16	16	0000					
		.0520						0000		18	
16		.0469									
		.0466		18	18						
		.0465	16								
	14	.0460								20	20
		.0420								22	
		.0410		20	20						
		.0406	18			000					
18		.0394									
	16	.0390									22
		.0380		22	22			000		24	
		.0360	20								24
		.0342		24	24						
20		.0331									
	20	.0328									
		.0320	22							26	26
		.0310		26	26					28	
		.0287	24			00		00		30	28
		.0282		28	28						30
25		.0280									
	24	.0276									
		.0275	26								
		.0268		30	30						
		.0257	28							32	
		.0248		32	32					34	32
		.0238	30								
30	28	.0232									34
		.0229		34	34	0				36	36
		.0223	32								
		.0213		36	36				0	38	38
		.0204	34								
		.0198		38	38					40	40
35		.0197									
	32	.0195									
		.0188	36							42	
		.0185		40	40					44	
		.0183		43	42						42
		.0178	38								
		.0172		46	44					46	44
40		.0165	40								
	35	.0164				1					46
		.0163		48							
		.0162			46						
		.0155		50				1		48	48
		.0153			48						

Table S.3 (*Continued*)

U.S. Std.	Tyler Std.	Aperture	Mill Screen (Tinned or S.S.)	Durloy or S.S. Bolting Cloth	Tuftex	Std. Silk	X Silk	XX Silk	XXX Silk	G.G.	XXX G.G.
		.0145		54	50					50	
		.0142	45			2				52	
45	42	.0138		56				2		54	50
		.0137			52						52
		.0132		58		3				56	54
		.0130			54					58	
		.0127		60	58						
		.0125	50			4		3			56
		.0122			60						
		.0121		62						60 & 62	58
50		.0117									
	48	.0116			62						60
		.0112	55	66							62
		.0111			64	5		4		64	
		.0106		70	66			5			64
		.0103			70					66	
		.0102	60	72							
		.0099			72						
60		.0098		74							
	60	.0097							6	68	66
		.0095		76	74	6				70	
		.0092			76			6			
		.0091		78			6		7		68
		.0088		80	78	7				72	
		.0085			80		7				70
		.0084		84							72
70		.0083									
	65	.0082						7	8		
		.0080			82	8					
		.0079		88	84		8				
		.0076			86			8			
		.0074			88				9		
		.0071		94	90						
80		.0070									
	80	.0069									
		.0067			92						
		.0066			94	9					
		.0065		105		10	9		10		
100		.0059									
	100	.0058					10	9			
		.0057		120		11					
		.0053					11	10	11		
		.0051		135							
120	115	.0049						11			
		.0047		145		12			12		
		.0042		165		13	12 & 13	12	13		
140	150	.0041									
		.0039				14	14	13	14		
		.0037				15	15	14 & 15	15		
170	170	.0035									
		.0034		200		16			16		
		.0032				17	16 & 17		17		
		.0031				18					
		.0030				19 & 20			18		
200	200	.0029		230							
		.0027				21					
		.0025				25					
230	250	.0024		270							
270		.0021									
325		.0017		325							
400		.0015									

Courtesy of Jabez-Burns-Gump Div., Blaw-Knox Co.

TABLE S.4

MEAN DIAMETERS

Mean Diameter	Symbol	Field of Application
Linear	$\bar{X}_a$	Evaporation
Surface	$\bar{X}_s$	Absorption (area involved)
Volume	$\bar{X}_v$	Distribution of mass in a spray
Surface diameter	$\bar{X}_{s-d}$	Adsorption
Volume, diameter	$\bar{X}_{v-d}$	Evaporation
Volume, surface (Sauter Method)	$\bar{X}_{vs}$	Mass transfer

Source: Mugele and Evans (1951)

drops would be the maximum size, X_m or less. The median diameter $\bar{X}$ is the point where 50% of the droplets (or some other variable) is included, and divides the spray into 2 equal portions. Table S.4 presents a recommended manner of designation and use of mean diameter which can be expressed by mathematical and statistical relationships (Marshall 1954). Most data presented pertaining to spray drying of milk and milk products are based on the mean diameter and do not include frequency distribution or the standard deviation from the mean diameter.

Dry Products

The size of dry product particles is designated by microns or mesh. A micron is 0.001 mm. Mesh refers to the number of screen openings per lineal inch. The opening also depends upon the wire size used in making the mesh material. The Tyler Sieve, the U.S. Scale sieve, and the BSS (British Standard Sieve) use different sizes of wires for making up the screen. Small particles will often stick together forming a larger apparent diameter of particle.

A 100-mesh Tyler sieve has an opening of 0.0058 in. or 0.147 mm which is equivalent to 147μ. The 400-mesh opening is equivalent to 38μ diam. For smaller sizes a microscopic analysis is made to determine the particle diameter.

Various methods may be used for representing the distribution of weight or distribution of size of particles involved. Excellent references covering these topics have been written by Lapple (1944, 1946).

Solids, Ground Products

The fineness of grind is usually designated as coarse, medium, or fine. The simplest term often used by manufacturers is called fineness. The fineness represents the initial diameter divided by the final diameter and whole numbers from 1 to 16 so obtained refer to the fineness. The recommended method is to designate the material by two numbers: (1) fineness modulus, and (2) uniformity index which represents the fineness of the material and the distribution of coarse, medium, and fine ingredients of the product.

A 1-lb sample of the ground grains or other dry products to be tested is placed on the top of 7 sieves and vibrated for 5 min with a Ro-tap machine. The 7 sieves are standard $^3/_8$ in. Tyler sieves of No. 4, 8, 14, 28, 48, and 100 mesh. After the test, the material remaining on each sieve is weighed and the percentage of material on each sieve calculated (Table G.3). The percentage of ground material accumulated on each sieve is multiplied by appropriate numbers from 7 to 0 and the products added.

The assigned number for sieve 8 is 5. For example, assume that the percentage of material collected on sieve 8 is 6%. Thus the product is 30. The products collected on the various sieves are added giving a total of 320, which is divided by 100 to give a fineness modulus of 3.2. A fineness modulus of 3.2 represents medium fineness. The fineness modulus gives no relationship of the proportion of coarse, medium, and fine materials in the product. It is possible to have two different samples of material with the same fineness modulus but with quite different constituents. The uniformity modulus was established to indicate the amounts of coarse, medium, and fine materials in the sample. The material collected on the top 3 sieves is considered as coarse, the next 2 sieves as medium, and the bottom 2 sieves and the pan as fine. The percentages collected in these groups are added making in the example given in Table S.5, 9.5% coarse, 67% medium, and 23.5% fine. The uniformity index is made up of 3 numbers, the sum of which is 10. Thus, the sum of the percentage on each sieve is divided by 10 to give a product which will add up to 100 divided by 10, or 10. The nearest whole number is assigned to the answer, so there is a relationship of 1:7:2 of coarse, medium, and fine in the example given in Table G.3. There are 66 different combinations for expressing the proportion of coarse, medium, and fine materials.

References

HALL, C. W. 1963. Processing Equipment for Agricultural Products. Edwards Brothers, Ann Arbor, Mich.

HALL, C. W., and HEDRICK, T. I. 1966. Drying of Milk and Milk Products. AVI Publishing Co., Westport, Conn.

LAPPLE, C. E. 1944. Mist and dust collection. Heating, Piping and Air Conditioning, *16*, No. 7, 410–414; No. 8, 464–466; No. 10, 578–581; No. 11, 635–640.

LAPPLE, C. E. 1945. Mist and dust collection. Heating, Piping and Air Conditioning, *17*, No. 11, 611–615.

LAPPLE, C. E. 1946. Mist and dust collection. Heating, Piping and Air Conditioning, *18*, No. 2, 108–113.

MARSHALL, W. R. JR. 1954. Atomization and spray drying. Amer. Inst. Chem. Eng. Monograph Ser. *50*, No. 2. New York.

MUGELE, R. A. and EVANS, H. D. 1951. Droplet size distribution in sprays. Ind. Eng. Chem. *43*, Part 1, 1317–1324.

Cross-references: *Grinders; Heat and Mass Transfer-Droplets.*

SLAUGHTER HOUSE DESIGN AND FACILITIES

Plant Location

Slaughtering and processing areas should be reasonably free from odors, smoke, ash, dust, etc. from other industry, dumps, or sewage. Adequate, dustproof access for shipping and receiving must be available. A slaughterhouse must be completely separated from any other building. When planning, give consideration to room for expansion when locating coolers, processing departments, etc. Facilities for handling inedible products should be in the rear of the plant.

Water Supply

Much cold and hot water (180°F) from a central heater will be needed. Mixing of steam and water at outlet is not acceptable for sterilizing contaminated material.

TABLE S.5

DIMENSIONS FOR SLAUGHTER HOUSE INSTALLATIONS

(Rail heights are measured from top of rail to highest part of floor)

Description		
	Vertical Distances	
	Ft	In.
Bleeding rail (distance from rail to point of application of shackle to shackled foot—48 in.)	16	0
Dressing rails (trolley length—15 in.)	11	0
Beef cooler rails (trolley length—15 in.)	11	0
Rails for beef quarters (trolley length—15 in.)	7	6
	Horizontal Distances	
Dry area in front of stunning pen	7 × 8 ft	
Curb of bleeding area to pritch plates (no header rail)	5	0
Line of drop-offs to line of half hoists (2 beds)	16	0
Line of drop-offs to line of half hoists (3 beds or more)	18	0
Line of half hoists to header rail leading to cooler (double rail)	14	0
Line of half hoists to header rail leading to cooler (single rail)	10	0
Between header rail and carcass washing rail, if parallel	6	0
Between header or washing rails and wall of slaughtering room	3	0
Between center lines of dressing beds	8	0
Between moving top table and dressing rail at inspector's platform	5	6
Area for sterilizing viscera inspection truck	7 × 8 ft	
	Vertical Distances	
Bleeding rails for calves (distance from top of rail to point of application of shackled to shackled foot—30 in.)	11	0
Bleeding rails if only sheep are slaughtered	9	0
Gambrels or leg hooks from which calf or sheep carcasses are suspended to floor or inspector's foot platform	7	6
Cooler rails, calf carcasses (gambrels, above floor)	7	6
Cooler rails, sheep carcasses on logs (hooks of logs, above floor)	6	6
	Horizontal Distances	
Vertical of rail to edge of viscera inspection stand	2	0
Length of rail from point of evisceration to point where carcass inspection is completed	6	0
	Vertical Distances	
Bleeding tail to sticker's platform	10	6
Extension of bleeding rail to top edge of scalding vat	9	0
Dressing rails	11	0
Gambrels (suspending carcasses) to floor (12 trolleys)	10	0
Rails in coolers for hog carcasses with heads removed (12 in. trolleys)	9	0
Rails in coolers for carcasses with heads attached (12 in. trolleys)	10	0
	Vertical Distances	
Bleeding rail	18	0
Dressing rails (trolley length 15 in.)	12	6
Cooler rails (trolley length 15 in.)	12	6
Cooler rails for carcasses in quarters	8	6

Table S.5 *(Continued)*

Description

	Horizontal Distances	
Line of drop-offs to line of half hoists	17	0
Clearance between walls, posts, etc., and adjoining rails in slaughtering rooms and coolers	3	0
Curb of bleeding area to pritch plates	6	0
Dry landing area (minimum)	7 × 8 ft	
	Vertical Distances	
Rails for sausage cages, etc.	7	6
Stationary or not readily movable equipment, from ceiling and from floor	1	0
	Horizontal Distances	
From vertical of rails in slaughtering rooms, coolers, etc., to walls, posts, and other fixed parts of the building	2	0
From vertical conveyor rails for sausage cages to stuffing tables	5	0
From vertical of carcass rails to edge of boning or cutting tables	7	0
Width of doors through which carcasses are railed	4	6
Width of doors through which product is conveyed in hand trucks	5	0
Truckways—unobstructed width	5	0
Stationary or not readily movable equipment, from wall	1	0

If water is from private wells, the wells must be on the premises and fully protected from pollution. If chlorinators are required, equip them with warning devices. Keep nonpotable water lines (for condensers or fire protection) out of edible product areas. Provide vacuum breakers on all water and steam lines.

Plant Drainage

Floors where wet operations are conducted must be drained with a uniform slope of about $1/4$ in. per ft (1 inlet for each 400 sq ft). Where limited water is used, the slope may be $1/8$ in. per ft. Drains are not required in freezer rooms or dry storage areas.

Unless floor drainage is carefully localized, drip valleys 2 ft wide are essential under dressing rails for cattle, calves, hogs, and sheep. Valleys must slope $1/8$ in. per ft to drains within the valleys. Drains inside the plant for cattle paunch contents should be cast iron or galvanized, 8 in. id, and for smaller animals, 6 in. id. All other drains must be at least 4 in. and trunk lines must be proportionately larger. Toilet soil lines must be separate from house drainage lines to a point outside the building and they must bypass the grease catch basin if one is present.

Every drain must be equipped with a deep seal trap, properly vented outside and equipped with rodent screens.

Where local ordinance permits, it is desirable to discharge into the municipal sewer system. If a private facility is used, it must be well-designed to prevent objectionable odors. No matter what system is used, a letter from the local health authority having jurisdiction indicating the system is satisfactory must be submitted to the inspector in charge.

Locate grease recovery basins away from edible products. Basins must have inclined bottoms and be without covers for easy cleaning. Provide suitable facilities for transfer and disposal of grease after it is skimmed from the basins. Blood, hair, and manure disposal must be provided for.

Plant Construction

Materials.—If a material is easy to clean, resistant to wear and corrosion, it is probably acceptable in edible product departments. Examples of unacceptable materials are plasterboard and acoustical tile.

Floors.—Two principal types of floors are used: (1) good quality vitrified brick, bonded with acid-resistant waterproof mortar laid on a waterproof concrete base, or (2) dense, acid-resistant waterproof concrete. Embedded abrasive particles in the surface, wood float (rough) surface and latex or synthetic base mortar will give good results. A cove radius of $1/2$ to 2 in. promotes sanitation at junctures of floors and walls in all rooms.

Interior Walls.—Use glazed brick, glazed tile, smooth Portland cement plaster or other nontoxic, nonabsorbent material for interior walls. Sanitary type bumpers (usually steel) will protect walls from damage by hand trucks and carcass shanks.

Ceilings.—Heights of 10 ft or more are desirable in workrooms. Use Portland cement plaster, large-size asbestos boards (sealed with flexible compounds), or other impervious materials. If joists are exposed, they must be at least 36 in. on center and without excessive crevices.

Window Ledges.—All window ledges should be sloped about 45°, with sills at least 36 in. from the floor to avoid damage from hand trucks or other equipment.

Door Widths.—Doorways for product transfer should be at least 5 ft wide. When 11-ft rails pass through doorways, then 4.5-ft doors may be used. Use metal or welded-seam metal covered wood doors and metal-covered jambs sealed with flexible compound.

Insect and Rodent Control.—Use screens on all openings and "fly chaser" fans on all outside entrances to food handling, shipping, and receiving areas. Except in the case of solid masonry walls, expanded metal mesh or wire screen ($1/2$ in. or smaller) should be embedded in walls and floors at their junction. This mesh should extend vertically and horizontally a sufficient distance to exclude entrance of rodents.

Other Interior.—Use dressed lumber for exposed woodwork, treated with nontoxic oil or plastic-base paint, hot linseed oil, or clear wood sealer. Stairs in edible product area shall be impervious, with solid treads and closed risers and side curbs of similar material, 6 in. high measured at the front edge of the treads.

Plant Lighting, Ventilation and Refrigeration.—All workrooms must have adequate ventilation and light with overall intensity of at least 20 foot candles. Where inspections are made, illumination must be at least 50 foot candles. Glass area of the skylights should be at least $1/4$ of the floor area. Use fixed windows and ventilate mechanically all areas subject to dust or objectionable odors. Use mechanical ventilation in refrigerated workrooms to prevent stagnation. Nonrefrigerated spaces ventilated entirely by mechanical systems must change the air six times hourly.

Equipment

All equipment must be constructed so that it can be cleaned readily. Surfaces contacting product must be smooth, free from pits, crevices, and scale.

Acceptable Materials.—Use rust-resisting metal, such as 18-8 (300 series) stainless steel, or plastic approved by U.S. Dept. of Agr. If galvanized steel is used in certain equipment it must be a high quality commercial hot dip.

Nonacceptable Materials.—Copper, cadmium, lead (except in the case of dairy solder not exceeding 5% lead), enamelware, and porcelain are not acceptable in any manner. Equipment with painted surfaces in the product zone is not acceptable.

Other Materials.—Plastics and resins must be approved by U.S. Dept. of Agr. before use. All gaskets and packing material must be nontoxic, nonporous, nonabsorbent, and unaffected by food and cleaning compounds.

Equipment Design and Construction.—Parts in the product zone must be easily demountable and readily accessible to sight and reach for cleaning and inspection. Quick opening devices and wing nuts on fixed studs are desirable for fast disassembly. Locate bearings outside the product zone with a readily removable seal at the food zone shaft entrance.

Interior corners should have a radius of at least $^1/_4$ in. The product zone must be free of open seams, gaps, ledges, threads, shoulders, bolts, rivets, or dead ends. Make welds smooth, even, and flush with adjacent surfaces. Where necessary for sanitation, equipment must be self-draining. Take care to avoid contamination by lubricants. Pumps and pipelines for edible product should be 18-8 type stainless steel or approved plastic.

Nonproduct Zone Construction.—Safety gear must be readily removable for cleaning and inspection. External surfaces must be free of open seams, gaps, and inaccessible recesses.

Equipment Installation.—Stationary or not readily removable equipment must be 1 ft from wall or ceiling and 1 ft above the floor (or completely sealed to the floor). Wall-mounted cabinets must be 1 in. from equipment or walls, or completely sealed. Water-wasting equipment, such as vats, sterilizers, and casing cleaners, must have drainage control without flowing over the floor. Drain valves must be easy to clean and flush with the bottom. Soaking and cooking vats need a 2-in. diam overflow with an open-end cleanout tee at the top. Design vent stacks (from cooking vats and hoods to preclude draining of condensate back into tank.

Work Tables.—Working surfaces should not be more than 34 in. above the floor. Higher work surfaces require metal foot platforms for employees to stand on. Tables having water on the working surfaces should be provided with turned-up edges of at least 1 in.

Cutting and Boning Boards.—Boards should be approved plastic or solid hardwood, not laminated. They should be in the shortest sections practical and easily removable for cleaning.

Cleanup Facilities.—For trucks, trays, tools, trees, or cages, provide a separate room or area with impervious floor, walls or ceiling, adequate drainage, light, and ventilating exhaust fan. Install approved lavatories in work areas and connect to drainage system. Sterilizers must be large enough to immerse knives or cleavers in scalding hot water. Provide drinking fountains in workrooms and dressing rooms. Sterilizers and fountains may drain into lavatory. Maintain hose connections and hose storage racks throughout plant. Avoid long hoses. All lavatories, sterilizers, fountains, and hose connections must show on drawings.

Edible Product Processing Facilities.—For efficiency, plan a proper flow without congestion or backtracking from receiving of raw materials to shipping of finished product. Boning and trimming, bacon slicing, pork cutting, sausage and frozen steak preparation require a temperature not higher than 50°F in rooms separated from carcass or holding coolers to avoid condensation and contamination by cleanup water. Product labeled "Frozen" must be frozen on the premises. Processed canned meat products require special retort tagging and incubation room.

Provide adjacent dry storage facilities (on racks 12 in. above the floor) for packaging materials and other supplies. Use 5 ft of unobstructed space for truckways. Use 7 ft if adjacent to overhead rail and indicate all truckways on drawings. Train and truck shipping areas must be concrete paved at least 20 ft from buildings, docks, or chutes.

Slaughtering Area

Livestock Pens.—Provide paved (concrete or brick) ramps, chutes, and holding pens large enough to hold the kill for one day. Use 12-in. curbs and provide a water trough next to or over pen floor drain. Have a watertight roof over part of the pen to include a well-lighted squeeze pen for antemortem inspection.

Holding and shackling pens must be outside of or separated from slaughtering by a full-height partition of impervious material. Use a power hoist for elevating animals to a bleeding rail.

Slaughtering Department.—Plan floor arrangement for sanitary, efficient operation with orderly inspection. An example of the sanitary aspect: truckways to coolers should not pass under dressed carcass rails. The degree of efficiency (size and type of equipment) will help determine the maximum rate of slaughter permitted. Specifications must indicate the rate of kill desired, also indicating if more than one species will be slaughtered simultaneously and if kosher method will be used.

CFR Amendment 67-14 dated July 27, 1967, U.S. Dept. of Agr. Manual of Meat Inspection—310.19 Contamination of carcasses, organs or parts. (b) Brains, cheek meat and head trimmings from animals stunned by lead, sponge iron, or frangible bullets shall not be saved for use as human food . . . alternative methods of stunning that do not produce contamination of edible product are approved for use . . . (captive bolt stunners).

Viscera Handling.—Provide space for separating and handling viscera with a power-operated lift and other approved equipment. Edible offal requires a separate cooler (or a separately drained part of a carcass cooler), directly accessible from the kill floor.

Maintain approved in-plant rendering facilities or use local plant. Special permission is necessary to move condemned material on public roadways. Check regulations if inedible animal or fish food manufacturing is planned.

Chill Coolers.—To protect walls, it is ideal to place cooler rails 3 ft from equipment columns, or walls, although 2 ft is permissible. Height of work rails vary with animals as follows:

	Ft
Halves of beef	11
Calves, headless hog carcasses (12-in. trolleys)	9
Beef quarters	7.5
Sheep, goats (hooks or gambrels)	6.5

Maintain an approved compartment for holding retained carcasses or parts.

Cattle Dressing Layouts.—Most modern kill floors use on-the-rail facilities, and because of improvements in efficiency and ease of inspection, U.S. Dept. of Agr. favors this system.

Provide for an efficient knocking pen with a dry landing area at least 7 ft wide. Use a partition 4 ft high to prevent escape of a revived animal, with a 16-in. opening for workers and rail suspended carcasses. Most use 2-in. galvanized pipe on 16-in. centers, imbedded in a 12-in. concrete curb.

Bleeding area must be curbed and located so the skinning and dry landing area will not be splashed. The bleeding rail top is 16 ft above the floor; dressing rail is 11 ft, except with a moving-top table it is 12 ft 3 in.

Provide suitable space and facilities for dehorning, flushing, washing, inspecting, and storing on approved equipment. Plan an efficient method for disposition of feet and udders and sanitary removal of hides through a vented (10-in.) hide chute or room.

Use a curbed and separately drained area (sloped $\frac{1}{2}$ in. per ft), equipped with nonslip elevating or stationary metal platform for washing and shrouding. Locate platforms so they will not touch skinned carcasses.

Header rail must be at least 3 ft from adjacent wall to clear carcasses during transfer or switching. Space dressing rail "stops" at least 5 ft apart to prevent contact between carcasses (use 8 ft if moving viscera inspection table is used).

Various dimensions are provided in Table S.5.

Viscera Inspection.—Approved stainless steel paunch trucks may be used for viscera inspection. A 7- by 8-ft cleaning room, walled to prevent splashing, is required. Floor is pitched $\frac{1}{2}$ in. per ft to a drain. Cleanup hose, with a dial thermometer, must have 180°F water from central supply.

Moving tables are required when the rate of slaughter is 40 or more hourly. The moving top is stainless steel with a vented washer-sterilizer in the end. It must be synchronized with the movement of the carcass conveyor and a stop-button must be in a location convenient to the inspector.

The moving table has a separate drain, foot platform, lavatory, hand tool sterilizer, boot washing cabinet, and boot storage locker.

Hogs

Location of Certain Operations.—Except for necessary openings, the equipment and operations listed shall be located in areas separated from carcass dressing: hoisting, sticking and bleeding; scalding vat; dehairing machine located within a curbed area having nonclogging drainage inlet; gambrelling table; facilities for depilatory dipping; and singeing.

Scalding Tub.—Provide a metal scalding vat with minimum lengths for the rates of slaughter indicated: 75 per hour, 20 ft; 150 per hour, 40 ft; 300 per hour, 60 ft; and 600 per hour, 90 ft. For slaughter of less than 20 per hour, a smaller vat may be used.

Space for Operations and Truckways.—Provide space for proper conduct of operations and inspection so it is not necessary to convey product through a line of suspended carcasses.

Floor Drainage.—A drip valley about 24 in. wide and integral with the floor should be provided. It must be pitched to drainage inlets properly located in the valley. The valley should extend from gambrelling table to where carcass inspection is completed. Floors may be sloped to drain in the drip valley.

Shaving and Carcass Washing Facilities.—It is essential to have a shaving rail of adequate length and a cabinet-type carcass washer with separate drain. Locate carcass washer beyond completion of shaving and before head dropping. No shaving is permitted after heads are dropped.

Inspection Facilities for More than 20 per Hour.—An approved moving carcass conveyor and a moving pan inspection-type table are required when the slaughter is faster than 20 hogs per hour. Hog viscera inspection conveyors must conform to specifications listed for cattle. A simplified system is suitable for inspection for 20 per hour or less.

Horses.—Construction requirements and facilities for horse slaughtering departments are essentially identical with those for cattle.

SOLIDS LEVEL CONTROL

To control the quantity of solid materials in hoppers and bins, an automatic sensing device which in turn activates a feeder, conveyor, or other materials handling system is necessary to reduce labor costs and achieve efficient operation. Solids level controls also protect conveyors from damage due to jamming if placed in transfer or discharge chutes. The control may sound an audio or visual warning signal in addition to stopping a conveyor system. Several designs of solids level controls are available, ranging from expensive devices utilizing radioactive materials to simple revolving paddles. Many of the designs depend on limit switches. A pendant cone or a diaphragm can serve as the sensing element against the material for activating the limit switch. The presence of material causing a pressure against the diaphragm or cone energizes the warning signal or perhaps a conveying system. Sketches in Fig. S.12 illustrate the pendant cone and diaphragm types of bin-level control units.

Specifications and Uses

A variety of sensing elements may be used to detect the presence of solid materials and may be utilized to automate storage and transfer of the product. Certain material level control devices are given in Table S.6.

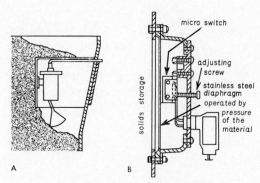

Source: Chemical Engineers' Handbook (Perry)

Fig. S-12.   Bin level control units: A—Pendant cone type; B—Diaphragm type

The selection of the proper sensing element will depend upon the type of material to be controlled. In general, the manufacturer's recommendations should be followed. Control devices may be used to indicate high and low levels in a supply bin. The diaphragm type of sensing element is constructed of a material suitable for the product. Rubber, Neoprene, and composition-coated fabric are in general use as diaphragm materials because of their sensitivity to pressure, wearing, and corrosion-resistant qualities. Hot or highly abrasive materials require stainless steel diaphragms and special applications. The diaphragm unit is usually mounted on the vertical sidewall of the bin or vessel and should be flush with the inner surface. This method minimizes damage to the unit and reduces buildup on the diaphragm.

Impeller Type Devices

The motor-driven paddle or impeller type of control devices may be mounted horizontally; however, top mounting on a bin is preferable. The paddle shaft is extended from the motor so that it is in the path of the angle of repose at the desired level for operation. The housing is totally enclosed and dusttight. When the material contacts the revolving paddle, the torque reaction created by the resistance of the material is detected through a spring controlled mechanism which in turn actuates the limit switch. There are variations of the paddle-type sensing device which include a pendulum type of control. The pendulum type is particularly useful where a long extension of the paddle shaft is required. There are advantages in applications such as extremely large bunkers where the maximum height of the material is a considerable distance from the top.

Pendant Float-Type Devices

Pendant float-type control switches are also available to achieve the same general results as the paddle or pendulum units. The float ball or float cone connected through a universal pivot operates the switch as material changes the position of the ball. Obviously, for high level control the float mechanism is placed near the top of the bin. For low level control, the float ball should be placed beneath a protective guard plate so it is not completely surrounded by the product. The protective guard must not interfere with the action caused by the normal angle of repose of the material. Vertical mounting adjustment is recommended to locate the device at the desired level of operation.

Electronic Type Devices

Level control devices of the electronic type are finding wider application in industry. The system employs a probe-type electrode which is mounted to sense the presence of material. The probe is a component of a high frequency circuit and is affected when inserted in the material to be controlled. In some cases, the probe need not be in contact with the material, therefore, it can be mounted outside the bin wall which should be of nonconductive material. Various types of electrodes are available for use on different applications. For example, the probe may be coated to withstand corrosive substances or it may consist of an insulated plate to withstand abrasion and shock as in coal bunker installations. The control box containing the relay for the electrode should be mounted for easy accessibility and where it is protected from

TABLE S.6

LEVEL CONTROL DEVICES

Type	Manufacturer	Design	Application Information	Operation
Mechanical Diaphragm	Richardson Scale Co.	6-, 12-, 18 in. diam sizes. Plunger, spring, switch	Adjustable to suit material. Recommended for general duty. Bin should be vented to relieve air pressure. Prefer use on vertical side of bin having two adjacent straight sides. Explosion-proof	Diaphragm connected to the plunger which operates the switch. Make point of switch occurs when diaphragm is depressed $1/8$ in. at the center. Break point of switch occurs $1/16$ in. before diaphragm returns to extended position
	The Bin-Dicator Co.	$10\frac{1}{4}$ in. OD, $5\frac{3}{4}$ in. OD sizes. Counterweighted lever system, switch, no springs	Adjustable to suit material. Available for general and special duty. Available for use under pressure or vacuum. Can be mounted on curved surface, and inside of bin as well as outside. Explosion-proof	Diaphragm is forced against the counterweighted lever system, tipping the lever plate and actuating the switch
	The Jeffrey Mfg. Co.	$4\frac{1}{2}$ in., 7 in. diam sizes. Counterweighted lever system, switch, no springs	Adjustable to suit material. Recommended for general duty. Can be mounted horizontally, vertically, or on curved or sloping surface. Weather and sparkproof	Counterweight operates the lever system and actuates the switch
	Tate & Roe Inc.	8 in. OD Diaphragm is free from switch. Unit does not contain counterweight. Diaphragm is backed up by pressure plate	Adjustable to suit material. Available for general duty. Can be used under high temperature. Can be mounted horizontally, vertically, or on a curved or sloping surface. Explosion-proof	$1/32$ in. diaphragm movement operates the switch
	The Fairfield Eng. Co.	10 in. OD. Diaphragm is free from switch. Unit does not contain counterweight	Adjustable to suit material. Available for use on coal and other lumpy, heavy bulk materials. Can be mounted in any position	Diaphragm movement operates the switch
Mechanical Pendant	Stephens Adamson Manufacturing Company	Pendant, universal pivot, switch.	Can be mounted vertically, or on a sloping surface. Available for normal and heavy duty. Explosion-proof.	20° movement of the pendant through the universal pivot collar operates the switch.
Electro-mechanical Paddle	Fuller Co.	Shaded pole induction motor, tension spring, spur gear train, cam, two switches. 6 in. long to 12 ft-0 in. long paddle shafts	Can be mounted vertically or horizontally. Available for general duty, also liquids. Protective guard recommended when used for low-level operation. Available for use under high temperatures. Requires alternating current	Paddle is constantly rotated by the motor. When paddle is restrained from turning, the motor and its mounting revolve about the drive shaft, actuating two switches. One switch operates the desired control. The other cuts out the level-control motor. A tension spring returns motor to its initial position

TABLE S.6 (*Continued*)

Type	Manufacturer	Design	Application Information	Operation
	Convair Inc.	$1/200$ hp motor, torsion spring	Available for use under pressure or vacuum. Recommended for general duty, also wet materials and slurries. Available in standard, heavy-duty, high-temperature, and explosion-proof models	Motor is connected to a shaft by a torsion spring. When the paddle stops, the motor keeps turning until the spring by torsion actuates the switch which cuts out the motor and actuates the desired control. The paddle turns the spring away from the switch and again starts up the motor
Electronic	Robertshaw Fulton Controls Co.	Relay circuit, two switches, cable, probe electrode	Can be used for operation under medium-high pressure and temperature. Available with special disc or plate electrodes to suit material characteristics. Recommended probe be installed horizontally. Available for general duty, also liquids. Weatherproof	A simple, highly stable-capacity relay circuit operates the two switches as a result of any slight change in electrical capacity at the probe electrode. One switch operates the signal control on front of the case, the other the desired external control
	Hewitt-Robins Inc.	Relay circuit, cable, probe electrode	Recommended for general duty. Recommend probe be installed vertically. Can be used under temperatures up to 140°F. Available for general duty, also liquids. Weather-resistant	A single-pole, double throw relay is acted upon by a high frequency field established by the tip of the probe. Disturbance to the high frequency field unbalances the relay circuit

Source: Bolz (1958).

moisture, dirt, and water. Electronic tubes should be replaced periodically. This type of sensing element is probably the most sensitive and accurate of any available. The initial installation cost, however, is usually higher than either of the mechanical systems.

Other Controls

Other controls which find use as level or quantity systems are photoelectric cells, strain gages, and atomic-type controls. The atomic level controls are finding increased applications, however, specially trained personnel are needed for servicing unless competent people are readily available.

References

BOLZ, H. A. (Editor) 1958. Materials Handling Handbook. Ronald Press Co., New York.
PERRY, J. H., CHILTON, C. H., and KIRKPATRICK, S. D. 1963. Perry's Chemical Engineers Handbook. McGraw-Hill Book Co., New York.

Cross-reference: *Level Measurement and Control.*

SPACE HEATING

Space heating normally refers to the process of providing the proper environmental temperature of the air in offices, laboratories, work areas, storages, etc. The quantity of heat provided to maintain a certain uniform temperature must make up the difference between the heat loss through the walls, floor, and ceiling, and heat loss through ventilation, less the heat produced in the space from people, processes, and equipment.

Degree-day

The average amount of heat needed is often estimated on a degree-day basis. For a particular day there exists as many degree-days as there are degrees Fahrenheit temperature difference between the mean temperature for the day and 65°F when the temperature is less than 65°F. The average degree-days determined by the Weather Bureau are Atlanta, 3,002; Boston, 5,943; Chicago, 6,287; Denver, 5,863; Detroit, 6,580; Minneapolis, 7,989; New Orleans, 1,208; New York, 5,306; San Francisco, 3,143; and Washington, D.C., 4,598. For an office building, about 1 lb of steam is required for heating per degree-day per 1,000 cu ft of heated space.

Components

Heating systems incorporate a combustion chamber in which the fuel is burned and heat transferred to a fluid, a fluid for carrying the heat, pipes for directing the flow of the fluid, and a method of moving the heat into the room.

Types of Systems

Most warm air systems use forced ventilation. Filters are often incorporated to remove particles. Temperature control is provided by operation of the furnace. Hot water systems carry sensible heat from the combustion chamber or heating element to the radiator where heat moves to the space. The temperature of the water is below boiling, and usually below 200°F, unless the system is under pressure. Control can be provided by the temperature of the water, speed of circulation of the water, and adjustment of the airflow around the radiator. Steam heating systems convey heat from a boiler through pipes to radiators. The heat transferred is principally latent heat. The steam condenses at the radiator and the condensate is returned to the boiler. The steam system provides positive circulation because of the steam pressure, can carry large amounts of heat, and is relatively inexpensive for large structures. Temperature control is provided by steam regulation and by adjusting the airflow over the radiator.

Space heating can also be accomplished by radiant or panel heating, with electricity widely used, although not exclusively for this purpose. Unit heaters, mounted on the wall, installed in the floor, or supported from the ceiling are also used. Unit heaters have a fan for circulating air within the space around the heater. Heat may be supplied from gas-fired units, steam, and electricity.

Cross-references: *Air Movement; Combustion; Fans; Filters; Heat Pump; Heat Transfer; Ventilation.*

SPECIFIC GRAVITY AND DENSITY

The density or specific gravity of a product is needed to determine the weight if the volume is known.   To apply the heat equation, it is necessary to know the weight of the product.   The density is the weight per unit volume, as in lb per gal., gm per cc, or lb per cu ft.   For a container of a given volume, the weight can be calculated if the density or specific gravity are known.   The equation

$$Q = cW(\Delta t)$$

$$Q = c\frac{1}{7.48} V(\Delta T)$$

where $\dfrac{1}{7.48} = \dfrac{\text{cu ft}}{\text{gal.}}$

c = specific heat, Btu/lb
V = volume in gal.
SG = specific gravity of product
$Q = c\,(SG)\,(\text{lb/gal.})$ water at $60°\text{F}$ (gal.) (Δt) = Btu

Definition

The specific gravity is the ratio of the weight of a product to an equal volume of water at $4°\text{C}$ as often used by physicists, or at $60°\text{F}$, as usually used by engineers. Specific gravity has dimensions of unity.   At $4°\text{C}$, water has a density of 1 gm per cc, so specific gravity and density have the same numerical value in the cgs system.   For a gas, the specific gravity is usually expressed in terms of hydrogen or air.

The values for specific gravity and density are affected by the temperature of the product.   In general, as the temperature increases, the specific gravity of the material decreases.   See Tables S.7, S.8, S.9, and S.10 for commonly accepted values of various materials.

TABLE S.7

DENSITY OF WATER (7.48 GAL. = 1 CU FT)

Temperature, °F	Lb/Cu Ft	Temperature, °F	Lb/Cu Ft
40	62.426	70	62.301
50	62.409	80	62.216
60	62.366	90	62.113
68	62.312		

TABLE S.8

COMMONLY USED VALUES FOR SPECIFIC GRAVITY

Air	0.0012	Condensed milk	1.16
Water	1.00	Evaporated milk	1.066
Water vapor	0.0006	40% cream	0.99
Milk, whole	1.032	Ice cream mix	1.08
Skimmilk	1.035	Ice cream (est.)	0.6 (100% overrun)
Milk fat	0.9	100% cream	0.54

TABLE S.9

CALCULATED DENSITIES OF GRAIN AND SEEDS BASED ON WEIGHTS AND MEASURES USED IN THE
U.S. DEPARTMENT OF AGRICULTURE

Grain or Seed	Unit Measure	Approximate Net Weight, Lb	Bulk Density, Lb/Cu Ft
Alfalfa	Bushel	60	48.0
Barley	Bushel	48	38.4
Beans			
Lima			
Dry	Bushel	56	44.8
Unshelled	Bushel	32	25.6
Snap	Bushel	30	24.0
Other			
Dry	Bushel	60	48.0
Dry	Sack	100	48.0
Bluegrass	Bushel	14–30	11.2–24.0
Broomcorn	Bushel	44–50	35.2–40.0
Buckwheat	Bushel	48–52	38.4–41.6
Castor beans	Bushel	46	36.8
Clover	Bushel	60	48.0
Corn			
Ear, husked	Bushel	70[1]	28.0
Shelled	Bushel	56	44.8
Green sweet	Bushel	35	28.0
Cottonseed	Bushel	32	25.6
Cowpeas	Bushel	60	48.0
Flaxseed	Bushel	56	44.8
Grain sorghums	Bushel	56 and 50	44.8 and 40.0
Hempseed	Bushel	44	35.2
Hickory nuts	Bushel	50	40.0
Hungarian millet	Bushel	48 and 50	38.4 and 40.0
Kafir	Bushel	56 and 50	44.8 and 40.0
Kapok	Bushel	35–40	28.0–32.0
Lentils	Bushel	60	48.0
Millet	Bushel	48–50	38.4–40.0
Mustard	Bushel	58–60	46.4–48.0
Oats	Bushel	32	25.6
Orchard grass	Bushel	14	11.2
Peanuts, unshelled			
Virginia type	Bushel	22	17.6
Runners, southeastern	Bushel	28	22.4
Spanish	Bushel	30	24.0
Perilla	Bushel	37–40	29.6–32.0
Popcorn			
On ear	Bushel	70[1]	28.0
Shelled	Bushel	56	44.8
Poppy	Bushel	46	36.8
Rapeseed	Bushel	50 and 60	40.0 and 48.0
Redtop	Bushel	50 and 60	40.0 and 48.0
Rice, rough	Bushel	45	36.0
	Bag	100	36.0
	Barrel	162	36.0
Rye	Bushel	56	44.8
Sesame	Bushel	46	36.8

TABLE S.9 (*Continued*)

Grain or Seed	Unit Measure	Approximate Net Weight, Lb	Bulk Density, Lb/Cu Ft
Sorgo	Bushel	50	40.0
Soybeans	Bushel	60	48.0
Spelt (p. wheat)	Bushel	40	32.0
Sudan grass	Bushel	40	32.0
Sunflower	Bushel	24 and 32	19.2 and 25.6
Timothy	Bushel	45	36.0
Velvet beans (hulled)	Bushel	60	48.0
Vetch	Bushel	60	48.0
Walnuts	Bushel	50	40.0
Wheat	Bushel	60	48.0

[1] The standard weight of 70 lb is usually recognized as being about two measured bushels of corn, husked, on the ear, because it requires 70 lb to yield 1 bu, or 56 lb of shelled corn. Agricultural Engineers' Yearbook, ASAE, St. Joseph, Mich.

TABLE S.10

SPECIFIC GRAVITY OF GRAIN AND PERCENTAGE OF VOIDS IN BULK GRAIN

Grain	Variety	Moisture Content, % (Wet Basis)	Air Space or Voids in Bulk, %	Kernel Specific Gravity
Wheat, hard	Turkey, winter	9.8	42.6	1.30
	Turkey, winter (yellow)	9.8	40.1	1.29
Wheat, soft	Harvest Queen	9.8	39.6	1.32
Oats	Victory	9.8	47.6	1.05
	Red Texas	10.3	55.5	0.99
	Iowar	9.7	51.4	0.95
	Kanota	9.4	50.9	1.06
Barley	White Hulless	10.4	39.5	1.33
	Svansota	9.8	45.4	1.21
	Coast (6 rows)	10.3	57.6	1.13
	Trebi (6 rows)	10.7	47.9	1.24
	Hannchen	9.7	44.5	1.26
Soybeans	Manchu	6.9	36.1	1.18
	Wilson	7.0	33.8	1.13
Grain sorghum	Yellow Milo	9.5	37.0	1.22
	Blackhull Kafir	9.9	36.8	1.26
Rye	Common	9.7	41.2	1.23
Rice	Honduras	11.9	50.4	1.11
	Wataribune	12.4	46.5	1.12
Flaxseed		5.8	34.6	1.10
Corn, No. 1	Mixed yellow and white	9.0	40.0	1.19
Buckwheat	Japanese	10.1	41.0	1.10
Millet	Siberian	9.4	36.8	1.11

Source: Zink (1935).
Agricultural Engineers Yearbook, ASAE, St. Joseph, Michigan.

Milk Density

The density of milk increases as the temperature is decreased. The density of whole milk at the time of production increases as the butterfat increases. It is a well-known fact that the specific gravity of butterfat is much less than the other major constituents. However, with whole milk, the solids-not-fat have a density greater

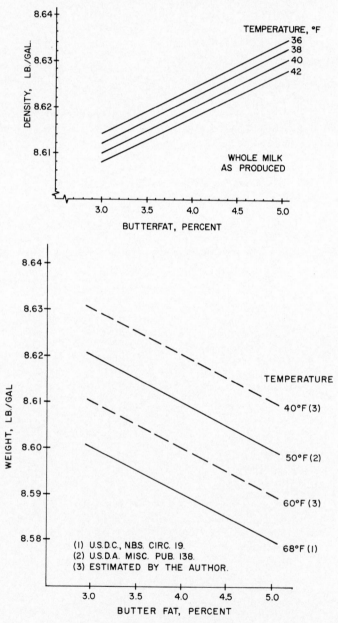

FIG. S-13.   A—Approximate density of whole milk as produced; B—approximate density of standardized milk

than 1, approximately 1.03 to 1.06, and in naturally produced whole milk, the solids-not-fat increases more rapidly than the fat, thereby, giving an increase in density with an increase in butterfat. This relationship is particularly important from the standpoint of calibration of bulk milk tanks where a naturally produced product is placed into the storage tank. On the other hand, for standardized milk product, as the butterfat is increased by adding fat to skim milk, the solids-not-fat remain constant and the density decreases as the fat increases (Fig. S.13A and B).

Hydrometer

The hydrometer is commonly used to determine the specific gravity of liquids. The hydrometer displaces a certain volume of fluid, depending on the weight of hydrometer and specific gravity (density) of liquid. The depth of submersion of the hydrometer can be measured on a calibrated scale which represents the specific gravity of the fluid. For known solutions, the specific gravity can be used to measure the concentration of solution. For example, the graduated scale on the hydrometer can be divided so that 1 division is equal to 1% sugar in solution, and is known as 1° Brix or 1° Balling. Other hydrometer scales are used, such as Baumé for salts and other solutions; alcoholometer for alcoholic solutions; oleometer for fats and oils; and Soxhlet's lactometer for milk.

The specific volume refers to the volume of product per unit weight, or the reciprocal of density, (L^3M^{-1}) where L represents a length dimension and M a weight dimension. The specific volume is often used to determine or to represent the quantity of steam in cubic feet to make a pound.

Reference

Zink, F. J. 1935. Agricultural Engineers Yearbook. Am. Soc. Agr. Engrs., St. Joseph, Mich.

Cross-references: *Cooling Milk; Density Control; Density of Milk; Fats, physical Properties; Grading.*

SPECIFIC HEAT

The specific heat, c, is a measure of the quantity of heat units required to change the temperature of a unit weight of product, either by heating or cooling, without change of state. Another definition, equally correct, is that the specific heat is the ratio of the thermal capacity of the product to that of water at 15°C. A heat unit is a British thermal unit (Btu) in the fph (foot-pound-hour) system or calories in the cgs (centigrade-gram-second) system of measurements. One Btu is equal to 252 cal. The quantity of heat to change 1 lb of water at 64°F by a temperature of 1°F is 1 Btu, or to change 1 gm of water at 15°C, is 1 cal, called a gram-calorie. The Calorie, called the kilogram-calorie, is often used to represent 1,000 calories. If a particular product requires 1 Btu to change 1 lb by temperature of 1°F, it has the same effect as for water at 64° and therefore, the product has a specific heat of 1. If less heat is required, the specific heat is less than 1.0. Most materials and products have a specific heat less than 1.0.

624. *Specific Heat*

The specific heat of a substance depends primarily on (1) the product, (2) the temperature, (3) the moisture content, and (4) the pressure. Because sufficient data are not available for specific heat as related to these variables, an average value is usually used for engineering calculations at a constant pressure.

TABLE S.11

SPECIFIC HEAT OF SELECTED PRODUCTS

Material	Moisture, %, Wb	Temperature Range, °F	Specific Heat, Btu/Lb-°F
Air		−22 to 50	0.238
Clay		68 to 212	0.22
Concrete		70 to 312	0.156
Cotton		32 to 212	0.362
Flour			0.397
Hay	20.0	60 to 100	0.4
	60.0	60 to 120	0.7
Ice		−30 to 32	0.505
Rice		50 to 100	0.44
Soybeans	17.7	75 to 129	0.47
	21.7	73 to 190	0.49
Starch (wheat, rice, and potato)			0.44
Sugar		68	0.274
Water		59	1.00
Wheat	0.4		0.302
	8.3		0.343
	13.0		0.377
	33.6		0.582
Wood			0.42
Wool		32 to 212	0.393
Butter, 15% water			0.50
Cream, 20% BF			0.88
Cream, 40% BF			0.80
Cream, 60% BF			0.75
Milk (3.5% BF)			0.93
Skimmilk			0.95
Ice cream mix			0.80
Ice cream			0.60
Condensed milk (plain)			0.94
Cheddar cheese			0.64
Sugar, liquid			0.30
Milk fat			0.56
Cottage cheese			0.78
Water			1.00
Water vapor at 212°F			0.47

A general rule-of-thumb is that the specific heat, SH,

$$SH = 0.20 + (\% \text{ water})(1\text{-a})$$

where a = 0.30 for carbohydrates.

= 0.40 for fats

or, more generally,

$SH = 0.20 + (\,008)(\% \text{ water})$

Source: Lange, N. A. 1967. Handbook of Chemistry, 10th Edition. McGraw-Hill Book Co.

The specific heats of gases are commonly available for a constant volume, c_v, or at a constant pressure, c_p. In general, the specific heat of a material increases, approaching one, as the moisture content increases. As the temperature of air and water vapor increases, the c_p and c_v decrease. As the temperature of a solid increases, the specific heat increases. The value of c_p is greater than the value of c_v for a gas, because some energy is required to expand the gas. Also, the specific heat c_p increases as the molecular weight of a gas increases. For example, the specific heat of helium He, and hydrogen, H, is 4.9 cal per mole-$°K$, and hydrogen, H_2, is 6.9, and carbon dioxide, CO_2, is 8.83.

The term thermal capacity or heat capacity may be used to represent 1 of 2 different relationships or concepts: (1) the thermal capacity represents the quantity of heat units moved per degree temperature change, and is equal to the specific heat times the weight of the product; (2) the thermal capacity can also be used interchangeably with specific heat, and is the quantity of heat required to produce a unit change in temperature for a unit mass.

Commonly used values of specific heat are given in Table S.11.

The quantity of heat involved in changing the temperature of the product is represented by Q, in Btu, and is equal to the specific heat, c

$$Q = c(W)(\Delta t)$$

where c = specific heat
W = weight, lb
Δt = temperature change

Apparent Specific Heat

The apparent specific heat incorporates the heat involved in a change of state, and usually represents values greater than 1.0. For example, when cooling butter, some heat is involved in a change of state of the product, which is difficult to identify or measure, so all of the heat is considered as sensible heat, providing a specific heat value greater than actual. For milk fat, the heat of solidification for the change of state from liquid to solid, is about 20 cal per gm. It is difficult to separate the quantity of heat removed as sensible and as latent heat when freezing ice cream. The apparent specific heat is often used for ice cream and its components (see Table S.12). The apparent specific heat can be predicted by using the specific heats of the ingredients

TABLE S.12

APPARENT SPECIFIC HEATS OF SUGARS

Temperature, °F	Sucrose	Lactose	Corn Syrup Solids
−20 to −15	0.647	0.516	0.439
−15 to −10	0.715	0.571	0.522
−10 to − 5	0.743	0.580	0.500
− 5 to 0	0.726	0.587	0.541
0 to 5	0.908	0.688	0.598
5 to 10	1.033	0.750	0.637
10 to 15	1.256	0.770	0.710
15 to 20	2.119	1.065	0.997

of the solutions.   The equation is similar to the parallel resistance of electrical circuits. The apparent specific heat is

$$c_p = \frac{\text{total parts of both components (sugar)}}{\dfrac{\text{parts of one sugar}}{c_{p_1}} + \dfrac{\text{parts of other sugar}}{c_p}}$$

Cross-references: *Btu; Fats, Physical Properties.*

SPRAY DRIER

The spray drier utilizes a product which is first condensed in a vacuum pan or an evaporator.   The product is then atomized inside a drying chamber of a drier.   The drying functions include: moving the air, cleaning the air, heating the air, atomizing the liquid, mixing the liquid in the hot air, removing the dry material from the air, additional drying of the product, cooling the product, and pulverizing and sizing the product.   Different methods of atomization may be used, but the most common procedure in the United States is to force the product by high-pressure pump through a nozzle to break up the liquid.   As the atomized product is introduced into the drying chamber, heated air is forced through the chamber.   The air furnishes heat for the evaporation of the moisture and the air is a carrier for moisture to be removed from the drier.   The air may be forced through the drier by either a pressure or suction system.   After drying, the product and air must be separated.   The product is then cooled and packaged.   Controls maintain the proper adjustment of the variables involved in drying.   Additional operations may be utilized to provide a product that will dissolve rapidly.   The capacity of commercial driers may vary from 500 to 5,000 lb per hr and higher of dried product, with 2,000 to 3,000 lb per hr being common (1965).   Proper management of a drier operation is important to provide good quality solid products from good quality liquid products.

Heating Air

Air for drying is filtered and heated before it passes through the atomized product. Filtering is normally done by mechanical means.   Future developments will probably involve more thorough filtering of the air.

Air may be heated with an indirect heater, such as steam; a direct-fired indirect heater, which burns the fuel with the heat transferred through the metal surface to the air; or with a direct-fired unit, in which the products of combustion enter the drier. Most spray driers have been of the indirect type, but many new installations are made with direct-fired units.   Radiators, with steam at 50 to 100 psi, have been quite common as a means of heating.

Direct-fired indirect heaters may burn liquid, solid, or gaseous fuels.   Fuels for the direct-fired units are limited to gas and light oil (No. 2) to avoid soot formation. The direct-fired units are more efficient due to less heat loss during heat transfer. With a direct-fired unit, the selection of fuel is based primarily on the cost and the effect of combustion products of the fuel on the drying product.   In laboratory units and in areas where electricity is competitive in cost, electrical heating may be utilized. Adequate heat transfer areas must be provided for heating the required quantity of air to the proper temperature.

The area of the heat exchanger surface must be determined for each installation, inasmuch as overall heat transfer coefficients vary considerably with the velocity of the air and the design of the heat exchanger or radiator. *U*-values for steam radiators for heating air vary from 0.5 to 10 Btu per hr sq ft °F.

Air is heated to about 300° to 500°F for drying milk products. The relative humidity of the drying air is quite low, even if the ambient air is of a high relative humidity. Air heated from 80° to 300°F and originally at 100% RH will have a relative humidity after heating of only 3 to 4%. However, air with a high relative humidity before heating does not have the same capacity to dry as low relative humidity air, although the difference is very small. The products of combustion for a direct-fired unit cause an increase in relative humidity of the drying air.

Interest has developed recently in using radiant heating to heat the air and the product by placing gas or electric infrared heating units opposite, but facing the atomizing units in the drier. As high a temperature as is consistent with obtaining a desirable product is used. The air may be forced through the drier by placing the fan ahead of the heater, providing a pressure system. If the fan is located at the discharge of the drier, the drier operates under a slight vacuum. Some driers use both fans with the neutral pressure zone approximately in the middle of the drying chamber.

Flow

The air must be properly and uniformly directed into and through the drying chamber. Otherwise, the heat in the air will not be utilized efficiently and a partially dried product may accumulate on the inside edge of the drier. Air straightening vanes are often used at bends in the ducts to direct the air into the drying chamber and to reduce pressure drops. Entrances to the drying chamber must be properly designed to permit and provide uniform airflow with a minimum loss of pressure drop. Each installation must be analyzed from a standpoint of airflow patterns and friction loss during airflow.

In a plant operation, a Niro spray drier was used for 6 months with air and milk streams flowing in the same direction followed by 6 months with flow of air and prod-

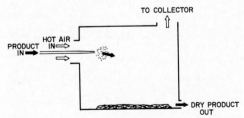

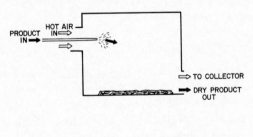

Fig. S-14.   Horizontal chamber dryers

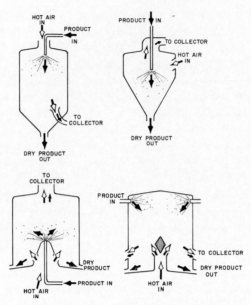

FIG. S-15.   Vertical chamber dryers

uct in opposite directions.   With flow in opposite directions as compared to parallel flow, there was (1) less tendency of the powder to stick to the drier, and (2) more particle aggregation with better wettability which was slightly less soluble.

The horizontal drier is in common use in the United States today.   These units usually use concurrent flow of air and product.   Centrifugal atomizers are not used in horizontal units (Fig. S.14).

The vertical drier is more flexible than the horizontal drier.   Spiral flow of air rather than straight flow permits a longer residue time thus permitting a unit wider and shorter than for straight-line flow (Fig. S.15).

The efficiency of a drier can be improved by using the heat in the air discharged from the drying chamber by preheating the incoming product and/or the incoming air to the drier using an indirect heat exchanger.

Steam Coil Versus Direct Flame Heating

Heating air for the drier is usually done with either steam for indirect heating using heating coils, or gas for direct flame heating.   It is easier to control a uniform low temperature with steam.   Steam provides a heat source which is relatively non-hazardous.   Higher efficiency is obtained with a higher temperature of inlet air, and direct heating with gas providing a more efficient operation than indirect heating. With direct heating, the products of combustion enter the heated air stream providing approximately 1 gal. of water for 1 gal. or equivalent of fuel.

Fuels

The heating value of fuels is the quantity of heat released by burning a unit weight or unit volume of fuel.   From 30 to 80% of the energy in the fuel may do useful work in a heater or drier.   The heating values (high or gross) for coal are from 11,000 to 14,000 Btu per lb; liquid fuels, 18,000 to 20,000 Btu per lb; gaseous fuels 500 to 1,000 Btu per cu ft; and fibrous fuels (wood, bagasse agricultural by-products) 8,000 to 11,000 Btu per lb.

A water droplet will dry or evaporate quite rapidly in a spray drier. The active evaporation in a drier occurs in 4 to 5 sec. As the drop diameter increases and as the temperature of air surrounding the droplet decreases, the length of time for complete evaporation increases. To evaporate the water in a 100μ droplet at $500°F$ takes approximately 0.3 sec. The time the droplet and the resulting dry product is in the drier is much greater than the theoretical time to dry a water droplet. The droplet and resulting dry particle is in the spray drier from 10 to 30 sec. The time may be much greater if the product is not immediately removed from the drier.

Air and Air Changes

Air moves into and through the drier at a velocity of from 1,200 to 2,000 fpm. If the droplet is not given an initial velocity, it will be carried by the high velocity air. If, on the other hand, the initial velocity is greater than the velocity of the air, the droplet velocity will decrease. The greater the velocity, the more likely the dry product will be carried from the drier. Air moving at 1 fps or 60 fpm will carry 100μ or smaller particles. The velocity which will support the particular size of particle is known as the terminal velocity. The terminal velocity increases with an increase in diameter of product.

The air supply to the drier may come from outside or inside the plant. With either source, the air should be filtered. An outside air supply next to roads, drives, or other conditions where dust or contamination may be present should be avoided. Inside sources might provide a more uniform temperature the year-round, but the practice makes it difficult to maintain uniform room temperature. It is usually easier to supply heat as needed to outside air to provide a uniform air temperature to the drier.

For a vertical spray drier, economy can be achieved by using warm air from the highest point in the building such as the top of the main drier penthouse. Using this procedure not only improves heating efficiency, but tends to maintain a more desirable temperature in the drying room.

The thermal efficiency of air utilization in the drier is enhanced by (1) high inlet temperature, (2) low outlet temperature, (3) high efficiency of heat exchanger for heating air, (4) use of outgoing exhaust air to heat incoming air, (5) insulated drier body to reduce heat losses, and (6) lack of air leaks. About 6 to 8% heat loss results from radiation from an insulated drier ($U = 0.5$) when operated at full capacity. Based on steam entering heater, the drier is about 40% efficient. Based on heat entering the drier, the drier is 55 to 60% efficient.

The use of gas engines to drive the supply and exhaust fans has proved satisfactory where natural gas is available. The heat from the radiator cooling water and from the exhaust gases is used to preheat incoming air. Also, the gas engine might be sized to drive an electric generator in addition to the fans. The electricity generated can be used to drive smaller motors in the drying system or in the plant.

The steam or vapor formed by the evaporation of 1% water from the product is 17 times the volume of the particle. The first 1% moisture evaporated surrounds the product with a layer of cool gas equal to about 5 times the radius of the particle.

The evaporation of 5% of the water from the water particle will lower the temperature 50°F.

Separation of Air and Powder

As the product is dried it is necessary to separate the dried product from the air. Without special design features the product will be carried by the moist air from the drier. It is necessary to remove the particles (1) to get a maximum yield from the drier by saving all powder product, and (2) to avoid air pollution surrounding the drying plant.

Location

The powder may be separated from the air primarily either (1) inside the drier (internal separation), or (2) outside the drier (external separation). In both cases it is necessary to use an additional device or component outside the drier to remove the fines or small particles which will not normally settle out in the drier. External separation devices are used on all driers.

Methods

The product which is separated from the air in the drier can be removed from the drier by: (1) an air brush by which air from outside the drier, either at room temperature or conditioned to a lower temperature, is used to direct a jet of air to move the product from the bottom of the drier; (2) a rake or broom which is pulled across the bottom of the drier; (3) a conveyor, flight or auger type; and (4) a gravity system.

Vibrators are often attached to the sides of the drier to prevent or reduce sticking of the powder and to move the product rapidly from the drier.

Variables

The variables affecting separation of powder from the air are particle size, concentration, nature of the material, and quantity of the product. In a drier, where most of the powder is removed internally, the quantity of air handled by the separation system will be the same as for external separation, but the quantity of product will be much less. The product nature or characteristics such as fat, moisture, cohesion, and friction greatly affect the efficiency of separation or collection. The efficiency of collection is designated as the ratio of the output divided by input times 100% with the product at the same moisture content at the 2 locations. Some manufacturers rate the efficiency of collection or separation on the basis of pounds of dry matter input. If all of a product at 3% moisture is collected, an efficiency of 103% would be claimed using this method of rating.

Types

Three types of air-product separators are commonly used for milk driers. The cyclone or multicyclone, which is a type of inertial separator, is most commonly used. Cloth collectors or bag filters have been used for many years. The material may be cotton, wool, or plastic. Approximately $1/3$ to $1/2$ sq ft of bag or cloth surface per cubic feet per minute of airflow is provided for external separation. Losses generally range from 0.2 to 0.5%. The wet scrubber or liquid device may be used where the fines passed through other separation devices are removed from the exhaust air and returned to the incoming product for redrying. From 1 to 16 gpm of milk are used for each 1,000 cfm of air for a wet scrubber. The wet scrubber provides for a high recovery of product.

Other methods of separation not now commonly used in the milk industry to separate fine solids from the air stream consist of the use of electrostatic, sonic or ultrasonic, electrical, and packed beds of granular or fibrous materials.

Cyclone Separators

The cyclonic separator is most commonly used for removing the dry product from the air. Air at a high velocity moves into a cylinder or cone which has a much larger cross section than the entering duct. The velocity of the air is decreased in the cone, thus permitting the settling of the solids. The velocity of the air decreases near the wall of the cylinder or cone, and the product falls by gravity and is removed from the bottom. Cyclones may be used for storage of product before packaging to provide for a more efficient packaging operation.

Efficiency of Separation

The efficiency of separation with a cyclone unit is based on product, cyclone design, and on the size of particle to be removed, but losses range from 0.5 to 3% and average 1%. The cyclone is normally used for separation of material between 5 to 200μ. As the size of particle decreases the efficiency of the cyclone decreases. A properly designed cyclone will remove 99% of the solids larger than 30μ (Brown *et al.* 1950), 98% of material larger than 20μ, 90% of material larger than 10μ, but only 50% of the material smaller than 5μ. One can see particles of about 10μ and larger with the eye.

A qualitative evaluation of the efficiency of the separator in operation can be obtained by placing a receptacle filled with water on the roof of a building under the outlet. Collection should proceed at intervals for about one month. The receptacle will catch particles over 1μ in diameter.

Drying in Tall Towers Without Added Heat

Towers 200 to 250 ft high and 50 ft in diameter can be used for drying with dehumidified air at normal atmospheric temperatures of about 86°F. The product falls through the tower by gravity in about 1.5 min. The air used for drying is dehydrated to about 3% RH by using silica gel. The air enters at the bottom and rises at $^1/_6$ to 3.0 fps leaving the top at nearly 90% RH. A cyclone separator is used. Up to 13,000 lb per hr of water can be removed and the product is dried to 2 to 4% moisture. The product has a rapid solubility and good flavor because there are no high temperature heating effects.

Effectiveness of Spray Drier

Two terms are used to describe the operation or effectiveness of spray driers. The evaporative capacity is the pounds of water evaporated per unit of time under standard operating conditions. The thermal efficiency is the percentage of total heat utilized for heating and evaporating the water

$$\text{Thermal efficiency} = \frac{(1 - R/100)\,(t_1 - t_2)}{t_1 - t_2}$$

where R = radiation loss, % of total temperature drop in drier
t_0 = atmospheric air temperature, °F
t_1 = temperature to which air is heated, °F
t_2 = temperature of air leaving drier, °F

A high efficiency is promoted by a high inlet temperature, a low exhaust temperature, reduced radiation loss, and recovery of heat from exhaust gas beyond the drying zone. The exhaust gas can be recirculated to the drying chamber, used to preheat fresh drying air, or can be used to preheat and concentrate the product. In practice, 2.2 to 3.2 lb of steam are required to evaporate each pound of water in the drier.

Cooling the Powder

The dried product should be removed from the drier as quickly as possible after it is produced to minimize the effect of heat damage on the product. The product and air may be removed together from the drier and separated outside of the drier to reduce heat effect.

Product cooling is done to prevent clumping, sticking, and heat damage to the product. Prolonged heating causes staleness in nonfat dry milk. Prolonged heating causes the fat to melt and move to the surface of whole milk powder. With more of the fat on the surface of the powder, the product will not keep as well in storage. Warm powder will hold the heat for some time in a bulk container, thus increasing the heat damage. The thermal conductivity, or k-value, is estimated at 0.15 to 0.25 Btu per hr sq ft °F per ft, which is considerably lower than most food particles and very similar to insulation materials.

Some cooling of the product will take place in the drier when using an air brush supplied with cool air to remove the dried product from the sides and bottom of the drier.

Pressure Drop

The pressure through a drier increases as the velocity is increased for a particular drier. The pressure drop varies from 5 to 25 in. of water, depending upon the design of the unit. The pressure drop may be calculated on the basis of the drop in each of the components plus the pressure drop in the piping. The components responsible for most of the pressure drop of the system are the filter, heat exchangers, collectors, and the ducts.

References

HALL, C. W., and HEDRICK, T. I. 1966. Drying of Milk and Milk Products. AVI Publishing Co., Westport, Conn.

MARSHALL, W. R., JR., and SELTZER, E. 1950. Principles of spray drying. Chem. Eng. Progr. *46*, 501–508, 575–584.

SELTZER, E., and SETTLMEYER, J. T. 1949. Spray drying of foods. Advan. Food Res. *2*, 399–520. Academic Press, New York.

Cross-references: *Atomization; Cooling Powder; Foam Spray Dryer.*

SPRAY FREEZERS

Spray freezers are used in the quick freezing of fruits, vegetables, and fish. Freezing is accomplished by spraying a very cold liquid such as nitrogen or brine or sugar solution over the material to be frozen as it passes the spray station on a conveyor.

The main feature of spray freezing is that it provides extremely rapid heat transfer due to the rapid movement of the film of the cooling agent over the product, and under certain conditions can provide practically instantaneous freezing. Nitrogen spray freezing is an adaptation of this method.

The cold liquid which is sprayed over the product must be one which is compatible with the food product and one which either evaporates or is readily removed by simple process. The efficiency of a spray cooling installation can be quite high. The losses are radiation from the cooling unit to the atmosphere and the energy required to circulate the spray.

References

STAPH, H. E. 1949. Specific heats of foodstuffs. Refrig. Eng. *57*, 767–771, 829–830.

REIDEL, L. 1951. The refrigerating effect required to freeze fruits and vegetables. Refrig. Eng. *59*, 670–673.

ANON. 1965. Liquid nitrogen freezing seen pivotal to creation of IQF fillet industry. Quick Frozen Foods, Nov.

Cross-references: *Nitrogen, Liquid, Cooling and Freezing.*

STAINLESS STEEL

Stainless steels are described as that group of metal alloys consisting principally of iron, nickel, chromium, sometimes manganese or molybdenum, and other trace elements, which are particularly resistant to corrosion and rusting. Stainless steels are of great importance in the food industry because, in addition to their rust and corrosion-free characteristics, they do not cause off-flavors in food products. Stainless steels are also characterized by resistance to the action of cleaning compounds and solutions and by their bright shiny appearance. Most dairy and food equipment is now made with stainless steel as the material used where food products may be in contact with the surface.

The stainless and nonrusting feature of stainless steel is the result of the development of an oxide film which forms naturally on the clean surface of the stainless steel surface or it may be produced artificially by the process of passivation.

There are many types and specifications for stainless steel. Three principal types are of most interest to the food industry. These are the type 302 which is used principally for appearance; the type 304 which has excellent corrosion resistance; and the type 316 which has high corrosion resistance. In addition, there is the type 440 hardenable stainless steel which is used for gear rotors, seal rings, and places where the surface must be very hard to resist wear. All stainless steel is harder than ordinary steel, but only certain formulations can be hardened to the degree of ordinary steel through tempering. The less expensive 200 series stainless steel is available for surfaces not in continual contact with food products.

TABLE S.13

COMPOSITION AND PROPERTIES OF SOME TYPES OF STAINLESS STEEL[1]

Part I—Composition of Some Stainless Steels

Composition	Type 302	Type 304	Type 316	Type 430	Type 440C	Type 502
Carbon	0.08–0.20	0.08	0.10	0.12	0.95	0.10
Manganese	2.00	2.00	2.00	1.00	1.00	1.00
Phosphorus	0.04	0.04	0.04	0.04	0.04	0.04
Sulfur	0.03	0.03	0.03	0.03	0.03	0.03
Silicon	1.00	1.00	1.00	1.00	1.00	1.00
Nickel	8.00–10.00	8.00–10.00	10.00–14.00	0.00	0.00	0.00
Chromium	17.00–19.00	18.00–20.00	16.00–18.00	14.00–18.00	16.00–18.00	4.00–6.00
Molybdenum	0.00	0.00	2.00–3.00	0.00	0.75	0.00

Part II—Properties of Some Types of Stainless Steel

Mechanical Properties	Types 302 and 304		Type 316		Type 430		Type 440C		Type 502
	Annealed	Cold Drawn	Annealed	Cold Drawn	Annealed	Ann. and Cold Drawn	Annealed	Ann. and Cold Drawn	Annealed Bars
Tensile strength	75,000	100,000	80,000	90,000	75,000	85,000	110,000	125,000	65,000
Yield strength	35,000	60,000	30,000	60,000	45,000	70,000	65,000	100,000	25,000
Brinnel hardness	150	212	149	190	155	185	230	260	150
Rockwell hardness		C-33	78				B.97	C.24	B.75
Scaling temp., °F	1,650	1,650	1,650	1,650	1,550	1,550			1,150
Annealing temp., °F	1,900–2,000 and quench		1,900–2,050 and quench		Air cool from		Cool slowly		Furnace Cool
	1,650	1,650	1,650	1,650	1,500–1,400°F		1,550–1,650		1,600–1,525
Hardenable	No	No					Yes	Yes	Yes
Magnetic							Yes	Yes	Yes

[1] Percent iron not shown.

A special type 430 stainless steel is a less expensive formulation which can be used widely for structural and decorative purposes.

Table S.13 shows a comparison of the composition and the basic properties of the above mentioned stainless steel types.

Stainless steel must be kept polished and in the passivated condition in order to retain its corrosion resistant properties. In time, if stainless steel is kept highly polished it will develop a natural oxide film which gives it high resistance to corrosion. If improper handling occurs or if repairs are made on the materials, it is necessary to reestablish this film by the process known as passivation. To passivate, the surface should be cleaned; then either sprayed or otherwise put in contact with a solution of 20 to 30% nitric acid for about 30 min at a temperature of 140°F.

Corrosion

Five distinct types of corrosion are normally found in food processing equipment: general, intergranular, galvanic, pitting, and stress. General corrosion would indicate that a more resistant type of stainless should be used.

Intergranular corrosion is that type which penetrates into the metal between the grains or crystals. One solution for this problem is to use a type of stainless steel which has a low carbon content, such as type 316L in place of 316, or 304L in place of 304.

Galvanic corrosion takes place when two dissimilar metals are immersed in water or other solution which may act as an electrolyte. Prevention of galvanic corrosion can be obtained by making certain that only one type of stainless steel or metal is used in the particular system. Also it is important that stray electric currents be prevented from flowing in the equipment. This can be accomplished by proper grounding of the equipment. Concentration cell corrosion can occur in tanks or vessels where there are variations in the concentration of the product in the tank. Concentration cell corrosion occurs when there is a space between two loose plates or gaskets which allows the liquid to stagnate and thereby cause an electrical potential between the stagnated spots and adjacent areas to develop.

Pit-type corrosion is caused by dirt, scale, or rough spots on the surface of the material. Keeping the surface highly polished and cleaned is the best preventive for this condition. Allowing a chlorine sterilizing solution to remain in contact with the stainless steel for an extended period of time will cause corrosion and pitting. The same is true of calcium and salt brines, particularly if they are slightly acid and if considerable air has been entrained in the brine.

Stress-corrosion cracking can be caused by the presence of stresses set up in plates of a tank. Sometimes this is due to stress which has been unrelieved and due to strain set up during welding. Danger from this source can be minimized through stress annealing, through avoiding chloride impurities in the process fluid, or through the use of special stainless steel containing molybdenum.

Finishes

Finish on stainless steel is important both from the standpoint of appearance, ease of cleaning, and resistance to corrosion. The No. 4 finish is the most commonly used.

Cross-references: *Alloys for Processing; Cleaning of Equipment; Finishes, Metal; Electrolytic Corrosion; EMF Series; HTST Pasteurization.*

STANDARDIZATION

Operators are often confronted with the task of determining the amount of substance to add or remove to obtain a desired concentration. A unique procedure, sometimes called Pearson's Square method, can be used, in which the desired concentration is placed in the center of the square. To find the proportions of 40% cream and 10% cream to get 20% cream, place these values on the corner of the squares as shown below, and subtract across, obtaining on the right hand side 10 parts of 40% to 20 parts of 10% to provide 20% cream. This same approach can be used for protein, nitrogen, etc.

The same approach can be used to determine the removal of substance to reduce the concentration. To produce 3.0% milk, from 5% milk, 2 parts (lb) of 20% product needs to be removed from 17 parts (lb) of 5% milk. (This procedure yields 15 parts with .45 lb fat, or 3.0% milk.)

Equations representing these relationships are

to lower the test of milk by removing cream, C

$$C = M \frac{(q - r)}{(p - r)}$$

where M = milk, lb

q = original test, %

r = final test, %

p = test of cream, %

to increase the fat, by removing skimmilk, S

$$S = M \frac{(r - q)}{r}$$

STANDARDS, 3-A

The 3-A Standards are the result of many years of cooperative effort between various industry groups and the sanitarians to set standards of sanitary construction for dairy and food processing equipment. Manufacturers are authorized to use the 3-A Standard symbol providing their equipment meets certain specifications. Only those manufacturers whose equipment conforms to existing 3-A Standards and who are authorized to do so by the 3-A Standards Symbol Administrative Council may use the symbol. Since the standards themselves may be amended from time to time, manufacturers must apply annually for the privilege of using the symbol and must indicate annually that their product corresponds to published 3-A Sanitary Standards.

The sanitary standards are formulated by groups representing dairy processors, dairy suppliers and equippers, and municipal and state regulatory officials, with the advice and council of public health and sanitation specialists from the federal government. These standards are voluntarily met by fabricators and manufacturers. As a general rule, equipment which conforms to 3-A Sanitary Standards is accepted in the health officers jurisdictions in all parts of the country. The 3-A Symbol Council is an incorporated body that issues authorization to use the symbol. Of its eight trustees, four are appointed by the International Association of Milk, Food and Environmental Sanitarians (two represent dairy processors and are members of the Sanitary Standards Subcommittee of the Dairy Industry Committee; and two represent the equipment manufacturers who are members of the Technical Committee of the Food and Industry Supply Association).

There are currently 28 3-A Sanitary Standards that have been published in the *Journal of Milk and Food Technology* (from which one may obtain reprints at nominal cost). The Journal is the official publication of the International Association of Milk Food and Environmental Sanitarians located at Shelbyville, Ind.

The 3-A Sanitary Standards program has been of tremendous value to the food industry in providing improved sanitary construction and in assisting both the processors and health departments in the matter of selection and approval of equipment. The standards program has also been of great value to food equipment manufacturers in guiding them in the design of equipment.

Reference

FARRALL, A. W. 1963. Engineering for Dairy and Food Products, 3rd Edition. John Wiley & Sons, New York.

Cross-references: *Cleaning of Equipment; Sanitation.*

STATIC PRESSURE, AIR

A manometer is a device in which the difference in elevation of the liquid in the tube can be measured to determine the pressure developed. A convenient material to use for the liquid in the manometer is water, although liquids of lower density might be used for greater accuracy. When material of lower density is used the amount of change of liquid level is greater for a given pressure, thus providing greater accuracy. For small readings the U-tube may be inclined and the reading of the change in elevation of the fluid taken along the U-tube at R

$$h = \Delta P = R \sin \theta$$

It is advisable to calibrate the gage because of possible variations in the diameter of the tube and inclination of the two legs.

The draft gage is commonly used for low pressure heads of gases and consists of a U-tube arrangement in which one leg of the tube is a reservoir of large diameter as compared to the diameter of the tube that forms the inclined leg. Small variations in the level of the inclined tube produce very little change in the level in the reservoir of large diameter. Commercial draft gages are usually designed to be provided with a liquid other than water. It is necessary to follow the instructions of the manufacturer for zeroing the instrument before use and leveling it while in use.

For very precise measurements a micromanometer is used. Basically, it operates on the same principle as a regular manometer, but is provided with an accurate method of reading.

A swinging vane meter may be used in which the impact of the moving air hits an air vane which is connected to a calibrated static pressure scale. These are quite useful for field work and should be calibrated against manometer readings for research work.

Cross-references: *Air; Air Movement; Fans; Manometers; Orifice.*

STEAM

Steam is water in vapor form. Steam may be produced under vacuum such as in a vacuum pan, or at atmospheric pressure and above, as in a boiler, and is known as live steam. Steam is a major source of thermal energy for food processing plants. Steam is used for cleaning, sanitizing, pasteurizing, sterilizing, and related heat processing operations.

Properties

As the pressure over the boiling water is increased, the temperature of evaporation increases. The latent heat, Btu per pound, decreases with an increase in temperature. The total heat in Btu per pound, increases with an increase in temperature of evaporation.

There are three classifications of steam; dry or dry saturated; wet; and super-heated. Dry saturated steam is preferred as the process for most applications. When heat is added to dry steam at constant pressure, superheated steam results. When heat is removed from dry saturated steam, wet steam results. Superheated steam is identified as the degrees of superheat, °F, the amount of temperature above saturation

TABLE S.14

PROPERTIES OF SATURATED STEAM, 0 TO 200 PSI GAGE

Psig	Temp, °F	Specific Volume, Cu Ft per Lb	Heat of the Liquid	Latent Heat, Btu/Lb	Total Heat of Steam, Btu/Lb	Psig	Temp, °F	Specific Volume, Cu Ft per Lb	Heat of the Liquid	Latent Heat, Btu/Lb	Total Heat of Steam, Btu/Lb
0	212.0	26.79	180.0	970.4	1,150.3	76	320.9	4.86	291.1	893.4	1,184.5
1	215.3	25.23	183.4	967.2	1,151.6	78	322.4	4.76	292.7	892.2	1,184.9
2	218.5	23.80	186.6	966.3	1,152.8	80	323.9	4.67	294.3	891.0	1,185.3
3	221.5	22.53	189.6	964.3	1,153.9	82	325.4	4.57	295.9	889.5	1,185.7
4	224.4	21.40	192.5	962.4	1,154.9	84	326.9	4.48	297.4	888.7	1,186.1
5	227.2	20.38	195.3	960.4	1,155.9	86	328.4	4.400	298.9	887.5	1,186.4
6	229.8	19.45	198.0	958.8	1,156.8	88	329.8	4.319	300.4	886.4	1,186.8
7	232.4	18.61	200.6	957.2	1,157.8	90	331.2	4.241	301.8	885.3	1,187.1
8	234.8	17.85	203.1	955.5	1,158.6	92	332.5	4.166	303.2	884.3	1,187.5
9	237.1	17.14	205.4	954.0	1,159.4	94	333.9	4.093	304.6	883.2	1,187.8
10	239.4	16.49	207.7	952.5	1,160.2	96	335.2	4.023	306.0	882.4	1,188.1
11	241.6	15.89	209.9	951.1	1,161.0	98	336.0	3.955	307.4	881.1	1,188.5
12	243.7	15.34	212.1	949.6	1,161.7	100	337.0	3.890	308.8	880.0	1,188.8
13	245.8	14.82	214.2	948.2	1,162.4	102	339.2	3.826	310.1	879.0	1,189.1
14	247.8	14.33	216.2	946.8	1,163.0	104	340.4	3.765	311.4	878.0	1,189.4
15	249.7	13.88	218.2	945.5	1,163.7	106	341.7	3.706	313.5	876.2	1,189.7
16	251.6	13.45	220.1	944.2	1,164.3	108	343.0	3.648	314.1	875.8	1,189.9
17	253.5	13.05	222.0	942.9	1,164.9	110	344.2	3.591	315.3	874.9	1,190.2
18	255.3	12.68	223.9	941.6	1,165.5	112	345.4	3.538	316.6	873.9	1,190.5
19	257.1	12.33	225.7	940.4	1,166.1	114	346.6	3.486	317.8	873.0	1,190.8
20	258.8	11.99	227.4	939.3	1,166.7	116	347.8	3.435	319.1	872.0	1,191.1
21	260.5	11.67	229.1	938.1	1,167.2	118	348.9	3.385	320.3	871.0	1,191.3
22	262.1	11.38	230.8	936.9	1,167.7	120	350.1	3.338	321.5	870.5	1,191.6
23	263.7	11.09	232.4	935.8	1,168.2	122	351.2	3.292	322.7	869.1	1,191.8
24	265.3	10.82	234.0	934.8	1,168.8	124	352.4	3.248	323.8	868.8	1,192.1
25	266.9	10.67	235.6	933.7	1,169.3	126	353.5	3.204	325.0	867.3	1,192.3
26	268.3	10.32	237.2	932.5	1,169.7	128	354.6	3.160	326.2	866.4	1,192.6
27	269.8	10.00	238.7	931.5	1,170.2	130	355.7	3.118	327.3	865.5	1,192.8
28	271.3	9.86	240.1	930.5	1,170.6	132	356.7	3.078	328.4	864.6	1,193.0
29	272.7	9.65	241.6	929.5	1,171.1	134	357.8	3.039	329.5	863.8	1,193.3
30	274.1	9.45	243.0	928.5	1,171.5	136	358.9	2.999	330.6	862.8	1,193.5
32	276.8	9.07	245.7	926.6	1,172.3	138	359.9	2.961	331.8	861.9	1,193.7
34	279.4	8.72	248.4	924.7	1,173.1	140	360.9	2.925	332.8	861.1	1,193.9
36	281.9	8.40	251.0	922.9	1,173.9	142	362.0	2.890	333.9	860.3	1,194.2
38	284.3	8.10	253.5	921.1	1,174.6	144	363.0	3.856	335.0	859.4	1,194.4
40	286.7	7.82	255.9	919.4	1,175.3	146	364.0	2.823	336.0	858.6	1,194.6
42	289.0	7.56	258.3	917.6	1,175.9	148	365.0	2.790	337.1	857.7	1,194.8
44	291.3	7.32	260.6	916.0	1,176.6	150	365.9	2.758	338.1	856.9	1,195.0
46	293.5	7.09	262.9	914.3	1,177.2	152	366.9	2.726	339.1	856.1	1,195.2
48	295.6	6.88	265.1	912.7	1,177.8	154	367.9	2.695	340.1	855.3	1,195.4
50	297.7	6.68	267.2	911.2	1,178.4	156	368.8	2.665	341.1	854.4	1,195.5
52	299.7	6.50	269.3	909.6	1,178.9	158	369.8	2.635	342.1	853.6	1,195.7
54	301.7	6.32	271.3	908.2	1,179.5	160	370.7	2.606	343.1	852.8	1,195.9
56	303.6	6.14	273.3	906.7	1,180.0	162	371.6	2.578	344.1	852.0	1,196.1
58	305.5	5.98	275.2	905.3	1,180.5	164	372.6	2.551	345.1	851.2	1,196.3
60	307.3	5.83	277.1	903.9	1,181.0	166	373.5	2.524	346.0	850.5	1,196.5
62	309.1	5.69	279.0	902.5	1,181.5	168	374.4	2.498	347.0	849.7	1,196.7
64	310.9	5.56	280.8	901.2	1,182.0	170	375.3	2.472	347.9	848.9	1,196.8
66	312.6	5.43	282.6	999.8	1,182.4	172	376.2	2.447	348.9	848.1	1,197.0
68	314.4	5.30	284.4	998.5	1,182.9	174	377.1	2.422	349.8	847.4	1,197.2
70	316.0	5.18	286.1	897.2	1,183.3	176	377.9	2.397	350.7	846.6	1,197.3
72	317.7	5.07	287.8	895.9	1,183.7	178	378.8	2.373	351.6	845.9	1,197.5
74	319.3	4.97	289.5	894.6	1,184.1						

TABLE S.15

SUPERHEATED STEAM

Pressure, Psia[1]		Temperature, °F					
		250	300	350	400	450	500
14.7 (212°F)	sh	38.00	88.00	138.00	188.00	238.0	288.00
	v	28.44	30.52	32.61	34.65	36.73	38.75
	th	1,169.2	1,192.0	1,215.4	1,238.9	1,262.1	1,285.4
30 (250°F)	sh		49.66	99.66	149.66	199.66	249.66
	v		14.82	15.87	16.89	17.91	18.92
	th		1,189.2	1,213.4	1,237.4	1,260.6	1,284.2
45 (274.5°F)	sh		25.55	75.55	125.55	175.55	225.55
	v		9.79	10.50	11.20	11.89	12.57
	th		1,185.9	1,211.1	1,235.8	1,259.1	128.30
60 (292.7°F)	sh		7.29	57.29	107.29	157.29	207.29
	v		7.26	7.81	8.35	8.82	9.39
	th		1,181.8	1,208.5	1,234.0	1,257.7	1,281.8
75 (307.6°F)	sh			42.4	92.4	142.40	192.40
	v			6.21	6.64	7.08	7.49
	th			1,205.8	1,232.2	1,256.2	1,280.6
90 (320.3°F)	sh				79.7	129.73	179.73
	v				5.5	5.87	6.22
	th				1,230.0	1,254.75	1,279.3
105 (331.4°F)	sh				68.6	118.62	168.62
	v				4.69	5.01	5.32
	th				1,227.6	1,252.9	1,278.0

sh = superheat, °F
v = specific volume, cu ft per lb
th = total heat, Btu per lb
14.7 psia = 0 psig
[1] Psia = pressure per sq in. absolute, i.e., above a perfect vacuum.   Normally 14.7 lb/sq/in. absolute is equivalent to 0 lb gage pressure at sea level.

temperature.   Wet steam is identified by the dryness in terms of percentage by weight of dry steam in the wet steam based on latent heat.   The steam tables present these relationships based on no-heat in water at 32°F (Tables S.14 and S.15).   Heat added or removed for a process can be determined using the steam table.   The pressure may be designated in absolute pressure, psia, or gage pressure, psig.   The gage pressure is 14.7 psi above absolute pressure at sea level.

Practices and Principles

(1) Dry saturated steam is usually desired for processing operations.

(2) By producing superheated steam at the boiler, heat may be lost in moving from the boiler to the process, and steam can be delivered to the process as saturated steam.

(3) Superheated steam is normally used for driving turbines.

(4) Pounds of steam required for a process is usually calculated based on the process needs and the quantity of heat in the steam considering efficiency.

(5) For quick calculations, as a rule of thumb, assume 1,000 Btu per lb of heat in steam at low temperatures below 300°F.   Consider the specific heat of water at 1.0 and of steam as 0.47 Btu per lb °F.

(6) Steam which is to be used for product contact should be safe from contaminating substances such as boiler treatment compound. Instructions on treatment of boiler water and its relationship to the product are available from the Food and Drug Administration.

(7) Culinary steam producers which are essentially indirect heat exchangers use steam produced by a regular boiler as a heat source and potable water as the heated water which becomes steam for the process.

(8) Spent process condensate should be returned to the boiler as feed water. This water is heated and treated and is less costly to reuse in most cases than using fresh feed water.

(9) Piping should be properly insulated to prevent heat loss and of the proper diameter to carry the quantity of steam involved (Table S.16).

TABLE S.16

STEAM CARRIED BY PIPE OF DIFFERENT SIZES, POUNDS PER MINUTE

Psig.	Pipe Diam Size, In.					
	1	$1\frac{1}{2}$	2	3	4	5
0	1	5	10	25	48	80
10		7	12	33	61	100
30		9	18	40	78	128
50		10	21	50	92	150
75		12	23	55	105	172
100		14	27	62	118	190
150		17	31	72	138	230

(10) Steam should be properly trapped to maintain pressure in the system and to prevent loss of heat by loss of steam to the environment without going to the process.

(11) Approximately 20 lb of steam are required in the dairy plant for each 100 lb of milk processed. The cost of steam will vary from $2.50 to $6.00 per 1,000 lb of steam. The fuel cost can be estimated using Fig. S.16.

(12) To reduce cost of steam consider the following. (a) Reduce losses of steam which occur. (b) Reduce steam requirements of the equipment by analyzing operation. (c) Minimize cost of producing steam at boiler.

Reference

BABCOCK and WILCOX Co. 1955. Steam, Its Generation and Use, 37th Edition. Babcock and Wilcox Co. New York.

Cross-references: *Boilers; Feedwater Heater; Insulation; Piping; Water Supplies.*

STEAM INJECTOR

The steam injector is a simple hydraulic device by means of which steam from a boiler is used to force feed water into the boiler against the pressure of the boiler and the steam.

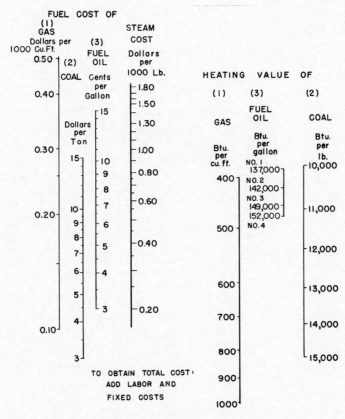

FIG. S-16.   Chart for determining fuel cost of producing 1000 lb of steam with boiler operating at 80% efficiency

Principle

The principle of operation is that a high velocity steam jet in combination with a venturi tube will provide suction and at the same time develop a greater pressure on the discharge than that of the steam which supplies the injector (Fig. S.17). The steam is supplied at 100 psi pressure and is forced through a constricted nozzle which greatly increases its velocity. Immediately below the high velocity tube, is a second tapering tube called the combining tube. As the high velocity steam leaves the steam nozzle a vacuum is created on the water feed supply chamber and draws in water which is subjected to the high velocity steam. The water is given a very high velocity in the combining tube. The velocity of the combined steam and water at the bottom of the combining tube is such that it will pass into the delivery tube, which is an expanding tube, and in which the high velocity of the water and steam is changed into pressure sufficient to force the water into the boiler.

At the beginning of the operation, before the balance has been established, some of the water will leak out between the combining tube and the delivery tube and go back to the water supply through the overflow line. When in operation, the velocity of the water as it reaches the end of the combining tube is such that it passes without loss directly to the delivery tube and into the boiler.

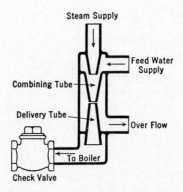

Fig. S-17.   The steam injector

Utilization

The simplicity and low cost of the injector make it widely used on small systems or small boilers.   An injector is not as dependable or as steady in operation as is a good feedwater pump, either steam or electrically operated.

In the operation of the injector it is very important that the feed water supply be cool.   The injector does not work well if the feed water is too warm, because it does not quickly condense the steam from the steam injector.

Impurities in the water such as small sticks or leaves also interfere with good operation of an injector.   In time the injector will also accumulate deposits of solids from the water and may have to be cleaned.

Reference

FARRALL, A. W.   1963.   Engineering for Dairy and Food Products, 3rd Edition.   John Wiley & Sons, New York.

Cross-references: *Boilers; UHT Equipment; Water Supplies; Vacuum Pump.*

STERILIZERS

A pressure sterilizer is a device in which food products can be sterilized or placed in contact with hot water or steam for a certain time and temperature treatment.

The basic principle of this device is to bring a moving container of food material into continuous contact with a heated liquid, usually water.

Atmospheric

The simplest form of this sterilizer is a tank of hot water at atmospheric pressure through which cans to be sterilized are carried on a conveyor at a certain rate of movement.

Pressure

To obtain high temperatures with water, it is necessary for the unit to be under a pressure greater than atmospheric, usually 30 psig or more.   This is accomplished by the use of water tight valves which allow the cans to enter and leave the unit or it may be a batch operation in which the batch is heated for a certain length of time in a retort type of chamber and then removed.

Continuous

The continuous pressure sterilizer is very widely used. One type consists of a rotary carrier under which the cans are automatically fed and passed through the apparatus usually under pressure. The feature of the unit is that it makes a continuous operating system with excellent heat transfer due to the movement of the cans on the carriage, as they pass from the feed end of the unit to the discharge usually in a spiral pattern.

The feature of the continuous sterilizer is excellent temperature control, excellent heat transfer rates, and particularly with the spiral continuous type, a low cost of operation.

Figure S.18 shows the construction of a continuous rotary pressure sterilizer.

Hydrostatic

The hydrostatic sterilizer, a type of pressure sterilizer, utilizes the same basic principles mentioned above; however, it uses hydrostatic pressure to automatically maintain the pressure in the sterilizing chamber, and at the same time permit cans of product to enter and leave without the need of a special valve. Referring to Fig. S.19, note that unsterilized product cans enter the unit on a continuous chain which carries the cans down through warming chamber C which is filled with water; they then pass to chamber (A) where they are subject to steam pressure as desired, usually 15 to 30 psig, then the product passes to chamber B where they are cooled. The holding time is determined by rate of movement of the chain. The time for the product in chamber (A) is usually 15 min or so but varies with the product.

Note that when steam pressure is built-up in chamber A, it pushes the water up in chambers B and C, thus obtaining an automatic pressure control and a removal of condensate; all without need for special valves to maintain pressure. The top of the chambers B and C are open to the atmosphere.

Courtesy of FMC Corp.

Fig. S-18.   The continuous milk sterilizer

raw product   sterilized product

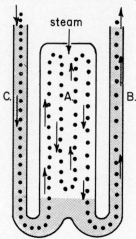

Fɪɢ. S-19.   Hydrostatic continuous sterilizer for cans
Dark area represents water level when operating. Steam pressure forces water
down in chamber A and up in chambers C and B. A continuous chain moves the
product can through the warming chamber C into the steam chamber A and out
of the cooling chamber B.

This is a very efficient and trouble-free sterilizer.   It requires considerable height
as, the height of water in chambers B and C must be sufficient to balance the steam
pressure.

Cross-references: *Aseptic Processes; UHT Equipment.*

STORAGE DESIGN

Satisfactory operation of a commercial storage depends greatly on the handling
facilities.   The grain should be checked regularly for heating, infestation, and damage
from rodents and weather.

A charge of 1 to 1.5 cents per bushel per month is usually made for storage.   It is
often more economical to store grain than to sell it at harvest to take advantage of the
increase in price after harvest.

The lateral pressure, L, lb per sq ft, for a shallow bin under 20 ft deep can be
calculated from Rankine's equation

$$L = wy \frac{1 - \sin \phi}{1 + \sin \phi}$$

where w = weight of material, lb per cu ft (40 to 50)
   y = distance from top to point in question, ft
   ϕ = the angle of repose, (25° to 35°)

The lateral pressure for a bin which is 15 ft deep, with material at 50 lb per sq ft
and a 30° angle of repose, is

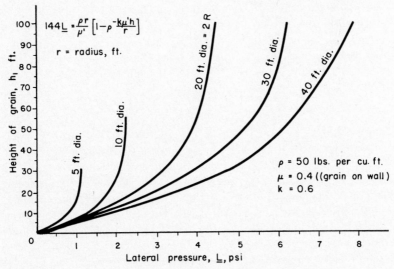

$$144L = \frac{\rho r}{\mu'}\left[1 - \rho^{-\frac{k\mu' h}{r}}\right]$$

r = radius, ft.

FIG. S-20.   Lateral pressure in cylindrical bin (or equivalent rectangular bin) based on Janssen's equation

$$50(15)\frac{(1 - 0.5)}{(1 + 0.5)} = 250 \text{ lb per sq ft or } 1.7 \text{ psi}$$

The lateral pressure in deep storages can be estimated from Janssen's equation (Fig. S.20)

$$L = \frac{wR}{\mu}\left(1 - \rho\frac{-K\mu h}{R}\right)$$

where L = lateral pressure of grain, lb per sq ft

w = weight of grain, lb per cu ft, (40–50)

μ = coefficient of friction of grain on walls (0.30–0.48)

R = hydraulic radius of bin, (area of cross section, sq ft/circumference, ft)

h = depth at any point, ft

Y = vertical pressure of the grain, lb per sq ft

K = ratio of lateral to vertical pressure, $\frac{L}{Y}$, (1.60)

Cross-reference: *Conversion Values.*

STORAGE, SEALED CORN

Hermetically sealed units can be used for storing wet shelled corn at 25 to 30% moisture content (wb). Oxygen is excluded so that the spoilage microorganisms, which are principally aerobic, cannot live. The air surrounding the shelled corn at time of storage is quickly depleted of its oxygen which is replaced by carbon dioxide through respiration. The corn can be crushed or ground before storing to decrease the oxygen surrounding the stored product and improve storage conditions.

Corn stored at 18% moisture developed a sour odor and darkened in 1 yr of storage. Corn at 27% moisture developed a sour odor and darkened in less than 1 month. The viability of the corn decreased to zero in from 1 yr to 3 months for 18 and 27% moisture corn, respectively. There was no great loss of dry matter during storage.

The use of shelled corn stored in sealed bins is limited to feeding when removed from the storage. A white powdery mold will develop on corn stored above 14.5% moisture within 24 hr after removal from storage.

STRAINERS

Strainers are regarded by most as coarse separation of particles from fluids, e.g., juice from fruit or cheese curd from whey. Simple strainers remove free liquid utilizing a screen or perforated metal with gravity flow. Strainer design and hole size of perforated metal is dependent upon the product and separation requirements.

A circular outlet strainer commonly used in a cheese vat and the inverted "V" type are illustrated in Fig. S.21. The greater area provided by the inverted "V" strainer increases capacity.

Dewaterers may be regarded as a strainer and discussed as a separate topic. A revolving cylinder installed on an incline extending from a vessel serves as an excellent strainer for separating juice from fruit. The elements of this type are shown in Fig. S.22. Soft fruit is not severely mashed by the gentle handling of the revolving strainer (Fig. S.23).

Cross-reference: *Dewaterer*

STRONTIUM 90 REMOVAL FROM MILK

The possibility of radioactive fallout increases the potential contamination of milk and other food products with strontium. A procedure for emergency treatment of milk has been developed to remove up to 98% of the radioactivity. An ion exchange principle is employed where resins containing chlorides of calcium, magnesium, po-

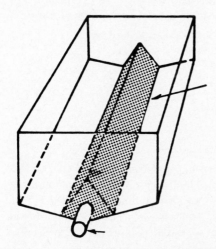

FIG. S-21.   Round or semicircular and inverted "V" strainers in cheese vat

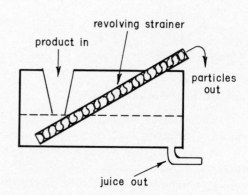

FIG. S-22.   Revolving cylinder strainer

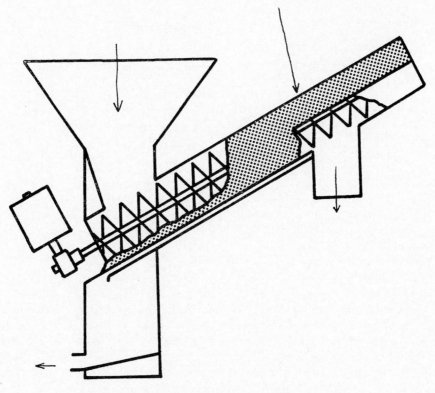

FIG. S-23.   Typical strainers used in food industry

tassium, and sodium are used for removing the radioactive components. Before passing through the ion exchanger, the milk is reduced to a pH of about 5.3 using citric acid.   This is done at a temperature below 80°F in order to obtain maximum removal.   The product is then passed through the ion exchanger.   As it leaves the exchanger, the pH is adjusted to 7.0 by addition of potassium hydroxide.   Following neutralization of the product, it can be pasteurized, homogenized, and deodorized. The ion exchanger is regenerated by one rinsing with warm water, washing with non-ionic cleaning solution at 140°F, sanitizing with hypochlorite (50 ppm), and removing the strontium from the column with a solution of salts of calcium, magnesium, and sodium.   On a pilot model basis, the cost of removal is approximately 5 to 10 cents per quart.

STUFFING BOXES

Stuffing boxes are used to seal a shaft or piston which leads out of a pressure or vacuum chamber.   Figure S.24 shows a simple stuffing box used on water pumps and ammonia compressors.   The stuffing box consists of a chamber that is filled with packing material of resilient nature and has a movable part called the follower which can be pushed by packing nuts or a screw to compress the flexible packing material as needed.

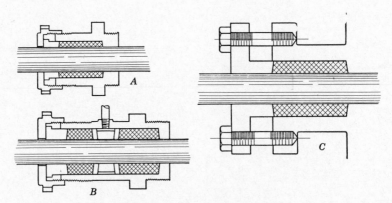

Fig. S-24.   Stuffing box design
A—Plain threaded nut with follower.   B—Threaded nut with follower and lubricator.   C—Double stud-type follower.

High-pressure installations may require several rings of packing.

Packing may be in a rope-like form or for high pressure use, it may be in the form of rings which are cut to an accurate shape and form.

It is customary to use packing material which is adapted to the liquids or gases which are to be held.   Normally, for water service a graphited cotton or flax material is used; for ammonia, a graphited cotton is normally used; for steam, a graphited cotton and asbestos mixture; for milk, a rubber compositioned or "O rings"; for brine, graphited square flax or cotton is used.   Homogenizers and extremely high pressure machines use special rubber, leather, plastic, or composition O rings.

Rings of packing must be inserted in such a manner that the joints are staggered.   Also it is important that the rods or shafts be kept very smooth as a scored surface will quickly wear out the best packing.

Tightening the stuffing box too much is the usual cause of scoring of rods and excessive wear of packing.   Usually, it is desirable to pack packing a little tighter than necessary and then back off slightly.   It is essential to draw packing evenly to prevent the follower contacting and rubbing the shaft.

One of the most satisfactory means of packing joints which do not move appreciably is the O ring.   The O ring is simple and inexpensive and the higher the pressure the tighter the hold.   O rings are usually made of rubber, synthetic rubber, or plastics.

The new material called Teflon is quite widely used for a packing on flanged joints. It is practically impervious to the flow of liquids of any kind and lasts well.

For packing joints which are in contact with food products the modern procedure is to use a rotary seal, if possible.   The rotary seal, can be perfectly cleaned and is long wearing and trouble-free if properly adjusted and cared for.   Rotary seals are also widely used on refrigeration equipment.

Cross-references: *O-Ring; Rotary Seal.*

SUMP PUMP

A sump pump is designed to pump liquid out of a low place such as a pit or basement, when the liquid such as water, waste, or sewage exceeds a certain depth.

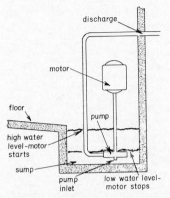

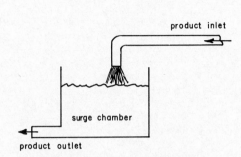

Fig. S-25.　Sump pump installation　　　Fig. S-26.　　Surge chamber

Usually a small pit called the sump is made at a level lower than the room or main area to be drained, and the sump pump is placed in this sump, although it is often found advisable to place the pump in a dry chamber, and to the side of the sump. The pump is fed by a pipe passing through the wall of the wet sump to the pump.

It is important that the pump be self-priming. Usually a sump pump is connected to a level control, so that whenever the level of liquid in the sump reaches a predetermined point, it will start, and run until the liquid is removed down to a predetermined level.

The capacity of the pump should be sufficient to handle the drainage into the sump under adverse conditions, but not so large that it will cycle on and off every few minutes. A larger sump capacity will remedy short cycling.

If the actual pump is at all times submerged it should handle either hot or cold liquid successfully, however if the liquid to be pumped is hot, the pump should be submerged deep enough to provide several feet head on the pump inlet. The discharge of the pump should be to atmosphere to prevent vapor lock (Fig. S.25).

Reference

Hicks, T. G. 1957. Pump Selection and Application. McGraw-Hill Book Co., New York.

SURGE CHAMBER

A surge chamber is defined as an enlargement of a fluid conduit or a vessel in a fluid line which accomplishes two main purposes: (1) permits the fluid to slow down and reduce its velocity; and (2) provides a vessel in which a certain quantity of the fluid will be caught in order to prevent overloading of lines or equipment beyond the fluid chamber (Fig. S.26).

Surge chambers are frequently used in refrigeration systems to provide a means for preventing slugs of refrigerating liquid from going into the compressor. Surge chambers are also widely used in product feed lines supplying fillers.

In many continuous processes, surge chambers are necessary to prevent overloading of lines and to provide for holding the fluid for short periods of time such as when the filler operation might be stopped due to a short-time emergency which would not be sufficiently long to require shutting down the entire production line.

Surge chambers must be properly sized to accommodate the maximum additional flow that is encountered in the operation of the system. Surge chambers may be enclosed or open to the atmosphere depending upon the type of service and the material which is being handled. Surge chambers may be fitted with automatic controls which will shut down the line in case certain conditions of operation are exceeded.

Other names for surge chambers are ballast tanks, accumulators, and surge tanks.

Cross-reference: *Accumulators.*

SYRUP SYSTEMS

The addition of syrup to canned material such as apples, apricots, berries, cherries, pears, peaches, and pineapple, and the brining of carrots and string beans are important in canning operations. Cans are syruped to a preset headspace from brimfull to as much as $\frac{1}{2}$ in. clearance regardless of quantity of fill of the other ingredients.

Syruping is accomplished by a special type of filler with a disc plate on the valve which gently holds the product down in the can without bruising. This action prevents the product from floating, thus permitting maximum fill area and rapid escape of air from the vent tube to the filler.

The machine is very similar to a standard gravity type milk bottle filler except for the special hold-down plate which is used to keep the solid material from pushing up, so that the syruper or briner follows a special filling machine which has placed the solid matter in the can. Syruping is followed by a lidding and sealing operation after which the cans may go to another processing station.

Syrup Storage Tanks

Tanks for storing liquid sugar and other food materials of similar nature are normally made with a built-in heating coil which uses a heating fluid or electricity to warm the contents of the tank, so that it has sufficient fluidity that it can be readily withdrawn. Most tanks of this type are cylindrical and can be either horizontal or vertical. They may be insulated or not as required for the process.

Many plants use railroad tank cars for transportation of the product and the tank car itself provides temporary storage.

Stainless steel is the preferred material of construction.

Reference

Botz, H. A. and Hagemann, G. E., Editors. 1958. Materials Handling Handbook. The Ronald Press, New York.

T

TEMPERATURE

All thermodynamic and heat transfer relationships involve temperature. Heat flows from high to low temperature bodies. Inasmuch as the flow of heat cannot be measured directly by a Btu-measuring device, it must be measured indirectly through temperature differences.

The difference in temperature between two locations represents the driving force for the movement of heat. The temperature difference is used to determine the amount of heat gained or lost by a particular body.

Scales

The centigrade scale often called Celsius, for each °C is $^1/_{100}$ of the difference between the temperature of evaporation of water at 100°C and the freezing of water at 0°C. Each degree Fahrenheit is $^1/_{180}$ of the difference between the boiling point of water at 212°F and the freezing of water at 32°F. On the Réaumur scale, freezing point is 0° Ré and the boiling point 80° Ré with 80 equal divisions. Or, stated another way

Temperature boiling minus temperature freezing of water at sea level =

$$100°C = 180°F = 80° (°Ré) \text{ Réaumur}$$

or a difference of

$$1°C = 9/5°F = 0.8° \text{ Ré}$$

The common scales for temperature are the centigrade scale in the cgs system, and the Fahrenheit scale in the British system. These are related by

$$°C = 5/9 (°F - 32)$$

$$°F = 9/5°C + 32$$

$$°Ré = 4/9 (°F - 32)$$

The temperature at which molecular movement of a body ceases is absolute zero temperature. The absolute zero temperature has been approached but has not been reached. One of two scales are commonly used for representing the absolute temperature. In the cgs system, absolute zero is equal to $-273°C$, and in the British system, $-460°F$. The absolute temperature scale on the cgs system is in degrees Kelvin (°K), which is equal to °C plus 273. In the British system, the absolute temperature is given in degrees Rankine (°R), which is equal to °F plus 460.

The relationship between these two temperatures is given by the following equation

$$\text{Degrees Kelvin (°K)} = °C + 273$$
$$\text{Degrees Rankin (°R)} = °F + 460$$
$$\frac{F - 32}{9} = \frac{C}{5} = \frac{Ré}{4}$$

The absolute temperature is used particularly for calculations involving heat transfer by radiation, and for volume changes of gases based on the gas laws. Where temperature differences are involved, the same value exists in the cgs system whether the absolute or regular scale is used, and likewise, in the British system. For equations involving temperature, t is commonly used for the regular temperature and T for the absolute temperature. Some authors use θ for temperature, but it is more common to use θ for time.

The freezing point and/or boiling point of water or other liquids are often used to check the accuracy of thermometers or other devices for measuring temperature.

Measurement by Expansion

The expansion of gases or liquids is often used as the principle on which a device for measuring temperature is based. For example, a thermometer element may consist of alcohol, mercury, or other liquid which expands upon heating and contracts upon cooling. The change of volume can be correlated to change of temperature and the device used as thermometer. With some thermometers, only the bulb is immersed, and with others, a 3-in. length or other specified length, including the total length may be immersed to get the proper temperature. The glass, metal, or other material holding the liquid also expands with the change of temperature, so that the thermometer must be used in exactly the same manner in which it was calibrated to establish the temperature scale.

Filled Systems

In addition to the bulb and stem type of thermometer, filled systems are commonly used in the food industry, in which the indicating element is a Bourdon tube or spring. The system consists of a bulb which is located where the temperature is to be measured, a capillary tube for transmitting the response of the filled medium, and a Bourdon tube which moves according to the expansion or contraction of the filled material. The movement of the end of the tube indicates the temperature. Filled systems may be classified as liquid, vapor pressure, gas filled, or mercury filled thermal systems. These work on the same principle as a thermometer except that with the vapor-liquid systems, a liquid is present in the bulb, and the vapor to the Bourdon tube transmits the response. Thus, the vapor pressure of the liquid is involved in measuring the temperature.

Other Methods

There are many methods of measuring the temperature. The cost usually increases with the accuracy desired. Some of these systems are thermocouple, resistance thermometers, radiation pyrometers, and thermistors. Different materials are available for each of these, depending on the temperature, temperature range, response, accuracy, and cost involved. The effect of the food product on the sensing element must be considered. Stainless steel, monel metal, and glass surfaces are often used for food applications. The speed of response of temperature sensing devices decreases with an increase in their mass.

Cross-references: *Thermocouples; Thermometers.*

THERMAL DEATH TIME (TDT)

A time-temperature relationship at which certain microorganisms can be killed or enzymes inactivated can be plotted on semilogarithmic paper, with time on the log scale (Fig. T.1). An equivalent effect is secured at other points on the time-temperature line. The principles involved were first developed to sterilize food so that processes are often expressed in terms of that effect at 250°F. The time to destroy the microorganism at 250°F is known as the F_0-value, which is 10 min for the example in Fig. T.1, and which becomes 1 point on the thermal death time (TDT) curve. The slope of the curve is represented by z, and is the temperature range traversed by the TDT curve in 1 log cycle, for which $z = 18$. Thus, a heat treatment of 268°F for 1 min gives an effect on the microorganism in question equivalent to 250°F for 10 min. The alignment chart (Fig. T.2) can be used to compute time-temperature values for different F_0 and z-values based on 250°F. In general, the following relationships

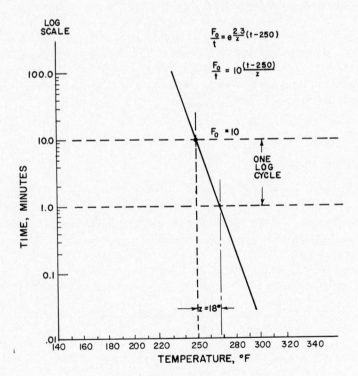

$$\frac{F_0}{t} = e^{\frac{2.3}{z}(t-250)}$$

$$\frac{F_0}{t} = 10^{\frac{(t-250)}{z}}$$

$F_0 = 10$

ONE LOG CYCLE

$z = 18°$

FIG. T-1. Representation of z and F_0 values

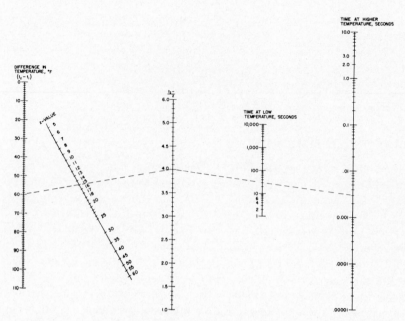

Fɪɢ. T-2.   Nomograph for determining equivalent heat treatment

exist.   (1) A higher F_0-value represents a greater heat treatment to obtain sterilization.
(2) A higher z-value represents a flatter slope of the TDT curve and a more difficult
organism to kill.   (3) The concept can be applied to enzyme activity as well as microorganisms.   (4) The concept can be applied to destruction of a certain percent of the
organisms or enzymes, as well as to total (or 99.99%).

The z-values of many enzymes in milk and other foods products are greater than
the z-values for destroying the microorganisms.

Cross-reference: *Pasteurization.*

THERMAL EXPANSION

During heating, gases, liquids, and solids usually increase in length or volume.
The notable exception is liquid water, which will decrease in volume until a temperature of approximately 4°C is reached and then increase in volume with the temperature
increase.   The total change in length of a solid from absolute zero temperature to the
melting point is about 2% of the total length.   The ratio of the change in length per
°C to the length at 0°C is known as the coefficient of linear expansion.   The equation
representing the relationship is

$$1_t = 1_0 (1 + \alpha t)$$

where 1_0 = length at 0°C

t = temperature, °C

α = linear coefficient of expansion, 1/°C

Likewise, the coefficient of volumetric expansion can be expressed by the equation

$$V_t = V_0 (1 + \beta t)$$

where

V_0 = volume at 0°C

t = temperature, °C

β = cubical coefficient of expansion, 1/°C

These equations can also be expressed in terms of the Fahrenheit temperature scale. The cubical or volumetric expansion is approximately three times the linear coefficient of expansion. The cubical coefficient of expansion for water vapor is 0.0042, of water is 0.000207, and of ice is 0.000113 The coefficient of volume expansion for gases is about the same, and is 0.00367 per 1°C. To obtain the coefficients in terms of °F, it is necessary to multiply by 5/9. Thus, the cubical coefficient of expansion of gases is 0.00204 per °F. For engineering purposes, the cubical expansion of most liquid foods like milk can be considered the same as for water.

TABLE T.1

ELECTROMOTIVE FORCE IN MILLIVOLTS WITH REFERENCE JUNCTIONS AT 32°F

Temperature, °F	Chromel-Alumel, Mv	Iron-Constantan, Mv	Copper-Constantan, Mv
−200	−4.29	−5.76	−4.111
−150	−3.52	−4.68	−3.380
−100	−2.65	−3.49	−2.559
− 50	−1.70	−2.22	−1.654
− 40	−1.50	−1.96	−1.463
− 20	−1.10	−1.43	−1.072
0	−0.68	−0.89	−0.670
20	−0.20	−0.34	−0.254
40	0.18	0.22	0.171
60	0.62	0.79	0.609
80	1.06	1.36	1.057
100	1.52	1.94	1.517
120	1.97	2.52	1.987
140	2.43	3.11	2.467
160	2.89	3.71	2.958
180	3.36	4.31	3.458
200	3.82	4.91	3.967
220	4.28	5.51	4.486
240	4.74	6.11	5.014
260	5.20	6.72	5.550
280	5.65	7.33	6.094
300	6.09	7.94	6.647
350	7.20	9.48	8.064
400	8.31	11.03	9.525
450	9.43	12.57	11.030
500	10.57	14.12	12.575
600	12.86	17.18	15.773
700	15.18	20.26	19.100

Source: U.S. Dept. of Commerce (1955). Reference Tables for Thermocouples, Natl. Bur. Stds. Circ. *561*.

A steel or wrought iron or cast iron pipe expands upon heating or contracts during cooling. Pipe installations are normally made at room temperature. Pipe expands when steam is added. For steel or wrought iron or cast iron installed at 32°F, the pipe would lengthen approximately ½ in. per 100 ft of length at 100°F; 1.3 in. per 100 ft of length at 200°F; 2.2 in. per 100 ft of length at 300°F; and 3.0 in. per 100 ft of length at 400°F. Joints must be provided or the design made to permit expansion of the pipeline without breaking. Expansion joints made of flexible material, slip joints, or loops in the pipe may be utilized to permit expansion of the pipe. Similar arrangements can be made for construction at low temperatures. Considerable force is exerted upon expansion or contraction during temperature changes. An iron bar 1 sq in. cross section, heated from 0° to 100°C will exert a force equal to the weight of about 13 tons on the supports.

Cross-references: *Fats, Physical Properties; Piping.*

THERMO-COOLER AND DEAERATOR

This system is used to chill mixtures of syrup and water from 78° to 35°F and inject the proper volume of carbon dioxide (CO_2) into high-speed filling lines of carbonated tanks. Figure T.3 shows the construction and principle of operation of this system. (1) The syrup and water from a premixer enters at the top of the unit and flows down over the side of refrigerated plates into a collecting chamber. (2) CO_2 gas is injected into the upper part of the chamber and is absorbed by the liquid as it cools. (3) The finished cooled and carbonated product is fed from the bottom of the

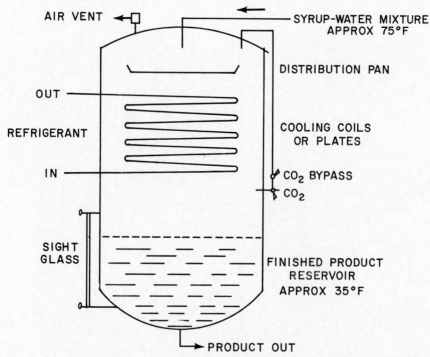

Fɪɢ. T-3.   Cooler for syrup and water carbonation

tank into the filling line. (4) Automatic controls of the cooling, the inlet of the various liquids, and of the CO_2 are provided.

An important attachment is the spray balls at the top of the chamber in such position that automatic CIP cleaning of the apparatus can be carried out.

The capacity of this apparatus is 2,000 to 4,000 gph with a tank 48 in. in diameter by 6 in. high.

The automatic control of the ratio blending of the water and the syrup utilizes the Brix principle. This analyzes the concentration of the product by a continuous measuring refractometer which indicates the Brix of the mixture on a continuous indicating recorder and feeds a signal to the proportioning system to maintain the specified Brix of the final solution.

Thermo Deaerator

Removal of air from filtered city water is necessary for effective carbonization of syrup and water mixtures. Figure T.4 shows a diagram of a deaerator. Water from the feed line enters the unit and is allowed to seep down through a bed of 1 in. chemical porcelain intalox saddles on which the water is exposed to vacuum. A typical unit will remove air and some other dissolved gases including carbon dioxide and oxygen.

Cross-reference: *Vacuum Treatment.*

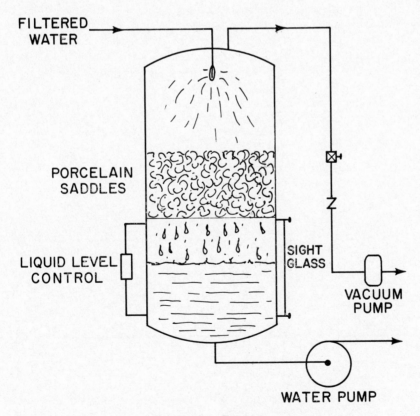

Fig. T-4. Deaerator

THERMOCOUPLES

A thermocouple is a device made of two metals which provide a current flow through or voltage change across the conductors which is dependent upon the temperature of the metals at their point of contact.   One leg of the thermocouple is positive and the other negative.   For temperature measurement, wire is usually used, with sizes between No. 8 to 28 gage.   It is necessary that a reference junction be used so that the change in voltage produced due to temperature is with respect to some constant voltage or emf produced at a reference junction (Fig. T.5).   The reference junction may be at 32°F as often used in manual operations with ice water, 75°F for many manual and recording devices, to as high as 212°F for some automatic units.   Lead wires connect the thermocouple and reference junction to a device for measuring the change in voltage.

Potentiometer

A potentiometer, either of the manual or automatic recording type is used to measure the millivolts which can be related to the temperature of the thermocouple.   It is necessary to compare the millivolt readings to charts or tables to determine the temperature with different tables for different thermocouple materials, Table T.1.   Recording potentiometers are often calibrated in °F for particular thermocouple materials, with conversion units available when using the unit with different thermocouple metals.   These recorders may be for a single point thermocouple recording, or multipoint recording by means of a stepping switch in the unit which measures and records the temperature at several thermocouple locations.   In specifying the recorder, it is necessary to specify the thermocouples involved and the speed of recording these temperatures. For recording units, tables are also used which give not only the temperature at each thermocouple, but the time at which the temperature is obtained.

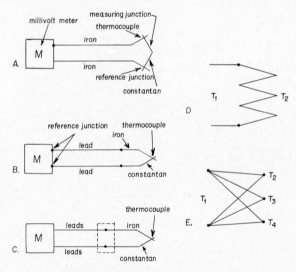

Fig. T-5.   Thermocouple connections
A, B, and C—Thermocouples.   D—Series thermocouple connector $T_2 = 3T_1$.
E—Parallel thermocouple T_1 will give average over the area.

Calibration

Thermocouple installations should be calibrated, i.e., the thermocouple should be immersed in ice water and other temperatures over the range of use, and compared to the value shown by the recording unit.

Making Thermocouples

Thermocouples are formed by twisting, soldering, or welding the dissimilar metals together. Generally, terminals near the thermocouple are provided so that lead wires connect the thermocouples to the potentiometer. Lead wires are usually copper and less expensive than the thermocouple wire itself. For low temperature applications, solder or silver solder is sometimes used.

The principles and practice of thermocouple use include the following: (1) The smaller the wires, the faster the response for temperature measurement. No. 28 gage wires are used where response is important. (2) The appropriate combination of wires must be selected for the temperature range involved. For low temperatures down to $-300°F$, copper-constantan; ambient temperatures, iron-constantan; up to $2300°F$ Chromel-Alumel; and up to $2700°F$, platinum-rhodium. (3) Copper wires are usually used for lead wires. To save on copper and simplify the circuit, a common ground wire may be used if the thermocouples are placed along a single line. A recording is only made from one thermocouple at a time, even if there are several thermocouples, when using a multipoint recorder. (4) The effect of corrosion by the product on the thermocouple and on the product must be considered. Chromel-Alumel is quite resistant to oxidation at high temperatures. Iron-constantan has only a minimum of corrosion resistance; the thermocouple can often be welded in place on a liner opposite the product side to avoid placing the thermocouple in the product. (5) It is important to protect the leads and to protect the thermocouple from damage by abrasion, breaking, or shorting of the circuit; the thermocouple must be shielded against radiation for high temperature applications.

Connections

Various arrangements can be used for connecting thermocouples to the potentiometer (Fig. T.5A, 5B, 5C, 5D, and 5E). In addition to having one thermocouple for each temperature measurement and each lead wire, series or parallel connections can be used. If a very small emf is normally provided for 1 thermocouple, 2, 3, or more thermocouples can be connected in series to increase the emf reading. The reading obtained is then divided by the number of thermocouples. Paralled connections can be made to provide an average temperature over an area.

Cross-references: *Temperature; Thermometers.*

THERMOMETERS

A thermometer is used to measure the relative energy level of a liquid, gas, or solid, but not the amount of heat. The amount of heat must be calculated based on the temperature.

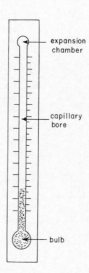

FIG. T-6.   Typical glass indicating thermometer

Indicating

The indicating glass stem thermometer is among the simplest instruments for measuring temperature (Fig. T.6).   The glass tube is filled with mercury, alcohol, toluol, or other liquid, which expands when heated into a capillary bore, appropriately marked for temperature.   Inert gas may be placed above the thermometer fluid.   For accurate temperature measurement, it is important that the thermometer be used in the same manner in which it was calibrated.   Thus, a thermometer may be designed for total or partial immersion.   The amount of immersion is designated by an etched line on the stem.   By appropriate constructions in the capillary stem, minimum or maximum thermometers can be designed.

When specifying or selecting a thermometer, the following factors should be considered: accuracy, sensitivity, speed of response, temperature range, and danger of breakage.

Filled System

Another category of temperature measuring devices is filled system thermometers (Fig. T.7).   The filled system units consist of a bulb, which is placed at the location of temperature measurement, a capillary tube which transmits the expansion or contraction of fluid in the bulb, and an indicating or recording device, such as a bourdon tube, on the opposite end of the capillary which transmits the signal.   These units are normally used where the temperature measurement and temperature indication location are separated as much as 250 ft.

Filled systems are classified according to the material and state of material in the bulb-capillary-bourdon tube volume.

Class I is a thermal system filled with any liquid except mercury.

Class II is a thermal system filled with vapor.

Class III is a thermal system filled with a gas.

Class IV is a thermal system filled with mercury.

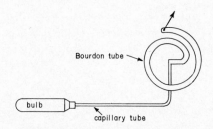

Fɪɢ. T-7.   Filled tube thermometer system

Class I System

Since the temperature along a capillary tube may affect the liquid, compensating devices are often used to assure greater accuracy than would otherwise occur. The speed of response is likely to be slower with a Class I system because of the thermal capacity of the fluid unless a small bulb is used. The fluid is often organic in nature. The response of the system is linear.

Liquid-Vapor

The Class II system is designed so that a liquid-vapor interface exists, always within the bulb. The Class II instruments are most widely used of the filled systems. They are lowest in cost. They respond quickly to temperature changes. The accuracy is not affected by changes in temperature along the capillary tube, as long as the ambient temperatures along the capillary do not fluctuate across the process temperatures at the bulb. A nonlinear relationship exists at the output. Temperature ranges can be selected to use the most accurate portion of the scale for reading the temperature.

Gas

Class III systems can be used for relatively high temperatures up to 1,000°F. The pressure (absolute) change in the system is proportional to the temperature change. Compensating devices may be used to correct for ambient temperatures. A fast response can be obtained if a small bulb is used. The stem, chart, or dial divisions are equal.

Mercury

Class IV systems can be used for low to high temperatures up to 1,000°F. Compensation devices are used for the capillary and case. The response is intermediate as compared to the other systems. A dual capillary and bourdon may be used for capillary compensation. The spirals are coupled so that the indicated temperature is that due to the bulb only. A linear response results.

Resistance

The resistance thermometer consists of electrical conductors which change in electrical resistance with a change in temperature. Nickel, copper, and platinum are a few of several metals used for resistance thermometers. The electrical resistance increases as the temperature increases, nearly in a straight line. The resistance thermometer bulb is connected to an electric bridge circuit with which the resistance is measured, thereby indicating the temperature.

Thermistors

Thermistors are elements which change in resistance with a change in temperature. The sensing element is a semiconductor which responds to temperature differently than metal conductors used in resistance thermometers. As the temperature of a thermistor is increased, its electrical resistance decreases, generally a straight line relationship between the log of the resistance and the temperature. The electrical output from the thermistor is directed to an appropriate electrical measuring unit, from which the temperature can be determined. These units must be calibrated occasionally because thermistors may increase in resistance with time. Thermistors come in a wide variety of sizes, shapes, and materials.

Cross-references: *Holding Methods of Pasteurization; HTST Pasteurization; Temperature; Thermocouples.*

TIN

Tin is a silvery white relatively soft nonmagnetic metal widely used in the food industry in the form of tin plate over iron or copper, in bearings, as an ingredient of

TABLE T.2

MELTING POINT OF SOLDER

No.	Use	Chemical Composition, %		Melting Range Liquid, °F
		Sn	Pb	
70-A	Coating metals	70	30	378
60-A	General (fine)	60	40	374
50-A	General purpose	50	50	421
Pure tin	Repairing dairy equipment	100	0	449.6

Source: ASTM Spec. *B-32-49*.

TABLE T.3

FUSABLE ALLOYS OF TIN

Melting Point, °F	Composition, %				
	Bi	Pb	Sn	Cd	Other
117	40.9	22.1	10.7	8.2	Indium 18.1
158	49.4	27.7	12.9	10.0	
203	52.0	32.0	16.0		
256	55.5	44.5			
281	57.0	43.0			
351			67.8	32.2	
462		84.0	4.0		Sb 12.0

Source: Intern. Tin Research Council (1937), Booklet *B.5*, Fusable Alloys Containing Tin.

solder, and for reusable plugs. Tin is an excellent metal for contact with food products since normally it does not affect the flavor of the product. Tin plate which makes the greatest use of tin in the food industry is applied to steel sheets by dipping in a bath of molten tin; however, electrodeposition is now most widely used, since it can give a very thin coating (about 0.1 lb of tin per base box of 112 plates 14 by 20 in., as compared to 1.0 to 1.5 lb for hot dipped sheets). For many years tin surfaces were considered to be the most satisfactory metals available. Tin has a tensile strength of 4,000 psi; resistivity at 20°C of 11.5 ohm-cm; a density at 20°C of 7.30

TABLE T.4

SUGGESTED LIST OF TOOLS FOR SMALL FOOD PLANTS

For Pipe Fitting

1 24-in. Stillson pipe wrench
1 18-in. Stillson pipe wrench
1 12-in. Stillson pipe wrench
1 8-in. Stillson pipe wrench
1 adjustable pipe vise to take $^1/_8$- to 2-in. iron pipe
1 adjustable pipe die and stock to take $^1/_8$- to $^3/_4$-in. pipe

1 adjustable pipe die and stock to take $^1/_2$- to 2-in. pipe
1 pipe cutter to cut $^1/_8$-in. to 2-in. pipe
1 pipe reamer to take $^1/_8$-in. to $1^1/_2$-in. pipe
1 lb white lead
1 lb powdered graphite

General-purpose Tools

1 12-in. monkey wrench
1 12-in. crescent wrench
1 6-in. crescent wrench
1 set socket wrenches to take $^1/_4$- to $^3/_4$-in. hex nuts
1 set Allen set screw wrenches to take $^1/_4$- to $^3/_8$-in. set screws
1 1-lb ball-peen hammer
1 light punch
1 heavy punch
1 hack saw and blades
1 center punch
1 4-in. screwdriver
1 6-in. screwdriver
1 10-in. screwdriver

1 set easyouts
1 set twist drills $^1/_8$-in. to $^3/_4$-in.
1 bench drill press
1 12-in. level
1 carpenter's brace
1 set wood drill bits, size $^1/_4$ to 1 in.
1 24-in. by 18-in. carpenter's square
1 6-ft folding rule
1 carpenter's 24-in. hand saw
1 standard claw hammer
1 set electrician's pliers
1 pair ordinary pliers
1 6-in. heavy-duty bench vise
1 tin snips

Soldering Equipment

1 blow torch
1 heavy soldering copper (2 lb)
1 electric soldering copper

1 portable bottled gas torch solder
1 box noncorrosive soldering flux

Miscellaneous Items

1 test pressure gage, 0 to 150 lb pressure
1 box fine valve grinding compound
1 set packing hooks
1 assortment of sheet and special packing to fit equipment in plant
1 large vise grip wrench
1 heavy duty $^5/_{16}$-in. electric drill
1 18-in. crowbar

1 portable tool box
1 set ammonia leak detectors (sulfur sticks)
1 assortment of machine bolts, screws, nails, washers, etc.
1 gas mask
1 small vise grip wrench
1 30 in. crowbar

Sources: Gunn (1967). Nailen (1967). Trickler (1966).

gm per cu cm; a thermal conductivity near 20°C of 0.155 (cal-cm/cm²-°C-sec) = 0.12 Btu-in./ft²-°F-sec; and a melting point of 231.9°C.

Tin bearing solders or the so-called soft solders are very widely used. They are composed of principally tin and lead. Table T.2 shows the composition and melting point of the various types of tin as listed by ASTM.

Another important use for tin alloys is a fusible plug such as are used for sprinkler heads and for safety plugs in boilers. A wide range of melting points of fusible alloys may be obtained as shown in Table T.3.

TOOLS AND SERVICE

It is essential that every food processing plant have a well-organized tool and service system. Such a system can pay for itself in a short time in savings in repair bills and in better production from the plant.

The key to a successful system is to have a man who is interested in charge, and a clean place for storage and use of the tools. It is also important to keep the tools sharp and in good working condition and every tool in its place so that it can be found when needed. A color code system to identify tools is very helpful. Many plants find it desirable to paint the outline of the tool in the cabinet so that it will call attention to a missing tool.

Some machines require frequent adjustments so that it is necessary to have special tools immediately available. Here, again it is possible to organize the storage of such tools (Table T.4). It is usually desirable for the operators of special machinery to be trained in the adjustment and care of their specific machine. Small plants usually depend upon the superintendent and individual machine operators for minor service adjustment. Large plants have a highly trained service group who are responsible for maintenance.

References

GUNN, A. J. 1967. Gaskets and packing materials. Plant Eng. *21*, No. 1, 152–154.
HITCHCOCK PUBLISHING CO. Hitchcock's Machine and Tool Directory. Wheaton, Ill.
NAILEN, R. L. 1967. Reduce vibration prolong motor life. Plant Eng. *21*, No. 1, 152–154.

TABLE T.5

SOME RELATIONS OF DRUG TOXICITY IN EXPERIMENTAL ANIMALS COMPARED TO MAN[1]

Animal	Weight in Kilos	Wt. Ratio Anim./Man	Drug Dose Ratio Anim./Man	Sensitivity Drug Dose Ratio/Wt. Ratio
Man	60	1	1	1
Cow	500	8	24	Man is 3 times as sensitive
Horse	500	8	16	Man is 2 times as sensitive
Sheep	60	1	3	Man is 3 times as sensitive
Goat	60	1	3	Man is 3 times as sensitive
Swine	60	1	2	Man is 2 times as sensitive
Dog	10	$1/6$	1	Man is 6 times as sensitive
Cat	3	$1/20$	$1/2$	Man is 10 times as sensitive
Rat	0.4	$1/150$	$1/15$	Man is 10 times as sensitive

[1] The values in these tables are average figures, drived from numerous sources.

TABLE T.6

CHEMICALS, THEIR POTENTIAL HAZARD

Chemical	Flash-point, °F	Underwriters' Lab. Classification	Explosive	Special[1]	Ingestion	Inhalation	Skin Contact
		Inflammable			Toxic		
Acetic acid	115	·	·	·	X	·	X
Acetone	0	90	X	·	X	X	X
Amyl acetate	77	55–60	·	·	X	X	·
Amyl alcohol	100	40	X	·	X	X	·
Aniline	168	·	·	·	X	X	X
Benzene (benzol)	12	·	X	·	X	X	·
Bromine	—	·	·	·	X	X	X
Butyl acetate	72	·	X	·	X	X	·
Butyl alcohol	82	40	X	·	X	X	·
Carbon disulfide	−22	110	X	·	X	X	X
Carbon tetrachloride	—	0	·	·	X	X	·
Cellosolve	104	·	X	·	X	·	·
Cellosolve acetate	124	·	X	·	X	·	·
Chloroform	—	·	·	·	X	X	·
Chromic acid	—	·	·	A	X	X	X
Cresol	178	·	·	·	X	X	X
Dichlorethylene	43	·	X	·	X	X	·
Ethyl acetate	24	·	X	·	X	·	·
Ethyl alcohol	55	70	X	·	X	X	·
Ethyl chloride	−58	·	X	·	X	X	·
Ethyl ether	−49	100	X	·	X	X	·
Ethylene dichloride	56	60–70	X	·	X	X	·
Formic acid	130	·	X	·	X	X	X
Glycerin	320	·	·	·	·	·	·
Hexane	−15	·	X	·	X	·	·
Hydrochloric acid (muriatic)	—	·	X	·	X	X	X
Hydrocyanic acid	0	·	X	·	X	X	X
Hydrofluoric acid	—	·	·	·	X	X	X
Hydrogen peroxide	—	·	·	A	X	·	X
Mercury	—	·	·	·	X	X	X
Methyl alcohol	52	·	X	·	X	X	·
Methylene chloride	—	·	·	·	X	X	·
Nitrobenzene	190	·	·	·	X	X	X
Nitric acid	—	·	·	A	X	X	X
Pentachlorethane	—	·	·	·	X	X	·
Sulfuric acid	—	·	·	A	X	X	X
Tetrachlorethane	—	·	·	·	X	X	·
Tetrachlorethylene (perchlorethylene)	—	0	·	·	X	X	·
Toluene (toluol)	40	75–80	X	·	X	X	·
Water	—	·	·	·	·	·	·
Xylene (xylol)	63	·	X	·	X	X	·

Key: X = considered a hazard. · = not especially a hazard. A = nonflammable, but may cause fire if it comes in contact with organic substances.

Sources: National Fire Protection Association; U.S. Department of Labor; Associated Factory Mutual Fire Insurance Co.

Cross-reference : *Maintenance.*

TOXICITY

Toxic substances are classified relative to their degree of toxicity based on certain animal tests. This applies to food additives or compounds taken internally, as well as from tests by means of a skin patch. Definitions of highly toxic and toxic substances including irritants and corrosive compounds are classified under the Federal Hazardous Substances Labeling Act which is in the U.S. Federal Register, August 12, 1961, Part 191, Chapter I, Title 21, Code of Federal Regulations.

Most all research work pertaining to drug toxicity is conducted with experimental animals. Virtually all experimental animals are less sensitive to drugs than man as shown in Table T.5.

Toxic Substances

Many chemicals including gases and vapors are considered toxic. Based on the degree of hazardous effects, the toxicity of several chemicals for ingestion, inhalation, and skin contact is shown in Table T.6.

Contaminates in the air which may affect people are given threshold limit values based on the judgment of a committee appointed by the American Medical Association. The values of various contaminants involved in air pollution are based on industry experience and from experimental studies. These values are reviewed and revised from time to time as more knowledge is gained concerning threshold limits. The threshold limit should not be regarded as a fine line dividing safe and dangerous concentrations. The threshold values represent only those conditions under which it is felt that workers may be exposed day after day without adverse affect on their health. The levels given refer to weighted average concentrations of an 8-hr day rather than a maximum which is not to be exceeded even momentarily. A workman may be exposed for short periods during the work day to higher concentrations; however, the intensity of the contaminant which may be tolerated would depend upon the nature of the pollutant, whether the results are cumulative, the frequency with which high values occur, and whether high concentrations produce acute poisoning. All of these factors must be considered in arriving at a decision as to whether or not a hazardous situation exists. The values given by the committee are not intended for use or modification for use in evaluating or control of community air pollution problems.

With increased emphasis upon cleaner air, all industry will be asked to minimize air pollution. Scrubbers on exhaust systems from processes for control of odors and other pollutants may be used. The amount and type of control desired will determine the type of exhaust air scrubber to be used.

Equipment Construction

Food processing equipment must be so constructed to avoid introducing toxic substances into a food product. Gaskets, shaft seal materials, as well as equipment contact surfaces themselves must be made of impervious noncorrosive material. Stainless steel is rated as the most satisfactory material for general equipment construction. The type and stage of a process, however, determines which materials are acceptable. Synthetic rubber, neoprene, Hycar, and others are satisfactory for contact with foods in most plants. Nickel alloy fittings may be satisfactory for contact with food products, however, over a period of time they corrode when in contact with hot detergent solutions during cleaning-in-place operations. Copper bearing metals are generally not regarded as satisfactory in food plants. Part of the problem is an adverse effect on food quality and flavor rather than production of a toxic effect.

References

Assoc. Food & Drug Officials U.S. 1959. Appraisal of the safety of chemicals in foods, drugs, and cosmetics.

Natl. Acad. Sci-Natl. Res. Council. 1964. Principles and procedures for evaluating the toxicity of household substances. Publ. *1138*. Washington, D.C.

Cross-reference : *Safety*.

TRIGONOMETRIC FUNCTIONS

The trigonometric functions represent the relationships of the length of the sides to the angle with 1 angle of the triangle of 90°. The various trigonometric functions can be represented in terms of the sine of angle A, represented as sin A, and cosine of angle A, represented as cos A. The sin A is equal to the length of y divided by the length of r, which is represented by sin $A = y/r$.

$$\sin A = y/r$$

$$\cos A = x/r$$

TABLE T.7

SOME TRIGONOMETRIC FUNCTIONS

Angle, $\theta°$	Sin θ	Cos θ	Tan θ
0	0.0	1.00	0.00
5	0.0872	0.9962	0.0875
10	0.1736	0.9848	0.1763
15	0.2588	0.9659	0.2679
20	0.3420	0.9397	0.3640
25	0.4226	0.9063	0.4663
30	0.5000	0.8660	0.5774
35	0.5736	0.8192	0.7002
40	0.6428	0.7660	0.8391
45	0.7071	0.7071	1.000
50	0.7660	0.6428	1.1918
55	0.8192	0.5736	1.4281
60	0.8660	0.5000	1.7321
65	0.9063	0.4226	2.1445
70	0.9397	0.3420	2.7475
75	0.9659	0.2588	3.7321
80	0.9848	0.1736	5.6713
85	0.9962	0.0872	11.43
90	1.000	0.00	0.00

$$\tan A = y/x = \sin A/\cos A$$

$$\text{cotangent } A = x/y = \cos A/\sin A$$

$$\text{secant } A = r/x = 1/\cos A$$

$$\text{cosecant } A = r/y = 1/\sin A$$

The tables of trigonometric functions provide the ratio of the length of sides of given angles. Thus, knowing the angle and the length of one side of the triangle, it is possible to calculate the other sides. Or knowing the length of the sides the angle can be determined easily (Table T.7).

In a circle there are 360°. Also, there are 2π radians in a circle of 360°. Pi is 3.14, so there are 57.2957° in 1 radian.

Some of the simple trigonometric relationships are

$$A + B = 90°$$

$$x^2 + y^2 = r^2$$

$$\sin A = \cos (90° - A) = \cos B$$

$$\sin^2 A + \cos^2 A = 1$$

Vector

In Fig. T.8, point 1 may be identified by rectangular coordinates, such as (x, y); and point 1 may be identified by polar coordinates by the radius vector, usually represented by ρ and the angle θ, which is (r,A).

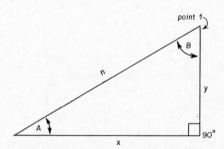

Fɪɢ. T-8. Trigonometric functions

A simple vector is a line, the length of which represents the magnitude (such as force in pounds, weight in pounds, velocity in feet per second, etc.), the direction of which represents the direction of application (or movement of the force, weight, velocity, etc.). In Fig. T.8, line n could represent a vector, with direction of $A°$ from the base.

Cross-reference: *Friction.*

TRUCKS FOR FOOD HANDLING

Food handling trucks, as contrasted to large motor trucks, are small tanks or chambers set on 3 or 4 wheels, and designed to be pushed usually by the operator from one location to another to carry food items.

Meat trucks are designed to handle from 225 to 1,000 lb of meat per load. The tank or body of the truck is usually made of stainless steel, fiber glass, or galvanized iron. Stainless steel is recommended for easy cleaning, and freedom from undesirable flavor effect on the product. The stainless steel truck usually costs about twice that of the galvanized iron truck.

There are many forms of hand trucks used in the fruit and vegetable industry. some of which are merely a flat platform with wheels and a handle for pulling.

An important part of the truck is the wheels. Usually either three or four wheels are used. Usually the wheels have solid rubber tires; some now use nylon wheels.

Forklift trucks are important in food handling in many plants and are available in many sizes from a couple thousand pounds capacity up to 4 or 5 tons or even greater. The fork truck is a tremendous time saver if used in connection with a pallet system. Usually the fork lift trucks are driven by a small gasoline or propane engine. Many users, however, use electric storage battery operated trucks. These have the advantage of quietness and freedom from objectionable fumes. Improvements in batteries and controls have almost doubled the hours of service which can be obtained from an electric driven forklift truck over the past 5 yr. The SCR control plus improved batteries are the important developments that have increased the range and efficiency of these trucks.

Trucks

Large over-the-road trucks for handling food products are both of the refrigerated and nonrefrigerated type. Most of these trucks are gas engine or diesel engine driven, however, in Great Britain thousands of electrically driven trucks are used. For heavy duty long distance trucking, the diesel driven truck will usually result in important savings in cost. For over-the-road trucks the state highway regulations for width, length, weight (usually per axle), and operating hours must be considered.

The cooling of refrigerated trucks can be accomplished by several different methods. One of the most popular methods is to use a small direct expansion Freon refrigeration unit driven either by a power takeoff from the truck or by a separate small gasoline engine. Using the separate small engine drive gives greater flexibility.

The second widely used method of refrigeration is to use so-called cold plates in the truck. These are filled with an eutectic solution which is refrigerated and frozen when the truck is connected to a suitable refrigeration system at its terminal. The frozen solution in the plates provides the necessary refrigeration to keep the truck cold for a number of hours. This is a very simple system and is very dependable, but lacks the flexibility available by using a separate small compressor driven system mounted on the truck.

A third system used is the expansion of nitrogen through pipes into the truck body storage space. This system has the advantage of extreme simplicity, however, it can only be used where there is a supply of liquid nitrogen available. The cost of the entire operation under favorable conditions will be comparable to that of other systems; however, this cost is dependent very largely upon the price which must be paid for the liquid nitrogen.

Cross-references: *Forklift Trucks; Nitrogen Liquid, Cooling and Freezing; Refrigerated Storage.*

TUBULAR HEATERS

Tubular heat exchangers consist of tubes, singly or in multiple units, through which heat passes from the hot to the cold product. Tubular units may be used for heating, holding, or cooling operations. A common procedure in using these units is for heating and cooling with tubular heat exchangers and holding in a vat.

The two principal tubular heat exchangers are the individually jacketed tubes and group jacketed tubes. In the former, a sanitary tube of from 1 to 2 in. diam is surrounded by a tube, forming concentric cylinders. Several tubes may be connected in series to obtain sufficient heat transfer surface.

The heating medium, usually water, is forced between the two tubes, and is circulated in the opposite direction, providing counter-current flow. The water is heated externally to the heat exchanger and pumped through the unit.

Several tubes may be surrounded by one jacket. Usually the tubes are mounted one above the other. The water may be heated by steam as an integral part of the unit, with the steam circulating the water.

Reference

HALL, C. W., and TROUT, G. M. 1968. Milk Pasteurization. AVI Publishing Co., Westport, Conn.

Cross-references: *Heat Exchangers; UHT Equipment.*

TUNNEL DRIER

The tunnel drier (Figs. T.9 and T.10) is widely used in the food industry to dehydrate cereals, grains, starches, gelatins, potatoes, vegetables, fruits, berries, crumps, yeast, and similar products. The tunnel drier is a versatile unit which can

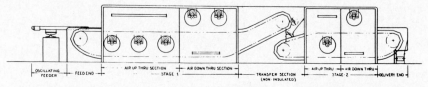

Courtesy of National Drying Machinery Co.

FIG. T-9.   Continuous industrial drier

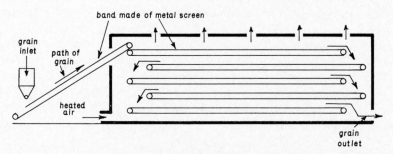

Courtesy of Institute of Agr. Machinery, Saitama, Japan

FIG. T-10.   Continuous grain drier

be accurately controlled and easily adapted to various uses. The cost of this type of drier is moderate. Tunnel driers are not adapted to drying of materials which must be exposed to the drying temperature for only a few seconds.

Principle

The basic principle of the tunnel drier is that material to be dried is spread evenly upon a perforated traveling conveyor or screen, and heated air is forced through in contact with the product. Most tunnel driers are of the continuous type although there are many variations some of which are batch type. Batch units employ trays or containers in a tunnel. Drying in the tunnel drier utilizes the same basic principles of heat and mass transfer as are found in spray driers.

Driers of this type can be atmospheric or may be placed under vacuum or pressure to meet the specific requirements. Heating may be by steam, gas, or electricity. Automatic controls are available to maintain temperature and humidity. The conveyor may be a flexible chain, a belt, or in some cases a stainless steel belt.

Feeding and unloading of the conveyor belt are important. The feeding is usually done by a vibratory or oscillating feeder, although the material may be sprayed on the belt or may be in the form of pellets against the belt.

The temperature of the drying air must be adapted to the product which is being dried. This may be anywhere from a few degrees above 0°F in a case of vacuum driers to 400° or 500°F.

Efficiency

The efficiency of tunnel driers varies from a low of 20% up to 70%. This efficiency depends very largely on the temperatures of operation, the amount of insulation on the drier, the percentage moisture to be removed from the product, and the type of product. The temperature at which the product enters the drier and the discharge temperature are also important elements in the cost of operation. In general, continuous operation provides a more efficient operation. Figure T.11 shows the variation in drying characteristics of certain grains.

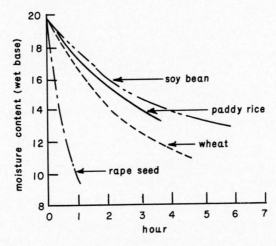

FIG. T-11.   Comparison of drying characteristics of some grains

TABLE T.8

YIELD OF DRY PRODUCTS PER 100 LB OF FRESH MATERIAL

Description	Wt. in Lb.
Apples	
Late autumn and winter varieties	12 – 15
Summer Varieties	10 – 12
Apricots	16 – 18
Blackberries	16 – 20
Beans	11 – 13
Beets	14 – 17
Cabbage	8 – 10
Carrots	10 – 12
Cauliflower	12 – 14
Celery	8 – 9
Cherries	
Pie	17 – 21
Sweet	22 – 26
Corn, sweet	26 – 33
Figs	18 – 23
Loganberries	17 – 22
Okra	10 – 11
Onions	9 – 11
Parsnips	20 – 22
Peaches	13 – 16
Pears	18 – 22
Peas, garden	22 – 25
Potatoes	
Sweet	30 – 35
White	23 – 25
Prunes	30 – 33
Pumpkin	6 – 8
Raspberries	17 – 23
Spinach	8 – 10
Squash	7 – 9
Tomatoes	$6^{1}/_{2}$ – 9
Turnips	7 – 8

Source: Farmers Bulletin *984*.

Table T.8 shows the yield of dry products per 100 lb of fresh material.

References

BAN, TOSHIZO. 1965. Drying of rice in Japan, special paper. Drying and Storage Equipment Lab., Inst. Agr. Machinery, Saitama, Japan. June.

Cross-references: *Air; Air Movement; Psychrometric Chart; Driers (Various).*

TURBIDITY METER

Evaporated water if not contaminated from the final effect of a multiple effect evaporator can be returned to the boiler or used for washing in a plant. Carryover of the product into the exhaust vapors can occur if (1) the evaporator is started too quickly, or (2) the level of liquid in the evaporator is too high.   In order to reduce the level in the evaporator, it is better to reduce gradually the water to the condenser instead of letting in air to reduce the foam.   This practice will reduce carryover.

Automatic units are available for diverting the flow if the product is contaminated. A turbidity meter can be used for direct divert.   If the connection is to the boiler and the return is diverted, it is desirable that other water be directed to the boiler.   The contaminated product is often referred to as "cow water."

Reference

HALL, C. W., and HEDRICK, T. I.   1966.   Drying of Milk and Milk Products.   AVI Publishing Co., Westport, Conn.

Cross-references: *Evaporation; Evaporators.*

U

ULTRACENTRIFUGE

"Super centrifuge" is a name applied to a type of ultracentrifuge which is able to develop a centrifugal force over 15,000 times gravity in commercial models and over 60,000 times gravity in special laboratory units.

Centrifugal equipment is made in both batch and continuous types, and is used for (1) separating solids from liquids, to clarify the liquid, recover the solid, or both; (2) separating mixtures or emulsions of two immiscible liquids; (3) separating three-phase systems in a single step—simultaneously removing solids and separating two liquids; and (4) classifying by particle size solids suspended in a liquid.

Ultracentrifuges have proved advantageous in a variety of applications. Ultracentrifuges are used by (1) food processors for clarifying and standardizing soups, jellies, juices, pastes, purées, and many other products; (2) vegetable oil refiners to gain increased efficiency and yield in refining and degumming; and (3) pharmaceutical manufacturers to clarify agars and broths, to produce penicillin, to prepare serums and vaccines, to separate blood and fractionate plasma, and to purify and harvest microscopically small viruses and bacteria.

Principle of the Centrifuge

A moving body tends to continue in the same direction in which it was started. If it is forced to change direction—to follow a curved path, for example—it resists the change and exerts a force against whatever keeps it from following a straight path. This force, which is applied outward from the center of curvature, is called centrifugal force.

The application of centrifugal force many times greater than the force of gravity makes possible both a more complete separation of the materials and a reduction of separation time to a mere fraction of that required for gravity settling. In many industrial separation problems, the difference in the specific gravity of the materials is very slight. In addition, the "settling" or separation time can be greatly affected by the size, shape and physical nature of the solids, the viscosities of the liquids, and other factors. High centrifugal force enables efficient, economical separation to be achieved even when separation by any other method is a practical impossibility.

Continuous Centrifuge

If a hollow "rotor" is equipped with an inlet at the bottom and discharge ports at the top, and is appropriately lengthened, a continuous flow of mixture may be subjected to high centrifugal force (Fig. U.1). The separated liquids are displaced by the

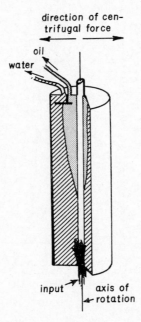

direction of cen-
trifugal force

oil

water

input

axis of
rotation

FIG. U-1.   Principles of the continuous centrifuge

incoming mixture, and are discharged through respective ports.   The solids accumulate in a layer or "cake" on the inner wall of the rotor, and can be periodically removed.

Many special types of centrifuges are available including open type, totally enlosed, and sludge discharge, which can be operated at refrigerated or heated temperatures.   Major considerations in the care and operation include leveling, lubricating, and installing on a firm foundation.

Cross-references: *Bactofugation; Centrifugal Separators.*

ULTRAFILTRATION

Ultrafiltration may be referred to as final filtering in obtaining sterile fluid or sterile air.   The filtration may be used to clarify a fluid possessing a haziness due to the presence of dead microorganisms or colloidal particles.   These filters are particularly useful in laboratory work or in the production of extremely high quality water or other liquids.   Some of the requirements of ultrafilters are: (1) possess sufficient strength to withstand necessary filtering pressure; (2) ability to retain particles within the stated limits; (3) filtration must be sufficiently rapid; (4) possess the ability to handle an adequate volume before developing undesirable resistance; (5) must withstand heat of sterilization or other sterilization procedure; and (6) satisfactory cleanability unless designed for single service.

Ceramic candles, so-called because of their shape, were the first submicron filters manufactured.   These were made by careful blending of ingredients followed by low temperature firing to produce a uniform porosity.   These units are tubular in shape and available in various size and pore diameters.   They are somewhat fragile for industrial use but have been useful in the laboratory.

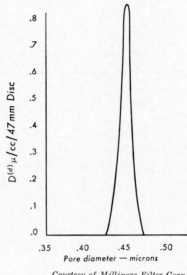

$D^{(d)} \mu / cc / 47 mm\ Disc$

Pore diameter — microns

Courtesy of Millipore Filter Corp.

FIG. U-2.   Pore size distribution curve for the type HA membrane filter

More recently the single service membranes composed of biologically inert cellulose esters are finding widespread use in industry. Ultrafiltration procedures for
determining the bacterial content of water or similar fluids with this type filter are
common. The filters are of several types with pore sizes from 5 to 10 μ. Each type
retains on its surface all particles, and bacteria whose size exceeds the pore diameter.
Pore size uniformity is important and varies no more than $\pm 0.02 \mu$ for a filter with a
designated pore size of 0.45μ. A typical pore size distribution curve is shown in
Fig. U.2.

The pore size and flow characteristics of some available filter membranes are presented in Table U.1. Many of the filters of this type enhance filtration of air and gases

TABLE U.1

PORE SIZE AND FLOW CHARACTERISTICS OF SOME FILTER MEMBRANES

Type Code	Pore Size, Microns	Flow Rate, Ml/Min. Cm² at 25°C and 70 Cm HgΔp.	
		Water	Air
SM	5.0 ± 1.2	560	35,000
SS	3.0 ± 0.9	400	20,000
RA	1.2 ± 0.3	300	14,000
AA	0.80 ± 0.05	220	9,800
DA	0.65 ± 0.03	175	8,000
HA	0.45 ± 0.02	65	4,900
PH	0.30 ± 0.02	40	3,700
GS	0.22 ± 0.02	22	2,500
VC	100 mμ ± 8 mμ	3.0	1,000
VM	50 mμ ± 3 mμ	1.5	700
VF	10 mμ ± 2 mμ	0.5	300

Source: Millipore Filter Corp.

through electrostatic charges which are generated. This negative charge prevents passage of particles smaller than the filter pores.

A typical small capacity filtering system to produce exceptionally high quality water is illustrated in Fig. U.3. This system incorporates a prefilter ahead of deionization followed by the ultrafilter. Final filter for the system is available in pore sizes of 0.65, 0.80, and 1.2μ.

The pleated membrane cartridge is also satisfactory for submicron filtration. A cartridge porosity of 0.45μ is recommended for bacteria removal. The replaceable

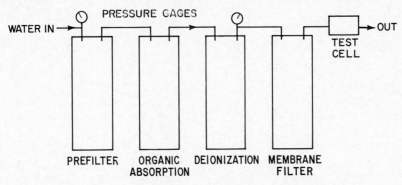

FIG. U-3.   Extra high quality modular water treatment system

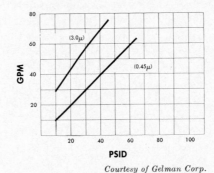

Courtesy of Gelman Corp.

FIG. U-4.   Water flow rate through stainless steel housing and pleated membrane at room temperature

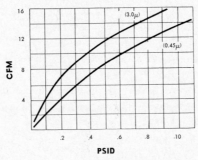

Courtesy of Gelman Corp.

FIG. U-5.   Airflow through plastic housing and pleated membrane at room temperature

cartridge of 2.59 in. diam by $9^{13}/_{16}$ in. length has a flow rate capacity of water with a stainless steel housing as illustrated in Fig. U.4. Capacity for this unit in both the 3.0 and 0.45μ pore size for air is shown in Fig. U.5.

Ultrafilters are valuable for obtaining exceptionally clean liquids and gases, and for microbiological analysis.

References

WEBB, F. C. 1964. Biochemical Engineering. D. Van Nostrand Co., London.
MILLIPORE FILTER CORP. 1962. Detection and analysis of contamination. Bedford, Mass.
GELMAN INSTRUMENT CO. 1968. Gelman pleated membrane cartridges make submicron filtration in your production line or lab practical! Bull., Ann Arbor, Mich.

Cross-references: *Air Filters; Filters.*

UHT EQUIPMENT

Vacreator

The vacreator consists of three stainless steel chambers connected together for continuous product flow and treatment with steam and vacuum. The product enters the first chamber where pasteurization occurs. This chamber is operated under a vacuum (5 in. Hg), to maintain a temperature of 194° to 205°F, while dry saturated steam at 40 psi is fed into the chamber at the top and falls by gravity to the bottom. Then the product and some free steam move from the bottom of the first chamber to the top of the second chamber. In the second chamber a temperature of 160° to 180°F is maintained under a vacuum of 15 to 20 in. Hg. A portion of the steam previously added is removed and the product moves down through the chamber. Some of the off-flavor causing substances are removed by the heat treatment and vacuum. Continuing, the product moves to the third chamber of 110°F, and by maintaining a vacuum of 26 to 28 in. Hg, more water and some off-flavors are removed. A multistage centrifugal pump removes the milk from the third chamber. See Vacuum Treatment.

The U.S. Public Health Service has accepted the vacreator method for pasteurization of milk (at a temperature of 194°F in properly operated conventional equipment), as being equivalent to conventional pasteurization. A total time of about 10 sec is required for the product to move continuously through the unit.

An ejector condenser produces the vacuum for the chambers and condenses the vapors and removes noncondensable gases. The water used for the condenser should be 90°F or below. The large size vacreator has a capacity of 12,000 lb per hr with water at 60° to 65°F, and requires 19,000 to 20,000 lb per hr of water at 70 to 75 psi at full load for the ejector condenser.

Steam of uniform pressure must be provided, normally assured by a pressure reducing and regulating valve. The steam must not contain any boiler compounds which may contaminate the product.

Roswell Heat Exchanger

The Roswell annular heat exchanger consists of a hollow stainless steel tubular unit, 4 in. in diam. and 68 in. long (Foote 1956). The tubular unit is encircled by a

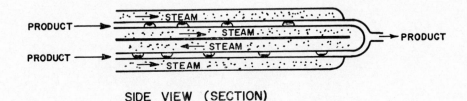

SIDE VIEW (SECTION)

FIG. U-6.   Roswell heat exchanger

spiral band of $^1/_8$ in. height so that the $^1/_8$ in. film of product must move around the tube.   The tubular unit slides into a cylindrical chamber.   The unit is made of type 316 stainless steel.   The product moves through the unit, a distance of 18 ft, at a velocity from 8 to 18 fps.   At a flow rate of 1,200 gph or 11,600 lb per hr the linear velocity is 12 fps.   Thus, the product is in the heat exchanger for 1.5 sec.   About 1.5 pt of product are required fo fill the heat exchanger unit.

The film is heated from both sides by using desuperheated steam.   (Fig. U.6). Approximately 13 sq ft of heating surface is provided for each heat exchanger tube. The unit is designed to heat the product through 70°F per tube at 1,200 gph capacity. The heat transfer rate is from 600,000 to 750,000 Btu per hr per tube.   A common arrangement uses two tubes obtaining double the heat transfer.   A U-value of 350 Btu per hr sq ft °F, is obtained.

To prevent burn-on and product damage the product must move through the heater rapidly and uniformly.   The unit is designed to use steam pressures up to 200 psi, with 100 to 125 psi steam pressure normally used.   For lower heat transfer rates it can be operated at 70 psi steam pressure.   More rapid heat transfer is obtained by using desuperheated steam.   A vacuum treatment may be placed ahead of the Roswell unit to remove air and to increase throughput.

Most of the steam moves in the same direction as the product flow.   The unit has been approved by the U.S. Public Health Service for pasteurization at 200°F with a calculated holding time of 3 sec.   When used without a designed holding time the effective holding time for a flow rate of 6,000 lb per hr is 0.5 sec for heatup, 0.2 sec for discharge from heater, and 0.1 sec for cooling, thus making a total of 0.8 sec effective holding at 187°F for Z-values equal to 8.9° and 10.2°F.

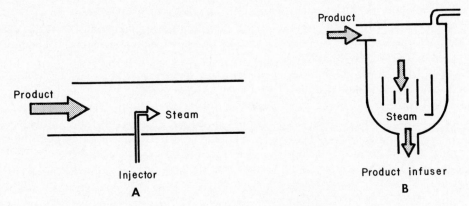

FIG. U-7.   Direct steam heaters

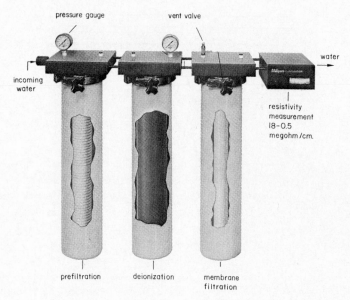

Courtesy of Millipore Filter Corp.

FIG. U-8.   Filtration and deionization system for water

Injection Steam Heating of Product

Steam heaters may be installed, injecting steam directly into the product ahead of the temperature control. The steam may be admitted by either an injector or infuser, (Fig. U.7 A and B), if local and state codes permit. With the injector the steam is admitted directly into the product, generally in the direction of flow of the product. With the infuser the product moves into a chamber to drop vertically through a steam bath, generally with the steam moving upward and the product moving downward. Direct-steam heating is used widely and is the basis for the uperization process developed in Europe.

Uperization is derived from the term ultrapasteurization and is a process by which steam is used for heating milk continuously to 300°F for less than 1 sec (reported as 0.75 sec). In this process the product is preheated and deaerated before moving to the uperization tube. Here the product is heated with high pressure steam at 140 to 195 psi. After heating, the product moves into an expansion chamber which is near atmospheric pressure and therefore permits some evaporation of moisture. The product then moves to a cooler and to storage.

If steam is injected into a product, the mean temperature difference between the steam and the milk should be reached. For example, dry, saturated steam at 70 psi pressure is discharged into a vat of milk heating it from 60° to 178°F. The mean temperature difference between the heated milk and steam is 191.9°F. The heat delivered by the steam is 1,089.1 Btu per lb, and the pounds of steam required to heat the milk through a stated temperature range can be calculated.

When the steam is discharged directly into the milk, the water of condensation is added to the milk. When exhaust steam is used instead of live steam, the quantity of water added is considerably higher, because exhaust steam contains a greater amount of water. To heat 1,000 lb of milk from 60° to 178°F, 103 lb of water are added, or 10.3%.

Reference

HALL, C. W., and TROUT, G. M. 1968. Milk Pasteurization. AVI Publishing Co., Westport, Conn.

Cross-references: *HTST Pasteurization; Heat Exchangers; Pasteurization; Sterilizers.*

UNSCRAMBLERS

Bottle unscramblers are widely used in large breweries and bottling plants of large capacity for soft drinks, dairy products, and certain juices. The unscrambler is a sizable labor saving device particularly when used in conjunction with an uncaser and bottle washer feed unit. Capacity in excess of 500 bottles per minute are handled with the unscrambler equipment. An unscrambler places bottles on flat top feed conveyors supplying the unscrambler sized to fit the full width of the bottle washer. An oscillating bar with vertical separators arranges the incoming bottles in such a way that they are channeled through feed lanes directly in line with each row of pockets in the bottle washer. Bottles are unscrambled in a vertical position; however, they are tipped over curved feed bars to enter the pocket in a horizontal position. The tipping of the bottle to the horizontal position is a function of the washer loader rather than of the unscrambler. The unscrambler consists of parallel flat top bottle conveyors the number of which is determined by the width of the washer. This bed of feed conveyors in the unscrambler run continuously carrying bottles to the oscillating bar with the separators. The unscrambler is a comparatively simple machine and is a feasible investment especially for large volume plants.

Unscramblers are also used in food canning plants to feed metal cans stored haphazardly in bins or hoppers on to conveyors for casing or labeling. A conveying chain or belt operating in grooves is one of the unscrambling principles employed to accomplish unscrambling.

V

VACUUM COOLING

Vacuum cooling is specialized precooling suitable for such crops as lettuce, cabbage, celery, cauliflower, and spinach. Some studies have shown the method to be satisfactory for garden peas and mushrooms. Water essentially boils at 32°F when the atmospheric pressure is reduced to $1/165$ of the normal 14.7 psi. This rapid evaporation dispels the heat from the product. The process of rapid evaporation under greatly reduced pressure allows a small quantity of water to reduce the temperature to the desired level, particularly of leafy type crops. A product with a large surface area in proportion to its volume will cool quickly through rapid evaporation without excessive drying of the surface. For this reason lettuce and other leafy products are especially suited to vacuum cooling. If sweet corn is vacuum cooled, it must be sprinkled with water before and after cooling to avoid drying of the kernels.

Vacuum cooling of lettuce is done in about 20 to 25 min in a vacuum vessel where the pressure is gradually reduced to a final reading of 4.6 mm Hg. By reducing the pressure to 3.8 mm Hg, lettuce can be satisfactorily cooled in 15 min. The saving in time is an advantage during the peak of the harvest season.

The operator of vacuum cooling equipment should not rely on a wet-bulb thermometer for temperature determination when the pressure is less than 4.6 mm Hg. At the low pressures the wet-bulb thermometer responds slowly and the surface water tends to freeze.

Cooling does not occur until the vacuum is increased to the "flash point" which should be reached as fast as possible. After reaching the "flash point," most products should be held about 15 min, and during this time the pressure should be reduced to a final 3.8 mm Hg. These conditions are especially suitable for cooling lettuce with an average temperature of 60°F.

Mushrooms are being successfully vacuum cooled under a pressure of 0.2 in. Hg. The product is reduced from 55° to 35°F in 15 min in the vacuum cooler. Water at 35°F is at the equilibrium temperature when exposed to water vapor at a pressure of 0.2 in. Hg. The weight loss of mushrooms cooled by this method averages about 3%.

A typical vacuum cooler is a long cylinder of heavy construction and designed especially to withstand high vacuums (Fig. V.1). The chamber may be opened on each end for loading and unloading of product. Chambers may be loaded with several pallets of produce and handled with a fork truck.

Two vacuum chambers may be connected with piping so that the freshly loaded chamber may be used to partially break the vacuum of the other. This arrangement permits alternating operation of the chambers in an efficient manner.

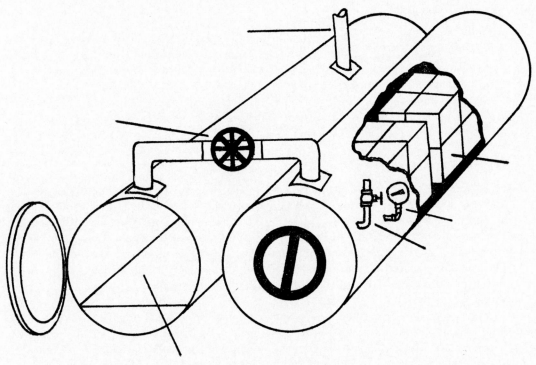

Fɪɢ. V-1.   Vacuum coolers

Vacuum for cooling may be produced by various systems.   The high barometric condenser is satisfactory when used in conjunction with steam jet vacuum units.

References

Cook, J. A. 1960. Precooling fruits and vegetables. Mich. State Univ. Exten. Folder *F285*. East Lansing, Mich.

U. S. Dept. Agr. 1962A. Precooling celery. Agr. Marketing Serv. 7, No. 12, Dec.

U. S. Dept. Agr. 1962B. Rapid vacuum cooling of lettuce. Agr. Marketing Serv. 7, No. 8, Aug.

Cross-reference: *Refrigerated Storage of Fruits and Vegetables.*

VACUUM DRIER

One method of vacuum drying is to meter nitrogen into concentrated whole milk after homogenization. The product is then cooled to 35°F in a scraped surface heat exchanger. The concentrate is placed on a solid stainless steel horizontal belt 12 in. wide (small model). It goes through a heating drum, then a cooling drum, each 2 ft diam for heating and cooling. Heat is supplied by 19 banks of 2 kw radiant heaters. A vacuum of about 50 mm Hg abs is supplied. Scraper blades remove the product from the belt.

Cross-reference: *Drum Drier.*

VACUUM FILLER

The filling of glass bottles particularly in the food industry is an exacting operation. The bottles must be filled accurately, capped automatically, and there must be no loss of liquid in case of a broken bottle or faulty operation. Operations must be done without contaminating the product.

Gravity fillers and pressure type fillers of various types have been used. Vacuum fillers for glass and rigid containers are widely used to minimize leaks, reduce foam problems, and to assure more uniform filling.

Types of Vacuum Fillers

There are two types of vacuum fillers. The simple type of vacuum filler valve shown in Fig. V.2 maintains a slight vacuum on the bottle filler bowl at all times and by that means prevents spilling of a broken bottle or one that is not fully indexed. The vacuum also draws off foam and thus assures a more properly filled bottle. The construction of the valve is very similar to that of the ordinary gravity type filler. The vacuum required for the operation of the filler is usually supplied by a suction blower or a high speed fan. About 4 in. Hg vacuum is normally used on this type filler.

The other type of vacuum filler (such as manufactured by Mojonnier) uses a very different type of filling device (shown in Fig. V.3). With this type of filler, the piping arrangement is such that the bottle acts as a trench to catch the milk as it comes through the filling orifice. If no bottle is under the valve or if the bottle is cracked and allows air to enter, the fluid is not raised to a sufficient elevation to fill the bottle and therefore passes unfilled. If no bottle is under the valve, the same thing happens.

Reference

FARRALL, A. W.   1963.   Engineering for Dairy and Food Products, 3rd Edition.   John Wiley & Sons, New York.

Cross-reference: *Bottle Fillers.*

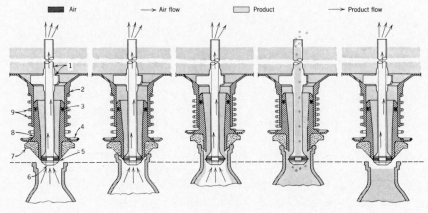

Courtesy of St. Regis Corp.

FIG. V-2.   Vacuum-filler valve action

VACUUM PACKAGING

The shelf-life of many foods is increased when stored or processed in an atmosphere of reduced oxygen content. Thus, attempts have been made to maintain a low oxygen content by various means. Vacuum packaging through the use of a hermetically sealed container, which serves as an oxygen barrier, is a technique successfully used, especially in packaging meats.

Quality factors of vacuum packaging as applied to the meat industry include: (1) packaging costs are slightly increased, (2) visibility of the product is enhanced to improve merchandising, (3) bacterial growth is substantially inhibited with resultant increased shelf-life, (4) sanitary conditions in the handling and packaging of the prod-

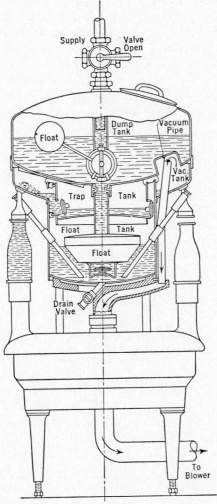

Courtesy of Mojonnier Bros.

FIG. V-3.   Cross section view showing principle of operation of the vacuum-type bottle filler

uct are maintained because packaging is done at the processing plant, and (5) red beef darkens in the vacuum package, however, the flavor is retained and the red color usually returns when the meat is later exposed to the atmosphere. (Oxygen is needed to produce red color in red meat.)

Processed meats usually require a package which will maintain a 25 mm abs pressure, which is equal to 1 psi under standard conditions. Vacuum packed cheese slices require a package which will maintain 15 mm abs pressure. Requirements for vacuum packaging include the following: (1) oxygen level within the package must be reduced to prevent spoilage, (2) package must be made from a film or other material which can be tightly sealed and serve as an adequate oxygen barrier, and (3) a satisfactory package must also be practical from a cost standpoint. Generally, those materials use extremely low oxygen permeability, are higher in cost, and for some products may not be practical. In selecting the package material, the shelf-life desired must be balanced against package costs. Additional shelf-life may be obtained in some cases but the cost is prohibitive. (4) Packaging materials must be sealable without wrinkles at the sealing point. Wrinkles at the seal usually result in inadequate sealing.

Oxygen transmission rates through flexible packaging materials are of interest to those packaging foods requiring low oxygen levels. Some of the commonly used plastics or laminates have the following oxygen transmission characteristics

Oxygen Transmission Rates of Flexible Materials
(Average varies under refrigerator display case conditions)

Material	CC per 100 Sq In per Day per Atmospheric Pressure Differential
Polyacrylonitrile, 1 mil	0.03
Saran, 1 mil	0.5
Saran (polymer) coated cellophane	1.0
Saran (polymer) coated polyester	1.0
Cellophane (MSAD or MSB) Laminated to PE (dry conditions)	2.5
Nylon, 1 mil	6.0
Polyester ($1/2$ mil uncoated, bioriented) laminated to PE	8.0
PE, 1 mil	250.0[1]

New developments are occurring regularly with one of the newer packaging innovations by the use of polyvinyl chloride (PVD). This material gives good product visibility, adequate flexibility, a high resistance to oxygen passage, and has Food and Drug Administration approval. PVC will undoubtedly find wider use in the food industry. A second new development involving vacuum packaging includes peelable seals suitable for reclosing a package, as well as an initially easy opening feature. Most vacuum packaging materials must be hermetically sealable to themselves. Aluminum foil is frequently used especially as a component of a laminate because of its low oxygen

---

[1] This material, when used in flexible vacuum packs, contributes properties other than gas barrier. It is shown for purposes of comparison. Most vacuum-packaged perishable foods will not tolerate a rate much above 5 cc and may require a rate under 1 cc to ensure 3-week shelf-life.

transmission properties. Aluminum foil is difficult to manufacture without developing pinholes especially in lighter gages. Aluminum foil upon creasing will frequently crack resulting in smaller openings and loss of barrier properties. Saran is a relatively inexpensive plastic with excellent barrier characteristics. Another product which may be receiving more attention in the industry is polyacrylonitrile. This material is said to possess approximately 20 times the barrier resistance as Saran. Combinations of Saran and vinyl are suitable for packaging bacon, frankfurters, and similar products. It is possible to extrude and form the laminated film at the processing plant at the time of packaging. The system requires considerable volume because of the initial cost.

Cellophane coated with Saran is a widely used material for vacuum and gas pouches. Two other materials used as laminates are a Saran film between two layers of polyethylene and nylon which has replaced polyester films in certain applications requiring deep draw which is the most thermoformable of the substrates used for vacuum packaging.

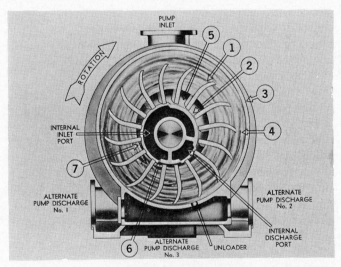

Courtesy of Nash Engineering Co.

Fig. V-4.   How a typical rotary vacuum pump operates
A rotor (1), in dynamic balance, revolves freely, without metallic contact, in a circular casing (3) containing a liquid, usually water (4). This rotor (1) is a circular casting consisting of a series of blades projecting from a hollow cylindrical hub through which the shaft has been pressed. These blades are shrouded at the sides and form a series of chambers. Note that the curvature of the blades is in the direction of rotation. Starting at point A, the chambers of the rotor are full of water. This water rotates with the rotor, but follows the contour of the casing (3), due to centrifugal force. The water (4), which entirely fills the rotor chamber at A, recedes as the rotor advances, until (at 5) the rotor chamber is empty. The converging casing forces the water back into the rotor chamber, until (at 6) it is full again. This cycle occurs once in each revolution. As the water is caused to recede from the rotor chamber (at 7) it is replaced by air entering through "Inlet Port" in conical casting (2), connected with the "Pump Inlet." As the rotor turns 360°, and the water is forced by the casing back into the rotor chamber, the air that has filled the chamber is forced through the "Discharge Ports" provided in the conical casting (2), to the Pump Discharge.

Other Uses for Vacuum Packaging

An example of vacuum packaging is for frozen vegetables containing butter sauce for boil-in-pack heating of the product. The vacuum packaged product does not float in the water assuring submergence with rapid and uniform defrosting and heating. Frozen fruit packed in this manner is also more easily thawed in warm water.

Reference

YOUNG, W. E.   1967.   Vacuum and gas packaging.   Mod. Packaging *21*, No. 9, 236–239.

Cross-references: *Oxygen-Effect on Foods; Packages; Packaging.*

VACUUM PUMPS

Vacuum pumps are very widely used in the food industry in vacuum evaporating systems and for the operation of automatic lifting devices.   Vacuum pumps are of the so-called high and low vacuum types.   High vacuum pumps are normally used with a condenser in connection with vacuum evaporating systems.

The vacuum pump must handle an extremely large volume of material such as gas or air, since the product is under less than atmospheric pressure and the volume of air expands greatly under these subatmospheric pressures.

The simplest type of vacuum pump which is used for low vacuum purposes is a rotating vane or lobe pump which is liquid sealed (Fig. V.4).   This pump is relatively inexpensive and performs very satisfactorily for vacuums up to 15 to 24 in. Hg.   It must be oil-sealed or water-sealed to work properly.   It is very steady and trouble-free in its operation.

The second type of vacuum pump is the piston type pump which is built much like the standard water pump except the clearance at the end of the cylinder and around the valves is kept as small as possible and the valves themselves are as lightweight as can be made and still withstand the operation.

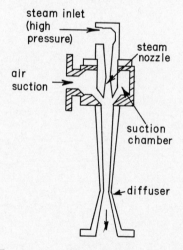

FIG. V-5.   Single-stage air ejector

The third type of vacuum pump is the so-called steam jet ejector (Fig. V.5). This pump is used on evaporating equipment, particularly if it is to be used at a real high vacuum, 29 in. Hg or higher. This type ejector is made in multistages from 1 to 4 and is very efficient in large sizes and at a high vacuum. It has no moving parts and very little service is required. It is necessary that no moisture go through the jet, and also that it is properly balanced relative to the pressure and size of the jet and orifice.

Cross-reference : *Vacuum Treatment.*

VACUUM TREATMENT (DEAERATION)

Milk may be subjected to a vacuum to improve flavor and odor by removing the low-boiling point volatile components. This practice was developed in New Zealand and Australia and in the southern states of the United States, particularly where onion and garlic milk flavors were encountered. A vacuum treatment after high temperature treatment also reduces burned or heat flavors. The purpose of vacuum treatment or deaeration is to provide an acceptable beverage with uniform quality with a minimum of off-flavors or taints throughout the year.

The off-flavor substances found in milk vary in volatility and vapor pressure. Volatility may vary according to whether or not steam is used with the vacuum, other factors remaining the same. Butyric acid has a higher boiling point than formic acid, but is more steam-volatile. Gas chromatography provides a method of evaluating the effectiveness of vacuum treatment by studying the liquid-gas phase.

Equipment

The equipment for vacuum treatment may be placed in three categories: (1)

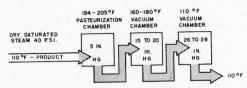

Fig. V-6.   Vacuum treatment for HTST pasteurization for milk

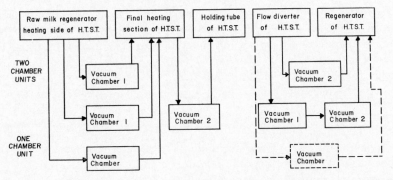

Fig. V-7.   Method of attaching vacuum treatment equipment to HTST system

simultaneous vacuum treatment and pasteurization in a single unit, (2) batch vacuum treatment, and (3) continuous vacuum treatment in remote units separate from the pasteurization equipment.

The first type used since 1940 is primarily for the treatment of cream as well as milk. The process involves steam injection followed by flashing of the product into one or more chambers to cool it and remove water. Volatiles are removed during the flashing of product. The product is then heated to 194°–205°F with 5 in. Hg vacuum in the pasteurization chamber, and then to the first vacuum chamber at 15–20 in. Hg at 160°–180°F, and a second vacuum chamber at 26–28 in. Hg at 110°F (Fig. V.6).

The batch vacuum treatment system consists of applying a vacuum during heating, holding, and cooling of the milk in a process vat. In commercial units now available up to 10 in. Hg vacuum may be used. This equipment is not used extensively in the United States, where batch pasteurization is not of major importance in processing plants.

Continuous vacuum treatment in remote units placed ahead of or following conventional HTST pasteurization has gained in importance. The equipment may be further classified as 1-chamber or 2-chamber, and as live (open) steam or flash steam units. These units can be placed in various positions in the HTST system (Fig. V.7).

Flash steam is produced by increasing the temperature of the product above the boiling point corresponding to the pressure of the product. The water which evaporates is known as flash steam. In some locations the introduction of live steam is prohibited, because the steam may contain undesirable chemicals from water treatment which will affect the product. A heat exchanger is available to produce culinary steam.

Steam Flow

As the product moves to the vacuum chamber, steam may be added to increase the temperature of the product. Heat may be taken away to reduce the temperature of the product by evaporation of water and volatiles. Heat loss from the walls of the chamber will occur, reducing the product temperature. Typical temperatures for a two-chamber unit using steam injection are as follows: 10,000 lb per hr milk at 162°F flows from the HTST unit to the first vacuum chamber at 9.5 in. Hg. Steam is added at the rate of 341 lb per hr which heats the milk about 34.1°F if there are no heat losses or evaporation. At 9.5 in. Hg evaporation takes place at 194°F, so that the temperature will not exceed that value. A heat loss of 8050 Btu per hr may occur from the first chamber, which is equivalent to reducing the temperature at full flow by 0.8°F. The product then moves to the second chamber at a vacuum of 22 in. Hg, where the product is cooled to 152°F by evaporation. With a heat loss of 6900 Btu per hr, a temperature drop of 0.69°F will occur making a total temperature drop of 1.49°F for full flow. The temperature drop would be greater for a lower flow rate.

Control

The proper control of steam flow, milk flow, and the vacuum is necessary to avoid either concentration or dilution of the product. With steam heating, the change in product concentration is determined primarily by the ratio of steam condensed in the first chamber to water evaporated in the second chamber. To avoid change in con-

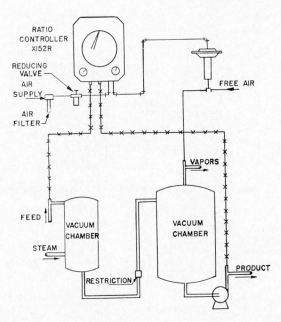

Fɪɢ. V-8.　　Control of two-vacuum chamber treatment unit

centration, assuming no heat loss, equal addition of steam and removal of water are obtained if the temperature rise in the first chamber with 100% quality steam is equal to the temperature decrease of the product in the second chamber. It is necessary in practice to have a lower outlet temperature than inlet temperature to provide heat for vaporization of components and heat losses. To remove more water in the second chamber, the temperature of evaporation is decreased by increasing the vacuum by means of automatic control devices which sense the inlet and outlet temperatures (Fig. V.8). The outlet is kept at 3° to 5°F below the inlet temperature to ensure that there is no change in density of the product.

Water

A direct water condenser (ejector condenser) may be used for condensing vapors in a chamber after the steam injection chamber (Fig. V.9). Condensables are removed with the water by a vacuum pump. A vacuum is pulled on the condenser to remove noncondensables. This unit is usually used if only noncondensables and low temperature volatiles are removed from the final chamber.

A plate condenser (Fig. V.9) with cold water for cooling is often used. The noncondensables are discharged with condensables by the vacuum pump. The plate condenser is usually used when considerable vapor is to be condensed after steam injection.

About 4 gal per min of water are needed for each 100 lb per hr of vapor for the direct water condenser. In a vacuum treating chamber separate from the pasteurization unit, 100 lb per hr of vapor can be handled for each 5000 lb per hr of product capacity. If no steam were added, this would provide a concentration of product of 2%.

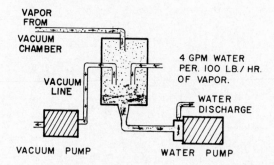

A. DIRECT WATER CONDENSER FOR VACUUM UNIT

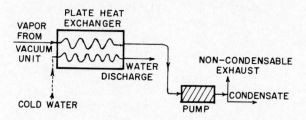

B. PLATE CONDENSER FOR VACUUM UNIT

FIG. V-9.   Condensation of vapor from vacuum unit

Off-Flavor Diffusion

The movement of the off-flavor or taint-producing substances from the milk is based primarily on the diffusion constant which is on the order of 1×10^{-5} sq ft per hr, and the vapor pressure difference between the off-flavor substance in the product and in the steam. The steam will absorb the off-flavor substance until it is at equilibrium with it. Thus, fresh steam must be supplied to continue removing the taint.

The equilibrium constant might be expressed by "m," the ratio of off-flavor concentration in the outgoing steam to the concentration in the outgoing product. The m is a property of the off-flavor and the product. The following relationship represents the effectiveness, E, of a vacuum system

$$E = \frac{mV}{L} \tag{1}$$

where m = equilibrium constant
V = flow of steam, lb per hr
L = flow of the product, lb per hr

Increased effectiveness is not obtained for V/L beyond 0.20.

For a single chamber without change in concentration of milk the reduction of off-flavor concentration based on the material balance is given by

$$\frac{X_f}{X_o} = \frac{1}{1 + (mV/L)} \tag{2}$$

where X_f = final off-flavor concentration of the product, ppm

X_o = original off-flavor concentration of the product, ppm

For poor quality cream, $m = 5$ (low volatility); for good quality cream, $m = 20$; for milk, m is much higher, perhaps 30 to 50, and for lactose solution, $m = 60$ (quite volatile). An equilibrium constant of $m = 10$ is used in New Zealand in design of deodorizers for cream.

When steam is not used, filtered air may be bubbled through the product to release the volatile materials. The vapor pressure difference principle is used for one commercial unit. In it the product at 162°F is forced through a venturi through which additional product is picked up and a thin film is sprayed inside the large vacuum cylinder. The noncondensable gases are carried from the system by a cold water spray. The product may be circulated through the venturi system several times.

Cross-references: *UHT Equipment; Vacuum Pumps.*

VALVES

Valves are devices for shutting off or modulating the flow of fluids such as air and liquids, and in some cases powdered or granular material. Valves are widely used in the food processing industry both in the power plant and in connection with the various processes for handling food products. The simplest type of valve is probably a plug valve and from this simple device there is a range to very complicated and sophisticated electronically or air operated valves.

Valves are either of the sanitary type or the nonsanitary type with respect to cleaning.

The principal criteria for the selection of valves are that they must be dependable, durable, and controllable.

Nonsanitary valves of dozens of configurations are made for general industrial use, however, Fig. V.10 shows the typical nonsanitary valves—plug valve, the globe valve, and the needle valve. A check valve is a special type of valve which will allow the fluid to pass only in one direction.

Figure V.11 shows an assortment of sanitary valves.

Sanitary valves are made according to the 3A Standards, and are quite highly standardized in the United States.

Materials of sanitary valves are usually stainless steel; however, some so-called white metal valves are still used.

Many special types of valves are used in the food industry, for example, the flow diversion valve (see pasteurization systems); in addition there are valves which are operated by air pressure or electromagnetic means.

Valves can be made reverse acting or direct acting.

Special valves called leak detector valves are used widely in the food industry, particularly as a part of pasteurization systems. These valves are so made that if there is any leakage from the pasteurized product or the unpasteurized product through the valve, it will be directed onto the floor, and it is therefore impossible for any unpasteurized product to leak into the pasteurized area.

A special type of valve is used in milk powder plants to feed powder out of a hopper without loss of appreciable quantities of air. This valve has a series of pockets which collect the powder, rotate, and carry the powder out without loss of air.

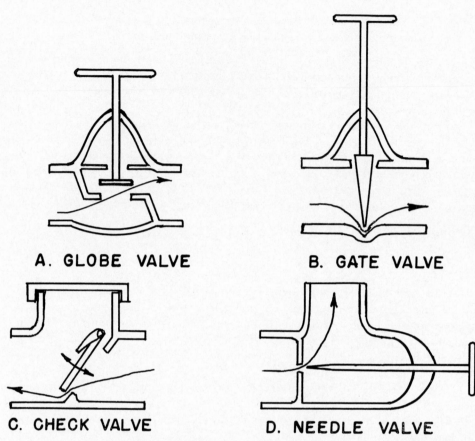

A. GLOBE VALVE   B. GATE VALVE

C. CHECK VALVE   D. NEEDLE VALVE

FIG. V-10.   Types of valves

Another special valve is used for feeding cans into or out of a pressure chamber continuously. This valve also has a series of pockets into which the cans fall and are carried in or out of the pressure chamber without loss of pressure.

Cross-references: *Pasteurization; Piping; Standards, 3A; Sterilizers.*

VAPOR PRESSURE

Vapor pressure concepts are important in understanding and designing systems for drying, air conditioning, ventilating, etc. Vapor pressure is due to the water vapor in the air or material. Vapor is produced from a liquid by the higher velocity molecules which escape the surface of the liquid through vaporization. Molecules have different velocities within the liquid and those with sufficient velocity overcome the surface tension, and escape into the space above the liquid forming a vapor. The temperature is the principal parameter affecting the vapor pressure. The energy level of the liquid is reduced upon the escape of the higher velocity molecules, and is illustrated by an accompanying reduction in temperature. The total pressure of a mixture of gases, such as the atmosphere, is made up of the sum of the pressures of the separate gases. The vapor pressure exerts its own individual pressure separate from that of carbon dioxide, oxygen, nitrogen, etc. in the air.   The flow of vapor is from high vapor pressure to low vapor pressure.

Vapor in the air is steam at low pressure.   Furthermore, except when the air is saturated with water vapor, the air at normal atmospheric conditions is superheated.

The relationship of pressure and volume of vapor pressure can be represented by the equation, $PV = WRT$, where P is the absolute pressure, lb per sq ft; V the volume, cu ft; W the weight, lb; R, the gas constant, which is 85.8 for water vapor; and T, the absolute temperature, °R.

Determination of Vapor Pressure

The vapor pressure is usually determined indirectly by measuring any 2 of the following 3: wet-bulb or dry-bulb temperatures, or dew point. By knowing 2 of

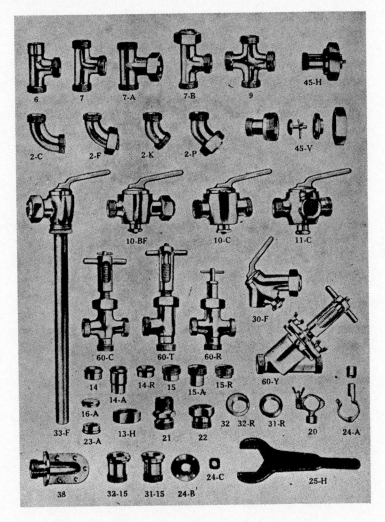

Fig. V-11.   Types of sanitary pipe fittings

these 3 temperatures, it is possible to determine the pressure of water vapor in the air from a psychrometric chart. The psychrometric chart is an organized method of relating the dew point, wet-bulb or dry-bulb temperatures, relative humidity, density, and vapor pressure. With the dry bulb temperature of 90°F and 50% RH, the vapor pressure is approximately 0.38 psi. The vapor pressure can also be represented in centimeters of mercury, millimeters of mercury, inches of water, and other equivalent relationships. The vapor pressure at saturation, that is at 100% RH of the atmosphere, is constant for a given temperature, with 0°C is 4.6 mm Hg; at 30°C is 31.8 mm Hg; at 60°C is 149.4 mm Hg. If the relative humidity is known, the percent relative humidity times the vapor pressure at saturation gives the vapor pressures at the given relative humidity.

Dew Point

The dew point is the temperature at which moisture will condense from the air. The dew point is a horizontal line of the psychrometric chart and represents a constant vapor pressure regardless of the dry-bulb temperature. The wet-bulb line represents the temperature of a thermometer with water evaporating from a cotton or cloth cover over the tip of the thermometer. As the relative humidity of the surrounding environment and as the vapor pressure decrease, the amount of vaporization from the wet bulb increases giving a cooling effect and a lower wet-bulb temperature, and for a given dry bulb temperature identifies a particular vapor pressure. The wet-bulb lines angle across the psychrometric chart from the upper left to lower right hand side. The wet-bulb lines should not be confused with the specific volume lines. The dry-bulb temperature is obtained with an ordinary thermometer.

The relative humidity is often determined from the wet-bulb, dry-bulb, or dew-point relationships. The relative humidity might be determined by indirect means using a material which is affected by the moisture content in the air which can be used as a measure of the relative humidity and/or vapor pressure. Materials which change dimensions or resistances upon absorption or desorption of moisture may be used for sensing the relative humidity. These can be designed and calibrated to provide relative humidity and/or vapor pressure values.

Vapor Pressure of Dry Milk

The vapor pressure of dry milk in relation to the vapor pressure of the surrounding

TABLE V.1

VAPOR PRESSURE OF LOW HEAT DRY MILK BASED ON EQUILIBRIUM VALUES FOR DESORPTION

Moisture Content, Dry Basis	Nonfat, at 100°F	13% Fat, at 100°F	26% Fat, at 100°F	Nonfat, at 86°F	Nonfat, at 60°F	Nonfat, at 35°F
2.5	0.07	0.05	0.03	0.04	0.03	0.03
5.0	0.17	0.11	0.09	0.10	0.08	0.07
7.5	0.49	0.38	0.23	0.22	0.19	0.17
10.0	0.64	0.60	0.51	0.40	0.39	0.29
12.5	0.72	0.68	0.63	0.63	0.59	0.55
15.0	0.76	0.73	0.69	0.69	0.67	0.65

air can be used as a means of determining whether moisture will be absorbed or desorbed should dry milk be exposed to its environment. If the vapor pressure of dry milk is below the vapor pressure of the atmosphere, the dry milk will gain moisture. Values of the vapor pressure of various dry milks are presented in Table V.1.

Evaporation of Moisture

The vapor pressure relationships are involved in evaporation of moisture from liquids and solids. The conditions which assist in the vaporization of moisture are as follows.

(1) Low moisture content of the air. The lower the moisture in the air, the more readily moisture moves into the air from the product. (2) High temperature of the liquid and the air or of the solid in the air. The higher the temperature of the liquid, the greater the pressure exerted by the vapor within the liquid or the solid. The higher the temperature of the air, the greater the capacity of the air for holding water vapor. (3) Large surface area of the solid or the liquid. The greater the surface area available for moisture and heat transfer, the greater the rate of vaporization. (4) Low boiling point of the liquid. A liquid with a low boiling point will have a greater vapor pressure at the same temperature. (5) Low pressure surrounding the product. A decreased pressure facilitates the escape of vapor molecules from the surface of the solid or liquid. (6) High velocity of airflow over the surface being dried. The vaporization from the surface increases as the velocity of flow over the surface increases and is generally considered to be proportional to the 0.8 power of the velocity, $(V^{0.8})$.

Maintaining Vapor Pressure

The relative humidity or vapor pressure of air may be controlled by using (1) saturated salt solutions, (2) acid solutions, (3) nozzles to disperse water droplets in the air, and (4) cold surfaces to remove excess moisture in the air. By appropriately

TABLE V.2

RANGE OF RELATIVE HUMIDITIES FOR SATURATED SALT SOLUTIONS IN THE NORMAL TEMPERATURE RANGE 32 TO 105°F

	%		%
Lithium chloride	11–12	Cobaltous chloride	57–65
Potassium acetate	22–23	Barium chloride	90–91
Calcium chloride	35–44	Potassium chromate	86–87
Magnesium chloride	32–33	Potassium nitrate	88–97
Potassium carbonate	43–44	Potassium sulfate	96–98
Magnesium nitrate	50–57		

controlling or utilizing these mechanisms, it is possible to obtain the relative humidity or vapor pressure desired. Vapor pressure or relative humidity control is more difficult than temperature control. Thermostats are readily available which operate within ±1°F. Humidistats normally operate within ±5% RH.

By adding an acid or a salt to water, the vapor pressure or relative humidity above the solution is decreased as compared to water alone. Saturated salt solutions are used for controlling the relative humidity with different salts used for different relative humidities (Table V.2).

Acid solutions may be used to obtain the desired relative humidities above a solution. The percent relative humidity, or vapor pressure, is changed by varying the percentage of acid. Sulfuric acid is commonly used which at 68°F, with 20%

TABLE V.3

SATURATION VAPOR PRESSURES OF WATER

Barometric pressure = 14.7 psia = O psia

Temp., °F	Pressure, Psia	Temp., °F	Pressure, Psia	Temp., °F	Pressure, Psia	Temp., °F	Pressure, Psia
32	0.08854	75	0.4298	134	2.4712	218	16.533
33	0.09223	76	0.4443	136	2.6042	220	17.186
34	0.09603	77	0.4593	138	2.7432	222	17.861
35	0.09995	78	0.4747	140	2.8886	224	18.557
36	0.10401	79	0.4906	142	3.0404	226	19.275
37	0.10821	80	0.5069	144	3.1990	228	20.016
38	0.11256	81	0.5237	146	3.365	230	20.780
39	0.11705	82	0.5410	148	3.547	232	21.567
40	0.12170	83	0.5588	150	3.718	234	22.379
41	0.12652	84	0.5771	152	3.906	236	23.217
42	0.13150	85	0.5959	154	4.102	238	24.080
43	0.13665	86	0.6152	156	4.306	240	24.969
44	0.14199	87	0.6351	158	4.519	242	25.884
45	0.14752	88	0.6556	160	4.741	244	26.827
46	0.15323	89	0.6766	162	4.971	246	27.798
47	0.15914	90	0.6982	164	5.212	248	28.797
48	0.16525	91	0.7204	166	5.461	250	29.825
49	0.17157	92	0.7432	168	5.721	252	30.884
50	0.17811	93	0.7666	170	5.992	254	31.973
51	0.18486	94	0.7906	172	6.273	256	33.093
52	0.19182	95	0.8353	174	6.565	258	34.245
53	0.19900	96	0.8407	176	6.868	260	35.429
54	0.20642	97	0.8668	178	7.183	262	36.646
55	0.2141	98	0.8935	180	7.510	264	37.897
56	0.2220	99	0.9210	182	7.850	266	39.182
57	0.2302	100	0.9492	184	8.202	268	40.502
58	0.2386	102	1.0078	186	8.567	270	41.858
59	0.2473	104	1.0695	188	8.946	272	43.252
60	0.2563	106	1.1345	190	9.339	274	44.682
61	0.2655	108	1.2020	192	9.746	276	46.150
62	0.2751	110	1.2748	194	10.168	278	47.657
63	0.2850	112	1.3504	196	10.605	280	49.203
64	0.2951	114	1.4298	198	11.058	282	50.790
65	0.3056	116	1.5130	200	11.526	284	52.416
66	0.3164	118	1.6006	202	12.011	286	54.088
67	0.3276	120	1.6924	204	12.512	288	55.300
68	0.3390	122	1.7888	206	13.031	290	57.556
69	0.3509	124	1.8897	208	13.568	292	59.356
70	0.3631	126	1.9955	210	14.123	294	61.201
71	0.3756	128	2.1064	212	14.696	296	63.091
72	0.3886	130	2.2225	214	15.289	298	65.028
73	0.4019	132	2.3440	216	15.901	300	67.013

solution provides 87.7% RH, 40% acid, 56.7% RH; 60% acid, 16.3% RH; and 80% acid, 4.8% RH. The relative humidity above the solution increases slightly as the temperature is increased. With acid solutions it is necessary to maintain the percentage of acid in the solution to maintain the relative humidity. If there is the chance of water escaping or being added to the solution, the relative humidity above that solution will change. It is necessary to meter either water or acid into the solution to maintain the relative humidity, whereas with a saturated salt solution, there is an excess of salt to begin with, and if moisture is evaporated from the solution, it will remain saturated. However, if too much water is added to the solution, it is necessary to add additional salt.

Moisture Carrying Capacity

The moisture carrying or holding ability of the air increases as the temperature is increased. In general, for a 20°F increase in temperature, the moisture carrying capacity is doubled. For example, at 55°F, air will hold a maximum of 64 gr of water vapor in 1 lb. At 75°F, air will hold approximately twice or 131 gr of water vapor per pound of dry air. Similarly, the vapor pressure approximately doubles by increasing the temperature of the air by 20°F.

The saturation vapor pressures of water for 100% RH are given in Table V.3. By multiplying the saturation vapor pressures and the relative humidity, the vapor pressure of a particular atmosphere can be determined accurately and easily.

Movement of Vapor

Vapor flows from high to low vapor pressure. Under normal conditions, the vapor flows from high temperature to low temperature areas, such as through an insulated or uninsulated wall. Thus, the vapor pressure is higher in an 80°F room outside of a 35°F refrigerated room. Some materials, e.g., plastics, metals, and asphalt base materials, are more or less impervious to the flow of moisture and may be used as vapor barriers. Vapor barriers should be placed on the warm side of insulated walls to intercept the flow of moisture. Some insulation materials are impervious to the flow of moisture and serve as vapor barriers.

Cross-references: *Equilibrium Moisture Content; Humidity Chart; Moisture Content.*

VEGETABLE FREEZERS

The frozen food industry has grown to be a four billion dollar per year industry in the United States. There are 2,823 types of frozen food, including 639 types of frozen vegetables (1968). In addition, there are 448 types of sea foods, and 446 ice creams and desserts frozen. Also, 58% of the volume of frozen foods is in fruit juice and vegetables; soups account for 11.4% and baked goods for 10.1%. The basic process of freezing is designed to preserve products for long periods of time. Freezing temperatures may be only a few degrees below zero, or −60°F, or as low as −320°F which is obtained from using liquid nitrogen.

The basic principle of freezing of fruits and vegetables is to solidify the moisture which is present by extracting the latent heat of fusion.

The freezing process involves blanching before freezing to destroy certain enzymes which could cause off-flavors and deterioration.

Another important factor is freezing the material quickly so that a more natural structure is obtained when the material is thawed. Slow freezing causes the formation of large ice crystals in the product and disrupts many of the cells.

Cold Plates

Freezing of fruits and vegetables can be done by placing them either in a packaged or unpackaged condition on shelves and subjecting them to high velocity air at temperatures of $-20°$ to $-40°F$. The Birds Eye process improved upon this by placing the products in packages or in paper between extremely cold plates, thus greatly increasing the rate of heat transfer and causing very rapid freezing. The development of rapid freezing methods has become the basis for an extremely large industry in quick frozen foods. A complete freezing setup containing a more recent development in rapid freezing is shown in Fig. V.12. In this system, the product enters a glazing area chamber at 15°F where a frozen glaze is developed over the product. The glaze prevents dehydration. The product then passes to a 0°F freezing chamber where extremely high velocity air is passed over the product. In from $\frac{1}{2}$ to 2 hr, depending upon the size of the particle, the freezing is completed.

Liquid Nitrogen

A third type of quick-freezing device for fruits and vegetables involves the use of liquid nitrogen. See Nitrogen, Liquid. In this system the basic arrangement of the machine consists of a product conveyor mounted within a double wall, vacuum insulated open end cylinder. The liquid nitrogen sprays over the product located in a

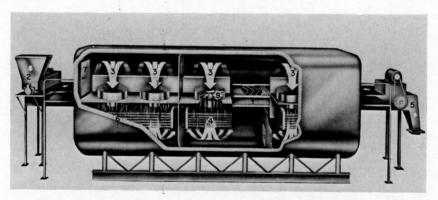

Courtesy of Frick Co.

FIG. V-12.   Rapid freezer for fruits and vegetables

In operation, the product is usually washed, dewatered and distributed to the freezer conveyor belt (1) by a shaker spreader located at the loading station (2). As the loose wet product enters the freezer, it is quickly glazed by an updraft of cold air (3) preventing product dehydration, sealing in the natural flavors and assuring maximum yield. Freezing is completed as the product is conveyed through the tunnel enclosure where low temperature air at $-25°$ to $-30°F$ is circulated evenly at high velocity from the refrigerated coil (4) up through the entire belt area. The high velocity of the cold air passing up through the belt fluidizes the product and assures IQF freezing with no clusters. The frozen product at 0°F, or lower, is discharged from the conveyor belt at the unloading station (5) ready for bulk storage or packaging.

central section of the unit, and includes spray nozzles above and sometimes below the product. Blower fans found on either end of the main chamber circulate the cold gas which is directed to nozzles and suction parts within the freezer chamber. The nozzles are positioned to direct high velocity cold gas over the surface of the product. The gas recirculators are located between the entrance and the spray zone chamber occupying the greater portion of the length of the unit. The machines operate continuously and automatically. A centrifugal pump and external reservoir pressurizes the liquid nitrogen now at $-320°F$ and at atmospheric pressure to 5 to 7 psig, and pumps the liquid into spray headers above and below the pump. Most of the liquid flashes to gas when it comes into contact with the product and the liquid which does not contact the product is recollected in the collector pan and flows back to the external head for recirculation.

Liquid Nitrogen Immersion

A somewhat different method of freezing is by means of a conveyor system which moves continuously and carries the product to be frozen through a tank of liquid nitrogen. This system provides extremely fast freezing and is said to have given excellent results with tomatoes and peaches, which cannot be successfully frozen by usual methods.

Quantity of Refrigeration

The capacity of freezing equipment depends upon the type of fruits and vegetables and upon the temperature to which the product is frozen. The formula for calculating the amount of refrigeration needed to freeze a product is:

Refrigeration, Btu, required to freeze vegetables, etc.
(1) Sensible Heat
Wt of product $\times$ % solids $\times$ (sp ht solids) $\times t_1 - t_2$ = Btu
Wt of product $\times$ % moisture $\times$ 1.0 (sp ht) $\times t_1 - t_3$ = Btu
Wt of product $\times$ % moisture $\times$ 0.5 (sp ht ice) $\times t_3 - t_2$ = Btu

(2) Latent Heat
Wt[1] of product $\times$ % moisture frozen $\times$ 144 = Btu

(3) Total Heat = Sensible plus Latent Heat
where t_1 = original temp. of product, °F
t_2 = final temp. of frozen product, °F
t_3 = freezing point of product, °F (usually slightly under 32°F)

In addition to the actual refrigeration required to freeze the product there is always a certain amount of refrigeration loss due to heat radiation through the walls of the freezer.

References

RIDEL, L. 1951. The refrigerating effect required to freeze fruits and vegetables. Refrig. Eng. *59*, 670–673.
TRESSLER, D. K., VAN ARSDEL, W. B., and COPLEY, M. J. 1968. The Freezing Preservation of Foods, Fourth Edition, 4 Vols. AVI Publishing Co., Westport, Conn.

[1] This assumes all moisture is fully frozen which may not be the case.

Cross-references: *Immersion Freezers; Nitrogen, Liquid; Cooling and Freezing.*

VENDING

Introduction

Vending is defined as the self-service mechanical distribution, metering, or portioning of services, merchandise, edibles, and beverages upon the insertion of a coin or coins into a slot. Vending machines were developed in their simplest form around 1900. The early form of motion picture was a vendable type of entertainment which was viewed through a box and activated by a crank. The slot machine or "one-armed bandit" is an example of vended gambling produced by a mechanical device without human assistance. Bulk vending equipment employed to dispense candy, peanuts, chewing gum, and a variety of sundry items has been used commercially for over 60 yr.

The vending of food and beverages, which forms the backbone of the modern day vending industry had its start with the advent of The Horn and Hardart Automats, just prior to World War I. This mode of service took hold rapidly and became an immediate success in the New York and Philadelphia marketing areas.

World War II Gives Birth to a New Industry

During and after World War II a major industry built entirely around the vending machine emerged. Industrial and in-plant feeding formed the focal point for this method of mechanical food service. Shortages of restaurant employees and the necessity for quick snacks within defense plants located away from urban areas were the essential elements involved in the creation of mechanical feeding facilities. Advances in electronics were responsible for the development and design of sophisticated devices, and complete cafeterias that were fully contained and automatic were constructed.

Modern Day Vending a Multiple Service Industry

The present vending industry covers a wide range of products and services. Labor shortages and the high cost of labor for menial tasks coupled to the development of convenience foods are responsible for the continued sharp growth of vending throughout the world. Although the growth of automated feeding services in Europe has lagged behind that of the Western Hemisphere, Europe's retail vending industry is successful and popular. Vending machines can be found at almost every street corner offering a variety of retail goods for sale.

Classification of Vendable Services

The vending industry, because of its diverse application and complex operation, can best be understood when divided into three service categories: (1) the hiring or leasing of services by mechanical means, (2) the dispensing of edible or personal services, and (3) the dispensing of sundry items and nonedible services, packaged foods, and bottled beverages.

The hiring or leasing of services by mechanical means includes telephone pay stations, juke boxes, public toilets, radio and television for hotel and home, auto parking meters, luggage storage lockers, and laundry washing machines and manglers.

The dispensing of edible or personal services includes shoe shiners, foot and hotel bed massage machines, soap and towel dispensers, electric and gas meters, perfume and toilet water dispensers, weight scales, ice machines, and all vending machines that dispense portioned food or beverages, e.g., hot and cold drink dispensers, hot and cold food units, and ice cream dispensers.

Dispensing of sundry items, nonedible services, packaged foods, and drinks includes stamps; subway and bus tokens; miscellaneous items, e.g., newspapers, paperback books, magazines, combs, cosmetics, handkerchiefs, postcards, stockings, and contraceptives; flight insurance policies; cigarette and cigar machines; bulk confectionary dispensers; and retail packaged food dispensers, e.g., bread, milk, canned goods.

Operating Principles of Vending Machines

Basically, the operating principles of vending machines or dispensing services are identical regardless of the product or service sold. A coin is the medium of payment which acts as the key to unlock a mechanism setting the dispenser in operation. Unlocking mechanisms that activate vending equipment are divided into two categories; (1) mechanical or manual operated, and (2) electrical activation.

Mechanical or manual operation uses the coin to bridge the lever or button to the interior controls allowing the product to be released. By moving an exterior lever or push button after the coin is inserted into the machine and accepted by it, the pressure exerted by the customer acts as the power source to set the dispenser in operation. When the external pressure is released the coin drops into the money storage box and the machine cannot be operated again until a new coin is inserted in the slot. This type of vending equipment can be placed in any location as no external power is required for its operation. The earliest forms of dispensing equipment employed these principles. Bulk vending units dispensing nuts, chewing gum, candy bars, sundry items, and cigarettes employ the mechanical system.

Electrically activated dispensers were made possible during and after World War II from the development of electronic components necessary to create operating systems that were fully automated. Machines were built containing a labyrinth of electrical circuits, encompassing microswitches, timers, fractional HP motors, and solenoids. Depending on the product dispensed, interior designs vary. Generally the design of the coin acceptor, coin counter, and change dispenser follow the same basic design. After the coin is deposited into the slot by the customer and the selection of an item made, a master switch is activated that sets the interior components in operation.

Parameters of Vending Machine Design

Modern vending machines must meet certain basic design criteria to satisfy the demands of the consumer, vendor, and if they are used to dispense food or beverages, governmental sanitation codes. Depending on the product or service rendered, the following items number 1 through 6 apply to all vending machines; items 7 to 10 apply to those dispensers serving food and beverages.

(1) Compactness
(2) Attractive and appealing exterior design and decoration
(3) Attractive and presentable display of merchandise
(4) Mechanical reliability and efficient operation
(5) Ease of loading
(6) Ease of repairs and servicing so that a semiskilled employee can perform on location minor repairs and adjustments
(7) Ease of sanitation and full accessibility to all interior parts for cleaning purposes
(8) If the vending unit dispenses perishable products or ingredients, the machine must be capable of maintaining a temperature of 45°F or below with necessary temperature controls as required, and shutoff controls should the temperature rise above 45°F.
(9) If the vending unit dispenses hot or heated food of a perishable nature, the machine must be capable of maintaining products at or above 140°F with necessary temperature controls, and shutoff controls should the temperature drop below 140°F.
(10) If vending machines are designed to dispense food or beverages, they must meet those regulations set forth by the U.S. Public Health Service 1965 sanitation ordinance and code under the title "The Vending of Foods and Beverages." This code was developed in cooperation with the National Automatic Merchandising Association (NAMA) in 1957 and revised in 1965. In addition, the National Sanitation Foundation (NSF) has also promulgated basic and specific criteria for the evaluation of vending machines for food and beverages.

Classification of Vending Machines

There are three classifications of coin operated vending machines: (1) vending machines for beverages, (2) vending machines for confections and foods, and (3) vending machines for sundry and miscellaneous products.

Vending machines for beverages
  Coffee
    Instant, freeze-dried or liquid concentrates
    Fresh brew (batch)
    Fresh brew (single cup)
    The above are manufactured in combination with hot chocolate, soup, and tea
  Soft drinks
    Bottle or canned
    Cup service (postmix)
    Cup service (premix)
  Milk
    Packaged (indoors and outdoors)
    Milk (bulk or cup service)
Vending machines for confections and food
  Bulk
  Candy bar

Hot canned foods and soups
Cold foods
Fresh fruit
Pastry, crackers, cookies, and popcorn
Chewing gum
Ice cream
Vending machines for sundry and miscellaneous products
Cigarette and cigars
Postage stamps
Ice
Cosmetics, toiletries, novelties, detergents, newspapers, and books

Solid Pack Vending Machines

Solid pack vending machines are manufactured in a variety of shapes, designs and are adapted for many products, both edible and nonedible.   They handle confections, solid food, sundries, and miscellaneous products.

Column and Drawer Dispensers

These machines store their products in stacks.   Each stack is set above a drawer. When the machine is filled the bottom package falls into the drawer.   Upon activation the machine mechanism allows the drawer to be opened.   After the product is withdrawn and the drawer pushed back into place a subsequent package falls into it. These units dispense cigarettes and candy bars.

Drop Flap Machines

Similar to the column and drawer equipment, packages are stored in columns. Instead of resting one on the other, each package rests on a hinged drop flap or leaf. When the machine is filled all the leaves or flaps are extended so that each package has its own shelf.   When the machine is activated the lowest shelf drops on its hinge and allows the package to drop by gravity onto the vending chute.   These machines are adaptable to cigarettes, candy, and packaged sundries.

Cupboard Machines

Cupboard dispensers consist of a number of small rectangular receptacles or storage spaces covered with a hinged glass door.   When the unit is activated the customer can observe the item desired, open the door, and withdraw the merchandise. Only one door is allowed to open at a time and once the item is withdrawn the storage space remains empty until reloaded.

Rotary turntable dispensers are available that increase the capacity of a machine. Where a turntable is provided, each shelf, which is divided into segments, can hold up to eight selections.   After a sale is completed, the closing of the vend door causes the turntable to move one segment.

There are many variations of the cupboard machines. Some are made with conveyors fitted with slots or pockets. The customer presses a button which activates the conveyor. As the conveyor moves each item is brought into view for selection.

These vending machines are available with refrigeration systems for the dispensing of cool foods or with heating units for hot or perishable foods.

Cigarette Vending Machines

Cigarette dispensers cover a wide capacity range. Some hold up to 1,200 packs of varying sizes. The cigarettes are loaded into columns, numbering up to 36 columns per machine. Horizontal conveyor type units are available. In these dispensers the package is laid flat. When the machine is activated the conveyor moves one package length releasing the merchandise into the chute. Because of the differences in price range of the king, 100, or regular size package, these dispensers require a flexible pricing capability for each size.

Canned Food and Beverage Machines

These dispensers consist of a series of runways or chutes. When the machine is activated the can is released and rolls or drops to the takeout shelf. Machines of this type can be adapted to heat canned food or for the cooling of canned beverages. Packaged ice cube dispensers operate on the same principle.

Ice Cream Dispensers

Dispensers that vend ice cream bricks or pops are completely refrigerated and insulated cabinets, constructed to maintain the product at its proper consistency. In addition, safety controls are incorporated that shut off the machine in the event of refrigeration failure.

Generally, packages are stored in column type magazines which revolve within the cabinet. When the dispenser is set into motion and the selection made by the customer, the ice cream package is released from the bottom of the column and drops through a double door. The double door is an added precaution to ensure that the inner cabinet is never exposed to the atmosphere.

Coffee Dispensers

Coffee dispensers are manufactured to dispense the beverage by four methods: (1) Instant crystals or powder and freeze-dried powder, (2) Liquid concentrates, (3) Fresh brew, batch brewing, and (4) Fresh brew, single cup brewing.

Method four, single cup brewing, is the most popular form of vended coffee. This method is presently the most widely used as the number of single cup brewers sold over the last 10 yr far exceeds all others. Because of this trend the single cup vending method will be discussed in detail. Most coffee machines have provisions to dispense hot chocolate, soup, and tea.

Figure V.13 shows the interior of a Seeburg hot beverage vender, model M7C5D. When a customer deposits a coin or coins, the Coin Switch is momentarily closed, energizing the Add Solenoid, see Fig. V.14. The Add Solenoid releases the Totalizer

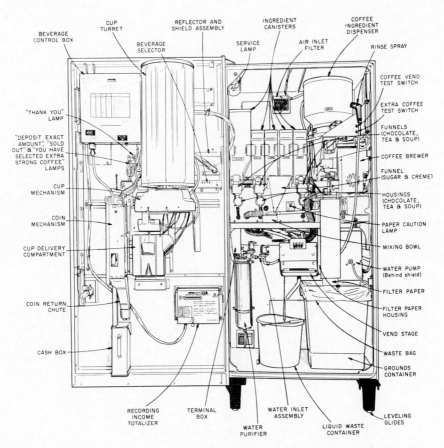

BEVERAGE CONTROL BOX

CUP TURRET

REFLECTOR AND SHIELD ASSEMBLY

INGREDIENT CANISTERS

COFFEE INGREDIENT DISPENSER

BEVERAGE SELECTOR

SERVICE LAMP

AIR INLET FILTER

RINSE SPRAY

COFFEE VEND TEST SWITCH

"THANK YOU" LAMP

EXTRA COFFEE TEST SWITCH

"DEPOSIT EXACT AMOUNT", "SOLD OUT" & "YOU HAVE SELECTED EXTRA STRONG COFFEE" LAMPS

FUNNELS (CHOCOLATE, TEA & SOUP)

COFFEE BREWER

FUNNEL (SUGAR & CREME)

CUP MECHANISM

HOUSINGS (CHOCOLATE, TEA & SOUP)

COIN MECHANISM

PAPER CAUTION LAMP

CUP DELIVERY COMPARTMENT

MIXING BOWL

WATER PUMP (Behind shield)

FILTER PAPER

COIN RETURN CHUTE

FILTER PAPER HOUSING

VEND STAGE

CASH BOX

WASTE BAG

GROUNDS CONTAINER

RECORDING INCOME TOTALIZER

TERMINAL BOX

WATER INLET ASSEMBLY

LEVELING GLIDES

WATER PURIFIER

LIQUID WASTE CONTAINER

Courtesy of The Seeburg Corp.

FIG. V-13.   Interior view of a fresh brew single cup brewer

Mechanism. Actuation of the Totalizer Mechanism operates the Credit Transfer Switch and the Add Motor Switch. The Add Motor Switch completes a circuit to the Add Motor. As the Add Motor operates, it resets the Totalizer Mechanism and adds the established credit to the accumulated total.

The Credit Transfer Switch completes a circuit to energize the Coin Relay. Once the Coin Relay is energized, the customer can make his selection. When a selector button is pressed, a circuit is completed to energize a solenoid which mechanically holds the selector button depressed. This same solenoid also completes a circuit to the Vend Timer Assembly and, if coffee was selected, to the Brew Timer Assembly.

The Vend Timer Assembly controls and times the entire vending sequence except the brewing cycle. One of the first functions is to complete a circuit to the Cup Dispenser to drop a cup to the Vend Stage. Other circuits are completed to Ingredient Dispensers and water valves as selected by the customer.

The Brew Timer Assembly controls and times all functions involved in brewing a single cup of coffee. The motors of this assembly are also used to power the mechanical functions of the Brewer and Paper Drive Assembly. At the conclusion of each

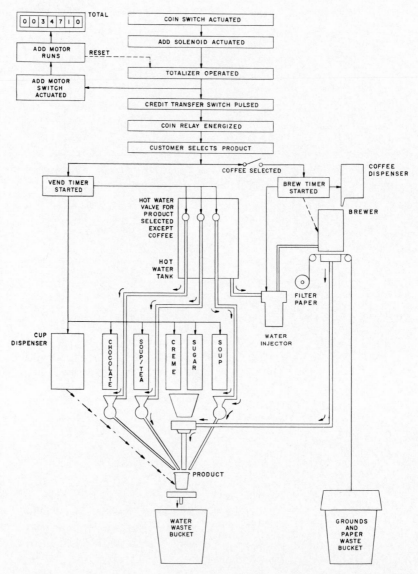

Courtesy of The Seeburg Corp.

Fig. V-14.   Schematic drawing of the operating sequence, fresh brew coffee vender

brew cycle, the Paper Drive Assembly advances the filter paper so that a clean filter is used for each cup.   The total vend time is about 10 sec with coffee starting to be delivered within 4 sec.

Ground coffee is stored in hoppers, which holds from 8 to 12 lb.   A volumetric measuring feed is built into the lower section of the hopper.   When the unit is activated, a screw type mechanism or worm gear pushes the coffee out into the brewing chamber.   The amount of coffee, measured in grams, is regulated by setting the controls on the hopper.   Depending on the brew strength, about 7 to 10 gm are used per cup. A very fine grind coffee is used. The short brew cycle makes this property mandatory so that full extraction can be obtained. Although many of the principles of essential brewing techniques apply to vending machines, those that were tailor-made to meet the unusual conditions, are extra fine particle size, short brew cycles, and blend components which ensure full wettability. About 6 oz of water are added to the coffee at a temperature of $200°F \pm 5°$. Depending on the manufacturer, the water may be heated in open or closed tanks. In any event, a constant source of hot water is necessary, especially during peak serving periods.

One of the major drawbacks of vended coffee is a lack of proper sanitation, so that off-flavors result from accumulated resins and dirt. Some equipment have provisions for self-cleaning. However regardless of the machine design, full sanitation is necessary for the vending of a clear uncontaminated brew.

Courtesy of The Vendo Co.

Fig. V-15.   Exterior view of a post-mix cold drink vending machine

Soft Drink Vending Machines

Of the three types of soft drink vending machines in current use, the postmix unit is the most popular (see Fig. V.15). These machines are completely automatic and contain all the components, including ice making equipment, to produce a finished beverage of high quality. This equipment is the result of man's ingenuity applied to the development of efficient automated dispensers. Postmix cup machines are those that dispense a finished soft drink in a cup with or without ice from a choice of flavored syrups, either carbonated or still. Dispensers of this type are available in a number of sizes and capacities, varying from 500 to 1,500 cups of 7-, 9-, or 10-oz capacity. Carbonation may be adjusted for high, low, or none, depending on the syrup used in the unit. Flavor selections range from 4 to 8.

Depending on the machine's design, flavor selections can be made before or after the coin is accepted by the unit. As with other venders, these machines are equipped with coin changers. After selection is made and the unit activated the finished beverage is ready for the consumer in about 10 sec. Activation starts a train of events. As the cup falls into place from its storage rack, syrup, carbonated water, and ice are metered and delivered to the cup. The amount of each ingredient is controlled by a cam or electrical sensing device.

Premix soft drink machines dispense individual cup size servings. Their use is limited to locations that do not have a water supply or where temporary installations are required. Portable tanks are filled with syrup and water and the mixture carbonated. These prefilled tanks are then installed into the machine and hooked into a refrigeration system. Carbonation can also be performed within the dispenser if it is equipped with a carbon dioxide injection system. Although greater uniformity is achieved with this type of equipment, since the filling operation can be controlled more carefully, a major drawback is their limited capacity.

The Effect of Water on Vendable Beverages

Water problems that affect beverages also pertain to those that are dispensed from vending machines. Manufacturers of beverage vending units are building into their machines strainers or screens and activated carbon water purifiers. However these do not eliminate problems emanating from brackish or hard water.

Screens and strainers will rid the water of solid particles, such as metal, coarse sand, and dirt. Activated carbon filters are effective in removing chlorine, metallic tastes, plant life, and sulfur dioxide. Brackish water can be successfully treated by the use of a reverse osmosis filtration system.

Hard water conditions can be corrected by a number of methods including the ion-exchange process. The ion-exchange process cannot be employed on water fed into coffee brew dispensers. The side effects will give a finished brew that is bitter and unpalatable. In addition, inconsistency and short-fill cups will also result. The ion exchange system produces sodium bicarbonate which forms a gel and binds the coffee particles together thus preventing a full and quick extraction. A polyphosphate system is recommended for the treatment of water fed to fresh brew vending equipment.

The following illustrates the respective effects on soft drinks:

Water Problem	Effect on Drink and Vending Machine
Iron	Imparts metallic taste
Dirt, cloudiness, chlorine mustiness, fishy tastes and odors	Excessive foaming, reduces carbonation, destroys flavor
Hard water (lime scale)	Plugs valves, reduces cooling efficiency, plugs lines, affects flavor
Acid	Corrodes pipes, causes metallic tastes
Sulfur	Imparts rotten egg odor

The Automated Cafeteria

The automated cafeteria and snack service account for the major dollar volume of the vending industry. A typical automated cafeteria may contain the following equipment.

(1) Pastry dispenser[1]—doughnuts, cakes, cookies, pie
(2) Dessert dispenser—puddings, fruit salad, fresh fruit
(3) Soft drink[1] dispenser—postmix, premix, bottles or cans
(4) Hot food dispenser—stews, prepared dishes
(5) Soup and canned food dispenser
(6) Sandwich dispenser
(7) Cold food dispenser, salads
(8) Ice cream dispenser[1]
(9) Milk and chocolate milk dispenser[1]
(10) Coffee, tea, hot chocolate, soup combination vender[1]
(11) Cigarettes and cigars dispenser[1]
(12) Candy dispenser[1]

Auxiliary Equipment

(1) Change maker
(2) Microwave oven
(3) Condiment table
(4) Can opener
(5) Stirrers, plastic spoons, forks, knives, and napkins
(6) Trash receptacle
(7) Water fountain
(8) Utility and storage closets, slop sink, mops, and buckets
(9) Water treatment system if required
(10) Tables and chairs

[1] Basic needs for a snack services.

Prepared by Marvin E. Thorner

References

ANON. 1963. Sanitation practices for vending routemen, Parts 1 and 2. National Automatic-Merchandising Assoc., Chicago, Ill.

ANON. 1965. Vending of Food Beverages. U. S. Dept. Health, Educ., Welfare, Washington, D. C.

ANON. 1968A. The soft drink market. Vend. *23*, No. 10, 29–42.

ANON. 1968B. Vending machines for food and beverages, Standard *25*. The National Sanitation Foundation, Ann Arbor, Mich.

ANON. 1968C. A profile of the vending operator today. National Automatic Merchandising Assoc., Chicago, Ill.

ANON. 1969A. Vending Machines, Industrial Rept., Ser. *MA-35U(68)-1*. U. S. Dept. Commerce, Washington, D. C.

ANON. 1969B. Tobacco spotlight. American Automatic Merchandiser *11*, No. 12.

ANON. 1970. Annual sales study and fact file. American Automatic Merchandiser *12*, No. 1.

LONGREE, K. 1969. Sanitation in food vending. J. Am. Dietet. Assoc. *54*, No. 3, 215–220.

MATZ, S. A. 1965. Water in Foods. AVI Publishing Co., Westport, Conn.

POTTER, N. N. 1968. Food Science. AVI Publishing Co., Westport, Conn.

ROGERS, J. L. 1958. Automatic Vending. Food Trade Review, London.

THORNER, M. E., and HERZBERG, R. J. 1970. Food Beverage Service Handbook. AVI Publishing Co., Westport, Conn.

Service Manuals

Seeburg Cold Drink Vender Manual 806604. The Seeburg Corp., Chicago, Ill.

Seeburg Hot Beverage Vender Manual 55524. The Seeburg Corp., Chicago, Ill.

Vendo Soda Shoppe Vending Machine, Service and Parts Manual. The Vendo Co., Kansas City, Mo.

VENTILATION

The movement of air by natural or mechanical means usually designated in terms of quantity of air is known as ventilation. The quantity of air is designated by air changes per unit time or velocity of the air. If environmental factors such as temperature are involved, the procedure is called air conditioning. The airflow may be designed to carry heat from the room or enclosed space to remove undesirable or toxic products, such as gases, dust, or moisture.

The heat produced by workers varies considerably with different people, various tasks, age distribution, etc. An office worker gives off approximately 500 Btu per hr; a person doing light work gives off about 1,000 Btu per hr, and for heavy tasks, up to 4,500 Btu per hr. A 1-hp motor in the ventilated space would give off 3,412 Btu per hr. A pound of steam condensing would give off a little over 1,000 Btu per hr. If the purpose of ventilation is to remove the heat, the heat given off by people, products, and equipment would cause only a very slight temperature rise, perhaps less than 1°F.

The comfort zone for humans varies with the temperature, relative humidity, and airflow. In general, the comfort zone is between 30 to 70% RH and 66° to 71°F for an airflow of 15 to 25 fpm. Velocities above 50 fpm are uncomfortable to many people and should be avoided.

The design of a particular system involves determining the movement of a minimum amount of air properly distributed to provide desirable conditions for people, equipment, product, and building. The ventilation system may be classified as general, or a special system directed to moving the air through a particular work or process area (Tables V.4 and V.5).

TABLE V.4

SYSTEM VENTILATION UNIT FAN AND DUCTWORK CONNECTED TO HOOD OR SLOTTED INTAKE

Process Activity	Type of Intake	Avg Intake Velocity, Fpm
Chemical laboratory	Enclosed hood, front open	100–150
	Down draft, table type	150–200
Flour, grain	Canopy hood	500
	Side slots	3–4 in.

TABLE V.5

VENTILATION—AIR CHANGES SUGGESTED

Minutes per Air Change		Minutes per Air Change	
Bakeries	2–3	Salesroom	2–10
Boiler room	1–5	Toilets	2–5
Dairies	2–5	Warehouse	2–10
Kitchen, home	2–5	Welding shop	1–3
Kitchen, restaurant	1–3	Laboratory	2–8
Offices	2–10	Cafeteria	3–5
Packing houses	2–5		

Source: Maintenance Engineering Handbook, McGraw-Hill Co. (1957).

The friction of airflow in the pipes must be carefully calculated to be sure that fans are properly selected and that the airflow is delivered and distributed most economically in appropriate areas (Table V.6).

Practices and Principles in Ventilation

(1) Determine air change and flow requirements on basis of use of the area and process involved.

(2) Select fans based on airflow, static pressure, and other conditions. Calculate pressure drop of the system based on duct system, filters, and room conditions.

(3) Use pressure system for rooms to be used for processing to avoid contamination by inflow of air. Filter incoming air to the fan.

(4) Fans should exhaust in the direction of prevailing winds. Intake areas should utilize pressure of the wind.

(5) Select dustproof motors for hazardous conditions. Also be sure the electrical equipment is properly grounded.

(6) Proper insulation is important to avoid condensation problems.

(7) Consider noise of (a) caused directly from the fans, and (b) caused indirectly from ducts and grill due to vibration of the fan and motor and from velocity of air.

(8) Minimize pressure drop by designing radius of elbows of ducts 1.5 to 2 times the diameter of the pipe duct.

(9) Air velocities above 50 fpm are uncomfortable for workers.

(10) A normal adult at 70°F will give off 300 Btu per hr due to radiation and convection, 100 Btu per hr due to evaporation, and will evaporate 665 gr per hr of moisture.

TABLE V.6

FRICTION OF AIR IN PIPES, IN. OF WATER PER 100 FT

Q Cfm	Diameter, In.								
	6	9	12	15	18	21	24	27	30
1,000	8.3	1.3	0.28	0.084	0.035				
5,000			5.0	1.7	0.68	0.32	0.17	0.09	0.052
10,000			6.0	2.5	1.1	0.58	0.31	0.14	
20,000				9.1	4.1	2.2	1.2	0.72	
40,000						8.0	4.3	2.7	
80,000									

Q Cfm	Diameter, In.							
	33	36	39	42	45	50	55	60
1,000								
5,000								
10,000	0.12	0.07	0.05		0.026			
20,000	0.38	0.28	0.18	0.14	0.09	0.056	0.033	0.023
40,000	1.5	1.0	0.68	0.47	0.34	0.20	0.12	0.055
80,000					1.3	0.72	0.46	0.30

Source: Heating, Ventilating, Air Conditioning Guide (1949).

(11) Another method of designating air supply for ventilation is in terms of cubic feet per hour per occupant. In general, about 1,500 to 2,000 cu ft per hr is supplied per occupant where several people are involved.

(12) Ventilating systems should be designed for a maximum resistance to flow of about $1^3/_4$ in. water.

Cross-references: *Air Movement; Fans; Fluid Flow; Friction; Humidity Chart.*

VENTING

Venting in the food industry usually refers to that step in the canning operation of removing air from a retort. All heat process determinations for canned foods are made in "pure" steam (free of air). Air in a retort decreases the effectiveness of the process and acts as an insulator around the cans. Considerable underprocessing and spoilage can result when retorts are not vented sufficiently to remove all of the air. Steam burning and rusting may occur on the cans when retorts are not completely vented.

Measurements have shown that a fully loaded horizontal retort contained 80% air, whereas a vertical retort had over 60% air.

The temperature at 15 psi shown on a gage with varying amounts of air removed from the retort is as follows:

Degree of Air Removal	Temperature in Retort, °F
Complete (allsteam)	250
$^2/_3$ of air removed	239
$^1/_2$ of air removed	234
No air removed	212

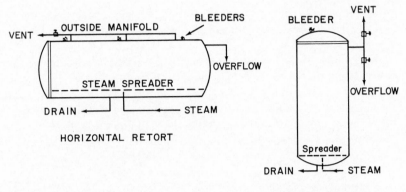

Fig. V-16. Retort steam and venting systems

The necessity for complete air removal is clearly indicated. The danger in operating a retort by a pressure gage reading or pressure controller instead of a mercury thermometer is also apparent.

Vent piping arrangements for successful venting must be determined for each individual operation. Outlet pipes for venting should be as free from bends and obstructions as possible. The best results are obtained when the vents are located in the extreme opposite wall of the retort from where the steam enters. A gage reading higher than that for steam at the observed temperature indicates the presence of air. Inadequate venting is responsible for this condition.

Venting arrangements for various types of retorts have been suggested and are presented together with the steam or water spreader hookup and venting method (Fig. V.16).

A minimum time limit is needed for the come-up time for adequate air removal during venting. The length of this time over and above the minimum venting requirements depends upon the steam system for the retort. The size of steam inlet, regulating valves, steam pressures, and others would be influencing factors.

Some vacuum packed cans must be heated sufficiently to dissipate the internal can vacuum to eliminate possible can distortion before applying any appreciable steam pressure in the retort.

References

Bobk, J. H. 1957. Retort Installation, Equipment and Operating Procedures. Continental Can Co., Chicago, Ill.

National Canners Assoc. 1959. An Information Bulletin on Retort Operation, Bull. *32-L.* Berkeley, Calif.

Cross-references: *Canning; Retorts.*

VESSELS, PRESSURE

Any vessel which is used under pressure must meet certain safety standards. This may be a boiler which is covered under ASME Code for boilers, or if it is unfired it is covered by the ASME Unfired Pressure Vessel Code.

There are many special types of cookers, sterilizers, and pressure treatment vessels used in the food industry, and even if the jacket alone is under pressure, it must meet certain specifications.

Low pressure vessels are usually considered as having a working pressure of 15 psig or lower. High pressure vessels may operate above that point.

The bursting strength of a pressure vessel is very greatly affected by its diameter, thus a vessel of 30 in. diam will have a theoretical bursting strength of twice the pressure of a 60 in. diam shell made of the same thickness and quality of steel.

The relationship of the bursting strength to diameter is given by the equation

$$S = RP/T$$

where S = tensile stress, in the metal of the pipe or tank cylinder, psi
R = radius of cylinder, in.
P = internal pressure in the vessel, psig
T = thickness of the wall, in.

Steel commonly used for pressure vessels has a maximum tensile strength of 55,000 psi.

Also, allowance should be made for seams. A double rivet seam has only 70% the strength of the base metal, so a factor of 70% should be allowed.

A minimum overall factor of safety of 4 is desirable for the vessel, thus if its operating pressure is 60 psig, it should be constructed to withstand a minimum of 240 psig.

All pressure vessels should be tested with water pressure from time to time using a test pressure as demanded by the local safety code, but in all cases 50% above operating pressure. The use of water pressure for testing is important because if the vessel should fail under test, there will be no explosion, as might occur if air or steam were used.

VISCOSITY

The viscosity of a fluid refers to the resistance of the fluid to flow. The reverse is known as fluidity. Viscosity is produced by the shearing effect of moving one layer of the fluid past an adjacent layer. Viscosity is present in ideal fluids as well as real fluids. Ideal fluids are usually called Newtonian fluids, and are described by the relationship that the rate of flow of the fluid is proportional to the stress, and there is zero flow at zero stress. Viscosity can be represented as the absolute viscosity, the kinematic viscosity, or relative (specific) viscosity. The absolute viscosity is represented by poise or centipoise. A poise is 1 dyne-sec per cm² or 1 gm per sec cm. A Reyn viscosity unit, lb_m per ft-sec or (poundal) (sec) per sq ft, is obtained by dividing centipoise by 1,488. The kinematic viscosity is the absolute viscosity divided by the density of the material and is represented by a stoke as 1 sq cm per sec or sq ft per sec. The relative (specific) viscosity is the ratio of the viscosity of a substance to that of water usually at 20°C, because the viscosity of water at 20°C is approximately 1 centipoise.

In general, for a liquid there will be an increase in viscosity with an increase of solids and with a decrease in temperature. Thus, for moving a product such as fat or butter, it might be economical to add heat to reduce the viscosity to reduce the pumping costs.

The viscosity in centipoise may be obtained by multiplying lb-mass per ft-hr by 0.413.

The viscosity of gases increases with an increase in temperature, or the opposite of the effect with liquids. The viscosity of air at 0°C is 173×10^{-4} centipoise, and at 100°C is 220×10^{-4} centipoise. For water vapor, the values are 90×10^{-4} and 132×10^{-4} centipoise, respectively.

With solids such as butter, the viscosity of the surfaces are often important, particularly for considering the pumping or flow of butter over a surface or through a surface of pipe. Butter at 70°F has a viscosity of 3.1×10^6 centipoise at a velocity of rotation of a Brookfield viscometer of 1 rpm; 1.4×10^5 centipoise at 2.5 rpm; 0.75×10^6 centipoise at 5 rpm; and 0.15×10^6 centipoise at 20 rpm.

Products with a high viscosity are more difficult to heat, to pump, to stir, and to mix than products of low viscosity. For lubrication, a petroleum with a high viscosity may not adequately cover the surface to be lubricated. The lubricant with too low a viscosity will not adhere to the surfaces to provide the reduction in power desired.

Cross-references: *Air Movement; Butter, Physical Properties; Density of Milk; Fluid Flow; Friction; Heat and Mass Transfer; Ice Cream, Physical Properties.*

VORTEX DRYING

The vortex method has been used in the laboratory for drying casein. The vertical drying cylinder has three overflow holes through which the dried product is discharged. The cylinder has a conical base and contains a horizontal sieve that supports the column of product and a dividing wall. The raw casein is fed in at the top; the drying air is fed in from the base causing intensive agitation and rapid drying of the particles. The air enters at 265°F and the casein column is heated to about 113°F. The drier used 1.9 lb steam per pound of water evaporated, as compared to 3 to 5 lb per lb for table driers.

W

WASHING AND BLANCHING

In the canning and freezing of fruits and vegetables the product flow is usually through the following operations: (1) clipper-cleaner, (2) washer, (3) sizer, (4) picking table, (5) blancher, and (6) processing such as freezing, sterilizing, canning, etc.

Washing of the product is to remove dirt and extraneous matter such as sand, stones, and sticks.

The blanching operation is for the purpose of inactivating enzymes which if not destroyed, would cause loss of flavor or color in the product. Blanching is done by exposing the product to water near 212°F from 2 to 3 up to 6 min depending upon the type of product. Blanching also breaks down the stems of spinach and eliminates volatile gases.

Washing

There are many different types and designs of washers, some are for general purpose and others are highly specialized. In general, washers utilize a conveyor which moves the product into contact with sprays of warm or cold water. Through cert_in screens and grids, the sticks, dirt, sand, stones, etc. drop through into a lower compartment. Usually the product is given a final treatment of clean water before the blanching operation.

Preliminary Washers.—These washers are of rather simple construction for the purpose of taking out the rough foreign material and also providing a hydraulic dump box for receiving the product at the beginning of the processing line. Such washers are made to handle products including beets, turnips, tomatoes, potatoes, apples, etc. They have a combination dump tank and soaking tank. A conveyor lifts the product out of the soaking tank and carries it up to a position where it is given a high pressure cold water spray, and then passes it on to the next operation. The capacity of these washers is about 7.5 to 10 tons per hr.

Flood Washing.—The so-called flood type washer is constructed with a false bottom and screen which allows sand and refuse to drain through. The material to be processed is carried forward in a rotary type of drum with perforations which act as a conveyor and at the same time allows water to fall through. It is provided with a fresh water overhead spray.

Eccentric Drum Water.—This is used for washing leafy vegetables such as spinach. It consists essentially of a soaking tank with a device which alternately submerges and releases the product in the water to assist in the loosening of dirt, etc.

Standard Rotary Washer.—This washer has a rotating drum made up of $^3/_4$ in.

round bars with about $^5/_8$ in. spacing. Water is sprayed over the product and the product never comes in contact with dirty water. This type of washer is widely used.

Rotary Combination Washer.—This is widely used for apples, pears, etc., and is designed to give a gentle scrubbing and washing action. It is often used to follow a steam, chemical, or high pressure steam peeling treatment. The rotating "rod and perforated drum" sections which carry the product continuously from one end out the other provide gentle washing and excellent peel removal.

Corrugated Drum Washer.—This is a rotary device which gives excellent scrubbing and washing action on peaches and vegetables. It gives high pressure fresh water sprays. The corrugated surface of the washer drum gives excellent but gentle movement to the product as it is subjected to the sprays.

Rotary Pea Washer.—This is similar to the regular rotary washer except that it has $^1/_8$ by $^5/_8$ in. slot perforations in the rotating cylinder. It is excellent for corn or peas.

Rotary Rod Washer.—This is a heavy duty type of machine used for potatoes, turnips, beets, etc. The rotating element is in effect a rod squirrel cage. It is fitted with lifting flights to provide product tumbling.

Wire Cylinder Leafy Vegetable Washer.—This can also be used as a dry cleaner. It has about 3 to 8 tons capacity per hour. The product is subjected to medium pressure sprays of fresh water. The wire surface of the cylinder makes it adaptable to leafy vegetables.

Blanching

The blancher is a rotary type cylinder which operates inside a heavy metal boiler-like drum, which is filled with boiling water so designed that the conveyor moves the product through the hot water treatment to give a predetermined blanching time and temperature treatment. The speed can usually be varied from 1 to 7 min.; 3 min is an approximate blanching time.

A special type of blanching equipment is designed for leafy products such as spinach, broccoli, and swisschard. In this particular machine, the hot water drum is fitted with two drapers. The lower draper carries the product through at a predetermined rate during the blanching period. The upper draper moves at the same rate but serves to hold the product under the surface of the hot water.

Cross-references: *Blanching; Grading.*

WASTE DISPOSAL

A program of prevention in the control of processing plant wastes is the most effective means of reducing the load on a stream or treatment plant. Waste prevention programs not only reduce the amount of waste, but result in a saving through greater product utilization within the plant. Product leakage and spillage can amount to many dollars during the year.

To prevent waste in plant operation, the following should be considered.

(1) Keep all sanitary fittings, sanitary valves, and filler valves in good repair

(2) Liquid level controls should operate so as to avoid overfilling vats, etc.

(3) Cheese whey should be collected and processed.

(4) Avoid bottle breakage as much as possible.

(5) Repair or replace leaky containers.

(6) By-products should not be flushed into the sewer.

(7) Adopt a definite waste prevention program.

(8) Thoroughly instruct personnel in operation and handling of equipment to prevent waste.

(9) Study the plant operations to determine where losses occur.

(10) Prevent product spoilage using ample refrigerated storage capacity and good processing methods.

(11) Prevent foaming as much as possible.

(12) Provide drip savers or collectors where practical.

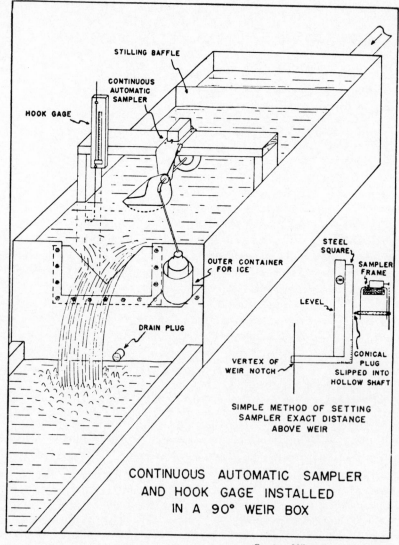

Courtesy Milk Industry Foundation

FIG. W-1.   Continuous automatic sampler and hook gauge

Flow

When using a 90° V-notch weir (Fig. W.1), the reading of the head in inches converted to gallons per minute flow at various levels is as follows:

In. Above Vertex	Flow Gal. per Min
1	2.4
2	13.6
3	36.9
4	75.0
5	129.6
6	204.5
7	299.0
8	415.6
9	555.9
10	720.6

The weir plate should be $\frac{1}{33}$ to $\frac{1}{16}$ in metal (noncorrodible) as brass, copper, or stainless steel.

The stilling box may be equipped with automatic samplers which are more accurate than hand sampling because of the regularity of obtaining the sample. An automatic sampler will take a sample about every 4 or 5 min, which are obtained by a gear reduction unit and motor. A scoop with a curvature is used which is designed to pick up the sample in proportion to the rate of flow. In determining the amount of waste, samples must be taken for several consecutive days at regular intervals. The strength of the waste must also be determined. Tests generally made on liquid waste are temperature, pH, dissolved oxygen in ppm, and the biochemical oxygen demand (BOD) at 20°C(68°F). In natural waters dissolved oxygen usually varies from near zero to 14 ppm; the average is about 8 ppm. Waste waters from a processing plant generally contain very little dissolved oxygen. The effluent from a waste treatment plant should have some dissolved oxygen upon being discharged to a stream.

BOD Test

BOD is a test for determining strength of a waste in terms of the amount of dissolved oxygen used up by the sample under standard conditions. These conditions are incubation for 5 days at 68°F of suitable sample in standard dilution water of known oxygen content and suitable microorganisms, but having no toxic substances.

WASTE TREATMENT

Introduction

The disposal of wastes from a food processing plant is an integral part of the total production system. To reduce costs associated with conventional waste treatment, recycle, reuse and by-product recovery and utilization should be studied as alternatives to waste disposal and as mechanisms for prevention of intrusion of undesirable degradable materials into the environment. The importance of in-plant efforts to reduce the total waste load can hardly be overemphasized. In many cases the reduced losses, improved product recovery, and reduced water usage have more than offset the cost of the treatment facilities.

The capital and operational costs of waste treatment facilities are closely related to the volume of waste that must be treated. Reduced waste volumes will reduce significantly the size of treatment units and the overall cost of treatment, and may reduce plant heat loss. Because excessive use of water often occurs in processing plants, the processor should examine every point of use to determine where water may be conserved or reused.

Water Reuse and Conservation

Reuse of process water reduces both waste load and water usage. A large percentage of the process water does not require biological treatment before reuse; however, care must be taken to assure that anaerobic biological decomposition does not occur, or decomposition products can accumulate which are corrosive, odorous, and

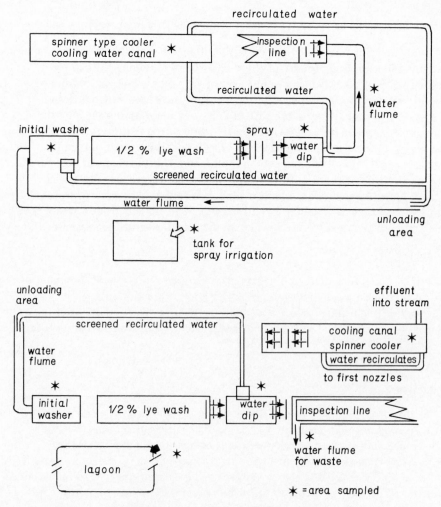

Fig. W-2.   (A) Flow diagram for two tomato processing plant layouts.

capable of affecting the quality of the final product. Bacterial growth can be controlled by disinfection and by changing environmental factors such as pH and temperature. Screening, settling, and velocity control can be used to remove particles from recycle waters prior to reuse in the process. In other instances, secondary biological treatment described below may be prerequisite to reuse for some process streams.

Studies of four tomato juice processing plants indicate considerable variation in the strength and amount of effluent from each of the plants. A study of waste water from various operations revealed that considerable saving of water and waste can be achieved through good water management and utilization methods. Figure W.2 shows the processing system as related to water use and effluent from 2 tomato processing plants and 2 sweet potato plants. The data in Tables W.1 and W.2 depict the condition of water at various stages of processing.

In evaluating reuse, the processor also should consider countercurrent flow. In this system, water from the last product fluming or washing operation, instead of being wasted, is collected and passed back in a countercurrent manner to be used in the preceding washing and fluming operation. The overall effect is that the product is moved forward after each washing operation into water which is cleaner than that used in the preceding operation.

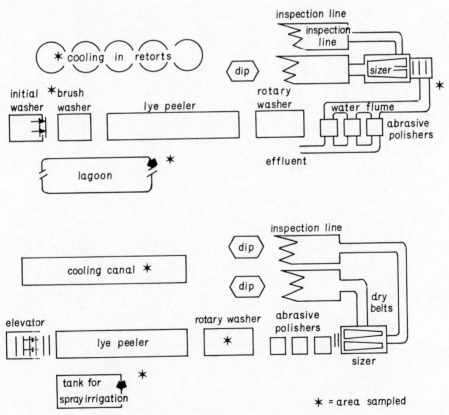

Fig. W-2.   (B) Flow diagram for two sweet potato processing plant layouts

TABLE W.1

ANALYSIS OF WASTE WATER FROM TOMATO JUICE PROCESSING PLANT "A"

Date	pH	Temp. °F	DO Ppm	BOD Ppm	Solids Total Ppm	Solubles Ppm	Insoluble Ppm	Thermo-acidurians Counts/Ml
				Effluent from Plant				
9/8	5.6	80	0.5	850	1,447	1,311	336	154
9/24	5.7	82	0.0	555	1,309	854	455	36
9/30	9.2	83	2.2	475	1,288	1,072	216	40
Avg	6.8	82	0.9	626	1,347	1,078	335	77
				Initial Wash Water				
9/8	6.2	76	3.5	348	814	540	274	247
9/24	5.2	79	0.0	425	693	534	159	59
9/30	6.9	79	0.0	287	870	532	338	285
Avg	6.1	78	1.2	353	792	535	257	197
			Wash Water Subsequent to Spray Rinse Subsequent to Lye Wash					
9/8	5.4	73	0	1,200	2,763	2,272	491	364
9/24	6.6	78	3.1	363	699	599	100	86
9/30	7.1	72	3.5	32	710	585	125	49
Avg	6.4	74	2.2	531	1,389	1,150	238	166
			Flume Water Conveying Tomatoes to the Inspection Line					
9/8	6.7	83	3.0	92	474	384	90	92
9/24	7.6	86	2.6	233	538	417	121	68
9/30	7.3	102	2.9	220	358	280	78	23
Avg	7.2	91	2.8	181	456	360	96	61
				Cooling Canal Water				
9/8	6.2	82	3.1	191	634	471	163	174
9/24	8.3	84	6.9	18	195	182	13	28
9/30	8.1	94	4.5	28	204	203	1	20
Avg	7.5	87	4.8	79	344	285	59	74

ANALYSIS OF WASTE WATER FROM TOMATO JUICE PROCESSING PLANT "B"

Date	pH	Temp. °F	DO Ppm	BOD Ppm	Total Ppm	Solubles Ppm	Insoluble Ppm	Thermo-acidurians Counts/Ml
				Effluent from Plant				
9/16	4.6	87	0.0	1,800	4,082	2,783	1,299	50
9/22	5.1	78	0.0	2,513	4,254	4,075	179	812
Avg	4.9	83	0.0	2,157	4,168	3,429	739	431
				Initial Wash Water				
9/16	4.6	72	0.0	913	2,855	1,475	1,380	141
9/22	4.7	65	0.0	2,038	3,790	2,638	1,152	426
Avg	4.7	69	0.0	1,476	3,323	2,056	1,266	284
			Wash Water Subsequent to Spray Rinse Subsequent to Lye Wash					
9/16	6.5	80	4.4	248	584	539	45	51
9/22	6.2	76	3.8	449	828	777	51	550
Avg	6.4	78	4.1	349	706	658	48	301
			Flume Water Conveying Tomatoes to the Inspection Line					
9/16	6.7	71	3.6	223	505	504	1	9
9/22	7.1	60	3.0	204	553	567	−14	531
Avg	6.9	66	3.3	214	529	536	1	270

TABLE W-1 (*Continued*)

| Date | pH | Temp. °F | DO Ppm | BOD Ppm | Solids | | | Thermo-acidurians Counts/Ml |
					Total Ppm	Solubles Ppm	Insoluble Ppm	
				Cooling Canal Water				
9/16	8.0	92	6.0	12	371	341	30	0
9/22	8.2	110	6.5	54	304	339	−34	163
Avg	8.1	101	6.3	33	338	340	10	82

Source: Md. Food Proc. Rept. *12*, 4, Sept. 1966.

Process Control and Modification

Proper operation of process equipment can reduce both waste load and product loss. In some cases adjustments in process require evaluation of treatment cost versus trimming cost or product quality. Good housekeeping, avoidance of spills, and education of personnel working on the process line to the magnitude of the waste problem can all work to reduce waste handling costs.

Although processors are not always able to take full advantage of new and improved equipment and methods, numerous possibilities exist for redesign and modification of existing equipment to reduce the waste load. Utilization of process by-products in a manner that provides income will reduce the total cost of waste treatment and eventually the cost of the final product. Waste solids should be evaluated as sources of food for plants and animals and as fuel with the possibility of financial return.

In many cases waste streams from different process steps should not be combined. Large savings in treatment costs may result from keeping dilute and concentrated waste streams separate. Dilute waste water can often be reused or disposed of after little or no treatment. Also, since the size of treatment units generally is determined by the waste volume rather than the strength, concentrated wastes will require smaller treatment units at lower capital investments. Waste streams with extreme pH values should be carefully considered because of their effect on biological treatment. The combination of acid and basic waste streams may result in neutralization, and if possible, cooperation between adjacent industries may be very beneficial.

Preliminary Treatment

Sand and silt from washing raw foods should be removed prior to transmitting waste waters to primary treatment units. Stones and gravel in flume water can be removed by sand traps, riggles, or grit chambers. A variety of separation equipment is available and shallow ponds can sometimes be used to treat silt laden wash waters.

Screening is an effective and extensively used method for removing larger solids and floating debris. Three types of screens are in use: fixed or stationary, rotary, and vibratory screens. Screens are discussed further in Guttormsen and Carlson (1969). Removal efficiencies vary greatly with type and number of screens employed, and the bar spacing or mesh sizes of the screens. Talburt and Smith (1967) have summarized waste characteristics from several operations prior to and after screening.

TABLE W.2

ANALYSIS OF WASTE WATER FROM SWEET POTATO PROCESSING PLANT "C"

					Solids		
Date	pH	Temp. °F	DO Ppm	BOD Ppm	Total Ppm	Soluble Ppm	Insoluble Ppm
Effluent from Plant							
10/19	11.8	89	0.0	>1,980	7,340	5,697	1,643
10/26	11.8	92	0.0	2,100	8,396	6,578	1,818
11/3	11.5	88	0.0	>1,675	4,860	4,139	542
Avg	11.7	90	0.0	1,916	6,858	5,465	1,333
Initial Wash Water							
10/19	6.6	65	4.3	3,375	962	316	610
10/26	7.8	63	6.6	400	1,452	314	1,138
11/3	7.7	68	6.6	175	442	257	185
Avg	7.4	66	5.8	1,315	951	295	644
Wash Water from Abrasive Peeler							
10/19							
10/26							
11/3	6.1	100	5.5	4,250	8,227	5,610	2,617
Avg							
Flume Water Conveying Sweet Potatoes to the Sizing Apparatus from the Abrasive Peeler							
10/19	4.6	86	5.5	1,258	2,384	1,817	567
10/26	7.6	91	4.3	355	703	541	162
11/3	7.4	75	3.1	950	659	580	79
Avg	6.5	84	4.3	853	1,247	978	269
Cooling Water from Retort							
10/19	8.1	105	0.8	50	148	106	42
10/26	8.1	110	0.8	100	184	197	−13
11/3	8.0	110	1.4	200	186	202	−16
Avg	8.1	108	1.0	117	172	168	14
ANALYSIS OF WASTE WATER FROM SWEET POTATO PROCESSING PLANT "D"							
Effluent from Plant[1]							
10/19[2]	11.0	79	3.2	375	2,796	1,790	1,006
10/26	11.8	84	0.0	2,513	9,601	7,757	1,844
Avg	11.4	82	1.6	1,444	6,199	4,774	1,425
Initial Wash Water from Carrots							
10/19[2]	6.7	65	3.9	1,500	995	168	827
10/26	No initial wash used on sweet potatoes						
Avg							
Wash Water from Rotary Washer Subsequent to Lye Peeler							
10/19[2]	11.2	89	0	>1,980	7,520	5,803	1,717
10/26	11.5	104	0	4,163	10,192	8,234	2,858
Avg	11.4	97	0		8,856	7,019	2,288
Cooling Canal Water							
10/19[2]	5.9	87	7.2	50	161	104	57
10/26	6.1	97	10.0	115	76	88	−14
Avg	6.0	92	8.6	83	119	96	29

[1] Waste water from carrots, sweet potatoes, and spinach.
[2] From carrot line.

Source: Md. Food Processors Rept. *12*, 4, Sept. 1966.

Primary Treatment

Although secondary treatment will be required by many authorities in the near future, primary treatment will become no less important. Secondary treatment is more expensive, and the maximum degree of primary treatment should be obtained to reduce the load on the secondary system. Primary treatment is used extensively with good results, but much can be done to improve its performance.

Primary treatment includes such treatment processes as settling or plain sedimentation, flocculation, flotation, and centrifugation. Settling facilities range from simple settling ponds to sophisticated clarifiers designed specifically for the particular waste stream involved. Settling ponds can provide good removal of suspended solids until they become filled and must be drained or dredged. Dredging can be an expensive odorous operation which makes the use of manufacturers' clarifiers seem more desirable.

Conventional clarifiers are either rectangular or circular; the circular is more common. Most clarifiers are designed on the basis of overflow rates in the range of 800 to 1,000 gal. per day per square foot of surface area and depths of 10 to 12 ft. Most of the settleable solids will be removed from the effluent, and chemical oxygen demand (COD) removals of 50 to 70% may be expected if the plant effluent has been properly screened.

Corrosion protection is an important consideration in clarifier design, since bacterial decomposition of the settled sludge can lower the pH as low as 3. Two or three heavy coats of epoxy tar paint have been found effective in protecting both steel and concrete structures submerged in the clarifier.

Flocculation has been found to increase the removal efficiency of clarifiers markedly when treating both domestic and industrial wastes. Mechanical flocculation is accomplished by gently stirring the waste with rotating paddles, thus causing the finely divided particles to coalesce into larger flocs with improved settling characteristics. Flocs so produced are easily broken up by too rapid stirring, and the most efficient peripheral speed of the flocculator has been reported to be 1.4 fps (Klein 1966). Hurley and Lester (1949) obtained 20% increase in clarifier removal efficiency by mechanical flocculation prior to sedimentation. Return of some of the settled sludge may be beneficial in some cases (Klein 1966).

Chemical flocculation or coagulation is used extensively in waste treatment. The addition of certain chemicals to the waste when followed by gentle stirring results in the formation of an insoluble flocculent precipitate, which adsorbs and carries down suspended and colloidal matter. Chemicals commonly used include lime, aluminum sulfate, copperas, and various ferric salts. The cost of the chemicals makes this method considerably more expensive than mechanical flocculation, but higher removal efficiencies are obtained.

Another process for solids removal is flotation in which the waste or a portion of clarified effluent is pressurized to 50 to 60 psi in the presence of sufficient air to approach saturation. When this air-liquid mixture is released at atmospheric pressure, minute air bubbles are released from solution. The rising bubbles adhere to or are trapped by the suspended solids and sludge flocs, and float them to the surface where they can be removed by skimming. The process is used by the potato processing plant in Presque Isle, Maine, and the removal efficiency of settleable solids has been reported to be as high as 86%. However, since the calculations are based on a volume per unit volume measurement (ml/l), it is difficult to compare this result with removal efficiencies based on weight per unit volume measurements (mg/l) (Ballance 1965).

TABLE W.3

PE AND BOD OF SOME DAIRY PRODUCTS, LB

	PE	BOD
Whole milk	61	10.3
Skimmed milk	43	7.2
Dry skim milk	442	73.9
Cream	239	39.9
Ice cream mix	175	29.2

Dickinson (1965) pointed out the advantages of treating potato waste, particularly flume and wash water, by centrifugation. A centrifuge conserves space and delivers the solids in a relatively dry state. Furthermore, any risk of anaerobic decomposition in settling tanks is avoided. An investigation carried out in Idaho did not find centrifugation a feasible replacement for conventional clarification (Grames and Kueneman 1968).

Secondary Treatment

As waste water effluent requirements become more stringent, the use of biological treatment to follow primary treatment is frequently a necessity. Biological processes are considered secondary treatment and involve such systems as activated sludge, aerobic trickling filters, anaerobic filters, spray irrigation, and a variety of ponds.

The activated sludge process consists of discharging the primary effluent into a large aeration basin where atmospheric oxygen is added either by mechanical surface aerators or under pressure from diffusers under the waste water surface. In addition a heavy concentration of a mixed culture of organisms is cycled through the tank for the purpose of biologically degrading the entering organic wastes.

There are a variety of modifications of the basic activated sludge plant. These systems include contact stabilization, extended aeration and the oxidation ditch. The oxidation ditch, for example, is commonly a ring-shaped ditch with aeration and circulation provided by one or more partially submerged rotors. The ditch can be loaded up to 34 lb biochemical oxygen demand (BOD)/1,000 cu ft ditch liquid volume/day and still provide good oxidation of the waste.

TABLE W.4

BOD LOADS WHICH MAY BE EXPECTED FROM CERTAIN DAIRY PROCESSES

Process	Lb BOD per 10,000 Lb Milk
Receiving and cooling milk	2
Tank truck delivery, milk	1
Cream separating	2
Pasteurizing, cooling, bottling (glass)	8
Pasteurizing, cooling, bottling (paper)	6
Ice Cream mix making	1
Skim drying spray process	1
Skim drying roller process	16

The volume milk handled in a plant can be estimated in terms of BOD in the waste using the above values.

Biological processes, such as activated sludge, rely on the maintenance of reasonable environmental conditions in the treatment unit for the process to work properly. Thus contact time, pH range, and nutrients would be of concern. Such ingredients as phosphorus and nitrogen may have to be added, and pH may require adjusting prior to stabilization of wastes in a biological system.

Trickling filters are a system of 3- to 4-in. rocks or plastic media piled inside a wall on screen and over which the waste water is distributed by a rotating arm. Air breathes naturally up through the voids between the rocks, and a mixed flora of microorganisms grow in a slime attached to the rocks. The mixed biological culture stabilizes the organic material in the wastes as the waste water passes down over the rock or plastic support media. As the organisms continue to grow there is a sloughing of excess growth that must be separated from the effluent water by sedimentation, which is the same system used to separate organisms from effluent in the activated sludge system. A variety of flow patterns and rates are used with trickling filters.

Mercer *et al.* (1964) used a pilot plant trickling filter with plastic support media for secondary treatment of peach and pear canning waste. The influent and effluent samples were settled for 15 min to simulate primary and secondary clarification. The raw waste had a pH of 10.5, and the effluent pH was 6.2. The results of the study are presented in Table W.5.

Norman *et al.* (1965) compared the use of the activated sludge process and the plastic media trickling filter as roughing treatment for beet sugar waste. Overloading the activated sludge unit to obtain only 50% BOD removal caused the formation of bulking sludge, and it was concluded that this process was not feasible for such treatment. The trickling filter gave BOD removals of between 33 and 50% on once through passes at loadings of 400 to 230 lb BOD/1,000 cu ft/day.

The anaerobic filter offers promise as a prospective treatment facility for certain potato processing wastes. Whereas conventional anaerobic digestion is limited to wastes of high strength and solids content at relatively high temperatures, the anaerobic filter has performed well at nominal temperatures with relatively dilute, soluble wastes.

The anaerobic filter, which is similar to the aerobic trickling filter in appearance, has upward flow so that the rock media is completely submerged. The anaerobic organisms are attached to the stones as well as suspended as discrete particles in the interstitial spaces. High solids retention time (SRT), which is an important operational parameter in anaerobic treatment, is easily obtained in the anaerobic filter,

TABLE W.5

TRICKLING FILTRATION OF PEACH AND PEAR CANNING WASTE

Flow, Gpm/Ft²		BOD, Mg/L		BOD, Lb/1,000 Ft³/Day		Percent BOD Removal
Raw	Recycle	Influent	Effluent	Loading	Removal	
0.14	2.0	4,033	580	316	273	86
0.42	2.0	3,200	1,395	730	410	56
0.72	2.0	2,700	1,800	1,060	350	33
1.0	1.0	3,210	2,040	1,760	630	36
1.0	1.0	2,750	1,515	1,510	680	45[1]

[1] Nutrients added (20 lb diammonium phosphate per 24 hr).

and is on the order of hundreds of days (Carlson 1968).   A gradual accumulation of solids may occur to the point where solids wasting may be required.

Recent studies have indicated the feasibility of the anaerobic filter.   Young and McCarty (1968) obtained BOD removals ranging from 60 to 99% when treating either simple volatile acids or complex protein-carbohydrate wastes.

Ponds.—Pond treatment of domestic sewage as well as industrial wastes is common around the world, and there are several reports of application of this treatment method to potato processing wastes on a pilot plant basis and in full scale ponds.   Ponds often are designated by various names, such as lagoons, oxidation ponds, stabilization ponds, and waste conversion ponds.   Dugan and Oswald (1968) classified the different types of ponds as follows:

Aerobic ponds—Those ponds in which only the reactions above the point where dissolved oxygen becomes zero (termed the oxypause) occur that provide aerobic oxidation and photosynthetic oxygenation.

Facultative ponds—Ponds in which an aerobic zone exists in the surface strata and an anaerobic zone exists in the lower strata.

Anaerobic ponds—Ponds in which the anaerobic reactions below the oxypause are the predominant ones.

The aerated lagoon is a fourth type where oxygen is supplied by diffused or mechanical aeration systems which also cause sufficient mixing to induce a significant amount of surface aeration.

Aerobic and facultative ponds depend upon the photosynthetic capabilities of algae to provide the oxygen required to satisfy the BOD applied.   Some surface aeration from wind action also occurs.   Since sunlight is essential for algae, the depth of the ponds is limited.   In aerobic ponds the waste material is stabilized wholly through aerobic oxidation.   The depth is therefore limited to that through which sunlight will penetrate.   For most wastes this will not exceed 18 in (Eckenfelder 1966).   Extremely large surface areas are therefore required.   Most existing ponds are facultative.   In facultative ponds, settled solids undergo anaerobic decomposition in the bottom layers, while aerobic oxidation takes place in the upper layers.   Serious odor problems will not develop if adequate depth is maintained and an upper aerobic environment is predominant.   The depth of facultative ponds is seldom greater than 5 ft.

Since both aerobic and facultative ponds are highly dependent upon algal photosynthesis, the environmental factors affecting the growth rate of algae must be considered carefully in pond design.   Gloyna (1968) has presented design criteria for the various classifications of ponds.

Active microbiological populations in anaerobic ponds are facultative and anaerobic bacteria which utilize chemically bound oxygen in the form of carbon dioxide, nitrates, sulfates, or organic molecules.   Anaerobic ponds have been used for treatment of food processing waste although odor nuisances can be associated with them.   Odors from anaerobic processes can be removed by the use of soil filters which can oxidize the objectionable polar gases.

Spray Irrigation.—Spray irrigation has been used successfully by many processors as a method of final disposal of waste water from fruit and vegetable processing.   Successful operation of spray irrigation fields is dependent on the capacity of the receiving site to absorb the waste water.   Among the variables influencing soil receiving

From Food Science, AVI Publishing Co.

FIG. W-3.   Waste treatment plant of aeration type

capacity are type of soil, stratification of soil profile, depth of ground water, initial moisture content, and cover crop.   Waste water chracteristics also are important.

General design criteria or recommendations cannot be stated for spray irrigation because of the variables involved, and most systems must be designed with considerable flexibility.   For a discussion of successful applications of spray irrigation see Guttormsen and Carlson (1969).

Tertiary Treatment

As reuse of treated waste water becomes more essential, tertiary treatment of these waters will become increasingly important.   The biological treatment methods, as presently used, leave significant residues in the effluents, and several physical and chemical treatment methods have therefore been investigated as a means for polishing effluents before reuse.   These methods include adsorption, foam separation, electrodialysis, evaporation, reverse osmosis, coagulation, chemical oxidation, and freezing.

Disposal of Solids

Solid wastes from food processing operations include sand and grit, peelings, trimmings, and pulp.   Solids also are one of the end products of nearly all waste treatment processes.   Effective solid waste disposal is essential for the waste treatment process to be successful.   Depending upon the method used, solids disposal may result in economic return or additional treatment cost.

Complete utilization is the ideal solution to the solids disposal problem, and fortunately a large fraction of the solid waste from potato processing is suitable for use as animal fodder and even for processing into by-products of commercial value (Shaw 1965; Dickey *et al.* 1963).   However, large amounts of solid waste are disposed of by other methods for economic as well as practical reasons.   In some areas the demand for the solid waste products is not sufficient to warrant the capital investment.   Furthermore, pesticide residues and high alkaline content may limit the usability of raw solid waste. Microbiological spoilage of food wastes presents another problem, since no economical method of preservation has been discovered (Rose 1965).

Some processing plants discharge solid wastes as well as liquid wastes directly to a municipal sewer. Generally, larger solids are comminuted prior to discharge. From the processor's standpoint this is a most convenient solids disposal method. The obvious disadvantage is the greatly increased waste load to the receiving treatment facility or waterway. In many instances solid waste discharge would not be permitted or would be economically unsound because of increased treatment cost.

A widely used method for disposal of solid wastes is by land disposal. Strict control is essential to prevent ground water contamination, fly breeding, and odor nuisances. An important requirement is that the waste be covered with a soil layer within 24 hr. (The Cost of Clean Water 1967). Primary and secondary sludges have a very high water content and generally must be dewatered prior to disposal. The dewatering step can be omitted by applying the sludge to the land in a thin layer. The same method may be applied to the solid waste from the processing operations. This method provides low cost oxidation of organic matter, providing sufficient low cost land is available. In many instances agricultural and forest soils are improved. Odors and fly breeding may cause problems (Anon. 1967).

Composting processes long have been used as a method of converting putrescible plant residues to more stable organic materials of value as fertilizers or soil conditioners. Composting also has had application as a method of solid waste disposal. Decomposition of the organic materials may proceed aerobically or anaerobically, depending upon the availability of oxygen. Anaerobic processes are slow, and offensive odor production is difficult to control. Aerobic composting is a much more rapid process and no offensive odors are produced. The process may be carried out in outdoor piles or in high-rate mechanical units (Rich 1963).

Incinerators currently are used in municipal treatment plants to burn solid organic wastes (Hindin and Dunstan 1965; Anon. 1967). To avoid objectionable odors from the volatile organic acids, temperatures of about 1,400°F must be maintained. Two basic types of open-air sludge incinerators are in use. These are the flash drier-incinerator and the multiple hearth incinerator.

Anaerobic digestion of solid waste decomposes the organic liquids and solids to inorganic matter and organic gases. Methane is the principal organic gas formed.

Pulp, peelings, and primary sludges offer possibilities for providing cattle feed. Processing, handling, and transportation costs should be evaluated in terms of providing a salable product in the region of the food processing plant.

Environmental Impact

The impact of the food processing industry on the total environment will be an area of vital concern in the seventies. It is not sufficient to consider only the growth and production of the product and the treatment of emanating waste streams. Concern must be directed as well to the chemicals, materials, and energy and ecological balances involved in the production system, and perhaps some of the most important plant evaluations will deal with the effect of production on these balances. Although the problems are not unique to the food processing industry, they are part of the total responsibility of mankind in maintaining the quality of the environment.

The loads of salts, pesticides, and herbicides dumped into the environment should be evaluated carefully in terms of their insult capacity to the environment, and alternative methods should be considered for growing and processing where the method used is not compatible with maintaining the quality of the environment. Other methods of growing, harvesting, and processing should be studied to explore mechanisms for providing greater amenability with the use and preservation of resources. Increases in receiving water temperature resulting from waste discharges can disrupt biospheres and create system imbalances which may have perturbations in other industries and water uses.

It is incumbent on the food processing industry to be cognizant of its societal impact and the legal and regulatory aspects of waste treatment including incentive systems, planning, and agricultural basin development. The expanding role of industry in relationship to man's needs and the maintenance of a quality environment must be considered in modernizing existing plants and planning for the processing systems of the future. Prepared by DALE A. CARLSON

References

ANON. 1967. Cost of Clean Water, Volume III, Industrial Waste Profile No. *6*, Canned and Frozen Fruits and Vegetables. Federal Water Pollution Control Admin.

BALLANCE, R. C. 1965. Review of Primary Treatment Processes. Proc. Intern. Symp., Utilization and Disposal of Potato Wastes. New Brunswick Research and Productivity Council, N. B., Canada.

CARLSON, D. A. 1968. Recent Developments in Anaerobic Waste Treatment. Proc. Symp. on Potato Waste Treatment. FWPCA and University of Idaho.

DICKEY, H. C., BRUGMAN, H. H., HIGHLANDS, M. E., AND PLUMMER, B. E. 1965. The Use of By-products from Potato Starch and Potato Processing. Proc. Intern. Symp., Utilization and Disposal of Potato Wastes. New Brunswick Research and Productivity Council, N.B., Canada.

DICKINSON, D. 1965. Treatment of Effluents from Potato Processing. Proc. Intern. Symp., Utilization and Disposal of Potato Wastes. New Brunswick Research and Productivity Council, N. B., Canada.

DUGAN, G. L., AND OSWALD, W. J. 1968. Mechanisms of Anaerobic Waste Treatment. Proc. Symp. on Potato Waste Treatment. FWPCA and University of Idaho.

ECKENFELDER, W. W., JR. 1966. Industrial Water Pollution Control. McGraw-Hill Book Co., New York.

GLOYNA, E. F. 1968. Basis for waste stabilization pond designs. *In* Advances in Water Quality Improvement. Univ. Texas Press, Austin.

GRAMES, L. M., AND KUENEMAN, R. W. 1968. Primary Treatment of Potato Processing Wastes with By-product Feed Recovery. Paper presented 41st Ann. Conf. Water Pollution Control Federation, Chicago, Ill.

GUTTORMSEN, K., and CARLSON, D. A. 1969. Potato Processing Waste Treatment Current Practice. FWPCA, U.S. Dept. Interior.

HINDIN, E., and DUNSTAN, G. H. 1963. Anaerobic Digestion of Potato Processing Wastes. J. Water Pollution Control Federation *35*, No. 4, 486.

HURLEY, J., and LESTER, W. F. 1949. Mechanical Flocculation in Sewage Purification. J. Inst. Sewage Purif. *2*, 193–202.

KLEIN, L. 1966. River Pollution, III. Control. Butterworths, London.

MERCER, W. A. *et al.*, 1964. Trickling Filter Treatment of Liquid Fruit Canning Waste. Progr. Rept. Prepared by Western Res. Lab., National Canners Assoc., Berkeley, Calif.

NORMAN, L. W. *et al.* 1965. Waste water treatment studies at Tracy, California. J. Am. Soc. Sugar Beet Technologists *13*, 5.

RICH, L. G. 1963. Unit Processes of Sanitary Engineering. John Wiley & Sons, New York.

Rose, W. W. 1965. Treatment and Disposal of Potato Wastes. Proc. Intern. Symp., Utilization and Disposal of Potato Wastes. New Brunswick Research and Productivity Council, N. B., Canada.

Shaw, R. 1965. Potato Specialties from Edible Potato Wastes—A Review, Proc. Intern. Symp., Utilization and Disposal of Potato Wastes. New Brunswick Research and Productivity Council, N. B., Canada.

Talburt, W. F., and Smith O. 1967. Potato Processing, 2nd Edition. AVI Publishing Co., Westport, Conn.

Young, J. C., and McCarty, P. L. 1968. The Anaerobic Filter for Waste Treatment. Techn. Rept. *87.* Dept. Civil Engineering, Stanford Univ.

Cross-references: *Lagoon; Waste Disposal; Water Supplies.*

WATER SUPPLIES

The water supply for a food plant is very important and essential for cooling purposes, equipment cleaning requirements, production of steam, refrigeration, condensing pans, and general sanitation. The purity of water is of utmost importance and is always subject to possible pollution which may cause an outbreak of disease or seriously decrease shelf-life of food products.

Plant operators are concerned with the requirements and utilization of water dealing with heat transfer and other general uses. The hardness of water is very important for prolonged efficiency in heat transfer, and therefore, most water requires treatment. Water hardness is generally expressed in terms of equivalent calcium carbonate measured either as grains per gallon or as parts per million. One grain per gallon is equal to 17.1 ppm. The hardness of water is measured often by the so-called sudsing power of the water with a soap solution which has been standardized against a calcium salt solution of known strength.

The U.S. Geological survey classifies water on a basis of hardness as follows:

	Ppm
Soft	0–60
Moderately hard	60–120
Hard	120–180
Very hard	Over 180

About 85% of the nation's water supplies are hard enough to require softening for greatest utility. In the United States, water hardness will vary from about 1 gr per gal. (gpg) to 350. The usual range will be from 3 to 50 gpg.

Hard water is the chief cause of scale formation in boilers which reduces heat transfer efficiency and is a serious problem. Hardness can also be troublesome in bottle washing and other cleaning operations, as well as in air conditioners, condensers of refrigeration systems, and in process cooling equipment. Corrosion of lines and equipment may also occur. This is especially true of steam condensate lines because of carbonic acid formed by the liberation of carbon dioxide from the bicarbonates.

Interpreted broadly, hardness is the presence of dissolved minerals in water. But for the usual treatment purposes, hardness is considered to be the effect resulting from dissolved salts of calcium and magnesium. The most common of these are calcium bicarbonate, magnesium bicarbonate, calcium chloride, magnesium chloride, and magnesium sulfate. The bicarbonates of calcium and magnesium are very soluble and are often referred to as "temporary hardness." When water is heated, these bicarbonates decompose into carbonates which are relatively insoluble thus forming deposits of scale.

Bicarbonates are often the principal hardness salts found in water. They are formed by the action of water and carbon dioxide on such substances as limestone. As water from rain or snow percolates through the ground, it picks up the carbon dioxide from decaying vegetation.

An approximation of the degree of hardness can be obtained with the soap or sudsing test. A soap solution is prepared by standardization against a calcium salt solution of known strength. Some variations are found in the actual use of this test; however, best results are obtained by using a 50-ml sample of water in a 250-ml bottle as outlined in *Standard Methods for the Examination of Water and Sewage.* Little or no reaction with magnesium will sometimes lead to inaccurate results with the soap test.

A more reliable method of determining water hardness is with the EDTA (disodium ethylene diamine tetraacetate) test. This is a titration procedure at controlled pH using Chrome Black T as the indicator. At pH 8.0 to 10.0, EDTA forms soluble complexions with calcium, magnesium, and other ions. A change in color (end point) from red to blue occurs when free calcium ions no longer exist. An accuracy of ±2 ppm is usually achieved with this hardness test.

Silica in Water

Silica can be found in all water supplies in concentrations ranging from 1 to 100 ppm. This is the result of the water flowing through sand and rocks. For most purposes the presence of a small amount of silica causes no trouble. However, a very hard silica scale which reduces fuel to steam efficiency may be formed in high pressure boilers. Corrective measures for boiler operation consist of adequate blowdown to hold the silica concentration at a sufficiently low level. For severe cases, continuous blowdown is recommended.

Hydrogen Sulfide in Water

The odor and taste of water containing 1 ppm or more of hydrogen sulfide is pungent and once experienced will always be remembered. Hydrogen sulfide in water is also objectionable because it promotes corrosion and tarnish on silver, and in high concentrations disrupts the action of an ion exchange softener. The quantity of hydrogen sulfide can be determined by titrating with a standardized solution of iodine using starch as the indicator.

Treatment.—Corrective measures for removing hydrogen sulfide from water generally involves conversion of the gas to elemental insoluble yellow sulfur powder which is filtered out. The type of treatment depends upon the concentration of the gas. Where only a trace exists, the gas can be absorbed on the surface of an activated carbon filter bed. For low to medium concentrations, an oxidizing filter such as is used for controlling iron is effective. The elemental sulfur precipitate which is formed tends to clog the filter; therefore, it is necessary to change the filter medium at intervals.

When hydrogen sulfide exists in high concentrations, chemical treatment by 1 of 2 methods is required. One method involves feeding chlorine solution (with a feed pump) into the water at a rate which provides no less than 2 ppm of chlorine for each ppm of hydrogen sulfide. The water must be mixed in a tank and then passed through an activated carbon filter to remove the insoluble sulfur and excess chlorine.

In the alternative treatment, potassium permanganate is fed into the water After mixing in a storage tank, the water is passed through an oxidizing iron filter. The excess potassium permanganate keeps the filter bed in a "regenerated" state which has the advantage of providing some reserve capacity.

Gases in Water

Although several gases may be found in plant water supplies, carbon dioxide and oxygen are the most common. Carbon dioxide varies in concentration ranging up to 50 ppm, and well water will frequently contain 4 ppm oxygen. Surface water supplies usually contain more of these gases than ground water. Occasionally, however, well water has enough CO_2 to cause bubbling when drawn. Depending upon the purpose for which the water is used, a certain amount of dissolved carbon dioxide and oxygen may be desirable. Carbon dioxide tends to give water a sparkle and sometimes improves the taste. Oxygen is, of course, necessary for marine life. However, both of these gases have a corrosive effect on iron, zinc, and brass, especially in enclosed systems at elevated temperatures.

Treatment.—Corrective measures for removing oxygen and carbon dioxide are preheating or chemical treatment. Preheating of boiler feedwater using exhaust steam not only removes free oxygen and CO_2, but will save fuel in most cases. The boiler capacity is also increased by preheating feedwater especially where only a portion of the condensate is returned. By rule of thumb estimates, boiler efficiency and capacity are increased 1% for each $11°F$ rise in the feedwater temperature.

Sodium sulfite and sometimes other chemicals are added to water to reduce the free oxygen content. Carbon dioxide may be controlled by a process involving the addition of soda ash to the water. Treating water with soda ash is practical for larger plants where sizable quantities of water are to be treated. The method has the advantage of removing CO_2 without increasing hardness.

Iron in Water

Iron is present in much of the ground water and exists in various forms. Most iron-bearing water contains less than 5 ppm of iron, but occasionally a concentration of 60 ppm can be found. In concentrations as low as 0.3 ppm, iron water stains nearly everything it contacts including equipment, walls, and floors. Therefore, an iron content in excess of 0.3 ppm is undesirable, particularly in final rinse and sanitizing solutions.

Freshly drawn ground water containing iron will usually be clear and colorless because the iron exists in the ferrous form. Upon exposure to air or available chlorine, oxidation occurs which converts the colorless ferrous salts into the familiar reddish-brown insoluble ferric compounds. Ferrous bicarbonate is the most common iron salt, but sometimes ferrous sulfide can be found, or ferrous sulfate in acid mine waters. By contrast, surface waters which contain iron will normally have the element in the ferric state. Both are objectionable.

Water systems have been known to have become clogged and badly corroded by the combination of "iron" bacteria growing profusely in iron-bearing water. Large quantities of a thick rust colored precipitate can be formed by the "iron loving" bacteria. When this condition exists, bactericidal treatment is necessary.

Because iron is likely to exist in water supplies in both the ferrous and ferric state, it is difficult to establish hard and fast rules for treatment. These irons may be naturally present or result from corrosion of iron or steel pipes of the plumbing system. For processing plants the usual treatment will involve oxidizing the iron to the insoluble ferric form followed by removal of these compounds by filtration. However, where the iron content is not excessively high and where removal does not seem feasible, it is desirable to add some hexametaphosphate to sequester the iron.

In certain cases where the iron concentration is very small, an ion exchange softner can also serve as the filter. Small quantities of ferrous ions will usually be removed by an active softener.

If the gelatinous ferric iron is present in sufficient quantity, it will coat the individual particles of the ion exchange medium and disrupt the normal operation of the softener. The ability of a softener to resist this action varies with its design, type of exchange medium, and operating conditions. For this reason, softener manufacturers specify a maximum tolerable iron content in the water to be treated. When the iron content exceeds the established maximum, some other corrective treatment must be used. An oxidizing filter is normally effective for medium iron concentrations. Oxidizing filters contain a base material which has been coated with manganese dioxide. Exposure to this substance will convert the dissolved ferrous ions to insoluble ferric compounds which can then be filtered out. These filters lose their effectiveness after a period of use and must be regenerated by a three-step process as follows.

(1) Back wash the unit to remove the precipitated iron.
(2) Flush a solution of potassium permanganate through the bed to restore the manganese dioxide surface coating.
(3) Rinse with fresh water and the unit is ready for use.

Water having high iron concentrations require treatment with chemicals such as a chlorine bleach solution to oxidize ferrous iron into the insoluble form. The contaminant can then be removed by running the water through a simple sand and gravel filter. Special chemical feed pumps should be used for the bleach solution in this process. A tank is desirable for proper mixing, and the solution must be in contact with the water for a minimum time (normally 20 min) to ensure thorough treatment. If these conditions are provided, the results are very good.

A filter in a water line is a good precaution to help prevent particles of rust and insoluble iron from entering food products. An in-line replaceable disc filter is inexpensive and has been found to be quite effective when installed near the water outlet.

Water Treatment for Hardness

When water hardness exceeds 5 grains per gallon (gpg), it usually pays to install a water softener. This is especially true for water to be used for cleaning purposes. Also, feedwater which has been softened generally requires smaller amounts of added chemicals to control scale buildup inside a boiler.

Several different methods may be used to treat or soften water. When selecting water treatment for a food plant, several factors must be considered but essentially the most economical method will depend upon water usage.   For example, water to be used in condensers and heat exchangers for cooling purposes need not be completely softened to control scale deposits.   The addition of 2 to 16 ppm of sodium hexametaphosphate (threshold treatment) is usually adequate.   Hard water is most often softened by one or a combination of two basic methods—chemical precipitation and base exchange.

The chemical precipitation processes have the advantage of reducing the total dissolved solids content of water.   This is achieved by precipitating and filtering out many of the hardness salts.   Two common types of chemical treatment are used.

(1)   For pretreating boiler feedwater for large plants, the Hot Process Lime-Soda method is quite satisfactory.   Hydrated lime and soda ash are mixed with hot water and after a settling period, softened feedwater may be drawn from the system.   Hardness can be reduced to about 1 gpg by this method.

(2)   The Cold Process Lime-Soda treatment is used to partially soften very hard water to about 3 to 5 gpg.   Municipalities will sometimes install these facilities as well as larger plants to improve water for general use.   With the modern detergents which are now available, water having about 5 gpg hardness can be used satisfactorily for most cleaning in food plants.   However, water with nearly zero hardness is preferred.

Passing water through a bed of base exchange material, such as zeolite, provides the most effective and practical method of obtaining soft water for cleaning purposes. The zeolites vary in composition but some common ones are synthetic resins or insoluble complex aluminasilicates.   As hard water flows through the zeolite material, sodium ions replace calcium and magnesium ions making the water ideal for cleaning. The residual hardness in the water will normally be less than 0.2 gpg.   Another advantage credited to this method of softening is the ability to adjust automatically to variations in the hardness of the supply water.   Regeneration with ordinary salt brine is simple and because the zeolite bed acts as a filter makes the base exchange softener practical for most plants.   One should recognize, however, that zeolite softeners do not reduce the total salts content of water.

About 3 yr is necessary to pay for zeolite softening equipment from savings in most food plants.   Direct savings come from lower requirements of cleaning compounds, fuel, water, maintenance, and a longer life for hoses and plumbing.   Zeolite softeners will not tolerate high temperature; however, some are affected more by heat than others.   To soften water having higher than usual temperatures, the manufacturer's recommendation should be followed closely.

For special uses including utilization in a laboratory, demineralized water is necessary.   So-called "demineralized water" is the result of passage through two ion exchange beds.   In the first, the calcium and magnesium ions are replaced by hydrogen ions.   This ion exchanger works on the hydrogen cycle.   The water then flows through a second exchanger where the sulfate, chloride, bicarbonate, and other negative ions are replaced by OH (hydroxyl) ions.   The resulting water is essentially mineral free.

Microorganisms in Water

Commercial water supplies are under close control to prevent the possibility of a disease outbreak caused by waterborne bacteria or viruses.   In the final stages of treatment before releasing into the municipal distribution system, chlorination is almost always done to make the water safe. In food plants it is necessary to have a water supply not only safe, but with a minimum number of food spoilage organisms. Water may show a negative coliform count, but still contain a variety of microorganisms which cause rancidity, putrefaction, or other spoilage.

Some food bacteriologists after studying the problem have suggested that water used in direct contact with foods should have a bacteria count of less than 50 ml as determined by the standard plate method. Preferably, the total count should not exceed 20 per ml and with a maximum of 5 proteolytic and/or lipolytic organisms per milliliter.

Studies indicate that in several plants bacteria counts increased as the water passed through the plant's distribution system. Bacteria counts in water mains at the entrance into the plant were often much lower than at the point of discharge at a churn or cheese vat. This suggests that it is important to check water quality at various outlets. Particular attention should be given to keeping hoses as clean as possible. Water which comes in direct contact with a food product should preferably be discharged directly from sanitary pipe which can be removed and cleaned rather than a flexible hose.

Food plants may use chlorination to control bacteria in water to fit their own requirements. Special uses for water will naturally require varying chlorine strength. It has been found in the sugar beet industry, for example, that 20 ppm chlorine for 25 to 30 min had little effect on certain spores. However, an exposure to 60 ppm was effective in destroying the spores.

The addition of 5 to 10 ppm of chlorine to water used for washing cottage cheese is generally recommended. The effectiveness of chlorination is dependent to some degree upon the pH of the water. Several common spoilage organisms are destroyed in water having 3 to 5 ppm of chlorine at pH 6.0. Although acidification combined with chlorination is effective, care must be taken to avoid reducing the pH below 5.0. If the pH is too low, there is the possibility of imparting metallic flavors and some danger of corroding pipelines. For best results, treated wash water should be held about 10 min in a sanitary tank before use.

Some plants may find pasteurization of water for certain purposes to be more feasible than chlorination. A temperature of 180°F for 20 min has been used in a cheese plant and found to be satisfactory.

Water Requirements

To estimate warm water requirements assume approximately 5 gal. per day per plant employee and 2 gal. per day for office employees. The figure usually used for a shower is 225 gal. per hr and the quantity for a wash basin, 12 gal. per hr. Each hot water hose should be figured at about 300 gal. per hr when used continuously. These values are useful in determining the size of the hot water heating system.

Estimates of the water usage in milk plants can be made with reasonable accuracy for planning. Average water requirements for dairy plants may be considered as follows.

Cleaning.—Water usage in gallons = $\frac{1}{2}$ cleaning time in minutes multiplied by 3. In modern clean-in-place systems, requirements may be much less than this depending upon equipment.

Cooling of Milk.—A ratio of 3 parts of water to 1 of milk.

Bottle Washing.—One gallon per minute washes approximately 4 bottles per minute.

Can Washing.—Approximately 2 gal. per can.

Refrigeration.—Small Freon units require approximately 1 gal. per min per hp. Larger ammonia systems approximately 2.5 gal. per min per ton of refrigeration.

Condensing Skim Milk or Milk.—Single effect condensing units require about 20 lb of water per pound of water evaporated. Double effect evaporators require approximately $1\frac{1}{4}$ gal. of water for each pound of water evaporated. By using thermocompression evaporators and triple effect evaporators, even smaller quantities of water are required for condensing.

Efficient Utilization of Water

The obvious steps needed to reduce water losses are readily detected. Some of these include excessive amounts of water running freely on the floor to wash wastes down the drain, and an unattended hose running freely. To minimize losses through hoses, a nozzle attachment is of considerable value. The nozzle also saves time by eliminating valve adjustments each time the hose is used. Solenoid valves on equipment operating intermittently will help in reducing water consumption. These valves may be used in the water supply lines of bottle washers, can washers, condensers, and other equipment. Water regulating valves are in common use in refrigeration systems where the volume of water needed is influenced by the system head pressure.

Refrigeration systems utilizing the shell and tube condensers require considerable volumes of water. These volumes become great unless the water is recooled and circulated through the condenser. Cooling may be done by means of cooling towers. One pound of water evaporated will absorb approximately 1,000 Btu. Cooling towers for recovery and reuse of water are very practical in many refrigerating systems. Water consumption for refrigeration may be reduced by as much as 95% through the use of an evaporative condenser. The amount of water evaporated in the evaporative condenser will be approximately 12 to 14 gal. per hr per ton of refrigeration, plus an additional 1 gal. per hr per ton for bleeding the tank. Spilled water from a shell and tube condenser will remove from 15 to 30 Btu per pound. The effect of water temperature will greatly influence the quantity required. An average amount of water from shell and tube condensers may range from approximately 2.5 gpm per ton with 65°F water to 4 gpm per ton with 85°F water.

Evaporative condensers vary somewhat in design, but are generally of two different types. One is known as the blow-through and the other the draw-through. The blow-through unit permits dry fan operation because the fans are located in the dry entering air rather than in the saturated discharge air. The draw-through unit is generally used indoors, although it is suitable for outdoor installation. With the fans located on the top of the unit, these condensers require slightly less floor space than do the blow-through units. As the draw-through unit may be used either indoors or outdoors some flexibility is given the operator for later equipment rearrangement.

Possibilities for Reducing Water Losses

Regeneration as used in the high-temperature short-time pasteurization system often eliminates the need for cooling water. When water is used for cooling purposes sometimes it may be collected for other purposes. Some uses may be for the washing of trucks and other vehicles. This water also has the advantage of being slightly preheated for the washing job.

The overflow rinse water from a bottle washer may also be used for case washing. It is usually advantageous to locate the case washer near the bottle washer to take advantage of this overflow water.

References

FARRALL, A. W. 1963. Engineering for Dairy and Food Products, 3rd Edition. John Wiley & Sons, New York.

MILK INDUSTRY FOUNDATION. 1967. Manual for Milk Plant Operators. 3rd Edition. Washington, D.C.

THE JOURNAL OF PLUMBING, HEATING AND AIR CONDITIONING. 1961. The Purification and Treatment of Domestic Water Supplies, A Handbook of Water Conditioning. Tarrytown, New York.

Cross-references: *Steam; Waste Disposal and Treatment Systems.*

WEIGHING

Weighing is an important activity in any food processing plant. Accurate weighing is necessary for proper cost records, product formulation, planning, and quality control. In addition to the simple beam scales, modern industry now has available many new weighing devices involving electronic controls, springs, and load cells. Many of these can be adapted to automation and give automatic weighing and totalizing figures. The dial type scale using weights is the standard for low cost dependable results for general weighing purposes. They can be used for measuring weights as little as a small fraction of an ounce up to hundreds of tons. The principal care and servicing involves periodic testing and lubrication of the bearings or points.

Load Cells

A second important type of weight device is the electronic load cell. The principle of this system is that one or more of the supports for the tank, for example, is fitted with a load cell whose resistance varies with the tension or strain on the cell. An electronic circuit from the load cell actuates an instrument which will give an indication of the weight or it can be used to give a totalized weight. Highly sophisticated automatic electronic weighing systems are built around these units. Equipment of this type is normally guaranteed to have an overall accuracy of 0.05% of indicator capacity. In combination with the hydraulic load cell system, this unit can be used in batching or other process weighing operations to indicate both the weight on the load cell, and to automatically activate a valve or other control when a preset weight is reached. With electronic load cell equipment, the principal service requirement is to periodically check the accuracy of the instrument.

A third type of weighing device is a hydraulic or pneumatic load cell, which is used to support the item being weighed. This cell through a hydraulic or pneumatic connection activates an indicator or recorder which may be at some distance from the load. The accuracy of these load cells is claimed to be 0.1% of load range.

A fourth type of weighing equipment utilizes one or more electronic load cells to measure the weight of product passing along a conveyor thus giving an over-or under-weight indication or control. The accuracy of this type of unit is also claimed to be 0.1% of applied load. These can all be tied in with a direct reading unit, a fully automated control system with printer, date logger, and card or tape punch to the computer.

Meter

A fifth method of weighing, an indirect method, a liquid meter, is quite widely used. This system is often used for a batch measurement and standardizer. Very accurate results can be obtained if the fluid is free from air and at reasonably uniform temperatures. A part of this system would be a counter, a progress pointer, a units totalizer and a batch totalizer.

Special exotic means of weighing can be designed using light beams and light sensitive cells. Air streams through proper auxiliaries can be used to indicate variations in weight.

Cross-reference: *Flow Meters.*

WELDING

Welding is the process of joining two or more pieces of metal using a fusion process in which another metal may or may not be added.

Acetylene Welding

This is a common type of gas welding where oxygen and acetylene are used to provide the fuel for combustion to heat the material. The two gases are placed in separate cylinders, are mixed and burned at a temperature considerably above the melting point of the metals being welded. Oxygen is stored at 2,000 psi at 70°F in the container and the acetylene at 250 psi at 70°F.

Considerable knowledge and skill are needed to (1) select the proper equipment including the tip of the welding torch, (2) select proper welding rod for the material, and (3) ensure proper preparation of the material for welding. References on properties of materials and methods of welding should be consulted with respect to specific welding jobs. For example, aluminum has a high rate of thermal conductivity and a low melting point. Thus, aluminum transfers heat quickly from the welding plane. Also, many metals such as aluminum develop an oxide layer on the surface. Manufacturers of welding equipment furnish tables and charts relating the proper welding rod with the material and procedure of operation (Fig. W.4 and W.5).

Brazing is another method of gas welding. Base metals are joined by the addition of a bronze filarod. The bond between 2 metals is formed by the bronze material at a temperature of about 1,000°F. A major advantage of brazing is that with the lower temperature there is less change in shape of the material and less heat damage to the material being welded. However, the joint is usually not as strong as one formed by fusion of the base materials.

A flux material is often used to cover the location of the weld to prevent the formation of oxides or other chemical reactions formed in the welding.

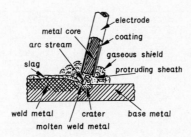

FIG. W-4.   Metallic shielded arc with gas and slag producing coating

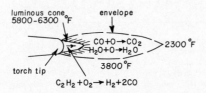

FIG. W-5.   The oxyacetylene flame: its related reactions and temperatures

Silver soldering is a special type of brazing alloy in which various percentages of silver, zinc, and copper may be used as the added material.   A major advantage to silver solders is that they are corrosion resistant.

Hard surfacing or facing of materials for abrasive wear can be carried out using acetylene for heating.

The safe use of acetylene includes the following.

(1) Cylinders and equipment which leak should not be used.   Torches or regulators which leak should be repaired and tested by the manufacturer.   Only hoses of high quality without leaks should be used.   (2) When lighting the torch, the acetylene torch heater valve is opened and ignited at the end of the tip with a spark lighter. (3) Eyes should be properly protected with dark glasses as specified, and hands protected with gloves.

Most welding operations in industry except for repairs are done by machine. Tubes, pipes, and plates can be directed through automatic machine welding.

Electric Arc Welding

This welding process consists of a method whereby the heat is provided by an electric arc formed either between the base metal and an electrode or between two electrodes (carbon arc).   Either alternating or direct current may be used.   Usually, the weld process is shielded by a material on the welding rod.   The shielding prevents the rapid oxidation of the high temperature material during the welding process (Fig. W.6).

The amount of heat provided by the electric welder is controlled by the voltage of the unit which normally varies from 20 to 95 v and the amperage which is adjusted by the operator.   The amount of heat desired or required depends upon the material, the thickness of the material, the speed of welding, and type of electrode.   In general, about 250 amp is required for a $1/4$-in. electrode used in a flat position.

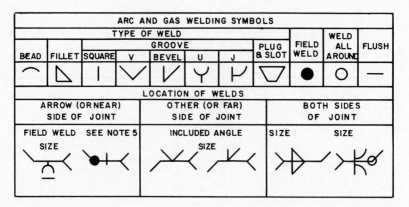

Fig. W-6.   Legend for use on drawings specifying arc and gas welding

Welding units generally have low power factors unless capacitors are incorporated with the units.   A high power factor is desired.

Of particular importance from the standpoint of safety and utilization of electric arc welding is the protection of the eyes.   Lenses must be used on the welding helmet which absorb at least 99% of the infrared and ultraviolet rays.   Also, for all types of welding, it is important that a proper welding booth be provided, and be well-ventilated so that fumes given off during the welding process are not inhaled by the operator.

Carbon electrodes are used for producing heating for cutting of material and for brazing.   A 100-amp current could be used for a $^1/_4$-in. carbon electrode.   The electrode itself does not enter the work but is used as a method of heating.

With electric resistance heating the material is heated and is joined under pressure. Simple spot welding is a method of resistance heating whereby one or more points of projection are heated and pressed into the opposite material.   Also, ridge welding may be practiced on the same basis.

WOOD

Wood is a versatile material used in the food industry for many purposes.   Wood is classified as hard and soft.   Typical hard woods are oak, chestnut, ash, maple, hickory, and poplar.   Soft woods include spruce, pine, hemlock, fur, cedar, and larch.

Wood is not used significantly in contact with food products, except for storage for grain and dry materials, and even here is being replaced by metal in many instances.

The softness of wood and its susceptibility to decay are problems.   The likelihood of picking up odors is also a problem.   There are, however, methods of treatment for wood which greatly improve its properties of resistance to weathering and rotting.

Wood is often used as a floor for storages.   Wood is being replaced in most instances by concrete due to the greater sanitation and better wearing qualities of the latter.

Plywood is widely used at the present time and it is of particular value in the food industry for building temporary structures, for wall partitions, and for base floors.

TABLE W.6

STRENGTH OF AIR SEASONED STRUCTURAL SIZE WOOD

Kind of Wood	Density Lb/Ft³ Oven Dry	Bending Lb/In.²-at Elastic Limit	Crushing Strength, Compression, psi		Shear, Lb/In.²
			Parallel to Fiber	Perpendicular to Fibers	
Longleaf pine	39	3,691	3,480	572	934
Douglas fir	28	4,563	3,271	639	822[1]
Redwood	22	3,442	—	525	671
Norway pine	27	4,069	3,047	924[1]	1,154

[1] Small pieces.

Source: U.S. Forest Service.

Wood is very susceptible to moisture changes unless treated and is also affected by the grain of the wood. Table W.6 shows the strength of air seasoned timber of commonly used varieties.

The thermal conductivity in Btu per hr °F per in. for Virginia white pine wood is 0.958; for standard white pine wood, 0.791; for oak wood, 1.000; and for balsawood, 0.350.

Woods such as mahogany or teak which are very heavy and dense are used for special purposes, as is also balsa wood which is extremely light and porous in structure.

Reference

U.S. DEPT. OF AGR. 1955. Wood Handbook, Agriculture Handbook 72.

Cross-references: *Building Materials; Fuels.*

X

XRAY

The Xray has become an important means for checking and testing materials in the food industry. Xrays are used for determining the strength and quality of welds in pressure vessels, for testing for the presence of blow holes in castings, and for locating imperfect seams and joints in cans or vessels or tubes. Xrays can be used for inspection of fruits and mixtures; to detect ripeness, excessive crystallization, etc., in oranges or lemons; and to detect the presence of foreign materials in fruits or vegetables.

The Xray is an electromagnetic radiation very similar to that of radio waves, infrared waves, and ordinary light, except that the wavelength of the radiation is much shorter, being in the range of 0.01 to 100 Angstrom[1] units (Å). Xrays are very penetrating and in fact can penetrate a number of inches of steel without difficulty. It is stopped quite effectively by a layer of lead. However, heavy walls of concrete also are quite resistant to radiation by Xray. Xrays are produced by the rapid moving charged particle given off by a filament striking a metal target in a vacuum tube and being reflected off.

Rays are designated as soft rays if they have a relatively light penetration and hard rays if they are capable of deep penetration as for example, in the use of Xrays for testing thick steel.

Type of Ray	Wavelength in Angstrom Units
Very soft	100–10.0
Soft	10–1.0
Hard	1–0.1
Very hard	0.1–0.01

There are several types of tubes. The earlier so-called Jackson tube is a gas-filled tube; the more recent method or type of tube is called the hot cathode tube which was developed by W. D. Coolidge of the General Electric Co. in 1913.

Xrays vary inversely in intensity as the square of the distance from the source of the Xray to the object it is striking. The absorption of the energy of the ray depends very largely upon the density of the material. For example, the Xray will travel great distances in vacuum or in ordinary air but only a short distance through lead which is very dense.

Four Principal Effects of the Xray

Activation of a Fluoroscopic Screen.—This is a screen which is coated with zinc sulfate. When Xrays strike the coated screen, they give a bright appearance on which the shadow of the X-ray picture can be very clearly seen.

Photo Effect.—Xrays striking a photographic film will cause it to blacken.

Ionizing Effect.—Xrays will ionize air through which they pass.

Biological Effect.—Xrays will destroy biological cells. This property is made use of in medicine for treatment of pathogenic cells. Elaborate scientific expriments have been carried on in this area, resulting in the development of very sophisticated application methods and equipment. By adjusting the intensity and time of treatment, remarkable results have been obtained.

In medical applications, the so-called soft ray of 100 kv or less is normally used; however, for industrial uses of x-raying heavy castings, voltages as high as 3 to 400 kv are frequently used. These rays are the so-called hard rays.

Future use in the food industry undoubtedly will continue to be in quality control, analysis, and testing of products and for use in determining the presence of undesirable components or materials in food packages.

Use will continue to be made on an even greater scale of X-ray methods of testing the quality of castings, tubes, sheets, welds, etc. used in food processing equipment.

Cross-references: *Electromagnetic; Irradiation; Ultraviolet.*

[1] 1 Angstrom Unit $= \dfrac{1}{100,000,000}$ centimeter.

Z

ZINC

Zinc is one of the very common nonferrous metals which is widely used in the food industry. It is useful as an alloy, as a coating to prevent corrosion, and is an element in bearings.

The ASTM specification B6-37 for slab zinc of high grade is as follows: maximum percent impurities: lead 0.07%, iron 0.02%, cadmium 0.07%, and sum of lead iron and lead cadmium, 0.10%. Commercial zinc has a temperature coefficient of resistivity near 20°C per °C of 0.0042. The density at 20°C is 7.14 gm per cu cm, and the melting point is 419.5°C. Zinc has an electrode potential of 0.7618 v which means that it will go into solution easier than iron which has a potential of 0.441v, and therefore is very effective as a means of providing a protective coating for iron. Zinc is resistant to atmospheric corrosion but is attacked by both alkalies and acids.

Zinc is not recommended for use in contact with food materials, since it is readily dissolved by both acids and alkalies. One important use for zinc is to use a strip of zinc submerged in a brine tank to prevent corrosion of the system, since due to its position in the electromotive series, the zinc will go into solution more readily than the iron parts of the brine system and will therefore protect the system.

Cross-references: *Alloys; Electrolysis; EMF series.*

INDEX